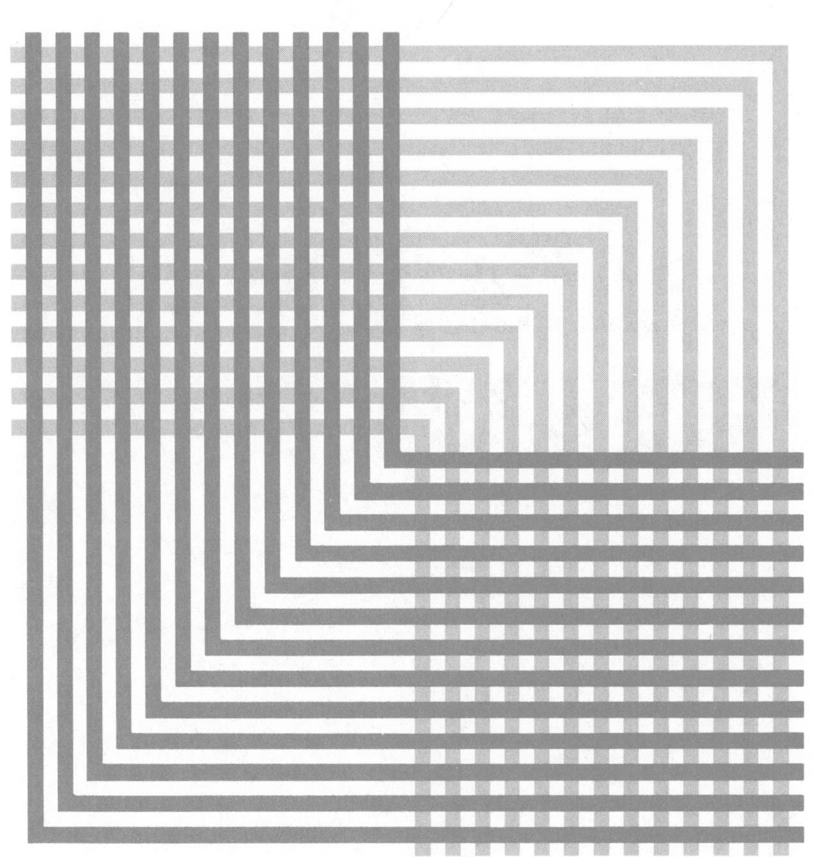

ADMINISTRATIVE OFFICE MANAGEMENT

6TH EDITION

John J. W. Neuner, Ph.D., C.P.A.

Baruch College of the City University of New York
Iona College, School of Business Administration
Formerly a partner of John B. Thurston & Company,
Management Consultants

B. Lewis Keeling

Associate Professor, Business Studies
Bucks County Community College
Newtown, Pennsylvania

Norman F. Kallaus, Ph.D.

Professor, Administrative Management
College of Business Administration
The University of Iowa
Iowa City, Iowa

G51

Published by

SOUTH-WESTERN PUBLISHING CO.

CINCINNATI WEST CHICAGO, ILL. DALLAS NEW ROCHELLE, N.Y.
BURLINGAME, CALIF. BRIGHTON, ENGLAND

ISBN: 0-538-07510-4

Library of Congress Catalog Card Number: 74-188154

2 3 4 5 6 7 8 K 0 9 8 7 6 5 4 3

Printed in the United States of America

Preface

In the past thirty years since this textbook was first published, office management has progressed from a minor supervisory clerical function to an important centralized, coordinating administrative function of modern business. In this revision, as in the previous five editions, the authors have attempted to keep pace with progressive changes in business management, but with added emphasis on information as the major product of the office.

This sixth edition meets the changing needs of today's college students majoring in business studies and of those executives and first-line supervisors in administrative management work who desire to update their knowledge in a rapidly changing social, political, and business environment. In this revision consideration has been given to both present and future problems of the administration of office work, based upon the experience and research of the authors as college instructors, business executives, certified public accountant, and management engineer. The material represents a comprehensive survey of the most acceptable methods and practices of office administration. Carefully planned questions, problems, and cases are included at the end of each chapter to facilitate the learning process.

More specifically this revision covers the following basic administrative office management areas:

1. Administrative Office Management in Modern Business, which introduces the student to the information management concept and automation in the modern office.

2. Organizing and Planning Administrative Office Services, with emphasis upon office layouts; office equipment; psychological and physical factors in the office environment; interoffice communication; information and records management; and auxiliary administrative services.

3. Leadership and Human Relations in Office Administration, covering the staffing and supervision of office activities and current personnel policies and practices.

4. Controlling Office Administrative Operations through cost reduction in such areas as systems and procedures analysis; forms design and control; mechanization of basic accounting procedures; job analysis; work measurement and standards; salary administration; budgetary control and report preparation; and the development of office manuals as a tool of cost control.

5. Business Information Processing Systems, such as punched-card systems, integrated data processing, and electronic data processing systems.

Underlying these five areas is a constant emphasis on two basic concepts of successful business management: *satisfactory human relations* and *continuous cost reduction.*

No textbook, especially one that has had five previous editions, is the product of the authors alone. Hundreds of business firms and executives, teachers, and students have contributed their ideas, experiences, and suggestions to make this one of the outstanding textbooks in its field, translated into several languages, with special printings for governmental agencies both here and abroad. To all of these valuable advisors, though unnamed, the authors are deeply grateful. Special appreciation, however, must be given to the following for their continued interest, help, and suggestions in making this new edition more successful: Dr. Abraham Klein and Dr. Jeanette Bely, both of the City University of New York; Mr. Jess C. Lang, Data Communications Manager, Northwestern Bell Telephone Company, Des Moines, Iowa; and Marion L. Clough, former Professor of Management at Bucks County Community College, whose teaching will continue to linger in the minds of his colleagues and students.

John J. W. Neuner
B. Lewis Keeling
Norman F. Kallaus

Contents

Part 1

Administrative Office Management in Modern Business

Part 2

Organizing and Planning Administrative Office Services

Part 3

Leadership and Human Relations in Office Administration

Part 4

Controlling Office Administrative Operations

Part 5

Business Information Processing Systems

1

The Information Management Concept

Tremendous advances in office technology, particularly relating to machines, have marked the past two decades. The computer and the copier, to name but two significant machine advances, have revolutionized many phases of office work and brought with them new specialists, new systems and procedures, and new problems. Alongside these technological strides have come pressing human problems as well as new advances in understanding human behavior. The usual office operation places people together—working together, planning together, and sometimes disagreeing together. The dynamics of human behavior, including the study of motivation of group interaction, has become basic to an understanding of the management process whether it be in the plant or in the office.

A highly accelerated pace in society, especially conditions in business, industry, and government, has given a new thrust to administrative office management. The traditional office concepts have generally given way to a more expansive network of information of enormous magnitude. Man's need for more information, better decisions, more regulation, greater speed and precision, and more communication has brought forth many new administrative concepts for solving present-day management problems.

To effectively control the collection, processing, storage, retrieval, and distribution of information is the responsibility of administrative office management. In addition to the basic office services over which he has exercised control, the office manager has been assigned new information responsibilities that have brought forth new systems for meeting these needs. The result has been a revolution of man and machine in the office as well as important new developments in coordinating these two key work components.

To meet this challenging and changing business scene, the office management student must study and understand management principles and systems and modern administrative practices. He must appreciate the role of man as the basic ingredient in the office function. Since the office manager is also a manager of people, successful office personnel practices must be studied. It is the purpose of this book to contribute to the knowledge of the student in these areas of study. Such knowledge will provide the basis and framework for intelligent and timely decision making as a participating member of the management team.

CHANGING CURRENTS IN THE OFFICE

In the long history of man, the office as we now know it has had a relatively brief reign. If one considers that the age of Lincoln had little staff or administrative organization and no telephones, typewriters, or copying devices which now typify office life, the newness of office work is obvious. Prior to this time much of the clerical work was associated with clerics or religious persons who performed paper-work and accounting functions required to "keep the books" of church organizations.

Industrial and technological progress in the 19th century generated a chain reaction in all parts of the economy. For example, the rise of the textile industry in the 1830's and the rise of the railroads later in the century caused the first real attempts to group people and to surround them with the services we now call offices. It was during this time and in the years following that the traditional office came into being.

The Traditional Office

To most people, even today, the office represents a place where the following activities and personnel abound:

Special Types of Work	*Special Types of Workers*
Pencil and paper work	Typists
Departmentation of work	Secretaries
Correspondence	Bookkeepers
Filing	File clerks
Preparation of forms, reports, and letters	Machine operators
	Supervisors
Record keeping	Managers

In such a setting too frequently the emphasis has been placed upon the physical product—the letters, memorandums, and reports being written; the budgets and bills being prepared; the notes taken and minutes recorded; the file cabinets bulging with carbon copies and duplicated materials. This type of office prevails in practice, but to the student of administrative office management this is a limited, fading, superficial picture of the office.

The Modern Office

In contrast to the older view of the office, a vastly different office world is taking form. It is an office much more comprehensive in nature, relying heavily on electronic machine systems and exerting far greater impact on the organization it serves. Some of the principal characteristics of the new office are listed in Figure 1-1, which is shown on the following page.

The modern office, as sketched above, is slowly but surely emerging. Emphasis in this new office is not upon the record or the form but upon the information contained within; it is not primarily upon the machine but upon the system within which the machine functions. Administrative office management, then, is a rapidly expanding, dynamic field of work comprising the world of administrative systems, data processing, records management, and information management. Its boundaries contain such associations as the Administrative Management Society, the Association for Systems Management, the Data Processing Management Association, the American Records Management Association, and the Society for Management Information Systems. In the final analysis changes taking place have brought greater specialization for most office personnel, but the administrative office manager must have much broader knowledges and understandings. A common denominator for all personnel, though, is their vital concern with and responsibility for processing information.

NEW FEATURES	ILLUSTRATION
Its broadening scope:	Within the decade terminology has indicated this sweeping change. (The National Office Management Association became the Administrative Management Society; the National Machine Accountants Association has become the Data Processing Management Association; the Office Management Division of the American Management Association has become the Administrative Services Division.)
Its expanding responsibilities:	Its office managers have become Administrative Vice Presidents, Controllers, Managers of Systems and Procedures or Data Processing or Administrative Services.
Its emerging concepts:	The total system views the office as an information network of jobs and people and procedures with increasing emphasis given to human behavior in the office function; the importance of information handling as the basic function of the office.
Its new technology:	The computer, integrated data processing equipment, data communications, and automated retrieval of information.

Fig. 1-1

Principal Characteristics of the New Office

THE FUNCTION OF MANAGEMENT

Any type of organization requires leadership and direction at various levels so that it may realize its objectives. In a business firm the man who leads and directs, who is in charge, is known as the manager or chief administrator. Typically he is responsible for organizing, planning, controlling, and combining all resources into a functioning, productive, unified organization. Essentially management becomes a process that involves all the activities related to decision making, coordination of group effort, and leadership. Management's function, then, is to blend in an effective way men, materials, money, methods, machines, and morale to set and achieve the goals of the firm. It, therefore, includes dealing with economic circumstances, with human and material resources, and, especially important, with directing people. In fact, Horace Greeley must have had management in mind when he defined a businessman as one who knows how to set other people's heads and hands at work, both to his profit and their own.

Management activities are performed at several levels in any organization, from the office of president to a first-line supervisor. Titles held by managers vary considerably, depending upon the nature of the work managed. Usually managerial levels are divided as shown in Figure 1-2.

MANAGERIAL LEVELS	MANAGERIAL TITLES	TYPICAL RESPONSIBILITIES
Top management	President Vice President	Developing long-range plans and policies; selecting and evaluating key executives.
Middle management	Controller Sales Manager Treasurer Production Manager Administrative Office Manager	Assisting top management in planning; developing intermediate-range plans; establishing departmental policies; initiating and reviewing operating systems.
Supervisory management	Office Supervisor Accounting Supervisor Foreman	Making detailed plans; supervising day-to-day operations; assigning tasks to personnel.

Fig. 1-2

Managerial Levels, Titles, and Responsibilities

THE ADMINISTRATIVE OFFICE MANAGEMENT FUNCTION

What has been said about management in general applies also to management of the office function. The administrative office manager, therefore, is responsible for the organizing, planning, coordinating, and controlling of all office activities in the firm. But this total-firm concept of the office has emerged slowly and recently.

Traditionally the office management function has been limited mainly to those basic services and personnel dealing with clerical work. With the passing of time and the development of new and more efficient methods of information handling came the demand for more information and for more decisions made at greatly accelerated rates. Management began to place greater reliance upon the office force, giving the office new importance and new responsibilities. The new technology with its greater power of communication and computation gave the office force greater processing power. The "one-department office" concept gave way to the broader company-wide administrative management concept in which the administrative office function becomes centralized in one administrative head.

During the period of the early 1960's the office function became the *information-management* function. This new concept gave to the office a company-wide responsibility for the collection, processing, storage, retrieval, and distribution of information. These activities represent a sequence of related procedures for handling the full information cycle; and when properly organized, they constitute a new area of study. As a result, information, or more properly the information system, has become a new academic discipline out of which will emerge new applications of information technology. Traditional office work, such as oral and written communication, computing and reporting, record keeping, accounting, and filing, however, remains, but in modified form.

Although in all organizations the offices are characteristically different from each other in specific duties and responsibilities, basically they are similar in function. Therefore, the principles of effective office management presented in this book are just as applicable to the small as to the large office.

The scope and responsibilities of administrative office management are presented in this book through an investigation and analysis of each of the managerial functions as applied to office activities. A logical sequence of these functions and activities may be outlined as shown in Figure 1-3.

As the first means of recognizing managers as "professionals," the Administrative Management Society inaugurated its Certified Administrative Manager (C.A.M.) program in 1970. Candidacy is open to all management personnel, and to achieve the C.A.M. designation and to gain membership in the Academy of Certified Administrative Managers, an individual must meet the following five program standards: (1) pass the five-part C.A.M. examination covering personnel management, financial management, control and economics, administrative services, and systems and information management; (2) have two years of experience at the administrative management level; (3) submit character references to certify high standards of personal and professional conduct; (4) provide evidence of leadership ability; and (5) show evidence of communication ability. The emergence of this certification program is further evidence

Fig. 1-3

MANAGERIAL FUNCTIONS	OFFICE ACTIVITIES
Organizing:	Applying basic principles of office organization in planning the working relationships among employees, equipped with the best physical facilities, to achieve the maximum profit.
Planning:	Coordinating the various office services, such as communications, records management, mailing, and reproduction; procuring a suitable office site; equipping the work areas with modern, functional, and efficient office furniture, machines, and equipment; staffing the office with qualified employees so that the work will flow smoothly and quickly.
Leading:	Directing and supervising effectively the office activities; adopting and implementing workable personnel policies that will maintain a desirable level of morale; training, orienting, promoting, and compensating office personnel; providing for static-free communications lines back and forth between employees and employer.
Controlling:	Developing, installing, and improving administrative office systems and procedures to be followed in completing each major phase of office work; supervising the procurement, preparation, and use of office forms and other supplies; measuring the work done and setting standards for its accomplishment; reducing the costs of office services; preparing budgets, reports, and office manuals as means whereby costs are reduced and controlled.

Managerial Functions and Office Activities

of the broadening scope and expanding responsibilities of the administrative manager in today's modern office.

SCIENTIFIC MANAGEMENT IN THE OFFICE

Like other types of specialized managers, administrative office managers have employed several approaches through the years in the management of their offices. Basically the efficient office reflects a perceptive supervisor—one who by training, experience, and intuition has sensed the need for improvement and has taken steps to effect necessary changes. The intuitive manager is still very much in demand at all managerial levels, for he is able to direct people effectively toward the firm's objectives. Unfortunately many people—perhaps most people—are not gifted with powerful intuition. Such a group turns to education to achieve the necessary technical, administrative, and human skills required to manage the firm.

During the late 19th century Frederick W. Taylor developed a logical, scientific approach to solving management problems in industry, a method that quickly gained support throughout the world. Education stresses this scientific approach to management—in fact, to all problem solving. The scientific method involves the use of logical, systematic steps to develop effective solutions to problems. It is utilized to solve problems in engineering and in the physical sciences, such as chemistry and physics, and can be employed in the solution of office problems.

To use the scientific method for solving office problems, logical steps are carefully formulated and followed:

1. The problem must first be recognized and carefully defined.
2. Information relating to the problem must then be collected, classified, and analyzed.
3. A tentative solution to the problem (sometimes called a hypothesis) is then developed and tested to determine its usefulness and validity.
4. On the basis of the test, modifications may be made in light of new findings or changed conditions after which the solution is put into practice.
5. A follow-up is made in order to check upon the effectiveness of the solution in meeting the objectives toward which the solution was applied.

The student of office management should study how these five steps are applied in the time-honored "Five Principles of Effective Work," illustrated in Figure 1-4, developed decades ago by William H. Leffingwell, a pioneer in office management. Although these principles relate to the proper management of all work, it is easy to apply them to the office. For example, any office manager must plan what work must be done and how, when, and where it must be done as well as by whom (Principle 1). He must recognize the total office plan of organization as to how the office product is developed so that he can coordinate the efforts of all men, machines, and information

Fig. 1-4

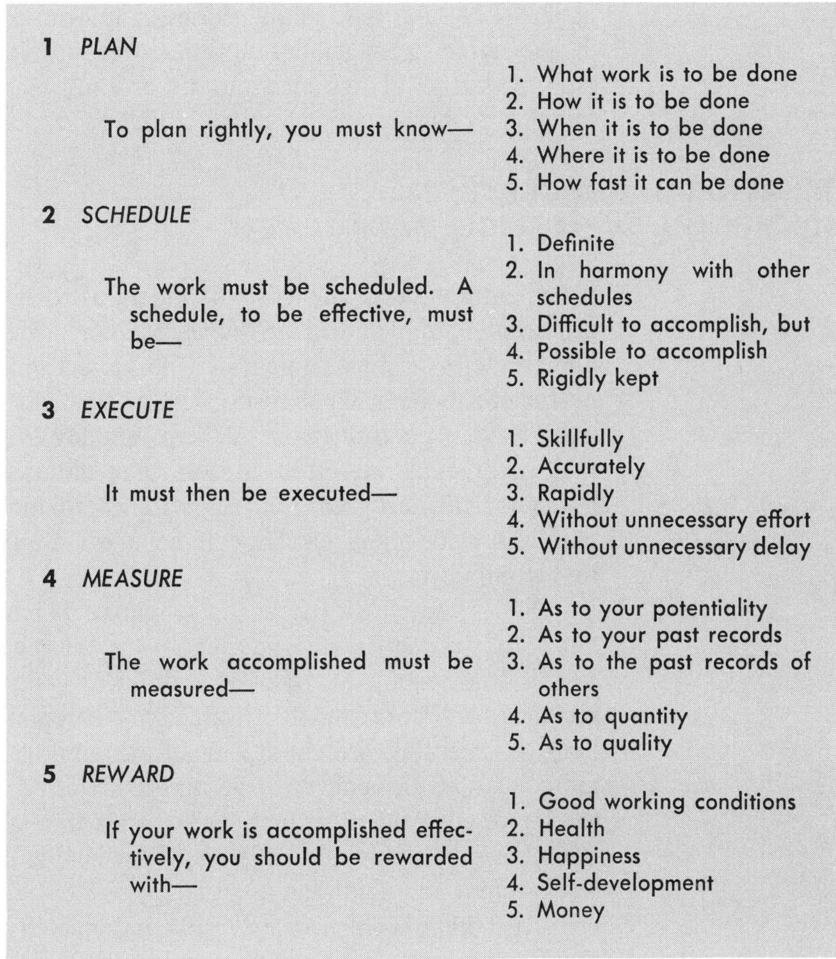

1 *PLAN*	
To plan rightly, you must know—	1. What work is to be done 2. How it is to be done 3. When it is to be done 4. Where it is to be done 5. How fast it can be done
2 *SCHEDULE*	
The work must be scheduled. A schedule, to be effective, must be—	1. Definite 2. In harmony with other schedules 3. Difficult to accomplish, but 4. Possible to accomplish 5. Rigidly kept
3 *EXECUTE*	
It must then be executed—	1. Skillfully 2. Accurately 3. Rapidly 4. Without unnecessary effort 5. Without unnecessary delay
4 *MEASURE*	
The work accomplished must be measured—	1. As to your potentiality 2. As to your past records 3. As to the past records of others 4. As to quantity 5. As to quality
5 *REWARD*	
If your work is accomplished effectively, you should be rewarded with—	1. Good working conditions 2. Health 3. Happiness 4. Self-development 5. Money

Five Principles of Effective Work

to formulate a proper work schedule to agree with the plan (Principle 2). Furthermore, he must develop proper operating systems, procedures, record-keeping practices, and methods for executing the plan as well as measurements, standards, and layouts for getting the work done effectively (Principles 3 and 4). Perhaps of most importance, he must select, train, motivate, and promote his employees to keep their interests and those of his firm at an optimum level (Principle 5).

Scientific management has been called doing that which is most logical; that is, using what is commonly called common sense. What is required in scientific management, however, is a higher order of common sense involving careful problem definition and development of plausible solutions. Many phases of information processing utilize the scientific management approach to problem solving. This is especially true of systems and procedures work, a common staff function in business firms today, which is discussed in Chapter 15.

BEHAVIORAL CONCEPTS IN ADMINISTRATIVE OFFICE MANAGEMENT

Scientific management is still widely used today to solve business problems. Coupled with it, however, is a growing concern for the human factor in management—to do more for workers than to post on bulletin boards euphemistic slogans such as "Be nice to people" and "Have a good attitude." There is today a clear-cut recognition that a worker is interested in more than money. He has social and psychological needs of great importance to him as well as to the man who is his manager. How he behaves on and off the job matters to his employer.

One of the classic studies in employee behavior occurred in the late 1920's at the Hawthorne plant of the Western Electric Company. In this study Elton Mayo of Harvard University sought to discover methods for improving the productivity of employees. He was primarily concerned with the aspects of the employee's physical environment, such as the effects of lighting and fatigue upon output. The results were confusing at first in that when the lighting was increased, output rose; but on the other hand, when lighting was decreased, work output still continued to rise.

After other such puzzling results an analysis of the study showed that the workers were highly motivated not by the degree of illumination provided but, rather, by their feelings of importance. It mattered to them that they were really making a contribution. Physical conditions, therefore, seemed to be of secondary importance in this study. From five years of research involving 20,000 workers, these two basic conclusions followed: (1) management needs an explicit skill for diagnosing human situations and (2) by means of this skill management should commit itself to the continuing study of human situations, both individual and group.[1]

From such studies as Mayo's come changing and sometimes conflicting philosophies of dealing with men. Douglas McGregor classifies the philosophies into two broad divisions, calling them Theory X and

---

[1] Gerald A. Lessels, "The Psychology of Supervision," Part I, *Chemical Engineering,* Vol. 71 (May 11, 1964), pp. 176-180.

Theory Y[2]—theories that are basic to an understanding of the two most prevalent approaches to studying human behavior in organizations. The characteristics of each approach are outlined in Figure 1-5.

THEORY X The Traditional View of Worker Behavior	THEORY Y The Current View of Worker Behavior
1. The average man dislikes work inherently. 2. The average man will avoid work if he can. 3. Most people must be coerced, controlled, or threatened with punishment to get them to work toward the achievement of organizational goals. 4. The average man prefers to be directed, to avoid responsibility. 5. The average man has relatively little ambition and wants security above all.	1. The average man does not inherently dislike work but, depending on conditions, may find work to be satisfying or punishing. 2. Man will exercise self-direction and self-control to achieve organizational objectives under certain conditions. 3. Man will seek to attain his firm's objectives if there are sufficient rewards provided. 4. Under proper conditions the average man will seek responsibility. 5. The capacity to use imagination and originality is widely found in the population. 6. In our modern society most people do not utilize all their mental potentialities.

Fig. 1-5

Traditional and Current Behavioral Theories

A third theory, called Theory Z, involves both behavioral and nonbehavioral aspects of organization theory. This theory is often called the systems approach to organization theory in which these six factors interact: (1) organization size, (2) degree of interaction, (3) personality of members, (4) congruence of goals, (5) level of decision making, and (6) state of the system. By analyzing the impact of each of these factors upon an organization, the student of administrative office management can better understand how to determine the most appropriate organizational structure and process for a given situation.[3]

---

[2] Douglas McGregor, *The Human Side of Enterprise* (New York: McGraw-Hill, Inc., 1960), pp. 33-57.

[3] For a thorough explanation of this theory, the reader is referred to Henry L. Sisk, *Principles of Management: A Systems Approach to the Management Process* (Cincinnati: South-Western Publishing Co., 1969), pp. 254-257.

The early view of man's behavior, Theory X, is based on limited experience and little or no scientific study. On the other hand, Theory Y outlines some critical features of human behavior and human motivation that spring from controlled experiments by highly trained researchers. In essence this theory points to the fact that man has wants or needs that are never completely fulfilled. Psychologists have repeatedly pointed out that these needs are organized in a series of levels. At the lowest level man develops *physiological needs* for food, rest, and shelter. When these needs are satisfied, he then recognizes his need for *safety*, for protection from danger. Accordingly, man gives priority to these physical needs.

Above these physiological needs come the needs to identify and to satisfy. All of us have a need for belonging, for acceptance by our fellow workers, for love; in short, a high-level *social* need. And at still higher levels are the *egoistic needs* (self-esteem, self-respect, personal achievement, status and recognition, appreciation, respect, and self-fulfillment). Continuing education brings this enlightened view of human behavior to the management of the office.

The perceptive manager is one who recognizes that a man is ill if he is denied a proper diet and that he is equally ineffective if he is denied the means for satisfying his mental needs. Since administrative office managers work closely with subordinates, it is vital for them to understand their own behavior as well as that of their workers so that conditions can be created which will enable each employee to meet his need fulfillments and which will enhance productivity as well as the organizational climate.

DECISION-MAKING CONCEPTS IN ADMINISTRATIVE OFFICE MANAGEMENT

Simply stated, decision making is nothing more than making a conscious choice between two or more alternative courses of action. While this definition is readily understandable, what is much more complex is how such courses of action are selected; that is, how a decision is made. For example, some students flip coins in deciding whether to study or to attend a movie. Businessmen of the old school make decisions on the basis of common sense or intuition, using a kind of educated guess. A consumer who is about to purchase a car is torn between conflicting desires for the economical aspects of the compact automobile and the aesthetic qualities of the higher priced luxury car. The *sound* decision, however, is made upon the basis of reliable information. To make such a decision, the series of events shown in Figure 1-6 occur.

Fig. 1-6

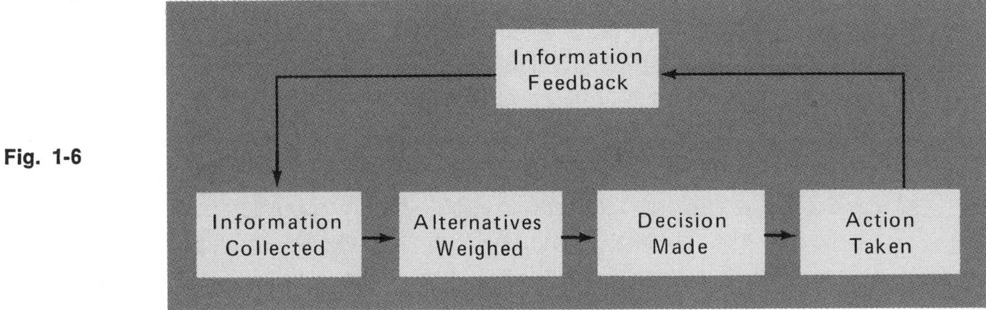

Information and Decision Making

Businessmen in today's competitive world face many decisions that deal with an uncertain, unpredictable future. In recent years attention has been focused on the use of reason or logic in the decision-making process in which as much objective fact (and as little subjective feeling) as possible is used. Technology has enabled businessmen to collect volumes of data to perform precise calculations and analyses as substitutions for judgment. Examples of such scientific methods for making decisions include sampling, factor analysis (used, for example, to determine whether advertising in newspapers, television, or radio has the greatest effect upon sales), linear programming, queueing or waiting-line theory (studying, for example, the behavior of waiting lines at a supermarket checkout counter), and game theory (such as studying the interactions of competitors in a manufacturing industry). Each of these sophisticated techniques of decision making employs the use of higher-level mathematics, and many depend for their increased use upon the rapid calculating ability and accuracy of the computer. The student of administrative office management is encouraged to understand these scientific approaches to decision making, for in the future they will be utilized in administrative management to a greater extent than ever before.

THE ROLE OF THE ADMINISTRATIVE OFFICE MANAGER

As a principal party in the collection, processing, storage, retrieval, and distribution of information, the administrative office manager plays an important role in the decision-making process. His task becomes one of providing the decision maker, at the least possible cost, with information that is accurate, accessible, and sufficiently current to be useful. Of course, each of these criteria for any information and communication system also applies to his own department where decisions must also be made.

No two office managers have the same job responsibilities. In one firm the office manager may be an accountant with the added supervision of correspondence, mailing, filing, and general administrative services. In another firm he may assume the chief responsibility of the personnel manager or the credit manager, with miscellaneous supervisory activities. In another firm he may be the office services executive; that is, he supervises and is responsible for rendering service to all office divisions. These services include mailing, filing, correspondence, messenger service, telephone and telegraph, and office maintenance.

The differences in responsibilities assigned the office manager are due to several factors among which the size of the organization is most important. Many banks in New York City, for example, employ 3,000 or more workers in their offices, and some insurance companies employ 10,000 or more. Naturally in such organizations where office work comprises the main output, the volume of the service activities is so great that their supervision and direction under an office manager are necessary. On the other hand, in many smaller organizations where the office force is not so great and where the factory staff is the primary source of business activity, the office service activities may come under the supervision and direction of the accountant, the controller, the treasurer, the credit manager, or the personnel manager.

Each year many studies are made showing the status of office employees and managers. Such agencies as the United States Department of Labor as well as private firms, such as the publishers of *Modern Office Procedures* and *Administrative Management*, analyze trends in the office world. Colleges and universities also engage in continuous research related to economic conditions and practices. One such study analyzed the office management organizational patterns in the Twin Cities of Minneapolis and St. Paul. The two clear-cut patterns found in this study are shown in Figure 1-7. Pattern 1 represents a traditional view of the office manager's role as reporting to the treasurer and having the typical responsibilities of filing, mailing, communication (largely correspondence), and duplicating. Pattern 2, however, is more noteworthy, for it reflects the broadening

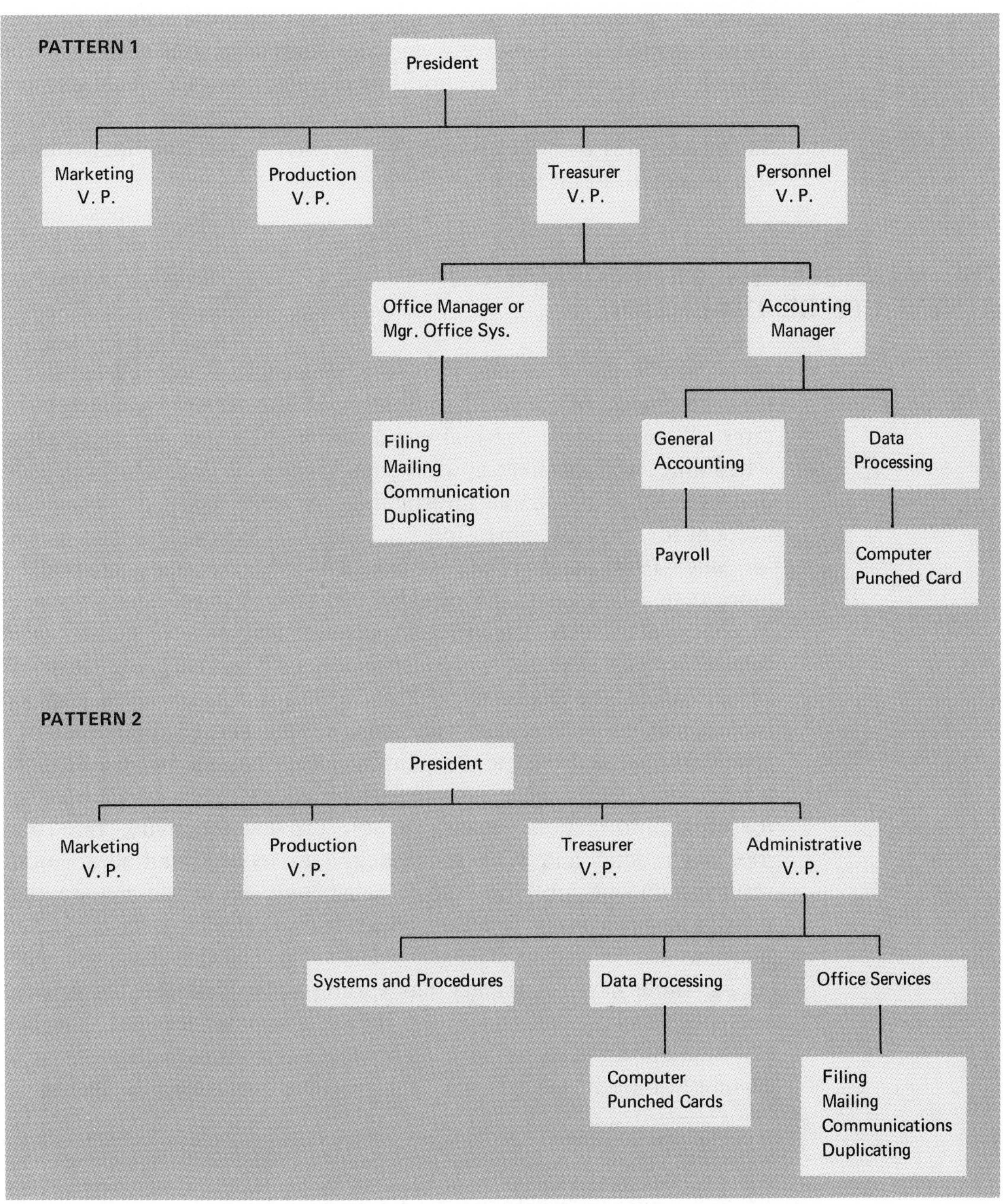

Fig. 1-7

Basic Organizational Patterns in Office Management

scope of the office and the recognition that the information management function is a top-level, vice-presidential responsibility. In the Minnesota study such a position has elevated the office management role to encompass all information processing connected with systems and procedures and data processing, as well as the traditional activities included in Pattern 1.[4]

THE MANAGEMENT OF INFORMATION: A NEW OFFICE DIMENSION

A newly added dimension of the management function considers it as the process of converting information into action. A manager is, after all, responsible for making decisions in planning, organizing, scheduling, and the like; and all such successful decisions are made upon the basis of reliable information. Several recent developments account for this new dimension.

Since 1960 the population of the United States has increased by more than 12 percent. Along with this growth have come increases in employment (16 percent), in personal income (57 percent), in retail sales (55 percent), in construction (70 percent), and in other key areas in the economy.[5] The world of business has become increasingly more complex with more people and more complicated relationships requiring more communication, more paper work, more power and energy, more taxes and regulations; in short, the need is for more information. Man can now provide too many facts and too much data; and with too much data, confusion and disorder result. Someone must be able to select only those useful data that relate to a problem or function. Such useful relevant data are called *information*.

A whole new vocabulary has sprung up to describe the present age. For example, one hears the terms "computer age" or "the age of automation" to describe a technological revolution in work processing. Similarly the phrases "information explosion," "paper-work

---

[4] Robert G. Benson, "An Analysis of the Office Manager's Role in Selected Automated Offices, with Implications for Collegiate Office Management Curricula," (Doctoral dissertation, University of Iowa, 1965). For another study whose purpose was to determine the requirements for the position of administrative manager and how the prospective manager should best prepare himself to assume this position, see Harold T. Smith and S. ElVon Warner, "Administrative Office Management Preparation," (Provo, Utah: Brigham Young University, College of Business, 1971).

[5] U.S. Department of Commerce, Bureau of the Census, *Statistical Abstract of the United States: 1969* (90th ed.; Washington: U.S. Government Printing Office, 1969).

explosion," and "paper-work jungle" are used to describe the changed conditions resulting from new machines and new systems. New machines, such as computers, microform devices, copiers, and data communication links, have made it possible to generate, process, and transport data in tremendous volume at great speeds. Such new machines and their related equipment have called for new systems and new personnel with more modern training to manage them.

A new breed of management specialist, the information manager, and a new information function are slowly emerging in many large companies. In addition to having expertise in managing administrative services, the information manager (sometimes called a Vice President of Information) must have some of the training and experience required of a systems analyst, a records management specialist, a data processing manager, and a communication specialist. To fill such a position calls for technical familiarity with machine systems and concepts, conceptual skills for visualizing better ways to manage, and supervisory skills for handling the combined technicians and clerical staff making up the information team. Such a management position requires broad experience and education to understand and manage the information-handling function in the business. Typical responsibilities of such a specialist include these special information activities in addition to those commonly assigned to any manager:

Activity	*Examples*
Collection and classification of data	Source data recorders
Processing (conversion of the data)	Calculating, typing
Data storage and retrieval	Microfilm, filing
Data communication (transportation)	Data-phones, letters
Control (monitoring the system)	Systems analysis, forms control

All of these activities and examples will be discussed in remaining chapters of this book. All of them, too, are directly connected with the information function regardless of the department involved.

The administrative office manager has always been a manager of facts and information, an informing manager. He has had the responsibility for developing and maintaining good systems, efficient personnel, and reliable equipment for his own department. With the advent of the new information technology of equipment, programming, and systems, his sphere of responsibility has extended companywide; for it can be said that information is information wherever it is found. A new total systems concept has developed, linking together all information functions of the firm into a company-wide information network. Such a network is illustrated in Figure 1-8 in which the coordinating function (the information center) represents the

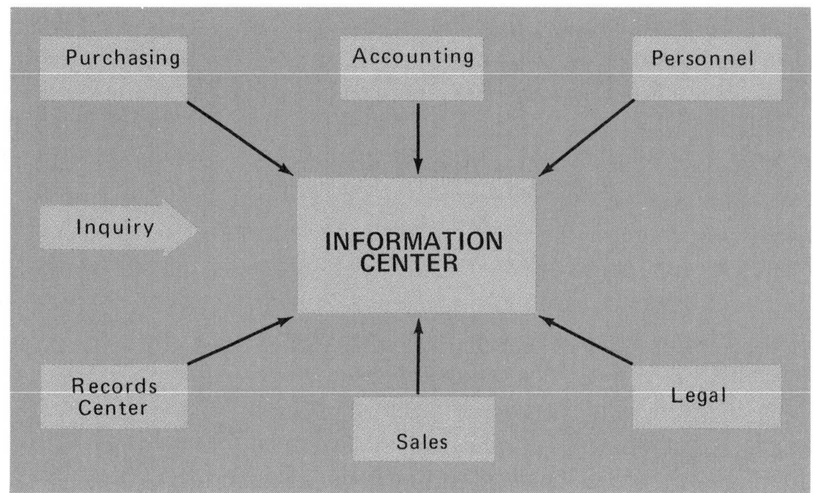

Fig. 1-8

A Company-Wide Information Network [6]

central intelligence center or data base for the organization. A network of this type can theoretically provide a single point of inquiry for access to all records and information anywhere in the company. It links together information sources on customers, sources of supply, and product information as well as market and financial information. Such information is ingested from the external environment as well as transmitted within the internal environment. At the present time this information function is being organized into a central information system by many large firms as well as governmental agencies. Since such a system is complex, involving many new positions, much new equipment, and reorganization in most cases, it is normally planned in stages to cover several years.

Traditionally the office has been considered as a place where facts and figures were collected, processed, and filed—usually on paper. As such it was considered a clerical record-keeping activity and storage location. This view is now being replaced by a more accurate

---

[6] Robert A. Shiff, "Information—Not Just Pieces of Paper," *Information and Records Management* (October-November, 1966), p. 21.

view of the office—as a function for managing information. In many respects, therefore, the office management function is synonymous with the information management function.

THE CHANGING OFFICE EMPLOYMENT SCENE

Since the meaning of the office function is rapidly expanding to include all information-processing activities in a firm, it can be expected that many new jobs will be added to the job titles usually found in the office. For example, increased use of the computer and its related equipment has created many new positions all of which are office positions. In its annual survey of salaries, the Administrative Management Society now includes both clerical and data processing job titles below the rank of administrative manager: [7]

Mail Clerk—File Clerk
General Clerk B
General Clerk A
Accounting Clerk B
Accounting Clerk A
Bookkeeping Machine Operator
Offset Duplicating Machine Operator
Telephone Switchboard Operator
Typist-Clerk

Stenographer
Secretary B
Secretary A
Key-punch Operator B
Key-punch Operator A
Tabulating Machine Operator
Computer Operator B
Computer Operator A
Programmer A
Systems Analyst

It is a foregone conclusion that in the future business information will be generated and processed to an even greater extent than ever before. Therefore, the information processors in our society, whether they have a clerical title such as typist-clerk or a data processing title such as programmer, will continue to grow in number and importance.

Composition of the Labor Force

Projections by the editorial staff of *Administrative Management* indicate that by 1980 the population of the United States will be 235 million.[8] It is further expected that the labor force will climb from 86 million in 1970 to 100 million in 1980 with the white-collar

---

[7] *Office Salaries, 1971-1972* (Willow Grove, Pennsylvania: Administrative Management Society, 1971).

[8] *Administrative Management* (January, 1969), p. 23.

work force constituting more than 50 percent of all workers. In 1971 white-collar personnel comprised 47.2 percent of the total labor force.[9] Many employees in 1980 will be working on machines and systems yet to be produced and will be relying on skills not yet developed. A large part of this projected increase will consist of younger workers and adult women. Since part-time work is prevalent among these groups, it is anticipated that the number of part-time workers will increase substantially. Employers will be provided with a flexible manpower supply, but jobs on a part-time basis will have to be rescheduled if the supply of workers is to be used effectively.

During the post-World War II period there has been a much greater growth in the number of white-collar occupations as compared with manual workers. An especially large increase has been noted in the number and proportion of professional and high-level managerial workers. In 1964 managers, officials, and proprietors numbered about 7.5 million, which represented an increase of more than one fourth since 1947.[10] It is estimated that the need for managers and other salaried officials, such as buyers, department store heads, and purchasing agents, is likely to continue increasing fairly rapidly in business organizations and government.

During this same period since World War II, the employment of clerical workers, such as typists, stenographers, secretaries, and clerks, has grown considerably—from 6.9 million to 10.7 million in 1964. Between 1964 and 1975 predictions indicate that the number of clerical workers needed will grow by about one third, a rate of increase that is greater than that for employment as a whole.

Educational Requirements

As a result of the changing occupational structure of the work force and the differing rate of growth among industries, the demand for workers with specific occupational skills and educational attainment will be significantly affected. Clearly there will be a rising demand for workers with a high level of education and training, while there will be a lessening of opportunities for the less skilled and less educated. The entire data processing field will offer great opportunity although clerical positions will remain firm.

---

[9] Lewis E. Lachter, "1971: Year of the 'Administrative Profit,'" *Administrative Management* (January, 1971), p. 18.

[10] Howard Stambler, "Manpower Needs in 1975," *Monthly Labor Review* (April, 1965), p. 380.

Because of the tremendous increase in college enrollments projected over the next decade or so, it is expected that the number of workers with a college degree may approximate the employment requirements for personnel with this level of training. Studies indicate that those whose highest level of educational attainment is high school graduation may also be adequate to meet the demands for workers with this amount of education.[11] Possibly enough new workers with a high school education will be available to permit employers to upgrade the requirements for many positions now being filled by persons with less than a high school education. Congressional acts, such as the Vocational Education Act of 1963 providing for a tremendous increase in vocational and technical training, will have a significant impact on the skill level of the work force.

The implications of these projections are that workers must obtain an adequate preparation for their work either by completing high school or college or through apprenticeship or other vocational training in order to find satisfactory and rewarding jobs. Further implications resulting from the increasing incidence of automated data processing installations are discussed in the following chapter.

QUESTIONS FOR REVIEW

1. Why is the administrative office manager an informing manager?
2. What are the six "m's" that must be organized and coordinated through the management process in order to ensure business success?
3. How may administrative office management be defined?
4. List the steps in the scientific method of solving problems. How is the scientific method related to administrative office management?
5. What are the five principles of effective work? How do these apply to the office? Which principle do you consider the most important?
6. What is the value of Theory Y to an administrative office manager?
7. How does an administrative office manager hold the key to decision making?
8. What is meant by the statement that no two office managers have the same job responsibilities?
9. How does the size of business organization affect the nature and number of responsibilities assigned the administrative office manager?
10. What are the projected trends for the (a) total labor force, (b) employment of office workers, and (c) educational requirements for workers? What are the implications of these trends?

---

[11] *Ibid.*

QUESTIONS FOR DISCUSSION

1. Offices are often classified in terms of the following sizes: (a) small, 1 to 25 employees; (b) medium, 100 to 500 employees; and (c) large, 500 or more employees. What personal qualifications, formal education, and experience should be considered when employing an administrative office manager for each of these office sizes?
2. Two schools of thought prevail in administrative management circles today: the behavioral or human relations school and the automated data processing school. If you were managing a modern office, which philosophy do you think should prevail? Why?
3. A well-known management professor has stated that today the office is a function and that it is meaningless to speak of the office as a physical place since there are many so-called offices in a firm. From your experiences with a large organization in your community, indicate some of the "offices." What basic factors do all these "offices" have in common?
4. A supervisor of office workers in an insurance company was asked to describe the requisite characteristics of a good executive. In his answer he indicated, among other things, that such an executive must be a self-starter, a highly motivated individual with the ability to see what is needed and the capacity to lay plans and then to follow through. If the right man is in the job, he will take his orders from the situation. Do these statements apply equally well to all office executives, including the administrative office manager? If the right office manager is in the job, how is he able to take his orders from the situation?
5. Women comprise the major portion of office workers, but at the managerial levels they are often discriminated against because of their sex. In fact, some women supervisors feel they must be twice as good as a rival male in order to obtain an administrative office management position. Do you agree with this opinion? What accounts for the fact that women aspiring to managerial positions must overcome what appear to be insurmountable obstacles?

PRACTICAL OFFICE CASES

Case 1-1 Reorganizing the Information Function

The California Savings and Loan Association was founded 35 years ago in Beverly Hills. Since that time it has grown in size to include 25 branch offices in each of the principal Los Angeles suburbs. The principal function of the Association is to serve as a banking facility for California residents. Presently it has demand deposits of $105 million on hand and approximately $87.5 million on loan.

To handle the growing volume of paper work accompanying the savings and loan functions, the main office employs the personnel shown in Figure A.

Fig. A

President's Office:	President Administrative Assistant Secretary
Vice Presidents' Offices:	Vice President (Savings) and Secretary Vice President (Loans) and Secretary Vice President (Trusts) and Secretary
General Office Personnel:	1 branch office coordinator 10 tellers 12 bookkeepers 8 accountants 14 clerk-typists 3 file clerks
Data Processing Department:	Manager, Data Processing Services 5 junior programmers 3 senior programmers 3 systems analysts 8 machine operators (key punch, tab machines)

Main Office Personnel

Each of the branch offices is organized in an identical fashion with these personnel: an office manager who also serves as the branch loan manager, an assistant loan officer, a secretary, and two tellers. All systems and procedures, forms, and reports are developed centrally in the main office although equipment and supplies are usually purchased from local office supplies stores in the immediate area of the branch office. No standard practices have been developed for the purchase of equipment, for the hiring or work performance of employees, or for office services, such as duplicating, transcribing, calculating, and correspondence.

The Savings and Loan vice presidents, as chief operating officers of the Association, have recently become aware of the great diversity of operating practices in the branch offices. After personal visits to each of these offices and a conference with the manager of data processing and the branch office coordinator, it became obvious that each of the information-handling activities lacked coordination and was in need of thorough study both from the standpoint of the branch offices and the Association.

Accordingly, J. B. Kingsley, the president, was advised to authorize such a study. From his office came the memorandum, shown in Figure B, addressed to the vice president (Savings), the senior officer under the president.

To: Mr. Baker
From: J. B. Kingsley Date September 17, 197-

It has come to my attention that the future success of our organization may well be hampered by the present status of our administrative office management setup. I believe, therefore, that a company-wide study should be initiated immediately in which all aspects of the information function be examined in depth.

You are hereby authorized to proceed as follows:

1. Select in-house or outside consulting help in order to provide an intensive review of our information activities.

2. Be alert and imaginative so that a total systems or unified organization will result.

3. Since the data processing installation (an IBM large-scale computer) is of recent origin, assume it is functioning satisfactorily and has the capability to handle our present and future needs. However, consult the data processing manager freely as a resource person.

Send me your recommendations as soon as possible.

Fig. B

Authorization Memorandum

■ Prepare a report for the president which contains your recommendations. The report should give attention to the following:

1. Define the information function for the firm.
2. What personnel would be required to handle a full-scale systems study of the paper-work and information functions? Elaborate.
3. What organizational and personnel changes would you recommend? Why?
4. Identify each of the key information-processing activities and show how each should be organized.
5. Clearly show your recommendations relative to both the main office operation and the branch office operation.

Case 1-2 Selecting an Office Manager

The Brooks Manufacturing Company, located in Los Angeles, California, owns a combined factory and office building. The fourth floor of the building, soundproof and air-conditioned, is used for the administrative and operating offices. Exclusive of top management, the firm has an office manager in charge of the office employees. All the accounting, credit, and personnel work and office services are handled in one large general office. The present office force is shown in Table A.

OFFICE PERSONNEL

Table A

Nature of Office Work	Men	Women	Age Group (Years)
Accounting Department	2		30 to 40
Accounting Department	6		24 to 30
Credit Department	1		30 to 40
Personnel Department	1		30 to 40
Personnel Department		2	20 to 30
Office Services	4		24 to 30
Office Services	2		30 to 40
Office Services		6	40 to 50
Office Services		10	30 to 40
Office Services		30	20 to 30

B. Ernst, the present office manager, is 58 years old. He has been with the firm for 30 years but has to retire within the next 30 days because of ill health. Although it is the policy of the company to promote from within whenever vacancies occur, in this instance the president of the company has decided to select someone from outside the organization to rejuvenate and bring the office systems and procedures up-to-date. The president feels that with the long period of service of the present office manager the office work has gotten into a "rut."

The starting salary of the new office manager will be $10,000. Ernst has been receiving an annual salary of $11,500. It is expected that the new office manager will be able to increase his salary beyond $11,500 within three years.

The applicants for the position have been narrowed down to three candidates, whose qualifications are listed in Table B.

QUALIFICATIONS OF CANDIDATES FOR OFFICE MANAGEMENT POSITION

Table B

Qualification	Candidate A (Male)	Candidate B (Female)	Candidate C (Male)
Age and marital status	28 years, married	35 years, single	40 years, single
Appearance	Good, but a little flashy	Executive type of personality	Excellent
Education	College graduate, major in accounting, minor in retailing and selling	One year of business college, and two years at university evening school (secretarial science, credit management, and personnel management)	Junior college associate certificate; three years in evening division of nearby university (accounting, office management, and economics)
Experience	**Junior accountant,** 1 year **Head bookkeeper,** small retail store, 1 year **Office manager,** textile office—10 employees, 2 years **Employment agency,** owner and manager, 1 year to present	**Stenographer** and **private secretary** to credit manager, 10 years **Credit manager,** 6 years to present	**Quartermaster,** U. S. Navy, 4 years **Bookkeeper,** small metal manufacturer, 4 years **Job placement** and **interviewer,** state unemployment office, 4 years **Office manager,** soft-drink distributor—10 employees, 10 years to present
Present annual salary	$8,500	$9,000	$8,200
Professional interests	Administrative Management Society and American Society for Personnel Administration	None	Data Processing Management Association
Reason for desiring a change	Greater stability and opportunity for advancement	Well satisfied with present position, but is "shopping around"	Lack of opportunity for advancement and personality conflict with his superiors

■ As advisor to the president, answer the following:

1. Which one of these candidates do you recommend that the president employ? Why?
2. For what reasons have you rejected the two other candidates?

2

Automation in the Modern Office

Since 1900, office practices have gone through several phases or cycles due to the growth in the size of business enterprises and the resulting increased volume of office work, the increased cost of services and materials, and the rapid technological and scientific progress of the modern age. Early in this period most of the office work was performed manually. A fine Spencerian handwriting was an important qualification for an office position. But manual office work was exceedingly slow and was soon to be supplemented by machines.

The invention of the typewriter and its use in the office were almost revolutionary in their effects upon business. Work could be done more quickly, more legibly, more accurately, and more economically. But the expansion of business activities demanded more office workers; hence, women were employed. The invention of the typewriter was followed by adding and calculating machines, cash registers, and bookkeeping machines. Because most office work was not directly income producing, great effort was made to increase the volume of work done by each employee. The simultaneous preparation of several forms or records with the use of mechanical equipment was one step in this direction. But the use of new office machines and methods also generated new business activities and new job opportunities. Improving the methods of business communication by expanding the uses of the telephone and telegraph opened up an entirely new set of business firms employing thousands of workers in jobs that never existed before the improvements and changes in these inventions.

Several wars stimulated the discovery of new products and methods and also increased governmental control over business through taxation and regulatory agencies. This phase of our everyday life, which has been affected increasingly by income taxes, social security laws, unemployment compensation laws, etc., has demanded of business many forms and reports not heretofore present. In addition to the record-keeping demands imposed by the federal government are those that continue to come forth from state and local governments. Thus, a heavier work load has been placed upon business offices without contributing to the firm's profit objective. Faster and more efficient methods and equipment had to be discovered so that more office work could be done without increasing the labor costs. The development of punched-card processing represented an almost unbelievable method of performing tremendous volumes of accounting and statistical work. The ensuing change in office systems and forms was an attempt to increase output without increasing the number of office workers.

Today the businessman is again faced with finding even better methods of doing a larger volume of office work at the same or less cost than before. The principles of automation, which have been applied in factory work and large-scale production, are now being effectively adapted to office work. In this chapter the nature of office automation is discussed, and its impact on business management is analyzed.

THE NATURE OF AUTOMATION IN THE OFFICE

Automation has been defined as "the entire field of investigation, design, development, application, and methods of rendering or making processes or machines self-acting or self-moving." [1] In the office automation refers to those self-regulating processes in which

---

[1] Martin H. Weik, "A Second Survey of Domestic Electronic Digital Computing Systems," *Ballistic Research Laboratory Report No. 1010, Ordnance Research and Development Project No. TB3-0007* (Maryland: Aberdeen Proving Grounds, 1957), p. 417.

work is completed with a minimum of human effort. Automation as a systematic philosophy takes form in the modern office through the techniques of automated data processing.

Automated data processing (*ADP*) can be looked upon as a self-regulating process in which information is handled with a minimum of human effort and intervention. In an automated data processing system, data are recorded in such a form that further use can be made of the data without need for any subsequent manual recording. Automated data processing is not truly automatic, however, for it demands outside direction and frequent interruption of the processes. Man is still the directing force; but once the step-by-step instructions have been carefully constructed, or *programmed,* the machines can do the work more quickly, more economically, and more accurately than manual methods. The punched-card system and the electronic computer system of automated data processing are briefly discussed in the following paragraphs. These systems are discussed in detail in Part V, Business Information Processing Systems.

The Punched-Card System of Processing Data

The *punched-card* or *unit record system* of processing data is based upon a code, or machine language, developed in the 1880's by Herman Hollerith and James Powers, two statisticians working for the Census Bureau. The Hollerith code, in which the data are represented by rectangular holes punched in cards, is reflected in products of the International Business Machines Corporation (IBM). The Powers code, making use of round punched holes, was formerly used with products of the Univac Division of Sperry Rand Corporation. Equipment now made by Univac uses the standard punched card with rectangular holes.

In the punched-card data processing system alphabetic and numeric data contained in typewritten or handwritten form on original source documents are known as *input,* and the punched cards upon which the data have been recorded are called *input media.* By means of sensing devices, machines can read and process electrically the data represented by the punched holes. The punched-card machines can be used to sort, collate, reproduce, and print the data as desired and to perform all types of arithmetic calculations. The processed data become the *output,* and the business forms upon which the processed data appear, such as summaries, tabulations, and reports, are called *output media.*

The Electronic Computer System of Processing Data

The most recent adaptation in the expanding field of data processing is in *electronic data processing (EDP)* through the use of electronic computers. The computer is simply an electronic machine that stores, calculates, and retrieves data with incredible speed, a speed that makes it superhuman. Electronic data processing refers to the use of electrical impulses, traveling at the speed of light, which record, compute, and transmit alphabetic and numeric data. Both the data to be processed and the instructions to process the data are stored in the memory cells of the computer.

The first completely electronic computer was developed in 1946 by John Mauchley and J. P. Eckert of the University of Pennsylvania. In this computer, vacuum tubes replaced the gears, wheels, and electric relays of earlier models. Although there are many brands and models of equipment, varying in design, construction, and capability, all aim toward the same objective—to handle information more quickly, more accurately, and more economically.

Like the punched-card system the electronic computer system depends upon a code, or a machine language. Alphabetic and numeric data appearing on source documents in typewritten or handwritten form must be recorded in code form on punched cards, paper tape, magnetic tape, or some other input medium. The coded data along with instructions for their processing are "fed" into the computer where they are stored in the form of electrical impulses. Computations are performed, comparisons are made, and summaries are prepared according to the instructions. Processed data are then written out of the computer in the form of punched cards, punched paper tape, magnetic tape, or printed business documents and reports.

PLANNING FOR AUTOMATED OFFICE OPERATIONS

By 1972 over 90,000 electronic computers were in use by business firms representing every major industry. Computers have proved very popular with banks and insurance companies whose routine operations are readily adaptable to programming. Computers are being used for accounting operations, inventory control, and the planning and control of production. According to a recent report in *Administrative Management*, developments in computer usage among the 500 leading companies in the United States indicate these trends:

1. Elevating the data-processing managers to the vice-presidential level, selecting them for their business judgment first and their computer knowledge second.
2. Expanding the accounting-type applications to many additional areas, such as project control, time reporting of manpower, and computer costing systems.
3. Extending the use of the computer beyond the handling of accounting problems to areas such as management control, selection of vendors, and simulation of a business environment to aid in decision making.[2]

Small companies, too, are reaping the benefits of electronic data processing. There are three alternatives open to these small companies: (1) they may utilize the services of a commercial data processing service bureau; (2) they may rent time on a large firm's computer during its idle hours; or (3) a rapidly expanding firm may choose to rent the new small-scale "mini-computer," such as IBM's System/3. Rent for the mini-computer ranges from $200 to $1,500 a month, depending on the complexity of the machine; a computer of this size may be purchased at figures ranging from $5,000 to $100,000. The mini-computer would be used to perform tasks that are too complex for the calculator and too simple for the large computer.

The Feasibility of Installing a Computer

A *feasibility study* is undertaken to determine whether specific office operations can be improved and if the installation of a computer is economically justified in order to bring about these improvements. The two basic questions to be answered in a feasibility study are: (1) Is a computer necessary? and (2) If so, which one is best?

Compiling all the data on present and proposed systems and methods, meeting with committees and subcommittees, working with the representatives of several computer manufacturers and studying their proposals, preparing all the specifications for the computer installation, and orienting employees to the new roles they will play may conservatively require two years or more. All of these activities are time-consuming and costly, especially for those, such as the office

---

[2] Frederik H. Lutter, "EDP Perspective: Danger or Opportunity," *Administrative Management* (January, 1970), p. 16.

manager, who are directly involved in the feasibility study. Often, however, the office manager will find that the investment in the computer study returns a dividend whether or not it is decided to install the computer. Some firms find that, as they commence to analyze their existing paper-work operations and then determine the costs of the labor and equipment presently used, procedural improvements are originated that more than pay for the computer study itself.

Guidelines for a Feasibility Study

Generally the installation of a computer is technically and economically feasible when office operations meet the following conditions:

1. Greater speed and accuracy are required in processing data and in preparing management reports.
2. Complexities of present data processing systems and procedures cannot be simplified without electronic assistance. The Research Institute of America suggests that if a company is spending as much as $500 a month to rent office machines or if the present office machine system is working at or near capacity, the firm might operate more economically with a small computer system.[3]
3. Investment in computer equipment is substantially offset by both quantitative and qualitative benefits. Offsetting factors include better customer service, lower costs to consumer, and improved control over internal operations, such as keeping inventory at desired levels.

To determine whether the office operations meet the requirements above and whether a computer installation represents the best solution to a company's data processing problems, the office manager or the person in charge of planning the feasibility study needs certain guidelines, such as those listed below:

1. *Select a qualified person to undertake the feasibility study.* Does the person have a thorough knowledge of company policies, accounting systems, and records retention? Does he possess the ability and interest to work with endless details and the persistence to see the job through? Has he the ability to organize, direct, and supervise others? Has he the ability

---

[3] John Medlin, "Small Computers—Stepping Stones to Large-Scale EDP," *Administrative Management* (March, 1968), p. 73.

to visualize the requirements of the installation and does he understand what costs are involved in operating the system?

2. *Assign the person initial responsibility for the feasibility study and provide him with adequate authority to complete the job.* Is he able to select, within reason, the resources needed to complete the study? Does he possess sufficient authority to perform his duties without being hampered by company policies or secondary responsibilities?
3. *Obtain the full cooperation of top management.* Is top management backing the feasibility study from the beginning so that the project is not doomed to failure before it starts? Does top management understand that the company organization may possibly have to undergo major changes, such as the elimination of a major unit, before the system can attain its full potential?
4. *Obtain the full cooperation of middle management and operating personnel.* Have the appropriate employees been assigned full-time responsibilities for certain phases of the study? Are personnel at the operating level involved in the initiation and planning of the computer project so that their support is obtained in carrying out the installation?
5. *Evaluate the need for outside help.* If there are no systems personnel in the company, is advice being solicited from the computer manufacturers' staffs or from private consultants?
6. *Determine the benefits to be realized from a computer system.* To what extent will clerical costs be reduced? Will the system accumulate data quickly and accurately enough to provide management with an up-to-date picture of internal operations at any time? Will the processing of payroll and other personnel data be completed more efficiently, accurately, and economically? Will the system provide for closer control over inventory as the result of being better able to estimate future needs? Will customers be provided better service as the result of a speedup in processing their orders?
7. *Consider all relevant factors in each computer proposal before making the final decision.* Does this computer offer the greatest anticipated return in clerical savings? What are the manpower requirements? How do the overall installation and operating costs, quality and speed of maintenance, and reputation of the manufacturer compare? Is the system compatible with existing systems? Can the system be expanded by adding on peripheral equipment as the company's needs change? Is it more economical to lease or to purchase the equipment? [4]

---

[4] See Chapter 5 for a complete discussion of renting or buying data processing equipment.

Insuring the Success of Automated Operations

After the feasibility study has been completed, the computer proposal approved and accepted, and the tentative installation date obtained from the computer manufacturer, much additional planning is needed to insure the success of the installation. The necessary tools for planning and controlling each long-range computer project must be provided so that management can determine how much is being spent on computer efforts and whether a particular application has been successful. Application of the computer to each project should be analyzed from the standpoint of costs and expected results. The estimated costs of each project must be provided for in the budget so that, when necessary, the actual costs and the progress to date can be compared with the planned costs and progress. With the high-speed processing and output of the computer, there lurks the potential danger that huge quantities of meaningless data may be generated with the result that management becomes flooded with too many facts. Therefore, adequate control systems, designed with the goals and values of the firm in mind, must be established so that irrelevant and unproductive activities do not creep into the computer operations.

All major changes in work flow, areas of responsibility, and manpower requirements must be planned well in advance in order to minimize the adverse effects upon the employees affected. As part of the changeover to computer operations, some of the jobs will be performed at isolated machine stations where the noise level is high and where constant attention to speed and accuracy is required for repetitive work. A "man to machine" relationship comes to be substituted for the "person to person" relationship to which employees had been accustomed. Since any change in the work environment gives rise to upset and restiveness among employees, the office manager should keep abreast of all proposed changes so that he can anticipate their effect upon employee attitudes. As part of the feasibility study, it was stressed that the full cooperation of the operating personnel should be obtained at the very beginning of the computer study. By serving on committees involved in studying the effect of changes upon present systems and procedures, supervisors and key workers come to realize that they are involved in the decisions being made. As a result, they can accomplish a great deal in working with their subordinates by "selling" a successful future for automated operations.

Following the announcement of the decision to install a computer, one of the most marked changes in employee attitudes comes about—the fear of a mass layoff. To deal with this fear, the administrative manager should utilize all available media—house organs, bulletin boards, departmental conferences, and personnel meetings—to inform the workers of the planned changes several months before the installation date. These measures have proved to be very effective in maintaining employee morale and displaying to the workers that management is interested in their welfare.

THE EFFECTS OF AUTOMATION IN THE OFFICE

With the ever growing number of automated data processing installations in business offices, management must give consideration to the effects of automation upon the office jobs, the education and training of office workers, the middle management, and the company operations. In its long-range planning, management must be aware of the human consequences of automation as well as the economic consequences. In purely economic terms automation will be successful and will work most effectively, according to former Secretary of Labor Wirtz, if "we take care of the human implications and the human concerns which automation creates." [5]

Effects upon Office Jobs

Society has been characterized by a certain amount of unemployment as the result of every major technological advance since the Industrial Revolution. Many of the jobs that man had been accustomed to performing fell by the wayside as the result of technological advances. In each instance, however, society adjusted itself and moved forward. Just as a new technology removed many jobs, it also expanded the level and variety of human wants. Most experts agree that automation abolished some types of blue-collar jobs, but the number of these jobs is unknown. There seems to be little evidence of job loss among white-collar workers, however. For the past 20 years office jobs have been growing at a faster rate than other types of employment. During the next 10 to 15 years it is estimated that "the employment of clerical workers will show a relatively large increase mainly because of the mounting volume of communications, record keeping, and other paper work which is likely to more than offset the laborsaving effects of electronic computers and other new office equipment." [6] Further estimates indicate that

---

[5] *Modern Office Procedures* (April, 1965), p. 16.
[6] *Ibid.*

by 1980 the white-collar work force will constitute more than 50 percent of the total work force as compared with a 47.2 percent share of the total work force in 1971.[7]

In many industries the installation of computers is rushing ahead at full speed, and in a dynamic economy it is difficult—if not impossible—to measure the sociological aspects of the changing employment picture. One group of experts states that, as the result of advances in automation, some 35,000 workers lose or change their jobs each week [8] and that some 250,000 "entry jobs" usually open to teen-agers are disappearing each year as the result of technological change.[9] Another group of experts has found that those industries which have automated the most have also expanded the most in employment. In one analysis of labor-efficient and labor-inefficient industries, it was found that the industries which invested the most money in plant and equipment in order to increase productivity enjoyed a 146 percent increase in pretax profits and a 51 percent increase in employment. This study also showed that those industries which invested the least money in plant and equipment and were the least labor-efficient sustained a 6 percent loss in pretax profits and a 7 percent decrease in employment.[10] A Bureau of Labor Statistics study shows that, even with the introduction of numerous laborsaving devices into the banking procedures, the number of banking employees in the past ten years has increased nearly three times as fast as employment in all nonagricultural industries combined.[11] The study concludes by predicting that, although banking will probably have a slower rate of growth in the future because of electronic data processing, some 400,000 new jobs will be created in the next 10 to 15 years as the volume of bank business grows. This same prediction holds true today.

For some industries the installation of computers has hardly affected the total unemployment picture; on the contrary, new skills have been required. In many companies the rate of turnover among

---

[7] Lewis E. Lachter, "1971: Year of the 'Administrative Profit,'" *Administrative Management* (January, 1971), p. 18.

[8] *Time* (April 2, 1965), p. 87.

[9] Stated by Eli E. Cohen, Executive Secretary of the National Committee on Employment of Youth, in "What Hit the Teen-agers," *Fortune* (April, 1965), p. 130.

[10] *The New York Times*, March 14, 1965, p. 55. (The report of a statement made by Dr. Louis T. Rader, Vice President and General Manager of General Electric Company's Industrial Electronics Division.)

[11] *Management Review* (November, 1963), pp. 33-34. This survey was reprinted by *Management Review* from *Dun's Review and Modern Industry* (September, 1963).

office employees continues to be high, with the result that proposed reductions in manpower requirements are compensated for by normal attrition. As noted before, many companies that are automating their office operations are also expanding rapidly their investments in plant and equipment. As a result many of the employees that have been released from routine, repetitive jobs are retrained and reassigned to other tasks or to other departments. Since the process of installing a computer may extend over two or more years, the replacement of office workers is usually spread over a period of time.

In an economic and statistical analysis conducted by *Fortune* magazine,[12] it was emphatically concluded that automation has made substantially less headway in the United States economy than the literature on the subject would suggest. Not denying that technology does change and does displace a substantial number of workers, it was noted that ten years after computers have come into common use no fully automated process exists for any major project in any industry in the United States. It was also pointed out that there is no prospect for such a fully automated process in the immediate future. This same statement clearly applies today.

When a firm converts to computer-controlled operations, there has not been so much an overall loss of jobs as a change in the nature of the jobs performed. As computers take over the repetitive clerical jobs, there is a demand for more highly skilled employees who can translate the vast amount of computer-produced data into useful information for management. The new jobs being created may cause a widespread dislocation among white-collar workers, however, and some labor economists feel that in the future reassignment may be as much a part of the office worker's life as periodic layoffs are of the factory worker's.

A recent study by the Administrative Management Society concluded that existing personnel are retrained and retained when a computer is installed. Generally no net reduction occurred in the work forces of the smaller companies; large companies did reduce their staffs on the average of 10-20 persons, while at the same time effecting a net increase in employment with new personnel as shown in Table 2-1.[13]

The divergent points of view and the differing statistics pertaining to the effects of automation upon office employment point up the

---

[12] Charles E. Silberman, "The Real News about Automation," *Fortune* (January, 1965), p. 125.

[13] "EDP Reduces Staff by 20 Persons: Survey," *Administrative Management* (January, 1970), p. 48.

NEW PERSONNEL REQUIRED BY COMPUTER INSTALLATION

Personnel	Net Increase	
	Large Firms	Small Firms
Programmers/Analysts	8 to 11	1 to 2
Key-punch Operators	7 to 9	1 to 4
Machine Operators	5 to 7	1
Supervisory Personnel	4 to 6	1
Library/Records Personnel	None	None

Table 2-1

impossibility of obtaining a complete and meaningful count of people immediately out of work as the direct result of automating office operations. The employment level prior to the automating of office operations cannot be used as a base for comparison, for this would require one to assume that in the meantime other unrelated factors had not affected employment. During the past several years, the total number of white-collar jobs has not been reduced as the result of automation, but the percentage of increase in such jobs has fallen. For example, in 1963 white-collar employment showed an increase of about one percent over the preceding year. However, this percentage of increase was much below the 2.6 percent rate of 1962 and the 2.8 percent rate of growth in the decade of the fifties.[14]

A recent study of 15 life insurance companies was conducted to determine employment changes at various job levels as a result of automation. Since computer-induced changes in employment are often hidden by changes in other factors (such as economic conditions, competition, and changing conditions that occur during the installation of the computer itself), these firms were asked to estimate the levels of employment that would be necessary to perform the current amount of work if these firms did not have the benefit of the computer. These companies believed that without the computer they would need (1) 60% more clerical personnel, (2) 9% more supervisory personnel, and (3) 2% more managerial personnel. This survey indicates that present levels of information-processing activity have been achieved with a decline in the number of human "inputs." Put in other words, while there may not be (and probably is not) a reduced number of office employees, more work is now

---

[14] Walter A. Kleinschrod, "Crossfire on Middle Management," *Administrative Management* (September, 1964), p. 30.

being done with electronic machines than ever before.[15] Even these statistics do not enable one to make any firm statements about how technology will alter the structure of office jobs. The large increase in the employment of clerical workers has been brought about not only because of technological change but also as the result of industries employing relatively large numbers of such workers (insurance, banking, transportation, communications) that have increased their output and share of the market much more rapidly than those industries employing relatively few workers.

Effects upon Education and Training of Office Workers

To meet the personnel needs of companies having or contemplating automated operations, there must be adequate liaison between school systems, industry, and government with respect to future job requirements. There is no way to measure with any degree of accuracy the net effect that automation will have upon the change in job requirements over the next decade. Undoubtedly automation will create new skilled jobs, alter the nature of others, and eliminate many unskilled jobs. For example, the job of key-punch operator is beginning to feel the effects of a definite trend. In the past few years key-punch operators have been in short supply, and as a result trade and vocational schools have emphasized key-punch training to meet the demand. Some experts now say that the need for key-punch operators will diminish, perhaps vanish, in the next ten years. This job, it is contended, will be replaced by source data automation such as optical character recognition machines that automatically read and feed written data into computer systems.

While this prediction may come true in a few years, much evidence exists to show that new forms of input other than the key punch are being used. A powerful new input medium utilizes a keyboard-to-magnetic-tape machine that bypasses the punched card, although the method of inputting data into the system is similar to the key-punch operation. Another replacement for key punching is the use of optical font sales registers and adding machines for entering numeric data. These machines make their entries on printed tapes in a series of stylized numbers and operating

15 Thomas L. Whisler, *Information Technology and Organization Change* (Belmont, California: Wadsworth Publishing Company, Inc., 1970), p. 38.

codes known as the National Optical Font (NOF), and the coded data can be read directly into computers through optical reading devices.[16] Other input devices (which in a sense will compete and tend to replace the key-punch operation) include couplers that move data by telephone to a central computer, point-of-sale recording of data in machinable form, as well as punched paper tape.

However, the key-punch machine still remains the principal method of coding and entering data into a computer system. In a survey of 500 managers across the country, it was found that employees work with punched cards in 87 percent of the companies. Other types of input-output media include magnetic tape in 47 percent of the firms and paper tape in 41 percent.[17] In another survey of 350 firms to determine how the use of computers had affected job categories, it was found that of all job categories that of key-punch operator had expanded the most (189), almost four times greater than the job of tabulating machine operator (49), the second job most affected by expansion. The survey also revealed that the job categories most often reduced were tabulating machine operator (197), payroll clerk (158), general clerk (155), and account clerk (120). The job categories most often replaced were bookkeeping machine operator (93), account clerk (35), and general clerk (34).[18]

The hierarchy of data processing positions is a common one with terms and duties known to many people. Figure 2-1 shows the most typical data processing positions. Of special concern in this group is the position of the programmer.

Presently more than 200,000 programmers and an equal number of systems analysts are required to meet the needs of electronic data processing installations. When computers were first introduced into offices, it was generally recognized that a qualified computer programmer should have at least a college degree. Many programmers, in fact, even held advanced degrees in such disciplines as engineering, mathematics, and business administration. However, with the continued progress in simplifying programming languages and techniques and with the ability to identify and measure the aptitude for programming work, many young men and women now enter the

---

[16] Malcolm K. Lee, "The Demise of the Keypunch," *Datamation* (March, 1968), pp. 51-52.

[17] "Manager's EDP Role: Select, Plan System," *Administrative Management* (January, 1968), p. 30.

[18] Edith H. Goodman, "Computer Use and Personnel Survey—1964," Part II, *Data Processing* (August, 1964), pp. 18-20.

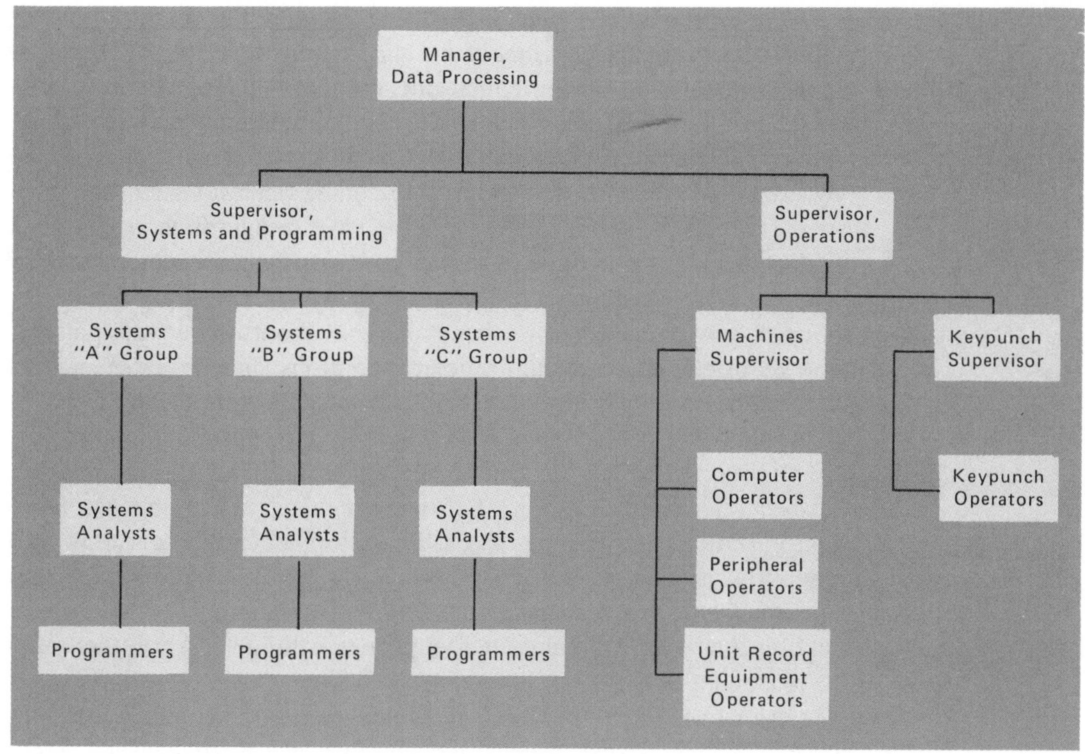

Fig. 2-1

Typical Data Processing Positions

programming field without a college education and achieve success on the job. As a rule, however, graduation from high school is the minimum educational requirement for data processing work.

The Department of Labor, in an occupational outlook study, predicts that as we look ahead to the creation of new jobs, three out of every ten new jobs will require persons trained in secretarial and stenographic skills.[19] During the past ten years the ratio of secretaries, stenographers, and typists to clerical workers as a whole has been rising and now represents about one fourth of this group. Many of these jobs will be upgraded somewhat as the result of new machines and equipment that make it possible to reduce the amount of time spent in routine clerical activities.

---

[19] "Education for Office Employment, A Program for Action," *Proceedings of a Problem-Solving Conference* held in Alexandria, Virginia (Willow Grove, Pennsylvania: Administrative Management Society, 1963).

Management has a role to play in presenting the current needs of office education at each level of the school system so that the goals of office education are well defined and related to the total educational program. For the great diversity of office occupations, training is needed at various educational levels. The office manager can aid by establishing clear-cut standards for office operations so that business teachers as well as personnel and training directors have a better picture of job classifications and job requirements that will help them in training students and employees more specifically for office employment. The changes that come about in the type, pattern, and requirements of certain office occupations should be reflected in the educational offerings of schools and in the training manuals of business firms. To accomplish this goal, there must be a continuous examination of office education subject matter and the methods of instruction. More and more the office manager is coming to realize that education and training are a life-long program. Training is continuously needed in basic skills such as English, arithmetic, and human relations—the ability to follow instructions, to respond to supervision, and to maintain the proper attitude toward the work to be done as well as to the employer.

Prior to the automating of office operations, the employees should be informed of management's plans and of the anticipated effect that automation will have on the number and types of jobs available in the company. For those workers presently employed who can be retrained to develop the new skills required, retraining programs should be provided. The person in charge of training may be helped by the computer manufacturer who in many cases will provide retraining programs on the company premises. Then, too, more and more public and private educational facilities are being expanded to include adult education retraining programs and upgrading programs for employees. Employees not possessing the necessary qualifications for retraining may be reassigned to other departments or aided in relocating elsewhere in the community.

Effects upon Middle Management

Middle management in one company may cover jobs far different from and at different levels than those in another company. For the purpose of this discussion, *middle management* is defined to include all managers below the highest level of policy making. Thus, in most business firms the administrative office manager and the production manager fall into the category of middle management.

As a result of the increasing utilization of computers, many writers now speculate that middle managers may be displaced—their jobs will be made easier, and as a result managerial personnel requirements will be restructured. At a world meeting of management leaders in Geneva in 1964, speakers told how computers were beginning to thin the ranks of office-based management, particularly middle management, as they have for years thinned the ranks of factory-based labor.[20] Interestingly, however, from the first part of 1961 to the third quarter of 1964 (three and one-half years) the employment of manufacturing production workers increased by one million. During the five years preceding 1961, there was a decrease of approximately 1.7 million production workers.[21] Thus, the speed with which machines are replacing blue-collar workers seems to be reversing itself and is presenting problems at this level as well as at the middle management level.

Since the advent of automation, many predictions have been made that middle management numbers will be severely reduced. In 1958, for example, Leavitt and Whisler postulated that the application of the computer would result in reductions in the middle management group.[22] Other writers often echoed their sentiments. Experience, however, has proven these predictions to be in error.

Since the early sixties, there has been a continuous demand for competent middle management personnel. With the growth of electronic data processing, there has developed an increased need for departmental managers to work with data processing personnel to make the types of operating decisions which involve advanced types of financial analysis, simulation, and improved information systems necessary to keep their organizations efficient.

A recent study confirms this new role of middle management. In this study Jackson surveyed 5 top executives and 20 middle managers in banking, chemical, steel, and oil industries. He found substantial evidence that the job content of the middle managers has expanded in scope and importance. In fact, 80 percent of the group stated that their job content increased, their decision-making capabilities expanded, and more decisions were required of them. At the same time, 75 percent indicated more time was spent with the planning function than ever before, due to the stress on long-term

---

[20] Kleinschrod, *op. cit.*, pp. 22-32.

[21] Silberman, *op. cit.*, p. 124.

[22] Thomas L. Whisler, *Information Technology and Organization Change* (Belmont, California: Wadsworth Publishing Company, Inc., 1970), p. 38.

planning and the need to make decisions with more foresight and on the basis of more up-to-date information.[23]

There are two major reasons why it is unlikely that middle management jobs will be dramatically decreased as the result of the computer. First, the managerial decisions made at this level involve far too many intangibles and too much abstract thinking to subject the problems to mechanical analyses. On the other hand, the manager is aided by the computer in making far more intelligent decisions. Much of the former uncertainty surrounding his job can be removed, and he will thus be better able to rely upon analyses than intuitive judgment. Many problems heretofore insolvable because of the time-consuming chore of dealing with a huge quantity of variable data can be converted into well-structured problems for the computer. In a matter of seconds or minutes, the manager is supplied with data that formerly may have required hours, months, or perhaps years for their calculation. Rather than reduce the degree of judgment required of middle managers, the increased emphasis upon programming of computer operations should result in a middle management position that is more highly structured. While some jobs requiring little skill and judgment may move down on the management ladder, other jobs requiring the compilation and interpretation of computer data will move upward. As a result there may be a tendency "to draw a line between top and middle management almost as rigid as today's line between hourly workers and first-line supervisors." [24]

Second, the availability of automatic equipment that can do a job more quickly than manual methods does not necessarily mean that the equipment will be automatically installed and used. If a company must spend perhaps $140,000 each year to cover the rental fee or the depreciation charges on a computer installation, the equipment should be able to accomplish, as a minimum, the work of seven $20,000-a-year managers. Automatic machines perform at their optimum level when performing routine, repetitive operations—tasks entirely unlike the unstructured problems facing managers. Thus, from the viewpoint of return on investment, the cost of applying computers to solving many managerial problems is prohibitive. The administrative manager must develop cost consciousness in the area of electronic data processing, for the absence of effective managerial

---

[23] Robert S. Jackson, "Computers and Middle Management," *Journal of Systems Management* (April, 1970), pp. 22-23.

[24] Auren Iris, "Middle Management and Technological Change," *Management Review* (October, 1963), pp. 55-58. This report was condensed in *Management Review* from *Chemical Engineering.*

direction over the EDP function has brought much waste and inefficiency into computer operations. A. T. Kearney & Company, management consultants, conducted a study of 89 companies and their 155 computer installations and found that: (1) only 48 percent of the available machine time is used productively, (2) computers are operated only 64 percent of the available time, (3) 25 percent of manned hours are wasted in idleness, reruns, machine maintenance, and down time, and (4) 42 percent of the companies surveyed do not maintain accurate records of computer performance.[25] Undoubtedly a great deal of the poor computer productivity, as evidenced in the findings above, is traceable to poor management practices. There is need for managers who deal with data processing functions to become intimately acquainted with EDP systems operations and for firms to consider the establishment of three shifts covering a 24-hour day as a means of maximizing productivity.

In an interview with 53 middle managers and 14 top managers in eight companies, it was confirmed that as a result of installing an electronic data processing system, (a) the job of the middle manager has become more complex, (b) the middle manager has a greatly increased volume of information to analyze in greater depth, (c) the middle manager is using more experience and judgment, and (d) electronic data processing has either added to his activities or has replaced some with more responsible functions.[26] When the findings of the interview are summarized by managerial function, these significant facts stand out:

1. *Planning:* 60 percent of the managers stated that they work longer on planning activities than they did before the electronic data processing system was installed.
2. *Organizing:* Practically no change was noted in the organization activities.
3. *Controlling:* About two thirds of the managers agreed that the computer had reduced the time required to spend on this function. More time was made available for other activities and previously neglected functions.

---

[25] "EDP Productivity at 50%? Three Shifts an Answer, Training Is Another," *Administrative Management* (June, 1971), pp. 66-67. Also see "Computers Make Management Efficient—But Who Makes Computers Efficient?" *Management News* (December, 1970), p. 7.

[26] Donald R. Shaul, "What's Really Ahead for Middle Management?" *Personnel* (November-December, 1964), pp. 8-16. All the managers in the companies surveyed, representing both manufacturing and service industries (aircraft, petroleum, governmental electronics work, radio and television, banking, life insurance, finance, and telephone), had at least two years' operating experience with their electronic data processing systems.

4. *Leading:* A high percentage of the managers have to spend more time on directing the work of their departments. A high-caliber manager is now required to fill the same positions, and additional time is needed to train people for the positions. There is an expansion in the number of contacts with subordinates, but contacts with the top echelon are no more frequent than before.

The results of the study above make it plain that the computer is a tool designed for use by the manager as an aid in the decision-making process. The computer is not the decision maker; it can accomplish only what it has been programmed to do. The successful use of the computer—like all management tools—will increase the need for and the importance of high-quality managers. To succeed as a middle manager in the future, however, the office manager will find it absolutely essential to have an understanding of the computer. According to Drucker, the computer will not eliminate middle managers but will force them to learn to make decisions and in turn will force corporations to develop managers who are trained and tested in making decisions that spell success or failure.[27]

Effects upon Company Operations

Automation is usually applied in two ways: (1) toward the processing of a product and (2) toward the processing of information necessary to produce the product. The core of automated operations—the computer—manipulates symbols, usually letters and numbers, and in this sense is largely an office machine. As a result, its use is of vital importance to the field of administrative office management. Since the advent of computers in business, several significant effects have been felt by business in general and by the office in particular.

Reorganization of Business. During the 1940's and 1950's many large firms expanded throughout the world, thus requiring them to decentralize operations. With the introduction of automation, however, companies such as General Electric and Westinghouse are recentralizing operations by using a central computerized information system at the home office to collect, process, and transmit

[27] Peter F. Drucker, "What Computers Will Be Telling You," *Management Review* (October, 1966), p. 32. This report was reprinted by *Management Review* from *Nation's Business* (August, 1966).

information throughout the world. Westinghouse with its Pittsburgh-based telecomputer center (merging the telephone system with the computer) is in continual communication with more than 300 locations, field offices, warehouses, and distributors, thus permitting rapid reporting and control over inventory, order processing, marketing, sales, and production activities. Accounting functions, too, are greatly speeded up as information is handled by machine. Similar applications in government, such as the processing of social security data, are now centralized.

In smaller firms a reverse trend, that of decentralizing operations, may be appearing. For example, systems planners expect a large number of specialized and localized data banks (large computerized libraries of filed data) to be functioning by the early seventies. Such data banks could be specialized for doctors, lawyers, credit agencies, employment agencies, merchants, and banks.[28]

Total Systems Approach. By reconcentrating control over its operations in a central headquarters, a firm is able to extend the influence of automation to many, if not all, of its functions—from inventory and payroll to production, sales, and personnel. In so doing, businesses visualize all the elements of the corporate function in their relationship to one another and to the overall objectives of the firm. From this total systems concept, companies learn that computers can accomplish much more than clerical and accounting jobs. Their capabilities can be tapped to perform the traditional applications (payroll processing, inventory control, accounts payable, and accounts receivable) as well as newer applications such as spotting deviations from planned programs (exception reporting), adjusting planning schedules, forecasting business trends, simulating market conditions, and solving production problems. Since the office manager is a manager of information and each of these applications revolves around the processing of data, he must take an active role in studying and improving the systems under his care.

New Systems Applications. Most office work is *batch-processed*; that is, facts are gathered and then worked upon in groups of orders or forms on a daily, weekly, or biweekly basis. By means of newer input devices on production and communication lines, however, data may be continuously fed into computer systems to give management

---

[28] Walter A. Kleinschrod (ed.), "The Office in Transition," *Administrative Management* (January, 1969), p. 25.

"instant information." This type of processing in *real-time* is the converse of batch-processing, for it records information by machine as the event or transaction occurs (for example, inventory files are updated as transactions and orders are received and processed). Such systems are also said to be *on-line.* While such examples are still limited, several widely known applications have been in operation for some years. Real-time reservation systems of American Airlines link computers in New York to input-output stations around the world. The SAGE (Semi-Automatic Ground Environment) system of the Department of Defense maintains a continental air command and warning system throughout North America. Other large companies have installed similar computer systems that are tied together by computers and communications equipment (telephone, teletypewriter, and the like).

Many firms, too small to maintain their own computer installations, participate in a time-sharing plan in which they buy time on someone else's computer. In such cases the firm uses the computer from a remote terminal at the same time other similar applications are taking place. The large-scale computer coordinates and schedules its own usage through its programmed instructions.

In a true operating sense, computers are merging with other types of office equipment to provide new systems applications. Such examples as these are now becoming more common:

1. Direct conversion of data from computer onto microfilm, thus bypassing the printout.
2. Transfer of data from computer to offset master for making multiple copies.
3. Storage and retrieval of information by computer.
4. Reading of many different types of print by scanner and converting to computer codes for storage and computation within the computer.
5. Sending data from a punched card over telephone lines to remote locations (the Bell System's Data-phone).

Future Applications. Present-day applications seem conservative when compared with anticipated uses of the computer in handling information. Being planned are: (1) large data bases or central computer repositories of information, (2) information utilities (such as electronic libraries of data that can be contacted by dialing a telephone), (3) home as well as office use of computer utilities on a city-wide basis, (4) advanced communication terminals including graphic and voice input and output, (5) many small central processors economically available to individuals as well as small firms, (6) three-dimensional color replication of living and moving objects, and (7) speech-recognition devices. The imagination of man as the master of the machine is the principal limitation to the use of the computer in and out of the office.

All these developments bring about a rethinking of the entire business structure and the concept of management. As a result of scientific advances and technological change, management is now able to regroup all the elements of control under a single roof. The centralization of information processing, the establishment of total systems and procedures, and the ability to project more accurately the company's goals, costs, and budgets all serve to justify the need for a full understanding of the managerial functions—organizing, planning, controlling, and leading. Automation in the office will never eliminate the need for men. They will be relieved of the repetitive monotonous functions of recording, transcribing, computing, and summarizing, however. People will still be required to generate data at the source, to prepare the input media for the machines, to program and control the machines, and most importantly to interpret the output of the machines. "The need is for the development of broad-gauge men in the office. Office managers must be *managers* in every sense of the word." [29]

QUESTIONS FOR REVIEW

1. What basic differences exist between the modern-day office and those offices that operated before the invention of information-processing machines?

2. Compare these terms:
   a. Automated data processing.
   b. Punched-card data processing.
   c. Electronic data processing.

3. Describe the basic flow of information into, through, and out of a punched-card data processing system.

4. How is a computer feasibility study made?

5. What are some of the specific questions that require answers in a feasibility study?

---

[29] H. W. Prentis, Jr., "Office Systems Are Not Enough!" *Men, Machines, and Methods in the Modern Office*, American Management Association Report No. 6, 1958, pp. 93-101.

6. How does the introduction of a computer into an organization affect the office staff?
7. On a national scale, what effect has the computer had on office employment?
8. In what areas of the office work force is the greatest growth anticipated? Why?
9. What is the advantage of bypassing the key-punch operation in an electronic data processing system?
10. Discuss some of the key operational and organizational effects of a computer upon a company's operations.

QUESTIONS FOR DISCUSSION

1. Automation has been called "a further extension of the hand." Explain the meaning of this symbolic phrase from the standpoint of administrative office management.
2. Consider carefully the comprehensive effects of automation as they relate to each of these components of our culture:
   a. Society.
   b. Business, industry, and government.
   c. The white-collar work force.
   d. The design and implementation of systems of processing information.
3. Computers today link large corporate headquarters with their many branch offices to provide "instant information" on such vital matters as sales, inventories, and production data. To the administrative office manager this information made possible by the computer actually improves the centralized control over all key business functions. Discuss.
4. In most management conferences where executives discuss the impact of computers, problems of machine usage, including programming, are assumed to be manageable. On the other hand, the more difficult and frustrating and less manageable factor is called the "people problem"—getting people to work well with machines and with new machine-based systems. In what ways can the administrative office manager assist top management to improve this situation?
5. Some technological developments tend to start a chain reaction with "ripples" extending throughout the economy. Do you believe that such a reaction will develop in the office work force with the demise of the key punch and the automating of source data?
6. Bernard Asbell, a journalist specializing in education, concludes in his book, *The New Improved American,* that, "Illiteracy rather than automation is the major cause of today's poverty." Discuss the

validity of this statement by analyzing the problem of unemployment in relation to the ever advancing technology of our age.

7. One of the major users of paper work and information handling is the banking system. To alleviate some of the mounting problems of dealing with the billions of checks written each day, systems analysts predict a "checkless society" in our future. Discuss the impact of this development on the general nature of such a society, the changes it would precipitate in the operation of bank offices, and the far-reaching influences of such a development on other sectors of the business society.
8. A continuing debate exists regarding the effect of computers on the general clerical force and on middle management. Defend the thesis that both levels of workers in business and industry will continue to grow in number despite the continuing encroachments of computers upon all forms of work.
9. The director of systems development for a large computer manufacturer has stated that the shortage of computer programmers is becoming so acute in this era of mounting computer sales that it is preventing many users from employing their computers to maximum advantage. What educational qualifications and type of background would you look for in the employment of a computer programmer?
10. Electronic computers make sweeping changes in the way that business data are handled and in the amount of information made available to top management. Do you believe that the selection of a computer is the top responsibility of the president of a company? Explain carefully.

PRACTICAL OFFICE CASES

Case 2-1 Planning a Feasibility Study

The following information relates to the administration of Palmer Plastics, Inc., a rapidly expanding manufacturer of novelty plastic toys and plastic kitchen and hardware utensils.

The growth of Palmer Plastics, Inc., parallels the rising expansion of the economy in general during the past 20 years. Starting as a partnership of 2 brothers in a converted brickyard in Pueblo, Colorado, it quickly prospered, expanding from a management team of 2 executives, an office staff of 5, and a factory work force of 40 supervisors and laborers to a management team of 32, an office work force of 15 supervisors and 78 general and special clerks, and a plant production force of 520. During this period of growth, annual gross sales have leaped from $400,500 to over $3,560,000, and expectations are for even greater growth in the future.

The novelty of the products and their durable composition have skyrocketed Palmer Plastics into the national spotlight. Advertising in national magazines and television and emphasizing the regional uses of the products (such as "Shoreline Toys" for the coastal and Great Lakes market and agricultural specialties for the rural housewife) have gained a wide sales margin for the manufacturer over old-line, more conservative competitors. Even as the home office was growing, sales offices (usually comprising a sales supervisor, several salesmen, and a small clerical staff) were opened in Denver, San Francisco, Omaha, Houston, Birmingham, Chicago, Cincinnati, Newark, and Worcester, Massachusetts.

During the short, fast-moving history of Palmer Plastics, total emphasis was placed on selling and promotion and perfecting the production function. The latest equipment, newest methods, and most highly trained engineering talent were procured. Extensive on-the-job training programs were held to assure that all production workers and their supervisors were properly meshing and working together as a team. Top management paid only passing attention to the office function, whose work force had grown much faster than the production force. Frequent suggestions, however, came from the more efficient sales offices for improving paperwork systems. These suggestions were acknowledged but never acted upon. No automated data processing equipment was used.

Presently the firm is divided into five divisions as shown in Figure A. Second largest in number of employees (behind the manufacturing division) is the general administrative division.

Each of these divisions has experienced decided growing pains: excessive worker turnover, many new staff members, increasing paper work, difficulty in meeting deadlines, and a feeling of desperation in keeping up with the work. Coordination among divisions (such as the relationship between sales, purchasing, inventory, and accounting functions) has not been achieved; and the forms, methods, and systems in use are geared to manual processing of information, the use of typewritten forms, out-of-date machines, and hand posting of accounts and inventory records. Briefly, the firm has geared its productive operation in the plant to the age of automation while its office operation remains in the "horse and buggy" age.

During the past two months several serious breakdowns in administration have occurred: (1) inability to update the inventory records resulted in a serious failure to order several of the key chemical components required to fabricate toys for the lucrative Christmas market; (2) due to a widespread epidemic of the Asian flu, over 60 percent of the office and payroll staffs were away from work on the average of ten days, thus resulting in long delays in paying the workers; and (3) the billing operation was found to be over two weeks late in processing all accounts, which resulted in delayed sales income for the firm.

Fig. A

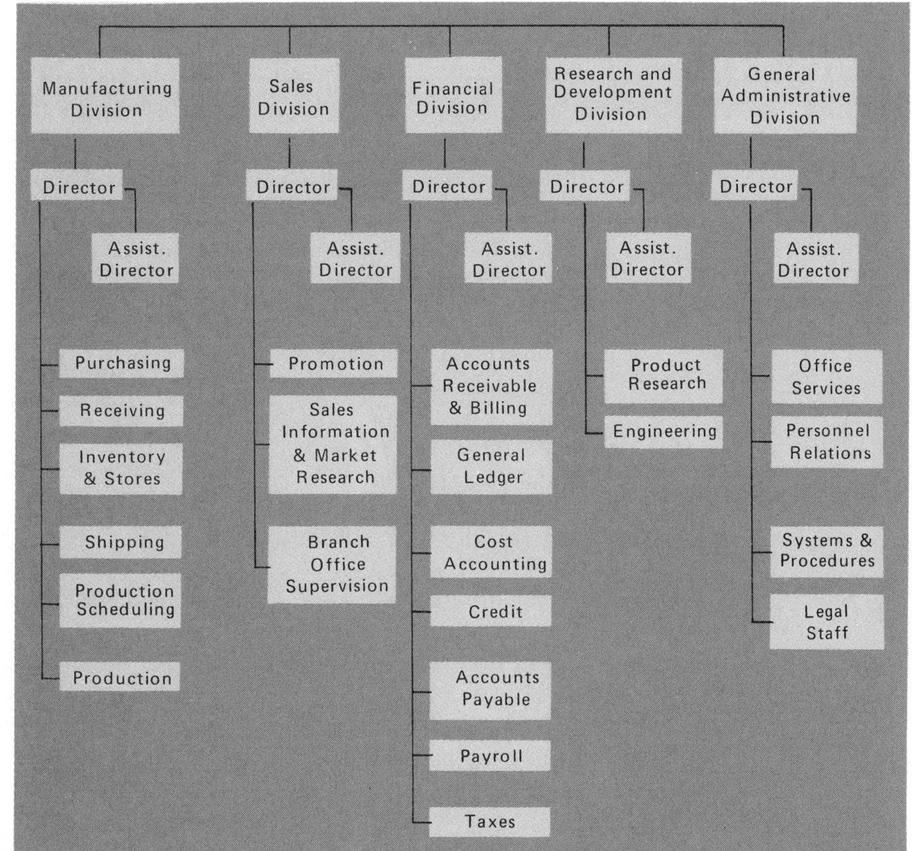

Divisional Structure of Palmer Plastics, Inc.

As a result of these crucial problems, the directors and assistant directors of each of the divisions held a series of meetings to evaluate or assess the cause of the problems. From these meetings and without further consultation came the following series of observations and proposals to the top management of Palmer Plastics, Inc.:

1. The information system of the firm is slow, unwieldy, and unfitted to meet modern processing needs.
2. A need exists for the immediate introduction of a medium-size electronic computer.
3. A separate and new data processing department is required. Due to the fact that the director of the financial division, a Certified Public Accountant, has had three years of punched-card processing experience and is responsible for all accounting work (an important use of data processing services),

it is recommended that he head this new data processing department.

4. The directors of the divisions, all highly trained in their fields and all college graduates, shall conduct their own feasibility study to be headed by the director of the financial division.
5. A service bureau (a data processing firm specializing in the processing of other firms' data) can satisfactorily handle all overload processing until a new data processing installation is installed. Such an agency should be contacted immediately to serve as an interim processing agent.
6. A functioning computer installation can be expected within 10 to 12 months.

■ Evaluate the feasibility approach recommended for Palmer Plastics. In this evaluation determine:

1. What type of information should have been presented and to whom?
2. Which are the faulty assumptions made by the divisional directors? Suggest substitute assumptions that spring from a more effective use of the scientific method.
3. Specifically, outline the most comprehensive method of solving the problem of considering the need for the mechanical processing of information. What part should the firm's top management play in such an approach? Their departmental managers and supervisors?
4. If you were the president of Palmer Plastics, what type of feasibility study would you insist on before committing the firm's resources to the procurement of an expensive computer?

Case 2-2 Introducing a Computer

The Casper Insurance Group represents a holding company of diversified insurance firms operating in the Pacific Northwest in the fire, casualty, and automobile fields. A Group Headquarters office of 120 employees is in Spokane, Washington, with large office staffs of 40 to 50 in each group-member location in each of the six northwestern state capitals. Sales staffs are controlled by each group-member office for that state. The insurance sales among Casper Insurance companies, as well as all other administrative requirements (underwriting, claims, actuarial work) peculiar to the insurance industry, are increasing by leaps and bounds.

At the present time the Group Headquarters office maintains a full-scale punched-card installation for handling payroll, premium billing, commissions accounting, and the like. To expedite central office processing, each office of the group member companies maintains its own key-punch machine (in some cases, several such machines), a sorter, and a tabulator-printer. Some of the firms have gradually expanded their use of these machines. A dynamic new president of Casper has recently been installed and has openly expressed the philosophy that he intends to centralize all data processing functions in the Spokane office for purposes of better control and to eliminate all data processing machines in the member offices in each state.

Fig. B

CASPER INSURANCE COMPANY

To: All Employees and Staff
From: James P. Thomas, President Date: December 11, 197-

As you know, our insurance sales are rising with insurance in force now exceeding $840 million, and growing more than 14 percent each year. In the insurance field much of our production is on paper, records, and forms; in short, data processing. The management of Casper has investigated the merits of bringing a computer system into the firm starting September 1 to handle centrally in the Spokane office all the firm's data processing and to provide much better service to our policyholders.

Accordingly, the following should be clearly understood by all:

1. The new computer system will be installed and functioning by September 1. A one-day orientation course will be provided for all central-office staff.

2. By October 1, all data processing punched-card machines will be removed from our offices.

3. No layoffs are expected at this time, though some retraining of clerical staff will be necessary.

4. Both senior and junior staff alike will benefit from the computer as a more efficient tool. Each of you will be challenged by this exciting and powerful machine.

Procedures Letter

Only four weeks after the new president joined Casper, the short, terse letter shown in Figure B was sent to all employees and staff of the headquarters office and each of the six member company offices.

■ As a member of the staff of a Casper office, answer the following:

1. What would be your reaction to this method of introducing a computer?
2. What steps should have been taken to give due consideration for the security of the workers and to provide for their full-scale acceptance of this important change in their work?
3. What are the social, operational, and training implications of this announcement? Discuss.

3

Basic Principles of Office Organization

Organizing is a management process by which people, functions, and physical factors are brought together to form a controllable (manageable) unit to accomplish specific company objectives. Such a unit is identified as an *organization*. Organizing occurs at all levels of operation—from the clerical employee who organizes his work around his skills and tasks to the executive who supervises the activities of complex units. To achieve the objectives of the organization, planning is performed by all levels of management. In the planning process relevant information from the present and the past is analyzed, and probable future developments are assessed so that a course of action—the plan—may be determined that will enable the firm to meet its stated objectives. The organizing of administrative office services is discussed specifically in this chapter, while the planning for these services is treated throughout the remaining chapters of this part, Chapters 4 through 9.

Since business is dynamic, its organization must be constantly studied. Over the years thoughtful leaders have put in statement form certain generally accepted and fundamental truths that are called *principles*. Thus, there are principles of marketing, principles of conduct, and principles of organization, to name but a few. Principles change, new principles are identified, and old principles are discarded when they no longer serve their purpose. It is imperative that managers have a keen understanding of basic principles pertinent to their field of speciality. Principles are much more permanent than practices. Principles are the backbone of decision making, the essence of intelligent planning, and the basis for evaluating situations. Therefore, a thorough understanding of the principles of organization is essential to good organization.

Good organization is based upon a careful planning of what is to be done, who is to do it, who is to supervise it, and how it is to be done most efficiently. Efficiency means speed, accuracy, and low cost. In other words, good organization results in the creation of well-balanced, low-cost teamwork that performs the necessary work. Through organization the duties of employees are planned and assigned so that responsibility may be fixed and so that more efficient work will be performed through greater specialization and better communications within the business firm. As the number of employees required to perform the work increases, the greater the need for integrating and coordinating the activities of each group of persons so that the firm may realize its objectives.

GUIDING PRINCIPLES OF ORGANIZATION

Good organization results in smoothly functioning business operations with a minimum of effort. The following principles underlie good managerial organization, and the effectiveness of these principles is measured by the results achieved.

Principle of Objectives

The objectives of a business or a group of functions within the business must be defined and understood.

An *objective* is an end or a goal to be achieved. Although objectives are usually specific and realistic, they may be broad and range from general, overall statements of an organization to specific, narrow statements about an individual's activities.[1] Objectives, usually established as part of the planning process for one-year and five-year

---

[1] M. Valliant Higginson, *Management Policies I, Their Development As Corporate Guides*, AMA Research Study 76 (New York: American Management Association, 1966), p. 17.

periods, are revised at regular intervals in order to adjust for any major changes.

There should be a policy, or guide for carrying out action, set up to define each one of the firm's objectives. The objective of a business firm may be to increase profits by increasing sales, and this objective determines the organization of the sales function in the business. Similarly the objective of the production function is to create a volume of products to meet the increased sales and to do this at the lowest possible cost. The objective of the administrative management function is to coordinate the activities of production and sales so that the unit cost of the product or service is reduced and productivity of the organization is increased. Here, administrative management is a facilitating function that is subordinate to the other functions.

Principle of Responsibility

Responsibility for organization exists with managers at all levels, beginning with top management and extending to the first-line supervisor.[2]

Overall responsibility for a sound structure definitely belongs to top management. The chief executive officer of the company must determine the major functions and responsibilities of individuals reporting directly to him. The company's long-range plans and objectives are formulated at this level, and proper organization by top management is essential to their accomplishment.

In the same manner as top management accepts its responsibility for organization, each succeeding level of management must complement this responsibility. Each level, therefore, should first approach its organization responsibility by:

1. Identifying major objectives and purposes for its department.
2. Determining activities in its department necessary to carry out those objectives.
3. Determining the best possible pattern of organization for its department.
4. Fixing responsibility within its department for the accomplishment of these objectives.

---

[2] Marion L. Clough, "Some Thoughts on Cardinal Principles for Setting Up an Organization" (From a presentation at the Thirtieth Annual Executives Conference, The Roosevelt Hotel, New York, December, 1959).

5. Establishing proper communications and relationships to unify all efforts and develop team spirit.

This same process is used at every level of management throughout the company. The only difference lies within the scope of responsibility and authority of the job and the direction of detail, as graphically illustrated in Figure 3-1. This figure shows that as one moves down the levels in the organization, there is less responsibility and authority and more direction of detail. As one moves up the levels, the reverse is the situation.

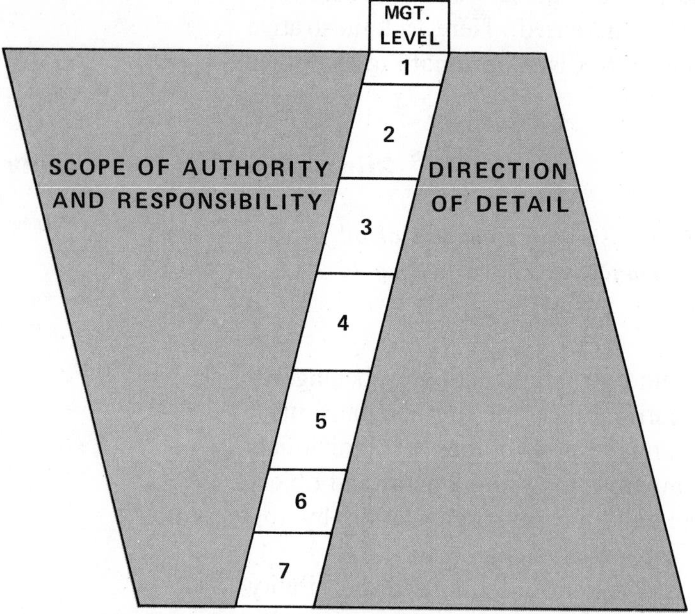

Fig. 3-1

The Change in Scope of Authority and Responsibility and the Change in Direction of Detail as One Moves Up and Down Management Levels

Principle of Unity of Functions

All business organizations are composed of functions that must work together to achieve the major objectives of the business.

The major functions of a business organization (production, distribution, finance, and personnel) may be likened to a system, and each of the functions may be regarded as a separate subsystem. The four functions are interrelated, and the effectiveness of any one function is dependent upon the execution of the other three functions. A survey undertaken by the Dartnell Institute of Business Research showed that the seven major functions performed by office administration executives are office management, credit and collection, purchasing, data processing, building supervision, employment, and accounting.[3] Like the circulatory system of the human body with its subsystems of arteries, veins, and capillaries, the needs, requirements, and objectives of each functional system and its subsystems must be clearly defined initially. Each of the component parts of the system must be considered in relation to the other parts of the system, expanding those activities as needed in terms of operations that will satisfy the overall objectives of the firm.

The principle of unity of functions requires that: (1) the various functions be in proper balance as determined by the relative importance of their contributions to the achievement of the company's objectives; (2) there be a certain amount of stability should changes in personnel occur; (3) there be flexibility to meet seasonal or territorial fluctuations; and (4) there be a possibility for growth and expansion to take care of future changes. As a result of building the organization around the main functions of the business, the need for people is decided. The organization must be designed to best serve the purposes of the firm; then workers are selected who are best qualified for the positions created.

The successful administrative office manager must accept the premise that his information processing work supports and coordinates every activity related to the organization. His problems are so closely interrelated that none of them can be considered without considering the others. The problem of providing transcription services must be related to the dictators' needs, records management, mailing, and supervision; and the problem of personnel relates to each of those just mentioned. In addition to this, the people in charge of the other functional units, such as production or distribution, must work with the administrative manager because in one way or another their activities are interrelated. Similarly, as the office organization is expanded and assistants or departmental heads are added, all must work together under the direction of the administrative manager as a coordinated team. This integration must be constantly kept in mind because it increases the efficiency of the information processing function by reducing the cost of the work.

---

[3] "Who Runs the Office?" *The Office*, Vol. 70, No. 3 (September, 1969), p. 26.

Principle of Simplicity

Effective organization is based upon simplicity and clear-cut interrelationships.

Because of its simplicity, an organization will be understood; because it is easily understood, it will be effective. Observing the principle of simplicity will aid in overcoming the phenomenon known as *Parkinson's Law,* which unfortunately does occur at times in all types of organizations. C. Northcote Parkinson, who formulated this "law," observed that work expands so as to fill the time available for its completion, work expands to fit the organization that is developed to perform that work, and there is a tendency for each unit within an organization to try to build up its importance by expanding the number of its personnel.[4]

Principle of Individual Relationships

Effective organization is made up of individuals who must perform the work.

This means that there must be a definite assignment of duties and responsibilities. Where similar but not identical assignments are given to several individuals, the similarities should be explained and the differences pointed out so as to prevent misunderstanding of assignments. Lines of authority must be established. Provision must be made for incentives (financial and nonfinancial) to do the work effectively, and each individual must know the interrelationship of the work within the function and among various functions. Good organization cannot exist without 100 percent participation. To bring about good organization, one should accept the fact that personnel are the keynote—the personnel available or that can be made available to the firm.

Principle of Delegating Authority Commensurate with Responsibility

Each individual in the organization must be given authority commensurate with his assigned responsibility so that he can be held accountable for the discharge of his duties.

Authority is the right to command or the right to act and the power to make decisions. *Responsibility* is the obligation and

[4] C. Northcote Parkinson, *Parkinson's Law* (New York: Houghton Mifflin Company, 1957).

accountability for properly performing work that is assigned. There must be a clear-cut flow of authority and responsibility from the top to the bottom of the organization so that managerial control can be effectively exercised, so that all functions will be covered, and so that there will be no duplication and overlapping of assignments. As an example of clearly delegated authority commensurate with responsibility, consider the position of supervisor of general services at American Standard of New York. The supervisor can approve purchase orders up to $500, but any orders over that sum must go to the corporate treasurer for his signature. The supervisor is also responsible for hiring, firing, and giving salary increases to his staff. If an exception to company policy is involved, the supervisor must obtain the approval of the treasurer and the vice president in charge of finance.[5]

In a study of the organization and administrative practices within 75 manufacturing concerns ranging in size from 40 to 600 workers, it was found that a leading cause for complaint by various members of management was the failure to delegate authority.[6] The delegation of authority is perhaps one of the most difficult jobs the supervisor has to learn. Some supervisors never learn to delegate but instead insist on handling the many details themselves. Other supervisors pay lip service to the principle of delegation but actually operate their departments like one-man offices. Some managers give their assistants many responsibilities but little or no authority. If, however, a supervisor is to manage his department successfully, he must delegate authority properly. As a minimum he should delegate enough authority to get the work done, to allow his key workers to take initiative, and to keep things going in his absence. Of course, the persons to whom responsibility and authority are delegated must be competent in the technical areas for which they are being held accountable.

Principle of Reporting to a Single Superior

So that each individual knows clearly to whom he reports, each employee should receive orders from and be responsible to only one supervisor.

Confusion results and morale and organization discipline may be eventually destroyed when an employee is accountable to several

[5] Lewis E. Lachter, "The Administrative Function," *Administrative Management* (August, 1966), p. 18.

[6] Rollin H. Simonds, "Are Organizational Principles a Thing of the Past?" *Personnel* (January-February, 1970), p. 17.

supervisors, each of whom may have varying standards in relation to the completed job. By reporting to only one supervisor, the worker knows exactly what is expected of him and the supervisor knows exactly who reports to him.

Each employee should be directly responsible to the individual who has been designated as the authority on a specific job or condition. Perhaps in one firm the administrative office manager should report to the controller because of conditions existing in that company; in another firm he may report to the vice president of sales if the office services are strictly sales oriented. What should be emphasized is that there is no cut-and-dried rule about who is to report to whom—it all depends upon the organizational structure, objectives, and conditions within the company. In fact, with today's emphasis on task forces and project teams, the middle manager or staff man may find himself reporting to half a dozen bosses.[7]

Principle of Supervision and Leadership

Effective supervision and leadership must be established so that the objectives of the business may be achieved.

The organization should permit and encourage each manager to exercise the maximum initiative within the limits of his delegated authority. Thus, ideas can be originated at lower levels of the organization and can flow by upward communications to the higher levels of management. A supervisor and leader must be able to plan and direct the work of others. For effective supervision the number of individuals for whom a supervisor is responsible must be limited. The employee must know how and to whom he must account for the responsibilities and duties assigned him. There must be cooperation and loyalty on the part of both the supervisor and employee.

Principle of Span of Control

For effective supervision and leadership, the span of subordinates under the immediate supervision of an executive or a supervisor should be limited.

Span of control refers to the number of employees who are directly supervised by one person. There is no predetermined formula

[7] See "Today's New Managers Are Changemakers," condensed from *Business Week* in *Management Review* (November, 1969), pp. 29-35.

that rigidly defines the span of control, for each situation must be carefully evaluated after an analysis of all factors involved. Among these factors are: (1) the capacity and skill of the supervisor and his subordinates, (2) the type of direction and control exercised over subordinates together with the latitude extended to them in decision making, (3) whether the operation is stable or dynamic, (4) the technical nature of the work, (5) the amount of time that the executive spends on other than supervisory work, (6) the type of organization, and (7) the number of interpersonal relationships inherent in each given situation. The most satisfactory span of control is one that avoids an over-long chain of command or levels and which does not overtax the executive's mental and physical capacities.[8]

Some management authorities have looked upon 12 to 15 subordinates as the maximum span at the lower levels in the organization, and early writers on organization stated emphatically that the span of control at the top level should not be more than five to six subordinates whose work interlocks. Later studies, however, show that many companies do not adhere to the recommendation of having five or, at the most, six subordinates report to each superior.[9] With the advent of the computer and today's management information systems, wherein subordinates are often performing similar kinds of work, it is possible by means of routine control procedures to increase further the number of persons supervised. For example, a Dartnell Institute of Business Research survey notes that the typical office services manager supervises 42 employees and has two assistants.[10]

FORMS OF ORGANIZATION

Organization is usually effected on a functional basis; that is, according to the basic functions of business—production, distribution, finance, and personnel. Within each of these basic groupings, the functions may be further subdivided. Four forms of organization may be set up to plan the work, to fix responsibility, to supervise the work, and to measure its results. These organizational forms are: (1) line, (2) functional, (3) line and staff, and (4) committee.

---

[8] Marion L. Clough, "Some Thoughts on Cardinal Principles for Setting Up an Organization" (From a presentation at the Thirtieth Annual Executives Conference, The Roosevelt Hotel, New York, December, 1959).

[9] Ernest Dale, *Planning and Developing the Company Organization Structure*, Research Report No. 20 (New York: American Management Association, 1952), p. 56.

[10] "Who Runs the Office?" *loc. cit.*

Line Organization

The earliest and simplest form of organization structure is the *line organization,* also known as the *scalar* or *military* type. In some offices a rather strict form of discipline and organization is carried on and the work is subdivided and delegated on a military line. Authority is passed down from the top management level to the various intermediate managers in charge of particular activities and from them down to supervisors who are directly in charge of workers at the operative level. As shown in Figure 3-2, authority flows in an unbroken line from the president to the worker.

The line organization is simple and easily understood by workers, for there is a clear-cut identification of duties and division of authority and responsibility. The performance or nonperformance of duties is directly traceable to a worker and his immediate superior in command. The line organization is characterized by a minimum of red tape in decision making, thus enabling action to be taken quickly. On the other hand, each supervisor is responsible for a wide variety

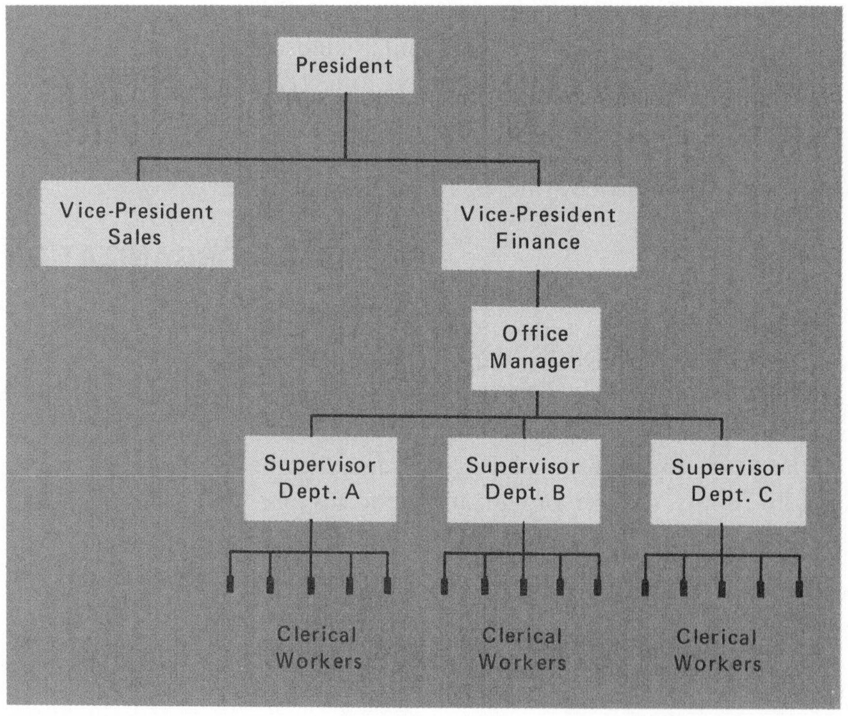

Fig. 3-2

Line Organization

of duties, in all of which he may not be expert. Thus, there is a lack of specialization at the supervisory level, an advantage of other forms of organization. At each succeeding level of organization, the wide and varied duties performed tend to overload intermediate and supervisory management, with the result that they are unable to tend to all matters requiring their personal attention.

The line form of organization is found in governmental offices, in the offices of military organizations, and in a few business offices. There are relatively few business offices that follow a "pure" line organization, but within large firms some phases of the work may be developed on a line organization plan of control and discipline. Within various departments the line organizaton plan of responsibility may be carried out quite rigidly, particularly in civil service divisions, banks, and insurance companies.

Functional Organization

The concept of *functional organization* was originally developed by Frederick W. Taylor to provide for specialized skills at the foreman level in the plant.[11] To handle the mental and clerical aspects of production, a clerical force consisting of a time and cost clerk, an instruction card clerk, an order of work and route clerk, and a shop disciplinarian was provided. The objective of functional organization was to provide for specialists at the supervisory level who would carry out each of the diverse duties of the foreman's position in the line organization. If applied to the office, the functional form might appear as shown in Figure 3-3. All matters pertaining to employment would be handled by the employment department; all payroll work, by the payroll department; all training and orientation, by the training department; all health, welfare, and morale problems, by the health and welfare department; and all employee counseling, by the employee counseling department.

In the functional form of organization, each supervisor grows in his own specialty and devotes all his time to one phase of work. Such specialization provides for increased efficiency since the workers are given specialized and skilled supervisory attention. However, with the development of so many kinds of independent specialists, the overspecialization causes confusion since there is overlapping of

[11] In 1880-1890, Taylor, looked upon as the father of scientific management, formulated fundamental principles, called duties of management, that challenged the traditional methods of management. See Frederick W. Taylor, *Scientific Management* (New York: Harper and Bros., 1947).

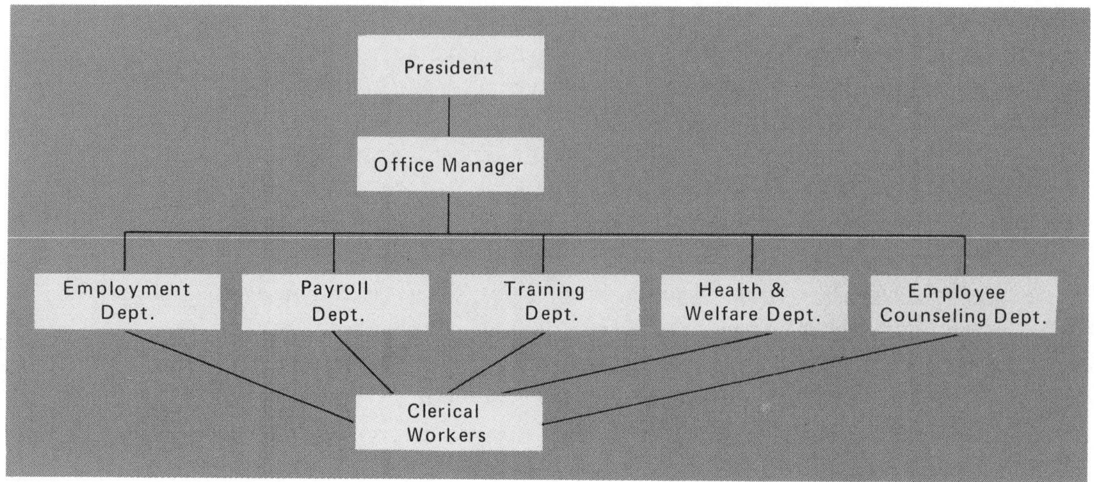

Fig. 3-3

Functional Organization Applied to the Office

authority and a lack of fixed lines of responsibility. As a result, the functional form lends itself to "buck passing." Since the workers must report to two or more supervisors, conflicting instructions are often given, which gives rise to friction. Because of all its disadvantages, a "pure" functional organization, like the line form, is rarely found in business today. As described below, however, the workable principles of the line form and the functional form have been brought together in the commonly used line-and-staff form of organization.

Line-and-Staff Organization

In a *line-and-staff organization,* near the top management level of a business firm, policies and practices are carried out on a line plan. Further down the line of authority and responsibility, the work is carried out on a functional basis, department by department. The staff feature comes in when a group of experts assists management as advisers to all the various departments. In many concerns the office manager becomes a functional officer covering certain business activities, but he acts as a staff officer to many other functional departments by advising on matters such as records management, correspondence, and other office services that may be performed in other departments.

As shown in the partial line-and-staff organization chart in Figure 3-4, there is a clear-cut flow of authority and responsibility from the top to the bottom of the organization. Operating efficiency through specialization is achieved since each supervisory manager, such as the assistant controller, directly controls the men under him and is

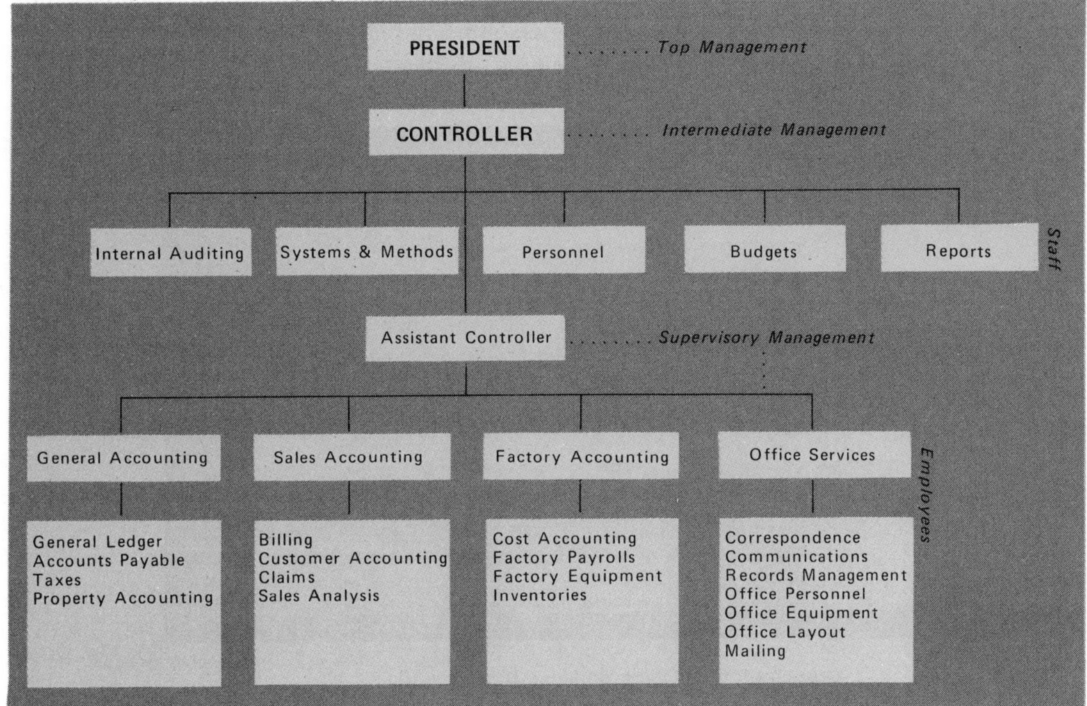

Fig. 3-4

Partial Line-and-Staff Organization

held responsible for specific activities. The supervisor, however, is not burdened with all the varied duties that he would have under the line form of organizaton. The personnel in the staff positions shown in Figure 3-4 (internal auditing, systems and methods, personnel, budgets, and reports) serve as advisers. They offer their counsel and recommendations to line officers throughout the organization (in Figure 3-4 only the relationship of the staff positions to the controller's department is illustrated). Traditionally staff officers do not give orders directly to line workers nor do they ordinarily have the authority to put their recommendations into action. The authority and responsibility for executing operations rests with the line officers.

Since the office is the focal point in a business organization for coordinating the work of production, distribution, finance, and personnel, office activities are in the nature of services to all other departments and to the business as a single unit. Thus, many offices are called by the title Office Services Department. Frequently, the supervision of the office services department comes under the direction of the administrative office manager, a controller (accountant), a credit manager, or a personnel manager. The organization of one office services department is illustrated in the chart in Figure 3-5.

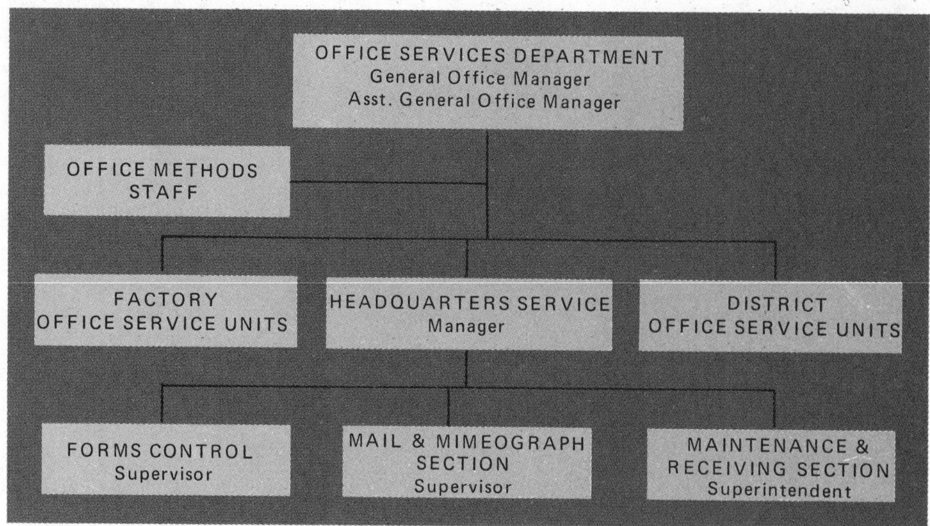

Fig. 3-5

Organization of Office Services Department

Committee Organization

The trend toward bigger and more complex enterprises has often necessitated interaction among executives and has increased the need for coordination. As a result "group executives" or "plural executives," whose authority is not always clearly defined, have emerged.[12] The committee form of organization is usually employed in conjunction with, or as a modification of, the line-and-staff plan. Experience has shown that, in some instances, people react more favorably to a group decision than to the dictatorial authority of one person.

Through the participative interaction of the members of the group, committee management brings better teamwork and makes supervisory personnel think of the company more as a unit than in terms

---

[12] Ambrose Klotz, "Line and Staff Today: We Need to Redefine Their Roles," *Administrative Management* (March, 1968), p. 22.

of their own individual departments. Committee management, however, is no substitute for individual authority and responsibility. Committee management helps develop broader views to improve the conduct of the business, to coordinate the programs and activities, and to develop decisions and discuss problems affecting more than one segment of the company's organization. In many instances the judgment of the group tends to be better than that of a single individual. As a result of pooling the knowledge and experience of all members on the committee, any plans developed may be executed more easily since all members participated in the development of the plans. Because of having participated in the decision-making process, committee members are further motivated to see the plan through to its successful culmination.

Sometimes the committee organization is expanded by the addition of a second echelon known as a *management council,* which enables as many of the supervisory personnel as possible to participate. The management council can be effective in handling specific problems pertaining to individual departments and in helping to sponsor new ideas and theories for consideration by top management. Other types of committee management sometimes found are: (1) the various executive and operational committees that are formed to obtain coordination among the primary functions of the firm, (2) special task forces consisting of representatives of several functions to handle difficult interfunctional problems, (3) staff groups whose primary purpose is to integrate a basic management activity such as planning within the firm, and (4) program or project management wherein each individual project is established as a distinct organizational element with a manager who integrates the functional groups beneath him into one operating unit to handle the various phases of the project.

Committee management is slower in reaching decisions than a one-man rule, but it has the advantage of eliminating snap judgments. In committee management the majority rules and thus no one individual is fully responsible for the decisions made, which leads to the disadvantages of divided responsibility and oftentimes a compromise decision that may not be of the best quality. Also, the use of committees requires many group meetings that can consume much valuable time in doing little more than displaying ignorances and exchanging prejudices. Successful committee organization results when companies do not put before the committee those problems that should be handled by individual executive decisions.

Informal Organization

Any series of principles for organization must be flexible. Business firms, products and services, and personnel vary. Generalizations may be made, but the reader must be able to adapt them. A wonderful plan of organization can be wrecked by a poor administrator, and a poor organization plan may be made effective by a top-rate administrator. Also to be kept in mind is the value to be gained from cultivating those working relations among people in the business firm which do not appear on the organization chart—those relations that make up the *informal organization.* No organization chart can portray the infinite person-to-person relationships that make up an informal organization, and no company can exist without it. The administrator must be acquainted with those individuals who have the power to help or impede him even though their names or positions do not appear on the company's organization chart. Often, an informal channel is more effective and efficient than the formal line in passing along information, solving problems, and revising procedures.

Because the informal organization is an ever-shifting and undefined structure, it is vulnerable to expediency, manipulation, and opportunity.[13] Among the abuses of informal organization are those vertical abuses that occur when the appropriate lines of authority and communication, up and down the organizational chain, are ignored or distorted. For example, vertical abuse occurs when a top-ranking executive, such as the vice president of finance, makes direct contact with and gives orders to someone far down his line of authority, such as a programmer, by skipping the intervening layer of supervision, the manager of the data processing division. With the manager possibly not having knowledge of the contact and the assignment of work given to the programmer, the responsibility of the manager deteriorates. Other abuses occur when two or more workers informally agree not to comply with an official pronouncement on policy or procedure. Substantial harm can result, and company policy tends to be seriously distorted.

THE ORGANIZATION CHART

Organization charts, such as those illustrated in this chapter, present graphically the line of authority, the span of control, and the responsibility for work in each function or department with as much

[13] Raymond F. Valentine, "The Pitfalls of Informal Organization," *Introduction to Business, A Contemporary Reader*, edited by Joel J. Lerner (Englewood Cliffs, New Jersey: Prentice-Hall, Inc., 1969), p. 88.

detail as possible. Oftentimes several charts may be necessary to give a complete and intelligent guide to company organization. Organization charts are an important tool of management in indicating the flow of work and the responsibility for its achievement. Merely because a chart is in existence, however, is no assurance that there is good organization.

Figure 3-6 presents ten suggestions for preparing organization charts.[14] These suggestions are not hard-and-fast rules, and they

Fig. 3-6

SUGGESTIONS FOR PREPARING AN ORGANIZATION CHART

1. Identify the chart fully showing the name of the company, date of preparation, and title of person or name of department responsible for preparation. If the chart is for one division of the company only, include such information as part of the title.
2. Use rectangular boxes to show either an organizational unit or a person. Plural executives and other committees should occupy one box.
3. The vertical placement of the boxes shows relative positions in the organizational hierarchy; however, due to space limitations, line units are frequently shown one level below staff units. (See Figure 3-3.)
4. Any given horizontal row of boxes should be of the same size and should include only those positions having the same organizational rank.
5. Vertical and horizontal solid lines are used to show the flow of line authority.
6. If necessary, use dotted or broken lines to show the flow of functional authority.
7. Lines of authority enter at the top center of a box and leave at the bottom center; they do not run through the box. Exception: the line of authority to a staff assistant or an "assistant-to" may enter the side of the box.
8. The title of each position should be placed in the box. The title should be descriptive and show function. For example, vice president is not sufficient as it does not show function. The functional area, e.g., manufacturing, should be included even though it is not a part of the official title. Titles should be consistent; if necessary, revise titles so they are both consistent and descriptive.
9. Include the name of the person currently holding the position unless personnel turnover is so great that revision of the chart becomes burdensome.
10. Keep the chart as simple as possible; include a legend if necessary to explain any special notations. When preparing a separate chart for an organizational unit, include the superior to whom the unit reports.

Suggestions for Preparing an Organization Chart

[14] Henry L. Sisk, *Principles of Management, A Systems Approach to the Management Process* (Cincinnati: South-Western Publishing Co., 1969), p. 377.

should be modified when the occasion demands. Often the organization chart is presented in the organization manual, which is described in Chapter 23. The organization manual explains in narrative form the organization, duties, and responsibilities of the various departments and their respective divisions.

CENTRALIZED vs. DECENTRALIZED ORGANIZATION

Theoretically centralizing the office work is desirable because it fixes responsibility under a capable executive, avoids duplication, and permits better supervision with a more even distribution of the individual work load. The nature of the office work in the business activity often does not permit such an acceptable theory, however, for office work does not permit as clearly a defined function as production or distribution. Office work is made up of a series of different activities such as dictation, correspondence, filing, mailing, and accounting. Furthermore, some firms have a number of plants and branch offices located throughout the country. Branch offices vary with different concerns. In many concerns the branch office is merely a branch sales office under the direction of a branch sales manager with such clerical and accounting assistance as necessary. For this arrangement the office manager in the home office has little to provide in the matter of guidance and control, except perhaps to issue some manuals or instruction sheets for certain clerical activities. The rest of the work is ordinarily directed by the branch sales manager. Some branches are established on a semi-independent basis with each branch acting somewhat like a separate unit. In such branches the office manager is faced with the same duties and responsibilities as any other office manager. In some concerns there is a greater volume of work than in others. In life insurance companies, banks, and brokerage firms, for example, the amount of office work looms greater than in a manufacturing or a retail organization. With all the foregoing variables in mind, the question of centralization versus decentralization naturally tends to become an individual problem for each firm.

Where all office work is confined to a single location or building, it is possible to centralize the bulk of the clerical work under a capable, experienced, and well-trained executive with assistants supervising the various activities. In such cases it is possible to maintain a centralized dictation and transcription department, using the latest and most efficient mechanical equipment. Also, centralized filing, mailing, and duplicating departments may be established. These activities can then be performed more expertly, at less cost, and with better supervision. There may still be some decentralized office work performed by private secretaries and others who maintain personal or confidential files.

A relatively new concept of centralization in today's offices is the *satellite administrative services center* or *substation.* The substation is a compact work station that handles many of the paper-work and clerical activities that are usually scattered throughout a number of offices. One of the major objectives of such a substation is to handle a growing work load with the same number of office workers. With the right person in charge, the center provides an organization with higher quality and lower cost services than conventional centralized services.[15] The administrative services substation, under centralized direction and control, links together the work stations in close proximity to the needs of the users of office services. A typical satellite services substation provides such administrative services as stationery and supplies, quick reproduction of copies, secretarial and clerical assistance, filing, records management, mail and communications, library, and information retrieval. A newly established substation may be organized to supply a minimum number of local administrative services such as mail, stationery supplies, and fast copies in a defined area that serves operations in close proximity. As the substation proves successful in meeting the needs of the users, additional services may be provided in a sort of building-block plan. Ideally all the substations are linked with other substations, with the central services unit, and with the computer information center.

Where a firm maintains plants and offices in several locations, many of the office services are often decentralized to permit more efficient operations. As a result, a certain amount of duplication of supervision and investment in equipment occurs, and the position of the office manager may become less responsible. However, where the office services are decentralized because of multilocation operations, the tendency has been to remove the accounting work from the office manager's authority and to centralize it in one location. This has been made possible by better means of communication and transmission of accounting data via teletypewriters, punched tape, punched-card systems, and the use of electronic data processing. Centralizing the accounting function is not only less costly but also more efficient. The work is done more accurately; and by means of more timely reports, management can make better use of the accounting and statistical information. As mentioned in the preceding chapter, some large companies (formerly decentralized) that have

---

[15] "Satellite Administrative Service Centers," *Administrative Management* (February, 1969), pp. 26-28.

installed a central computer system have recentralized their operations at a single headquarters.

Wherever possible, the office work should be centralized because of the following advantages, in addition to those discussed above:

1. The office manager's job increases in stature because of greater responsibility for all the office work.
2. Office methods and procedures can be standardized.
3. Training programs can be instituted to improve the work.
4. Cost studies and analyses of office work are possible.
5. A better distribution of the work load can be provided with a resulting savings in the cost of doing the work.

Nevertheless, there are certain disadvantages of centralization:

1. Time of personnel is lost going to and from the centralized activity to the department where the work must be done, as in the case of the centralized filing or centralized transcription department.
2. Supervision costs add to the total office costs. However, this disadvantage is offset by the economies effected by supervision. The economies include better selected personnel and better trained personnel.
3. Effort-consuming inconvenience results from centralization when the office organization is spread over a wide geographic area or is dispersed on several floors.
4. The confidential nature of some of the information and records makes it impractical to place them in a centralized location.
5. Work in a centralized organization may be performed in the order of receipt rather than in the order of importance.

QUESTIONS FOR REVIEW

1. What is organizing? Why must organization be constantly studied, changed, and improved?

2. Distinguish between authority and responsibility. What is the relationship of accountability to responsibility?

3. What are the major characteristics of a line organization?

4. "The functional form of organization lends itself to 'buck passing.'" Explain.

5. Describe briefly the line-and-staff form of organization. In this form of organization, is the position of office manager ordinarily classified as line or staff?

6. What organizational conditions suggest the use of a committee type of office administration?

7. What advantages and disadvantages are associated with committee management?
8. What is informal organization? What are some of the abuses to which informal organization is exposed?
9. Why is the organization chart an important tool of office administration?
10. What suggestions should be followed in preparing organization charts?
11. What are the advantages and disadvantages of centralizing office services?
12. Describe how office services are provided in a satellite administrative services center.

QUESTIONS FOR DISCUSSION

1. Nine principles governing the nature of office organization are discussed in this chapter. Which three, in rank order, do you consider to be the most important? Why?
2. Does Parkinson's Law have greater application in office work than in factory operations? Why?
3. What effect does each of the following have on the organization plans for office work?
   a. Geographic decentralization of the office work.
   b. Automation in the office systems and routines.
4. Two statements recently made with reference to the concept of systems are: (a) a business system is a social system, and (b) the machine is not a system. Explain the significance and interrelationships of these two statements.
5. Explain the significance of the following statements when applied to office administration:
   a. "It is not what we tell the employees that matters, but what they accept."
   b. "A clean desk indicates great executive ability."
   c. "Too much harmony in business operations is not always evidence of efficient business operations."
   d. "We are not really successful office executives until we learn to work with people we dislike and who dislike us."
6. How do the policies of "promoting from within" and "the use and training of understudies" affect office organization and administration?
7. Why are "levels of management" important in planning an organization? What effect do levels of management have on the functional phase of office organization?
8. The supervisor of the correspondence department has attempted on several occasions to make improvements in the dictation and transcription work in the office. Whenever changes are suggested to the

office manager, they are ignored or else the supervisor is stymied by the remark, "It has always been done this way, and your suggestions have been tried before without success." The supervisor feels that this is not a satisfactory answer and would like to go to some higher authority for approval of his ideas for change. Discuss how you feel the supervisor's problem should be resolved.

9. The DiMario Manufacturing Company has created a centralized Organization-Planning Division whose function among others is to constantly study the organization, supervision, and lines of authority with the objective of avoiding inefficiencies and duplication of effort. As a result of its work during the past two years, the Organization-Planning Division has prepared a comprehensive report that includes a detailed organization chart and a supplementary manual indicating specific authorities and responsibilities throughout the company. Discuss the favorable and unfavorable aspects of such a report and its preparation.

10. The Hampton Company recently initiated a management arrangement whereby a Junior Board of Directors consisting of the executives of the various operating departments was established. Membership on the Junior Board is carefully determined by the executive committee of the regular Board of Directors. Membership on the Junior Board is on a rotating basis, and each member serves only a one-year term. The Junior Board is made up of 15 members who meet every two weeks, at which time the following problems are considered:

a. Mechanization and automation of various operations.
b. Salary schedules, benefits, and revisions.
c. Sales and marketing ideas.
d. Quality and service control of sales.
e. Business expansion, working conditions, and employee grievances.

Discuss the advantages and disadvantages of such an organization-administration plan and the relationship between the participative and the conceptual action of authority, responsibility, and accountability.

PRACTICAL OFFICE CASES

Case 3-1 Reorganizing the Administrative Services Function

The Atlas Electronics Corporation started as a small postwar organization interested in television improvement devices. Over the past 20 years the company has expanded steadily and consistently and recently has received several large government missile orders. The office expansion that has taken place has been under three vice presidents each of whom is in charge of one of the functions of production, distribution, and finance. No one person has been in charge of administrative services.

Each functional vice president maintains his own filing, stenographic, mailing, and duplicating departments. Supervisors are in charge of the functional activities under the headings of production, distribution, and finance. Part of the organization chart indicates that there are supervisors in charge of purchasing, receiving, storing, accounts payable (voucher system), factory payroll, cost accounting, and shipping. Under the heading of distribution there are supervisors in charge of sales, advertising, credit, and accounts receivable accounting. Under the direction of the vice president in charge of finance are financial accounting, taxes, governmental reports, and office payrolls.

Many of the supervisors of these activities are persons who have been shifted into supervisory positions with little knowledge of systems or methods. The supervisors are hard pressed to get out the work because of inefficiency, lack of knowledge, and needless duplication of records and work. Office equipment has been ordered from time to time and placed where it was thought it would be used later.

The president of the company, Paul S. Chaney, has recently been overwhelmed by the fact that whenever he wants information he must go to several sources and waste much time in locating it. He is also beginning to notice the idle equipment in the offices and the delay in the preparation of certain operating reports.

Chaney has recently had a conference with the three executives in charge of the production, distribution, and finance activities and indicated his dissatisfaction. Neither the production manager, the marketing manager, nor the treasurer feels that he can give up or change any of his work routines or his present personnel.

■ Chaney feels that something must be done in the interest of a more efficient organization and lower costs. He has called upon you to find out how it might be possible to reorganize the office services so that a better utilization of present personnel and equipment might achieve the objectives of greater and faster output and reduced costs. You are asked to prepare a report, including a chart showing the reorganization of the work in this concern, and to indicate the changes in the organization that you would make. (Since many of the details of this concern are not given, it will be necessary to assume conditions prevalent in most manufacturing concerns having an office staff of 60 persons.)

Case 3-2 Preparing an Organization Chart of the Administrative Office Management Function

You have just accepted the position of administrative office manager of the Sutton Manufacturing Company, which has 175 office employees. It is planned to centralize as many of the office services as possible and to develop a staff department under a supervisor whose sole job will be to study and improve office methods, systems, and procedures. In addition it is your plan to organize the work so that it will be properly supervised and controlled. As administrative office manager in charge of the entire office organization, you report to the treasurer of the company, who in turn reports directly to the president.

The proposed supervisory setup includes the following personnel: (The estimated number of employees needed in each department, including the supervisor and/or the officer of that department, is given in parentheses.)

a. Howard Anness, who handles office space, office equipment, and reports. He has the title of assistant administrative office manager. (25)
b. Cornelius Holliday, chief accountant in charge of budgets, costs, and financial accounting. (25)
c. James Gorrell, who handles the factory personnel problems. As assistant personnel manager, Gorrell reports to the personnel director, Richard T. Dwyer who, in his staff position, reports directly to the president. (15)
d. John Byrd, in charge of office methods and procedures, a staff position. (4)
e. Louis Perrino, in charge of internal auditing, also a staff position. Perrino has the title of auditor. (5)
f. Carla Wilson, supervisor, who directs the transcription department. (50)
g. Beatrice Vetter, supervisor, who directs the filing and mailing departments. (30)
h. Frank Wold, supervisor, who is responsible for office communications, supplies, and duplicating work. (20)

■ On the basis of the above information, you are asked to prepare a partial organization chart showing the line-and-staff arrangements.

1. In this chart place the name of the person responsible for the direction or supervision of the work. Under each supervisor's name indicate some of the activities that will be directed by him.
2. Prepare a brief explanation of the line-and-staff authority as outlined on your chart.
3. Estimate the weekly cost of office salaries of all employees except the treasurer and the president. Assume a minimum salary of $105 a week for the 165 clerical office workers; for the 10 supervisors and officers, assume a salary commensurate with the responsibilities of their positions. Assuming that office salaries are five percent of sales, what would you estimate to be the minimum weekly sales volume required to justify the cost of this office work?

4

Space Management in the Office

In all cities the search for more office space for housing a growing clerical work force continues unabated. Skyrocketing costs of such space (as high as $8 to $10 a square foot), increased costs of labor for maintenance and cleaning, and the effort to solve production and status problems of employees through a better working environment are all factors that provide motivation for giving more attention to managing office space.

The space available for performing office work constitutes the "geography" of the office. Until recently the term "office layout" was usually used to categorize discussions as to how office space can be effectively utilized. Newer concepts with respect to space allocation for office work have led to substituting the term "space management" for "office layout." To understand newer concepts of space management, it is essential to recall that the function of the office is to process information. In the office, information flows in a manner like the flow of materials in a factory. In each there are routes or aisles of transport, in each the transportation time must be held to a minimum, and in each a strong need exists to keep the number of work stations for the loading and unloading of information (or materials) to a minimum without sacrificing the accessibility of the service or the product.

Regardless of the type of product (a factory product, a paper product, or simply oral communication), how space is planned and utilized affects the efficiency and productivity of the workers.

One should also consider as valid the traditional concept of the office as a service center of the firm. Robert Propst, President of Herman Miller Research Corporation and a qualified critic of the office function, suggests that the traditional purpose of the office was "to provide an environment that was conducive to work on the part of the individual."[1] That office, he believes, should grow with the individual and should be an extension of the individual and the work he performs.

The need to control space carefully is critical if (1) a new office building is being planned, (2) an old building is being renovated, or (3) the layout of a present building is being analyzed with a view toward reshuffling people, furniture, and equipment. The planning of a new office building or the renovation of an old building requires careful study to obtain the most efficient use of space. In this chapter the objectives and principles of space management are discussed, and applications of good layout are examined and illustrated.

OBJECTIVES OF SPACE MANAGEMENT IN THE OFFICE

Space management in the office involves five principal factors: (1) the physical features of the office, especially those relating to the design of the building (such as window locations, elevators, and the plumbing, heating, and electrical systems); (2) the needs of the organization including departmental locations, special facilities such as reference services, the computer installation, and executive office requirements; (3) the work being performed; (4) the nature of and the number of employees presently working as well as the number contemplated in the future; and (5) the equipment and the furniture required to complete the work assigned.

Space management in the office has these specific objectives:

1. To provide sufficient office space and to maximize its use.
2. To assure employees as well as customers and the general public of comfort and convenience.
3. To develop work flows that are effective and low in cost.
4. To design work stations that are conducive to good working methods and that are in keeping with the work-flow system.

---

[1] *Business Equipment Manufacturers Association News,* November 3, 1969, p. 11.

5. To coordinate the utilization of space with all related environmental factors (such as heat, light, color, and noise control).
6. To permit flexibility in layout for rearrangement or expansion.
7. To consider carefully the interpersonal communication needs of the office staff in providing an environment free of communication barriers.
8. To review periodically all aspects of the space management program and make improvements when necessary.

The principles of space management were developed with these objectives in mind. The remaining sections of this chapter use these objectives as a frame of reference.

THE PHYSICAL OFFICE: GEOGRAPHY OF THE SYSTEM

Planning and executing an efficient, economical space management program require careful and continuous study. If one considers simply the growth in the office work force of the United States (estimated conservatively as increasing by approximately 850,000 workers annually) and that space must be provided for this huge work force, the enormity of the space management problem is clear. In fact, in most corporations the increase in office personnel still ranges from 4 to 7 percent annually.[2]

When occupying a new building or renovating an existing building, management finds it advisable to consult reliable space planners and interior designers. Such specialists make recommendations based upon a complete assessment of economic, efficiency, and esthetic or appearance factors. Within the firm a team approach is normally required to help plan and approve the new office design. Working with the architect are the systems analysts, engineers, department heads, industrial psychologists, and industrial relations personnel. The administrative office manager should, of course, play a significant role in planning and outlining the work-flow needs of the office.

In planning a new office building, generally the essential physical features, such as supporting pillars, elevators, rest rooms, lockers, and cafeteria, can be located where they are most desirable. More frequently, however, the firm is moving into a new location in an existing building where these physical features must be accepted as they are. Planning the arrangement of departments and equipment and work flows, therefore, must be carried on around the present location

[2] Hans J. Lorenzen, "The Office Landscape: A Management Tool," *Journal of Systems Management* (October, 1969), p. 14.

of these fixed factors. Such an approach also typifies the firm that is making changes in its space management plan in its present location.

In analyzing the physical features of the building, it is well to keep in mind that:

1. Large, open spaces are usually more desirable than a series of small rooms.
2. Natural light should be used wherever possible. In so doing, the arrangement of office furniture, machines, and other equipment should take into consideration the location of windows.
3. The total environment must be considered. Such features as heating, lighting, air conditioning, acoustic treatment, and color schemes (discussed in Chapter 6) are all part of the physical features to be included in a space management effort.

ORGANIZATIONAL NEEDS IN SPACE MANAGEMENT

The organization of an office usually influences its layout. In many large firms, such as pharmaceuticals, industrial chemicals, and agricultural chemicals, the plant and office locations are separated. Many of these firms, too, have branch offices that are decentralized geographically.

Probably the most common type of organization, especially for small offices, is a departmental plan arranged according to the functions of purchasing, marketing, accounting, credit, and administrative services. In planning the best utilization of office space, factors such as the following must be considered: (1) the interrelationships existing among departments, (2) the number of persons located in each department, (3) the type and flow of information-processing work, and (4) the need for private offices. One basic principle must be observed—the space plan must follow work flows or work functions rather than preferences of personnel or purely esthetic considerations.

Work Flow

In an office *work flow* is the movement of information that flows from superiors to subordinates or laterally among workers at the same level. An optimum layout is not derived simply from a quick overview of an office operation. Rather it emerges slowly from an intensive analysis of information flows. Involved is a study of the division of labor, the nature and frequency of information-processing documents, and the distribution of documents within and, where applicable, outside the firm. An effort should be made to measure the frequency and quantity of documents processed as well as the number of work stations involved along with the total cycle time of each process.

Many offices function around a key (or source) document that contains the basic information, and most of the other records are offshoots of the key document. In an insurance company this document is an application for insurance; in an employment office, an application for work; and in a wholesale house, a customer's order. In studying information flows, it is necessary to trace the movement of each key document or set of documents from the time it enters the office until the time it is completely processed. From this study the work flow (with connecting functions along the way) can be plotted, and in this way the entire office function can be patterned. Since this processing takes place primarily among people, major emphasis should be given to the layout of each work station in the total work flow. However, computers and other data processing machines assist the workers to an increasing degree in the exchange of information. The interaction of all such components must be considered in an effort to create a true information processing center for the office.

Perhaps the most common method of analyzing information flows and organizational communication is to examine the organization chart. In the chart illustrated in Figure 4-1, the organization is depicted as a matrix. The most frequent communications, shown by the thick lines, are often not known formally by the organization but must be disclosed through systems studies of information flow. In space-planning programs interviews are usually conducted by asking the question "Who communicates with whom?" Figure 4-1 shows a top executive (such as a president), a subordinate line with three vice presidents, followed by six equal-level positions of, perhaps, department supervisors. Information flows into and out of each box. Such hidden processes of information exchange must be identified before a sound space management program can be completed.[3]

When office work flow is analyzed for efficiency, it will be found that the flow is most effective when it is continuous—that is, when intermittent storage stops are eliminated. Therefore, processing time at each work station must be identified and verified, transport time between work stations eliminated or reduced, and storage time decreased, if not omitted. A more extensive discussion of work flow and work efficiency is found in Chapter 15.

---

[3] *Ibid.*, p. 15.

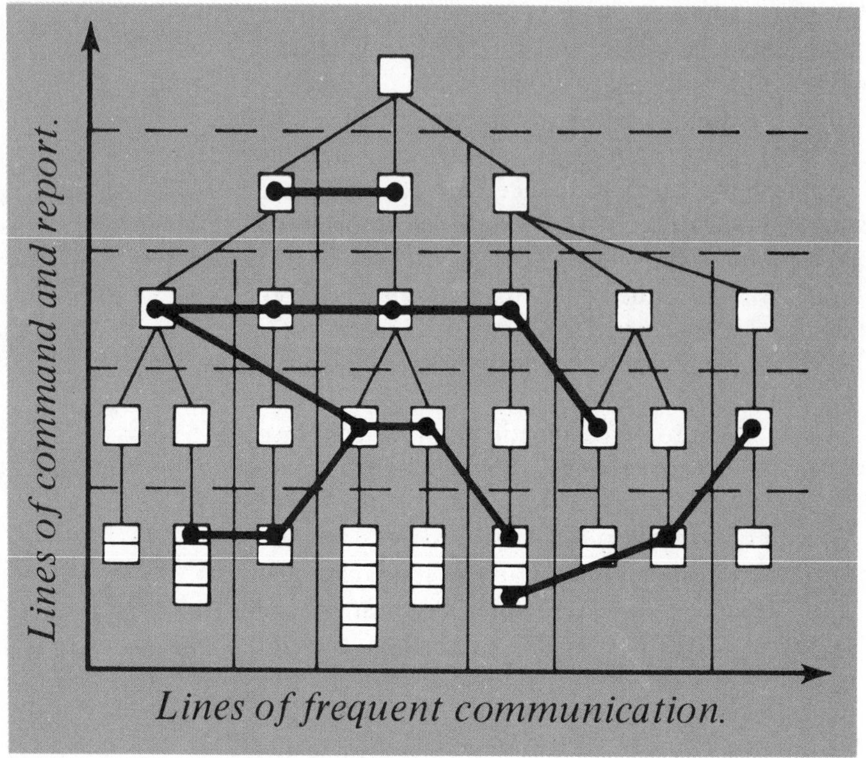

Fig. 4-1

Main Communication Flows in the Organization

Source: *Journal of Systems Management* (October, 1969).

Space Planning by Function: The Department

Although computers and other automated processing methods have caused changes in organizational patterns, the basic organizational unit of specialized functions continues to be the department. Departments should be arranged so that the work flow proceeds in an uninterrupted manner and so that the work passes through as few hands as possible. The planning of space will necessarily require a study of the office systems and procedures, the arrangement of furniture and equipment, and, of course, the personnel.

Certain principles should be followed in providing a layout for departments. Departments with constant or frequent contact with the public should be located near the reception area or have direct access to the corridors in order to minimize the traffic through open working areas. For example, the personnel and the purchasing departments have frequent contact with outside business representatives and should be located near the reception area. Operating departments, such as sales, should be near the executive and administrative area, whereas the controller's department may be remote from the executive area.

The Conventional Department Layout. The following description and Figure 4-2 indicate how departments are located in one conventional office layout.[4]

1. *Executive Suite.* This area is isolated at one end of the offices for maximum privacy. Note that it is self-contained, has its own access corridor, and is grouped around its own foyer.
2. *Sales Department.* Also relatively self-contained. Close to conference rooms for sales meetings. Adequate windows for highly paid personnel. Has its own access corridor close to executive suite, an important factor.
3. *Purchasing Department.* Has fairly close contact with sales at executive level. Considerable outside traffic, hence own corridor to reception area. Uses duplicating facilities heavily. Traffic department reports to director of purchasing.
4. *Accounting Department.* Provided with maximum window space for employees doing close and tedious work. Adjacent to data processing center, at least half of whose services it uses. Space for its own filing cabinets, frequently and exclusively referred to. Relatively isolated for minimum distraction. Located at extreme end of office since it has least contact with other departments.
5. *Comptroller.* An important executive, given a corner office. Typically this man is in charge of the accounting and data processing operations and supervises the office and personnel managers. While the comptroller has relatively close contact with the "policy" men in the executive suite, it is more important for him to be near the departments reporting directly to him.
6. *Office and Personnel Department.* In addition to being in charge of "housekeeping," this department originates forms and interviews and manages personnel. Has heavy traffic from outside so is close to reception area. Since mail deliveries, job applicants, and personnel with individual problems channel through the department, it is located near the service areas.

---

[4] Taken with permission of *Management Magazines, Inc.*, from *Integrated Office* (Fall, 1953), p. 16.

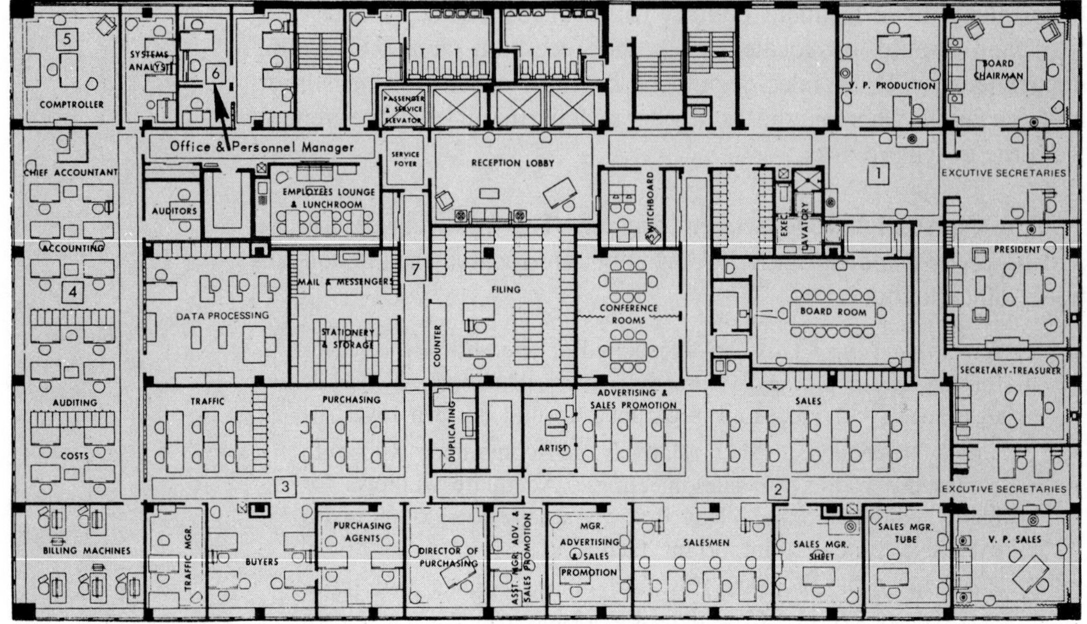

Fig. 4-2

How Departments Are Located in a Conventional Office Layout

The Office Landscape. The conventional departmental layout by function is characterized by isolated groups and wall barriers that uniformly enclose areas. Critics of this layout style suggest that it prevents or hinders interaction and communication and denies the existence of interdepartmental work flow. A space-planning authority comments on the effect of such conditions as follows:

> Activities which are prone to get messy or unsightly are never cleaned up and streamlined; they are enclosed in more walls! The end result is a cellular society in which the office workers spend their days in business boxes of varying sizes, depending upon their stations.[5]

To overcome the criticisms of the conventional layout plan, a new concept—the office landscape—has emerged. The *office landscape*, also referred to as *free-form clustering*, is an open plan in which

[5] Sydney G. Rodgers, "Modularity Versus Free-Form Clustering," *New Concepts in Office Design*, Business Equipment Manufacturers Association (Elmhurst, Illinois: The Business Press, 1968), p. 13.

functional, behavioral, and technical factors are all combined to determine the layout of individual work centers, work groups, and departments. This layout, illustrated in Figure 4-3, is characterized by

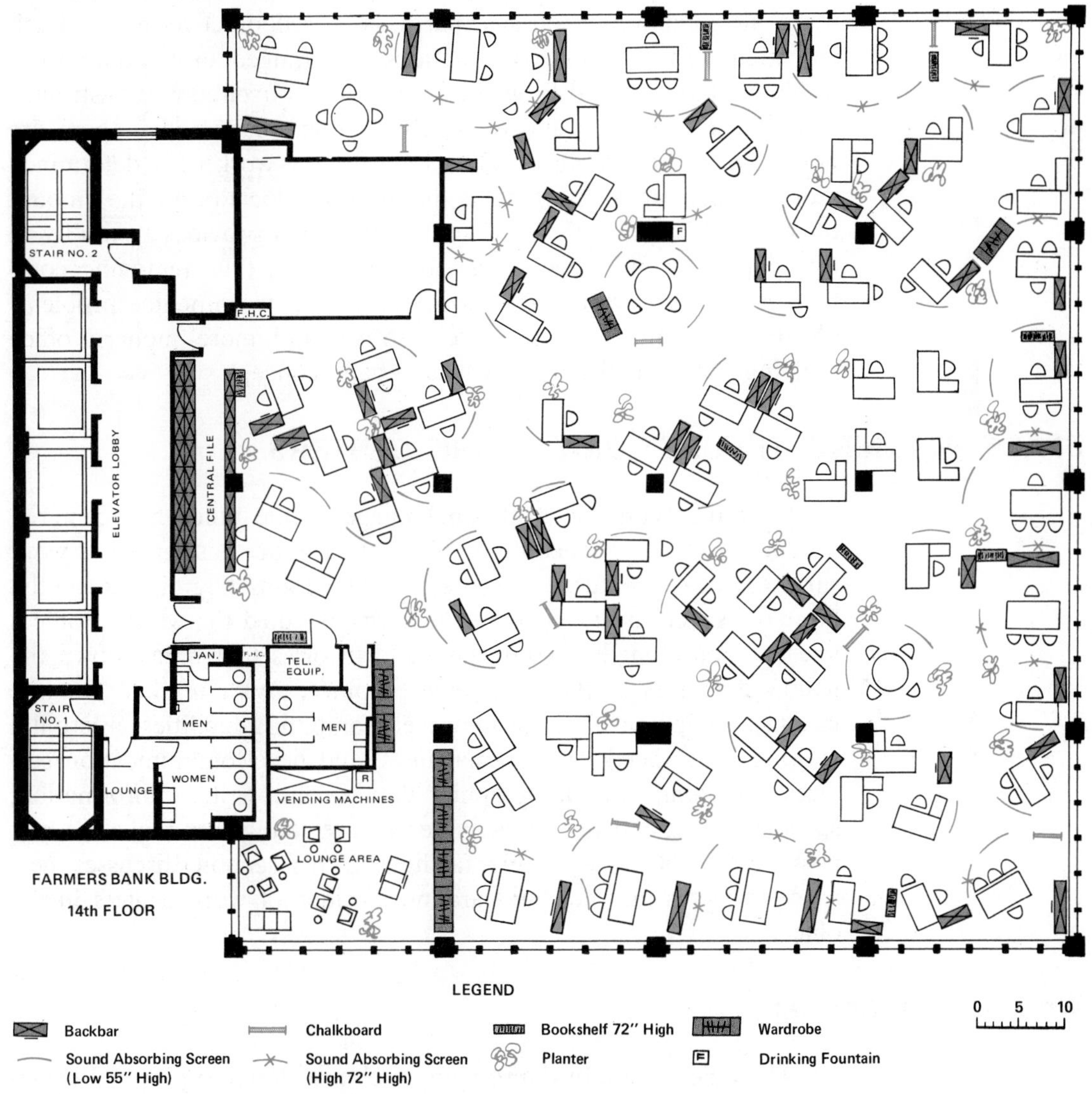

Fig. 4-3

Office Landscape Space Plan of Working Groups Arranged According to Their Communication and Information-Flow Requirements

Source: Freon Products Division, E. I. du Pont de Nemours & Co.

open planning; and privacy is provided by using movable, sound-absorbing screens and plants. The arrangement of work stations is accomplished by rearranging movable elements such as desks, chairs, screens, and planters without changing fixed installations (light fixtures, air-conditioning outlets, partitions, or floor coverings). Each individual grouping of work stations is arranged in a nonuniform fashion without regard to windows or other conventional constraints. Since the office landscape is largely an open-plan model, there are normally no private offices. The status of the workers is determined more by their work assignments than by their location or the amount of space allocated to them. Such an open plan provides flexibility in that partitions and screens are easily movable, thus removing communication barriers as well as minimizing environmental problems (heating, lighting, and the like). More and more modern office buildings are utilizing this open landscape concept.

SPACE PLANNING IN FUNCTIONAL WORK CENTERS

Over the years the traditional image of the office has centered around the desk. This common piece of furniture has served as work surface, storage center, and conference and counseling aid. Recently, however, space specialists have intensively studied the work in offices and have developed new concepts and theories that break down the hallowed images of the desk-centered office. With marked changes in office equipment through improved computing facilities, microfilm viewing, high-speed copying machines, and new communication services providing audible, graphic, digital, and written information, space-planning and work-flow patterns have changed to make the best possible use of all available facilities. This section discusses new space concepts that are built around the idea of work centers in the office.

Work Center Concept

The office is, more than anything else, a thinking place. Personnel must be placed at strategic locations for thinking—that is, for dealing with information from its collection through its transmission stages. In another sense the office may be considered as a place where work situations or tasks are generated. Related to these views is the recognition that most, if not all, office work centers around communication. In fact, behavioral scientists stress that better morale and more productivity can be expected if space planning makes adequate allowance for easy conversational exchange.

The basic unit of office space planning is the individual work station or work center where each employee performs the bulk of his assigned responsibilities. When all the work stations are combined, whether departmentally or in some other functional sense, the total work place or group work center is the result. Consideration of both the individual and the group work center concepts is necessary to achieve the optimum use of office space.

Individual Work Center. With most office employment comes the assignment of certain basic furniture and equipment at each work station. Such items as a desk or table for work surface and work storage, counters and shelves, files, machines, and seating facilities are normally required for each worker. Beyond the physical equipment necessary to each work station are certain functional requirements of all work stations. These functions and certain key questions concerning them are outlined in Figure 4-4.

With the exception of the one-man office, each work station must be designed so that it merges with the other work stations in the total working environment. In other words, groups of workers at groups of work stations must be coordinated in the space environment.

Group Work Centers. No one work station exists by itself or for itself. Rather it serves as one part of a larger group working toward a group goal. All the work centers, therefore, must be space-planned and coordinated to fit into a total work environment.

A department is the typical working environment for groups of workers. For example, everyone specializing in hiring, testing, evaluating, and training workers is housed in a personnel department or division. Each of the multiwork tasks and the work centers at which these tasks are completed must be planned and spaced so that it relates to the needs of the total personnel function.

The administrative office manager's responsibilities include coordinating all work centers into an arrangement that facilitates the combined teamwork of all the individual members. This responsibility requires that he bear in mind the following space requirements of group work centers:

1. Relationships between positions as well as relationships between the position and the total working environment must be recognized. This requires a knowledge of:

INDIVIDUAL WORK CENTER FUNCTIONS	KEY QUESTIONS
A. Duties performed at each work station	1. What work is performed? 2. By whom is the work performed? 3. How is the work performed? 4. How is the work performed related to the entire work effort?
B. Equipment requirements for work performance	1. What furniture is required? 2. What machines are required? 3. What equipment is available? 4. What future equipment will be available? 5. What equipment would be helpful (but is not required)?
C. Space requirements	1. How much space is available and how much is required for optimum work performance? 2. What are the space requirements for each item of furniture and machinery? 3. What should be the minimum allowance for each worker of each grade level? 4. How can employee comfort and concentration be maximized? 5. How can purposeful communications be encouraged and auditory and visual distractions discouraged? 6. What are the acoustical and esthetic requirements for the work station?
D. Economic feasibility	1. What will an effective work center cost? 2. How much money is available for the work center? 3. Where can reasonable compromises with costs be made?
E. Flexibility and future expansion	1. What are the future plans for the work station? 2. What equipment, space, and costs will be required? 3. How can the work station be closely tied to the expected changes in new office equipment? 4. How much interchangeability can be built into the work station's component parts?

Fig. 4-4

Functional Requirements of Work Stations

a. Each work center's total set of activities.
b. All exchanges of information and movement of documents and records.
c. All individual and joint uses of documents, equipment, files, and supplies.
d. All personnel interrelationships, skills, and understandings requirements.
e. Supervisory requirements.
f. Individual and group goals.

2. Individual and group work center placement must be coordinated. Normally this suggests that:

    a. Similar and/or identical work should be located at adjacent work centers.
    b. Individuals with the same basic skills and same job requirements should be located in adjacent positions.
    c. Work sequences should be reflected in similar position sequences in a work area.
    d. Joint use of files and equipment should be considered.
    e. Common supervision should be employed requiring close physical proximity of the supervised group.

3. The nature and frequency or volume of work and the requirements for maximizing efficiency should dictate how all work centers are grouped together. This means that:

    a. Standard work flows as well as variations in work patterns should be identified.
    b. Volumes of work (and their fluctuations) should be determined.
    c. Specialties of workers should be clustered or grouped.
    d. Peak and valley work loads, as well as their causes and effects, should be noted.
    e. The input (or inflow) of work and workers as well as the output (or outflow) of work and workers should be considered.

Effective group work reflects effective planning and coordination, whether it be the management of space or personnel. The administrative office manager is faced with several options as he faces the decision of how best to utilize the available space. Of primary concern is the question of whether to design private or large general office areas, or both, and how to provide for the special work centers commonly found in most organizations.

Private vs. General Offices

Several decades ago the private office was widely regarded as one very important status symbol of executive success. Today, however, with rising costs of office space as well as the realization that much of the office work can be done more efficiently while working with others, many questions must be answered before deciding whether to design private offices or general, open office spaces for office workers.

Management must weigh the relative advantages and disadvantages of using private offices. The reasons usually given for providing private offices are: (1) they create prestige in the eyes of employees and visitors for top management, department heads, and high-level staff people; (2) the nature of the work being done, such as research, planning, and financial report preparation, is confidential; and (3) the work, such as computer programming, requires a high degree of concentration. On the other hand, the private office makes efficient use of approximately 50 percent of the space allocated to it and consequently constitutes an expensive method of providing utilities, such as heating, lighting, and air conditioning. The private office is relatively inflexible, for its permanent partitions are expensive and difficult to remove; it provides barriers to supervision of employees as the supervisor is separated from the employees; and it sets up arbitrary barriers to oral communications in the office.

Movable partitions can be used to provide a certain amount of privacy in work without the disadvantages of the private office. The use of partitioning meets the needs of those workers who require work privacy and provides needed flexibility for changing work stations as work patterns change. The following are some of the types of movable partitions that are available:

1. *Ceiling height:* in wood, steel, and other materials featuring soundproofing and glass inserts. Commonly used for private offices, conference rooms, and corridors.
2. *Partial height:* similar to the ceiling height but more often with glass inserts rather than solid constructions. Commonly used for general offices and room and department dividers.
3. *Bank screen partitions:* usually 5′6″ to 5′8″ high. These have a solid base section 42″ to 54″ high, topped by a glass section 12″ to 24″, providing privacy and yet not interfering too much with lighting and ventilating conditions.
4. *Low rail or counter-height partitions:* 36″ to 42″ high, used to segregate units in large areas and prevent short cuts through

the departments. Commonly used for central files, mailroom, cashier stations, and reception areas.

5. *Folding walls:* available in wood or plastic material, receding in accordion style when necessary. These are ceiling high, providing complete privacy.
6. *Ceiling high glass walls:* sometimes used for decorative purposes, giving the effect of lightness and openness. Clear glass permits supervision from room to room.

In some office buildings the number of private offices is decreased in favor of large general offices controlled by bays. A *bay* is the unit of floor space used for control purposes. Its size varies from 300 to 450 square feet. The bays may be separated by lines drawn on the floor or by supports from ceiling to floor, or they may be shown only on the blueprints. Types of work as well as types of office equipment are often segregated in offices by means of bays.

In the Martin Company of Baltimore, Maryland, both floors of the two-story building are open; there are no interior walls nor room dividers. The only signs of top executive status are the corner areas which are occupied by the president and his vice presidents. All furnishings—desks, draperies, and carpeting—are identical. In this office it is felt that walls represent barriers to communications, and it is desired to make it impossible for a staff executive to avoid contact with other people who help run the business. Another reversal of the traditional layout for executives is seen in the Federal Aviation Agency in Washington, D.C. Executive offices are clustered near the center of each floor in the eight-story building. The status level decreases as one moves from the center of the office area toward the outside windows where the secretaries and clerks are located. In this building the elevator is centrally located throughout all offices. Since managers and supervisors attract more traffic than others, it is desired to concentrate the traffic near the central elevator core to avoid disruption of other workers. Also, since there are more secretaries and clerks than other workers, they have been placed near the windows where there is more usable space.[6]

Along with the use of bays in large areas, conference rooms may be provided for the use of those executives who do not need privacy too frequently. However, most top-level executives will always continue to need and prefer private offices.

---

[6] "Two New Fashions for Executives' Offices," *Business Management* (July, 1965), p. 58.

Special Work Centers

Many large firms have developed work centers that are somewhat different from the typical ones found in all businesses. The most common of these special work centers are (1) the reception center, (2) reference services center (sometimes called the library), and (3) the data processing center.[7]

The Reception Center. The reception center serves not only to promote efficiency in office operations but also as a promotional medium of the firm and its products or services. It is therefore important that this area be well arranged and kept orderly, for the visitor gets his first impression of the business when he steps into its reception center. The center should express honesty, reliability, and efficiency. It is the introductory chapter to the biography of the business.

The reception area should be located so that from it the visitors cannot see the main office. This will prevent interruption of the work, as the attention of the workers is often distracted by the flow of callers. In planning a reception center, at least ten square feet should be allocated for each visitor, in terms of the maximum number to be expected at any one time.

Reading matter should be supplied the visitors, who may have to wait until those upon whom they call are ready to receive them. As it may be assumed that many of the callers are interested in some product or service of the company, often some literature or a display of these subjects is provided. If reading matter or displays are provided, the lighting should be sufficient for comfortable reading.

The Reference Services Center. In an attempt to encourage their employees to be well informed on both general and special topics, many companies have established libraries or reference services centers. In planning the space for reference services, some firms design the area to serve a dual function—to serve as a reference area and at the same time to utilize the book shelves as room dividers.

Businesses also maintain special libraries as a service-rendering unit that makes available whatever knowledge and experience it can accumulate to further the activities of the organization. As such, the special library is really an information bureau, with a limited

[7] For a review of other special work centers, such as the files department, vaults, coat rooms, interviewing rooms, and conference rooms, the reader should consult *Office Standards and Planning*, Art Metal, Inc., Jamestown, New York.

number of reference books, technical handbooks, and other publications in the special field of the company.

According to The Special Libraries Association, reference services constitute a significant additional cost to the administrative budget. A survey by the Association shows the average reference librarian's salary alone to be $11,800, with salaries ranging upwards to more than $25,000 per year. When the total budget for the reference services center is prepared, it will, therefore, be useful to consider these accepted budget ratios: [8]

Salaries (professional and clerical)	70%
Books, pamphlets, documents; periodical subscriptions; society memberships (for publications)	25%
Binding, supplies, microform publications, photocopying expenses, etc.	3%
Professional association expenses and travel expenses	2%

Before deciding whether a company reference services center is feasible, the following questions should be answered: [9]

1. How much of the research done by executives and scientists in the company is unnecessary because someone else has already done it?
2. When a man is assigned to a market research, public relations, or other project, how much time does he spend on preparatory research?
3. How often are junior executives and secretaries sent out to "look something up" in a local library? How long does it take?
4. What is the cost of distributing multiple copies of business periodicals and little-used reports?
5. How much time and money do executives devote to telephoning around the country seeking information before making important decisions?

A firm may obtain assistance in setting up its reference services center by contacting The Special Libraries Association which will provide a library consultant free of charge (except for travel

[8] Ruth S. Leonard, *Profiles of Special Libraries*, Special Libraries Association, New York, reprinted from *Special Libraries* 57: (No. 3) 179-84; (No. 4) 227-31; (No. 5) 327-31 (1966), p. 7. (Firms considering the formation of a special library should contact The Special Libraries Association, 235 Park Avenue South, New York, NY 10003.)

[9] Peter R. Weill, "Are You Ready for a Company Library?" *Administrative Management* (August, 1963), p. 44.

expenses), if the visit does not require more than one day's time. The consultant will survey the company's existing facilities and offer recommendations on costs, techniques, space and equipment requirements, and staff requirements. The Association also makes available a listing of professional consultants who are experienced in the firm's subject field so that the firm can select its own consultant, determine the length of the consultation period, and agree upon the fee.

Data Processing Center. Many administrative office managers are faced with the problem of designing and constructing facilities to handle the space needs of programmers and systems personnel, as well as the data processing center itself. Although the computer is capable of an increasing number of applications, it still does not determine its own space needs.

Space Requirements for Programmers. Programming an electronic computer requires considerable concentration and thought in a setting free from noise and distraction so that attention can be given to the detail of the problem to be programmed. How to provide this type of space is a growing problem with the continual increase in programming and related systems personnel. One possible answer is provided by an executive of a large insurance company who describes how his firm, with a programming staff of nearly a hundred employees, handled this space problem:

> We did it by compartmentalizing with 54-inch-high, freestanding, glazed-rail partitioning. Each partition unit abuts the front of each desk and also has a return on two sides to separate desks in a row from each other. When seated, the programmer is effectively cut off from his neighbors and potential distraction. Yet when he rises to his feet, he does not feel he is in a huge maze of egg crates from which there is no escape. Lighting problems and problems of heating and air conditioning are avoided. Further, we can actually place more people in a given area than we otherwise could have. Expense-wise, we spent about $168 per unit for this job, including expenditure for a corkboard to replace the glazed rail on one of the return partitions and a built-in rack attached to the partition at the front of the desk to house manuals and program binders.[10]

[10] Walter C. Waddell, "Effective Space Utilization and Its Meaning to Employee Morale," *Developing the Total Office Environment* (Washington, D.C.: Thompson Book Company, 1967), p. 52.

Space Requirements for the Computer Center. The computer and its related peripheral equipment require a well-controlled environment if they are to operate at optimum efficiency. Typically the computer center must be a dust-resistant area with (1) rigidly controlled temperature and humidity, (2) nearby facilities for programmers, (3) fireproof tape storage vaults, (4) space for auxiliary equipment and furniture, and (5) an allowance for expansion.[11]

Fig. 4-5

Courtesy of Fimaco, Inc., Philadelphia

A Computer Center

Because of the cost and complexity of computers, their installation requires extensive planning. Although the location and size of the computer center will be greatly influenced by the particular computer system being installed, consideration must also be given the following factors: the flow of work within the firm; the location of key auxiliary areas such as the mail room, the supply room, and the

[11] H. E. Wriggelsworth, "Constructing a Computer Room," *Administrative Management* (April, 1964), p. 56.

maintenance area; the availability of air conditioning, electricity, fire protection, and other necessary services; and plans for future expansion.

If the computer center is to be located in a multistory building, the floor above the computer center should be watertight so as to prevent possible water damage to the equipment. Ordinarily basements are avoided as a site for the computer center because of their dampness and the possibility of flooding as the result of the weather or faulty plumbing. Noncombustible, fire-resistant walls, floors, and ceilings should be used in the construction of the computer center so that it is completely cut off from others parts of the building. The flooring should be sturdy, for medium and large-scale computer systems produce a loading of 100 to 250 pounds per square foot.

One of the most important elements to be considered in the computer center is the temperature and humidity control. Extremely high temperatures can cause malfunctioning within the component parts of the computer system, and low temperatures may cause condensation on the electronic parts. For most computer systems the ideal temperature is between 65° and 75° F. Too much humidity in the center can impair the operation of magnetic tapes and discs, paper tapes, and card readers, while too little humidity can cause electrostatic charges to build up on cards and tapes, thus causing them to stick and bring about errors. The recommended relative humidity in a computer center is between 40 and 60 percent. Although most computers and magnetic tape units have built-in dust filters, care should be taken to protect the computer from dust, smoke, and other particles that affect the computer system adversely.

In planning the site for the computer center another very important factor to be considered is the electrical installation. The wiring arrangements should be gauged to the system being installed and should follow the manufacturer's specifications. Unless careful provisions are made for the proper wiring needs, it may be necessary to undertake expensive rewiring of the area or to make wiring changes within the equipment.

Computer systems are extremely delicate, and down time can be highly costly. Therefore, prior to the layout of the computer center, extensive preinstallation planning must be undertaken. In planning and executing the computer installation, the administrative office manager is well advised to make full use of the expert assistance of the computer manufacturer and its sales representatives and outside consultants if necessary.

PRINCIPLES OF SPACE MANAGEMENT

In this chapter attention has been called to the fact that layout is a key factor in achieving office efficiency. As such, layout may be considered as a component part of the administrative office system. Other components of this system are the work methods and procedures that are executed in the office, the personnel in the office, as well as the furniture and equipment required to do the work.

Space Guidelines for Efficient Work

The following space guidelines will aid the administrative office manager in achieving work efficiency. A more intensive study of systems and procedures is contained in Chapter 15.

1. To reduce communication and transportation lines to a minimum, a straight-line flow of information (forms, records, reports, etc.) rather than a crisscrossing of lines is recommended.
2. Space should be conserved as much as possible without cramping individuals in work centers. Large sums of money can be saved by making better use of space, especially that space above the surfaces of desks and tables.
3. Those offices requiring considerable contact with the public should be located in a place accessible to the public. Conversely, those offices requiring confidential work or great privacy should be removed from the easy accessibility of the public. Purchasing, sales, and personnel departments fall into the former category; accounting and research and development offices are among the latter group.
4. Space allocation should be based on major work flows which normally function around major source documents such as the purchase order, the time card, and the sales invoice. This implies that departments having a great deal of cross-communication with other departments should be located adjacent to each other. Examples of this relationship are the personnel and payroll departments.
5. Future work requirements should be forecast. One guideline to use in such forecasts is the rate of increase in volume of work over several "bellwether" years.

The factors of lighting, ventilation, noise levels, and interior decoration, which also must be considered in planning a layout because of their effects on worker efficiency, are discussed at length in Chapter 6.

Space Guidelines for Personnel

The number of persons to be housed in a given area both at present and in the future has an effect on the amount of space to be used. Because there are so many variables in allocating space in an office, it becomes difficult to set standards of space requirements. Single-occupancy private offices may vary from 200 to 600 square feet, whereas those in open office spaces may require only 75 to 100 square feet each. In addition, allowance must be made for space allotted to reception centers, display rooms, filing rooms, and employee lounges. It becomes difficult to compute the average amount of space required for each employee. The best that can be achieved in setting space standards is to group employees and set minimum and maximum guidelines for each group. For example:

1. Private offices vary from 600 square feet for senior executives to 200 for senior assistants, and 75 to 100 square feet for cubicles in an open office space.
2. General offices should have 80 to 100 square feet per working area in smaller departments, or in units where there are high-level nonexecutive personnel, or where the visitor traffic is heavy. In large clerical work areas, the allowance can be reduced to 40 to 80 square feet per working area.
3. Aisles and corridors will probably require about 10 to 15 percent of the total area of private and general offices.
4. Conference and board rooms require 25 square feet for each person for rooms housing up to 30 persons and 8 square feet per person for areas housing 30 to 200 persons.
5. Central files require 5 to 7 square feet per letter-size cabinet and 6 to 8 square feet for the legal-size cabinet.
6. Coat room allowances are 1.5 square feet per person for two rows of racks with an aisle between.
7. Telephone switchboard requires 50 square feet for basic equipment per position.

Space Guidelines for Furniture and Equipment

The placement of furniture and equipment requires an inventory of the quantity, description, and size of each piece of furniture and equipment. In locating each item on the floor plan, some well-recognized guidelines are usually followed:

1. The width of main aisles may vary from 5 to 8 feet. Less important aisles should be 45 to 65 inches in width.
2. Aisle space between desks should not be less than 36 inches.
3. Space between desks facing in the same direction—that is, the space occupied by chairs—should not be less than 28 inches, preferably 36 inches.
4. If files open up front to front—that is, to an aisle—the width of the aisle, when the file drawers are open, should not be less than 30 to 40 inches.
5. Large open spaces are better than small room spaces cut out of the same area. Supervision and control can be more easily maintained, communication between individual employees is more direct, and better light and ventilation are possible.
6. Movable, modern partitions should be used rather than fixed walls as alternatives to private offices.
7. No workers should face the light. Whenever possible, desks and machines should be located so that light from the windows is at the left of the individual.
8. Desks should generally face the same direction, unless the employees work together.
9. No more than two desks should be placed side by side so that each desk will be on an aisle, thus permitting easy flow of traffic.
10. Desks should be arranged to give a straight flow of work—that is, so that a person will receive his work from the desk beside or in back of him.
11. Files should be placed against walls or railings if possible.
12. Persons who have the most communication with other departments should be located nearest the exits.
13. Those who must do the closest work should have the best light. Employees engaged in doing fine, close work should be placed nearest the natural light.

THE OFFICE SPACE STUDY: ALTERNATIVE METHODS

The importance of making office plans and revising the layout is recognized not only by administrative office managers but also by many manufacturers of office supplies and equipment. There are several methods by which a space study may be undertaken. All of these are usually based upon a floor plan, drawn to scale, of the office space available. Four methods of preparing a model of the office layout are described below.

1. The first method, shown in Figure 4-6, makes use of colored paper cutouts of all types of equipment such as desks, chairs,

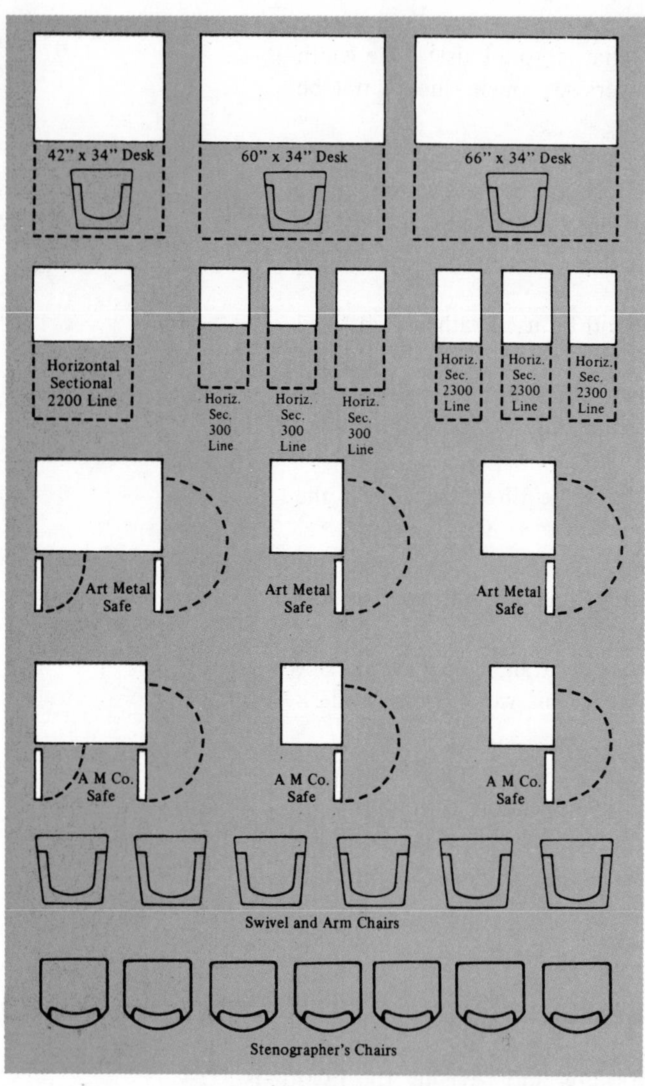

Art Metal, Inc.

Fig. 4-6

Colored Paper Cutouts Drawn to Scale for Use in Preparing Office Layouts

files, and safes. Each piece of furniture and equipment is drawn to the same scale as the floor plan so that proper relationships are maintained when the cutouts are pasted into position. This is the simplest and least expensive method of illustrating a proposed layout.

2. The second method, illustrated in Figure 4-7, makes use of a plastic template upon which the cutout areas indicate the size and shape of the various types of equipment and the special symbols that are used to prepare flow charts of the work within the office.
3. A third method, a rather expensive one, is to use a layout board drawn to scale, as shown in Figure 4-8. The top surface

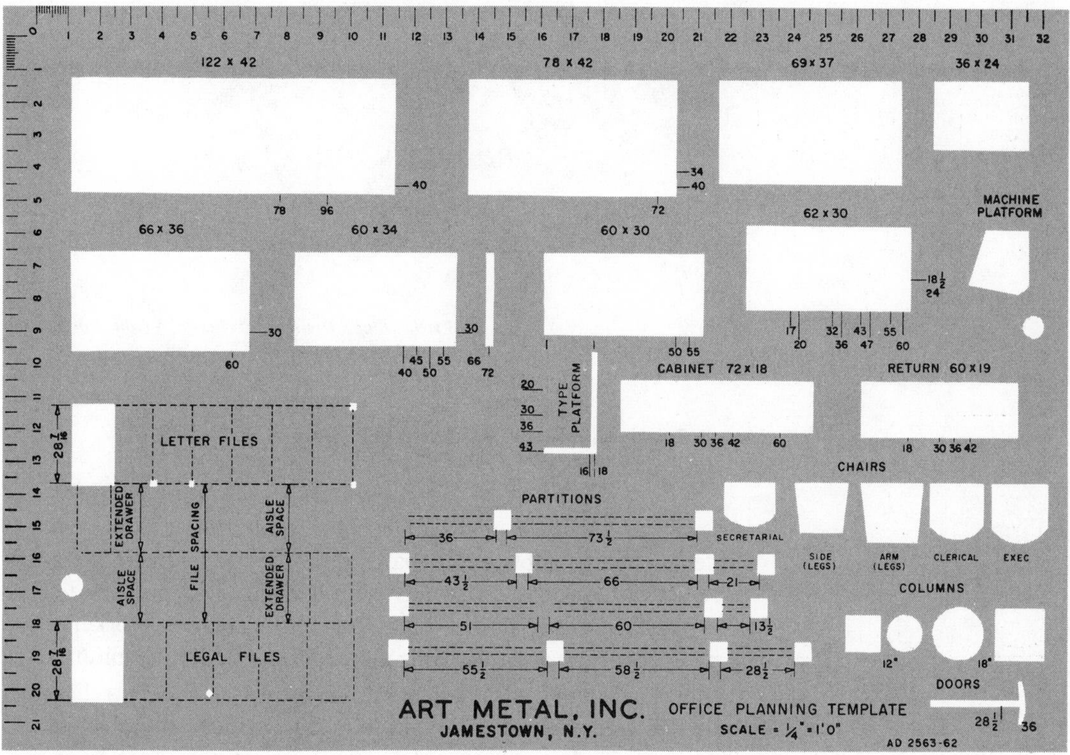

Art Metal, Inc.

Fig. 4-7

Plastic Template

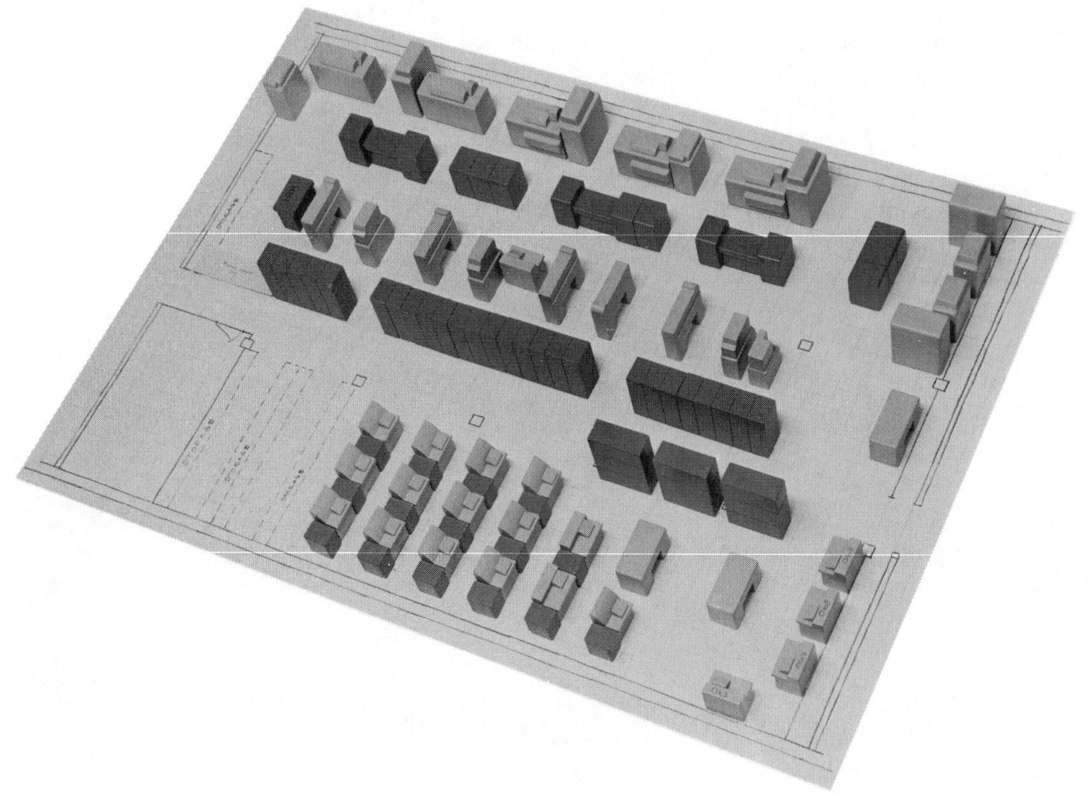

Wright Line, Division of Barry Wright Corporation

Fig. 4-8

Layout Board with Scale Models of Furniture, Machines, and Equipment

of this board may be made of cork so that the scale models of desks, chairs, tables, and partitions may be pinned down when set up. Once the plan has been laid out, it is possible to use it for the basis of discussion among executives and workers, or photographs may be made as a guide for installing furniture.

4. A fourth method (the simulated office space model) relies upon the actual construction of full-size replicas of selected office areas.[12] In such complete mock-up offices, executives and office workers can sit in their actual offices and know

---

[12] For additional information on the use of full-size replicas in planning the offices of Bristol-Myers and General Motors headquarters in New York, see "Complete Mock-Up Offices Used to Plan Real Ones," *Administrative Management* (April, 1969), pp. 30-31.

beforehand what their work stations will be like. They can examine and test all the various components as provided by different manufacturers. Colors and textures can be evaluated and examined together in the same proportions and arrangements in which they will be ultimately used. This method, the most expensive of all, is feasible only when large sums of money are to be spent on large quantities of space.

QUESTIONS FOR REVIEW

1. What is the significant difference in meaning between the terms "office layout" and "space management"?
2. How realistic and practical is the "office landscape" form of office layout? What disadvantages do you see in its development and implementation?
3. What are the principal factors to consider in the planning of an efficient individual work center? How may these factors be modified to make allowance for individual worker preferences?
4. Explain in detail the reasons underlying the trend away from the use of private offices. Under what conditions may private offices be necessary? What types of substitutes are available to be used for private offices?
5. The first glimpse that the visitor has of an organization is its reception center. How important is this area, and how may its space be properly planned?
6. Discuss the uses of a company reference services center that are not provided by an up-to-date metropolitan or university library.
7. The data processing center is receiving increasing attention by today's management. To plan properly the space allocated to this center, many environmental factors must be considered. Cite those factors that you consider most important and be prepared to defend your choice.
8. Identify four key space management principles and give an application of each principle.
9. Compare the four methods of undertaking an office space study, giving the advantages and disadvantages of each method.
10. How does each of the following factors influence office space management?
    a. Work flow.
    b. Supervision of work.
    c. Types of furniture and equipment.
    d. Number and location of entrances.

QUESTIONS FOR DISCUSSION

1. Assume you have been appointed by the Administrative Management Society to develop a set of criteria for making awards to the five best "space-managed" offices in America. What would your set of criteria include?

2. How important is the planning of vault and storage space for:

a. A manufacturer of sporting goods—three factories employing 500 employees and a central office force of 80 workers.

b. A savings bank having four branches in a large city, 200,000 depositors, 60 office workers and tellers.

c. A commercial bank having 60 branch offices located in a large city and its suburbs, employing 2,000 persons.

d. A life insurance company employing 3,000 workers, doing business on a national scale.

e. A New York brokerage firm having a main office and 15 branch offices, employing 250 office workers.

3. How would the space allocations in each of the following offices differ?

a. A payroll accounting office, staffed by seven employees, in a small manufacturing firm.

b. A branch office of a savings and loan company having four office workers.

c. A real estate office with eight employees.

d. A legal office with seven partners and ten clerical workers.

4. In the law offices of Jeremy, Blair, and Baer, there are 32 lawyers, a certified public accountant, and 24 clerical employees. The firm is now planning its new quarters, which will be ready late next year. The partners realize they have a lot to learn in their planning. What suggestions can you offer them in the area of initial planning to make sure that a satisfactory space plan is devised for the offices?

5. The Stewart Company is moving to a new building in which the office manager's work area is 28′ x 14′. This space will be occupied by the office manager, his assistant, a secretary, a typist, and a young man who works part-time. In this area there will be need for desks and chairs for all employees, chairs for visitors, two file cabinets, bookcases, a cabinet and rack for literature, and a coat rack. The office manager would also like to have some sort of partitioning around his area because he does a great deal of dictating. However, he does not want it to appear that he is appropriating the only two windows in the office, both of which are on one 14-foot wall.

What suggestions can you offer the office manager as he commences to plan his space requirements? Should the office manager be concerned that others will feel he is unjustifiably entitled to all window space? Sketch a rough space plan for the new area, in which you indicate the size of desk you recommend for each employee.

6. Figure A shows the area occupied by the credit department of the Triad Hosiery Company. The company is in need of providing additional work stations for its expanding work force and asks for your suggestions in increasing and rearranging the number of desks. Study the diagram carefully and make suggestions for a revised plan that will provide as many work stations as possible without changing the size of desks.

Fig. A

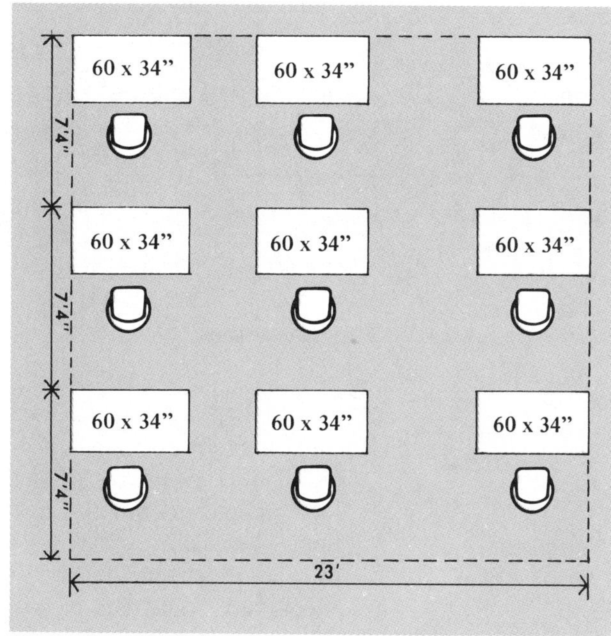

Credit Department of Triad Hosiery Company

7. In the filing department shown in Figure B, the east and west walls are solid (without windows); along the northern and southern dimensions, the space is open to permit entrance and exit to adjacent departments. Discuss how the five-drawer files in the department might be rearranged and additional five-drawer units added to provide the maximum number of file cabinets. The outside dimensions of each five-drawer unit are 57½″ high, 15″ wide, and 27″ deep. No provision should be made for tables or chairs since they are located in the departments adjacent to the filing department. If each file clerk can handle 60 file drawers, how many clerks will be needed in your expanded layout?

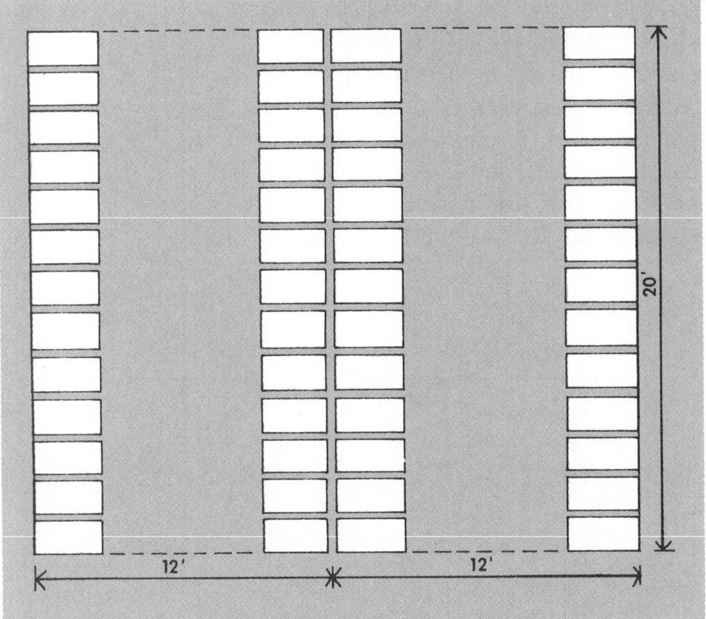

Fig. B

Filing Department

8. The data processing center of the Armstrong Department Store is converting from punched-card machines to a small-scale computer installation. Much of the same space (50′ x 42′) will be utilized for the computer as was utilized for the original punched-card machines, though parallel runs (using both computer and punched-card systems) will be in effect for one month while the new system is being "debugged." The data processing supervisor must come to some space management decisions as soon as he considers this information:

a. The staff of three key-punch operators will be retained. Three key-punch machines and one verifier machine also will be retained.
b. All other staff will be retrained and retained. They consist of five machine operators, two of whom will be retained for programming positions.
c. One additional programmer, as well as a senior systems analyst, will be obtained.
d. Appropriate space must be provided in the present quarters for the new equipment (a computer, the console, two tape drive units, the key-punch and verifier machines, one input/output card unit, one card-to-tape converter, and one printing unit), as well as for the supervisory personnel, the programming and systems personnel, and the machine operators.

Develop a plan of suggested space allocations, along with a list of unanswerable questions at this point in time. How can the space plan incorporate all machines required during the parallel runs?

PRACTICAL OFFICE CASES

Case 4-1 Revising an Office Space Plan

The Farmer & Luce Sales Company occupies the second floor of the suburban Cherry Grove Office Building. The size of the office, 30′ x 25′, provides adequate space for the employees' comfort. However, the office manager has become very much disturbed by the constant movement of workers around the office. A study of the work flow has been conducted and it is found that the incoming mail is handled as shown in Figure C. The administrative office manager notes especially the backtracking in the handling and routing of office correspondence.

Fig. C

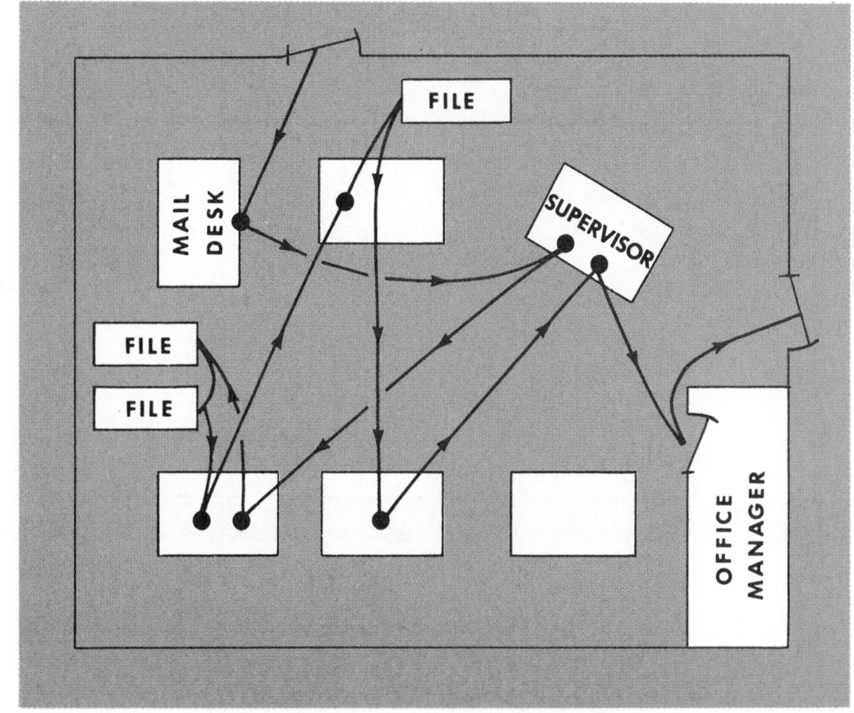

Office of the Farmer & Luce Sales Company

■ As administrative office manager of this firm, prepare a revised workflow chart and space plan, indicating the approximate area required for the workers. Show how the handling of incoming mail may be accomplished more quickly and efficiently and indicate how much savings in space will result from your revised space plan.

Case 4-2 Designing a Reception Center Space Plan

Doctors McGarvey and Schumacher, specialists in internal medicine, have moved to a new second-floor location in an urban office building. One of their last unsolved space problems is the reception center (shown in Figure D) where a limited amount of space is available in which to accommodate a growing number of medical patients. The size of the reception space (11′ x 22′9″) is small, and it is an inner office. Due to the construction of the building and the permanence of the wall partitions, no changes in basic building construction can be made. However, railings, movable partitions, and the like may be employed in the space plan in an effort to provide maximum seating and comfort, and space for the usual furniture and accessories for a waiting-reception room. Only one receptionist (also the administrative assistant) will be stationed in this area.

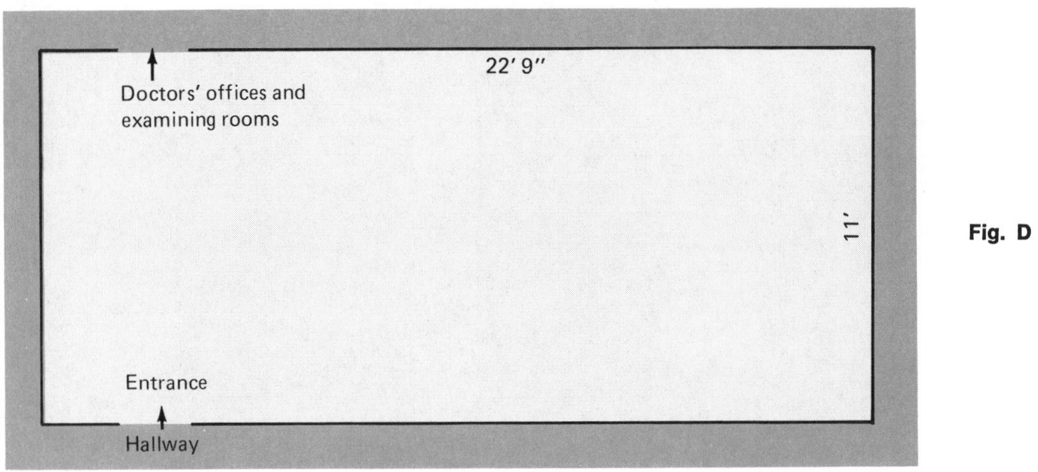

Fig. D

Doctors' Office Reception Center

■ As administrative assistant to the two physicians, design a new space plan for this area in which space is utilized efficiently for the maximum number of patients as well as for your work station. In your plan consideration should be given to types of furniture, furniture groupings, and environmental factors, such as color, lighting, and ventilation.

5

The Office Environment: Furniture and Equipment

One convenient way of describing the office environment is in terms of its physical and mental factors. In addition to furniture and equipment, or furnishings, the physical environment of the office includes its size or dimensions, types of surfaces (color of walls, type of floor, window coverings), the nature of the lighting provided, noise control and acoustical materials, air conditioning and ventilation, and background music. Each of these factors has physical characteristics that strongly affect the mental condition of the workers—their morale and overall attitude toward work and toward each other.

Management considerations regarding the selection, procurement, maintenance, replacement, and control of office furniture and equipment are important and complex responsibilities of the office manager. These will be discussed in this chapter. The psycho-physiological impact of the other factors that make up the physical office environment will be treated in Chapter 6.

SELECTION

No one can know everything about the physical environment in which he works. Yet, the office manager, as the custodian of the information center of the firm, is usually expected to have available a large body of facts and information about the office furniture and equipment required for the firm. In addition, he is expected to know what office furnishings are available for consideration by his firm. To provide such information, the office manager should have available, or should know where to obtain, information about each of the following items:

1. Principal types of furniture and equipment and reputable suppliers of each.
2. Reliable statistics for comparing the effectiveness of competing brands of equipment and furniture.
3. Current prices on all items and preferably catalogs representing each major supplier's merchandise.
4. Criteria for deciding on the need for such equipment and for selecting the equipment.
5. Knowledge about the impact of the equipment on the information system, particularly the training or retraining needed, new suppliers, and operating costs.
6. Possibilities for standardizing equipment throughout the firm.
7. Procurement alternatives (such as renting, leasing, or purchasing) and quantity purchasing options.
8. Maintenance, repair, and replacement considerations.

In a world in which technology is providing an almost endless array of new products and machines, the office manager must be constantly alert to make sure that he has the best equipped office environment possible. He should have a good understanding of the principal uses or applications of the various office furniture and equipment and be able to assist not only his own staff but also the staffs of other departments in his firm in choosing the most appropriate office furnishings.

Office Furniture

Modern office furniture manufacturers continue to expand both the types and the various styles of their products. Generally all such manufacturers include filing cabinets, desks, tables, and chairs as well as other related items in both executive or managerial lines and in clerical lines. Since filing equipment is discussed in Chapter 8, only the common types of furniture will be discussed in detail in this chapter.

The cost of office furniture constitutes a significant part of the overall cost of the space in which office work is accomplished. As a rule, furniture is purchased rather than leased or rented, for it is intended to last for a long period of time. Thus, the office manager should give serious attention to the selection and use of office furniture. If properly selected, office furniture can assist the office manager to increase employee productivity, to lower production costs, and to retain efficient people on their jobs.

Office Desks. The desk is a universal symbol of office work. Whenever a desk is found, paper work is performed. The desk fulfills many purposes in the office. Primarily it provides a suitable surface for processing information that is usually in written form. It is considered to be the central part of the office work station, frequently as a place on which (or along which) data processing or word processing machines are positioned. In all cases, too, the desk furnishes a useful storage place for supplies needed and data collected.

The cost factor is important in the selection of office desks. In most cases, even when a company owns its office building, estimates are made of rentals that should be charged against each department and division. Each component unit space and each department and division, in turn, is charged rental space. Desk space in offices in large cities may rent for as much as $10 a square foot on an annual basis. A desk 60 inches by 34 inches occupies a space of over 14 square feet. This space, at $10 a square foot, would rent for more than $140 a year. The rental for the chair space, which would approximate 60 inches by 30 inches, or 12½ square feet, would be $125, making a total of more than $265 for the desk and chair. However, a desk 48 inches by 30 inches would probably be satisfactory for many office workers. This desk and a smaller chair would occupy only 20 square feet of space, making the space rental amount $200 a year, or about $65 less than that charged in the case of the bigger desk and chair.

Types of Desks. Desks may be broadly classified into two types: (1) according to size and shape, or style, and (2) according to use, or function. Examples of both types are illustrated in Figure 5-1.

Desks classified as to style may take any one of the following descriptions:

1. Flat top, single pedestal, 40 to 60 inches wide, suitable for salesmen or clerks whose work does not require the use of large-size records. The term *pedestal* refers to the drawers

contained on one side of the desk (single pedestal) or on both sides of the desk (double pedestal).

2. Flat top, double pedestal, 50 inches wide, suitable for workers using many papers; 50 to 55 inches wide, suitable for workers requiring the use of many papers and their storage; 55 to 75 inches wide, suitable for supervisors or clerks using large records or books. Probably the 60 by 30 inch double pedestal desk is the most popular size for general office work.
3. Fixed bed, single or double pedestal, suitable for stenographers and clerks. The fixed-bed desk is full height except for that portion immediately in front of the occupant, which is constructed at the conventional height, with an adjustable base for raising or lowering the typewriter or office machine.

When classified according to use, or function, desks may be briefly described as follows:

1. Executive desks, with top, 66 to 78 inches wide, extending over a double pedestal.
2. Clerical desks, double pedestal, for employees not needing a typewriter.
3. Secretarial desks, double pedestal, 60 inches, with a typewriter contained in one of the pedestals.
4. Typist desks, with a fixed bed for the typewriter. The modular L-shaped desk, a single pedestal unit with an extension on either side containing the second pedestal, is becoming increasingly popular. In order processing and billing and traffic departments, typists commonly use fanfold desks, which have a metal compartment in the back for storing the unused portion of the continuous forms. The strip of forms feeds easily from the compartment into the typewriter.
5. Machine desks, specially designed for use with adding, accounting, and billing machines of various types. A well is provided at either end of the desk so that the machine sits lower than the standard desk height.
6. Special desks, such as those for card-punch operators, with pedestal units equipped with file trays for punched cards. Other specially designed units include those that accommodate copying machines and reproduction supplies, and those with a single pedestal and extended overhang for use by interviewers.

Modular Furniture. Many manufacturers have designed their office desks to meet more accurately the description of "the working tools" or the work centers of the office employees. This has been

Fig. 5-1

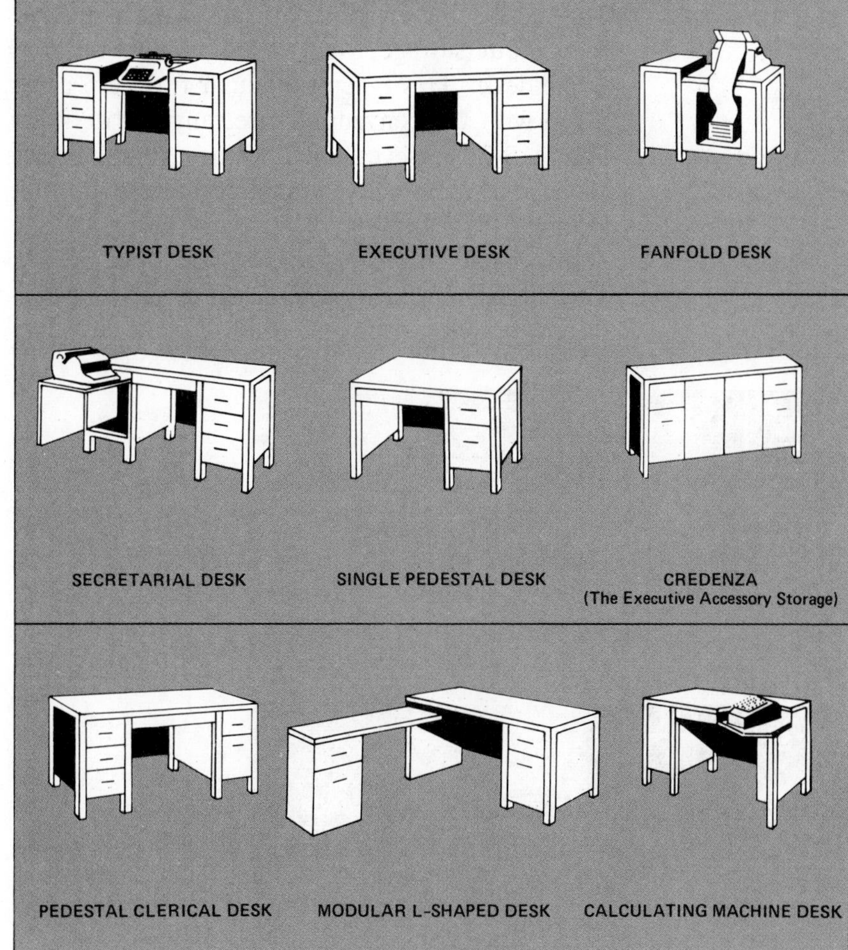

The Major Types of Desks

accomplished as shown in the following illustrations by: (1) reducing the floor space required for desk working area by approximately 20 percent; (2) providing interlocking, interchangeable units for greater ease and speed of output; and (3) fully utilizing the work area by building the desk complete with bookcase, file, and dwarfed partitions.

Functionally designed modular furniture, based upon motion and time studies of the work to be done, represents the trend in modern office design. Modular layouts combine separate furniture units that are designed according to the unitized or modular construction principle. The main advantages attributed to modular layouts include the conservation of floor space and more productive work motions. The most common modular unit is the L-return, a flat surface, with or without storage room below, which is attached at right angles to the desk. This type of modular furniture arrangement, when compared with the conventional rectangular desk arrangement shown in Figure 5-2, achieves not only a saving in space but also in work efficiency. (The conventional desk arrangement shown in the top of Figure 5-2 occupies 7,920 square inches. The modular furniture arrangement shown in the bottom occupies 6,468 square inches. Techniplan represents a trade name for an office furniture manufacturer's modular arrangement of work stations.)

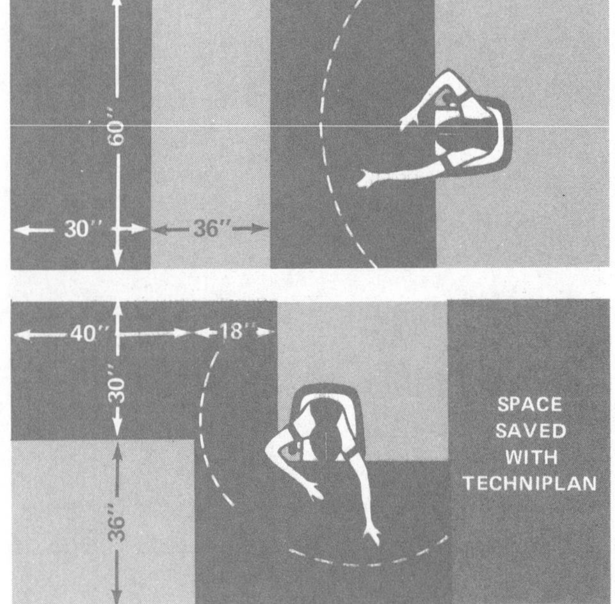

Fig. 5-2

Globe-Wernicke Company

Space Saved Using Modular Layout vs. Conventional Layout

A careful study of the diagrams in Figure 5-3 shows the relative space advantages offered by modular furniture arrangements over conventional furniture groupings. Note how the various furniture arrangements provide for flexibility in the use of this type of furniture. Many other groupings are possible, subject to both the imagination of the administrative office manager and the limitations of space.

Tables. Tables serve four purposes in the office: (1) as desks or desk-substitutes, (2) as a place for sorting when considerable flat

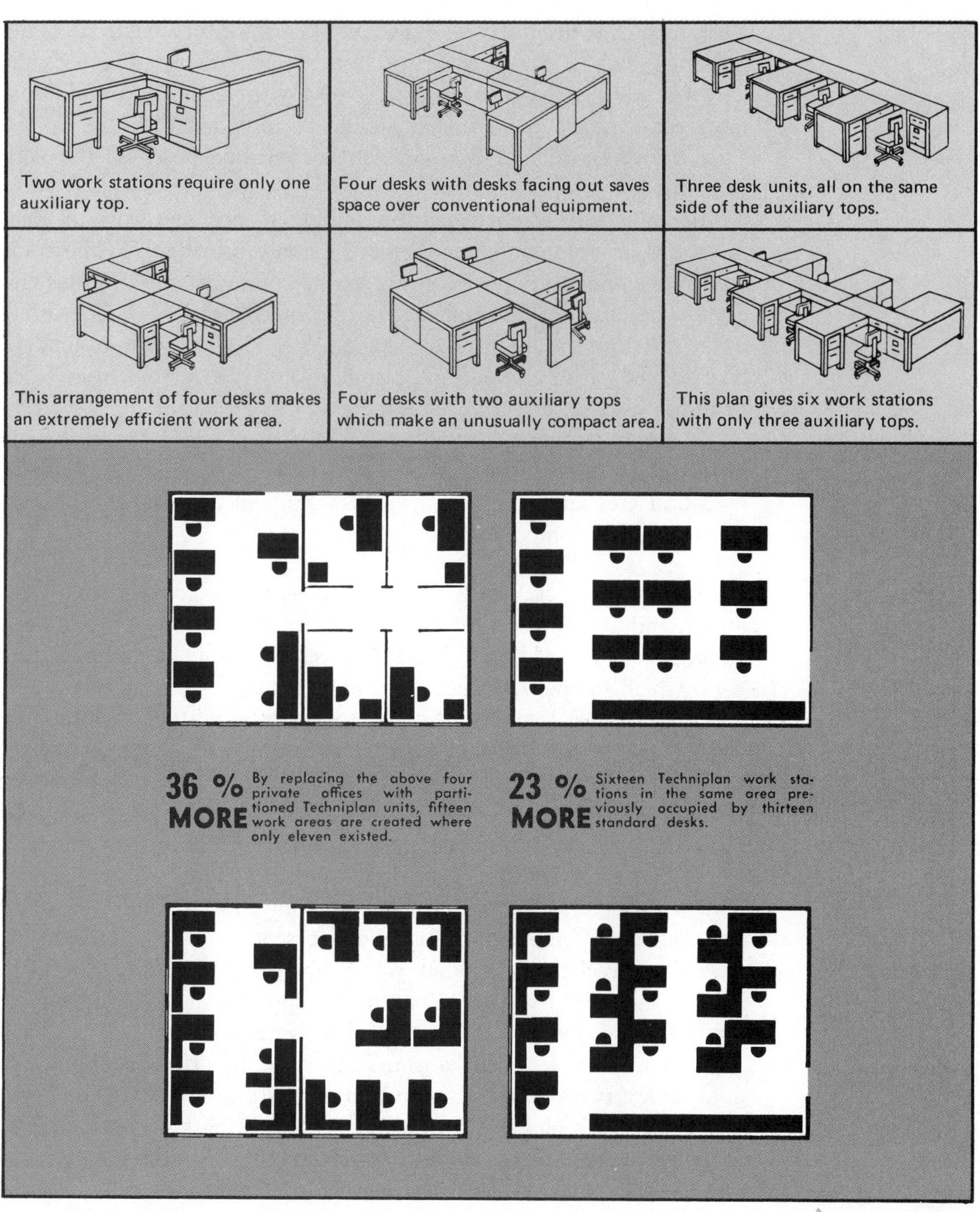

Two work stations require only one auxiliary top.
Four desks with desks facing out saves space over conventional equipment.
Three desk units, all on the same side of the auxiliary tops.
This arrangement of four desks makes an extremely efficient work area.
Four desks with two auxiliary tops which make an unusually compact area.
This plan gives six work stations with only three auxiliary tops.
36 % MORE
By replacing the above four private offices with partitioned Techniplan units, fifteen work areas are created where only eleven existed.
23 % MORE
Sixteen Techniplan work stations in the same area previously occupied by thirteen standard desks.

Globe-Wernicke Company

Fig. 5-3

Space-Saving Possibilities of Modular Furniture Layouts

work surface is necessary, (3) as a work surface for conferences and meetings, and (4) as a place for storage. For many office jobs the use of a table is preferred to a desk of any kind and is, in addition, more economical. Such a table should be provided with one or two small drawers, which will be sufficient for most purposes for the clerk using it.

In many firms where executives and others meet and work together in groups, a large conference table is usually provided. While some conference tables found in board rooms of large corporations are custom designed to harmonize with the office decor, a wide variety of styles (from the traditional rectangular shapes to the more modern boat-shaped, oval, curved, and round styles) is available from office furniture distributors in all large cities.

Many other types of tables are also available. These include machine stands (for typewriters, calculators, and other machines), reception area tables, and panel-end (enclosed end) tables for conferences or as companions to desks.

Chairs. The total work center for the typical office worker utilizes a desk and a chair, both of which contribute to his physical comfort. In turn, his physical comfort is closely related to his mental condition upon which his performance ultimately rests.

Where office workers sit for hours, it is important that they be comfortable so there will be no strained posture. The office manager can detect many signs of fatigue by taking a close look at the posture of his workers. He will find that many feet are entwined around the chair legs. He will find that many workers are humped over their work, because either the chair or the desk, or both, is not the right height. Such incorrect sitting positions may not be due to careless posture, but often result from defective seating.

All office chairs other than side chairs should be adjustable as to height and should revolve. The back support should be adjustable vertically and horizontally adjustable forward and back. If the back support is provided with a spring tension, the tension should be adjustable. If the worker has to bring his work to his eyes, he needs arm rests on his chair. If the worker has to bring his eyes and arms to the work, he does not need arms on the chair. Studies have proven that proper posture while working in the office not only reduces fatigue but also improves the health of the workers by making them less susceptible to colds and headaches. This, in turn, benefits the firm as a result of less absenteeism, fewer errors, and a larger volume of production.

Today many office chairs are designed to fit as closely as possible the contours of the body. Saddle seats are one example of the contour designs normally used in the construction of wooden chairs. Correctly contoured seats, especially those covered with foam latex, add to the worker's comfort. Many workers also like wooden seats supplemented with felt pads.

For the modern office the main types of chairs are classified as follows:

1. Executive chairs, completely adjustable to the physical characteristics of the executive, or in swivel and tilt-back styles.
2. Stenographer posture chairs, with or without swivel base.
3. Clerical posture chairs, with or without swivel base, with or without arms.
4. Side chairs, straight back and four legged, designed for use by visitors since these chairs are not suitable for all-day sitting.

Other Furniture and Accessories. The preceding discussion has indicated that desks, tables, and chairs are the key furniture items in any office. While this continues to be true, the forward-looking administrative manager will modify the working environment as conditions (particularly the layout), the financial resources, and the tastes of management dictate. It is becoming increasingly common to find extra furnishings such as sofas, end tables with harmonizing table lamps, coffee tables, art objects, credenzas, refreshment centers, bookcases, foliage and other plantings, office valets or coat racks, and magazine racks in the office. These accessories provide an environment that is more conducive to relaxed work, concentration, and enjoyment of the work hours spent on the job.

Principles of Furniture Selection. While it is obvious that office furniture should be selected on the basis of its contribution to the performance of office work, more specific selection criteria are required. The following principles should be considered in the selection of all office furniture:

1. The furniture should be attractive and modern in style and harmonize with the decor of the office—a feature that affects the volume, accuracy, and morale of the workers.
2. The furniture should be of good quality, solid construction, and suitable design to facilitate the work to be done. Furniture of good quality is usually more attractive and more economical to maintain.

3. The furniture should be suitable for the work that is to be done. Since each office has individual requirements, use by similar offices is not necessarily a strong reason for adoption of the furniture.
4. The furniture should be adaptable to multipurpose use wherever possible.
5. The quantity of furniture should be sufficient for the number of employees and the types of tasks performed.
6. Specialized items of furniture, such as sorting racks, revolving or modular desk combination units, and portable furniture pieces, should be installed only if savings in clerical costs and convenience can be justified.
7. The furniture should be fitted to the needs and preferences of the worker. He should always be consulted regarding new furniture purchases. Where his suggestions cannot be followed, reasons for the decision made should be communicated to him.
8. The alternatives of metal or plastic versus wood furniture should be carefully weighed. For superior durability under hard wear, metal office furniture should be considered. Normally metal furniture is more flexible, is constructed with interchangeable units or parts, and is used most widely in areas such as the general office where many units are required. On the other hand, wood furniture is also long lasting and has the added values of warm tone, rich appearance, and prestige that enhance the attitude of the office worker toward his job. Wood furniture is often found in executive offices.
9. The furniture should contribute to comfortable working conditions. This principle involves the nature of the work to be performed and the economy of physical effort as well as the speed of the various operations.

Office Equipment

In addition to the furniture required for the modern office, a great array of office equipment is available. The term office equipment, as used here, refers primarily to office machines and devices that are found in the office.[1]

Essentially an office machine is an information machine. Whether it is a typewriter, a rotary calculator, a photocopier, or an electronic

---

[1] For discussions concerning specific types of office equipment, see Chapter 7 (communication machines), Chapter 8 (storage and retrieval machines), Chapter 9 (mailing and reproducing machines), and Chapter 17 (accounting and calculating machines). Office equipment used in automated business information systems (such as computers and punched-card equipment) is discussed in Part V, Business Information Processing Systems.

computer, each of these machines deals with information. Then, too, office equipment is the intermediary between man and his work. It enables him to accomplish more work in fewer hours with greater accuracy and with better quality. Furthermore, some equipment, such as the teletypewriter, helps him to transmit the results of his work to others over long distances and to receive rapid feedback. Not only the types and brands of equipment but also the number of their possible uses continue to grow at an accelerated rate.

A modern approach to equipment selection starts with a feasibility study in which the entire information processing system is identified and the role of the equipment in such a system is clarified. Such a study requires concentrated and prolonged thought with well-documented answers to the key questions involved. A form for this purpose is illustrated in Figure 5-4.

To assist the administrative office manager in making equipment-selection decisions, the following basic principles should prove helpful:

1. Equipment should be chosen for any job or task for which it is more efficient than the worker. Where job monotony due to unchallenging, repetitive work tasks is found, a machine should be considered.
2. High-volume, rather than low-frequency or one-time only, applications point to the need for machines. From such high-volume applications can spring better service, more prompt report preparation, and other positive results.
3. Where equipment can provide higher quality of output, it should be utilized. For example, compare typewritten versus handwritten reports and offset printing versus more primitive forms of duplicating.
4. The need for accuracy should be determined, and where internal machine checks and controls can provide such accuracy, a machine should be selected.
5. Equipment should be installed whenever it will reduce the actual cost of performing office work. The costs of service contracts, of operation, and of layout alterations required must be considered in calculating the total cost of the equipment installation.
6. To handle urgent work, high-speed requirements, or peak loads in the office work schedule, appropriate equipment should be considered.
7. Not only the capabilities but also the limitations of equipment should be carefully considered. Included in such limitations are the digital capacity of numbers handled, size of forms and records, cycling speeds, numbers of copies

REPRODUCTION SERVICES CENTER

Machine Selection Guide

date: ______________

Salesman	Firm	Telephone
Machine type	Brand name and model	

	Comments
1. Availability lease/rent/buy available from (firm) available by (date)	
2. Work station requirements space electrical tables, etc. Storage equipment	
3. Portability	
4. Duplicating/copying capabilities size of copy enlarging/reducing length of run best suited color capabilities other:	
5. Speed of operation	
6. Ease of operation (operation requirements)	
7. Maintenance requirements	
8. Maintenance costs	
9. Copy paper and supplies required/recommended	
10. Operating costs (including per-copy costs)	
11. Machine specifications (size, colors, models available, etc.)	
12. Satisfied users of equipment (name, firm, telephone)	

______________ Rep. Center Supervisor

Fig. 5-4

A Form Used to Help Select Office Equipment

required, number of mathematic processes possible, number of storage registers, longevity of expected performance, and trade-in value.

8. Both operating and supervisory personnel involved with the equipment should be consulted for their machine preferences. In addition, the impact of training or retraining required for proper machine operation should be considered.
9. The availability of ready, reliable maintenance service should receive top priority in equipment selection. If equipment is not working properly or not working at all, this constitutes an added cost to office operations.

10. Assuming that usage of the equipment allows, effort should be made to procure equipment that has these features: simplicity (for ease of operation, of learning, and of maintenance); flexibility (for use in many situations); portability (for easier use in several office departments); and adaptability (for immediate integration into a present office system).
11. Before purchase, lease, or rental, equipment should be "test run" in the office situation where it is considered for installation. In some cases a one- or two-week trial period is recommended for smaller machines. For the larger, more expensive machines in the computer family, more intensive feasibility studies, as explained in Chapter 2, are carried out.
12. Standardization of office equipment is desirable. By standardizing on sizes, styles, and brands, it is possible:
    a. To obtain lower prices through larger purchases.
    b. To lower the maintenance costs by servicing fewer brands of machines.
    c. To develop, if necessary, the company's own service department more easily and more economically.
    d. To have one group of employees who can operate any of the machines, which may be a real economy.
    e. To train operators more simply and easily.
    f. To purchase and use more easily office forms to fit the brands of machines.
    g. To simplify the computation of depreciation and trade-in value of the equipment, which is important from the standpoint of both income taxes and disposition of equipment by trade-in.

PROCUREMENT

It has been shown that the selection of office furniture and equipment is an important and complex responsibility of the office manager. It has also been noted that office furniture, which is intended to last for a long time, is usually purchased. However, the same is not necessarily true of office equipment, which is subject to much wear and tear as well as to increasing technological improvements. The remainder of this chapter will be devoted to the other closely related managerial considerations of procuring, maintaining, replacing, and developing centralized procedures for assuring the proper control and utilization of office equipment.

Although office equipment may be purchased outright, in 1970 most companies with assets of less than $500,000 procured one half of all their new equipment by leasing. Almost all types of office machines and equipment—small office appliances, electronic data processing equipment, and reproduction equipment—can be leased.[2] Equipment can be leased from three sources: (1) directly from the manufacturer or through his distributor, (2) from the local office equipment dealer, and (3) from an independent leasing company organized for the specific purpose of leasing a variety of brands of office machines and equipment.

Advantages of Leasing

The advantages that accrue from leasing include:

1. Working capital is conserved for expansion and profit building since ordinarily only one or two months' payments are made in advance for the rental of office machines and equipment. Thus, the capital is freed for other revenue-producing investments.
2. Budgetary control is facilitated since the amount of regular payments is easily determinable. A hedge against inflation is also provided since the same dollar payments are spread over a period of years.
3. The risk of obsolescence can be hedged. Costly modern machines and equipment are made available to the lessee for relatively low rental payments. In many cases equipment can be replaced during the life of the lease; and at the end of the lease period, the company can take advantage of the latest advances in technology.
4. Tax benefits are realized since the rental payments are fully deductible for income tax purposes.
5. Rapidly expanding companies and those opening branch offices are aided by the package plans of some lessors, under which equipment can be added as the needs of the company grow.

Leasing Plans and Their Cost

Most leasing plans fall into four categories: (1) short term, (2) long term with renewal option, (3) long term with purchase option, and (4) sale-leaseback. Each of these plans is briefly described in the following paragraphs.

---

[2] For an in-depth four-year study of the opinions and experiences of some 300 lessors and lessees, see "Leasing in Industry" by Henry G. Hamel, a 1970 report available from the National Industrial Conference Board, 845 Third Avenue, New York, NY 10022.

Short-Term Lease. The short-term lease is used to obtain extra equipment, such as typewriters and calculating machines, for special peak workload jobs, such as year-end inventory. Ordinarily any furnishings or equipment can be leased under these terms for 3 to 3.5 percent of its purchase value. For example, a typewriter can be leased for as little as $5 a month. The major advantage of this leasing plan is that the needed equipment is immediately made available with the need for little cash outlay.

Long-Term Lease with Renewal Option. Under this plan the lease usually runs between 75 and 80 percent of the useful life of the equipment. On the average the leases run from three to five years. At the end of the rental period, the lease can be renewed at a reduced rate. During the period of useful life, the payments equal the original price plus financing charges. The annual cost of the long-term lease with renewal option, as well as the long-term lease with purchase option and the sale-leaseback, averages approximately 6 percent on the original purchase price.

Long-Term Lease with Purchase Option. This plan is similar to the long-term lease previously described, except at the end of the rental period, the equipment can be purchased for a small percentage of the original cost. This form of lease seems to have lost some of its popularity, perhaps because under income tax regulations the lease may be interpreted as a conditional sale and thus the company is denied tax deductions.

Sale-Leaseback. Under the sale-leaseback plan, the company purchases its equipment, sells it to a lessor, and then leases it back. Thus, the company receives almost 100 percent value of its fixed assets in the form of immediate cash. This plan may prove very useful when quick capital is needed.

Decisions on Procuring Data Processing Equipment

Because the procurement of data processing equipment involves a sizable expenditure as compared to the amount of money invested in other kinds of office equipment, a detailed discussion of this subject is presented in this section. Like the other kinds of office equipment mentioned earlier, data processing equipment may be purchased outright, rented from the manufacturer with an option to renew at the end of the rental period or with an option to purchase, or leased from a computer leasing firm. A company may also realize the benefits of automated data processing by utilizing a service center provided by the manufacturer or by purchasing processing time from another firm that has spare computer time available.

Most companies rent or lease their data processing equipment, such as card-punch machines, tabulating machines, optical scanning equipment, and electronic computers. With the increased experience and knowledge being gained in the field of data processing, however, management is inquiring more and more into the practicability of buying rather than leasing low-priced computers. Many of the advantages that accrue from leasing, as cited earlier, are being reappraised by users of computers in relation to rental payments that have already surpassed the original purchase price of the equipment. In some firms, increased applications of their present installations have caused the additional rental charges to become a greater cost factor than originally expected.

The advantage of renting electronic data processing equipment as a means of hedging against technological obsolescence has been somewhat weakened with the advent of *modularity*—the "building-block" concept of design in the manufacture of computer equipment. In installations using the building-block concept, individual pieces of equipment can be integrated into the present system or replaced as the needs of the data processing system change; there is no need to scrap the entire system as a result of increased workload. Prior to the availability of modular units, a firm had to provide for its eventual needs at the outset and had to bear the additional costs of unused capacity from the beginning.

In deciding whether to lease, to rent, or to buy electronic data processing equipment, a realistic analysis should be undertaken by the data processing staff. These individuals, because of their familiarity with the data processing activity, are the most knowledgeable and experienced in evaluating the future potential of electronic equipment in meeting the firm's needs. As a result of the staff's study, it may be found that the firm is not yet ready for a computer, or that considerable savings can be achieved by eliminating or combining jobs, or that more efficient and economical use can be made of the present equipment.[3]

If after a feasibility study it has been determined that there is need for a computer, the following factors should be carefully

[3] Other factors to be considered as part of the study prior to the selection and installation of a computer are discussed in Chapter 2.

analyzed and investigated before making the decision to rent, to lease, or to buy the equipment:

1. *Relative net cost of purchase and rental.* If the equipment is to be used for more than one shift a day, it may, in terms of direct cost, be economical for many companies to purchase the equipment. However, each firm should conduct its own study, as in the case of any other capital investment, perhaps by using a return-on-investment formula or determining the lease-buy break-even point.[4]
2. *Threat of obsolescence.* Companies concerned that their computer installation may soon be obsolete as the result of technological advances often decide to rent although it may be less expensive to buy. As mentioned before, however, modular installations have to a great extent overcome the threat of obsolescence. A greater threat for many firms may be that too small a computer has been purchased, with the result that in a few years the company will have outgrown its installation.
3. *Useful life of the data processing system.* The expected average utilization of the system—one-, two-, or three-shift operations and over how many years—must be determined. Although an analysis of useful life is very difficult, a realistic appraisal must be made of how long the equipment will serve the company's needs. In some companies long-range planners are at work developing great changes for the future that might radically affect the role of electronic data processing. To forecast the future, the data processing staff must analyze the company's plans and trends for sales, production, and purchases in order to determine the need for new or expanded automated processes.
4. *Amount of base rental fee.* Ordinarily a firm pays a base fee that entitles the company to operate the computer so many hours each month. Regular overtime usage requires the payment of additional rent, which is directly determinable with the installation of time recorders on the equipment. All terms governing the basic rental period should be spelled out in advance. For example, if the equipment breaks down for a few hours, is the company charged for these hours or does the manufacturer assume the loss?

---

[4] For an illustrative example of determining the lease-buy break-even point, see Frank B. Gardner, "EDP Equipment: Rent or Buy?" Administrative Management Society, Management Bulletin No. 10, Vol. 4, pp. 2-10. For a detailed comparative cost analysis of renting or buying electronic data processing equipment, see E. D. Wolf, "Rent or Buy?" *Management Services* (November-December, 1964), pp. 44-51.

5. *Maintenance services provided by the manufacturer.* The rental contract should clearly indicate the type of services—preventive and repair—that will be provided by the manufacturer. The availability of skilled help, when needed, should also be determined.
6. *Salvage value of equipment.* In making cost comparisons between renting and buying, often the salvage value of equipment at the end of its useful life is overlooked. With a growing market for used equipment, the business may realize a substantial trade-in value for that equipment which has a system life shorter than its productive life.
7. *Interest costs.* When placing the costs of leasing and of buying on a comparative basis, the firm should consider the rate of interest that it pays for borrowed money or the rate it expects to earn on an investment of the funds.

Aid in making a good decision on whether to purchase, to rent, or to lease a computer, or to utilize a computer service center may be obtained from the firm's own financial specialists and auditors, independent consultants, and equipment manufacturers, many of whom will prepare a detailed analysis of purchase and rental factors.

MAINTENANCE

Maintenance is an important factor to be considered by the office manager when purchasing equipment. Many office machines must be operated almost continuously each day. With automatic machines and equipment handling the bulk of data processing, the servicing of these machines becomes a factor of prime consideration. When machines and equipment get out of order, the office worker is unable to perform his work until repairs have been made, unless there is some unused standby equipment.

Depending somewhat upon the complexity of the equipment and the number of machines being used, service and maintenance of office equipment may be handled by one or more of the following methods:

1. Service contract with the manufacturer of the equipment or with independent servicemen.
2. Service by company's internal service department.
3. Use of manufacturer's servicemen or independent servicemen on a per-call basis with no contract.

Service Contract

It is estimated that American business spends $100 million each year on service contracts for the five main types of machines—adding machines, calculators, dictating machines, and electric and manual typewriters. Even so, by purchasing a service contract, a firm may be able to save money in the area of "hidden costs." For example, each time a serviceman on a per-call basis renders his service, an invoice must be processed and a check written to cover the fee charged. This office operation costs, on the average, from $5 to $7.50. If, however, a service contract had been purchased, only one annual billing would have been made, thus the need for processing only one invoice and writing only one check. A second hidden cost lies in the amount of downtime, a cost that can never be measured finely. Involved are not only the idle time of the machine operator but also the possible delay in operations being performed by a higher salaried supervisor. Preventive maintenance, which forms a part of every manufacturer's service contract, may reduce or eliminate the number of breakdowns.

Service contracts are also known as maintenance agreements, maintenance guarantees, and business equipment efficiency agreements. They range widely in price, from approximately $15 on a manual adding machine to $50 on some models of typewriters. Contracts on some machines, but not typewriters, include the cost of supplies such as ribbons and ink rolls. All service contracts include periodic cleaning, lubrication, three or four inspections per year, and replacement of worn out or defective machine parts. The increased use of electric typewriters has raised the question of maintenance and service more emphatically since such equipment needs special attention. Most of the typewriter manufacturers supply a service agreement similar to that used for accounting machines.

In a survey of 1,129 companies, the Administrative Management Society observed the following practices: [5]

1. The prevailing trend was to place the maintenance under contract with the manufacturer. Most of the companies expected to renew their contracts (including those held with independent agencies).
2. A majority of the machines were serviced on an average of every three months. Machine age was generally 10-12 years.

---

[5] Reported in *Management Review* (February, 1963), p. 64.

3. At first glance, the maintenance cost figures seemed to indicate that the contracts with the manufacturer were more expensive than those with independent servicemen. However, when factors such as the type of machine, provision for machine parts, and preventive maintenance are considered, it is possible that having contracts with the manufacturer is in many instances the least expensive of the policies considered.

In the servicing of typewriters, some firms, especially those in the smaller outlying communities, enter into an agreement with a local typewriter service firm. For a small fixed fee, the firm inspects, cleans, and repairs monthly each typewriter in the office. Any special calls for service or repairs are usually taken care of without extra charge.

Internal Service Department

Since typewriters are very important both from the viewpoint of the number involved and the amount of the investment, their care and maintenance are important. Many offices issue instruction sheets to all typists on how to care for their machines so that they will operate efficiently and require a minimum of servicing and repairs. If there are a large number of typewriters in use, it may be desirable to have several employees devote their time to servicing and repairing the machines.

To maintain its own service personnel, the company must be fairly large. Involved in the installation of a service department are the relatively high salary rates of trained service personnel, the hidden costs of their fringe benefits, the cost of retraining the personnel as new machine models appear on the market, and the cost of the space allotted to the servicing area.

Per-Call Basis

Some firms feel that it is more economical to pay for each individual service call as the service is needed. However, in the case of particularly troublesome and highly automatic equipment, repeat calls are often necessary. When a fixed-fee manufacturer's service contract is used, such calls become the problem of the manufacturer.

In a survey of 462 business firms using more than 250,000 adding machines, calculators, dictating machines, and electric and manual typewriters, the Buyers Laboratory, Inc., found that the cost of service contracts was about twice what the cost would be for servicing the machines on a per-call basis or by internal repair departments.[6] It was further noted that the annual cost of service contracts on electric typewriters averaged $34, while the annual cost of per-call service averaged $18. However, these average direct cost figures do not take into consideration the previously mentioned hidden or indirect costs of processing the invoice and writing the check for each service call nor the unmeasurable costs of machine downtime. Another interesting aspect of the survey revealed that in firms with fewer than 1,000 machines, the service contract is favored; in firms with more than 1,000 machines, the preference is for per-call or in-plant service.

REPLACEMENT

Equipment for office work becomes obsolete quite frequently because of newer and better models placed on the market. No office manager can keep up with all such improvements while he still has useful machines in his office. It therefore becomes necessary for him to buy the best machine available at the time of purchase and to use this machine until its efficiency lessens, at which time he may be able to replace the old machine with a newer model without too great a loss. This loss can be absorbed by the business if a sound depreciation policy has been established.

Ordinarily, office machines are depreciated over a period of ten years. Due to the factor of obsolescence, however, some special-purpose machines, such as accounting machines and automated data processing equipment, may be depreciated much sooner or at a much greater rate. Thus, most office managers would be wise to use a policy of five-year depreciation, that is, 20 percent of cost-less-scrap value. This practice permits a trade-in policy of obtaining new machines at least every five years and thus keeps the work of the office at top efficiency at all times.

As the result of inaugurating a planned replacement program for its machines and equipment, a firm is able to predict each year, with a high degree of accuracy, the exact cost of its equipment needs.

---

[6] "Service Contracts, Pro and Con," *Administrative Management* (August, 1964), p. 17. For an interesting rebuttal to the findings of the Buyers Laboratory, see "Why I Like Service Contracts," by Roy H. Olsen, Director of Purchasing, Avis Rent-A-Car, *Administrative Management* (January, 1965), p. 34. For the story of a firm that has eliminated the majority of its service contracts, see "Why I Have Eliminated Most Service Contracts," by H. B. Ward, Purchasing Manager, International Nickel Corp., *Administrative Management* (February, 1966), pp. 22-23.

The cutoff point of operating efficiency and economy can be established for each piece of equipment, the number of new items to be purchased can be forecast, and the amount for maintenance during the coming year can be budgeted. A planned replacement program also enables the firm to establish better control over its maintenance costs, especially those that tend to rise during the latter years of machine usage. By closely controlling the replacement schedule of office machines, the firm can avoid those additional expenses that arise during the period when the equipment is old enough to require extensive reconditioning, replacement of parts, and special cleanings. An intangible advantage in the area of prestige and morale also characterizes the company having a planned replacement program. By means of such a program, the company is able to present to its customers, visitors, and employees a modern image of a businesslike, well-equipped, up-to-date office.[7]

CENTRALIZED CONTROL

The procurement, maintenance, and replacement of equipment should be centrally controlled particularly in the large office where specialization of function is found and where enormous sums have been invested in machines and equipment. Usually this function is the responsibility of the manager of administrative services. Such a program of control is usually divided into the following categories:

1. Maintaining an up-to-date file of information on office equipment and equipment trends.
2. Setting up a central records control system that will show the following kinds of information:
   a. The equipment owned/leased/rented by the firm.
   b. Where the equipment is used.
   c. What the equipment is used for.
   d. Company and manufacturer serial numbers.
   e. Complete description of type of equipment.
   f. Date of purchase.
   g. Cost.
   h. Service history.
   i. Maintenance costs.

---

[7] For an interesting description of a typewriter replacement program and an analysis of typewriter costs over a ten-year period, see "A Plan for Replacing Typewriters," by Arthur Bajart, Assistant Vice President, Home Office Administration, Equitable Life Assurance Society of the United States, *Administrative Management* (July, 1964), pp. 62-64.

j. Accumulated and current depreciation costs.
k. Book value.

3. Establishing machine and equipment standards.
4. Controlling the selection and purchase of machines in line with use to be made of the machines.
5. Developing effective procedures for maintenance and replacement of machines.
6. Maintaining a periodic review of all equipment and machine installations.
7. Functioning as a central clearinghouse for all equipment needs within the firm and as the contact point for all vendors outside the firm.

The small office, too, has need for equipment controls. Although it is unlikely that much specialization of function will be found in the small office, the control of equipment should be assigned to one competent individual who can give it the attention it deserves.

QUESTIONS FOR REVIEW

1. What constitutes the "total office environment"? How does it influence and how is it influenced by today's unceasing demand for more information?

2. To be both up-to-date and able to provide the most service to his firm relative to the physical environment of the office, what types and sources of information should the administrative office manager keep handy?

3. If you were asked to provide a comprehensive set of criteria for selecting an office desk, what should your list include?

4. What is the meaning of a "total work center" as discussed in this chapter? How is such a center related to the total office system?

5. In what respects is modular office furniture more desirable than the more conventional forms of office furniture?

6. What are the characteristics of a good posture chair? Why is the selection of a good chair just as important as the selection of a suitable desk?

7. From the standpoint of machine usage, what factors must be taken into consideration before an office machine is properly selected?

8. What is meant by standardization of office machines and equipment? What are the advantages of standardizing office machines and equipment? In what respects do these advantages of standardization apply to office furniture?

9. Feasibility studies are commonly associated with decisions to acquire a computer. What factors of a feasibility study are also relevant when considering the acquisition of small-scale office machines such as typewriters?
10. What advantages may be realized by the business firm that leases rather than buys its data processing equipment? How has the advent of modularity affected the advantages to be realized from renting such equipment?
11. What is meant by a "service contract" for office machines and equipment? Discuss the need for such contracts in the modern business office.
12. Progressive offices develop and use a definite trade-in program for their office machines and equipment. Indicate the advantages of such a trade-in program.
13. For what reasons should the procurement, maintenance, and replacement of office machines be centrally controlled?

QUESTIONS FOR DISCUSSION

1. The Ritz Manufacturing Company has need for $10,000 worth of office equipment, which it can either purchase outright or rent. Over a ten-year period, the rental cost for the equipment would be $14,000. The rental cost includes insurance, but all maintenance costs must be paid by the lessee. At the end of the ten years, the estimated value of the equipment, if purchased, would be $2,500. If the equipment were purchased, the annual insurance costs would be $60. Discuss the advisability of renting the equipment, assuming the interest on the investment in the machines over a ten-year period would be $4,500.
2. The office manager of the Truesdale Farm Implement Company is finding it increasingly difficult to select office equipment because there are so many competing sources of supply from which to choose. Lately, the office manager has been faced with this problem in the matter of selecting office chairs, dictating machines, and other office appliances that seem to look alike and operate alike and that are competitively priced. The company has planned to standardize and replace some 300 office chairs at a cost of $18,000. The office manager wants to be sure that his selection of supplier will be correct. Discuss the procedure you would follow if there were seven competing firms interested in supplying these chairs to your firm.
3. As office manager for Globe Trucking, Inc., you have been given the job of trading in the old office furniture and purchasing new items. Since the trade-in allowance on the old furniture is practically the same with each manufacturer, the trade-in allowance is not to be

considered a competitive factor in your selection. Your survey of the office indicates the following needs to be considered in the selection of the furniture:

a. Two private offices in each of which a desk, an armchair, and two visitors chairs are to be provided.
b. Three secretaries, whose desks are located outside the private offices, are to be provided with new desks and chairs.
c. Four stenographer-typists, whose entire working time is spent in taking dictation and typing, are to be given new desks and chairs.
d. Five clerks, engaged in various clerical tasks (except typing), are to be provided with new desks and chairs.
e. Three accountants must have new desks and chairs.

Although it is possible to supply the clerks and the accountants with the same size desk, you believe that a more satisfactory arrangement will be achieved through the functional selection of desks and chairs. Therefore, you are asked to discuss the styles or types of desks and chairs that you think should be selected for each of the employees and for the two private offices. If you have access to office furniture catalogs, indicate the approximate cost of each desk and chair. The reasons for selecting a particular size, style, or type of desk and chair should also be stated.

4. A leading management consulting firm, with 65 offices in the United States, has recently centralized the purchasing of all office equipment through its New York office. Each of the branch offices selects its needed supplies and equipment from a manual published by the company. If, for example, one office wishes to purchase a calculator, the administrative manager investigates the equipment available in the company's catalog and requests the purchase of the calculator through the central purchasing unit. What advantages can you cite for this type of centralized procurement of equipment? What disadvantages can be anticipated?

PRACTICAL OFFICE CASES

Case 5-1 Selecting Service Contracts for Office Machines

The Arcadia Manufacturing Company is located in a small suburban community about 50 miles from Harrisburg, Pennsylvania. The company is engaged in the production of small parts and subassemblies for electrical appliances such as toasters, mixers, blenders, and deep fryers. Its products have received increasing acceptance among the appliance manufacturers for whom they are fabricated, and the result has been a continuing increase in production, personnel, accounting, and related activities.

One of the areas of deep concern to the president, Kenneth Milani, is that the administrative staff is growing at a rate almost twice that of the factory work force. With this growth in administration has come a repeated emphasis on keeping office costs in line and on trying to find the best means of providing all the available mechanization possible to supplement the clerical work force. At the same time the office machines must be kept up-to-date and in good operating condition.

Presently the company is wrestling with a problem concerning the servicing of its basic office machines and is delaying temporarily a decision to automate some of the common office systems such as inventory and purchasing. A recent count of the office machines shows that there are 40 electric typewriters, 10 of which are less than one year old; 20 are two to three years old, and the remaining 10 are four or more years old. In addition to the typewriters, there are three ten-key adding machines, each six months old, principally used for payroll and production work, and two accounting machines, each two years old.

A decision must be made soon as to the best method of servicing these machines. These options seem possible:

1. A local independent serviceman is willing to service all machines at these costs:

   Electric typewriters: $35 per machine, plus parts, each year

   Ten-key adding machines: $25 per machine, plus parts, each year

   Accounting machines: $90 per machine, plus parts, each year

   The service agreement on each type of machine includes a quarterly inspection (that is, one inspection per machine every three-month period) at which time the machines are cleaned and adjusted.

2. Two of the machine manufacturers' distributors are located in Harrisburg, about one hour's traveling distance away. The manufacturer's service agreement for the electric typewriters is $50 per machine annually, including a zone charge since the Arcadia Company is located beyond the radius point of the manufacturer's service office. This amount includes three periodic inspections each year, emergency service calls during regular working hours, and all parts except platens.

   The accounting machine manufacturer provides a similar service at a per-machine cost of $140 per year after the first year's use. This amount covers the replacement of all defective parts, except platens. Machines are examined every six months under this firm's agreement.

   A unique situation presents itself regarding the ten-key adding machines, which are import models, for there is no branch service office in Pennsylvania. Although these machines are relatively new and have performed very satisfactorily, attention must be given to their service. When contacted about the possibilities for servicing the machines, the manufacturer's representative recommended a local serviceman be contacted in case of machine malfunction. Otherwise, the machine would have to be returned to the nearest service representative on the East Coast, some 200 miles away. The warranty on the ten-key machine covers a one-year period during which all defective parts will be replaced free of charge, provided the defective machine is shipped direct to the East Coast office.

■ Prepare a report in which you outline clearly for Milani, the president of Arcadia, the best probable course of action, giving reasons to substantiate your recommendations for:

1. The type of service you recommend for the typewriters.
2. The type of service that would be preferable for the accounting machines.
3. How the servicing of the ten-key adding machines should be handled.

Case 5-2 Preparing a Layout of the General Offices

The Pineault Leather Goods Company has just leased office space on the sixth floor of the Queensgate Office Building, Omaha, Nebraska. The space, 50′ x 40′, rents for $6,600 a year.

There is one private office in which the president and the treasurer of the company have their desks. No other employees are located in this office. The accounting machine operators do not have desks for their work since they work continuously at their machines. The firm has 6 five-drawer letter-size files, a stationery and supplies storage cabinet 3′ x 6′, and one safe 3′ x 3′. In addition there are several pieces of miscellaneous office furniture such as visitors chairs in the president's office and in the reception area. Space is provided for ladies' and men's lounges, but these areas are comparatively small.

The office staff is composed of the following:

1 chief accountant and office manager—executive desk (66″ x 40″, double pedestal)

2 junior accountants—penwritten records with desks (60″ x 30″, double pedestal)

2 billing machine operators—no desks

2 posting machine operators—no desks, but four ledger card trays on stands

2 secretaries—secretarial desks (60″ x 30″, single pedestal)

2 stenographers—typist desks (60″ x 30″, single pedestal)

1 order pricing clerk who also serves as receptionist—clerical desk (50″ x 30″, double pedestal)
1 sales-credit manager—executive desk (60″ x 30″, double pedestal)
1 clerk (checking of invoices)—clerical desk (50″ x 30″, double pedestal)

On the north side of the building there are four large windows, each five feet wide and extending from radiator top to ceiling. On the east and the west sides there are no windows. On the south side of the office there are two doors, but only one is used by the public for entrance and exit. The other door is for the sole use of the employees.

▪ Using a sheet of graph paper, and making either template designs or a line drawing to scale of the desks and equipment, prepare a floor plan showing the layout of the desks, the private office, and the furniture and equipment. Prepare a report to accompany this in which you give the reasons for your layout.

6

Psycho-Physiological Factors in the Office Environment

Ecology (the study of man's environment and his interaction with it) is increasingly being recognized for its basic role in the successful progress of mankind. Man's affairs, ecologists maintain, are greatly influenced by his environment. This is true whether man is functioning in the classroom, in the manufacturing plant, on the athletic field, or in the office.

Office ecology is closely dependent upon the proper utilization of space and the effective arrangement of furniture and equipment, which were discussed in Chapters 4 and 5, respectively. Apart from such physical or tangible considerations, however, the administrative office manager has come to realize that his first consideration is the office staff. As a result, he must consider their working conditions, their preferences, and their weaknesses by providing a working environment that promotes productivity, teamwork, convenience, and comfort.

Such *physical factors* as lighting and acoustics, noise elimination or reduction, the effective use of color, and floor coverings in the office make up a significant part of the office world. However, each of these factors also has *psychological* implications in that it affects the behavior, attitudes, and morale of the worker, and hence his performance. The purpose of this chapter is to analyze the environment of the office from a combined psycho-physiological viewpoint as illustrated in Figure 6-1.

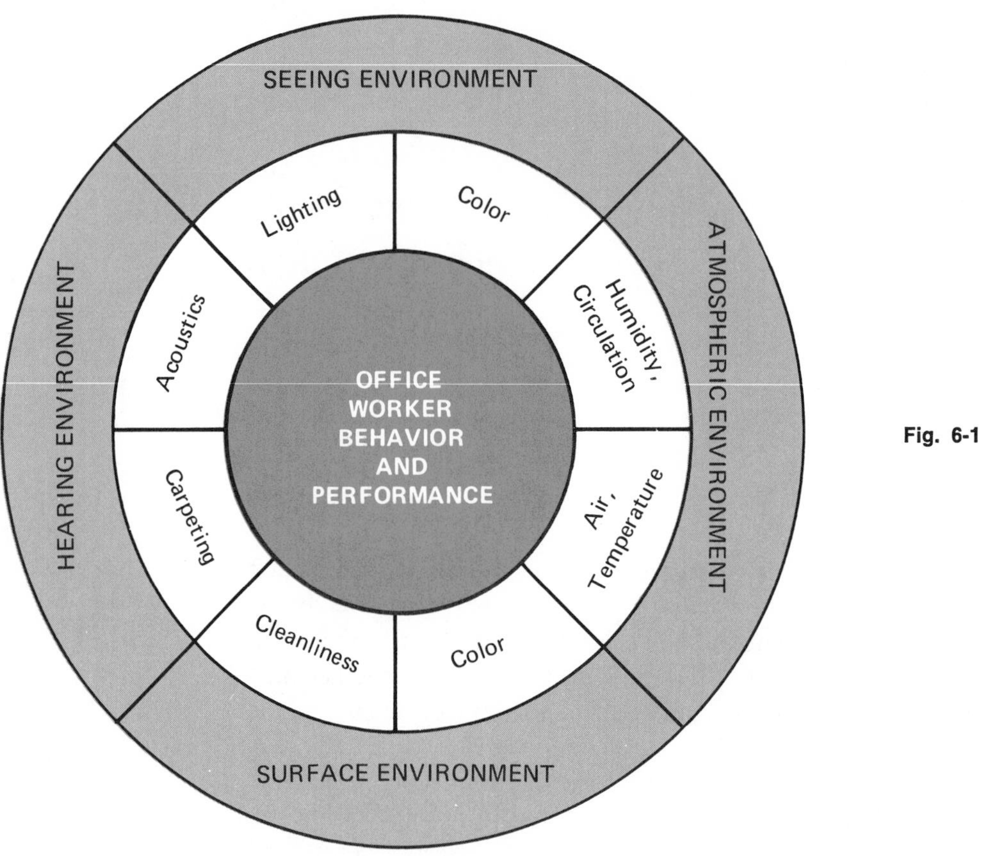

Fig. 6-1

Interaction of the Psychological and Physiological Factors in the Office Environment

THE OFFICE ENVIRONMENT AND WORKER BEHAVIOR

To assist management in its many complex responsibilities, industrial and social psychologists are examining the nature of man and his work assignments in relation to his surroundings. They examine his drives and needs, his motivations and frustrations, his satisfactions and his conflicts. At both the managerial and the worker levels, man has a complex network and hierarchy of needs that should be fulfilled if each person is to attain his optimum performance. It is, of course, management's responsibility to see that each person does optimize his work assignment, both for personal as well as for organizational reasons.

Human behavior is probably the most complex phenomenon faced by management because it is intangible and emotion-based to a large extent. As such it is subject to the widely varying perceptual interpretations of many people. While the study of human behavior constitutes the specialized field of study of psychologists, nevertheless any well-adjusted worker as well as any effective manager must possess a good working knowledge of the common-sense principles of practical psychology. He must be able to adjust to other people's personalities, recognize and solve personal problems, and motivate and challenge his subordinates.

The office environment plays a large role in the human behavior of the office staff. Although illustrations of this point are almost limitless, the following examples typify how *physiological* factors have a great impact on the *psychological* condition of the workers:

1. The executive private office "guarded" by a private secretary.

   The president of a highly regarded research corporation contends that such an arrangement inhibits person-to-person communication, isolates both manager and worker from each other, and gives the secretary a sentry role to play. Such an executive is removed from the main current of thought and action.

2. The across-the-desk "confrontation" of manager and worker.

   Behavioral scientists often regard this physical arrangement as pitting one worker against another. With the superior confining himself to the "boss" side of the desk, he often takes the role of an information sender; and the worker becomes an information receiver. Especially when the manager stays behind the desk during a conference does he occupy the dominant position, one in which feedback and the easy flow of information are prevented. Such a situation does not suggest a natural responsiveness on the part of the worker. In short, he is likely to be psychologically inhibited in part by the arrangement. His work and working relationships are affected.

3. The uniform, impersonal, institutional work stations for each executive and each worker.

   To the extent that the office contains row after row of desks, chairs, files, and tables, and to the extent that the office is depersonalized and institutional rather than personal, even "homey" in character, lacking interest, comfort and convenience, then the environment detracts from, rather than encourages, the development of good worker spirit and productivity.

4. A lack of definition of the unique personalities and job responsibilities of each employee.

   The employee's physical environment should promote concentration as well as easy communication, depending upon the particular job to be performed. A receptionist may well be provided with a highly interesting setting with bright colors, modern functional furniture, background music, and unusual displays of the firm's services or products. Her personality, too, should be in harmony with this public relations-information function.[1]

The office staff, as well as those customers and clients who also use a firm's office facilities, are sensitive to the office environment. As a rule, they attach *sensory* values to each facet of the office—that is, values attracted and assigned by each of the senses. This suggests that the main senses of seeing, hearing, touching, and feeling and their relation to the office environment should be given prior study in the management of any office situation.

Psychologically an office manager should design his environment with the following important criteria in mind:

1. *Responsiveness.* The environment of the office should be responsive to the needs of each worker in particular and of the entire work unit in general. First, it should support and enhance the character of the worker, recognizing his personality and job assignment. In so doing it helps the worker to express his own personality needs at work. It should also be adaptable and flexible so that changes in personnel and shifts in job functions can be handled easily without undue expense.
2. *Identification.* The office environment should also tell the visitor visually what is being done in the office—and do so with more than a sign on an entrance door. Through product displays in a sales office, bulletin board charts in a data center, and informal conference space in an executive suite, the environment should assist the worker to identify with his allotted space. An effort should be made, for example, to make the

[1] Robert L. Propst, "The Psychology of Sensory Values" (From a speech given before the Business Equipment Manufacturers Association, New York, October, 1969).

accounting department office unique and differentiated from that of the personnel office.

3. *Self-Renewal.* A key quality of a well-adjusted work schedule is the provision for self-renewal, for stimulation, for relaxation both during work and during work breaks. Adequate lounges assist in providing for off-work renewal; more comfortable work equipment serves a similar purpose while the employee is at work.

THE OFFICE SURFACE ENVIRONMENT

In the typical office the *surface environment* comprises the walls, ceilings, and floors as well as other basic building features such as windows and pillars. Other objects whose surfaces affect the environment are the furniture and the equipment items that make up the office facility. Each of these items has a pronounced effect on the psychological reaction of an office worker to his job.

Color in the Office

In planning the physical factors of the office, color must be considered first, because color has an effect on the lighting conditions. Different colors have different reflective capacities, and thus influence both the illumination level available for the various types of work and the visual comfort. According to the Illuminating Engineers Society, a change from light buff to white ceilings and the addition of light-tinted walls in one large building would have reduced annual lighting costs about $14,000. Good reflecting colors usually give the greatest worker efficiency and the lowest light bills.

In a survey of 500 executive offices conducted by the Color Corporation of America, it was found that the basic color preferences for office decor are beige, green, off-white, blue, yellow, orange, mauve, and blue-green. Most of those interviewed felt that color-coordinated offices aid morale, efficiency, and productivity, and greatly help to reduce tension.

Work assignments and, hence, color formulas differ for the receptionist and the bookkeeper; similarly, differences are noted in the conference room and the drafting department. Light colors are essential in offices where close work on white paper is done. Gray colors have the effect of putting workers to sleep. Strong colors often have such a stimulating effect as to cause headaches. If the walls, woodwork, and other fixtures in the office are the same color, a sleep-producing effect is created. If the office has windows, warm colors such as yellow, peach, pink, brown, and tan can be used for eastern or northern exposures. For southern exposures, cool colors such as green, yellow-green, blue-green, and blue can be used. Although deeper colors can be used opposite windows, they should not be used on the window side because the contrast between the window and the dark colors is too great for visual comfort.

Color Dynamics.[2] The use of color influences the following conditions in the office: (1) prestige, (2) health, (3) morale, and (4) efficiency.

Prestige. The prestige of a business firm is indicated by the impression outsiders receive, either consciously or unconsciously, from the appearance of its offices. Attractive, cheerful, and efficient appearing offices tend to inspire a feeling of confidence and trust; a drab, uninviting, or poorly painted office can induce a feeling of doubt or mistrust.

Health. The health and well-being of office workers are directly influenced by color, as many studies show. For example, the color of walls, equipment, and forms, as determined by an insufficient amount of light available as well as an improper reflective factor, often causes eyestrain. This may, in turn, cause headaches, feelings of tiredness, and other unhealthy effects that reduce the volume of work and increase the number of errors.

Morale. Color has a psychological effect on employee morale and attitudes of workers toward their colleagues and the firm. Color influences the emotions, moods, and dispositions, and, therefore, the thought processes of workers. Some colors, for example, are known as "warm" colors and create the effect of warmth and cheer; others are "cool" in effect and create an atmosphere of quiet, calmness, and restfulness.

Efficiency. Not only does color affect both the health and the morale of workers, but also it has a strong impact on their personal efficiency, as numerous surveys disclose. Some production engineers estimate that production increases 15 to 30 percent when colors are

---

[2] Adapted in part with permission from *Pittsburgh Color Dynamics,* Pittsburgh Plate Glass Company Bulletin.

selected scientifically. One firm estimated that absenteeism was reduced 20 percent as a result of a new color plan.

Other studies estimate the dollar value of a properly chosen color and correct illumination in an office.[3] A study made by the Public Buildings Administration and the U.S. Public Health Service measured the working efficiency of a group of employees using business machines. In the study three conditions were checked: (1) the original room, which had poor light and dark colors on machinery and floors; (2) the same situation with new fluorescent lighting installed; and (3) the same room but with new lighting plus light gray floors and equipment and pale green walls. The results of the study were reported as follows:

> From condition one to three, worker efficiency on one task improved 37.4 percent. However, a conservative figure of 5.5 percent was set for the general increase in productivity for the entire department. In cash value this was equivalent to a saving on gross payroll of $139.25 for each employee per year. So for ten employees, a hundred, or a thousand, multiply by $139.25 to determine the financial benefit to be derived from good illumination and good color, as against the drab conventions of the past.

Color alone, however, is not the influencing factor. It is the effect of the combination of color and light that is the basic consideration. Furthermore, color and light have dimensional influences. For example, long narrow offices can be made to seem wider by using darker, advancing colors on the end walls and lighter, retreating colors on long side walls. The impression of monotonous proportion can be avoided in square rooms by painting one wall, preferably the window or opposite wall, a color or value different than the others. High ceilings seem perceptibly lower when painted darker than the walls. The use of a dado (lower part of the room painted or decorated differently from the upper part) also appears to reduce the height of a room.

Reflection Factors of Color. An understanding of the reflection factors of certain surfaces and certain colors is of prime importance in controlling the brightness ratios. A *reflection factor,* sometimes called a *reflection ratio* or a *coefficient of reflection*, is the ratio of

---

[3] Faber Birren, "Impact of Color on Employee Morale and Productivity," *New Concepts in Office Design* (Elmhurst, Illinois: Business Press, 1968), p. 93.

the total light reflected from a surface to the total light striking the reflection surface.

Suggested surface reflectances for various parts of the office are given in Table 6-1. Since these figures are much higher than generally recognized, a study of them is important.

RECOMMENDED SURFACE REFLECTANCES FOR OFFICES

Table 6-1

Surface	Reflectance	
	"Center-Point" Value and Tolerances	Equivalent Range
Ceiling finishes *	.80 + 15%	80 — 92%
Walls	.50 ± 20%	40 — 60%
Furniture	.35 ± 25%**	26 — 44%
Office machines and equipment	.35 ± 25%**	26 — 44%
Floors	.30 ± 30%	21 — 39%

Source: Illuminating Engineering Society, 1956 Report.

* Recommended reflectances are for finish only. Overall average reflectance of acoustic materials may be somewhat lower.

** American Standard Office Reflectances X2.1.3, 1954.

The intelligent application of paint and simple decorations can accomplish truly remarkable results. Colors that are psychologically pleasant should be chosen. As a matter of general principle, office walls should be light enough to reflect light rather than to absorb it, but not light enough to produce annoying glare. Table 6-2 indicates the reflection factors for a wide range of colors.

REFLECTION FACTORS OF COLORS

Table 6-2

Color	Reflection Factor Percent	Color	Reflection Factor Percent
White	82	Golden yellow	51
Gray-white	76	Medium gray	46
Light cream	74	Dark orange	37
Very light green	70	Copper yellow	27
Lemon yellow	67	Medium red	21
Medium pink	60	Cadet blue	15
Very light blue	60	Dark red	12
Light gray	56	Dark green	10

Tints with a reflection factor between 40 and 60 percent have been found to be best for office walls. When the reflection factor is under 40 percent, too much light is absorbed, thus necessitating extra electricity, an expense that can be avoided by tinting the walls properly. Tints that reflect over 60 percent of light have a tendency to cause glare. Annoying glare may also be caused by the use of glossy paint. Flat paint should therefore be used for ceilings and side walls.

Furniture Colors. In general the same principles of color selection for wall surfaces apply to the surface colors of office furniture. Glare on furniture is often caused by the reflection of light from glass tops on desks or from metal or other highly polished surfaces. For this reason dark shiny tops are not recommended for desks at which a great deal of continuous close work is required. Instead, light-colored furniture with a nongloss finish is the best choice from the point of view of reflection. Manufacturers of floor tile and plastic and linoleum desk tops will furnish data on the reflectance qualities of their products. Reference to such information is helpful in developing and coordinating a complete color plan.

Floor Coverings

The total office environment requires the coordination of floor colors as well as wall and other surface factors. While considerable attention has been given to the ceilings in most offices, the floor coverings have traditionally been ignored or reduced in importance, even though they occupy a space equal to the ceiling. With added emphasis given to all phases of the surface environment in the office, the psychological importance of adequate floor coverings comes into play.

Several classes of floor coverings are available. The most traditional type of flooring, wood, is available in many styles (from random width planks to the square parquets) and lends itself to many decorating designs. Other commonly used floor coverings, such as vinyl asbestos tile, are durable and come in many colorful designs. Hard-surfaced coverings, such as marble, travertine, brick, and flagstone, are used to withstand heavy traffic in areas such as reception centers. In the past few years, however, a marked preference has developed for carpeting all areas of the office including the computer room. Carpeting creates a quiet, relaxed atmosphere in which to work. Through the use of carpeting, a feeling of luxury is created, which enhances worker satisfaction. The fact that carpeting is a much more comfortable floor covering on which to walk reduces employee fatigue. At the same time it is safer to walk on carpeting than high gloss, slippery, hard-surfaced tile or concrete. Carpeting also has considerable acoustical qualities and is easier to maintain than many other types of floor coverings.

THE SEEING ENVIRONMENT: LIGHTING CONTROL

Office workers must see to work. This truism, however, is too often taken for granted by simply providing standard fluorescent lighting. Since the office manager's principal concern is people, he must realize that proper lighting has both physical and psychological effects on workers. Both natural light (from daylight) and artificial lighting sources must be considered. In either case the goal is a sufficient quantity and quality of light that is well-diffused on working surfaces without the presence of glare or sharp shadows.

Inadequate and improper lighting contributes to eyestrain, which, in turn, may be the cause of many physical disorders such as muscular tension, eye fatigue, and an increased blinking rate. Unfavorable lighting conditions may cause poor workmanship, mistakes, and decreased production as the result of inability to see the work clearly and quickly enough, as well as leading to fatigue and irritability on the part of the workers. On the other hand, adequate and proper lighting assists in maintaining health and in increasing employee productivity. Figure 6-2 shows the physiological effects of increasing the illumination from 10 to 100 foot-candles. As a unit for measuring illumination, a *foot-candle* (F-C) is the amount of light produced by a standard candle at a distance of one foot. An increase in foot-candles

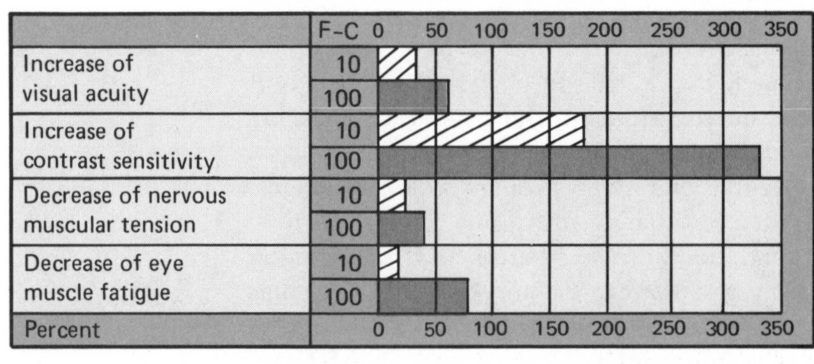

Fig. 6-2

Relative Benefits of Increased Illumination

from 10 to 100 on the working surface, for example, increases the ability to see clearly and distinctly from 30 to 60 percent; eye-muscle fatigue is decreased from 15 percent for 10 foot-candles to 70 percent for 100 foot-candles. The higher the foot-candle level of illumination attained, the better are the health, morale, and efficiency of the employees. If there is an absence of sharp shadows and glare, the seeability is better. Good lighting also increases production because the better seeability enables employees to see more clearly and more quickly and to work more safely.

Reflection and direct rays of sunlight and artificial light are not the only causes of eye discomfort. There are others that are all too common in offices today. A lighting fixture, or *luminaire,* that is insufficiently shaded or shielded when in the visual field causes eye fatigue. The luminaires should be shaded or lowered so as to emit no more than 400 foot-lamberts if more than one fixture is in the visual field. A *foot-lambert* is a unit of brightness, and is defined as a diffusing surface of uniform brightness reflecting or emitting one lumen (a unit of light) for each square foot when viewed from a designated direction. In effect, a foot-lambert is equivalent to one foot-candle emitted or reflected.

Another factor contributing to eye discomfort is *brightness ratio,* that is, the ratio of foot-lamberts between two surfaces such as the visual task and its surroundings. If the brightness of a visual task is 60 foot-lamberts and that of a dark desk top against which it is viewed is 5 foot-lamberts, the brightness ratio is 12 to 1. This amount of brightness may cause visual discomfort. Normally the brightness ratio should not exceed 3 to 1.

Natural Lighting in the Office

Although natural light can be put to use in many ways in the office, it must be controlled to some extent. Direct sunlight would, for example, produce glare, discomfort, and eyestrain; and on cloudy days, no sunlight would be available. But natural light can be "captured" as it comes in through the ubiquitous glass curtain of windows common to contemporary architecture. Unfortunately the cheerfulness of natural light is often lost by heavy draperies, venetian blinds, or partitions that obscure portions of the light. Proper use of casements that diffuse the light, deflect glare, and protect the view of nature is recommended.

Another product that can be used to prevent solar-ray penetration and yet admit light that is well diffused is a type of wire window screen that does not obstruct vision. Its greatest usefulness is for windows facing east, west, and south because it reduces considerably the amount of heat entering the office through solar radiation.

Artificial Lighting in the Office[4]

Artificial lighting systems may be classified as: (1) indirect, (2) semi-indirect, (3) general diffuse, (4) semidirect, and (5) direct.

Indirect Lighting. Indirect lighting produces a quality of lighting highly desirable for such visual tasks as are found in drafting rooms, general offices, and private offices. With this system 90 to 100 percent of the light from the luminaires is first directed to the ceiling and upper side walls, from which it is diffusely reflected to all parts of the room. In effect the entire ceiling becomes the light source, and shadows and reflected glare are minimized. Since the light source is the entire ceiling, it cannot be avoided by the observer; so care must be taken to keep the brightness low enough to prevent its being a source of glare. Because the ceiling constitutes an important part of such a lighting system, careful attention must be paid to having it as light in color as possible and to maintaining it in good condition. It should be given a matted finish in a color that has a high reflection factor.

Semi-Indirect Lighting. Semi-indirect lighting is defined as any system in which 60 to 90 percent of the luminaire output is emitted upward toward the ceiling and upper side walls, while the rest is directed downward. As this system also utilizes the ceiling as the main source of light, the same considerations as for indirect lighting should be observed with regard to ceiling finish and good maintenance characteristics. In general, semi-indirect lighting units give a little more light for the same wattage than do indirect units, but more attention may have to be given to the factors of direct and reflected glare.

General Diffuse Lighting. This classification refers to systems where the predominant illumination on horizontal working surfaces (40 to 60 percent) comes directly from the lighting units, but where

[4] This section describing and illustrating the five types of artificial lighting systems is taken from *Recommended Practice for Office Lighting,* Office Lighting Committee of the Illuminating Engineering Society (1960 Edition), pp. 14-15.

there is also a considerable contribution from upward light reflected back from the ceiling and upper wall areas.

One type of unit of this classification is the glass diffusing, enclosing globe. Another general type of unit in this classification is represented by the direct-indirect units, where little or no light is emitted in the normal fields of view.

While general diffuse lighting systems give more illumination for a specified wattage than do indirect or semi-indirect systems, shadows are more noticeable and some difficulty may be experienced with both direct and reflected glare.

Semidirect Lighting. In this classification 60 to 90 percent of the output of the luminaire is directed downward to the working surface. There is, therefore, some contribution to the illumination at the working surface from light that is directed upward and reflected by the ceiling and upper wall areas.

Direct Lighting. Units in this classification can be defined as those that direct practically all (90 to 100 percent) of the light of the luminaires in angles below the horizontal, i.e., directly toward the working areas. While, in general, such systems provide illumination on the working surfaces most efficiently, this may be at the sacrifice of other factors. For example, disturbing shadows may result unless the area of the lighting units is relatively large. Direct and reflected glare may be distressing unless the relative brightnesses are kept within the recommended limits. An appearance of dinginess may result unless some means of brightening the ceiling is provided, such as special provision for upward light from the luminaires or the use of light-colored floorings, desk tops, and furniture finishes.

Considerations in Artificial Lighting Systems

Human beings cannot be standardized, and in many respects neither can the lighting systems that are provided for their peculiar uses. Man's unique work assignments, his moods, his periods of intensive work activity and concentration—all of these must be given consideration. Since proper lighting includes more than avoiding eyestrain and providing sufficient light, its proper installation requires the technical skills of a lighting engineer who can advise the office manager on the best lighting system for his work areas.

Working as a team, the lighting specialist and the office manager must find reasonable answers to many questions such as the following:

1. How can comfortable brightness be provided—that is, how should luminaires be spaced?
2. What wiring and switch requirements are required, keeping in mind the need to supplement natural light to a greater extent in some areas than others?
3. What facilities (such as translucent glass in partitions and doors) are available for diffusing light and yet providing necessary privacy?
4. What types of lighting fixtures are most efficient and yet most economical and convenient to maintain and clean?
5. What are the relative advantages and disadvantages of incandescent and fluorescent lighting?

Incandescent light is produced in filament lamps or bulbs. The average life of a filament bulb is 1,000 hours of operation; 2,500 hours with special-service bulbs, which are lower in efficiency than general-service bulbs. Filament bulbs have a high-power factor rating, use much current, and emit a steady light in which they strengthen yellow, orange, and red colors. Incandescent lighting fixtures and lamps are less expensive than fluorescent fixtures and tubes. It is difficult, however, to provide the current recommended levels of general illumination because of the relatively low efficiency of incandescent lamps.

Fluorescent light is produced by the action of ultraviolet waves on coated phosphors on the inside of tubular bulbs. Fluorescent lamps do not emit nearly so much radiant heat as incandescent lamps and consume about one third of the wattages for an equal amount of light emitted. Their chief advantages are: low cost of operation, low radiant heat emission, resemblance to natural daylight in color, and ability to increase levels of illumination without the necessity for rewiring the building. Today lighting experts agree that the *luminous ceiling* in which the lighting is diffused evenly and indirectly over the entire work area is the most efficient system for general offices. An example of this adaptation is illustrated in Figure 6-3.

Guidelines for the Seeing Environment

Not only does the office manager bear the responsibility for optimizing the seeing environment of his own area, but in addition he is frequently asked to advise on the lighting requirements of other departments in his firm. For this reason it is incumbent upon him to

Fig. 6-3

Designed for United Financial Center, Los Angeles, by Welton Becker & Associates, Architects

Office Area Using Luminous Ceiling Lighting System

develop a set of working guidelines for improving or maintaining a good seeing environment. In such a list these items should be included:

1. Provide maximum illumination for each task, considered individually for each worker, and avoid the monotony of standard illumination for the entire office area.
2. Consider the recommended illumination levels outlined in Table 6-3 on the following page.
3. Emphasize seeing, rather than lighting, and the impact that good seeability has on employee mood and efficiency.
4. Measure lighting conditions with a light meter, available from the local light company.
5. Minimize (and eliminate if possible) all glare and shadows.
6. Shade office windows so that the direct sun rays are not permitted to shine directly on work surfaces.

RECOMMENDED ILLUMINATION LEVELS

Table 6-3

Type of Office or Work	Foot-Candles on Task *
Cartography, designing, detailed drafting	200
Accounting, auditing, tabulating, bookkeeping, business machines operation, reading poor reproductions, rough layout drafting	150
Regular office work, reading good reproductions, reading or transcribing handwriting in hard pencil or on poor paper. Active filing, index references, mail sorting, critical visual tasks in conference rooms	100
Reading or transcribing handwriting in ink or medium pencil on good quality paper, intermittent filing	70
Reading high contrast or well-printed material, tasks and areas not involving critical or prolonged seeing such as conferring, interviewing, inactive files and washrooms	30
Corridors, elevators, escalators, stairways	20 * *

Source: Adapted from *Recommended Practice for Office Lighting,* the Office Lighting Committee of the Illuminating Engineering Society (1960 Edition), p. 7.

* Minimum on task at any time.
** Or not less than 1/5 the level in adjacent areas.

7. Clean frequently all reflectors, lamps, windows, shades, or blinds used in connection with lighting. (Accumulated dust on lighting units can reduce the available light from an estimated 25 to 40 percent.)
8. Consult a qualified illuminating engineer for assistance in laying out an office lighting system. However, the following are some general suggestions that can be followed by the office manager alone:
   a. For indirect lighting, locate outlets about as far apart as ceiling height. Generally, the maximum spacing for uniformity is this distance plus two feet.
   b. Arrange the wattage capacity of electrical outlets used for lighting so that there will be available about 5 to 7½ watts for each square foot of floor area. The use of fluorescent lighting will reduce this figure.
   c. Consider that most fluorescent fixtures, except luminous side fixtures with glass or plastic sides, are more comfortable when viewed crosswise.
   d. Choose indirect luminaires which are as simple as possible both in construction and design to harmonize with

the interior decorative scheme. The efficiencies of luminaires may vary from 50 to 85 percent. Only those having efficiencies of 75 percent or more should be given consideration in the usual office space.

9. Provide supplementary lighting such as desk lamps to meet special seeing requirements by increasing foot-candles of work areas by 50 to 100 percent.

THE HEARING ENVIRONMENT: NOISE CONTROL

In the age of machines, from the telephone to the tabulating machine, an increasing tempo of noise has been generated, calling for strong measures to be taken for its control. The *decibel,* a unit for measuring the loudness of sound, is used to express the smallest change in sound that a human being can detect. For example, zero decibel (0 db.) represents the point at which the faintest sound becomes audible to the average ear; and from this point a decibel scale can be drawn at intervals of one or more decibels to represent increases in sound intensity detectable by the human ear. Such a scale appears in Figure 6-4 in which common sounds and noises are ranked.[5]

Fig. 6-4

SOUND PRESSURE LEVELS OF COMMON SOUNDS AND NOISES

	Decibels	Threshold of feeling
	120	
Deafening	110	Thunder, artillery, nearby riveter, elevated train, boiler factory
	100	
Very Loud	90	Loud street noises, noisy factory, OFFICE MACHINE ROOM, police whistle
	80	
Loud	70	NOISY OFFICE, average street noise, average radio, average factory
	60	
Moderate	50	Noisy home, AVERAGE OFFICE, average conversation, quiet radio
	40	
Faint	30	Quiet home or PRIVATE OFFICE, average auditorium, quiet conversation
	20	
Very Faint	10	Rustle of leaves, whisper, sound proof room
	0	Threshold of audibility

Common Office Sounds Compared with Other Noises of Varying Intensity

[5] "Stop, Look, and Listen to Your Office Environment," *Modern Office Procedures* (March, 1970), p. 18.

An important element to be considered in determining the level of noise is the pitch or the frequency of the sound. An optimum pitch lies within a range that does not exceed 6,000 cycles per second (about the level of an alto voice). The more vibrations per second of a sound, the higher the pitch. High sounds are most likely to be annoying and harmful.

Recommended maximum levels of noise for efficient office work are as follows: (1) for the private office, 40-50 decibels; (2) for the general office, 60 decibels; (3) for the accounting office, 65 decibels; and (4) for data centers, 80 decibels. It should be noted that these figures are approximations as well as recommendations, and permitting the noise levels to extend beyond these maximum levels will result in physical and psychological problems for the workers.

Sources of Noise

In the modern city where most offices are located, noise may well be the most common negative feature of the environment. Automobiles, airplanes, and trucks alone account for a sizable portion of this condition. These out-of-door elements of noise, of course, are carried into the office itself where the two key ingredients of office work—personnel and machines—are found. These two latter factors also constitute the principal sources of all internal office noise.

The universal office machine—the typewriter—is a key source of office noise; and as it has progressed from its manual to electric form, the level of noise generated by its use has been increased. In Figure 6-5 it is shown that a manual (or standard) typewriter measures 64 db. while the electric machine measures 68 db.[6] In addition this illustration shows criteria for noise control (NC) that have been developed. For example, NC-35, the lowest noise criterion curve, suggests the maximum noise that should be permitted in staff level offices; NC-45, the maximum noise that should be allowed in a work center where a conference must be carried on around a desk; and NC-55, the upper limit of noise in which satisfactory telephone usage is possible.

Typical of another common source of machine noise is the printer in the data processing department. Figure 6-5 shows that one printer's noise level (the original machine) was modified by acoustical treatment, thus permitting reliable communications to be carried on around the machine.

---

[6] Paul S. Veneklasen, "Modern Acoustics in the Office," *New Concepts in Office Design* (Elmhurst, Illinois: Business Press, 1968), pp. 81-82.

Fig. 6-5

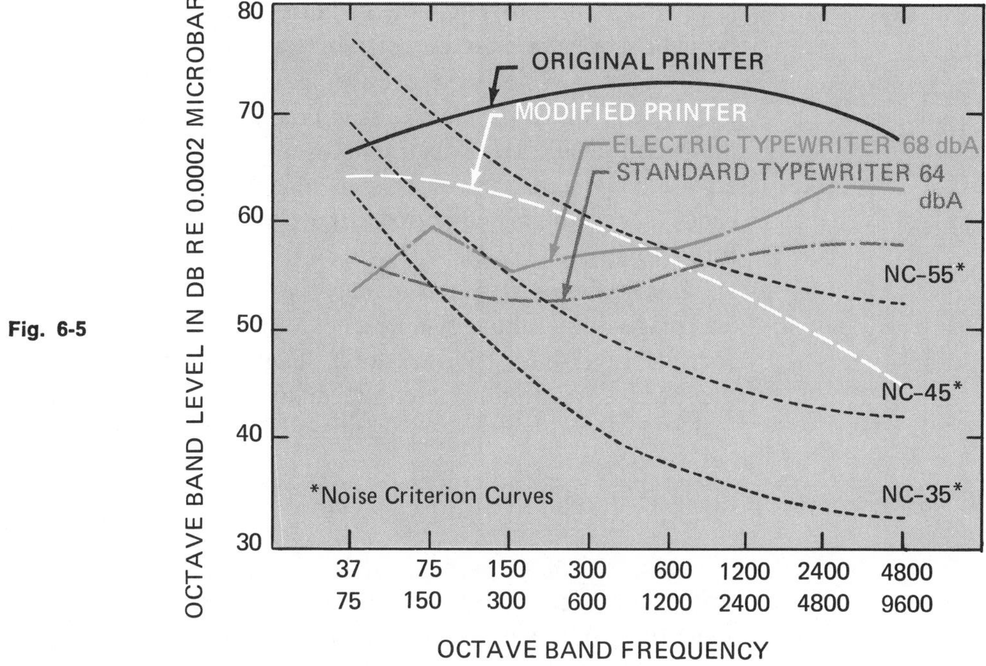

Criteria for Evaluating Noise Levels Generated by Typical Office Machines

While the machine is often considered the chief culprit of office noise, office personnel must not be overlooked. Conversation and gossip, conferences and telephone calls, and interpersonal work assignments all call forth vocal noise; the distribution of data, in another sense, calls forth transportation noise as workers move from one location to another.

The Effects of Noise in the Office

Noise in the office is more than unpleasant; it diminishes the worker's efficiency. It interferes with communication and makes concentration exceedingly difficult, if not impossible. High levels of noise may impair hearing, increase blood pressure, cause fatigue, and in some cases bring about neuroses. According to a five-year study made by the United States Health Service of the Department of Health, Education, and Welfare, in some cases the prolonged exposure to high noise levels can produce a permanent effect in hearing ability. The federal government sets 75 decibels as the critical range beyond which physical damage to hearing can occur. Experiments have shown that a reduction in noise levels from 50 to 35 decibels brought about a five percent increase in typewriting production.

The Aetna Life Insurance Company proved by actual test during a two-year study in their offices that sound conditioning increased the overall efficiency of their employees 8.8 percent, decreased typists' errors 29 percent, and decreased machine operators' errors 52 percent. The company also experienced a 47 percent decrease in their turnover rates.

In Oklahoma City the manager of a large tabulating department was plagued by an average absence of three to four days a month by each of his 14 to 16 operators. Then, the room was sound conditioned. Five months later the manager reported that absenteeism had been forgotten as a problem in his department.

Noise Control in Offices

One basic fact is involved in all noise control programs: hard surfaces reflect sounds while soft surfaces absorb sound waves. Therefore, initial noise control efforts are designed to eliminate the source of the sound or, if this is impossible, to utilize sound-absorbing materials to muffle or absorb the noise. Other techniques, such as moving offices away from noisy locations, are also effective, as reflected in the following summary of effective sound-reduction practices.

Personnel. To reduce the noise created by office workers, efficient layout is recommended to decrease the amount of required walking. For example, placing side by side two office workers required to do considerable work together can reduce telephone calls and cut down on frequent moving about. Conferences can be scheduled for private offices, and workers can be instructed to converse in low tones and to restrict informal personal interaction to break periods.

Layout and Location. Noises exterior to the office can in some cases be eliminated or reduced in intensity if the office is relocated. For example, there is considerably less noise on the tenth floor of a large building than on the first floor. Keeping doors and windows closed, if possible, also helps reduce unwanted sound. "Noisy" departments, such as those having many machines, can be segregated into a remote, corner location, thus isolating the noise from the departments requiring a more quiet working environment.

Floor Coverings. Uncovered concrete floors in the office are to be avoided at any cost. Such hard surfaces reflect rather than absorb sound. Such resilient coverings as rubber, asphalt, and cork tile, however, have considerable absorption qualities. Carpeting is now the preferred floor covering for reducing office noise from footsteps, the movement of chairs and desks, and the dropping of objects. Carpeting also aids in muffling other sound waves directed to the office area.[7]

Wall Coverings. Any room has considerable absorptive material in it—in the walls, furniture, ceilings, and floors, as well as in the people and their clothing! To achieve a reduction in the office decibel level, the absorption materials must be increased considerably. Fabrics in upholstered office furniture, as well as in draperies, have noise-reducing qualities and are used both for window and wall treatments and inner office partitions. Where used as draperies, they are spaced about three or four inches away from the windows to obtain the best sound absorption. Acoustical plasters can also be used but are not popular in offices due to the high cost of installation and difficulties encountered in redecoration.

Ceiling Coverings. Wall and ceiling surfaces in modern offices are often finished in hard gypsum plaster applied on concrete or hollow tile. Every sound produced in such offices is intensified and permeates the entire room unless some absorptive material is placed on the office surfaces. The material most frequently used as a ceiling covering to reduce noise is acoustical tile. Dozens of different styles and types are available, with one firm producing more than 70 different types for office use.

Machines and Equipment. Because of the increased use of automatic information-processing equipment, such as accounting and calculating machines and card-punch and tabulating machines, office noise can reach alarming proportions. As previously discussed, placing all these noisy machines in one soundproof location helps to reduce noise, although the effect of such noise upon the machine

---

[7] Information on flooring is available from two associations: Asphalt Tile Institute, 101 Park Avenue, New York, and the Vinyl and Rubber Flooring Division, the Rubber Manufacturers Association, 444 Madison Avenue, New York. Some major manufacturers, such as Armstrong Cork Company, will give free advice on materials relating to installation of flooring.

operators themselves has not been improved. The following possibilities are also available:

1. Muting telephone bells and typewriter bells.
2. Using rubber-tired casters on movable machines and equipment.
3. Using noiseless typewriters.
4. Placing sound-absorbing pads on desks and table tops.
5. Keeping swivel and tilting chairs properly oiled and adjusted.
6. Selecting filing equipment with well-built suspension drawers.
7. Using sound-engineered acoustical cabinets for data-processing machines. (See Figure 6-6.)

Gates Acoustinet, Inc.

Fig. 6-6

Acoustical Cabinets Enclosing Card-Punch Machines

THE ATMOSPHERIC ENVIRONMENT: AIR CONTROL

More and more office employees today work in air-conditioned surroundings—so much so, in fact, that frequently the general office atmosphere is equated with air conditioning. There are, however, other related factors such as air temperature and circulation, the relative humidity level, and the general conditions of cleanliness which affect the atmosphere and spirit of the office. The music-while-you-work concept, another important agent for providing a comfortable office environment, is discussed in Chapter 13.

Air Conditioning in the Office

Air carries heat and moisture, as well as foreign matter of many descriptions, including germ diseases. All these elements, except germ diseases, can be controlled with air-conditioning equipment. Air, when conditioned, is scientifically treated so that its temperature, humidity, cleanliness, and circulation are all accurately and constantly controlled.

Air conditioning in an office contributes to mental activity and boosts the efficiency of employees; its liveness gives one vigor. Bad, dry, and dust-clouded air reduces human efficiency and hampers production. This is especially true in work, such as office duties, that is largely mental in nature. It means lowered vitality, headaches, and "four o'clock fatigue."

The United States General Services Administration has conducted probably the most complete study of the impact of air conditioning on office workers. Two large offices—one air-conditioned, the other not—were studied for five months to compare employee performance. In the air-conditioned office it was found that productivity increased 9.5 percent; absenteeism decreased 2.5 percent; and clerical errors were down slightly, .9 percent.[8]

Temperature

Extended and scientific research by the American Society of Heating and Ventilating Engineers and the United States Public Health Service has determined the most healthful and comfortable air conditions for normal people, at both sedentary and active occupations, in offices, shops, and homes. Although there is no temperature level that will please everybody, the most comfortable and healthful temperature for work is below 70 degrees. This is true, however, only when proper humidity or moisture is maintained. The normal body temperature of the human being remains constant, winter or summer, so long as health prevails.

---

[8] "Does Your Office Need Air Conditioning?" *Modern Office Procedures* (March, 1961), p. 26. This article describes several other surveys in which the findings show increases in efficiency of 24 to 51 percent and decreases in absenteeism of 25 to 30 percent after the installation of air conditioning.

Along with the outside temperature, office heat may be created as a result of the number of lighting fixtures, the number of workers in the office, the number of windows and the direction they face, the number of large office machines, the height of the ceiling, and the material used in constructing the building. The development of *space conditioning*, or *heating with light*, which combines air conditioning and heat, captures this heat and puts it to use. Cool air is brought into the office to cool the lighting fixtures and prolong their life; at the same time the fixtures warm the air. During the summer the warm air is blown out of the building, thus helping to reduce the air-conditioning load; in the winter the air is recirculated to help heat the office. Some lighting systems often provide enough heat to warm offices without the need for additional heat and in some instances the heat from the air is drawn off into storage tanks for later use when the lights are off. In other systems the lighting fixtures are tied in with thermostats that turn on the lights during the night to help heat the offices.

In the 60-story First National Bank of Chicago, regular fluorescent lights provide both illumination and the major source of heat. When heat is needed in the offices, air warmed by the fluorescent tubes is drawn into ducts and distributed through the building by the ventilating system. An estimated 35 percent of all major building construction makes use of the "heating with light" method.[9]

Air Circulation

If the air were not circulated, each person would tend to become encased in air that would approach skin temperature and the saturation point. Ten cubic feet of outside air per person, per minute, makes for an ideal working atmosphere. The air motion should be gentle and not drafty. Air movement in winter should not exceed 50 feet a minute. A movement of 25 feet a minute is preferable. Air in motion has a cooling effect, even though its temperature may be high, because it accelerates the evaporation of everpresent body moisture.

A method of keeping air in motion, which can easily be used to satisfaction in smaller offices, is the fan. It is an inexpensive piece of equipment, but a useful one. There are two types of office fans. The

---

[9] For additional examples of present and proposed "heating with light" installations, see "Let 'em Burn: More Firms Rely on Lights to Cut Heating Bills," *The Wall Street Journal,* July 26, 1965, p. 1; "Building," *Time* (August 6, 1965), p. 51; and "Let Your Light Heat Your Building," *Business Week* (August 21, 1965), pp. 137-138.

older type, which circulates the same air, may be placed anywhere within the office. The newer type, sometimes known as an electric ventilator, is placed at a window, facing the outdoors. This provides a complete change of air every few minutes. Stale air and odors are pushed out by these fans and new air is admitted. However, in the use of fans, the circulation of air is not coordinated with temperature and moisture control.

Air may also be kept in motion through blowers, which are used in the larger office buildings, schools, and public buildings. Each blower consists of a motor-driven fan, enclosed in a chamber, with large tubes leading away from it. These tubes are distributed throughout the building, with openings in different rooms. The fan pushes air through the tubes. This air escapes through the openings in the rooms, forcing the other air to move.

Humidity

Air-conditioning equipment adds or removes moisture from the air. It humidifies the air during the winter and dehumidifies it during the summer. The removal of moisture from the air is accomplished by condensation. The temperature of the air is lowered below its dew point, thereby causing the excess water to condense and fall into the tank of the conditioning machine.

Ventilation must always be considered from three standpoints: entrance of outdoor air, heating of fresh air, and exit of used air. Ventilation should not be left to chance. The opening and shutting of windows to suit someone never secures proper air conditions in an office.

The control of air is a science in itself. If the relative humidity of the atmosphere is high, it makes one feel colder on a cold day and hotter on a hot day. One is more comfortable in a room with a temperature of 65 to 70 degrees if the air is reasonably moist than in a room where the air is dry and the temperature several degrees higher. The relative humidity should be approximately 50 percent for comfort and health.

Atmospheric Cleanliness in the Office

Not only must the air in the office be maintained at the proper temperature, be properly circulated, and contain a comfortable relative humidity; it must also be kept clean, that is, free of dirt, dust, odors, and other unpleasant, uncomfortable, or harmful conditions.

Several types of machines are available for providing a clean atmosphere. For example, ultraviolet lamps are available that destroy a large percentage of airborne bacteria in large work locations, often reducing the incidence of common colds. Mechanical air filters, too, are used to strain foreign particles out of the air through cloth, felt, cellulose, glass fibers, or other filtering materials.

When one considers the office atmosphere to be more pervasive than the sphere of air within it—that is, to cover the total environment—cleanliness can take on an added meaning. All of the environmental factors, therefore, should be maintained in a clean, neat manner in keeping with the desired office image and the preferences of employees. This suggests, too, that a program of periodic evaluation and renewal of the total environment is a sound practice, probably resulting in more benefits than out-of-pocket costs. Included in such a program would be the following factors:

1. Floors: scrubbing, polishing, mopping, waxing, buffing, sweeping; carpet vacuuming, stair cleaning.
2. Restrooms: cleaning and servicing.
3. Lighting: cleaning and replacing fixtures and bulbs.
4. Lobby and corridor policing.
5. Paper and trash collection: with the objective of reducing air pollution and dumping-ground contamination by selling waste paper to paper mills for recycling and by purchasing recycled paper and paper products for office use.
6. Windows: washing inside and out; window shade and/or drapery maintenance.
7. Elevators: cleaning and maintenance.
8. Outdoor factors: lawn maintenance; driveway cleaning; landscaping.
9. Miscellaneous factors: general utility work (moving, rearranging equipment; repainting; extermination control for insects).

THE IDEAL OFFICE ENVIRONMENT

The total office environment is a complex phenomenon that includes all the physical and psychological factors discussed in this chapter. To provide the best environment for any given group of people in any firm, both employee preferences and available resources must be considered. Administrative office managers planning new offices or considering changes in existing offices would be well advised to consider the results of a study by Lawrence Wheeler, head of the behavioral research department of Ewing and Miller, Associates.[10] In this study 358 office personnel composed of managers and nonmanagers in 18 organizations were interrogated regarding their environmental preferences for an ideal office. In general these findings emerged from the study:

1. The most bothersome noise in the office is the human voice.
2. Managers are more sensitive to typewriter and office machine noises than are nonmanagers.
3. The ideal office has extensive carpeting, true daylight equivalent lighting, quiet colors, and adequate work surface for each employee. Managers prefer additional work space behind them rather than off to the side.
4. In general office areas, workers do not like to face each other but prefer working side by side or one in front of the other.
5. Windowless offices tend to make people feel uncomfortable.
6. Executives prefer an office arrangement with a partition between them and their secretary, but not cut off completely from one another.
7. Carpeting is the most desired floor covering by all groups, and natural wood finishes on walls are most preferred.
8. Most popular ceilings are light colored, covered with acoustic material, and illuminated by fixtures.
9. Most people prefer quiet colors with a few bright or strong colors. Second preference is a cool blue or green color in large areas with a near neutral but not gray color close to them.

QUESTIONS FOR REVIEW

1. Define the term "office environment." What is the relationship of this term to productivity in the office?

2. How can it be maintained that "the office environment has sensory values"?

3. In what way does color influence the following conditions in the office: (a) prestige, (b) health, (c) morale, and (d) efficiency?

4. Color dynamics is a more important psychological problem than most office managers realize. Explain the physical and psychological

---

[10] "The Offices of the 70's," *Modern Office Procedures* (January, 1970), pp. 22-23.

effects of the following: (a) warm colors, (b) strong colors, and (c) having the entire office area and the fixtures the same color.

5. What is meant by the reflection factor of colors? How does this factor affect the problem of color dynamics?

6. Identify the various alternatives for floor coverings in the modern office, and compare the relative values of each to the improvement of the office environment.

7. What is a "foot-candle"? What are the recommended foot-candles for various office jobs?

8. Name the several causes of eye discomfort in office work. Which of these causes probably brings about the greatest amount of eyestrain?

9. What advantages may be realized from the use of fluorescent lamps in the office? Do these same advantages characterize incandescent lighting?

10. What term is used as the unit of measure for the loudness of sound? Discuss several methods of noise control that can be used in an office.

11. What effect has the increased use of automatic data processing equipment and other types of machines had upon the noise problem in offices? How may the administrative office manager reduce the decibel levels of sound generated by these machines?

12. Several factors affect the conditions of office space. Discuss the nature of these space conditions and what technological developments are being utilized in modern building and maintenance programs to control the space environment of the office.

QUESTIONS FOR DISCUSSION

1. A recently constructed office building in New York City is characterized by a large number of windows. No space in the building is more than 18 feet from any window exposure. Do you think this is a good lighting plan? What effect will this construction factor have on the office work?

2. The owner of a small jewelry manufacturing company in a midwestern city recently stated, "Air conditioning is an expensive luxury. All it does is coddle the employees." As office manager of this company, how would you proceed to convince the owner of the need for air conditioning?

3. In an interview a design consultant remarked, "Offices that lack human qualities dull the senses, slow the mind, reduce the ability to discriminate, and increase the chance of error." He went on to say

that when the individuality of workers is not recognized in the planning and design of offices, the workers become bored and, as a result, less efficient and productive. Discuss several techniques that may be employed to overcome the feeling of boredom on the part of employees, thus making the offices more human.

4. In the offices of the Tyndall Supply Company, a survey is being made of the lighting conditions. The office employees have complained that in some offices they make many mistakes because there does not seem to be enough light and in others because there is too much light or glare. By means of a light meter, the following light conditions have been found in the various offices:

a. In the general offices where 20 men work constantly at their desks, there are 500-watt filament lamps, in indirect luminaires, spaced 10 feet apart. These provide 25 foot-candles.

b. In the transcription department where there are 10 girls transcribing shorthand notes, the indirect luminaires contribute 80 foot-candles.

c. In the filing department where there are three clerks, the light offered is 50 foot-candles.

d. In the drafting room which faces north, there are 100 foot-candles of light.

e. In the three private offices occupied by the officers, the use of fluorescent lights gives them 50 foot-candles. These officers are in and out constantly, some working in the factory, others in the office, and some out of the building entirely.

Criticize the lighting conditions in these offices. Suggest the improvements you would make and give the reasons for your suggestions.

5. The staff headquarters of the Ransom Sales Corporation is located in Atlanta, Georgia. This office is the firm's southernmost branch. No customers use this office since it is the staff headquarters. The manager of this office wants to air condition his office, even though his branch has been losing money on its operations during the past year. How should this air-conditioning problem be handled?

6. The McKenna Manufacturing Company is planning to move its plant and offices to a city in the Tennessee Valley district because of cheaper power and a good trainable labor supply. The city selected has a population of 20,000. Very little manufacturing has been done heretofore in this city. The firm will require space for 1,400 factory workers and 400 office employees. The temperature in this city varies from 5° F. in the winter to 108° F. in the summer. In addition to providing space for the needs of the plant and the office, the site selected has sufficient area for ample parking.

As the office administrator of this firm, you are asked to recommend the physical factors that should be considered and the facilities to be installed so that the employees will be able to work in a healthful environment which promotes good morale and encourages high productivity.

PRACTICAL OFFICE CASES

Case 6-1 Renovating the Office Environment

The Casper Corn Products Corporation, located in an upper midwestern city of 120,000, is engaged in the processing of corn and cane for shipment throughout the country. Its principal products are syrups, molasses, and cooking supplies to complement the waffle and pancake products produced in another smaller subsidiary. The firm was started by a conservative midwestern family more than 90 years ago and has steadily grown from a work force of 5 (the Casper family alone) with annual sales of $750 to its present size of 1,150 with annual sales totaling approximately $14 million. The firm is still a close corporation, headed by a member of the founding family, Joseph Casper. As president, he seems to reflect the industrious, conservative point of view of the founder.

The office occupies the entire three-story brick building located due south and within 100 feet of the two huge processing plants. This building was constructed 35 years ago. Nearby is a trunkline of the railroad used in shipping packaged products as well as carload lots to large institutional users of the firm's products. Due to its north-central geographic location and also due to the fact that the prevailing summer breezes usually blow from the south, the building has not been renovated since it was built. No sizable environmental changes, such as air conditioning, have been installed, although the building has been maintained in a spotless condition and has been painted every four years.

The building is laid out according to the following plan:

First floor: mail room and duplicating services (near the elevator); records center; purchasing department; sales and advertising departments; engineering department; shipping services.

Second floor: financial offices; accounting department; data processing.

Third floor: general office services; executive offices.

Traditionally the general office function has been the responsibility of the accounting department, which has been highly cost conscious. As early as 1915, a cost accounting system was installed to control the plant's processing operation; and in the office a detailed cost accounting system was put into operation in 1938. As a result it is generally believed that costs have been contained and that the major effort toward maximizing profits for the firm has been satisfied.

The office services group is responsible for general office work for the entire firm. Although each of the department executives and their assistants have secretarial help for departmental work, the bulk of the office work, such as correspondence, reproduction work, and typing of reports and forms, is handled by the stenographic pool on the third floor. Other responsibilities of the office services group are centralized filing, ordering office supplies, designing and procuring office forms, and other related clerical services. Included in the general office services group are the office services manager; his secretary, Dorothy Binnall; a stenographic pool of 15 girls supervised by a veteran employee, Gertrude Erickson; and a general clerical pool of 12 who are responsible for filing and other clerical tasks, headed by Prudence Robillard.

Recently Neil Sylvestre, a young, ambitious senior accountant, has been transferred from the accounting department to replace Roger LeBlanc, the office manager, who has retired after 32 years in his position. Sylvestre is approximately the same age as Casper and was chosen for the position because of his fine performance in the accounting department, his overall knowledge of the firm, and his educational background in general management, data processing, and information systems. It appeared to Casper, to whom Sylvestre reports, that Sylvestre could integrate the many information-processing activities of the firm into a workable system. He is already knowledgeable concerning the firm's combined punched-card and small-scale computer system on the second floor, a unit that has recently expanded so that its six key-punch operators have been forced to take temporary quarters in one section of the general office services area.

Within three months after assuming his new position, Sylvestre conducted an intensive office audit to determine the scope and condition of his area of responsibility. In this audit the following significant facts came to light:

1. A "total systems" approach should be considered in which data processing systems are developed for each of the departments in the firm.
2. While the entire office environment needs modernization to reflect a more progressive image for the firm, immediate attention should be centered on the general office area and executive suites. Specifically:

   a. The entire building should be air-conditioned. Although meteorological records indicate that, on the average, only 20 days each summer have temperatures above 90° F., an offsetting feature is the fact that 80 of the 90 days during the summer season have relative humidity levels above 75 percent. In addition, the girls in the office have complained repeatedly about the open windows in the summer which let in sickening odors from the corn processing operation, dust, and soot from the close proximity of plant and railroad. For these reasons several of the new girls have been leaving work at 3 o'clock due to nausea and complications. Clothing bills (for laundry and dry cleaning) and building maintenance costs are considered to be extraordinarily high. Circulating fans are available for moving the air, but succeed only in drawing the plant odors and dust throughout the office.

b. With 30 typewriters plus additional machines, such as a stencil-duplicating machine, three ten-key adding machines, and the six key-punch machines in the general office area, a noise factor of serious consequence has developed. Space is not a problem, so it would appear that some segregation and acoustical treatment would be possible. The original vinyl asbestos tile floors and plastered walls and ceilings are found throughout the entire office building.

c. An open landscape plan for the open general office area should be considered.

d. Transportation of finished correspondence and typed reports to the first and second floors entails noise and disruption of work on the third floor.

e. While traditionally the office staff has shown intense loyalty to Casper, of late the new additions to the office staff are more concerned with comfort and convenience and recognize that their general office skills have a ready market in other expanding businesses and industries in the same city.

f. Sylvestre's absentee records indicate that during the three months' tenure in his position, 82 percent of the general office clerical staff have taken both of the sick days permitted each month. Four of the girls under the age of 25 have indicated a desire for other employment unless working conditions were more competitive with other modern firms.

g. Several talks with the veteran office supervisors, Dorothy Binnall and Gertrude Erickson, indicate that both feel that conditions are satisfactory; but they do indicate some anxiety with a change in leadership, both from the standpoint of Sylvestre and Casper, who assumed the presidency nine months ago after a transfer from another family interest in a neighboring state.

3. The executive suite consists of Casper's office; an office for his secretary, Julie Cunningham; and a two-room suite for the

executive vice president (and nephew of Casper), Donald Hanekamp, and his secretary. This suite is small, plain, and furnished with the same steel furniture found in the general office area. Casper's overall conservatism, it was assumed, accounted for this situation, although all the equipment and furniture except the data processing machines was inherited from his father who preceded him as president.

4. Sylvestre has contacted three firms dealing with office environments who have submitted bids for renovating the general office, for air conditioning the entire building, and for ideas on conducting the office operation without interruption during the renovation process. Recently Sylvestre has discovered that Casper, who is quiet, though pleasant, is himself a Certified Public Accountant as well as a chemical engineer, a fact that causes Sylvestre to hesitate to submit the results of his audit or any recommendations to Casper.

▪ After considering the above situation carefully, analyze the problems involved and answer the following:

1. What key behavioral problems are involved in this situation, and what are their likely effects on office productivity? What can be done about them without a general overall revamping of the office environment?
2. What inferences can Sylvestre draw from Casper's background that will assist in the improvement of the general office and executive suite environments?
3. What should Sylvestre do to correct the situation? If your answer to this question is to submit an audit report with recommendations, what main points should this report include?
4. On a person-to-person basis, what can be done to improve the rapport between Sylvestre and Casper?

Case 6-2 Reducing the Tensions of Office Workers

Alice Pendery, office manager of Mid-Twenty Styles, has become very much concerned about the increased absenteeism in her office and the number of errors that are costing the company time and money. Alice has consulted the MacDowell Company, a firm of office planning experts, from whom she has learned that much of the trouble in her office is due to unnecessary sounds, harsh lighting, glaring texture of the walls, and intense colors. The design specialists have presented evidence that poor lighting causes eyestrain and that hard, brittle surfaces make the noises bounce off the walls and affect the efficiency of workers. The atmosphere of discord in many offices results from the noise of typewriters and office machines, along with the voices of workers trying to be heard above the din. The conclusion reached by the planning experts was that Alice's workers are unconsciously using up their energies to block out the office noises and the confusion, with the result that by the middle of the day the workers have a feeling of complete fatigue.

■ Assume you are one of the office planning experts who has counseled Alice Pendery. What specific steps would you recommend that she take to reduce the tensions of her office workers? List your steps for building a better office environment in their order of importance so that Alice can implement your recommendations gradually over a period of several months.

7

Communication Services in the Office

Communication is the one basic activity of all managers. Repeated studies show that as much as 75 percent of a manager's time is devoted to the communication function. Such activities vary from the use of mechanical devices to human communications involving morale and motivation and dealing with subordinates in the form of instructing, reprimanding, and conferring. Much of this type of communication is task-oriented—that is, given to the user of information for solving problems, for making decisions, and for meeting organizational objectives.

The principal functions of the office staff are the gathering and processing of information. However, the processed information is usually used by personnel other than the processors themselves. This suggests that the typical office worker must transport the processed information to the location of the user, whether he be employed within the firm or in another organization. Thus, *communication services* are the means and media utilized by a firm to move its processed information to the ultimate user.

THE OFFICE COMMUNICATION SYSTEM

In this chapter the office communication system is restricted to the means and methods by which information is distributed from sender to receiver. Today there are many media and forms of communication and many alternative means by which messages may be sent. Due to the growing complexity of communication needs and functions, communication activities must be organized and planned to provide optimum service within and outside the firm.

In setting up an effective communication system, the following conditions are essential:

1. Information must be transmitted quickly enough to be current.
2. Information must be accessible—that is, easily retrieved for use.
3. Information must be provided on an economical basis, bearing in mind the volume of messages sent and the urgency with which each must be sent.
4. Information should be accurate and should be received in a usable condition.

Traditionally, written or other recorded communications have received major emphasis and have been considered the most accurate or acceptable media, accounting for about one third of the office activity. However, trends indicate greater use of oral communication, especially as the computer and the human voice interact to a greater degree.

COMMUNICATION MEDIA IN THE OFFICE

An office communication system involves a host of activities for sending and receiving information. As shown in Figure 7-1, all communications involve the transmittal of messages from a sender to a receiver. These communications are classified as written or voice and may be transmitted internally or externally. The administrative office manager must be familiar with the many media and forms of communication and with the equipment available for improving the distribution of information. In addition, he should be aware of the various factors involved in the installation of equipment or in the transmission of communications if the system has already been installed.

Unfortunately office communications have often just grown with the business and therefore have been established in a hit-or-miss fashion, rather than being based on a scientific analysis and study of the problem. To improve present methods or to install a new system of office communications, the office manager must analyze the problem in a logical manner. This can be done, first, by making

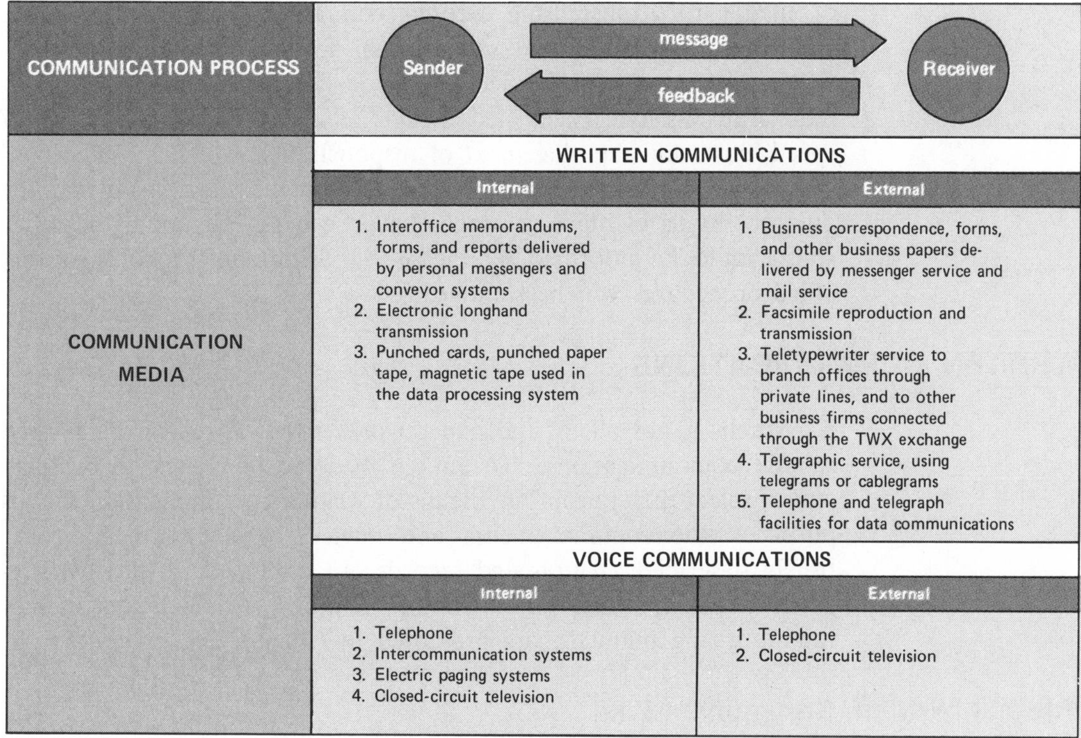

Fig. 7-1

The Communication System Within the Office

a study of what communications must be transmitted to the outside public and what communications must be sent to workers in the organization.

The second problem that must be considered in this analysis is which of the communications must be in writing and which can be transmitted orally. Those that should be transmitted orally can be grouped into those which are urgent and those which can be delayed; those which will be used frequently and those for which the use is infrequent. A list of the media of transmitting oral communications should then be prepared—by telephone, intercommunication systems, electric paging or announcing systems, closed-circuit television, or in person. Each method must be studied from the viewpoints of cost, speed, and effectiveness.

The same process of analysis is relevant for selecting written communications but should be extended to include the form in which communications must be transmitted. From this analysis a selection of media for transmitting written communications can be made from the following: by messenger, mail, facsimile reproduction, teletypewriter, telegraphic service, conveyor system, and electronic longhand transmission. Each medium has its comparative advantages of speed, cost, and the placement of responsibility, which must be considered in the final decision. Once the media of transmitting the different kinds of office messages have been agreed upon, the office staff should be informed by means of written instructions so that office procedures will be standardized.

WRITTEN COMMUNICATIONS

Much, if not all, of the paper work in an office can be termed written communications. To enable the office manager to evaluate and to select the appropriate means of written communication for his purposes, the common media and devices of communication are briefly described. Automated records are discussed in Part V; suggestions for improving written communications, such as letters, memorandums, and manuals, are presented in Chapter 23.

Internal Written Communications

The internal phase of written communications is concerned with the transmission of the following types of documents:

1. Interoffice or interdepartmental memorandums and letters.
2. Special forms and reports and many other kinds of working papers. For example, the work of an insurance company requires that a vast number of applications, affidavits, and vouchers pass through a series of departments for clerical and managerial attention.

The volume of communications under each heading will help to determine whether the use of personal messengers, conveyor systems, an electronic longhand device, or a combination of these, best fits the needs of the organization.

Personal Messengers. The use of numerous mechanical devices has largely supplanted the use of office messenger service, although such service is still maintained in some offices to save the time of executives in interoffice communications. Frequently other office duties are assigned to the messenger so that he really becomes an office clerk. Many concerns find that messenger service is more expensive than the mechanical means of communication. However, the difference in cost can be charged to the expense of training workers for the more responsible positions to which messengers are commonly promoted as they become more familiar with the methods of the business. Minimum wage and hour laws have further discouraged the use of messenger service so that today it is looked upon as more or less of a luxury enjoyed only by the larger offices. Some smaller concerns, however, such as printing and photoengraving establishments, find messenger service the best method of picking up copy and delivering the finished product.

In evaluating an office messenger service, the following questions should be considered:

1. Is the personal messenger the best means of transmitting the messages or records?
2. If so, is the messenger properly supervised and controlled?
3. Are there checks to ascertain whether the required number of stops or calls are made by each messenger?
4. Are efforts made to train messengers in more effective work and to help them assume more responsible duties as they become more mature?

To facilitate the control of the personal messenger service, many firms use cards on which are noted the time a messenger started from the central station and the time of his arrival at the various desks. Another method of control is to use varicolored or varinumbered cards. The messenger is given cards containing certain numbers for each trip through the office. At each stop he turns in a card in exchange for one left there previously. Upon his return to the central station, he will hand in the same quantity of cards with which he started, but not the same group. Different cards are used each day.

Office Conveyor Systems. Whenever large amounts of paper are circulated on a continuing basis and whenever such paper work can be distributed to fixed locations, *conveyor systems* should be considered. Such systems help to maintain an efficient flow of work by preventing the buildup of papers. Office conveyor systems minimize the movement of office personnel and, therefore, increase worker productivity by decreasing wasted manhours spent away from the work station.

Conveyors, often called "automatic office boys," are available in several types. The most popular types are as follows:

1. The *pneumatic tube* for swift transport of paper in a pneumatic container between two points.
2. The *multichannel conveyor* for transmitting paper work horizontally between work stations.
3. The *vertical lift conveyor* for moving paper vertically between floors, like an automatic dumb waiter. This device moves at a rate of up to 16 trays per minute, with some models receiving and discharging the trays continuously and automatically.
4. The *flatbed* for moving papers, parcels, and other materials on a moving belt.
5. The *chain conveyor* for moving papers attached by a clip to a chain. This device is not designed for the office, but it is often used in warehouse operations.
6. The *sandwich belt* for carrying papers between two canvas belts that can be arranged to move vertically, horizontally, around corners, over aisles, and across ceilings. Pulleys and weights provide the tension necessary for holding the papers between the belts; when the tension is lessened, the papers drop out automatically at established dropout points.
7. The *drag belt* for transporting messages, newspaper copy, proofs, and other papers, primarily found in communications firms.

Brief descriptions of the two most frequently used systems—the pneumatic tube and the multichannel conveyor—follow.

Pneumatic Tubes. Use of a pneumatic tube system is ordinarily confined to the largest companies, where speed and accuracy of transmission are more important than cost or where the volume of transmission is so enormous that the cost of maintaining a large staff of messengers would be greater than the cost of a tube system. In addition to the cost of installation, the expensive procedure of making structural changes is involved, unless the equipment is installed during the erection of the building.

In pneumatic tube installations each department may be connected with a control station, to which all papers that must be distributed are sent in a pneumatic container large enough to hold dozens of papers of ordinary business size. There they are sorted by hand, placed in a container, carried by conveyor belt to the appropriate dispatch tubes, and routed to the proper departments. The delivery job is completed in a short time, with no loss of time on the part of the employees who otherwise would be called upon to travel from one department to another.

Multichannel Conveyors. These conveyors are used to transport papers horizontally between work stations, as shown in Figure 7-2. The papers travel continuously, as sheets, file folders, or small batches, in an upright position between two stationary vertical guides that are moved by a motor-driven belt beneath them. The conveyor is fast (200 to 300 feet per minute), quiet, clean, safe, and less obtrusive than most other types of conveyors. The major disadvantage of the multichannel conveyor is that it cannot climb vertically from one floor to another.

Fig. 7-2

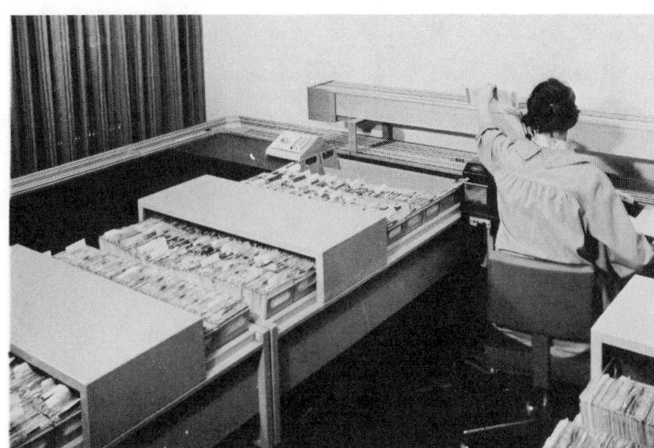

Novak Company

A Multichannel Conveyor

Electronic Longhand Transmission. *Electronic longhand transmission* is a means of electronically sending messages in one's own handwriting whereby the messages are received almost simultaneously with the writing. The system is used almost exclusively for communications within the firm—between departments, warehouse and office, branch offices, and main offices.

In using the electronic longhand machine, such as the *TELautograph,* the writing made by a pen is converted to electrical currents of varying intensities. At the receiving end, these currents pass through coils that move up and down according to the strength of the current and thus duplicate by means of a receiving pen the same movements made by the sending pen. One excellent application of the electronic longhand machine is made in the telephone order-processing procedure. A machine is installed on the desk of the telephone order clerk and a second machine is placed in the shipping or packing department. As an order is received on the telephone, the clerk can write simultaneously on both machines. Thus, before the customer has completed the call, the processing of the order can be under way in the shipping department. Figure 7-3 illustrates the TELautograph's sending (left) and receiving units (right).

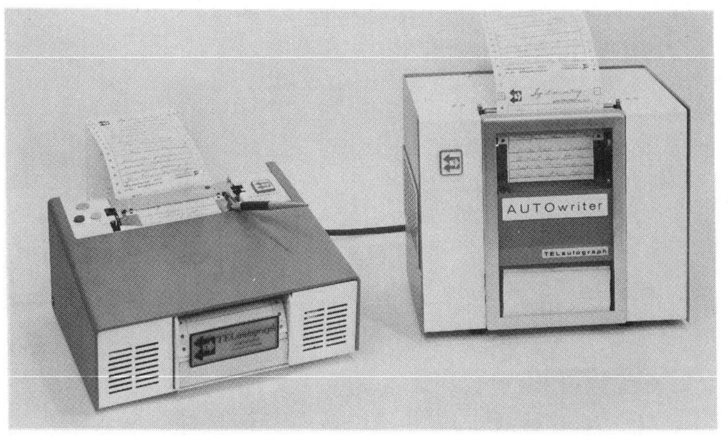

TELautograph Corporation

Fig. 7-3

TELautograph Sending and Receiving Units

External Written Communications

External written communications are required for the distribution of information to all points outside the office and its immediate environment. The following media are used for this type of communication: office correspondence, facsimile reproduction and transmission, the teletypewriter, and telegraph and telephone services.

Correspondence (Letters). Even in the age of automation, the letter remains the most important and most common medium of formal business communication. The letter serves as an official record of information as well as a substitute for person-to-person conversation. Because of the importance and cost of the correspondence function, organizing, planning, and controlling this function are of vital interest to the administrative office manager.

Organizing the Correspondence Function. Requirements of the business firm determine whether the correspondence work shall be decentralized or centralized. In a decentralized plan, correspondence is dictated by the executives in the departments affected. For example, letters affecting credits and collections are dictated in the credit department; the sales and the advertising departments prepare and mail sales letters; and so on throughout the entire organization. The stenographers and typists may be centralized, or they may be located in the departments for which they are preparing the correspondence.

In an effort to improve the caliber and effectiveness of correspondence, many companies centralize the correspondence function. Under one method of centralization, specially trained correspondents, concentrated in one department under the direction of a correspondence supervisor, are designated to handle all the company's dictation, with the exception of that of top-level managers. The individual departments are thus relieved of all responsibility for handling correspondence. Such a central correspondence department receives all letters, obtains from the files the necessary information for the departments affected, dictates all correspondence, makes any adjustments that may be necessary or refers the correspondence to the proper department, and systematically follows up all letters that may require later attention. This method of centralized correspondence aims to develop the concept of individualized service to the customer and the retention of his goodwill. Furthermore, workers in such a central department become very proficient since they specialize in the handling of correspondence only.

In large offices, however, there is a disadvantage in the centralization of the correspondence function because the correspondents must necessarily interrupt the workers in those departments in which such letters would ordinarily originate in order to verify or check information needed for answering the letters. Letters based on secondhand information may be weak and inaccurate, and may require a referral to the individual department in order to complete promised adjustments. This also complicates matters and may be the cause of lengthy correspondence between the customer and the department before the matter is finally settled.

In another system, the handling of correspondence may be partially decentralized. One or more correspondents are assigned to each department and are directly responsible to the department head while under the general supervision of a correspondence supervisor.

In small offices the correspondence function is placed under the immediate direction of the office manager. Where office correspondence looms important because of its exclusive contact with customers of the firm or because many business transactions are completed by its use, the supervision of this work may be placed in charge of an assistant. One business organization with many branch offices has a correspondence supervisor whose responsibilities include supervision of correspondence in all the branches as well as in the home office. In order to effect uniform correspondence procedures, the supervisor prepares bulletins from time to time that are sent to all the correspondents. The bulletins discuss the form of the company letters, the vocabulary, the tone, and the proper way to handle adjustments, especially those that are particularly difficult. The bulletins also contain correspondence problems that are to be solved and returned to the correspondence supervisor, who gives their correct solutions in the next issue of the bulletin.

Organizing Office Dictation. Dictation may be given in one of the following ways: (a) to a shorthand-writing stenographer, (b) to a machine-writing stenographer, (c) to a dictating machine, or (d) directly to the typist. Good dictation procedure is equally applicable to all four methods, and careful procedures in dictation will save thousands of dollars in many offices. Dictation procedures cover the office work from the moment the executive receives his morning mail until each letter has been dictated.

Efficient dictation requires that attention be given to the following: (1) collection of all relevant information necessary to organize, compose, and dictate the message; (2) preparation of the information in a form that facilitates the dictation process; (3) control of the dictation by providing for proper sequence of the thoughts to be communicated, by eliminating distracting mannerisms, and by effectively using the voice; and (4) assurance of appropriately quiet physical surroundings.

One large firm utilizes the following approach for training its dictators:

1. The dictator is asked to write out and then read the material to a machine or a secretary, avoiding the temptation to read too fast or to slur his connectives and word endings.
2. Once this is mastered, he is taught to dictate from an extensive, written outline of the key thoughts in each paragraph.
3. This is followed by dictation from a very concise outline in which emphasis is placed on good preparation and reducing the amount of writing to a minimum.
4. As the dictator improves in technique and experience, he gradually becomes able to dictate from a mental outline alone.[1]

[1] Glenn R. Coleman, Jr., "Du Pont's Engineering Department Has a Practical Program for Dictation Training," *AMS Professional Management Bulletin: Administrative Services* (December, 1969), p. 18.

Organizing Transcription. Transcription is usually completed on a typewriter. Electric typewriters, because of their increased efficiency, are fast replacing manually operated machines. Figure 7-4 shows clearly an eight-year trend in typewriter buying preferences in the United States.[2] Reasons given for the increased popularity of the electric typewriter include: (1) increased output with less human effort and energy being expended by the typist, (2) need for high-quality copy that can be reproduced on an office copier or photographed, and (3) capability of producing multiple copies, each of which is legible.

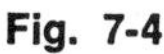
Fig. 7-4

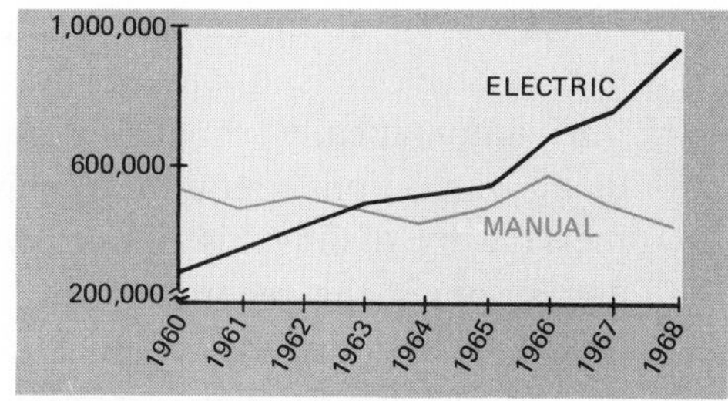

A Comparison of Manual and Electric Typewriter Sales in the United States

Source: Reprinted from the November, 1969, issue of *Modern Office Procedures* and copyrighted (1969) by Industrial Publishing Company, Division Pittway Corporation.

In addition to the use of electric typewriters, the use of dictating and transcribing machines has increased at a rapid pace due to their lower cost of letter production. Dictating and transcribing machines using plastic belts, plastic discs, or magnetic tape vary in size and capability—from a handsize, shirt-pocket model costing under $100 to the central office system costing thousands of dollars.

Plastic belts, discs, and cartridge tapes are commonly used because they permit dictation by remote control. Dictation by remote control is possible by means of combining a telephonic type of arrangement for the dictating microphones of a number of executives with a centrally located series of recording machines. The proper use of these devices permits either a centralized or a decentralized plan of organization. Under the decentralized plan, used in smaller offices, each department retains a staff of transcribers for that

[2] "Machines That Speed Written Communication," *Modern Office Procedures* (November, 1969), p. 33.

department, with one transcriber usually being assigned to serve one or more executives. Often the transcribers may be called upon to do other clerical work as well as to transcribe dictation. In larger offices greater efficiency is obtained by centralizing the transcription work under a trained supervisor. This arrangement, commonly termed a *stenographic* or *transcription pool,* results in a more uniform and equitable distribution of work; in better supervision of each employee's production; and in a standardized, more efficient, and less expensive way of doing the work.

Large firms use private telephone links to connect dictators with transcribing equipment. One insurance organization uses the telephone system to link its 450 dictators to two secretarial centers with banks of dictation units. When the dictator contacts a unit and finds it busy, he is automatically switched to the first vacant recorder, thus automatically equalizing the workload. Such a dictator can make corrections, request a playback, and indicate the end of a message by dialing his phone, with his voice automatically starting and stopping the recording unit. This same system is automatically linked to a timing device that turns the recorders on at 7:00 a.m. and off at 10:00 p.m. seven days a week. Thus, after-hour and weekend dictation becomes possible, although transcription must be delayed until the next workday. Another firm, also linking its dictators to the dictation equipment by telephone, finds that a typing pool of 20 girls, using 8 transcribers, can handle the transcribing needs of the 90 dictators.[3]

Supervising the Dictation-Transcription Function. The supervision of dictation includes the training of executives and correspondents in the best methods of writing business letters and a systematic review of the quality of the letters written. Among the methods used are: (1) issuance of special bulletins covering such topics as "Sales Value of Letters," "Cutting Correspondence Costs," and "Mechanics of the Letter," (2) periodic conferences with the correspondents, correspondence supervisors, and the transcription supervisor, (3) developing and using a correspondence manual to guide the executives and employees in improving their work and standardizing their output,[4] and (4) analyzing each dictator's work by means of a transcription report, such as that shown in Figure 7-5.

---

[3] Diane Wendt, "Management Communicates When It Dictates," *Business Automation* (July, 1969), p. 42.

[4] See Chapter 23 for a discussion of the correspondence manual, a table of contents of a typical manual, and a partially illustrated manual.

Supervising the transcription starts with the selection of an experienced, well-trained person who can obtain the cooperation of both the dictators and the transcribing personnel. This person may have a full-time supervising job that involves training transcribers, setting standards, and measuring the output of each employee, as well as analyzing the quality of output.

Fig. 7-5

TRANSCRIPTION REPORT

To ______________________ Date ______________

Difficulty was encountered in transcribing for the following reason:

____ Dictated before disc was in motion.
____ Dictated beyond end of disc.
____ Dictated too fast. ____ Too slow. ____ Too loud.
____ Enunciation not clear.
____ Failed to spell proper names or unusual words.
Examples: ______________________________
____
____ Failed to indicate corrections.
____ Failed to indicate length of letter or memo.
____ Failed to distinguish between numbers or letters of like sound.
____ Failed to indicate that paragraph(s) or tabulation was to be inserted.
____ Failed to indicate extra copies on indicator slip, requested copies at end or in middle of memo or letter.
____ Failed to give proper instructions on how to set up.
____ Failed to indicate beginning or end of quotation, indentation, or tabulation.
____ Failed to enclose correspondence.
____ Failed to indicate number of disc when dictation is continued on two or more discs.

Any questions on this report should be discussed with the Stenographic Supervisor.

____
Operator's Number

INSTRUCTIONS TO OPERATOR: Prepare this report in duplicate. Return one copy to dictator with the transcribing folder and one copy to Stenographic Supervisor.

A Transcription Report

Facsimile Reproduction and Transmission. In the *facsimile reproduction and transmission system,* an exact duplicate of anything written, drawn, or typed is transmitted between two distant points. With one type of facsimile machine, shown in Figure 7-6, exact reproductions of business documents are sent and received by telephone. The original document is placed in the transceiver and the send button is pushed; a telephone call is then directed to the receiving party, who in turn engages the receive button on their machine. Transmission takes place automatically, and in minutes the recipient has an exact copy of the original document.

Teletypewriter Service. The *teletypewriter,* illustrated in Figure 7-7, is a machine used for transmitting written conversations just as the telephone is a means of transmitting oral conversations. The teletypewriter, similar to a typewriter, transmits electrical impulses over telephone lines, which cause a simultaneous reproduction of the message in typewritten form on machines in neighboring or distant offices. Through the use of punched tape, there has been a great expansion in the use of the teletypewriter as a means of data communications.

Two illustrations of the many applications of this medium of communication are given. One large shoe manufacturer teletypes orders on specially designed forms from the sales offices directly to the plants. One teletyping of an order at the sales office produces sufficient copies locally for the use of the sales office. At the same time the necessary copies are produced at the plant, thus enabling it to plan for immediate production. As a result of this installation, the firm was able to eliminate several days in the time required to produce and ship an order. Another firm has its receiving machine equipped with a duplicating typewriter ribbon and special duplication stencil paper, so that as the information is received, a stencil is prepared. The stencil is then used to make copies without the delay of retyping. Both of these applications represent the first step in an integrated data processing system, as explained in Chapter 24.

Telegraphic Services. Telegraphic services meet the need of modern business for a fast, accurate, and dependable means of communication in written form. Telegrams compel attention, assure a careful reading, and get quick action. Through the telegraph office and its connections, telegraphic communications serve virtually every community in the United States and Canada. Through extensive cable systems, communications may be sent to any part of the world.

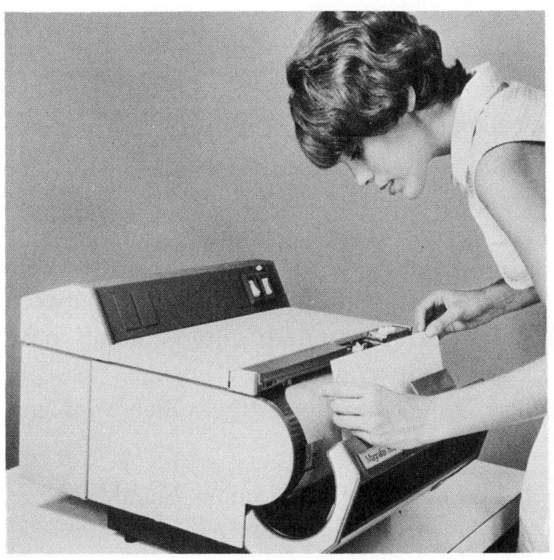

Magnavox Systems, Incorporated

Fig. 7-6

The Magnafax Desk-Top Facsimile Unit

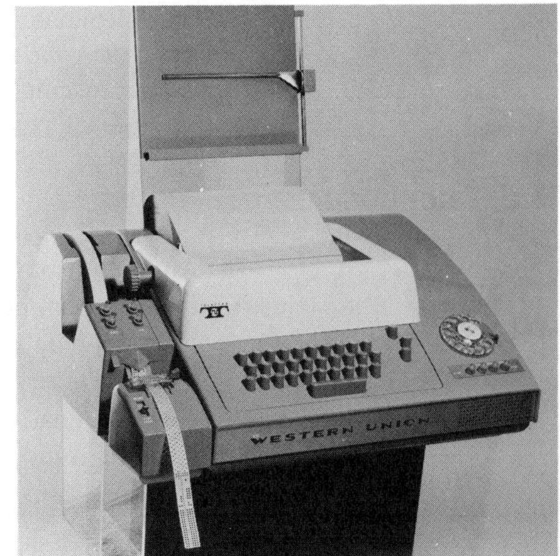

Western Union Telegraph Company

Fig. 7-7

The Teletypewriter

Underlying the use of telegraphic services are the principles of economy and speed.

No one pattern of telegraph service will fit all companies irrespective of size and nature of business. For this reason, the telegraph companies employ specialists whose services are offered without obligation to make analytical studies of the communication needs of customers. Such studies develop information as to how the customer can obtain the fastest telegraphic service at the lowest cost. In the use of telegrams, for example, there are certain short cuts which, if the customer will only take time to learn, will result in savings and in a general improvement in the efficiency of the business. Since telegraphic communications are highly technical in nature, the office manager should seek assistance from experts in solving his telegraphic problems so that he may receive the best service at the greatest saving.

VOICE COMMUNICATIONS

In this section the following means of voice communication will be described. (The telephone and closed-circuit television are considered as both internal and external media in this discussion.)

1. The telephone.
2. Intercommunications systems.
3. Electric paging system.
4. Audiovisual communication systems.

The Telephone

In American business the telephone is the most widely used instrument for communications both within an office and between offices that are widely separated. Many modern improvements have been made in the type of equipment available for business use. In planning this phase of office communications, the office manager should keep in mind the following points:

1. Enough telephones and switchboard connections should be provided so that business with outside firms may be transacted without delay.
2. Intraoffice calls should be freed from the switchboard that is connected with outside lines by either purchasing or renting a separate internal, automatic dialing system. The installation of a paging system should be investigated in order to reduce the internal load placed upon the switchboard.
3. Well-trained switchboard operators should be employed.
4. Expanded use of the telephone service for transmission of data communications should be studied.
5. Modern, up-to-date switchboards, which pay for themselves by providing better service in greater volume, should be installed.

Types of Telephone Systems. Except for very small offices, the telephone systems in most firms require the use of a switchboard so that several incoming or outgoing calls may be handled simultaneously. The number of the simultaneous calls will determine the kind and size of system needed. Three types of telephone systems in use are: PBX, PAX, and CENTREX.

PBX. *PBX*, or *private branch exchange,* is a telephone switchboard or console in offices where there are frequent interoffice and outside calls. This system enables a person in one department to call a person in another department without having to place the number through the central telephone exchange. The switchboard may be operated by one or more persons, depending upon the number of extensions and the number of calls. Where traffic is heavy, the cord-type switchboard is sometimes used; where calls are less numerous, the key-type console is installed.

PAX. *PAX*, or *private automatic exchange,* is a dial system that is used when there is extensive communication between departments. Thus, its use is more or less restricted to large business concerns. Under one form of PAX, the telephone company frees the business concern of all responsibility for the operation of the system. Both interoffice and outside calls may be made by dialing, with a switchboard and operator being provided to sort the incoming calls. The true PAX, however, is used entirely for internal calls, with no attendant operator or connection with the central telephone exchange. Calls are made in the same manner as in public telephone booths, merely by dialing the number of the department or person wanted.

CENTREX. *CENTREX*, or *central exchange,* is a relatively new concept in telephone service. Under one feature of this system, Direct Inward Dialing (DID), incoming calls from almost anywhere in the country can be dialed directly to any CENTREX station, without the need of an operator. CENTREX station users can also dial their own outgoing calls, both local and long distance, as well as calls to stations in the same organization, without assistance from a switchboard operator.

Automatic Dialing Equipment. In planning the installation of one of the telephone systems described earlier, the administrative manager should investigate the timesaving automatic dialing equipment that will guarantee 100 percent accuracy in dialing, free the operator for other duties, and overcome the need for remembering frequently used numbers.

The *Card Dialer* consists of a six-button key set and an automatic dial unit with storage pockets accommodating about 40 dialing cards. Up to 14 digits can be punched into each card to identify the number called. To place a call, the appropriate card is inserted into a slot of the instrument, the receiver is lifted, and the start bar is pushed. The Card Dialer, illustrated in Figure 7-8, is available on standard dial telephones as well as on the Touch-Tone telephones (with 10 decimal-digit keys for the rapid registration of numbers into the telephone).

The *Magicall dialer* is a separate dial unit that can be tied in with any telephone instrument. The digits of each telephone number are

Northwestern Bell Telephone Company

Fig. 7-8

The Card Dialer

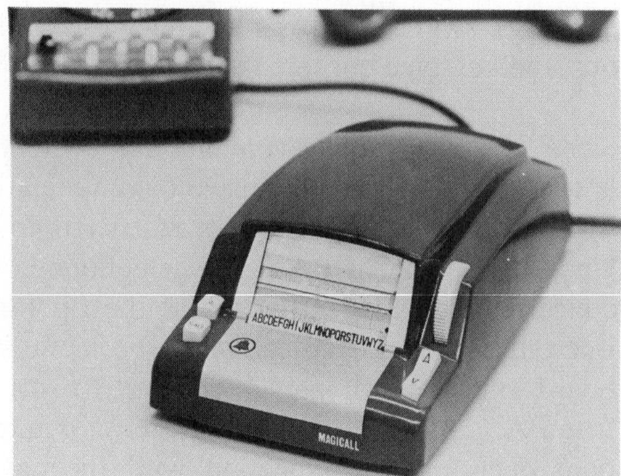

New York Telephone Company

Fig. 7-9

The Magicall Dialer

stored on a magnetic tape that holds up to 1,000 numbers. To place a call, the knob on the dial is turned to the desired name, the receiver is lifted, and the automatic dialing button is pressed. Figure 7-9 illustrates this unit.

The ease and simplicity with which the telephone can be used often leads to a waste of time and money. A discussion of cost-reducing measures that may be followed in the use of the telephone is presented in Chapter 21.

Intercommunication Systems

Communication equipment other than the regular telephone that is used to connect or tie together the departments of an organization is called an *intercommunication* (or intercom) *system.* The internal voice communications relieve the telephone switchboard of the many intraoffice communications and are available in many forms, from the old "squawk box" speakers to the miniature telephonic systems with sophisticated switching mechanisms.

Intercommunication systems fall into three categories: (1) electronic systems that utilize the principles of radio, in which individual speakers are connected directly through master units; (2) private telephone lines that operate through a central switching system by means of a dial or a Touch-Tone keyboard; and (3) loudspeaker intercoms that operate like private telephones with central automatic exchanges.[5] Each of these systems, in turn, utilizes equipment that is available in many forms. Included are desk units, paging horns, central telephone consoles (or switchboards), two-station units, multi-station units, equipment permitting "listen only" as well as "talk only," and standard intercommunication systems.

Since intercommunication machines connect two or more departments within a firm, an interdepartmental systems study must be conducted to determine the most effective equipment installation required. For example, after one large insurance firm installed a new central filing system, it became clear that new communication services would be required since telephone requests for files would be delayed due to other uses of the telephone system. As a result, a private intercom system was installed so that files could be requested without disturbing the regular telephone conversations.

As technology develops new equipment and systems analysts improve their ability to utilize such equipment, many new inroads into communications services are made available for the small and the large offices. It then becomes possible to provide the office manager with services such as the following:

1. One or more master or executive stations, connected with as many as 80 staff stations. Control buttons enable the executive stations to have right of way over staff stations when urgent use is desired.
2. One- or two-way conversation arrangements between executive and staff, or between staff members, or simultaneous conference calls to a number of staff stations.
3. Connection of the intercom to loudspeakers throughout the office and plant so that individuals may be paged.
4. Tie-in between intercom system and central dictating pool, which enables all dictating machines and typists to be located in one place. By dialing a number on the intercom set, workers can dictate letters and have them typed without leaving their desks.
5. Noise reducers on intercom equipment located in noisy work centers.
6. Hands-free equipment to answer intercom equipment without picking up a handset.

---

[5] Marvin J. Bevans, "Communications: Internal and External," *Administrative Management* (October, 1968), p. 72.

Electric Paging Systems

In many large organizations such as department stores, manufacturing plants, banks, and insurance companies, executives sometimes move about the offices regularly. When urgent matters arise, to locate executives by telephoning the various departments may waste valuable minutes. To avoid this, electric paging systems that operate through the telephone switchboard have been developed. Each important executive is given a number. The switchboard operator, who also operates the central station of the electric paging system, "plugs in" or makes the electrical connection for the number of the executive being called. Throughout the office or plant, a signal corresponding to the executive's number will sound. When the executive hears his signal, he picks up the nearest telephone, calls the switchboard operator, and receives the message. In another type of paging system, the switchboard operator or the receptionist speaks into a microphone and summons the attention of the paged person through loudspeakers distributed throughout the area. This system is one-way only but covers large areas. More than one paging location can be provided and music or other signals can be transmitted through the loudspeakers.

For maintaining voice contact with people who are often away from their offices, pocket-size paging systems have been developed for receiving voice messages up to two miles away from the central transmitter. No wires or external antenna are needed. Whenever communication is desired with an executive anywhere within the transmitting area, the clerk signals him by radio, after which the person paged can either communicate by radio or go to the nearest telephone to receive the message.

Audiovisual Communication Systems

Both voice and written documents, including facsimile copies of records, may be transmitted over long distances. Voice and pictures can be simultaneously transmitted via the more advanced equipment provided by the communications industry. Two of these services —closed-circuit television and the Picturephone—are discussed in this section.

Closed-Circuit Television. The medium of television has uses far beyond home entertainment, extending even to the office. For as little as $1,500, a closed-circuit television system can be installed to provide two-way sound arrangements along with the transmission of a picture.

Banks, in particular, make use of closed-circuit TV. In one installation, as shown in Figure 7-10, the closed-circuit TV system makes signature verification between the bookkeeping department and the bank's four drive-in windows fast and easy. The teller simply phones the bookkeeping office and asks for a certain signature to be placed on the monitor. The bookkeeper does so, and the teller needs only to glance at her monitor for a large, sharp picture of the signature. Mechanized files make the signature card almost instantly available, thus keeping transaction time to a minimum. The system is also used to alert tellers on new stop-payments, holds, and lost checkbooks.

Fig. 7-10

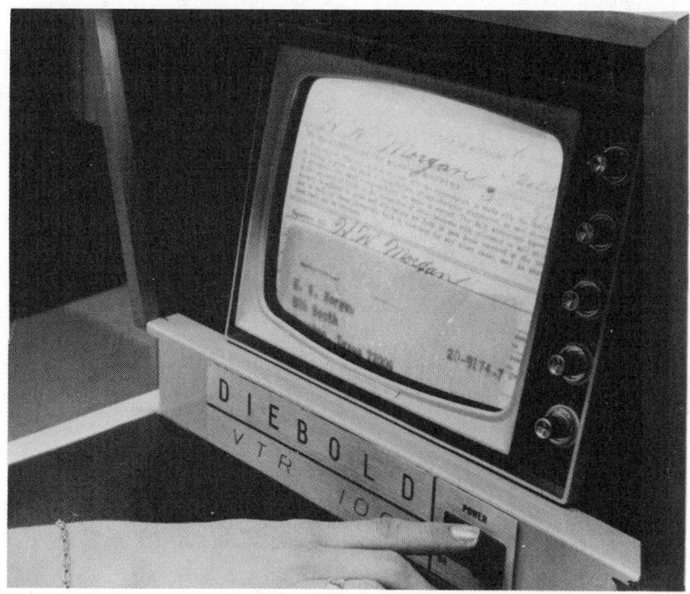

Diebold, Incorporated

Verification of Signature by Means of Closed-Circuit TV

The Picturephone. The Picturephone, a product of the Bell System, combines the television screen with the telephone, thus enabling the user to see as well as to talk with the person at the distant end. (See Figure 7-11 on the next page.) This service, first installed commercially in Pittsburgh in July, 1970, promises to have a profound effect on communication habits and practices. It can be expected to influence out-of-town travel, conference scheduling, sales and advertising techniques, as well as the communication systems within and between organizations.

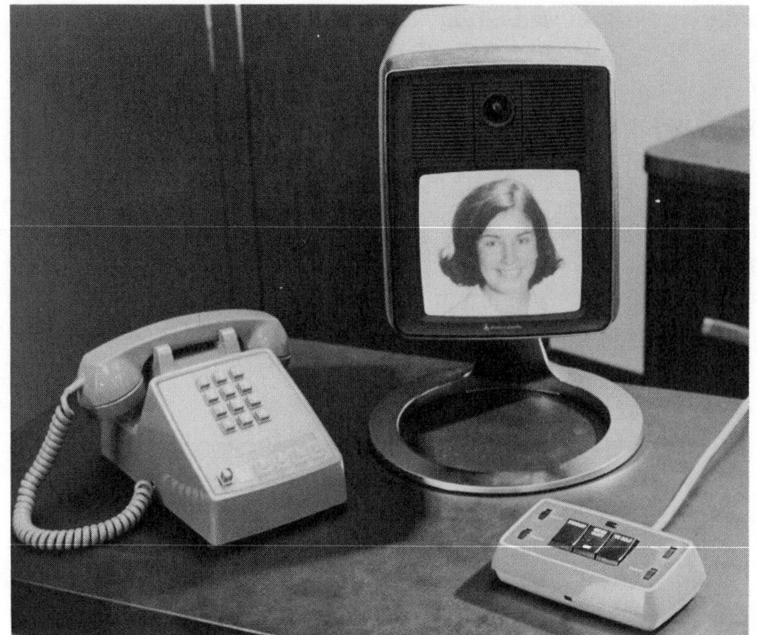

American Telephone and Telegraph

Fig. 7-11

The Picturephone

DATA COMMUNICATION SYSTEMS [6]

In this age of computers, a need has arisen to develop equipment for transmitting data over long distances at electronic speeds. Men and machines have combined to form *data communication systems* to move information for making decisions and for controlling business operations. Before such data can be processed, however, they must be gathered from various sources, some of which are in decentralized locations miles away, such as a warehouse or a distant branch office.

To meet the requirements of a modern management information system, existing communication facilities are used to transmit data from several different locations to a central processing point. By merging the computing, telegraphic, and telephone facilities, a worldwide communication system is developed to supply management with

---

[6] For an excellent discussion of data communication concepts and applications see *Data Communications in Business: An Introduction,* a publication of the American Telephone & Telegraph Company. Copies are available from local telephone companies.

timely and accurate reports. While the term "data communications" is most frequently applied to an overall system that permits one or more users access to a remotely located computer, in this context the term will be used more broadly to refer to all aspects of mechanized data transmission over long distances.

Data Communication Media

Both the computing and the communication fields utilize complex machines to fulfill their respective functions in business. Therefore, an understanding of their technical makeup is a job for engineers and other highly specialized personnel. But for management—and especially for the administrative office manager—what the hardware will do must be understood so that it can be considered for possible use in the firm.

The administrative office manager must find answers to the following questions:

1. What are the various ways of transmitting data over long distances at fast rates of speed?
2. In what form can the data be sent and received?
3. What are the equipment requirements for data communications?

Beyond these basic questions are a host of related considerations such as cost of installing the system; training, displacement, and retraining of personnel; and redesign of existing systems. Due to the specialized nature of the communications field, only a brief discussion of possible answers to such questions will be given here.

Transmitting and Receiving Data: Terminal Equipment

A *terminal* refers to any input/output device attached to a computer system whose primary purpose is to transmit and receive data from one location to another. The most prevalent types of terminals, some of which are shown in Figure 7-12, are typewriters, paper tape and magnetic tape transmission machines, microfilm equipment, and cathode ray tube devices employing the use of a television-like screen for information display. Through the use of a typewriter terminal, for example, the executive can enter into his keyboard input requests for up-to-the minute information on sales, inventory, and costs, bypassing the time-consuming channels of a data processing center. In

Victor Comptometer Corporation

Punched Card Transmission Terminal

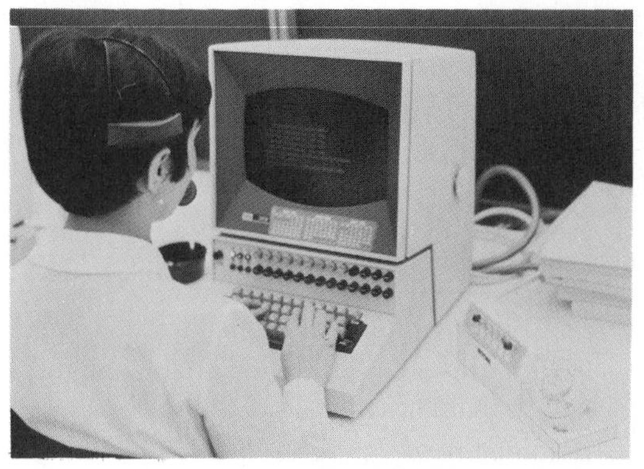

American Telephone and Telegraph

Visual Display Terminal

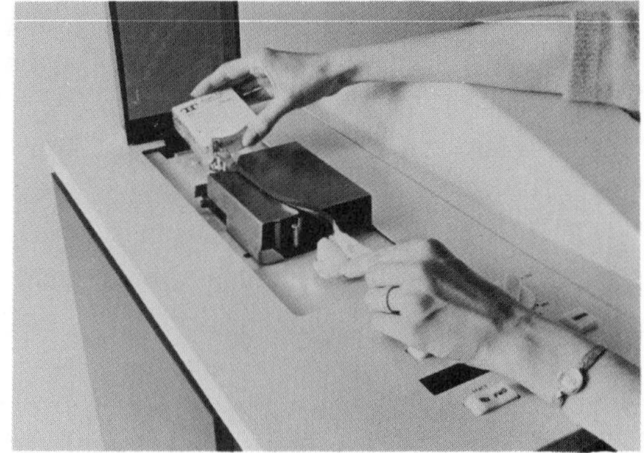

American Telephone and Telegraph

Magnetic Tape Terminal

Victor Comptometer Corporation

Keyboard Printer

Fig. 7-12

Terminal Equipment

return, he can receive in his office as output an answer from the computer system displayed on a cathode ray tube, on his own typewriter terminal, or in some other medium such as the punched card.

Most data can be transmitted over standard telephone lines. In order to transmit the information, two broad types of transmission systems are used: (1) the point-to-point communication system by which data are transmitted at varying speeds over private, leased, or regular telephone lines between two or more terminals; and (2) the computer-based networks that permit a large number of people located throughout a wide area to communicate via telephone lines with each other and a central computer. Typical of the latter type of system is the large firm in which the computer links the headquarters office, the plant, and the regional and warehouse facilities with all orders and other messages sent by telephone to the computer center at the headquarters office. Such close linkage within a large firm brings about better control, faster processing of orders, tighter inventory systems, and other benefits. The revolutionary advances of such communication systems have been cited as follows:

> Retail store salesmen receive voice response approval of a sale to a credit card holder within microseconds of tapping out a number on a Touch-Tone telephone. This allows the salesmen to complete the transaction without risk of fraud.
>
> Shortly after the close of business, a corporate headquarters has on record the day's details of inventory levels, sales figures, and production in all its branches and can order an action by the time work resumes the next morning.
>
> A contract drawn up by a manufacturer's lawyer in New York is transmitted within minutes to Los Angeles for consideration by a distributor. A few minutes later, a hard copy of the original contract, with the distributor's comments and changes marked on it, is back on the manufacturer's desk in New York.[7]

With such powerful communication facilities, instant information is available to the office on a continuing basis. Other uses of terminal equipment are discussed in Chapter 25.

Communication Services of the Common Carriers

Public utilities such as the telephone company and the telegraph company are *communication common carriers.* Since the early days

[7] Anthony D. K. Carding, "New Ways to Transmit Data," *Administrative Management* (May, 1970), p. 56.

when simple long-distance or local telephone calls or standard telegrams were transmitted, a wide range of communication services has been developed by these carriers to meet the insatiable needs of society for processing and distributing information. Four services that are important to the office function are: leased lines, toll-switched networks, Wide Area Telephone Service, and Wideband Data Service.

Leased Lines. A *leased line* is a teletype or telephone line made available to the subscriber on a full-time basis between specific points. *Telpak* is the name given to the American Telephone and Telegraph service in which telephone lines are leased as a group between two points. Such services are useful for large-volume point-to-point transmission of data, voice, teletypewriter, and facsimile for a flat rate regardless of usage. Telpak rates are substantially lower than those for an equivalent number of single telephone channels.

Toll-Switched Network. The *toll-switched network* utilizes a line switching technique of temporarily connecting two lines for the direct exchange of information between stations that are not within the same local service area, thus involving a toll charge. Two services of this network are Telex and TWX; both employ a teletypewriter for transmitting written messages and/or data. The subscriber pays for this service only when it is actually in use. Telex time charges are computed in 1/10-minute increments; TWX time charges are based on 1-minute minimums.

Wide-Area Telephone Service (WATS). WATS is a telephone service through which an unlimited number of calls may be made for a flat monthly charge from a single point to any other subscriber within a specified area. The New York Telephone Company, for example, offers intrastate WATS service for about $650 per month. For calls made outside the home state, interstate WATS is provided with a choice of six prescribed areas that form banks circling the home state. The rates for interstate WATS vary from $500 a month for Band 1 to $1,900 a month for Band 6.

Wideband Data Service. Wideband Data Service automatically links two subscribers over transmission channels that are selected as best meeting their communication needs. By means of a pushbutton voice-data instrument, the user selects a broadband width that will furnish the optimum, economical data transmission. Thus, the user can select one width for transmitting punched-card data or for permitting computers to communicate with one another. These machines, with their greater capabilities, transmit at rates that cannot be satisfactorily handled over the narrow telegraph channels or voice bands. Transmission speeds in the band widths vary from the teleprinter speeds up to 4,800 words a minute by means of tape devices. Wider bands that would enable computers to communicate at rates of up to 240,000 words a minute are now available.

Wideband service provides for varying types of transmission. The equipment will transmit the voice alone or digital data contained in punched cards, punched paper tape, magnetic tape, or computer storage devices.

PLANNING COMMUNICATION SERVICES

The range of communication services in the office continues to expand, as do their cost and complexity. Furthermore, the power of communication facilities continues to increase, with the result that it becomes more and more difficult to realize the full potential of the machines available. Since modern-day communication systems normally involve many departments, a "total-systems" approach is necessary to study the entire firm's communication needs.

A committee of office personnel should be selected to study and analyze communications systems being perfected. Too many firms are satisfied with what has been used in the past and make little effort to study new media or methods just because they are new. Most manufacturers of communications systems are willing to survey free of charge the needs of a business firm. In fact, the willingness of a sales representative to perform this service may be used as a guide to his dependability and to the reliability of the company he represents.

Before moving toward the purchase of new or additional communication equipment, consideration should be given to the development of a Communications Department in the organization, which would have the authority and responsibilities of any other operating department. A person qualified in the area of communication services should be selected to supervise the department and charged with the responsibility for providing effective and economical communications.

QUESTIONS FOR REVIEW

1. Discuss the main considerations involved in setting up an effective communications program.

2. Why is the use of personal messenger service declining in offices today?

3. What are the principal media used in written communications? What are the main advantages of each medium?

4. Mechanical conveyor systems have limited, but at times very efficient, uses in modern office administration. Under what conditions can these systems be used most effectively?

5. What is the nature of electronic longhand transmission and under what conditions might it be used in business? What advantages does its use have over that of the telephone and personal messenger service?

6. Office correspondence continues to be the most common medium of external written communications. As an office supervisor, indicate the methods you might use to make this phase of office work more effective.

7. The teletypewriter has in recent years grown more popular as a medium of office communications. Explain the reasons for this increased use.

8. What improvements in modern telephone equipment have expanded the use of this medium in today's business office? How do these improvements aid in expediting office work?

9. What are the major features of the Direct Inward Dialing System of CENTREX?

10. What is the nature of an electric paging system? Describe one type of system.

11. What is meant by the term "data communication systems"? Explain the more common types of data communication systems in use today.

12. How do you account for the increased use of data communication systems in modern office procedures?

13. Prior to developing a communications department within the firm, what factors should be carefully analyzed and studied?

QUESTIONS FOR DISCUSSION

1. Use your imagination and ingenuity in projecting your thinking about the impact that the Picturephone will have on office work in the future.

2. Many executives feel that machine dictation is less efficient than shorthand dictation since the transcriber must listen to or "preview" all material dictated before she commences to transcribe. Explain your agreement or disagreement with this statement.

3. The Kendall Company has been receiving a number of complaints from both within and without the organization relating to its correspondence. Among these complaints are the following: (a) customers have to wait too long for answers to their inquiries, (b) many letters are too long, (c) letters are sometimes too complicated with peculiar or technical expressions, and (d) customers have to write in for replies to their letters.

In order to improve the efficiency of the company's correspondence department, discuss how you think these difficulties should be remedied.

4. The administrative manager of the Rollins Company is overworked, for in addition to his regular duties, he supervises the clerical force, the accountants, the billing clerks, two secretaries, and six stenographers. Because of the irregularity in the volume and the timing of the dictation work for the credit manager, the chief accountant, and the two corporate officers, along with routine correspondence, there are delays and confusion in completing the necessary correspondence. The administrative manager is considering the installation of machine dictation to improve the situation.

Discuss the advisability of installing the following methods of machine dictation, assuming that in each case a transcriber will be able to double her output as the result of using the equipment:

a. Use of dictating and transcribing machines, each costing $450, with plastic discs, containing 15 minutes of dictation on each side and costing 10 cents each. The discs are not reusable. A separate machine must be used for dictation and for transcribing.
b. Use of magnetic tape recorders costing $400 each. The same machine may be used for both dictation and transcription. Tapes containing 15 minutes of dictation cost $4.50 each and can be erased and reused indefinitely.
c. Use of a centralized recording system whereby each executive or group of executives may use a telephone connection for dictation to centrally located recording machines. Two central recorders would be needed. Total cost of installation, including four transcribing machines, is $1,400.

5. A group of seven physicians, incorporated as the Medical Associates, have come to you for advice on their record-keeping operations. Over the last year they have noticed that their patient-billing procedures as well as the ordering of routine medical supplies have been greatly delayed due to the expansion of their medical practice and their inability to increase their own clerical staff or physical office layout. In describing their problem they indicate that all patient care and the resultant billing are generally routine, normally consisting of such information as a code number for the type of treatment or examination, the date of the visit, the charge made, and a repetition of the patient's name and address on the billing form. Similarly, the supply ordering procedure includes largely standard supplies that are coded by the supply house, the amount or quantity to be ordered, an order number, the extended amount of the order, and the transcription of the vendor's name and address.

Presently the medical practice of these cooperating physicians has grown to the point where 120 patients are "seen" each day. At the same time ordering at least 25 items daily constitutes an impossible workload for the present staff of five secretaries. In seeking your advice to resolve these problems, the physicians have asked the following key questions:

a. What alternatives are available to the Medical Associates office, including the use of outside agencies, to handle the growing burden of paper work?
b. How can they simplify the record processing problems so that the doctors can devote the maximum amount of time to patient care?

PRACTICAL OFFICE CASES

Case 7-1 Reorganizing a Data Communication System

The Tri-State Manufacturing Company has its main administrative offices in St. Louis, Missouri, with branch offices and warehouses in Buffalo, New York; Trenton, New Jersey; and Harrisburg, Pennsylvania. The office manager has been faced with mounting telephone costs that are resulting from the increased sales volume. He feels that the present system of having one main switchboard to handle all incoming and outgoing calls in the main office, and similar arrangements in the branch offices, is not up-to-date and efficient. In addition to the voice communication within the firm as well as from the outside, thought must be given to the movement of alphanumeric information from each branch office to the headquarters in St. Louis and vice versa. Presently each of the branch offices processes its records on a decentralized basis. The large-volume operations connected with sales, purchase order processing, the maintenance of inventory, customer billing, and creditor payments are handled locally in each branch.

Recognizing the improvement in data communication and computing facilities, the firm is contemplating the recentralization of all its accounting data in the main office in order to reduce a certain amount of duplication in office work, but more importantly, to provide management with up-to-the-minute operating data from which decisions can more easily be made. As a result of the proposed move toward centralization, it is expected that the present medium-scale computer system can accommodate the extra load by operating on three eight-hour shifts and by reducing some of the unnecessary administrative reports that are presently being prepared.

▪ On the basis of the information given above, suggest how the company can develop a data communication network that will handle effectively the following:

1. Daily interoffice telephone calls for the office staff of 120 employees in the ten departments in the St. Louis main office.
2. Long-distance telephone calls from St. Louis to each of the branch offices, normally occurring many times each day (although no accurate record has been kept).
3. Interbranch calls which occur from five to ten times daily for each branch.

Case 7-2 Centralizing the Transcription Function

Fair Oaks Leather Products is engaged in the manufacture of specialty leather goods. The company employs 20 stenographers in the three departments in its plant offices. You have been recently employed as office manager, with a base salary of $11,000 and the promise of a $1,500 bonus after the first year if you can reduce the costs of office work at least $10,000 a year.

You feel that one of the first possibilities for reducing costs is to centralize and mechanize the dictation and transcription work. In order to estimate the savings that might be effected, you have made a survey of the cost of the work as it is presently done and what it would cost if it were mechanized. The survey of the stenographic and transcription work for a period of one month (four weeks) is shown in Table A. The work is done on a decentralized basis.

SURVEY OF STENOGRAPHIC AND TRANSCRIPTION WORK

Table A

Kind of Work	Time Spent in		
	Department I (Minutes)	Department II (Minutes)	Department III (Minutes)
Dictation	10,400	6,000	8,800
Transcription	26,000	16,000	24,000
Clerical work (filing)	16,000	23,000	10,800
General typing	20,800	20,000	1,800
No work	1,500	160	250
Totals	74,700	65,160	45,650

Department I (8 stenographers) transcribed 33,000 lines of dictation.
Department II (7 stenographers) transcribed 20,000 lines of dictation.
Department III (5 stenographers) transcribed 28,500 lines of dictation.

After consulting with several sales representatives of dictating and transcribing equipment firms, you learn that a transcribing machine operator can transcribe, on the average, 5,000 lines of dictation per week. After some preliminary thinking, you feel that it would be advisable to form a centralized transcription department. In this department there would be several general-copy typists, in addition to the transcribing machine operators and general clerical workers. Assume that the following weekly salaries would be paid: stenographers, $100; typists, $85; general clerical workers, $75; and transcribing machine operators, $90. Employees work an estimated 154 hours each month (four weeks).

The centralized transcription department would serve 15 executives. A remote-control telephonic dictation system with 12 stations would be required, since three of the executives would double up with the others. The equipment would be depreciated over a period of six years. The total installation cost for three recording stations and four transcribing machines is estimated at $6,000, with an annual service maintenance cost of $360. It is estimated that the annual cost of supplies will be $250.

■ On the basis of this information, you are asked to prepare a report for the office manager that will prove conclusively the savings that can be effected by mechanizing and centralizing the dictation and transcription work. This report should include:

1. Time spent in dictation under the present method.
2. Time spent in transcription under the present method and the number of transcribing machine operators that are needed.
3. Time spent in general typing under the present method and the number of general-copy typists that are needed.
4. Time spent in clerical work under the present method and the number of general clerical workers that are needed.
5. The savings that would be realized (a) during the present year and (b) during the next five years.
6. The effect upon the conditional bonus arrangement with the office manager.

8

Information and Records Management

The phrase "red tape" has common acceptance in society today. Along with this term have appeared other closely related figures of speech, such as the "information explosion," the "paper-work jungle," the "flood of forms," and an accurate description of American offices as being "adrift on a sea of paper." To bring the great tidal wave of records under control is indeed an increasing challenge to business management.

Business cannot survive without records and the information these records contain. In a sense paper work is the sole office product. Yet the problem of overrecording becomes clearer when it is realized that the uncontrolled creation of records leads to confusion, mounting administrative costs, and administrative inefficiency. Too often office supervisors leap to the conclusion that an increased output of paper work is an indication of clerical efficiency, and this, of course, is usually not true.

THE RECORDS CYCLE

In most offices these common records are found: (1) correspondence, including letters and memos; (2) business forms; (3) reports and summaries; (4) standard practice instructions and procedures; and (5) handbooks and manuals. Greenlaw classifies these common records in terms of their administrative functions:

> Administrative records comprise approximately 10-15 percent of any company's records collection while the remaining 85-90 percent are operational records. The latter fall into volume groupings such as purchase orders and requisitions, claims, bills of lading, maps and blueprints, personnel and individual medical records, legislative bills, construction records, invoices, cancelled checks, and the like.
>
> Administrative records are those such as agenda and minutes, articles and bylaws, secretarial records, financial and planning records, rules and regulations, policy and procedures manuals, executive reference material, or anything that a management staff needs for making its decision in a competent, progressive, and profitable manner.[1]

Each of these records takes proper form; each, therefore, is a tangible document. But a new dimension in record keeping entered the business world when the punched-card and computer systems were applied to information storage and retrieval. While pieces of paper may serve as input and output to the computer, intangible information in magnetized form on tapes, discs, drums, and cores within the computer system has greatly expanded the modern information system and given new responsibilities to the administrative office manager.

The storage and retrieval of records and information is commonplace in everyday life. Whether it is a dictionary, an inventory-control system, or a worldwide airline reservation computer network, all such systems are comprised of records to which one may address a variety of questions with a reasonable expectation of retrieving either a record or information from a stored document in response to each question. Following identical paths or cycles, all records and information are (1) created, (2) classified, (3) stored, (4) retrieved when necessary, and (5) returned to storage or destroyed. To manage records and information, each of these phases in the records cycle must be studied and controlled.

RECORDS MANAGEMENT PROGRAMS

Frequently the term records management is considered to be synonymous with filing. This is a serious misconception. Filing,

---

[1] Terry Greenlaw, "Basic Filing Systems for Administrative Records," *The Office* (November, 1964), p. 89.

the storage and getting-ready-for-storage operations dealing with records, represents but one small phase in the life-span of a record. *Records management,* on the other hand, is a program that encompasses all those activities dealing with the creation, maintenance, and disposition of records. Representative of a larger firm's concept of the well-developed records management program is the chart shown in Figure 8-1.[2] This industrial view of the program compares favorably with the overall programs for managing records as developed by the federal government's General Services Administration (GSA). In the GSA, where a continuing education program in paper-work simplification is maintained, records management includes these basic areas:

1. Forms management (sometimes called "forms control").
2. Reports management.
3. Administrative issuances (directives and memorandums).
4. Correspondence management.
5. Paper-work simplification.
6. Records disposal, storage, and protection.

Fig. 8-1

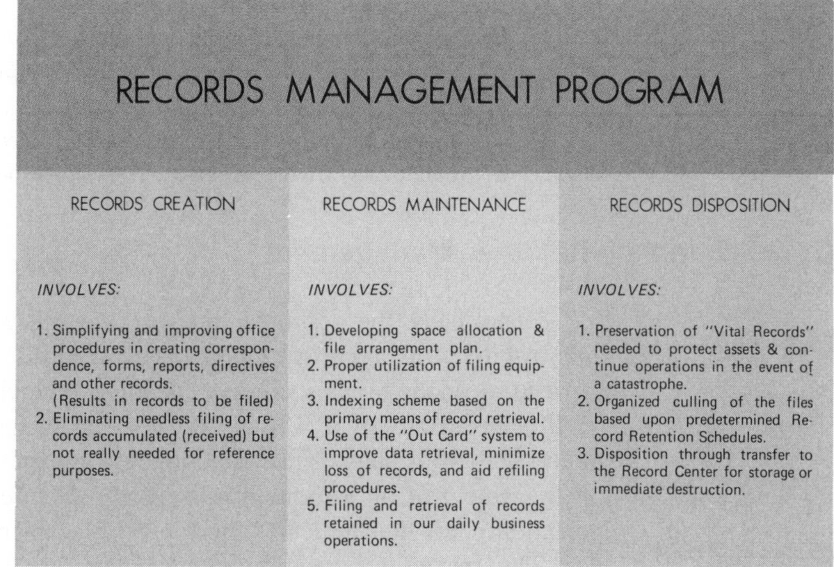

Records Management Program in a Large Manufacturing Company

[2] Richard E. Wolff, "Information Management and Retrieval," *Systems Management Bulletin* (Administrative Management Society, 1965), p. 8.

Objectives of Records Management Programs

It would be an oversimplification to say that the main goal of records management programs is to assure that there are fewer and better records. Yet this is a very basic goal. The well-integrated program normally encompasses these basic objectives:

1. To develop a proper appreciation for the information function of a business organization as well as for the records function and to work for significant cost savings through the efficient use of the office force, equipment, and space allocated to records production and control.
2. To determine what records and information are to be filed and for how long (resulting in a records retention schedule of active, semiactive, and inactive files) and to develop a sound depository (archives) for storing inactive records.
3. To develop a systematic procedure for storing and protecting records, for retrieving them when needed, and for disposing of all unnecessary records. Frequently a filing manual is a corollary development along with this procedure. (See Chapter 23 for a discussion of the filing manual.)
4. To improve clerical performance in all activities related to the creation, maintenance, and disposition of records. (This objective involves the management of forms, correspondence, reports, manuals, and procedures.)
5. To set and maintain efficient standards for equipment, personnel, and procedures relating to records management.

Organization of Records Management

Historically the responsibility for the office function, including control over its records, has been assigned to the controller, the treasurer, or the firm's secretary, usually at the vice-presidential level. With the advent of a formal records management program, it was natural for this same office function to be expanded to embrace the management of information and records. Figure 8-2 shows an organization chart that indicates the typical placement of these functions.

The setting for records management as shown in Figure 8-2 places the function in a natural environment of related activities. The service function of administration has a keen concern for personnel and information-processing services, as opposed to the decentralization of this function under each department or division. This

Fig. 8-2

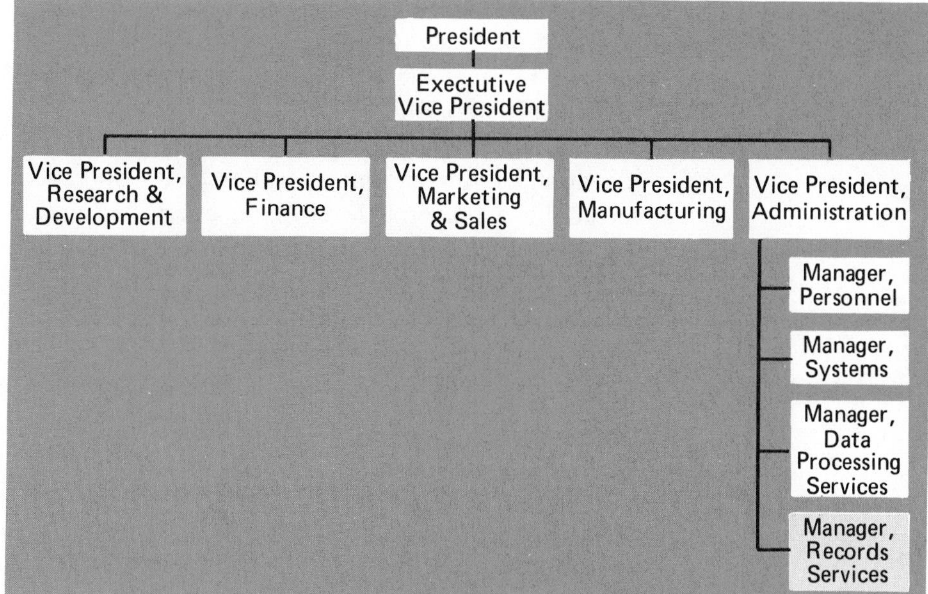

Records Management Organization Chart

same degree of specialized administration cannot be found in small companies. Nevertheless, the functional responsibilities still remain. For example, in the small firm a personnel director may be required to handle administrative services, such as systems and data processing. In another firm, the office services manager may handle personnel selection, placement, training, and general office management functions including records and forms control, while the systems and data processing services may be the responsibility of another person. Most important is that related work be grouped together and assigned to those individuals who by aptitude, interest, and training are most highly qualified for such assignments.

Information and Records Management Personnel

A records manager is in effect an information manager, whether the information exists in tangible (paper) form or in intangible form on magnetic tape. As such, he is concerned with:

1. What information an organization needs to accomplish its objectives.
2. Where this information can be found.

3. How this information can be economically processed or reduced to usable form.
4. How to store and retrieve this information in minimum time at minimum cost.[3]

To shoulder this enormous and essential operation requires personnel at the managerial level, files supervisors and clerks, records analysts and archivists, and records inventory specialists. While it is not necessary that records managers be data processing specialists, nevertheless they should understand the concepts and applications of the information-processing equipment.

Reporting to the records manager most typically are the filing personnel shown in Figure 8-3. The supervisor would normally report to the records manager or his equivalent. In many firms new records management positions are being created as the nature of the records system becomes more highly automated. Such positions as tape librarian, program library records clerk, and documentation clerk are becoming more common in larger offices such as banks, insurance companies, and utilities.

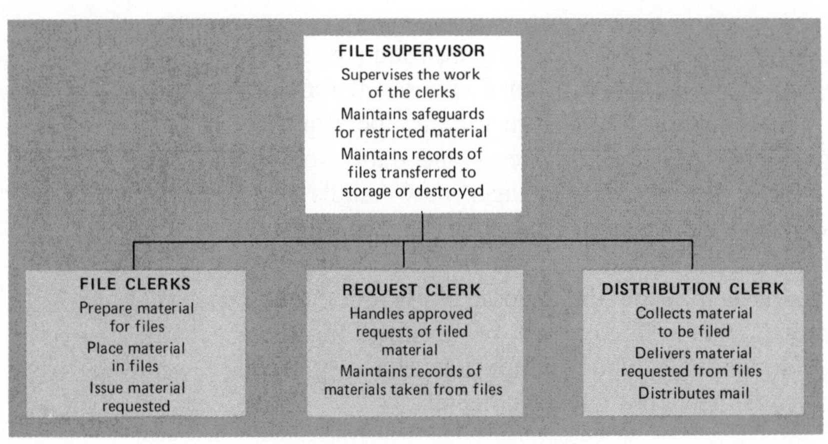

Fig. 8-3

Hierarchy in a Files Section

Cost of Records Management

For many years cost accountants have been successful in defining, recording, and reporting factory operating costs. As a result, they

[3] Milton Reitzfeld, "The Records Manager as Information Scientist," *Records Management Journal,* Vol. 1, No. 4 (Winter, 1963), p. 2.

can pinpoint to a marked degree the unit costs in producing a product at varying volumes, including both direct and indirect costs. Office costs, however, have remained shrouded in mystery, often being grouped together under the catchall term "overhead." However, with rising costs in a so-called cost-squeeze economy and with the realization that administrative work is taking more and more of its share of the profit dollar, increased effort is being directed toward controlling office costs. The paper-work costs that apply to any administrative operation are identified in Figure 8-4.[4]

Fig. 8-4

COST FACTOR	RELATED PAPER-WORK COSTS
1. Personnel	a. Clerical salaries b. Those portions of salaries of other personnel engaged part-time in the use of records
2. Equipment	a. Depreciation b. Rentals
3. Space	a. Rent b. Maintenance c. Taxes
4. Miscellaneous	a. Stationery and supplies b. Postage c. Telephone and telegraph d. Printing

Paper-Work Costs Applicable to Administrative Operations

Apart from these overall administrative expenses, the cost of maintaining a four-drawer file, excluding supervisory costs, would break down into the following approximate percentage distributions:

File clerk's salary	75%
Space (5¾ sq. ft.)	10%
Supplies	10%
File cabinet (10 year life span)	5%

Salaries constitute the greatest percentage of money spent on keeping records and the area in which urgent steps must be taken

[4] Victor Lazzaro (ed.), *Systems and Procedures: A Handbook for Business and Industry* (2d edition; Prentice-Hall, Inc., 1968), p. 217.

to control costs. Record-keeping salaries may be controlled through the establishment of performance standards for the filing and processing of each record, the development of a cost consciousness among all workers, and, very importantly, through the use of more convenient and efficient equipment and supplies. Chapter 21 discusses effective cost control over all office services in more detail.

Evaluation of Records Management

Periodically the records should be examined and audited to determine how well they are fulfilling their objectives and to determine, too, how efficient the filing system is. In such an audit the questions shown in Figure 8-5 should be answered. As soon as weak spots have been identified, principles of forms design and control, work simplification, and information systems management can be brought to bear on the problems.

GENERAL CHARACTERISTIC	SPECIFIC DETAILS
Scope of the records system	How many file drawers and shelves in use? How many duplicate systems are detected?
Type of filing system	Method of filing. Types of controls (charge-outs, cross-references, etc.). Nature and extent of confidential and private files.
Filing personnel	Who does the filing and finding? How are they supervised? What kind of performance standards are in effect?
The user of the records	Who uses the files? What access does he have to the files?
Standard procedures	Are filing policies and procedures set up? Availability of a filing manual. Creation of standards and retention and destruction systems.
Record activity	How many records are filed daily? How many records are requested daily? How many requested records cannot be found?

Fig. 8-5

Records Audit Checklist

Two common guidelines or rule-of-thumb ratios for evaluating the efficiency of the files have been developed: (1) the *reference ratio,* and (2) the *accuracy ratio.* The reference ratio may be expressed as follows:

$$\frac{\text{number of records requested}}{\text{number of records filed}}.$$

To illustrate, whenever a records management system shows 600 documents requested out of a total file of 12,000, the reference ratio would be .05, or 5 percent. A reference activity of 5 percent or less is normally considered low and points to the need for transferring records from active storage to the archives or possibly even destroying them.

Even though records are requested frequently—that is, actively used—the filing system is not serving its purpose if the records cannot be found when needed. As a yardstick for measuring the difficulty of locating requested records, the following accuracy ratio has been developed:

$$\frac{\text{number of records found}}{\text{number of records requested}}.$$

If, for example, 9,250 records out of a possible 9,500 requested are located, this means that there is 97.37 percent accuracy for the filing system and that the files are in excellent operating condition. Industry practices show that if this ratio falls below 97 percent, the files should be studied carefully, especially for these suspicious problems: (1) too many private files (as in the executives' desks); (2) improper indexing and coding; (3) poor charge-out procedures; and (4) insufficient cross-indexing and referencing.

FILES MANAGEMENT

The files represent the archives, or storage centers, of information for the firm. To manage the files properly requires attention to these factors: (1) decentralizing versus centralizing the filing operations, (2) developing efficient filing systems, (3) procuring filing equipment and supplies, and (4) evaluating the filing equipment.

Decentralized Filing

Under a decentralized filing plan, each office division maintains its own filing system and equipment; and the work is performed by one or more employees who may have other types of office work to do. Such an arrangement often results in needless duplication of equipment; less efficient personnel to do the filing work, since such employees may also perform other office duties; and possibly a confused filing system, since in one department the filing methods may be entirely different from, if not inconsistent with, those of some other department.

The main arguments for decentralized filing are:

1. The confidential nature of the material filed suggests that it be kept from the majority of the employees.
2. Unnecessary delay in getting papers from the centralized department is avoided.
3. The papers filed will not be required by any other department.

Centralized Filing

The advantages of a centralized department for any of the office services, be it filing or duplicating, ideally result in more and better work at less cost. In filing, this result has greater significance when all filing work is done in a centralized department. Centralized filing means that all filing equipment is located in a single area of the office, accessible to all departments by personal messengers and office conveyor systems and controlled by a centralized indexing plan.

The advantages of a centralized filing system are:

1. The elimination of needless duplication of equipment. Where each department has its own filing system, each will require cabinets, file folders, and supplies. Fewer cabinets will be required if the work is centralized, and these will be used to greater capacity.
2. The elimination of needless duplication of records. If files are departmentalized, it may be necessary to make several copies of orders, invoices, or statements to be sent to different departments for their retention. This procedure is unnecessary where records are centralized.
3. More rapid delivery of filed material, which saves the time of persons requesting the materials. This rapid delivery results from a uniform method of filing, greater accuracy, and more skilled specialized personnel.
4. A lower cost of doing the filing work. Having a specially trained force of clerks who do filing work only, under capable supervision, will reduce by 25 to 50 percent the number of employees required.

5. A constantly and continuously functioning department. There will be no delays or interruptions in the filing work due to lunch hours, coffee breaks, vacations, or absenteeism.

Record-keeping requirements differ from office to office, depending on the size of the office staff, the nature of the business operation, and such factors as competition and governmental regulation and control. As the firm expands in size and the volume of information to be processed and stored increases, there is a tendency to centralize the records management and filing work. However, even where a centralized filing system is found, some of the work may be decentralized.

The administrative office manager must weigh carefully the advantages of one filing plan against the disadvantages of the other. No doubt a compromise will have to be reached, but only on the matter of the confidential nature of the filed material. The records to be filed departmentally should be kept to a minimum and, if possible, filed only temporarily in departmental files.

Filing Systems

A basic system of rules and regulations for classifying and storing records is necessary if the records are to be located when they are needed. All filing systems, therefore, are maintained in order to provide quick access to and adequate protection for information.

The term *filing system* refers to the steps and factors involved in storing and finding records. Such steps normally are considered as classifying, arranging, and storing records for fast accessibility when needed. Basically there are but two such systems, *alphabetic* and *numeric,* each of which can be subdivided in this manner:

1. Alphabetic Systems.
   a. Correspondence filing (by name).
   b. Geographic filing.
   c. Subject filing.
2. Numeric Systems.
   a. Numeric filing.
   b. Chronologic filing.

While various combinations and versions of each of these systems are found, most firms will use all of these systems, each having a particular advantage for a type of record-keeping function. For example, a credit office may maintain accounts receivable files in name (customer) order; a purchasing department, in order sequence (numeric); a personnel department, in files by type of position (subject); or a traffic department, in files by delivery dates or perhaps by a time-of-day scheduling chart (chronologic).

Filing Equipment and Supplies

Careful studies of storage and retrieval patterns and needs within the office should be conducted before a decision is made to procure filing equipment. Of particular importance in the selection of equipment is filing efficiency, for frequently the type of filing operation is greatly affected by the efficiency of the equipment. Among the many questions that require answers before purchasing filing equipment and supplies are the following:

1. What kinds of records will be filed?
2. What volume of materials will be filed during a specified period—a month, six months, a year?
3. How frequently are the records called for?
4. How many people ordinarily refer to one record that is taken, i.e., how extensively does one record travel?
5. How many people have access to the files?
6. What methods of filing are best for the records to be filed?
7. What methods of charge-out and follow-up are best suited to the operation of the filing department?
8. Are the records kept in a central location, departmentally, or a combination of the two?
9. What are the policies of the company toward transfer, retention, and disposal of the filed records?
10. What kinds of equipment are on hand?
11. How much space is available for the records and how much additional room is available for expansion?
12. Does the office layout provide for the most efficient use of space and flow of work? If not, can changes be made?
13. Are economic factors taking precedence over efficiency factors? (Equipment and supplies are tools of efficient filing, and rigid economies can seriously hinder that efficiency.)
14. What types of equipment and supplies are locally available without special order?
15. What services do local equipment and supply firms offer in connection with filing needs? [5]

---

[5] Mina M. Johnson and Norman F. Kallaus, *Records Management* (Cincinnati: South-Western Publishing Co., 1967), p. 293.

Primary attention in the selection of such equipment should be given to cost and the savings possible through standardization. However, there are other factors to consider before a commitment is made to spend money for filing equipment: (1) its appearance and design, (2) the space it conserves, (3) its construction and durability, and (4) its capacity for time-saving efficiencies.

Filing equipment may be classified as: (1) vertical, (2) horizontal, (3) visible card, (4) rotary, and (5) mobile (see Figure 8-6).

Vertical Filing Equipment. Vertical filing equipment, the most commonly used type of equipment for record keeping, can be obtained in units of one to six drawers. Papers are filed on edge in as nearly a vertical position as possible. The average width of standard letter-size files is 15 inches; for the legal-size materials, 18 inches. The depth of the file ranges from 24 to 28½ inches. This means that the floor space occupied by one file drawer is about 2.55 square feet. To provide working area when the file is opened, at least six square feet of floor space are required for each file drawer unit. Increasing the number of file drawers without increasing the amount of floor space required results in a better utilization of office floor space as illustrated in Figure 8-7 on page 221. Also, less stooping and walking around are required on the part of the file clerks with the result that the filing work is accomplished more quickly.

Variations of the vertical filing equipment include: (1) the *rock-a-file* in which the drawers rock open sideways, thus requiring less floor space; (2) the *roll-out file,* called a lateral unit, in which the drawers roll out sideways, thus exposing all the records in half the aisle space required by vertical drawer files; and (3) the *open-shelf file* in which the file folders or other filed materials are arranged on shelves. Open-shelf filing permits unlimited visibility, provides a high degree of compactness, and aids in completing the filing work faster and more efficiently than the use of vertical drawer files. To utilize space to the fullest, these files often run to the ceiling; however, experience shows that file personnel do not like to use ladders.

Horizontal Filing Equipment. Horizontal filing equipment is used for storing papers or records, such as maps and drawings, in a flat position. Often, horizontal filing equipment of counter-high design is purchased so that, at no extra expense, the files may serve the dual purpose of providing a file and a counter-high working area.

Open-Shelf File

Horizontal File

Remington Rand Office Systems Division, Sperry Rand Corporation

Visible Card File

Acme Visible Records, Inc.

Rotary Card File

Remington Rand Office Systems Division, Sperry Rand Corporation

Motorized Card File

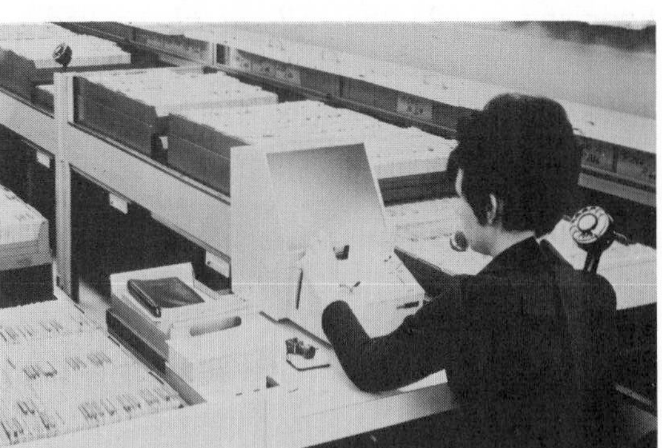

Watson Manufacturing Company

Mobile File

Fig. 8-6

Types of Filing Equipment

Fig. 8-7

Space-Saving Filing Equipment

Visible Card Filing Equipment. Visible card filing equipment provides for retaining records, such as accounts receivable and personnel data, in a fairly permanent position for frequent reference. The speed with which the cards can be located and entries made justifies the use and cost of this type of equipment. The main characteristic of the visible card file is the visibility at all times of all the names, numbers, or other reference data recorded on the edges of the cards. Visible files are available in the form of trays that lie flat horizontally in a cabinet, on revolving racks, or in loose-leaf book binders. Signaling devices such as metal tabs, plastic strips, or color indicators may be used with the cards to indicate such conditions as past-due accounts, accounts exceeding the credit limit, type of merchandise purchased, and classification of accounts.

Rotary Card Filing Equipment. Rotary card filing equipment is a variation of the visible card equipment whereby cards are attached to a belt or a series of rings that surround the core of a rotating wheel. Cards may be inserted or removed quickly by rotating the wheel to the desired location. Wheels may be kept in a vertical or a horizontal position in specially constructed desks.

Motorized card files are a variation of rotary card filing equipment developed to make card filing more efficient. The motorized card file consists of a cabinet that houses a motorized, push-button, chain-driven arrangement of fixed cradles on which trays of record cards or papers are revolved vertically in either direction to bring the desired tray to desk or counter height.

Mobile Filing Equipment. This type of equipment consists of specially constructed files used for very active records. In one type of installation the files operator sits in one position at a mobile desk-chair work station and in front of her has access to all divisions of a file by merely sliding back and forth on the work-station track. The work station can be wired for electricity and a telephone, and these items move with the desk. Some forms of mobile filing equipment resemble doughnut-shaped desks in which the clerk sits in the center opening of the desk and locates the records by rotating the desk. Equipment of this type is designed with the principle in mind that it is more efficient and less fatiguing to have the work brought to the worker than to have the worker go to the work.

Evaluation of Filing Equipment

An objective appraisal, as opposed to an educated guess, should be made before purchasing file units. The experience of one large firm, as shown in Figure 8-8, demonstrates how such an appraisal is made and what its values are.[6] Each time the firm conducted similar tests, the five-drawer cabinet was judged the most efficient for high-speed filing operations. On the average this type of study, as well as complete time and motion studies of cabinet and open-shelf file operations, showed a 58 percent increase in production for all file operations in the cabinet file area as well as greater installation costs. On the other hand, open-shelf filing saved 27 percent in floor space with a lower cost of installation.

MANAGEMENT OF AUTOMATED RECORDS

Before the time of the computer, a punched card or a printout from a punched card served as an understandable, tangible kind of record. However, there is a growing trend to record information in magnetized form on tapes, discs, and drums. What is produced might, therefore, be called an "invisible" record, although still a record and still requiring a schedule of retention and other record controls. One unique feature of the magnetic record, of course, is that the data can be erased, thus permitting the tape to be reused.

The automated record has certain features that differentiate it from the tangible paper record as well as some features that it shares with paper work. For example, to control and protect the data on automated records, frequently two tapes—one a duplicate of the other—are prepared. Accuracy is required and is controlled through internal machine checks within the computer, the careful

[6] Richard Tarrant, "Selecting Filing Equipment," *Records Management Journal*, Vol. 1, No. 3 (Autumn, 1963), p. 13.

Fig. 8-8

After the operator had gained somewhat more than two months' experience with the test unit (a shelf file with a capacity of 4 five-drawer cabinets), timings were made at the test unit and at four of the present drawer files to have a comparable number of total folders so that the walking factor would be made a part of the test for the operations of finding and pulling folders, returning folders to file, and inserting papers in the folders. These timings are shown in Exhibits A and B.

Exhibit A

Four 5-drawer cabinet files (100% efficiency)

1. insert time	0.014 min/insertion
2. file time	0.011 min/case
3. find time	0.108 min/case

Exhibit B

Test unit (a shelf file with a capacity equivalent to the files in Exhibit A)

1. insert time	0.25 min/insertion
2. file time	0.25 min/case
3. find time	0.21 min/case

Allowing an experience factor of 75%, these timings are adjusted to

1. insert time	0.188 min/insertion
2. file time	0.188 min/case
3. find time	0.158 min/case

Time Study of Filing Operations

debugging and testing of a computer program, and the verification of input data prior to entrance into the magnetic tape file. To serve as a check on the information flow through the data processing system, printouts from the tape records can be effected. Since printing out is a relatively slow process in routine operations, the hard or printout copies are normally not required in checking the accuracy of the records. Accountants in fulfilling their auditing function can trace the reports back to the source documents on file and the corresponding tape can be printed out as needed.

As time goes on, more and more records will be kept in "invisible" form, thus requiring close cooperation among the records manager, the systems personnel, the data processing managers, and the operating departments. Records managers are cautioned to make sure that all information recorded automatically represents reliable data, that they retain records for a sufficient period of time to be able to prove past transactions and events, and that the retention and destruction of all records satisfy administrative requirements. Close contact, too, should be maintained with the legal counsel regarding federal and state retention requirements as well as interpretations relative to automated records.

Records in Microform

The term "microfilm" is well known in business and industry. When the word is used, typically it conveys the impression of a cure-all for space problems as it is said to reduce filing space by over 98 percent. Microfilm also has value as a means of protecting vital records and as a compact method of grouping and systematizing records.

The first records that were microfilmed were greatly reduced in size, producing very small (or micro) records. Reduction ratios of 10:1 are common; that is, the microrecord is one tenth the size of the original record. Some reduction ratios may even go as high as 2,400:1. Later the same photographic and reduction processes were expanded to include other forms of microrecording. Today the film formats illustrated in Figure 8-9 are commonly found.[7]

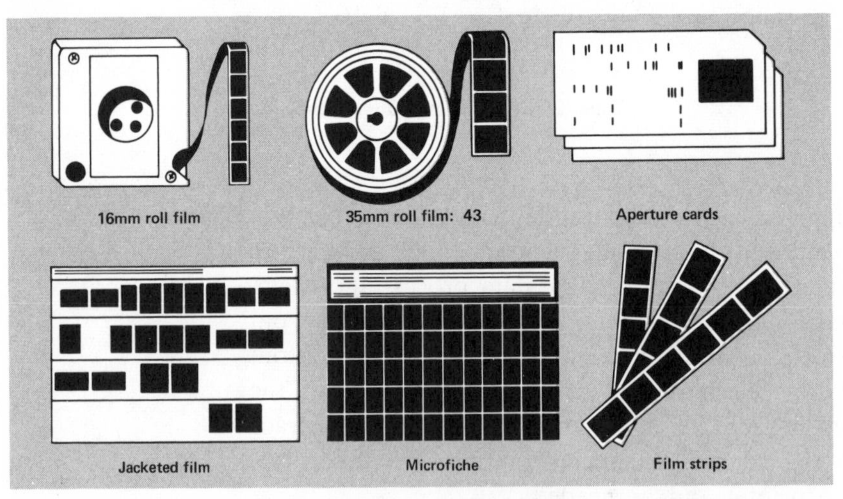

Fig. 8-9

Business Automation

Common Formats for Microrecords

[7] Edward J. Menkhaus, "Microfilm Captures More of the Action," reprinted from *Business Automation,* May, 1969, copyright Business Press International, Inc.

Selecting the proper microform format requires considerable study and visits to present users of the equipment, as well as securing the advice of consultants and systems personnel. The records administrator faces many pressing problems before he decides to microfilm his records. One office executive cites the need to group similar items in like retention schedules to provide an orderly sequence for microfilming the records. The condition of the records, too, must be considered, for poorly prepared records are difficult to photograph for later enlargement and reading or printout. In some states microfilm may not be admissible in court, while in other states corrections on film can be certified and added at the end of a reel. To assure that the documents in film form will stand up in court requires a planned, well-defined program with proper records retention schedules that are accepted by the court. It is possible, of course, that certain records may be overlooked during the photographing process. Management may never be aware of the possible loss of some of the records because of bad film, improper filming operations, or actual failure to photograph the particular records.

Microform Equipment

Whether the microform chosen is film, microfiche, aperture card, or some other medium, certain basic equipment is required. To film the records in black and white or in color requires a camera, and to read the microrecord requires a reader. In addition, there are other types of equipment, such as reader-printers that print out hard copy of the document being displayed on the screen, enlarger-printers, processors, film duplicators, magnetic-tape-to-film recorders, and many other forms of automated retrieval units.

With the exception of the readers, all the machines in the microform operation require specially trained operators for proper use. Readers and reader-printers, such as the reader shown in Figure 8-10, are designed to be used by the general office staff, and their proper operation can be learned in a few minutes' time.

INFORMATION AND RECORDS RETRIEVAL

The fast retrieval of records hinges upon accurate indexing and storage procedures. Such procedures have special relevance and take on new meaning when considered in an automated age when machines assume some of the storage and retrieval functions of information handling.

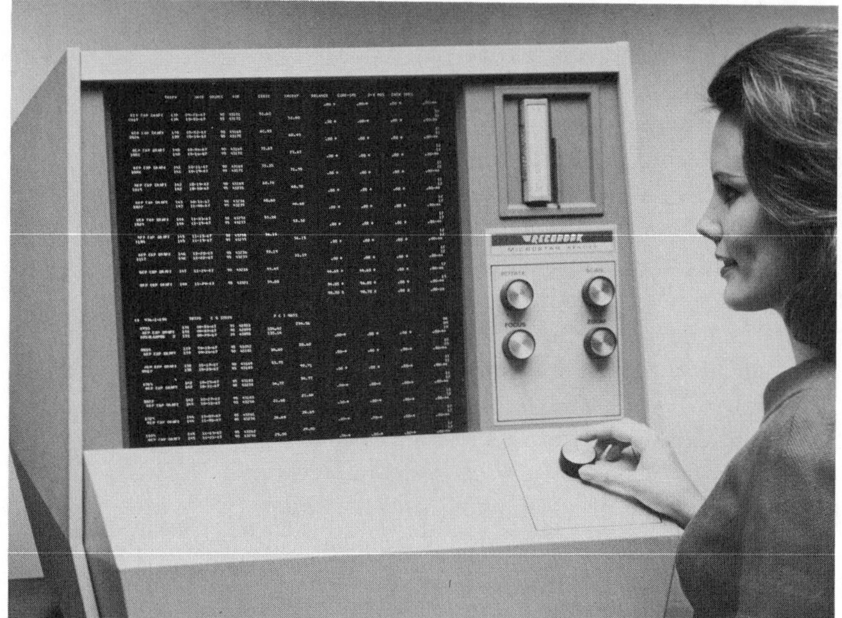

Fig. 8-10

Eastman Kodak Company

A Microfilm Reader for General Office Use

What Retrieval Means

The retrieval process in any filing system begins with a request for information or for a document. This request or inquiry is then followed by a search or scanning operation. Locating or not locating the requested record involves a comparison of the record found with another record or with some characteristic of the record in the searcher's memory or mind. There is implied in any retrieval process the ability to recognize the important features in a record by which comparison is made. Whether the files be correspondence systems, accounting systems, inventory documents, directories, or the like, all are examples of systems for storing and retrieving data.

The manual system of retrieval is simple to understand, though not necessarily simple to operate effectively. When the retrieval function is turned over to a machine, however, considerable complexity and difficulty occur. This is true because retrieval is, in the final analysis, a process of communication in which someone asks somebody to find something. To convert such a verbal request into a machine-managed system is indeed difficult.

Information Retrieval by Machine

With problems of space, time, and volumes of information facing the businessman, new efforts to solve these problems have been made. Microfilming has been shown to meet the space problem effectively; the computer and punched-card machines, too, are meeting the problems of faster processing and storage of larger and larger quantities of data. These machines are the principal technological media for retrieving information. Each of these media is briefly discussed as it relates to information retrieval. First, however, to understand the machine retrieval of information, one must remember that the machine handles data in the following ways:

1. Data are stored in coded form in computers and in most data processing machines.
2. Machine programmers or coding clerks index and code the data by subject matter.
3. The subject matter code appears adjacent to the stored information so that the code can be searched by machine.
4. An inquiry is made in code form into a keyboard inquiry station asking the machine to search its files or its index.
5. The coded information or document (if in microform) is found.
6. The document or information is retrieved and takes one of these forms:
    a. The document is decoded and printed out in readable form (hard copy).
    b. The contents of the document may appear on a display screen.
    c. The document may be retrieved in microform and taken to an enlarger (reader) for viewing and use.

Retrieval from Microforms. There are many ways to retrieve information from microforms. Normally the use of the document or the manner in which the record is requested specifies how the record is retrieved. If, for example, the March 30, 1965, issue of *The Wall Street Journal* were requested, it could be found in a microfilm reel by checking the label of the contents on the cartridge box. After the reel of film is inserted into the reader, the operator advances the film manually or by mechanical means to the point on the film where the desired document is stored.

With a retrieval system such as that illustrated in Figure 8-11, both microfiche and aperture cards, separately or combined, may be retrieved by having a request entered into the system from keyboards either in the file area or a remote location. When a document is desired, its code number is located in an index file, and the number is entered into the keyboard and transmitted to the information system. Within the system the search is made, and, depending upon the request, the document's contents may be projected on a screen and printed out (hard copy) or may bypass the screen and be printed out. Such a system, costing approximately $170,000, automatically stores up to 200,000 microforms; and it retrieves, duplicates, transmits, and copies both alphabetic and numeric text and graphics—each in less than ten seconds after the request is made.[8]

Retrieval by Punched-Card Machines. The aperture card is a punched card with an opening (aperture) for inserting a microphotographed record. A description of the contents of the card,

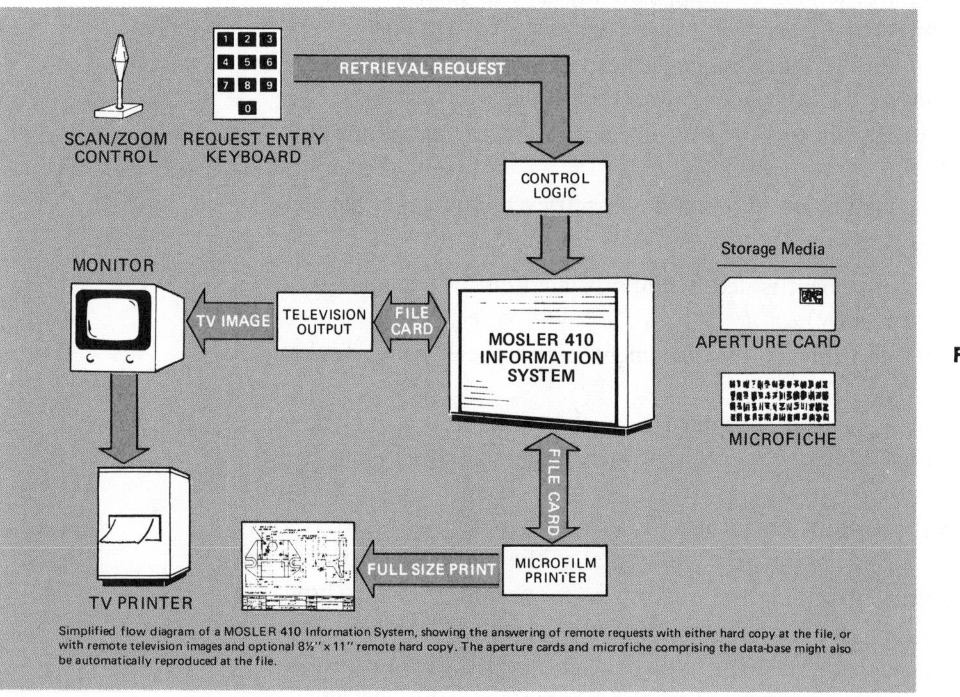

Simplified flow diagram of a MOSLER 410 Information System, showing the answering of remote requests with either hard copy at the file, or with remote television images and optional 8½" x 11" remote hard copy. The aperture cards and microfiche comprising the data-base might also be automatically reproduced at the file.

Fig. 8-11

Courtesy of Information and Records Management

Retrieval from Microforms

---

[8] "The Mosler 410 Information System," *Information and Records Management* (April-May, 1969), pp. 67-68.

either in abbreviated form or in code form, can be punched into the card. For example, the card appearing in Figure 8-12 shows one single frame of microfilm that contains eight pages of historic information. Punched into the card is a concise description of the contents, thus permitting the card to be mechanically retrieved by means of a sorter or a collator. To permit hand retrieval and hand filing of this card, the words "U S HISTORIC PATENTS" appear in decoded, plain-language form at the top of the card.

Fig. 8-12

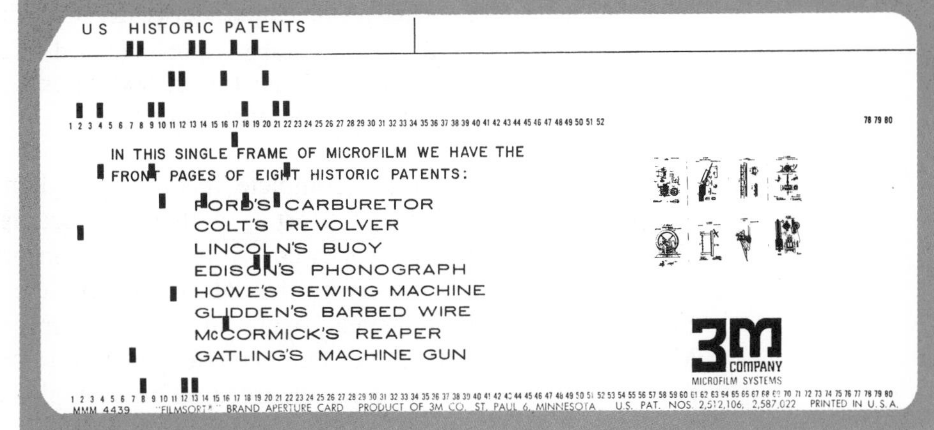

Courtesy of 3M Company

An Aperture Card Showing the Storage of Eight Historic Records

Retrieval by Computer. The computer system stores information internally and externally. Internally, data are stored on magnetic drums, magnetic cores, and magnetic discs. Externally, but connected with the computer, are other means of storage, such as magnetic-tape devices, paper-tape devices, and punched-card machines. While the computer can store information internally or externally, it must also have the capability of finding what has been stored. To do this requires a proper search (retrieval) program in which the computer is instructed how to search a collection of machine-readable records. Since the machine can recognize in a record a specific code, word, or phrase, it can seek out the pertinent records and list them, copy them, compile them, or cause them to be physically retrieved or transmitted.

The development of computer output microfilm (with the acronym COM) merges the space-saving features of microfilm with the speed and machine accessibility of the computer. The equivalent of

16,000 pages of computer-generated information can be converted to microfilm in about an hour, and the result fits in the palm of a hand. Simply stated, the following procedure is required:

1. Data are put on magnetic tape, usually by way of the punched card though not necessarily. Such data serve as input to the computer.
2. These data are converted by the computer into alphanumeric or graphic form for display on a cathode ray tube similar to a television screen (an output device for the computer).
3. The display of data on the tube is photographed at a rate of 7,000 to 30,000 lines a minute (about 300 pages a minute). Output appears as 16mm or 35mm film.[9]

It is possible to have a complete records cycle handled by the computer and the microfilm, starting with the recording of data in visual form (microfilm), followed by reading the information into a computer, and then modifying the data using computer techniques. Finally, the new data appear again in visual form on microfilm. Many applications of this development to complex information and records retrieval systems have emerged. For example, New York's Equitable Life Assurance Society operates a system in which over two million pages of data are microfilmed. Prior to the installation of the system, a tape file consisting of all the records involved with more than three million policies passed through a computer daily in order to process inquiries. This procedure required separate microfilming operations that now can be merged with the updating and inquiry functions of the computer. Considerable time and labor savings have ensued.

New Retrieval Systems

A relatively recent principle of information retrieval maintains that records can be indexed and summarized on the basis of certain words which they contain. Furthermore, if such key words are truly representative and descriptive of the record's contents, they can serve as the vehicle for the storage and location of information. While the idea is old (filing by book title and report title has long used this technique), what is new is that descriptive words can be used to extract specific information from a larger body of printed matter.

[9] "Here Comes the C.O.M.," *Information and Records Management* (October-November, 1968), p. 46.

The Keyword in Context (KWIC) indexing system is an example of the new retrieval systems. In this system a clerk reads an article or record and underlines key phrases, subtitles, or headings. Each document is given an arbitrary code number, and each key phrase with its code number is keypunched into a punched card. The card is fed into a computer which, through manipulation of the data according to the computer program, prints out a list of phrases. Copies of the keyword lists can be circulated throughout the firm to show at a glance the general contents of the record as well as the record number. Retrieval can be quickly effected by using the number assigned to the record.

RETENTION OF RECORDS

Even though the files are efficiently handled for storing and retrieving records, over a period of time the human tendency to hoard records will prevail. As a deterrent against this fatal disease of paper-work systems, the concept of records retention has been developed.

What Retention Means

Retention is the condition or process of retaining or keeping records. But in a records management program, much more is implied. Specifically, *records retention* involves the survey of all existing records, the development of schedules for retaining these records, and the systematic transfer from active files to inactive storage or disposal of all those records no longer needed.

The Records Retention Schedule

A definite policy should be developed and approved administratively as to the procedure to be followed in keeping material in the files, in microfilming papers, in placing materials in the vaults of a records center, and in destroying papers and records. In large offices the approval of records retention schedules very often involves top management and the accounting and the law departments in conjunction with the heads of the departments who hold the records. In small and medium-size offices top management ordinarily has the responsibility for approving the records retention schedules. Even though most companies may have retention and destruction schedules, in many instances the creation of records far surpasses the ability

LEGEND FOR AUTHORITY TO DISPOSE

AD—Administrative Decision
ASPR—Armed Services Procurement Regulation
CFR—Code of Federal Regulations
FLSA—Fair Labor Standards Act
INS—Insurance Company Regulation

*After Disposed
**Normally
† Govt. R & D Contracts

LEGEND FOR RETENTION PERIOD

AC—Dispose After Completion of Job or Contract
AE—Dispose After Expiration
AF—After End of Fiscal Year
AS—After Settlement
AT—Dispose After Termination
OBS—Dispose When Obsolete
P—Permanent
SUP—Dispose When Superseded

TYPE OF RECORD	RETENTION PERIOD YEARS	AUTHORITY
ACCOUNTING & FISCAL		
Accounts Payable Invoices	3	ASPR-STATE, FLSA
Accounts Payable Ledger	P	AD
Accounts Receivable Ledgers	5	AD
Balance Sheets	P	AD
Bank Deposits	3	AD
Bank Statements	3	AD
Bonds	P	AD
Budgets	3	AD
Capital Asset Record	3*	AD
Cash Receipt Records	7	AD
Check Register	P	AD
Checks, Dividend	6	
Checks, Payroll	2	FLSA, STATE
Checks, Voucher	3	FLSA, STATE
Cost Accounting Records	5	AD
Earnings Register	3	FLSA, STATE
Entertainment Gifts & Gratuities	3	AD
Expense Reports	3	AD
Financial Statements, Certified	P	AD
Financial Statements, Periodic	2	AD
General Ledger Records	P	CFR
Labor Cost Records	3	ASPR, CFR
Magnetic Tape and Tab Cards	1**	
Note Register	P	AD
Payroll Registers	3	FLSA, STATE
Petty Cash Records	3	AD
P & L Statements	P	AD
Salesman Commission Reports	3	AD
Travel Expense Reports	3	AD
Work Papers, Rough	2	AD

TYPE OF RECORD	RETENTION PERIOD YEARS	AUTHORITY
PERSONNEL		
Accident Reports, Injury Claims, Settlements	30 AS	CFR, INS, STATE
Applications, Changes & Terminations	50	AD, ASPR, CFR
Attendance Records	7	AD
Employee Activity Files	2 or SUP	AD
Employee Contracts	6 AT	AD
Fidelity Bonds	3 AT	AD
Garnishments	5	AD
Health & Safety Bulletins	P	AD
Injury Frequency Charts	P	CFR
Insurance Records, Employees	11 AT	INS
Job Descriptions	2 or SUP	CFR
Rating Cards	2 or SUP	CFR
Time Cards	3	AD
Training Manuals	P	AD
Union Agreements	3	WALSH-HEALEY ACT
PLANT & PROPERTY RECORDS		
Depreciation Schedules	P	AD
Inventory Records	P	AD
Maintenance & Repair, Building	10	AD
Maintenance & Repair, Machinery	5	AD
Plant Account Cards, Equipment	P	CFR, AD
Property Deeds	P	AD
Purchase or Lease Records of Plant Facility	P	AD
PRINTING & DUPLICATING		
Copies Produced, Tech. Pubs., Charts	1 or OBS	AD

Record	Retention	Authority
ADMINISTRATIVE RECORDS		
Audit Reports	10	AD
Audit Work Papers	3	AD
Classified Documents: Inventories, Reports, Receipts	10	AD
Correspondence, Executive	P	AD
Correspondence, General	5	AD
Directives from Officers	P	AD
Forms Used, File Copies	P	AD
Systems and Procedures Records	P	AD
Work Papers, Management Projects	P	AD
COMMUNICATIONS		
Bulletins Explaining Communications	P	AD
Messenger Records	1	AD
Phone Directories	SUP	AD
Postage Reports, Stamp Requisitions	1 AF	AD
Postal Records, Registered Mail & Insured Mail Logs & Meter Records	1 AF	AD, CFR
Telecommunications Copies	1	AD
CORPORATE		
Annual Reports	P	AD
Authority to Issue Securities	P	AD
Bonds, Surety	3 AE	AD
Capital Stock Ledger	P	AD
Charters, Constitutions, Bylaws	P	AD
Contracts	20 AT	AD
Corporate Election Records	P	AD
Incorporation Records	P	AD
Licenses – Federal, State, Local	AT	AD
Stock Transfer & Stockholder	P	AD
LEGAL		
Claims and Litigation Concerning Torts and Breach of Contracts	P	AD
Law Records – Federal, State, Local	SUP	AD
Patents and Related Material	P	AD
Trademark & Copyrights	P	AD
OFFICE SUPPLIES & SERVICES		
Inventories	1 AF	AD
Office Equipment Records	6 AF	AD
Requests for: Services	1 AF	AD
Requisitions for Supplies	1 AF	AD
Film Reports	5	AD
Negatives	5	AD
Photographs	1	AD
Production Records	1 AC	AD
TAXATION		
Annuity or Deferred Payment Plan	P	CFR
Depreciation Schedules	P	CFR
Dividend Register	P	CFR
Employee Withholding	4	CFR
Excise Exemption Certificates	4	CFR
Excise Reports (Manufacturing)	4	CFR
Excise Reports (Retail)	4	CFR
Inventory Reports	P	CFR
Tax Bills and Statements	P	AD
Tax Returns	P	AD
CONTRACT ADMINISTRATION		
Contracts, Negotiated. Bailments Changes, Specifications, Procedures, Correspondence	P	CFR
Customer Reports	P	AD
Materials Relating to Distribution Revisions, Forms, and Format of Reports	P	AD
Work Papers	OBS	AD
LIBRARY, COMPANY		
Accession Lists	P	AD
Copies of Requests for Materials	6 mos.	AD
Meeting Calendars	P	AD
Research Papers, Abstracts, Bibliographies	SUP, 6 mos. AC	AD
MANUFACTURING		
Bills of Material	2	AD, ASPR
Drafting Records	P	AD†
Drawings	2	AD, ASPR
Inspection Records	2	AD
Lab Test Reports	P	AD
Memos, Production	AC	AD
Product, Tooling, Design, Engineering Research, Experiment & Specs Records	20	STATUE LIMITATIONS
Production Reports	3	AD
Quality Reports	1 AC	AD

Electric Wastebasket Corporation

Fig. 8-13
Records Retention Timetable

of these companies to house the records in the space set aside for this purpose.

A large part of the material filed is of a temporary nature and should be destroyed as soon as practical. Most companies retain records far longer than is legally necessary. Their most impelling reasons for doing so are the federal, state, and local laws that set up minimum—and often conflicting—retention periods for specific papers. State and federal regulatory bodies have handed down instructions as to the length of time that certain records should be kept in insurance companies, banks, railroads, and telephone companies. For example, the Interstate Commerce Commission has over 250 separate retention regulations for railroads, airlines, and other carriers to follow. The Internal Revenue Service has ruled that, generally, records bearing on income taxes must be kept five years; however, the loss or destruction of older records is not recognized as a valid excuse for failure to produce them. The statutes of limitation in the various states also affect the decision of how long records and correspondence should be kept. A suggested schedule for the retention of business records is presented in Figure 8-13.[10]

DISPOSITION OF RECORDS

After the active period of use has passed, many records are transferred to lower-cost storage locations. Other records, having ceased to have any further usefulness, are destroyed. Procedures for the transfer of records to inactive storage as well as for their destruction are discussed in this section.

Transferring and Storing Inactive Records

Having determined what to retain and what to transfer to inactive files in low-rental storage areas, the next step is to determine the method of transfer and storage. Under the *duplicate equipment method* last year's materials are kept in file cabinets located next to the present active files. At the end of the year, the contents of last year's files are placed in transfer cases, and the present fiscal year's file becomes the "back" file. Although this method is fairly

[10] Abstracted from "Records Retention Timetable," reset and printed by Electric Wastebasket Corporation, 145 West 44th Street, New York, NY 10036. (Affiliated with Michael Lith Sales Corporation, 1967). For the provisions of federal laws and regulations relating to the keeping of records by the public, see *Guide to Record Retention Requirements* (Washington, D.C.: U.S. Government Printing Office, January 1, 1971).

expensive from the viewpoint of investment in equipment, it is very efficient. In the *periodic method,* at fixed intervals of six months or one year the material in the files is examined and all inactive material is placed in transfer cases that duplicate the arrangement of the regular filing equipment. A disadvantage of this method is that the periodic inspection of the files is a laborious job and may interfere with the regular filing procedures. Under the *continuous method* of transferring inactive records, which is characterized as being rather inefficient, the filed materials are continuously examined and transferred as soon as they reach a certain age.

Transferred materials should be kept in that part of the office or storage area that is least desirable for general use. The files should be of inexpensive but practical construction and kept in an orderly manner so that desired information may be located without too much delay. Figure 8-14 presents ten points for the office manager or files supervisor to keep in mind at the time of transferring the files.[11]

In medium-size and large offices, a *records center* is often established to provide for the storage of records. In the records center or archives (a specially designed building or storage place) the inactive records of all departments are centrally stored. Large companies that have established records centers cite the following advantages of keeping their noncurrent records in a separate specially designed storage center:

1. Savings in space and equipment costs.
2. Better utilization of space. In offices the ratio of cubic feet of records to one square foot of floor space is usually 1:1. In records centers it is possible to achieve a ratio of up to 5:1.
3. Increased efficiency and easy finding. If the retention of records is uncontrolled, much time is spent in finding materials. The records center eliminates this problem by maintaining an accurate index of all records and by providing for an orderly storage system of records under a defined responsibility.

Protecting Vital Records

In planning the location and layout of the vital records files, each firm must appraise the risks involved and decide for itself the degree of protection desired for its operating records. Since data about a

[11] "Today's Files Offer Space-Saving Design and Easier Access," *Administrative Management* (February, 1965), p. 60.

TEN TIPS WHEN PLANNING FOR "T-DAY"

The approach of "T-Day" (transfer time) to a file supervisor or the file operators is usually looked upon with apprehension because of the confusion and inconvenience accompanying such a task.

Transfer is to business what thorough housecleaning is to the home. It upsets normal procedures. Thus, planning should be done several weeks in advance of the transfer date. Here are a few tips to make the process easier to cope with.

(1) Determine and tabulate by number of inches the amount of material that can be destroyed.
(2) Remove this material from the old files or transfer cases.
(3) Rearrange the transfer files in such a way as to provide empty drawer space within the immediate proximity of the next year's files.
(4) Prepare a list of the names for which folders or folder labels must be prepared. Analyze the files to be sure you include folders for new customers, and break down bulky folders with chronological folders.
(5) Indicate on the label list which names are most active so that special name guides and chronological folders in the proper size breakdown may be obtained.
(6) Determine the number of folders needed, both individual and chronological.
(7) Place the order for labels, folders, and other supplies 60 to 90 days before they are to be used.
(8) Type the labels from rolls or pads and keep in alphabetical order.
(9) Apply the labels to the folders and place in cartons in front of the miscellaneous folders in the same order as they will be placed in the active file.
(10) On transfer day merely remove what has been current material to its new location and place the newly prepared material in the space provided for the current files.

Fig. 8-14

Suggestions for Transferring Inactive Records

company's customers, creditors, inventory, and sources of supply are all entered on records, their loss could very well mean the discontinuance of the business with a substantial loss of property and means of livelihood. Yet the real value of records is not always recognized by management until after a disaster has struck and the records are no longer available.

In protecting themselves against the risk of loss of business records, companies should not attempt to depend on insurance alone. Although extended coverage may be obtained to cover the expense of reconstructing business records after a disaster, no protection is available for the loss of information contained in such records. Fire insurance policies require that a proof of loss be submitted for the collection of insurance after a fire. An insurance company cannot afford to pay for losses that cannot be proven. Thus, long and costly delays may be expected when records are destroyed.

After a company has appraised and classified its records as to those that must be protected in the event of disaster, it should next determine the manner in which the records will be protected. The three main means of protecting vital records are:

1. *Special facilities:* housing records in fire-resistive vaults, safes, storage rooms, or buildings.
2. *Dispersion:* evacuating essential records and documents to locations away from the place of business. Multiplant companies can exchange records between the various offices to assure adequate protection. Single-plant companies with sales offices located off premises also can exchange valuable records. Other companies can establish depositories for their records at other locations or use the facilities of other companies on a lease or rental basis. Small business firms can pool their resources and establish cooperative vital records storage centers to spread the expense of such an undertaking and to reduce the outlay required for any one participant. Business records storage centers, such as Bekins Van & Storage Company in Los Angeles and Leahy and Company of New York, are established in major cities across the country to provide records storage space for rent by those firms not wishing to establish on-premises protection measures.
3. *Duplication:* reproducing vital documents so that duplicates become the security copies which are stored in remote locations away from the disaster area. As a means of protection, for example, nearly all large institutions rely upon duplication of their records by microfilming, especially if the records management program involves consideration of nuclear attack.

Destruction of Records

Stored records no longer required should be destroyed. The date of destruction should be determined when the records are put into storage and this date should be properly labeled on the transfer cases. Top management must decide what materials can be destroyed and when they should be destroyed. To avoid carelessness and errors in this matter, a destruction calendar and storage instruction sheet is often used. One such program for the destruction of records is given as part of the illustrative filing manual presented in Chapter 23.

QUESTIONS FOR REVIEW

1. What are the steps that make up a typical records cycle? In your opinion, which of these steps requires the greatest study and control by the administrative office manager?
2. Differentiate between records management and filing. What are the specific objectives of a records management program?
3. Although each records management program has its own individual characteristics, it also has many similarities with other such programs. What are some of the important organizational features of records management, and why are these features significant?
4. What personal characteristics, knowledge, and skills should be possessed by a records manager? How would these position requirements differ in a machine-based records system as opposed to a manual records system?
5. What evaluation techniques are available for assessing the efficiency of a filing system? How does each technique contribute to the overall program for managing records?
6. Compare the relative merits of decentralized filing and centralized filing.
7. Define *filing system.* For what purpose is a filing system installed?
8. What legal implications do you see for the firm whose information system relies upon retention of records in an "invisible" or magnetized record form?
9. Outline the process of retrieving a record from (a) a manual storage system and (b) a machine storage system.
10. One of the basic components of a records management program is records retention. What steps should be followed to develop a retention program in order to insure that only essential documents are kept in the files and protected against loss?
11. Compare and contrast the three methods of transferring and storing inactive records.

QUESTIONS FOR DISCUSSION

1. "The manager of the records in a firm actually controls to a certain extent the decision-making process." Why is this statement made more often today than ever before, and what are some of its implications?
2. Design a model records management program in which you show all the relevant and essential components for controlling all aspects of paper work in an organization.
3. One of the first steps in the management process (records management included) is the development of the goals and objectives of the department. Discuss the objectives for a records management function and indicate how they differ when you view records broadly (such as paper-work management) as opposed to the narrow view (such as filing procedures.)
4. Assume that you are called in by a businessman to design a filing system for his relatively small office of one secretary, three typists, and five process clerks. In addition to this clerical staff, the businessman, his assistant, and three junior executives constitute the entire office staff. The office is not departmentalized and is located in one large general office room with no partition or privacy provided. How would you proceed? What key questions would you ask? What type(s) of filing system(s) would you prescribe and why?
5. If you were employed as supervisor of a centralized filing department, what information would you consider essential in an annual report of your departmental operation?
6. In a large metropolitan hospital the hospital administrator is searching for better methods of handling his expanding volume of records. He has compiled a list of his most urgent problems as follows:

   a. 150 X-rays are developed and processed daily (none of which are destroyed).
   b. 300 outpatients' and 2,500 inpatients' records must be handled daily with Medicare forms adding to the problem by 10 percent each year.
   c. 15,400 health insurance forms were processed during the past six months.
   d. No central depository of records is available.
   e. Physicians are growing more impatient with the slow retrieval of medical records from the files but are resisting the use of microfilmed records.
   f. The hospital administrator himself is in charge of all records, assisted on a full-time basis by three file clerks.

   Assuming the accuracy of these facts and the existence of other equally pressing problems, recommend to the hospital administrator a comprehensive plan for improving his records management practices including records retention and protection programs.

7. A philosophical problem among executives relates to their lack of concern about the importance of managing the entire information-processing function including the records. To clarify the issues involved, such questions as the following should be answered:

a. What contribution does the records management function make to top management?
b. How can a firm first recognize and then organize this company-wide responsibility?
c. What basic knowledge and attitudes should executives possess in order to give the top-level sanction to the program that is vitally necessary to its success?
d. Does a modern executive need any knowledge of information storage and retrieval methods, or is this purely a clerical responsibility? If yes, what knowledge is needed and where can it be obtained?
e. For a typical executive (such as a sales manager, a corporate controller, or a vice president of administration) what responsibilities would commonly be found that directly relate to the organization and administration of a records system?

Assume that you as an executive must find answers to these fundamental questions.

8. The filing work of the Frenchly Tool & Die Company has always been confused and spread throughout the various departments, with each department maintaining its own group of files. The firm has recently decided that the volume of work and the cost of maintaining the files have become large enough to justify the hiring of a files supervisor and the necessary assistants to do the work efficiently. It has been proposed to centralize all the filing operations, with the exception of the following:

a. Accounts receivable records will be kept on visible card files in the accounting department.
b. Credit files of customers will be kept on visible card files in the credit department.
c. Purchasing catalogs will be housed in the purchasing department.
d. Confidential financial reports will be kept in the treasurer's office.

Discuss: (a) the proposed organization of the centralized filing department; (b) a recommended method of standardizing the filing procedures and routines; (c) a plan for effective supervision of the filing work; (d) the filing system to be used for filing sales invoices, purchase orders and invoices, correspondence, and catalogs; (e) how costs may be reduced through the elimination of material from the files; and (f) a policy of destruction of filed materials and transferral of inactive materials to storage.

PRACTICAL OFFICE CASES

Case 8-1 Reorganizing the Filing Function

When you accepted the position of office manager of Carroll's Mercantile, Inc., five months ago, several serious record-keeping and filing problems immediately came to your attention. Equipment used in storing records is outdated; the old wooden file cabinets painted an olive green are difficult to operate. Presently there are 30 four-drawer file units crammed with records dating back as far as 15 years. No retention schedule is in effect, no filing manual in existence, and the present system for storing and retrieving documents is done on an informal, intuitive basis. Three general clerks do most of the filing, although all office employees have full access to the files. Each clerk is paid a weekly salary of $80. No one has been given formal training for designing or operating the filing system. Ninety percent of the records involve correspondence and invoices.

After studying the filing system in depth for several months, you have become convinced that the growing volume of records and other anticipated factors (such as firm growth and a larger office work force) point to the need for a reorganization of the entire filing function. Accordingly, you have proposed that Evelyn Krebs, a careful, experienced worker and a senior employee of the firm, be appointed as files supervisor with the responsibility of coordinating all filing activity, procuring the necessary filing equipment and supplies, and designing whatever new filing systems that she deems necessary. One full-time files assistant, to be chosen, would work closely with the files supervisor, thereby assuming centralized control over all the records.

Evelyn Krebs knows the firm and its problems and has the full cooperation of the entire office staff. Her close, intensive examination of the problems has confirmed your suspicions about the serious condition of the filing system. She has, accordingly, recommended to you that the old file cabinets be replaced with modern steel five-drawer units and corresponding supplies. In addition, she has proposed a transfer-of-records procedure known as the duplicate equipment method from active to inactive storage. During the first year of operations, the present four-drawer file units will be used as the "back" file. At the end of this first year, the contents of the old four-drawer units will be analyzed and most records will be destroyed. At the end of the first year, the four-drawer units will be discarded with no salvage value. The very small amount of correspondence remaining in the four-drawer units will be combined with the correspondence in the five-drawer units and these files will serve as the "back" file during the second year. At the end of the second and each succeeding year new single-drawer transfer cases will be purchased to be used in storing inactive correspondence in the atmosphere-controlled basement of the warehouse.

For the past two months Evelyn has worked with you in studying the correspondence patterns for the office. Approximately 4,000 incoming letters and 3,000 carbon copies of outgoing correspondence require filing each week. Each 26-inch drawer in the standard-size file cabinet holds approximately 5,000 papers. To handle the file or storage requirements, she consulted three filing equipment manufacturers who provided the following quotations for new equipment:

five-drawer filing units, letter size	$200.00 each
2 file shelves (attachable to either side of file drawer)	7.50 each
2 filing stools	20.00 each
transfer cases, single-drawer unit, letter size	17.50 each
1 sorting tray with guides	35.00 each

Two of the three equipment representatives submitted proposals for open-shelf filing (as an alternative to five-drawer filing cabinets) in which the following quotations would apply:

Open-shelf filing units, letter size (7-shelf, each 36″ long)	$50.00 each
Filing ladder	20.00 each

The equipment representatives suggested that during the first year the present four-drawer files be used as the "back" file. At the end of the first year, the four-drawer files would be discarded and new five-drawer files could be purchased to serve as "back" files during the second and succeeding years.

In addition to the filing equipment, Evelyn's report shows that the following supplies will be needed the first year for the active files:

Alphabetic file guides, pressboard (20 to each file drawer or 25 to each shelf)	$25.00 per C
File folders, heavy weight (100 to each file drawer or 130 to each shelf)	37.50 per M
100 out guides (manila)	10.00 per C
1,000 cross-reference sheets	17.50 per M

The forms and supplies are required and are available for cabinet as well as for open-shelf filing. However, the assumption should be made that the 36-inch open shelf can accommodate about 35 percent more records than the 26-inch cabinet drawer. For the active files 1,000 additional cross-reference sheets will have to be purchased each succeeding year. For the transfer files after the second year, only file folders will be used in each file drawer.

It is planned to pay the supervisor of the filing department $120 each week. The assistant in the filing department will be paid $90 each week.

▪ Since it is necessary to obtain a more objective analysis of costs in order to substantiate these proposals, you are asked to prepare a report showing the cost of operating and equipping the centralized filing department during the next five years. This report is to become part of the office manager's recommendation to the president of the company for the centralization of the filing department. In your report cover each of the following items:

1. Present and proposed payroll costs in the filing department.
2. Annual savings in payroll costs.
3. Investment in equipment and cost of supplies for first year.
4. Investment in equipment and cost of supplies for second year.
5. Investment in equipment and cost of supplies for the third, fourth, and fifth years.
6. Savings to be realized over a five-year period as the result of reducing the number of filing personnel and the installation of the new equipment in the centralized department.

Case 8-2 Retaining Records

Midland Insurance Company is a relatively new fire and casualty company organized in 1955 with headquarters in Omaha. During the past 15 years, small sales offices have been set up in Topeka, Des Moines, Aberdeen, and Cheyenne to cover the expanding sales territory of the firm. Because of large overall increases in sales and in staff, a fine new five-story office building was built in Omaha in 1971. Future plans provide for the air-conditioned basement of the new building to be utilized as an inactive records storage center.

Because of the large volume of record-keeping activities, a centralized filing unit was set up three years ago under the jurisdiction of the Systems and Procedures Department. This filing unit is located on the fourth floor with the following staff: a records supervisor and 10 file clerks to serve an office staff of 20 underwriters, 32 claims men, 25 general office executives, and a clerical home-office staff of 90, including a data processing installation.

Although no actual count has been made of the papers flowing into and out of the office, careful estimates have been made in each department during the past year. As a result, the records supervisor outlined the following as typical paper-work activities in his department:

500 outgoing letters each day
350 incoming letters each day
Approximately 350 copies of general office paper work (such as invoices, purchase and sales invoices, applications, and promotional literature) and interoffice memorandums
Only 25 percent of the file drawers contain active files. (Magnetic tape and punched-card records are kept on file in the data processing department.)

The records supervisor further estimates an annual 15 percent increase in the volume of record-keeping and filing activities. If this rate is maintained, the fourth floor records department will soon lack sufficient storage space for records, excessive budgeting for file equipment will be required, and many records will be retained in active storage that are not essential to day-to-day activities. He comes to you requesting assistance in answering some key questions dealing with the problem of retention of records.

■ Study the questions below and report your answers to the records supervisor.

1. How can objective evidence be secured for justifying the need for a records retention schedule?
2. What steps should be taken to develop a records retention schedule? Whose responsibility is the development of such a schedule?
3. Indicate how the activity of the files can be determined and how filing activity standards are related to the records retention problem.
4. What budgetary appropriations would be required to handle the volume of records presently found in the firm?
5. Should microfilming play any part in the development of a company archive? If so, what?
6. Approximately how much space and what equipment costs would be necessitated if an inactive records center were established? What additional responsibilities (and what personnel) would be required of the records department staff?

9

Auxiliary Administrative Services

Supplementing the communication services previously discussed are several related administrative services, each of which must be carefully organized and planned before the administrative office function can be effectively executed. Two main activities comprise auxiliary services: (1) mail services and (2) reproduction services. In order to develop and maintain a high level of productivity in the office, each of these auxiliary services must be understood and managed by the modern administrator.

MANAGEMENT OF MAILING SERVICES

The constantly increasing amount of paper work calls for increasing use of services to disseminate the forms, reports, and letters generated in the office. For many years the mailing operation was considered a necessary, though relatively unimportant, phase of office operations. The mailroom all too often was a secondary responsibility of a general clerical staff without formal organization, planning, and training for their responsibility. In general the costs of the mailroom operation were considered to be insignificant. This narrow mailroom concept has given way to a more comprehensive concept of mail management; for in order to administer the mailing function, the men, machines, materials, money, and other related factors must be organized and their work planned, coordinated, and directed. Without such management the mailing function is left to chance and to intuitive handling by a clerical supervisor. For the small and large firm alike, mailing services must exist; and to be effective, they must be managed.

PRINCIPLES OF MAIL MANAGEMENT

A business organization is generally defined in terms of such major functional systems as marketing, finance, and production. Accordingly, to manage each of these functions, basic principles have been developed and tested through the years. As described in earlier chapters, principles are general statements or rules that have universal application. Consequently, the principles of management should be extended to include administrative services such as mailing services. The principles of mail management that are basic to an effective mail operation are concerned with these functions:

1. Planning the mailing services.
2. Organizing the mailing center.
3. Defining and assigning responsibilities to trained personnel.
4. Establishing operating controls.
5. Providing adequate space for the mailing center.
6. Developing efficient mailing procedures.
7. Procuring efficient mailing equipment.
8. Carefully controlling costs.
9. Maintaining periodic reviews.

Planning the Mailing Services

Planning is the first phase in the management process, as it must be in the management of the mailing services. Basic to the planning of the mailing function are these considerations:

1. The entire organization must be considered in planning the mailing center's functions. Particular importance should be attached to such factors as size and complexity of the firm, type of mail, and location of buildings as well as building design and layout. (In several newly constructed skyscraper

office buildings, rapid transportation of incoming mail is provided by electronically controlled conveyors that deliver mail from the lower floors of a building to the upper-floor occupants at predetermined time intervals.)

2. No single standard pattern of operation will be found effective, though ideas and practices are often borrowed from other firms and adapted to the local needs of the office.
3. Greatest priority should be given to developing a mail routing pattern that provides the quickest and most direct flow of mail from sender to receiver.
4. Thought should be given to personnel requirements and areas and assignments of responsibilities, developing proper operating controls, procuring adequate space, developing efficient mailing procedures for incoming and outgoing mails, procuring efficient mailing equipment, working within a carefully designed cost structure, and periodically reviewing the mailing center's operations.

Business mail may be classified as *internal* (intradepartmental or interdepartmental mail) and *external* (incoming and outgoing mail). Since mailing services exist for all departments of a business, the mail department or *mailing center* has developed as a central reservoir of information and service for all mailing activities.

The purpose of the mailing center is to handle the various classes of mail in the most efficient manner consistent with the needs of the organization. While the principles of planning the mailing services are equally applicable to the small as well as to the large business organization, in general the larger the organization, the greater the degree of work specialization.

Organizing the Mailing Center

When setting up a new or revised service function, management typically considers whether to centralize or to decentralize the function. While there are strengths and weaknesses for each of these organizational patterns, the general trend has been and continues to be a centralized organizational plan for mailing services.

The main purpose of organizing the mailing center is to bring about control over time and costs to enable this service unit to perform its functions efficiently and economically. Proper organization effects savings in these two items not only in the mailing center but in other departments as well. This latter economy is achieved because higher paid clerks, stenographers, and secretaries are released from the time-consuming necessity of interrupting their regular duties to attend to matters that can be handled more efficiently by the mailing department.

Advantages of a Centralized Mailing Unit. In some offices both internal and external mail are handled through a centralized mailing department. In other offices incoming mail is handled centrally by one person or department and outgoing mail is taken care of by the department in which it originates. In the small office one person may handle both incoming and outgoing mail.

Handling Incoming Mail. The individual requirements of a business may require departmental handling of mail; but generally when the volume of mail warrants, the mailing services should be centralized because of the following advantages:

1. The responsibility for handling the important details of incoming mail is placed with one experienced person.
2. The careful opening and the proper distribution of mail are insured.
3. Stamping the accurate time of receipt on each piece of incoming mail is made possible.
4. Enclosures are carefully checked and clipped to the correspondence to which they belong.
5. Mail of a confidential nature is routed unopened to the addressee.
6. The detection of correspondents who continually neglect to pay full postage on their mail is made possible.
7. Time is saved by a more prompt distribution of incoming mail to all departments.

Handling Outgoing Mail. For handling outgoing mail, the advantages of a centralized mailing center are:

1. Operations are systematized, and duplication and errors are reduced by combining all the scattered mailing operations.
2. The centralized unit is brought under the direction of management so that the mailing services receive the executive attention that their importance demands.
3. The important details of mailing are assigned to one capable supervisor.

4. Postage costs are reduced by placing the supply of postage under the control of one responsible individual, thus making it possible to keep a proper accounting of all postage purchased.
5. The centralized mailroom can be located so that it will be accessible to the departments that it serves. For example, in the offices of the Standard Oil Company of Indiana, which occupy 15 floors of a 17-story building, the mailroom was located on the seventeenth floor before the mailing activities were reorganized. Moving this room to the eleventh floor resulted in saving a day in the mailing services. This was partly due to the fact that half of the building's 12 elevators served floors one to eleven, and the other half expressed from one to eleven and served the upper floors individually. The revised central location of the mailing activities eliminated the endless elevator changing that was necessary when the mailroom was located on the seventeenth floor. Above and below the central mailroom were smaller mailrooms on each floor that served as headquarters for the floor messengers.
6. Clerical work is saved. Stenographers can devote their full time to correspondence if they are relieved of the details of dispatching their mail and if it is systematically sent to the mailing room at regular intervals.
7. Congestion is avoided by eliminating rush work in the various departments at the close of business hours. The mailings are staggered so that the day's correspondence is not received at the post office in one bulk mailing during the peak hours when congestion prevails there also.
8. The economical use of automatic laborsaving devices, such as the postage meter, is made possible.
9. Better control over presorting of second- and third-class mail can be accomplished by large-volume mailers. All mail going to a particular ZIP code area can be sacked by the centralized department and placed on the shipping dock ready for transport to the final distribution center.

Defining and Assigning Responsibilities to Trained Personnel

In the small organization a part-time office employee may combine the duties of mail clerk with that of messenger, file clerk, or another related job. On the other hand, the large organization will doubtless appoint one person as mailing center supervisor and provide sufficient additional help to handle the operation satisfactorily.

Normally it is necessary to analyze the entire communication system within the firm in order to make basic decisions regarding the mailing center. Other matters such as government rules and regulations must also be considered. In both small and large firms, the following procedures should be considered carefully before duties and responsibilities are defined and assigned to mailing center personnel:

1. Determine the nature and scope of authority in the mailing center. Frequently this service is a responsibility of the director of administrative office services or the office manager. Such an officer should clearly indicate the authority and responsibilities of the mailing center for the entire organization to observe.
2. Select the mailing center supervisor. The supervision of the mailing center requires an experienced person who is thoroughly familiar with the routines of mailing work and with the rules and regulations of the U.S. Postal Service. The supervisor must be one who can command the respect of his subordinates and who is willing and able to train them in the proper performance of their duties. In addition to possessing these leadership qualities, the supervisor should be capable, aggressive, and constructive. The last quality is especially necessary when the supervisor is called upon to make suggestions regarding standardization of correspondence routines, correspondence forms, and envelopes.
3. Survey the firm's departments to determine their mailing needs, the nature of their mail, and their deadlines and schedule preferences. In addition local post office, airmail, and other mail transmission agencies should be studied in order to develop efficient mail procedures.
4. Procure appropriate mailing center personnel and assign their duties. The following duties are frequently assigned to the mailing center:

   a. *Mailing duties*
      Handling incoming mail
      Handling outgoing mail
      Developing schedules for pickup and delivery of internal and external mail
      Providing inside messenger service
      Developing training programs for workers on postage matters
      Coordinating mailing services with the post office authorities
      Providing informational services for all postage matters

Selecting personnel for the mailing center
Training personnel for the mailing center
Obtaining equipment

b. *Nonmailing duties*
Providing outside messenger service
Performing housekeeping duties
Maintaining petty cash funds
Collating and merging mailing pieces
Filing correspondence
Rendering duplicating services

Since much of the work in the mailing center is manual in nature, manual dexterity is important in all mail personnel. In the sorting activity, for example, both manual dexterity and reading and coding abilities interplay. Proper orientation to the firm and understanding of postal rules and regulations must also be achieved, in addition to instructing employees in the methods and schedules of handling incoming and outgoing mail. To aid the supervisor in his job of training, some of the large firms use mailing manuals for instructing mail center personnel. (Departmental practice manuals are described in Chapter 23.)

Establishing Operating Controls

The mailing supervisor and his staff should have a well-developed plan for executing their responsibilities. This objective includes establishing controls over incoming and outgoing mails as well as developing schedules for pickup and delivery of mail. Particularly important are the following control procedures:

1. Early delivery of mail to the firm by the post office or by firm vehicles and convenient pickup of mail for transmission from the firm.
2. Time stamping of all mail and the identification of all first-class mail for early, if not immediate, delivery to the addressee.
3. Developing straight-line routes for mail within the firm.
4. Designing and implementing a receipt log or register for all important mail such as telegrams, classified or secret documents, and registered or classified mail.
5. Controlling postage to prevent "shrinkage" resulting from such factors as accidental loss, mutilation, pilferage, or improper rating of the mails.
6. Random sampling of mailing center operations to assure proper conformance to the center's standard operating procedures.

7. Assuring proper use of special mailing equipment. When debating the purchase of any special equipment, the mail supervisor should question whether time will be saved by the machine and, if so, how important is the time saved.
8. Discouraging the handling of personal mail except under extraordinary circumstances. The time spent on handling personal mail places an extra burden on mailroom personnel who will have, accordingly, fewer minutes to give to official duties.
9. Setting up work schedules. One schedule guideline is that mail be processed and delivered within one hour after its receipt or one hour after the beginning of the normal workday. Similarly, outgoing mail received in the mailing center during working hours should be dispatched the same day. To achieve these scheduling requirements, the mailing center supervisor should consider establishing staggered or split shifts.

Providing Adequate Space for the Mailing Center

The location of the mailing center is of great importance to a firm. The mailing center should be accessible; that is, located in such a spot that heavy mail sacks and packages can be conveniently transported to and from postal trucks. A central location also will minimize the distance that messengers must travel and will promote more efficient messenger service, which is often a responsibility of the mailing center.

Within the mailing center itself, the principles of office layout discussed in Chapter 4 should be applied. Pomrenze recommends these specific layout details regarding mailing center layout:

1. Provide two doors for the mail center: one for the entrance and one for the exit of messengers.
2. Arrange the flow of incoming mail so that the mail is received at a point close to one door and processed for dispatching near the other.
3. Place furniture and equipment in the mail center in such a way that there is little or no backtracking in the flow of mail.
4. Provide for more than one person to work at a table, sorting rack, or other equipment. In this way personnel can be readily shifted from one job to another to assist in handling peak loads.[1]

---

[1] S. J. Pomrenze for the General Services Administration, "Instructional Materials on Mail Management" (Washington, D.C.: U.S. Government Printing Office, undated).

In addition to the layout suggestions just mentioned, other features of the working environment, such as air conditioning, acoustical materials for sound control, and lighting factors that are available for improving working conditions, should be given consideration when space is allocated for the mailing center.

Developing Efficient Mailing Procedures

The following questions require answers before the mailing operation can work satisfactorily:

1. Who picks up the mail?
2. When is the mail picked up and delivered?
3. What route does the messenger or conveyor equipment take?
4. Who opens what class of mail?
5. What equipment is used for what purposes?

To answer these and other related questions requires setting up standard operating policies and instructions, or *mailing procedures,* by which all mail is distributed upon arrival at the mailing center and picked up at each distribution point. These procedures involve both incoming and outgoing mail routines, which must be carefully designed, installed, and periodically reviewed for effectiveness and efficiency.

Incoming Mail Procedures. The principles underlying the procedures for handling incoming mail are those of *speed* and *accuracy*. An efficient mailing center does all that is physically possible to see that mail is distributed quickly and accurately so that no department can later excuse itself for inaction by a charge of lateness and inaccuracy against the mail clerks.

To carry out these principles, all but the very small firms have their mail picked up at the post office by company messengers. After the personal letters are sorted from the company correspondence, the latter is opened either by hand, by a hand-operated opener, or by an electrically operated machine. If the mail is opened by hand, a systematic procedure should be followed to increase the speed of operations. The inefficiency of opening one envelope at a time, removing the contents, and placing them on the proper departmental pile is readily apparent. Lost motion and time are saved by performing the same operation on many pieces of mail before turning to the succeeding step. Some firms combine the sorting of the opened mail with the time stamping of each piece of incoming mail, a procedure that definitely establishes responsibility for delays in answering correspondence. In a large business the job of sorting mail should be assigned to a person who is thoroughly acquainted with the company, its products, and the work of the operating departments so as to insure accuracy of distribution.

All letters containing remittances should be placed in a separate pile after it has been determined that the amount enclosed corresponds to the amount indicated in the accompanying letter. Under a good system of internal control, a mail clerk lists the names of the customers sending remittances, together with the amounts enclosed, and sends the remittances directly to the cashier and a duplicate list of enclosures to the controller. Some firms also keep a record of incoming registered, special delivery, and insured mail, and a record of mail expected when a letter indicates that something is being forwarded under separate cover. Letters not containing remittances are sorted by departments or by specifically named addressees. The last step in the procedures of handling the incoming mail is its distribution to the departments by company messengers or other means.

Outgoing Mail Procedures. Handling outgoing mail is a much more complex service than that of incoming mail because the former involves the question of centralization of the mailing unit, a thorough understanding of postal rules and regulations, a knowledge of dispatch times by the post office, and other factors. In some concerns the outgoing mail is handled departmentally in which case each department seals, stamps, and mails its own correspondence. But even where there is a centralized mailing unit, the procedure varies. Some firms may deliver mail to the mailing center with the letters folded and inserted in envelopes, leaving only the sealing and stamping to be done by the mail clerks. Many business organizations merely deliver the addressed envelopes with enclosures, giving the mailing department the additional duties of folding and inserting.

In collecting the outgoing mail from the various departments, messengers may make periodic trips throughout the offices and pick up mail from baskets labeled "Outgoing Mail." Some concerns have regularly scheduled messenger service, while others determine their pickup schedules in relation to train, plane, and boat connections.

After the mail reaches the mailing room, it is sorted as to that for branches or other company units, if any, and that for outside firms and individuals. It is then folded, inserted into envelopes, sealed, and stamped unless the first two operations have already been taken care of departmentally. In performing these operations, clerks must be guided by two important rules: (1) the number of enclosures must agree with the number indicated in the letter; (2) each operation must be performed carefully so that addressees will gain a favorable impression of the company.

The outgoing mail is next dispatched to the post office in time to make the necessary carrier connections. Printed schedules, showing the time that mail should leave the department in order that connections may be made, should be prepared and posted by the supervisor of the mailing center. When a transportation schedule is changed, the supervisor should immediately make the necessary corrections in the posted schedules.

Procuring Efficient Mailing Equipment

With the steady rise of office labor costs, management is forced to turn to greater use of machines and other equipment to process the mail. No longer is it feasible or practical to stamp, seal, sort, and address mail by hand. Instead machines are available for folding, gathering, sorting, addressing, and stamping mail.

The purpose of installing mailing equipment is to save the time of certain employees and to expedite the business of the office, even though this means that the equipment may be idle part of the day. A good measure of the need or worth of a machine is whether or not the value of the employee's time saved is greater than the depreciation and cost of the machine used. If the time saved is worth more than the cost of the machine, considering depreciation, then the use of the machine is worthwhile. Stated another way, the volume of mail handled must be substantial enough to warrant the capital expenditure for highly specialized equipment.

Some types of equipment that are available for expediting the mailroom work are briefly described below.

Postage Meter Equipment. Postage meter equipment generally consists of two parts: an office mailing machine and a detachable postage meter. The meter is licensed for use by the U.S. Postal Service. The meter, which prints the amount of postage and accounts for government revenue under official lock and key, is leased from the manufacturer who is held responsible to the post office for its proper operation and replacement when necessary. To purchase postage, the meter is taken to the nearest post office where it is "set" for one convenient lump sum. The postage is paid in advance just as when buying ordinary stamps.

Most of the large business firms in the United States use postage meter equipment. Among the advantages attributed to this equipment are: speed in sealing, stamping, and stacking the mail in one operation; elimination of waste and misuse of postage; and better control over postage costs. Also, by means of the postage meter, the firm's trademark, slogan, or advertising message can be imprinted on the mailing piece at the same time the postage impression is made.

Postage meter machines are available in various sizes and models to meet the varying needs of any office. Attachments include feeding hoppers, stackers, inserters, sealers, check signers, and United Parcel Service metering. Machine metering speeds vary from hand-operated machines with variable metering speed to the most complex machine that meters 200 envelopes per minute. The smallest manual machine permits maximum postage purchase of $99.99, while the automatic metering machines most frequently allow a maximum postage purchase of $9,999.99.

Addressing Machine. Whenever a considerable amount of repetitive addressing of envelopes and packages is to be done, the mailing center supervisor should give thought to an addressing machine. These machines can write a complete name and address on a label or envelope faster than a typist can type a single line. Models are available that imprint account numbers, district or territory codes, and salesmen's code numbers. These machines range from hand-operated, portable models to large, electronic models. The computer, too, may be used for printing out addresses in label form that can then be attached to the mail and documents. On some computers up to 1,000 addresses per minute may be printed. Optical scanning addressers are also used to prepare labels at rates up to 18,000 addresses per hour. By optically scanning programmed instructions on a punched card, these addressing machines perform specific functions such as print/skip, sort, count, and stop. In selecting such machines the size of the mailing list, the frequency of the mailing, and the size and variety of forms used should be considered.

Other addressing features include the following: (1) a label-listing attachment that writes addresses on continuous rolls at high speeds, often used in addressing magazines; (2) counters; (3) automatic form feeders that permit continuous feeding of envelopes, postal cards, and brochures, thus eliminating separate handling; (4) automatic selection which selects and imprints addresses in selected classes; (5) mail-zone signals, which stop the machine at the end of a ZIP code zone to simplify sorting and grouping by codes; (6) sheet listers that print names or data in vertical columns on sheets; (7) multiprint and repeat which allows the machines to duplicate, triplicate, or do repeat printing; and (8) numbering devices.

Mail Inserter. For volume mailings, such as advertising and promotional mail, routine billings, or bulletins, inserting machines are necessary. Today's inserters handle an insert (from one to eight pieces) at 165 inserts a minute—20 times faster than could be done by hand. An inserter can gather eight pieces, insert them, and seal 5,000 such mailings in 30 minutes. When the inserter is used with a postage meter, all 5,000 will be stamped and stacked at the same time.[2]

Mail Opener. Mail-opening equipment is manufactured in various models, from the hand-operated opener that shears each envelope edge by means of depressing a lever, up to the high-speed automatic model that feeds, opens, and stacks more than 500 envelopes a minute.

Mailing Scale. Studies have revealed that the overpayment of postage due to inaccurate scales is one of the major causes of high mailroom operating costs. The accurate weighing of mail eliminates the wasteful overpayment of postage that results from "playing it safe" by guessing at the amount of postage required and minimizes the underpayment of postage that delays the mail and risks customer goodwill with its annoying "postage due." Modern mailing scales are characterized by built-in charts that provide foreign as well as domestic postage rates.

Date and Time Recorder. With this equipment a record of all incoming mail can be maintained in order to avoid costly misunderstanding with customers and suppliers. The mail is stamped with the date and time of receipt as fast as a clerk can insert it into the recorder. Electric clocks automatically change the time and date, thus leaving no room for error.

Miscellaneous Mailing Center Equipment. Among the many timesaving pieces of equipment that speed the flow of mail are:

---

[2] "Four Important Mailroom Tools," *Modern Office Procedures* (June, 1969), pp. 32-33.

(1) sorting and folding machines; (2) automatic gathering and sealing machines that pick up most enclosures, stuff them into envelopes, and seal them ready to stamp, sack, and mail; (3) separators that electronically separate the mail by ZIP code, town, state, or zone in combination with high-speed labeling or addressing; (4) tying machines; and (5) nonmechanical items such as mailbag racks and mail carts that speed up the distribution of the mail.

Controlling the Cost of Mailing Services

It is almost a truism to say that the cost of the mailing activity is constantly rising, but this fact must not be ignored. With postage and messenger costs rising, as well as that of costs of equipment and personnel, the planning function must give extra attention to reducing costs.

Mail authorities today estimate that in an eight-hour workday an average of 8,100 mailings occur each second, or 486,000 each hour. The U.S. Postal Service reports that approximately 79 billion pieces of mail were handled during 1968, an increase of 1.5 percent over 1967.[3] If only 25 percent of this volume were first-class mail, the cost to business firms would be at least $4.74 billion.

To receive, open, time stamp, read, sort, record and log, route, distribute, deliver, and follow up mail items—all necessary incoming mail control activities—costs, on the average, 21 cents per piece of mail. Three of these activities alone—time stamping, channeling of mail, and poor routing instructions—often result in slow mail delivery, added costs, and action delays.[4] A successful mail management program can keep these costs and inefficiencies at a minimum.

In addition to the costs mentioned above are the hidden costs related to personnel time, space, equipment, and overhead costs that can easily drain the office budget. The control of these costs is discussed in Chapter 21.

Maintaining Periodic Reviews

Effective management of the mailing center involves a periodic review and evaluation of the work being done and a study of how the work can be improved. To assist in such a review, use of a form similar to that shown in Figure 9-1 is recommended.

---

[3] *Ibid.*, p. 32.

[4] S. J. Pomrenze for the General Services Administration, "Instructional Materials on Mail Management" (Washington, D.C.: U.S. Government Printing Office, undated).

MAILING CENTER EVALUATION

	YES	NO		YES	NO
Administration			16. Are messenger runs adequate?		
1. Are all mailing services centralized?			17. Do the messenger schedules coincide with post office deliveries and pickups?		
2. Are all duties and responsibilities clearly defined?			18. Is a log or register of incoming and outgoing mail available and used?		
3. Has a communication explaining the operation of the mailing center been disseminated?			19. Are important documents (e.g., those having monetary contents) time stamped and logged?		
4. Is modern mail equipment available?			20. Before the mail is opened, is it sorted to separate that which needs prompt handling?		
5. Is the equipment being properly used?			21. Is internal mail sent in envelopes which easily distinguish it from external mail?		
6. Is the equipment in good working condition?			22. Are letters and enclosures that are sent to the same addressee consolidated in the same envelope?		
7. Are working conditions in the mailing center satisfactory?			23. Are incoming mail schedules as well as outgoing mail schedules and postal regulations posted or made readily accessible?		
8. Is the space properly laid out for good straight-line work flow?			24. Are postal rules and regulations publications available to each department?		
9. Are periodic mailing center reviews made?			25. Is postage expense controlled and assigned as the responsibility of one individual?		
10. Are good personnel practices observed regarding selection, orientation, and training of the mailing center staff?			26. Is postage expense charged to each department as incurred?		
Operating Practices			27. Are window envelopes used for letters whenever possible?		
11. Is a manual available and in use that describes the entire mailing center's operations?			28. Are there as few sizes of stationery and envelopes as possible?		
12. Do the mailing center personnel report early enough to assure mail delivery soon after working hours begin?			29. Are all outgoing communications reviewed at least once to check for enclosures, signatures, date, and the number of copies?		
13. Do some mailing center personnel remain after regular working hours to dispatch the mail received at the close of business?			30. Are efficient work methods utilized by mailing center personnel?		
14. Do messengers have established schedules that they follow?					
15. Are messenger schedules maintained?					

Fig. 9-1

Mailing Center Evaluation Form

MANAGEMENT OF REPRODUCTION SERVICES

One of the continuing needs in the modern office is the "extra copy," varying in degree from one carbon copy of a business letter to the hundreds or thousands of copies of promotional literature produced by the offset machine. In earlier days two processes—spirit and stencil—constituted the bulk of all multiple-copymaking in the office and were known largely as *duplicating*. Today, however, the field of duplicating machines and supplies has broadened beyond these two processes, covering such supplies as carbon paper, spirit, stencil, and offset machines, and embodying photographic processes such as the copier. This broad expanse of copymaking technology is now generally classified as *reproduction services*. The management of these services is an important responsibility of the administrative office manager. Each of the three major classes of reproduction services, duplicating, copying, and imprinting, is discussed in this section.

Duplicating Processes

Duplicating machines—especially the spirit and the stencil processes—have long been a part of the office scene. Within the past few decades, a third process—offset—has been achieving great successes in office work. Together this triad of machines constitutes the duplicating processes in the office (see Figure 9-2). Each process has its advantages and disadvantages, and no one process is ideal for all purposes. Frequently the typewriter and carbon paper also are considered. a form of duplicating extra copies of documents.

Stencil Duplicating. In this process, popularly called *mimeographing,* a stencil is first prepared on the typewriter, with the ribbon in nontype position, or it is written or drawn with a stylus. As the coating on the stencil is penetrated by the typewriter key or stylus point, a porous tissue is exposed which permits ink to pass through. Next the stencil is attached to the duplicating machine; and as the paper is fed through, the ink in the machine cylinder is forced through the openings of the stencil onto the paper. After a "run," the stencil can be stored for reuse at a later time.

The stencil process is the least expensive and best suited duplicating method for moderate-length runs. Since the equipment is relatively inexpensive and requires no skilled operator, it is practical

Courtesy of Heyer, Inc.

Stencil Duplicator

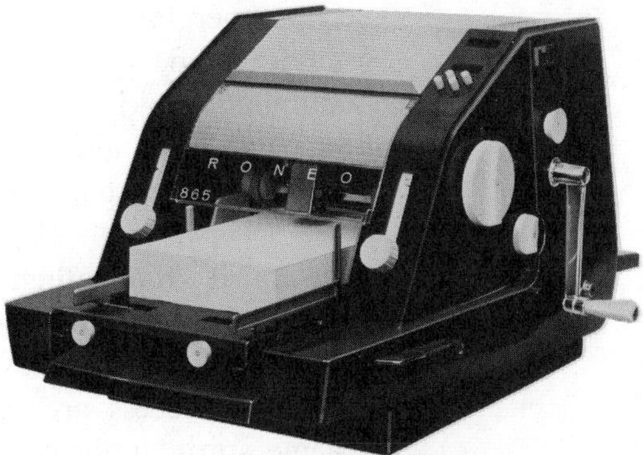

Courtesy of Roneo Machines Company Division of Comperipherals, Inc.

Spirit Duplicator

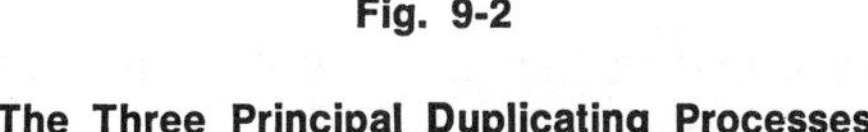
Fig. 9-2

The Three Principal Duplicating Processes

Courtesy of Rex-Rotary America Division of Bohn Business Machines, Inc.

Offset Duplicator

for the small firm in which its most widespread applications are forms preparation, report preparation, and copying.

Stencils are available in various quality grades and for purposes including *photostencils,* which permit the transfer of photographs, artwork, and drawings, and *electronic stencils,* upon which straight copy and halftone illustrations are automatically copied by means of an electronic eye that scans the original and cuts the stencil at the same time. A maximum of approximately 5,000 copies may be run from a good quality stencil on machines that operate from 60 to 200 cycles per minute, depending upon the type of manual or electric model used. New improvements on these machines include fully automatic inking systems, variable speed controls in which the machine stops automatically after a preset number of copies are run, and automatic paper feeding.

Spirit Duplicating. As the most inexpensive duplicating method for short runs (300 copies or fewer), *spirit duplicating* is one of the most popular and flexible processes today. Other common names for this process are *liquid, fluid, fluid duplicating,* and *ditto.* The name spirit duplicating comes from the use of alcohol as a solvent for the aniline dye used on the special carbon master sheet. To duplicate materials by this process, first the paper master is prepared by typing, printing, using a thermal copier, or by writing with a stylus, pencil, or ball point pen. As an impression is made on the face of the master, the back of the top sheet of the master picks up a spirit carbon impression from the carbon backing sheet. The master sheet is then clamped on the master cylinder of the machine and the duplicator moistens the master with fluid, which in turn picks up part of the carbon impression of the original master and transfers it onto the copy paper.

Considerable variety is permitted in the spirit duplicating process, both in terms of grades of master sets and in terms of machines. On the average, about 300 clear copies can be made from one high-quality master on both manual and electric machines with cycle rates of 60 to 150 copies per minute. All spirit masters can be easily stored and reused.

Besides its fast, inexpensive, and flexible applications, the spirit duplicating process has other advantages. Presently it is the only duplicating method that permits as many as five colors to be used during a single run. Each color is obtained at the time of preparing the master by switching the color of the carbon transfer sheet. New features of these machines include the use of odorless spirit liquids and an automatic fluid supply providing the correct amount of fluid for all kinds of copy.

Offset Duplicating. This process, sometimes called *multilith,* utilizes offset duplicators which are increasing at a faster rate than any other duplicating process. *Modern Office Procedures* predicts that the number going into offices will increase 71 percent by 1976 due to such new developments as higher speeds, lower per-copy costs, excellent quality of copy, and more automated operating features.[5] Present offset machines range in size from desk-top models to large floor presses and provide the closest representation of printing possible from a duplicating machine.

The offset principle of duplication is based on the fact that ink and water do not mix. The material to be duplicated is either typewritten, handwritten, or drawn on the offset master or even directly photographed from the original copy. Since water and grease do not mix, the image attracts the ink but the water in the blank spaces repels it, thus making a copy when paper is brought into contact with the image.

The number of impressions range from 5,400 to 10,000 copies per hour. By running two letter-size pages side by side, 10,800 to 20,000 copies can be produced in this same period of time. While the principal advantage of the machine has been the near-printing quality of the product, new advantages incorporating counters and quantity-to-run selectors, automatic machine stops, faster drying inks, automatic insertion and ejection of masters, automatic machine cleaning, and production of multiple colors in one run make this machine a very important consideration for the modern office.

Typewriter Duplicating. For a limited number of copies, at the most 8 to 10 on a manual typewriter and 10 to 20 on an electric typewriter, carbon-copy duplicating still represents the most common duplicating method. The principal disadvantage of this method is the need to correct not only the original but each copy as well. Platens (or typewriter rollers) are available in a variety of hardness for different numbers of carbon copies. For ordinary office work in which four or five carbons may be required, a relatively soft platen is satisfactory. But the platen must be harder when more carbons are needed.

In addition to manual typing, automatic typewriters are available, operating from one of the following input media containing the message to be duplicated on one or more electric typewriters:

1. *Punched tape.* Correspondence and systems data are punched into the tape by the tape punch on the typewriter. When fed through the typewriter's reader unit, the tape mechanically activates the keys to type a letter or form or to produce another tape in the punch unit.

---

[5] "A Guide to Offset," *Modern Office Procedures* (February, 1969), p. 43.

2. *Punched cards.* Three kinds of cards—edge punched, file, and tabulating cards—may be used. The typewriter reads the punched cards mechanically or pneumatically. Individual cards can be used for form paragraphs, lines of copy, or nonvariable systems data.
3. *Paper rolls.* Rolls come in varying widths, depending on equipment. Punched paper rolls are read pneumatically to activate the keyboard.
4. *Precoded photoelectric cards.* The standard Teletype code is printed on the back of the card in the form of ink bars; a black bar equals a space and a white space equals a character. A photoelectric reader senses the difference and output is prepared as a printed message and a standard paper tape.
5. *Magnetic tape.* While the operator is typing a rough draft, a magnetic tape record of the material is being prepared. If a wrong key is struck, the operator simply backspaces and types over the error; simultaneously the tape is automatically corrected. After the rough draft has been typed, the magnetic tape is used to reproduce one or more copies of the typed material at about 175 words per minute, with no errors and no further proofreading required.

In preparing paper rolls to be used in activating electric typewriters, first the letter or data to be reproduced is cut on a perforating machine. Each perforation corresponds to a character on the standard typewriter keyboard. The perforated roll is attached to the typewriting machine in front of the keyboard of the automatically equipped machine. As the machine is started, the perforated roll takes the place of a typist and operates the keys. Personalized letters are secured by means of stops, which check the machine and leave a space in which any variable personal matter desired can be inserted manually by the operator. On some models a number of form letters may be stored in the "memory unit." By means of push-button selectors, the operator can select a certain letter and interchange paragraphs automatically. Upon the completion of one letter, the operator removes the sheet and inserts another. Automatic typing is fast and error free, with typical speeds ranging from 100 to 150 words per minute. Some machines can operate much faster, depending on the kind of electric typewriters being used. Automatic typewriters are capable of producing typewritten letters at three times the speed of ordinary typing; or, if a battery of four of the machines is used, one typist can produce as many typewritten letters as would ordinarily take ten or twelve typists to produce on manual typewriters.

Copying Processes

Studies of office work through the years have shown that about 40 percent of all typing work in offices represents copying. Such work is time-consuming, costly, and prone to error and may also result in monotony for the typist. Several years ago when the first copiers came on the market, not many managers saw a very extensive use of these machines, yet today they have become indispensable office tools.

In a national study of companies employing 100 employees or more, 157 executives reported using the following number of copiers.[6]

Number of copiers in each company	*Percentage of companies with this number of copiers*
1-3	69%
4-6	17%
7-10	6%
11-19	4%
20 or more	3%

The primary types of copying processes are: (1) diffusion transfer, (2) dye transfer, (3) diazo, (4) stabilization, (5) thermography, and (6) electrostatic. New processes representing combinations of these main types (such as the copier/duplicator) are being perfected and placed on the market each year.

Diffusion Transfer. The diffusion transfer process, also known as the *phototransfer* or the *photocopying* process, is the basic copying method used in most office copiers. The document to be copied is placed against a light-sensitive sheet and then exposed to light. The light passes through the negative, hits the original, and bounces back from the unprinted parts of the original to strike the silver-halide surface of the negative, causing these areas to be made insoluble. The printed sections of the original receive no reflected light and these portions of the negative remain soluble. The negative is next placed against a chemically treated positive paper and both are run through a solution of developer and silver-halide solvent. The soluble printed section on the negative then diffuses to the positive sheet, where it turns black to form the copy.

---

[6] "What Users Say About Their Copiers," *Modern Office Procedures* (June, 1969), p. 24.

Diffusion is not the fastest of the copying processes and does require an operator who knows how to use the equipment efficiently and economically. The process does offer copies with good contrast and the unit is compact, when compared with other copying equipment. The relative advantages and disadvantages of this process and the other processes discussed below are outlined in Figure 9-3.

Dye Transfer. In the dye transfer process, also referred to as the *gelatin transfer* process, the original document is placed against the surface of a negative. As light passes through the negative, it bounces off the unprinted areas of the original and reacts with the silver-halide coating on the negative. The exposed parts become hard on the negative coating, which contains a gelatin substance, as the negative is passed through an activator solution. The unexposed parts remain soft and in the solution turn dark, thus forming a dye. The negative and copying paper are then passed through a pressure roller and the soft dye is transferred from the master negative to the copying paper.

A single master negative can be used to make six or seven copies in rapid succession. However, as the master dries, it becomes more difficult to transfer the dye; and as the dye is used up, the copies become fainter. In this process it costs considerably less for the second and succeeding copies after the first copy has been made.

Diazo. In this dye process the light passes through a translucent original that may be typewritten, handwritten, or printed on one side only. The translucent original is placed against a diazonium-coated copy sheet and both are exposed to ultraviolet light. The printed areas of the original block the light rays while the unprinted areas permit the rays to pass through and deactivate the coated copy sheet. The blocked areas of the coated sheet remain activated and, when joined with another chemical, form a visible dye. A copier using the diazo process is shown in Figure 9-4.

The diazo process cannot be used to copy two-sided originals directly. Such documents must first be converted to translucent originals by some other copying process. Manufacturers of diazo copying equipment claim the lowest cost per copy of any copying process, and in some high-volume installations the cost per copy may run as low as one-half cent.

Stabilization. In the stabilization process a light-sensitive sheet of paper and the original document are exposed to light. The sensitized sheet is then run through a developer bath and a fixing solution,

**OFFICE COPYING PROCESSES—
THEIR ADVANTAGES AND DISADVANTAGES**[7]

Process	Advantages (A) and Disadvantages (D)
Diffusion Transfer	(A) Produces sharp, high-contrast copies; can copy all colors; machines are compact and relatively inexpensive; equipment requires comparatively little maintenance.
	(D) Uses wet chemicals; usually involves a relatively large amount of manual operation, although newer models are fairly automatic; copies come out damp and must be dried; usually the cost per copy is relatively high.
Dye Transfer	(A) Can make a number of copies (usually up to seven) from a single negative; if several copies are produced from a single negative, the cost per copy is low; can copy all colors.
	(D) Uses wet chemicals; usually requires a good deal of manual operation, although newer models are more automatic; copies usually come out damp and must be dried; cost of single copy is high.
Diazo	(A) Lowest cost per copy of any copying method; can produce copies in any one of a variety of colors; copies are permanent.
	(D) Normally does not copy opaque originals or originals printed on both sides; involves handling of ammonia or alkaline liquid, unless thermal process is used; does not copy some blues and purples and other colors transparent to ultraviolet light.
Stabilization	(A) Requires only one type of coated paper; can copy all colors; reproduces photographs well.
	(D) Requires wet chemicals; first copy is white on black, unless direct-positive papers are used; copies may gradually deteriorate.
Thermography	(A) No liquid chemicals needed; copies are made easily and rapidly; equipment requires little maintenance.
	(D) Will only copy inks that absorb infrared radiation—inks containing carbon black or a metallic compound; copies made on treated paper usually darken if exposed to heat; copies are often made on lightweight paper that becomes brittle with age.
Electrostatic	(A) Uses no liquid chemicals; can copy all colors; copies are made on ordinary untreated paper and are permanent; excellent reproduction of printed type.
	(D) Machine is too expensive for low-volume user; does a fair job of copying photographs and large solid areas; complex machine requires more than usual amount of maintenance; uses a coated drum that must be replaced periodically (usually after about every 40,000 to 50,000 copies).

Fig. 9-3

Advantages and Disadvantages of Office Copying Processes

---

[7] Adapted from a special report of *Chemical and Engineering News,* July 13, 1964.

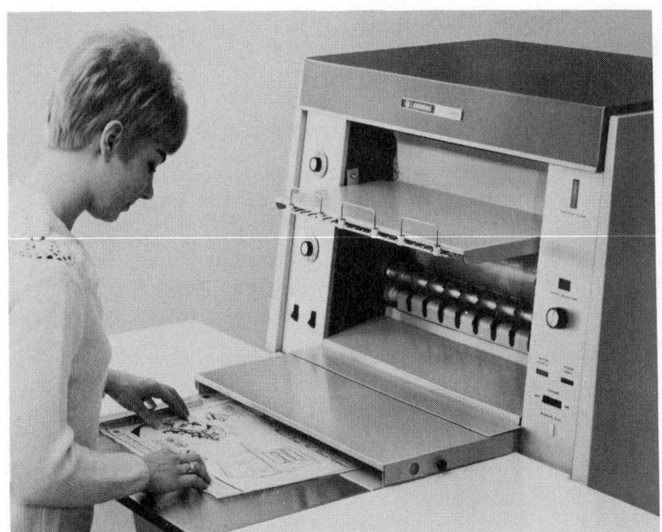

Courtesy of Charles Bruning Company a Division of Addressograph-Multigraph Corporation

Office Copier—Diazo Process

Fig. 9-4

called a stabilizer, which makes the image permanent. The negative, which may be stored indefinitely, can be used to make as many positives as desired.

The stabilization process can be used to reproduce photographs very well and original documents printed in almost any color. When reproducing only one copy, however, the process is a fairly slow one.

Thermography. In this "dry" copying process, also known as *infrared* or *heat transfer,* heat is used to form the image. The original document and a heat-sensitive copy sheet are fed into the copying unit which exposes both to infrared rays. The rays pass through the copy sheet and strike the original printed material, which absorbs and holds onto the rays. The heat that is held in the image area causes the corresponding area on the copy sheet to turn dark, thus forming the copy image. A thermographic copier is shown in Figure 9-5.

Only four or five seconds are required for the entire thermographic process. Some thermographic copying equipment is relatively insensitive to certain inks and colors. Some copy papers tend to become brittle and to darken when exposed to heat. Manufacturers of the equipment and the copy paper have greatly overcome these basic problems and are continuing to make improvements. For speed

Fig. 9-5

Courtesy of 3M Company

Office Copier—Thermography or "Dry" Copying Process

and ease in copying, however, the thermographic process can be highly satisfactory.

Electrostatic. This copying process, for which there are several techniques in use, is based upon the law that opposite charges attract. In one electrostatic copier as the light strikes the original document, the charge remains where the light strikes the printed area. The light that strikes the unprinted areas is dissipated. A black powder carrying an opposite electrical charge is then spread over the electrical photograph that covers the plate. The powder adheres to the charged areas and produces a visible image, but in reverse. A sheet of paper is next placed above the plate and both pass beneath charging wires. As the paper receives a charge opposite to that of the plate, the powder image leaves the plate and clings to the paper where it is permanently affixed by means of heat. An electrostatic copier is shown in Figure 9-6.

The initial investment in many electrostatic copiers is high, and for this reason rental arrangements are very common.

Courtesy of Xerox Corporation

Fig. 9-6

Office Copier—Electrostatic Process

New Processes. Integrating copying equipment, such as thermographic, with duplicators is becoming very common. For example, many copiers have the ability to make masters for use in one or more of the duplicating processes. In addition, some copier/duplicator machines combine duplicator speeds with copier quality and operating simplicity. Essentially these machines are copiers that are fast enough to handle work previously undertaken only by duplicators. Required only is the insertion of copy (no special paper is required) and the selection of the number of copies needed, with the machine producing copies at the rate of 90 sheets a minute.

Other technical advances include the development of copiers that produce copies on standard bond paper, a console copier that is capable of reducing computer printout to standard letter size, and copiers that reproduce in color.

Imprinting Processes

Several imprinting devices are available that stamp or print information on a number of pages or forms. Included in this class of machines are impression stamps and numbering machines, addressing machines, and signature machines.

PRINCIPLES OF REPRODUCTION SERVICES MANAGEMENT

Administrative services share many principles of organization and management. Those principles and practices that relate particularly to the management of the reproduction services are described in this section.

Planning the Reproduction Services

The field of reproducing technology is far more complex than appears on the surface. For example, today a potential buyer of copiers may choose from about 140 models produced by 44 manufacturers. Consequently much planning is required before the reproducing function can be put into operation.

Establishing a reproduction services function begins with the decision to centralize or decentralize the unit. Since normally there is better control over the machines that are centrally located under specialized personnel, this organizational plan seems to be preferred. Other advantages of centralization include greater flexibility and variety in the selection of reproduction processes, a minimum investment in equipment by reducing duplicate equipment, better scheduling of work, and ideally, increased output. In addition, management should consider that a reproduction services center permits a wiser choice of equipment and supplies, a knowledge of the limitations and possibilities of the equipment as well as more specialized skill in the operation and care of the equipment. Improved quality of the work and greater service to the firm should be the result.

The planning phase also involves staff procurement, defining and assigning responsibilities, establishing operating controls, allocating space, and developing efficient procedures as well as controlling and selecting good equipment.

Organizing the Reproduction Services Center

The term *reproduction services center* has broad and important connotations. Essentially it implies centralized organizational control over all types of equipment, supplies, procedures, and personnel responsible for any and all types of reproducing in the office even though a physical decentralization of some machines may be permitted. In the small office the center may be a small corner with one duplicating machine; in the large office, an entire department with many methods of reproduction. In either case the basic objective is to provide the most economical and efficient methods of reproduction in keeping with the needs of the office.

To organize the center, a thorough investigation of the company's operations and a careful estimate of its duplicating and copying requirements must be determined. An effective technique to obtain this information is to survey the reproduction needs of each department. In such a survey answers to the following questions should be obtained:

1. How many copies are made of each form, report, bulletin, manual, etc.?
2. To whom is each copy distributed?
3. How is each copy used and stored?
4. In what condition or form is the original copy?
5. Who requests reproduction or copying in each department?
6. How long is each copy retained?
7. How frequently are copies requested for reproduction?
8. What is the size of each copy desired? Is it enlarged or reduced in size?

As soon as the survey is completed, preferably in person by the center supervisor, the data must be analyzed. From the study priority can be given to determining the nature of the equipment to be purchased, thus answering the question of how much in-house reproducing work can be done and how much must be purchased from outside reproducing firms. Unless the firm is very large, some critical limits must be established as to the kind and amount of work that will be "farmed out." Policy regarding priority scheduling and work responsibilities must be established and approved by management. Finally, the center must be offered as the firm's specialized information bank on all reproduction methods, and all departments must be invited to use its services.

Defining the Responsibilities for Reproduction Services

The responsibilities for operating a reproduction services center normally fall on the administrative office manager or office services supervisor who may supervise the clerical and communication services. In a small firm he may wear "many hats" and serve as the supervisor of the reproducing function. In such a setting the day-to-day reproduction work may be handled by secretaries and typists, with commercial printers handling the larger duplicating needs. In the large firm, on the other hand, a full-time, specialized equipment-oriented supervisor should be appointed. His main responsibilities are to select necessary staff, develop production schedules, purchase equipment and supplies, and develop all the necessary operating controls for maintaining a sound reproduction services program.

Establishing Operating Controls

The philosophy of "run me off an extra 50 copies" is difficult to control in any office. However, this disregard for reproducing costs and operating needs, along with other misunderstandings of the reproducing function, must receive high priority. In order to do so, the following factors—equipment, location, and accountability—should be carefully weighed.

Equipment. Information should be obtained from the equipment manufacturer regarding initial equipment cost, per-copy cost of operation, and maintenance costs and service contracts on the equipment. In addition, the possibility of renting or leasing vs. purchasing the machines should be considered. Only authorized center personnel should be permitted to use the equipment. If not, equipment misuse can be expected as well as a continuous drain on the budget and the production of "bootleg" forms.

Location. Strategic control over the equipment can be effected by the proper location of the machines. Some firms with a large volume of copying and duplicating work centrally locate one copier and spirit duplicator near those departments having the most need for such services. In other offices, such as those located on several floors, several decentralized copy stations may be provided. By decentralizing the location of desk-top machines, employees can remain at their desks, thus eliminating the travel time to the reproduction services center. The time consumed, including stops to chat on the way, is considerable. Misuse and malfunctioning of the equipment and improper use of supplies can be prevented by training one or more individuals in its operation and upkeep and in the control of copies made and quantities produced.

Accountability. The reproduction services center must develop its own communication system showing what work it does, how well it does the work, how much the work costs, and other related information. These data will be useful for internal controls within the center as well as for providing guides to top management on the values and efficiency of maintaining the center. Of particular importance are these matters:

1. Careful evaluation of all equipment additions.
2. Year-end reports reviewing equipment use, number of copies reproduced, total cost of operation, type of documents copied, experiences with departments (by department).
3. Separate expense classifications to isolate and identify reproducing costs to promote the cost-consciousness of department heads.
4. Optional counters affixed to reproducing machines to provide foolproof automatic auditing of departmental copy costs. Key- or switch-activated models will audit up to 24 departments with the copier being activated only by authorized personnel.
5. Policies regarding the acquisition, proper use, and cost reporting of all reproducing machines.[8]

Planning Adequate Space

Along with maintaining standards of good work layout, as discussed in Chapter 4, the reproduction services center should provide adequate storeroom space for the large quantities of copy paper and supplies required. Other needs include lavatory facilities for cleaning up after operating the machines, darkroom facilities if photographic equipment is used, and acoustical materials to reduce the noise of equipment which can be annoying to office workers in adjacent areas.

Developing Efficient Reproducing Procedures

Orderly, efficient procedures must be developed for the reproduction of copies. One tested and well-developed technique is the use of a requisition procedure after all departments (or office employees, in the small office) have been alerted to the reproduction services center and its functions. A requisition form that provides control data regarding such items of information as volume, use by departments, and comparative uses of reproduction methods, is shown in Figure 9-7. Small offices frequently provide a usage log for the copier work station which serves a similar purpose to the requisition procedure in that it accounts for usage of the machine, though use of the log is more difficult to control.

[8] Adapted from Otto P. Kramer, "How to Select and Control Office Copiers," *Systems and Procedures Journal* (September-October, 1968), pp. 40-41.

1. Complete form in duplicate.
2. Retain one copy in department.

REPRODUCTION REQUISITION

____
date

Copy Number*	Reproduction Method Preferred	No. of Copies	Date Needed	For Rep. Center Use Only	
				Machine Operator	Total Run Time (in hours)

To be completed by requisitioning department:

Department to be charged: ________________ Department code number: ________

For questions, call: ________________ Telephone number: ________

Deliver to: ________________

Approved by (name, title)

(Requisitioning Department)

*Number copies if more than one copy is to be reproduced.

Fig. 9-7

A Form for Requisitioning Reproduction Services

Personal, sometimes selfish, desires rather than actual needs for copiers must be carefully controlled in the office. As a general rule office workers (and management, too) take conservative views of their copying needs and ask for extra copies in case they are needed. This problem, as well as the following copying abuses, should be rigidly checked:

1. Misusing equipment (such as using a copier instead of making one or two more carbon copies when the original was typed).
2. Making extra copies ("interest" copies) for others instead of circulating a "reading copy" among the staff.
3. Copying blank forms that can be requisitioned from the stockroom.
4. Using a copier as a duplicator (for creating large numbers of copies) or a duplicator as a copier (for creating very limited numbers of copies).
5. Remaking copies due to small, unimportant imperfections in the copy.
6. Making copies of lengthy magazine articles when additional copies of the magazine would be significantly less expensive.

7. Making copies of materials for personal or any nonbusiness use.[9]

Without adequate supervision each of these problems will likely occur both in copying and in duplicating procedures.

Procuring Efficient Reproduction Equipment

This principle is closely related to, and dependent upon, the survey of the company's reproduction needs and desires. A well-experienced reproduction center staff should study the results of the survey and, in keeping with modern equipment trends, attempt to buy the equipment that will provide at least cost the reproduced material, keeping quality and volume in mind. Good work relationships with associations, such as the Business Equipment Manufacturer's Association, the Association for Systems Management, and the Administrative Management Society, and machines sales representatives as well as a close study of publications such as *Modern Office Procedures,* which highlights equipment, will assist in the careful procurement of equipment.

To facilitate equipment selection, use of a form similar to the Machine Selection Guide shown on page 124 of Chapter 5 is recommended.

Controlling the Cost of Reproduction Services

One of the most persistent problems in the office is the uncontrolled quantity of documents being reproduced. The myth that reproducing multiple or extra copies is inexpensive has been a principal cause of the paper-work or information explosion. To be sure, an inexpensive sheet of carbon paper that can be used from five to ten times under optimum conditions may cost no more than 1/10 of a cent and creates a new copy at the same time the original copy is prepared. But with today's more sophisticated copymaking, expensive reproducing machinery is involved along with expensive supplies and the cost of highly trained personnel. If 100 copies of a one-page original are required, a modern copier could be employed at a cost of $5 to $7. On the other hand, an alternative process might be selected that would cost but 50 percent of this figure.

With a growing emphasis on reducing clerical costs, the administrative office manager must stress the need for controlling office

[9] *Ibid.*, p. 41.

reproduction operations. He can do this successfully by pointing out the chief components of reproduction costs, which include the equipment and related supplies, personnel operator time, and the related overhead costs for maintaining the reproduction facilities.

To control the cost of reproduction services requires first of all that: (1) competent authority be exercised in approving or rejecting all records to be reproduced; (2) the organization's administrative staff be able to choose the best from the several alternative methods of reproducing available, depending upon the needs of the user; and (3) an accurate accounting of all copymaking costs be made with charges allocated to the requesting department. Controlling the cost of reproduction services is discussed further in Chapter 21.

Maintaining Periodic Reviews

Preferably once a year management should be provided by the reproduction services center with a full report of its operation and plans for improvement. Standards should be checked against operations, departmental usages determined and interpreted, quality and quantity runs appraised, production of center employees measured, and center records audited. Economies in operation can be effected and more efficient operating procedures developed from such a review.

QUESTIONS FOR REVIEW

1. Evaluate the requirements for a mailing center supervisor from the following points of view: (a) personal characteristics and (b) professional knowledge, skills, and experience.
2. How would you compare the overall complexity of the incoming and the outgoing mail procedures? Which would you consider the more important? Why?
3. In what ways has the mailing center become mechanized? In your answer point out areas in which mechanical limitations exist, thus requiring the retention of human skills.
4. Analyze the sequence of steps involved in the outgoing mail procedure. What space planning should be required in order to promote the efficiency of this procedure?
5. How much information and knowledge about the mailing function should the typical departmental manager possess? How can such knowledge be updated and kept current?
6. One principle of mail management states that the mailing function should be periodically reviewed. How should this principle be properly carried out and put into practice?

7. What arguments can be given *against* a central mail facility?
8. What basic semantic differences exist in the terms *duplicating* and *reproduction* as used in this chapter? Of what importance are these differences, if any?
9. Compare the differences in applications among the three duplicating processes: stencil, spirit, and offset.
10. What factors would seem to account for the rapid rise of the offset duplicating and copier industries in our economy during the past 10 to 15 years?
11. If you were an office administrator about to select your first copying machine, how would you proceed and what factors would you consider in the selection of the machine?
12. What advantages accrue to the physical decentralization but organizational centralization of copiers?

QUESTIONS FOR DISCUSSION

1. In the small office, mailroom activities typically represent but a part-time responsibility of one or more employees. What procedures would you recommend to keep the cost of these operations as low as possible, assuming there is no full-time supervisor of the mail?
2. If you were asked to develop an outline for a comprehensive mail management program for a firm occupying the top 12 floors of a 30-story office building, what would your outline include?
3. Assume that the duplicating department head of McBride Mail Order Fashions is repeatedly questioned by other departmental managers about the best method of duplicating various communications, some of which are large and some small in volume. Discuss the development of a set of guidelines that describe the relative values and optimum applications for each method.
4. A reproduction services center incurs many operating expenses in the course of its operations. To show management clearly the expenses involved in the work of the reproduction services center, what type of report would be advisable? What should be its contents?
5. The field of work methods is sometimes called "work simplification" or "efficiency" work. How could such a methods program be applied in the administration of a reproduction services center?
6. The mailing center supervisor of Candless Products recently noticed the following practices in his unit:
   a. Only rarely is outgoing mail sorted; the feeling seems to be that this is the function of the post office.
   b. Repeated requests from other departments come to the mailing center regarding mailing rules and economies. Each caller is referred to the U.S. Postal Service for answers.

c. Even though some of the firm's products are perishable and others breakable, no standardized labels have been set up by the mailing center to ensure that all such packages receive the special handling they require.
d. The firm's main office is in an industrial park area four miles from the city's post office. By utilizing the post office delivery trucks, first-class mail is delivered to the center at 9:45 a.m. and 2:45 p.m. daily.
e. The mailing center supervisor "thinks" that the volume of mail serviced by his unit has increased a good deal in the past five years since he came to the job. In fact, a bimonthly mailing to 30,000 selected households throughout the country alone taxes his staff of three full-time persons since all assembling of enclosures and other postal tasks must be done manually with the exception of affixing postage, which is done by meter machine.

Logically the mailing center supervisor knows that his unit is not using good mailing center practices. What are the implications of each of the present practices and what recommendations should be made for improving each of them?

7. The Sheldon Manufacturing Company has its headquarters office located on four floors of a modern office building in Chicago. Each day the company receives, on the average, 1,500 pieces of first-class mail, 120 pieces of third-class mail, and occasionally some fourth-class mail. The daily average number of pieces of outgoing mail is 2,800 pieces of first-class mail and a few fourth-class packages. Four times a year 10,000 pieces of advertising literature are mailed at the third-class rate. Most of the fourth-class mail is sent from ten sales offices and warehouses located throughout the country. Only about ten percent of the shipments from the warehouses are sent by parcel post; the remainder is shipped by express or truck.

On the basis of the information above, discuss: (a) a suggested plan for organizing the mailroom activities; (b) recommended routines for handling the incoming and the outgoing mail; and (c) the control of postage costs.

8. Each of the ten main departments of the Branson Wire and Steel Company has maintained its own duplicating machine, usually a spirit duplicator, and a copier for convenience in use. As a result, uncontrolled copymaking has occurred in about half of the departments, as indicated by an in-house study conducted by a systems analyst. Copying costs have spiralled and complaints are commonly heard in each department that only poor duplicating services are available even though an adequate budget is provided therefor. As a result, an analyst studied the problems at length and has made the following general recommendations to the Vice President of Administration:

a. Initially appoint a full-time supervisor of all reproduction services since the 300 office employees and the large office seem to warrant this move.
b. Temporarily appoint departmental representatives who will be responsible for controlling each department's copymaking and working with the new supervisor.
c. Leave the machines in each department, but develop a requisition order form for all copying required.
d. At the end of a six-month period, make a decision as to the organizational restructuring necessary to control reproduction services activities.

Discuss each of the four recommendations as to (1) employee and managerial reactions to anticipate, (2) the wisdom of the organizational changes, and (3) future new personnel to be trained.

9. The Neel Trucking Company requires the following materials for the month of February. Indicate which of these items might be prepared most economically and efficiently by the office force and which should be provided by agencies outside the office. Also, indicate the type of reproduction service (duplicating, copying, or imprinting) to which each job is best suited.

a. 200 copies of time cards for the office employees. The employee's name, clock number, and date are to be inserted on each card.
b. 20 copies of a two-page bulletin to be sent to each department head.
c. 5 copies of the minutes of the directors' meeting held on February 10 to be sent to board members.
d. 3,000 copies of a two-page form letter to be sent to prospective customers.
e. 500 copies of the eight-page house organ. The company paper, issued monthly, contains snapshots, illustrations, and reading material.
f. 250 copies of notices to stockholders announcing the annual meeting on March 15.
g. 20 copies of a sales analysis report, eight pages in length, for distribution to each of the 20 district sales managers.
h. 20 copies of bulletins to typists suggesting procedures to follow in improving their work. Similar bulletins are issued weekly to the typists, who keep them in binders for future reference.

10. Assume that all the communications in Question 9 are satisfactorily reproduced. What distribution method (mail, personal messenger, etc.) would be the most practical and expeditious for each type of communication?

Dear Mr. ______________:

I was happy to meet you last ____________ when you opened a CRESCENT NATIONAL account. I hope that the full facilities of the bank--the savings, lending, and trust facilities and services, especially--have been well explained to you.

The enclosed brochure has been written to give you additional information about our entire organization, including our computer services department. I urge you to study it carefully; and, if you have any questions of any kind, please call me at the telephone number listed on the bank letterhead or call my assistant, ____________________, at Extension _______.

Sincerely,

Enclosure

PRACTICAL OFFICE CASES

Case 9-1 Selecting a Reproducing Method

The Crescent National Bank operates from one large, modern urban bank building and fifteen suburban branch banks scattered throughout the Greater Boston area. From its beginning Crescent National's management has continued to promote a policy of close personal contact with all its customers, both borrowers and lenders. In fact, one of the standing policies in force through the years, rigidly adhered to by the present chairman of the board, F. Blair Carson, and required of all branch managers, is that top management personally meet and welcome all new customers to the bank. Wherever possible the chairman or his executive vice president attempts to follow this same practice in the home office. This policy is, of course, admittedly difficult with the great growth in banking services and personnel.

F. Blair Carson has been in charge of the bank for more than 27 years. During this time he has followed the practice of following up each of the personal welcomes with a short, friendly letter of appreciation to the new customer, normally the next day. The branch managers send out the same letter to each of their new customers from their branches. At the present time this form letter is being used:

When the thank-you concept was first initiated, personal handwritten letters were sent. As the banking business expanded, original typewritten letters were sent. Mimeographed letters came into use when the volume increased to its present rate of 185 new customers daily (on the average, about 35 new customers at the main bank and 10 new customers from each of the 15 branch banks).

Carson's administrative assistant, Jon Edmunds, has been asked to look into ways of improving the present stencil-duplicated letter system which requires all branches to maintain stencil duplicators, when in fact this is their main use. Then, too, copy quality varies greatly from branch to branch, partially negating the good image that the letter is intended to create. His task involves finding answers to these questions:

1. How can an original-looking form letter best be prepared and at what relative cost?
2. What equipment, space, personnel training, and systems changes would such an installation require?
3. How could the insertions of the variable information be made in the form letters?
4. Where can information on applications of the equipment, initial cost, per-copy cost, maintenance expenses, etc., be obtained on a trustworthy basis?
5. How much time is required before such a new system can be installed and functioning satisfactorily?

■ After carefully examining literature available from manufacturers of office machines and equipment and consulting current office management periodicals and journals, provide answers to the above questions.

Case 9-2 Evaluating and Reorganizing the Mailing Center

The Cassidy Rubber Company of Toledo, Ohio, has just appointed you as office manager. The company maintains ten branch offices located in key cities throughout the United States. In Toledo the offices are arranged in more or less a functional plan with the following departments:

Sales Order	Records Management	Purchasing
Billing	Manufacturing	Office Services
Cashier	Accounting	Data Processing
Receiving	Correspondence	Executive offices, such as President, Vice President
Shipping	Credit	

In evaluating the present systems and procedures, the methods of handling the mail seem to require top priority. The present system of handling mail is described on the following page.

Incoming Mail. The mail is picked up at the main post office at 8:30 a.m. and 12:30 p.m. by Frank Duke, one of the sales correspondents. Duke takes care of the incoming mail since his trip from home in the morning and his return from lunch take him past the post office. The mail is quite heavy, often numbering 4,000 pieces a day. For example, this morning's mail brought the following 1,741 pieces:

100 communications from the branch offices
50 order cancellations
10 letters from salesmen requesting price reductions
300 checks and money orders in payment on account
30 applications for jobs
50 credit references
1 letter from the Internal Revenue Service
160 invoices for goods purchased
200 advertising circulars
470 orders from customers
80 C.O.D. requests
40 complaints for orders not yet delivered
20 complaints of errors in invoices
200 inquiries for price lists and catalogs
30 letters stating inability to ship goods ordered

When the mail reaches the office, Duke, assisted by the switchboard operator and a file clerk, sorts the mail into two sacks—personally addressed and addressed to the firm. The personally addressed mail is sorted and delivered unopened. The mail addressed to the firm is opened by a hand-operated opener at the rate of 100 pieces a minute. Whenever there is an enclosure in a letter, it is clipped to the covering letter. After all the letters have been opened, their contents are sorted. This sorting is completed by the use of deep oblong wire baskets, each of which is labeled for one department. When the sorting has been completed, the mail is distributed, which is usually not before 10:30 a.m. or 2:30 p.m.

Outgoing Mail. The daily outgoing mail averages between 1,100 and 1,200 pieces, not including the printed advertising circulars. The circulars, numbering from 20,000 to 30,000 pieces, are sent out regularly on January 2, April 1, July 1, and October 1. The daily outgoing mail typically consists of the following:

400 sales invoices
200 letters enclosing price lists and catalogs
100 letters to the branch offices
400 letters acknowledging orders, answering complaints, etc.

Stamped window envelopes are used for the sales invoices and stamped envelopes for the letters, except those addressed to the branch offices. The latter are sent in specially printed envelopes that require the individual affixing of stamps. There have been numerous complaints that letters do not have sufficient postage when they reach their destination, a situation which has been creating poor effects on the customers.

Each department sends its sealed, stamped letters to Frank Duke's office by 4:00 p.m. All outgoing mail is taken to the post office by Duke at 4:30 p.m. on his way home.

▪ After carefully considering the facts presented, prepare a report in which you:

a. Criticize the present methods of handling the incoming and the outgoing mail.
b. Present your suggested methods for reorganizing the mailing work, including comments on personnel, equipment, and mailing routines. Give your reasons for recommended changes in the routine and estimate the cost of the equipment that should be purchased. (Prices may be obtained from equipment catalogs.) Assume that two mail clerks will be employed at $80 a week and that a supervisor earning $160 a week will devote half her time to the mailing work. Set up a schedule for handling the mail under the reorganized plan.

10

Staffing the Office

In the preceding part of this book, the managerial functions of organizing and planning have been examined in their relationship to the efficient, economical, and accurate accomplishment of office work. In this part, the third function—leading—is discussed by centering attention upon these areas: staffing the office; supervising the office activities; human relations; personnel policies and practices; and training, orienting, and promoting office personnel. *Leading* is concerned with motivating and directing workers so that the objectives of the company will be successfully accomplished. In exercising the leadership function, administrative office managers place special emphasis on man, an average amount of emphasis on machines and methods, and only a minimum on materials. Leadership is present at all levels of the organization—from the president who stimulates, directs, and coordinates functions assigned to his line-and-staff officers, to the supervisor of the data center who meets departmental goals by coordinating and directing the efforts of workers who have no supervisory responsibilities.

The cost of hiring an office worker with medium skills is about $700 for each applicant. This cost includes recruiting, interviewing, testing, placing, orienting, training, and supervising the newly hired worker until he reaches a production level commensurate with his wages. Thus, every turnover in an office represents a loss of at least $700 at the rank-and-file level, and more than $1,200 for the highest skilled office workers to $1,325 for similarly qualified machine production personnel. To keep turnover at the lowest level is one of the objectives of sound administrative management. Turnover can be kept at a minimum by an efficient selection process, adequate preliminary training, and a salary that is commensurate with the skill required and the competitive market conditions. Some firms have a separate department to fulfill the personnel function of employee selection. In others, the office manager must act as personnel officer for the employees. In firms such as commercial banks, insurance companies, and stock brokerage firms whose workers are primarily office personnel, a separate department may be set up as part of the administrative management function.

Struggling with the serious problem of how to preserve profits in the face of continually rising personnel costs, the administrative office manager finds that staffing the office is a vital phase of his daily job. Not only must the workers be hired, but also every effort must be exercised to keep, to promote, and to encourage the workers in their jobs. Salary costs, at their highest levels in history and representing an ever-increasing percentage of the cost of products and services, have climbed steadily at an average of four percent each year during the past ten years.[1] Fringe benefit costs, now rising more than twice as fast as salaries, average $1,500 per worker each year. Another important element that contributes to increased staffing costs is the processing and maintaining of employee records. One management consulting firm places the cost of calculating and issuing a payroll check at 72 cents. Noticeable increases have been noted in the federal and state reporting requirements, equal opportunity compliance records, legally required insurance and compensation forms, performance analyses, and job evaluations. All of these present substantial charges against a firm's profits. Recruiting new personnel has likewise increased in cost, for the cost of newspaper help-wanted advertising alone has been rising at an average of 14 percent each year.

The problem of obtaining and keeping well-qualified employees for office positions involves a knowledge of the sources of supply, interviewing and testing, maintaining the personnel records required by business and government, and keeping abreast of governmental regulations that affect the selection process. Each of these topics is

[1] *Planned Staffing for Profit* (Milwaukee: Manpower, Inc., 1968), pp. 2 and 3.

discussed in this chapter. The training, orientation, and promotion of office personnel are discussed in Chapter 14.

SOURCES OF OFFICE WORKERS

The first phase of the selection process, which may continue at regular intervals in large offices, is to determine the best sources of employees, without conflicting with the fair employment practices and age discrimination laws. A 1969 national survey, conducted by The Bureau of National Affairs, Inc., found that for employees with college degrees the most successful recruiting sources used by all companies (large and small) are, in rank order: (1) interviews at colleges, (2) employment agencies, (3) newspaper advertisements, (4) professional journals, (5) in-house referrals, and (6) college placement offices.[2] The leading recruiting sources for noncollege-degree employees are: (1) walk-ins, (2) newspaper advertisements, (3) in-house referrals, (4) employment agencies, (5) requests to high schools, (6) high school career conferences, and (7) unions.[3] Economic conditions, the status of general business activity, and geographic factors affect the relative advantages of the various sources. The sources used in securing employees vary with different companies, and often it is best to make intelligent use of more than one source, depending upon the type of worker desired. A good administrative manager or employer is careful in his selection both of sources and of employees. Only through a thorough examination of candidates from carefully selected sources can an efficient employment policy be developed that will avoid the maladjustment of employees and the waste of time and money in hiring others.

The factors underlying the use of the following sources of office employees are: (1) economy of time on the part of the employer in interviewing a minimum number of candidates, (2) a prompt and reliable source of qualified workers, (3) reduction of labor turnover because of careful screening by a reliable source and subsequent elimination by interview, and (4) the creation of a staff that is cooperative and progressive.

Employment Agencies

In recruiting office personnel, many employers make use of employment agencies, both public and private, for these agencies are

---

[2] *Recruiting Practices,* Personnel Policies Forum Survey No. 86 (Washington, D.C.: The Bureau of National Affairs, Inc., March, 1969), p. 4.

[3] *Ibid.,* p. 10.

in a position to put an employer in contact with a selected number of prospective workers. It is an economical procedure, since it enables the firm to contact a small number of qualified workers rather than a large number of individuals whose qualifications are uncertain.

Public Employment Agencies. The largest public employment agency is the United States Training and Employment Service (USTES), which is supervised by the Department of Labor. Each state has its employment service, sometimes called an employment commission or an employment security agency, which is affiliated with USTES. The 3,800 USTES offices are located in every metropolitan area throughout the country. The full-time state employment offices are generally equipped to offer employers the following services:

1. Recruitment of workers in all occupations and for meeting employers' personnel needs resulting from attrition, expansion, and staffing of new plants, establishments, and offices.
2. Locating qualified workers—not available locally—through a nationwide interarea recruitment service that includes a professional placement network of about 120 selected offices.
3. Selecting the best qualified workers through the modern interviewing and testing techniques. Aptitude test batteries have been validated for more than 500 specific occupations.
4. Testing (including the use of the General Aptitude Test Battery) and counseling of youths in the fields of work for which their aptitudes and interests best fit them.
5. Giving guidance in resolving employment problems, such as turnover and absenteeism, in maintaining an adequate work force, and assisting in personnel planning by use of job analyses and related techniques.
6. Providing information on labor supply and demand on local, state, and national levels.
7. Initiating training courses—under the Manpower Development and Training Act and other training programs—to help in alleviating existing shortages of qualified workers and in meeting expected needs for additional trained workers.
8. Relating veterans' service training to civilian occupations.[4]

Private Employment Agencies. In competition with public employment agencies are approximately 9,000 privately owned

---

[4] Louis Levine, *How the Public Employment Service Helps Small Business,* Management Aids for Small Manufacturers, No. 41 (Washington, D.C.: Small Business Administration, August, 1964), p. 1.

employment agencies. Private agencies charge a fee, depending upon local or state law, which may range from a week's pay to ten percent of the employee's annual salary. In a national survey of 247 firms, it was discovered that 92 percent of the companies use employment agencies—private and state—when hiring office personnel. The study showed that private employment agencies are utilized to a greater extent than the state employment agencies. Of the companies indicating their use of both agencies, 92 stated that they placed 50 percent or more "hires" through private agencies; 82 firms stated that they placed 50 percent or less of their "hires" through private agencies.[5] Practice varies according to company policy and geographic location as to whether the private employment fee will be paid by the job applicant or by the employer. In the study cited above, it was found that in the selection of clerical workers, 34 percent of the companies paid the entire agency fee; 45 percent paid the entire fee for supervisory employees; 48 percent for executives employed; and 38 percent for data processing workers hired.[6] In another survey of 371 firms, it was found that 60 percent of the companies pay the employment agency fee. Of those paying the fee, 11 percent pay only part—usually half—of the fee.[7] The National Personnel Consultants reveal that on all positions paying in excess of $8,000 per year, the employers pay the employment agency fee, the interview expenses, and the relocation costs on 83 percent of the placements.[8]

In selecting a private employment agency, the administrative office manager should make sure that the agency is professionally qualified to do its job. Evidence that an agency subscribes to professional and ethical standards may be obtained by checking to see that the agency has membership in its state and national employment agency association. More about the agency's standing and reputation in the community may be obtained by checking with the better business bureau and the chamber of commerce.

Temporary Office Help Agencies. Temporary office help agencies "rent out" office workers for a day, a week, or two or three months. Theirs is a highly competitive field, consisting of about 400 firms, with ten dominating the field, each having 100 or more offices across

[5] "Survey: 92% of Firms Hire Through Agencies," *Administrative Management* (September, 1966), p. 62.

[6] *Ibid.*

[7] "60% of Surveyed Companies Pay Employment Agency Fee," *Administrative Management* (March, 1968), p. 68.

[8] A. H. Sautter, "How to Use Private Employment Agencies," *Personnel* (July, 1966), p. 20.

the country and abroad.[9] Use of temporary office personnel has effected significant savings for many firms and enabled them to maintain a lower labor budget without lowering their pay rates.

In utilizing the services of part-time workers, the employer seeking additional help commonly pays a flat fee to the temporary office help agency. The temporary employee is interviewed, trained, and paid by the agency. The employee's bonding, social security records, tax deductions, accident and sickness insurance, and vacation, if earned, are all obligations of the agency. The client-company realizes its savings in the areas of record-keeping costs, payroll taxes, workmen's compensation, vacation and sick time, and use of the employee only when needed. Because of the tremendous increase in the payment of fringe benefits, a company is often able to realize considerable savings by relying on temporary help services for its ordinary business situations—not just for emergencies such as peak-load periods. Such savings were reported by the management consulting firm of Stevenson, Jordan & Harrison of New York, who found, for example, that a statistical typist in a Cincinnati insurance company costs that firm $2.54 an hour, 49 cents an hour more than a temporary employee. In a Houston firm, a duplicating machine operator ordinarily receives $2.33 an hour, while the temporary firm bills the company only $1.96 for the same type of worker.[10]

Another type of temporary office service, called "Dictation-to-go," is provided by a manufacturer of business communications machines and equipment. The firm supplies transcription service from any type of dictating machine recording including tapes, belts, and discs. The dictated matter is picked up and delivered twice daily, transcribed letter perfect on the client's letterhead. Usually the transcribed dictation is delivered to the client within 24 hours after pickup, but faster deliveries can be arranged. Each secretary employed by the transcribing service undergoes extensive testing designed to measure skills in grammar, spelling, punctuation, and general reasoning ability. If the dictation is of a specialized nature, it is transcribed by someone who has had experience in that field. The client is billed

---

[9] For an interesting sketch of the development of temporary help agencies, see Irwin Ross, "For Rent: Secretaries, Salesmen, Physicists, & Human Guinea Pigs," *Fortune* (October, 1968), p. 164.

[10] Allen K. Trueman, "Temporaries Can Reduce Overhead," *Administrative Management* (August, 1964), pp. 36-41. This article presents several helpful hints for the proper use of temporary employees and lists those temporary personnel organizations that have offices in more than one state. For further details of the study cited, see "The Economics of Using a Temporary Help Service" by Stevenson, Jordan & Harrison, Management Consultants, Inc., 19 West 44th Street, New York, New York 10036.

on a cost-per-line or hourly basis. If desired, the service is also available on a contract basis for long-term assignment in the client's office.

The administrative office manager contemplating the use of temporary office help is advised to keep the following guidelines in mind:

1. Determine in advance the manhours needed for clerical workload in the department needing help and compare the costs of part-time help on the company's own payroll with that of using temporary help.
2. When ordering help from the agency, give a good job description for each position to be filled so that if, for example, a receptionist is needed, a secretary will not be requested.
3. Have the work ready prior to the arrival of the temporary helper by preplanning complete step-by-step job instructions.
4. Make sure the permanent workers understand in advance that the temporaries are being brought in for special needs only and not for completing the work of the permanent workers. Ask that the permanent workers be helpful and cooperative in whatever way possible.
5. Make sure that the office equipment is in good working order, supplies are on hand, and space is adequate for the temporaries' needs.
6. Appoint one person to meet the temporary worker, to introduce the worker to others in the department, and to orient the worker briefly to the locations of the lounge, the cafeteria, and the work station.
7. The person in charge of supervising the temporary worker should make sure that the temporary understands the step-by-step instruction sheet by reviewing its contents with the temporary.
8. If possible, employ the temporary helper a day in advance so that she can become familiar with the duties of the person she is to relieve. Company procedures—time for lunch, coffee breaks, handling of personal incoming and outgoing calls, etc.—should be reviewed.
9. If a temporary should not be producing satisfactorily, contact the agency and explain the situation. Usually a temporary can be released after the first four hours and the worker will be replaced by the agency.
10. By reviewing the overall performance of each job with the temporaries, ways may be discovered to do the job better and at less cost.

Advantages accrue to the persons who pass the extensive proficiency tests of the temporary office help agency and thus qualify for temporary employment. Ordinarily the temporary employee pays no employment fee to the agency, is able to enjoy diversified surroundings and fellow workers, and may accept work from the agency as the home schedule permits.

Advertising

Another source of supply is through advertisements. Before placing advertisements, a careful study should be made of the most profitable form of advertising to use and the most appropriate medium. The type of position to be filled and the local conditions will influence the selection, but a little experimentation will show which is the most satisfactory medium. Care must be exercised in placing advertisements for help wanted to make sure that the wording and the positioning of the advertisements do not run afoul of the fair employment practices laws, which are discussed later in this chapter.

One disadvantage of placing help-wanted advertisements in newspapers is that a large number of replies may be received, of which it is possible to interview only a few applicants. This method proves very suitable, however, for the firm that has a personnel department adequately staffed to interview, screen, and test applicants.

A source of employees, often aggressive ones, is the "Situations Wanted" columns of local papers. Persons seeking a position often advertise their talents and availability by listing their qualifications in these columns.

Friends of Employees, Customers, and Officers of the Firm

Very often a firm obtains satisfactory employees through the recommendation of present employees, customers, and company officers. Great care must be exercised in the use of in-house referrals, however. If a customer or an officer recommends a person who is not suitable or qualified for the job, it may cause the firm some embarrassment if the applicant is not hired or is not retained for any length of time. Some firms make a practice of having their present employees recommend friends as possible employees because of the psychological effect on the employee and his increased prestige in the office. Some firms offer incentives, such as a United States savings bond, for in-house referrals after the newly employed worker has been on the job for a stipulated period of time.

Schools, Colleges, and Their Placement Offices

Representatives of many large business firms come to school and college campuses to interview members of the graduating classes about possible employment after graduation. According to The Bureau of National Affairs survey cited earlier, 57 percent of the larger companies recruit noncollege employees by using high school career conferences, while only 17 percent of the smaller firms use this source.[11] For selecting potential employees with college degrees, interviewing on college campuses is the most popular recruiting method, with 88 percent of the larger companies and 58 percent of the smaller firms conducting recruiting drives.[12] If it is not possible to send representatives, a firm may write to the placement offices of the schools, describe the types of job openings available, and arrange for an interview with interested job applicants. There are both favorable and unfavorable factors in the use of this source. One firm, for example, would hire graduates from a certain college only, because the president of the firm was a graduate of that school. Executive prospects coming from one school tend to provide only one viewpoint on managerial problems. While this may supply harmony, it may also lead to stagnation. On the other hand, some firms wish to hire only inexperienced employees so that they may train them in methods peculiar to their work. For these firms, this source may prove helpful, especially if they are hiring for long-term employment.

Many private business schools maintain a placement service for their students, some of whom have had office experience. A number of high schools, junior colleges, community colleges, and universities cooperate with industry by setting up apprenticeship and cooperative work-study programs in which students attend school part time and work part time. Some companies sponsor a summer-hire program in which during the junior or senior year the student works for the company during the summer months. If the student's work proves satisfactory, he is asked to return the following summer at an appropriate salary increase. Such cooperative training programs develop many good trainees who later become full-time employees of the participating companies. According to John E. Steele, director of placement for Harvard Graduate School of Business Administration,

---

[11] *Recruiting Practices, op. cit.*, p. 1.
[12] *Ibid.*

"Co-op and summer programs are among the best devices for giving companies a known product for managerial purposes and arousing interest in business among college students."[13]

Other Sources of Office Employees

Additional recruiting sources used by firms include applicants who walk in from the street and apply for a position and applicants who have written unsolicited letters of application. Sometimes firms consult the placement bureaus established by trade associations, fraternal organizations, and institutions for the rehabilitation of physically and mentally handicapped persons. Many companies recruit persons about to leave the armed services by maintaining relations with employment agencies that specialize in the placement of veterans, while other firms may schedule interviews at separation centers or advertise in military publications. Some manufacturers of office machines and equipment have established training schools and placement agencies to supply their customers with well-trained, efficient operators of their equipment. One New York bank, faced with a great need for clerks, has conducted intensive recruiting efforts among Negroes and Puerto Ricans in low-income neighborhoods in Harlem, as well as in the Bronx and Brooklyn. Today these groups make up about 30 percent of the bank's 18,000 employees in this country.[14]

PROCEDURES FOR EMPLOYING OFFICE WORKERS

The employment procedure in small offices is quite simple compared with that in offices having large staffs of workers. In small offices an interview is usually all that is necessary, followed by a statement that within a few days the applicant will be informed if he has been successful. In this way no decision need be reached until a sufficient number of candidates has been interviewed. In larger offices, however, the procedure becomes more formal and perhaps more complicated, since the larger the office staff, the more necessary records become.

Federal, state, and local laws affecting the employment process have stimulated the need for more complete and detailed records of

---

[13] John Kobliska, "Attracting the College Graduate," *Administrative Management* (May, 1969), pp. 39-40.

[14] "Banking on Blacks, Chase Manhattan Recruits in the Ghetto, and Results Are Mixed," *The Wall Street Journal,* December 28, 1969, p. 1.

employees. For the medium-size office, the employment records should include, as a minimum, the application blank and the employment record. Where the organization has become so large as to require the special services of a personnel manager, the other forms discussed below will become necessary in order to establish a definite procedure and adequate control over the employment and discharge of workers.

The forms used in the offices of most large firms are:

1. Personnel requisition blank.
2. Application blank.
3. Record of interview.
4. Record of employment.
5. Payroll change record.

The large amount of clerical work involved in handling all these forms would be justified only in a very large organization. These employment records can be adapted to smaller offices by eliminating all but the basic forms—the application record and the employment record—which, in turn, may be consolidated.

Personnel Requisition Blank

To many people, the application blank is probably the first office employment record of any importance. Its use in large offices, however, is sometimes preceded by the personnel requisition blank prepared by a department head. The form specifies the number of persons required and the kind of work to be done. If the office has prepared job specifications, they are studied in order to obtain specific information concerning the job requirements. This is preliminary to any search for a job applicant. If a list of suitable applicants is kept on file, reference is made to this list so that persons may be notified to call for an interview. If no such list is kept, the sources previously mentioned are consulted.

Application Blank

The second and probably the most frequently used form is the application blank, such as that shown in Figure 10-1. The information called for on an application blank is usually grouped under the headings of personal information, education, business experience, references, and general remarks. In designing their application

THE PROCTER & GAMBLE COMPANIES

PERSONAL DATA SHEET

PERSONAL

(PRINT) LAST NAME | FIRST NAME | MIDDLE NAME | TODAY'S DATE

PRESENT ADDRESS | NO. | STREET | CITY | STATE | ZIP CODE | TELEPHONE AREA CODE & NUMBER

PERMANENT ADDRESS | NO. | STREET | CITY | STATE | ZIP CODE | TELEPHONE AREA CODE & NUMBER

SEX | HEIGHT | WEIGHT | SOCIAL SECURITY NO.

MARITAL STATUS: SINGLE -------- MARRIED -------- ENGAGED -------- SEPARATED ------- DIVORCED -------- WIDOWED ---------- | NO. OF CHILDREN | TOTAL DEPENDENTS (INCLUDE SELF)

LIST ANY PHYSICAL DEFECTS OR HEALTH PROBLEMS

OCCUPATIONS OF BROTHERS, SISTERS | OCCUPATION OF WIFE OR HUSBAND

FATHER'S POSITION OR OCCUPATION IS ☐ WAS ☐ | POSITION | EMPLOYER

CAREER

IN WHAT DEPARTMENT(s) OR TYPE(s) OF WORK ARE YOU INTERESTED?

DO YOU HAVE ANY RESTRICTIONS AS TO LOCATION? | DATE AVAILABLE FOR EMPLOYMENT

EDUCATION

TYPE OF SCHOOL	NAME OF SCHOOL AND LOCATION	MAJOR FIELD OF STUDY	DATES ATTENDED		YEARS COM-PLETED	DEGREE (INCL. MO. & YR. GRANTED OR EX-PECTED)	APPROX. SIZE OF GRAD. CLASS	STANDING IN GRAD. CLASS (TOP 10%, 25%, 50% OR LOWER 50%)	SCHOLASTIC STANDING	
			FROM	TO					GRADE AVERAGE	OUT OF POSSIBLE
HIGH SCHOOL						X			X	X
COLLEGE OR UNIVER-SITY										
GRADUATE OR OTHER FORMAL EDUCATION										

PERCENT OF COLLEGE EXPENSES EARNED? (EXCLUDE GOV'T AID) | APPROXIMATE NO. OF HOURS PER WEEK WORKED DURING SCHOOL YEAR?

ACTIVITIES

LIST SCHOLASTIC HONORS AND ACTIVITIES, WITH OFFICES HELD, FOR EACH SCHOOL ATTENDED*

SCHOLASTIC HONORS (INCLUDING SCHOLARSHIPS AND HONORARY SOCIETIES):

ACTIVITIES -- OTHER THAN ATHLETICS (PUBLICATIONS, CLASS ORGANIZATIONS, OFFICES, CLUBS, ETC.)*:

ATHLETIC ACTIVITIES (UNDERLINE VARSITY SPORTS):

HOBBIES AND OUTSIDE INTERESTS (INCLUDING CIVIC ACTIVITIES)*:

* EXCLUDE THOSE WHICH WOULD DISCLOSE RACE, COLOR, CREED OR NATIONAL ORIGIN.

The Procter & Gamble Companies

Fig. 10-1

Application Blank (page 1)

blanks, employers must be very careful not to ask questions that may become the basis for charges of discrimination under the fair employment practices regulations. In some states there are departments of labor that examine application blanks to make sure they are prepared within the meaning of the law.

WORK EXPERIENCE

GIVE INFORMATION REGARDING PRESENT AND FORMER EMPLOYMENT.
INDICATE (X) WHETHER POSITION WAS FULL TIME, PART TIME, OR SUMMER EMPLOYMENT.
IF ON COMMISSION. ESTIMATE AVERAGE EARNINGS ON A MONTHLY SALARY BASIS.

NAME AND ADDRESS OF EMPLOYER	DATES	FULL	PART	SUM	NATURE OF YOUR WORK	MONTHLY SALARY	REASON FOR LEAVING
PRESENT OR LAST POSITION	FROM					AT EMPLOYMENT	
	TO					AT LEAVING	
SECOND LAST	FROM					AT EMPLOYMENT	
	TO					AT LEAVING	
THIRD LAST	FROM					AT EMPLOYMENT	
	TO					AT LEAVING	
FOURTH LAST	FROM					AT EMPLOYMENT	
	TO					AT LEAVING	

U.S. MILITARY SERVICE

ACTIVE MILITARY SERVICE
☐ COMPLETED
☐ PRESENTLY SERVING
ANTICIPATING:
☐ NONE
☐ 6 MO'S STARTING ___ 19___
☐ ___ YR'S STARTING ___ 19___

ACTIVE DUTY	PERIOD OF SERVICE ___ 19 ___ TO ___ 19 ___	BRANCH OF SERVICE	HIGHEST RANK	TYPE OF SEPARATION ☐ HONORABLE ☐ MEDICAL ☐ OTHER ☐ RELEASE TO INACTIVE DUTY

DESCRIBE PRINCIPAL DUTIES PERFORMED WHILE IN SERVICE

PRESENT SELECTIVE SERVICE CLASSIFICATION ___

RESERVE STATUS — DO YOU OR WILL YOU ATTEND MEETINGS AND/OR SUMMER CAMP? BRANCH OF SERVICE? WHEN COMPLETED? 19___

GENERAL INFORMATION

INDICATE CHANNEL OF APPLICATION — COLLEGE PLACEMENT OFFICE: ☐ ON CAMPUS INTERVIEW ☐ OTHER — VOLUNTARY: ☐ LETTER ☐ PERSONAL VISIT — ☐ EMPLOYMENT AGENCY (SPECIFY) ___ ☐ ADVERTISEMENT (SPECIFY) ___ ☐ OTHER (SPECIFY) ___

HAVE YOU PREVIOUSLY APPLIED TO ☐, OR BEEN EMPLOYED BY ☐, THIS COMPANY? WHERE? WHICH DEPARTMENT? WHEN?

NAME FRIENDS OR RELATIVES EMPLOYED BY THIS COMPANY — WHERE EMPLOYED?

APPROXIMATE MONTHLY SALARY REQUIREMENTS

PLEASE GIVE US ANY FURTHER INFORMATION WHICH MAY BE HELPFUL TO US IN CONSIDERING YOUR QUALIFICATIONS AND INTERESTS

SIGNATURE OF APPLICANT

PLEASE LEAVE BLANK

G 5018-B 10/63 SPW PRINTED IN U. S. A.

Fig. 10-1

Application Blank (page 2)

A company may extend the usefulness of its traditional application blank by including a battery of attitude-probing questions, among which some of the questions might be:

Why do you believe you would be a successful (. . . . . .)?
What do you like best (least) about this (previous) job?

What is your philosophy of work?
What do you like most about yourself?
What special or personal fact should the company know about you? [15]

An analysis by the interviewer of a series of unstructured questions such as those listed above should aid in revealing some personal attitudes before the interview commences and will be helpful in the interview and later in both placement and appraisal procedures.

Careful use of application blanks permits a preliminary screening of unqualified candidates for the position, thus saving the time of interviewers. Should the applicant be accepted, the application blank may be used as a permanent employment record. Sometimes the application blank is combined with the history of employment record.

The Interview and the Record of Interview

As a result of studying the application blank or the personal data sheet of a job applicant, it is possible for the interviewer to select specific areas that he wishes to explore more fully or to clarify during the interview. The interviewer should be on guard against arriving at immediate conclusions regarding the personality, intelligence, skills, and abilities of the job applicant. In many instances, especially during the early phases of the interview, the job applicant may not show himself at his best nor show the true kind of face-to-face impact he ordinarily makes. Possibly, only after the interview has been under way for several minutes and rapport has been built, does the applicant commence to loosen up and reveal some of his hidden feelings. Thus, the interviewer should try to remain as objective as he can and resist drawing conclusions about the applicant until the interview is well under way and plenty of evidence is available to substantiate the interviewer's feelings.

During the interview the personal appearance of the individual can be evaluated and related to the job opening and to any dress codes that the firm may have established. Some interviewers note that young applicants weaken their chances for employment when the female applicant appears wearing a miniskirt or the male applicant

[15] For an interesting study in the expanded use of the application blank at the Bulova Watch Company by means of including attitudinal survey questions, see Robert Hershey, "The Application Form," *Personnel* (January-February, 1971), pp. 36-39.

is wearing long hair and "mod" clothing. In many firms dress codes are flexible in relation to the job and the extent to which the job holder meets the public. For example, one insurance company prohibits any of its male employees from wearing beards if they meet and work with the public in the course of their workday. However, in departments such as data processing and accounting, beards are acceptable.

In the process of arriving at an opinion—positive or negative—regarding the suitability of the applicant for the job at hand, the interviewer should strive to preserve the applicant's sense of dignity and self-respect. At the close of the interview, the applicant should be able to leave with a positive feeling toward the company and its position in the community. In some instances, especially where more responsible positions are being filled, it may be advisable to schedule a second interview in order to check on impressions gained during the first meeting and to insure that the applicant still displays interest in the position. During the second interview, senior members of the firm may be called upon to interview the applicant to make sure that he is truly qualified for the position.

In eliciting information from the job applicant that relates to his education, training, and experience, there are several types of interviews, or approaches, that may be employed. Four of these types are briefly described below.

The Direct Interview. In this traditional interviewing technique, the job applicant is asked direct questions related to his qualifications and ability to fill the job. The direct interview can be completed relatively quickly since a concise answer is required for each specific question. However, use of this method limits the amount of information that can ordinarily be obtained. For this reason, the direct method is most commonly used when screening applicants for jobs of a fairly low level. In using this technique, the interviewer must be careful in wording his direct questions, for oftentimes he will learn no more than a specific answer to the question asked, or in his question, he will reveal the answer desired. Little opportunity is provided in this method for the applicant to reveal his innermost feelings, especially when he arrives at the interview well prepared to offer stock answers to stock questions.

The Indirect Interview. The indirect, or unstructured, interview rests upon the premise that more can be learned about an applicant by stimulating him to talk about himself than by asking him direct questions. By listening and being patient, the interviewer can learn much as the applicant elaborates on important points, such as why he left his former job. During this time the interviewer has an excellent opportunity to determine how well the applicant demonstrates his qualifications and to observe the self-expression of the applicant, along with other factors such as his manners, poise, and dress. The indirect interview is time consuming and requires an able interviewer who can keep the applicant from rambling too far away from the subject at hand.

The Patterned Interview. The patterned interview is also known as the guided, standardized, or structured interview. A printed form or questionnaire, containing specific key questions, is used by the interviewer as he asks questions and writes down the applicant's answers, either during or immediately after the interview. This technique is especially effective when many people are being screened to fill a number of jobs, usually at a lower level. Time is saved by obtaining the same type of information from all applicants. Also, more than one interviewer may be used at the same time, with the evaluations being compared and reviewed by a senior executive such as the personnel director.

The Stress Interview. The stress, or probing, interview, mainly used by the military and other governmental services, is carried on by one or more persons who fire questions at the applicant to keep him continuously on the defensive. The objective is to find the applicant's breaking point and to determine how much pressure he can take. Even in the hands of skilled interviewers, this technique is a highly controversial one, especially when relating its use to business and industry. If not properly handled, the interviewing situation may damage the employer from a public relations point of view, and, of course, ruin the ego of a very sensitive applicant.

Record of Interview. The record of interview contains in an organized form all the information that is acquired during the interview. The form aids the interviewer in remembering all factors and in making a thorough analysis of his final recommendations regarding the applicant's employment. If the personal interview has been favorable and there seems to be a possibility of early employment, a subsequent interview may result in further use of the interview record. This brief checkup of the personal characteristics of the applicant is then used in conjunction with the application blank in making a final decision. It should not be assumed, however, that the employment manager, office manager, or interviewer makes the final selection in any but a small number of cases. Usually the interviewer makes a preliminary selection from among all those who apply, but leaves the final selection to the executive in whose department the vacancy exists.

References of Applicants

Generally, many managers do not place too much confidence in references or letters of recommendation. First, if the person named as a reference were not favorable, his name would not have been given by the applicant. Second, most people hesitate to write unfavorable letters of recommendation. If information is requested from the references that are listed on the application blank, oftentimes the letters may not be answered. If answered, the letters are often vague, noncommittal, or incredibly glowing.

For those positions in which the employees must be bonded, an insurance company will make as thorough an investigation as possible and use formal inquiry blanks for this purpose. Some large public accounting firms use a printed inquiry blank for checking references. Although this is a routine matter, even for some large offices, many firms feel that it should be done, if only for its psychological effect. The following questions, taken from a widely used inquiry form, illustrate the nature of questions that may be asked of the reference:

1. Do you consider this person qualified for the kind of employment mentioned on the first page of this folder? If not, please indicate the line of his best talents and answer the remaining questions in the light of your recommendations.
2. a. How long have you known him?
   b. How well and in what connection?
3. a. If he has ever been employed by you or been under your supervision, please give details regarding the various duties he performed and the quality of his work.
   b. Would you reemploy him? If not, will you please give your reasons?
   c. Other remarks:
4. a. In what particular phases of his work has he shown extraordinary ability?
   b. In what particular phase, if any, has he shown weakness?

5. What is your opinion of his judgment and of the keenness and clearness of his thinking?
6. What is your opinion of his personal integrity and general character?
7. Does he suffer from any physical or other handicap that might impair his efficiency?
8. Is his personality normal, well balanced, and adaptable?
9. a. To what extent can he direct the work of others?
   b. Does he require close supervision?
10. a. Is he likely to get along well with those who supervise his work and those whose work he supervises?
    b. If not, what traits may produce serious friction?
11. a. To what extent and in what way would his wife and family be an asset or a liability?
    b. Has he demonstrated loyalty to present and former employers?

The questions above are rather comprehensive and may require more effort than the average reference may care to give. They should not necessarily be used as a model, but rather as a guide. Best results are usually obtained by using questions that require brief answers or simply a check mark, as shown in Figure 10-2.

When checking local references, the telephone may be effectively used if the interviewer is careful to establish a good state of rapport with the reference and to ask carefully phrased questions. In the conversation, the interviewer should strive to follow up on every hint or clue, or else he runs the risk of accepting biased information. Although long-distance calls may be expensive, they are an excellent means of checking references when time is of the essence and thorough information is essential.

In many communities there are reporting agencies, generally known as credit associations, that record such information as dates of employment, salaries earned, and civic offices held. Although these agencies are utilized primarily to provide credit ratings to businessmen, they can be used by the hiring firm to obtain factual, objective information about a prospective employee and to perform special field investigations. Under the Fair Credit Reporting Act of 1971, however, the employer is required to tell an applicant when a retail credit investigation is being made and whether the credit check is the result of the firm's rejection of the applicant.

Fig. 10-2

CONFIDENTIAL INQUIRY

The following person has given your name as a reference in his application to us for a position of employment. We would appreciate your reply to the questions below, for which a stamped, addressed envelope is enclosed.

Are you related to the person named above? Yes ☐ No ☐ If so, how? ________

How long have you known this person? ________

Have you ever employed or supervised the above person? Yes ☐ No ☐

Dates of such employment________ Give title of last position ________

Was he a supervisory employee? Yes ☐ No ☐

Reason for leaving ________

If discharged or forced to resign, was he notified as to the reason? Yes ☐ No ☐

To your knowledge, has he ever been discharged or forced to resign from any other position? Yes ☐ No ☐

If so, please give the name of the employer who discharged him ________
Reason for discharge ________

What is your estimate of this person's ability as to the following:

	EXCELLENT	GOOD	FAIR	POOR
Honesty				
Reliability				
General conduct				

On the basis of your knowledge, would you recommend him for a position with our firm? Yes ☐ No ☐

Signed________ ________ ________
NAME DATE POSITION

Form for Checking References of Applicant

Record of Employment

The record of employment consists of a brief personal status and a history of the applicant's employment. In addition to providing personal data and other information usually found on the application blank, this record may provide space for recording such information as progress of the employee, his attendance, and his promotions and salary increases. In some firms the employment records are kept in visible-card files so that signal devices may be used to indicate taxable status and other information.

Payroll Change Record

The payroll change record is used to notify the payroll department of a change in the employee's pay status because of transfer, increase in salary, leave of absence, or termination of employment. In large offices a separate employee transfer form may be used when an employee is transferred from one department to another so that all cost records reflect the correct data. In some businesses a separate change in payroll rate form is used to notify the payroll department of a change in pay status so that the rate increase is put into effect at the proper time and all records reflect the new rate. In most states employers are not required to file a termination of employment report unless the worker whose employment is terminated is not entitled to unemployment benefits. In a few states, however, a termination report is required whenever a worker leaves his place of employment. Along with the termination report, some businesses issue a form when an employee is released for any reason. The purpose of this report is to provide a written record for interested persons such as the personnel or employment department, the payroll department, and the employee.

THE USE OF TESTS IN SELECTING WORKERS

In a survey conducted by the Harvard School of Business, more than 50 percent of the companies that replied indicated that they were then using testing in the selection of personnel.[16] The increased use of tests in the selection of office workers has made employee selection for office positions more scientific and more reliable. The president of one large testing service states that testing gives "valuable insights into the intellectual and emotional resources of job candidates," but conceded that "it is a mistake to make decisions purely on the basis of test scores."[17] Some feel that testing discriminates against the person from a minority or a culturally deprived background. Many experts in favor of testing say that special norms can be developed on any test for every distinctive group likely to take an exam so that intercomparisons and intracomparisons could be made.[18] Others maintain that if tests are designed to predict the success of individuals in the broader scheme of the organization,

---

[16] M. J. Bevans, "To Test or Not to Test?" *Administrative Management* (May, 1969), p. 30.

[17] Reported in *The Wall Street Journal,* February 9, 1965, p. 1.

[18] Bevans, *op. cit.,* p. 28.

then it should be assumed that tests are doing their job if they actually do discriminate.

Among the charges leveled at tests are: (1) many existing tests do not adequately evaluate the capabilities of members of disadvantaged groups, and the disadvantaged may score poorly because of anxiety about the testing situation and because of low motivation; (2) most tests, especially verbal measures, emphasize middle-class concepts and information and are thus unfair to those who have not been exposed to such cultural influences; (3) test scores do not have the same meaning for the disadvantaged as they do for the advantaged; test scores of the disadvantaged, it is held, should be compared only with test scores of others similarly disadvantaged; (4) test items are often not related to the work required on the job for which the applicant is being considered.[19]

In meeting these criticisms, the following suggestions have been offered: [20]

1. Allay test anxiety by permitting an examinee who has failed to come back for one or more retests.
2. Reduce the role of the live examiner in the testing situation by using recorded directions to administer the actual tests, with both the reading of directions and the timing included on the tape or record.
3. Develop tests in which many of the terms are based on "culture-laden" experiences that are assumed to be quite common in the population.[21]
4. Investigate the use of bonuses to compensate the disadvantaged for the effects of deprivation they have experienced.
5. Establish separate norms so that test scores of the disadvantaged are compared only with scores of others similarly disadvantaged.
6. Make sure that test scores are appropriately used in job placement, keeping in mind, however, that tests which seem unrelated to immediate jobs may be useful in identifying those who can advance to higher levels at a later date.

---

[19] Jerome E. Doppelt and George K. Bennett, "Testing Job Applicants from Disadvantaged Groups," Test Service Bulletin No. 57 (New York: The Psychological Corporation, May, 1967), p. 2.

[20] *Ibid.*, pp. 3-5.

[21] See the description of *Fundamental Achievement Series* test on page 309. Also, Walter V. Clarke Associates of New York has developed a test known as the Activity Vector Analysis that will match applicants to jobs without respect to their race. To use the Analysis, it is first necessary to rate the job to learn what factors are essential for best performance. For more details about the Analysis, see "As We See It," *The Office* (July, 1969), p. 146.

The use of tests in selecting office workers is based upon two principles:

1. There is need for some unbiased, objective basis for selecting, placing, and promoting office employees.
2. The use of tests is not an exclusive device, but is *supplemental* to the use of judgment obtained through the interview and the application blank.

The increased use of tests seems to indicate that the larger offices use testing programs as part of the improvement of their personnel relations programs. Qualified employees can be selected, thus reducing the loss due to errors in office work, labor turnover, and unhappy and misplaced employees. Better promotional policies can be established by using a more scientific basis, with the greatest number of qualified employees.

Before a testing program can be installed properly, management must be sure that the program can be used successfully. The following conditions seem to indicate when a valid and reliable testing program can be used:

1. A firm either has in its employ or must hire a large number of persons doing similar work for which there are more applicants than positions.
2. An excessive turnover of office workers is traceable to inefficient hiring practices.
3. There is evidence of inefficient work as the result of low aptitude, training, or interest.

Whether the testing program should be part of the personnel administrator's activities or should be handled by a professional organization of industrial psychologists depends upon the number of workers that must be hired from time to time. The cost of tests and the trained personnel that must administer and interpret the tests is more than some firms wish to spend.

A test that is to be used in selecting individuals should have a high degree of *reliability*; that is, the test should measure consistently whatever it measures. The information that is published about a test should describe its reliability. Also, a test should be *valid*, in that it can be shown to serve the purpose for which it was intended. For example, the validity of an employment test rests on whether a score on the test predicts a level of performance on the job. If the test predicts performance, the test is valid. If the test does not predict performance, the test is not valid. The six commonly recognized steps in validating a battery of tests are:

1. Study the job.
2. Analyze the characteristics needed for success.
3. Determine which of these characteristics can be recognized by tests; then select or develop the tests required.
4. Administer the tests to job applicants and hire without reference to tests, and/or give the tests to a group of "good" and "poor" employees to determine test validity.
5. Determine the extent to which test results are related to job performance.
6. Test the results over a period of time.[22]

A test that has been used by one company successfully in predicting success for a certain job need not necessarily work elsewhere, even though the job designations may be similar. Jobs may seem the same, but often they are different in subtle but important and measurable ways. Furthermore, what constitutes job success is likely to vary from company to company. Too, many managers feel that a serious drawback to testing is the difficulty in validly predicting performance in jobs requiring abilities that are difficult to define and therefore to test.

Tests Used in Selecting Office Workers

Once a firm has decided to use a testing program for selecting or promoting its employees, the next question confronting the office administrator is: What tests should be used in this program?

The nearly 5,000 different personnel tests may be classified as:

1. *Intelligence* tests, which measure mental and reasoning ability to the extent that the one tested is able and willing to demonstrate it through the medium of a particular test. In present-day society, intelligence and educational achievement (which itself depends heavily on intelligence) tests are used to eliminate many candidates from consideration before they arrive at the employment office.[23]

---

[22] "Uses and Abuses of Psychological Testing," *Automation* (October, 1969), p. 10.

[23] Richard S. Barrett, "Guide to Using Psychological Tests," *Personnel Management Series,* reprints from *Harvard Business Review* (September-October, 1963), p. 27.

2. *Aptitude* and *ability* tests, which attempt to predict the measure of success for applicants with little or no experience for the job and for whom a firm may have to make long and costly investments in training and experience should the applicant be hired.
3. *Achievement* tests, which attempt to measure the degree of proficiency in a given type of work, whether this has been obtained in jobs with other firms or with the present firm, in anticipation of promotion.
4. *Personality, interest,* and *attitude* inventories, which measure personality traits.

Large organizations may develop their own tests or have them designed by a consulting firm of professional testers. In most cases small companies purchase ready-made tests from one or more of hundreds of test publishers in the United States.[24]

Test experts are not agreed upon what the tests should indicate. Some professional testers maintain that a battery of tests is necessary in order to test the variety of abilities required for a specific job; others feel that every job can be analyzed into certain basic requisites which can be discovered by a single test. Thus, many offices experiment with a number of the standardized tests on the market and supplement these by tests of their own creation, until experience has shown the testing practices and procedures to be valid and reliable.

Some of the employment tests used by business firms are briefly described below.

Intelligence Tests

1. *Alpha Examination, Modified Form 9*—revision of original Army Alpha; eight tests that yield subscores for numerical and verbal ability, in addition to a total score.
2. *Army General Classification Test (first civilian edition)*—a measure of general learning ability, including verbal comprehension, quantitative reasoning, and spatial perception; designed to classify the overall mental abilities of employees and applicants for selection and placement, or for their assignment to training programs.

[24] An invaluable aid in the selection of tests is Buros' *Mental Measurements Yearbook* series, which presents a listing of tests, critical evaluation of the tests, and a directory of test publishers. The *Yearbook* series may be obtained from The Gryphon Press, Highland Park, New Jersey, and from many public libraries.

3. *Otis Quick-Scoring Mental Ability Tests* and *Otis Employment Tests*—a special printing of the former without the words "Mental Ability" or reference to schools on the cover, for business and industrial use.
4. *SRA (Science Research Associates) Adaptability Tests*—consists of 35 items arranged in ascending order of difficulty to yield a single measure of mental ability.
5. *Thurstone Mental Alertness Test*—a general measure of learning ability of candidate; a verbal score gives an indication of ability to reason; a numerical score indicates the candidate's understanding of quantitative relationships and his ability to work under pressure.
6. *Wesman Personnel Classification Test*—a mental ability test that yields separate scores for verbal and numerical ability; used in the selection of employees for clerical, sales, supervisory, and managerial positions.
7. *Wonderlic Personnel Test*—designed to measure learning ability; most questions involve knowledge of words and use of reasoning in solving arithmetic problems; used with candidates for clerical, sales, and supervisory positions.
8. *Fundamental Achievement Series*—a set of two employment tests (verbal and numerical) covering the ability range from basic literacy to somewhat above the eighth-grade level; designed to give the disadvantaged a fair break, to assist in proper job placement, and to help define the kind and level of needed supplementary education; questions are based on experiences assumed to be familiar to both the disadvantaged and the advantaged.

Aptitude and Ability Tests

1. *Computer Programmer Aptitude Battery*—five subtests in verbal meaning, number approximation, letter series, reasoning, and diagramming; designed to evaluate experienced personnel or to select trainees for beginning or advanced courses.
2. *General Clerical Test*—provides three subscores to indicate abilities important in office work: clerical speed and accuracy; numerical ability; and verbal facility; entire test may be given when applicants are being considered for variety of jobs, or specific sections may be used for stenographic applicants, routine clericals, payroll clerks, etc.
3. *Minnesota Clerical Test*—measures speed and accuracy in matching 200 pairs of numbers and matching 200 pairs of

names; used largely to select clerks and other types of employees whose work requires quick perception and quick recording of numbers, letters, names, and symbols.

4. *Short Employment Tests (SET)*—integrated battery of three five-minute tests designed to produce scores that experience has shown to be most effective predictors of satisfactory performance in office work.
5. *SRA Clerical Aptitudes Test*—for checking on applicants for general office work; test measures applicant's office vocabulary and gives some idea of his skill in office arithmetic and of his ability to understand work problems and to check and discern details quickly.
6. *SRA Typing Adaptability Test*—provides a measure of the ability to type special materials such as edited manuscripts, forms, tables, and addresses in block form.
7. *Survey of Working Speed and Accuracy Test*—helpful in selection of personnel for various kinds of office positions; useful in routine clerical positions involving number checking, code translation, finger dexterity, and counting.
8. *How Supervise?*—useful in training or upgrading candidates for supervisory positions, in evaluating the results of supervisory training programs, and in counseling supervisors; test deals with problems of supervision and human relations common to most business organizations and has three sections: Supervisor Practices, Company Policies, and Supervisor Opinions.

Achievement Tests

1. *Seashore-Bennett Stenographic Proficiency Test*—five business letters without technical words make up test; two letters are short and slow; two are medium in length and average in speed; one is long and rapid. The test is available in two formats: one 33⅓ rpm LP record or two tape recordings.
2. *SRA Typing Skills Test*—for checking on typing skills; measures speed and accuracy of typing from straight copy and differentiates between the careless but rapid typist and the accurate but slow typist.
3. *Typing Test for Business*—to help appraise an applicant's skill in any or all of the several kinds of typing needed in business; in less than 10 minutes the test can be used as a screening test to separate good, fast typists from slow, inaccurate candidates; in 45 minutes, the test provides a thorough assessment of the five kinds of typing skill commonly required of professional typists.

Personality, Interest, and Attitude Inventories

1. *Bell Adjustment Inventory (Adult form)*—aids in discovering the extent and sources of personal maladjustment in five areas: home, health, social, emotional, and occupational.
2. *Kuder Preference Record*—measures interests in activities related to specific jobs; recommended for use in selecting, placing, or promoting to a specific position.
3. *Strong Vocational Interest Blanks*—an inventory of interests and preferences designed to aid in predicting chances of success and satisfaction in a variety of occupations.
4. *Thurstone Temperament Schedule*—measures seven personality traits: active, vigorous, impulsive, dominant, stable, sociable, and reflective; to be used in appraising and selecting job applicants.
5. *Thurstone Interest Schedule*—a paired-comparison checklist in which subject expresses his preference or liking for each of 100 pairs of vocations or job names; schedule yields a profile of preferences for occupations in ten fields: physical science, biological science, computational, business, executive, persuasive, linguistic, humanitarian, artistic, and musical.

Trends in Employment Testing

Many large companies have experimented with testing programs for office workers because they feel that such programs will reduce costs. Many of these firms find that they must use tests in selecting sales and industrial employees, so they expand their programs to include office workers. The larger the number of employees concerned, the more elaborate and costly the testing program may be.

To indicate the nature and the popularity of employment tests being used, the following summary of a survey undertaken by the Administrative Management Society is given.[25] Although only 88 companies responded to the survey, it is felt by the Society that this number represents a fairly good sample of those firms using tests in the selection of their employees.

Very few companies reported that they test prospective employees for their general interest, and the testing of temperament and personality is relatively rare in business. Two observers, studying the validity of personality measures in personnel selection, concluded that ". . . taken as a whole, there is no generalizable evidence that personality measures can be recommended as good or practical tools

[25] For more details of this survey of employment testing, see the AMS Report, *Administrative Management* (July, 1965), pp. 44-45.

for employment selection."[26] Doctor Joseph Tiffin, a well-known industrial psychologist and highly regarded in the field of psychological testing, has said that:

> More often than not, the use of personality "tests" in an employment department is not only a waste of time but borders on being a dangerous practice. Many studies have shown that anyone who can read can fake these "tests" to make himself appear to be just the kind of person the company is seeking. Using personality "tests" thus often results in employing the wrong men and in passing up the more promising candidates.[27]

Barrett offers another indictment of personality tests: "There have been a few scattered successes with some modern techniques, but on the whole the typical personality questionnaire, test, or inventory has not proved to be useful."[28]

In the area of skills testing, as evidenced by the AMS survey, about 75 percent of the firms surveyed reported that they use typewriting tests. Over half of those companies giving typewriting and shorthand tests reported the use of their own tests.

In the selection of employees from high school graduating classes, the Wonderlic test was found to be the most popular, with 40 companies reporting its use. In the selection of college graduates and in the testing of professional employees, the Wonderlic test was also found to be most commonly used.

In its study of 384 manufacturing companies, the National Industrial Conference Board found that the kinds of tests shown in Table 10-1 are given to white-collar employees, to blue-collar employees, and to both white-collar and blue-collar employees.[29]

This study shows that of all types of tests given white-collar employees, the clerical ability or aptitude test is by far the most popular, with approximately three fourths of the companies reporting its use. Approximately 17 percent of the companies surveyed made use of interest tests. These findings appear to parallel those of the Administrative Management Society, cited earlier.

In the National Industrial Conference Board study, it was found that of those companies with one or more tests used, 65 percent used

---

[26] Robert M. Guion and Richard F. Gottier, "Validity of Personality Measures in Personnel Selection," *Personnel Psychology,* Vol. XVIII, No. 2 (1965).

[27] With permission of Everett M. Christensen, Personnel Director, Farmers and Mechanics Savings Bank of Minneapolis, from an unpublished manuscript.

[28] Barrett, *loc. cit.*

[29] "Personnel Practices in Factory and Office: Manufacturing," Personnel Policy Study No. 194, National Industrial Conference Board, 1964, p. 14.

Table 10-1

TESTING PROGRAMS IN MANUFACTURING

Type of Test	No. of Companies	White Collar Only	Blue Collar Only	Both White and Blue Collar
Clerical ability or aptitude	357	290	5	62
Intelligence	283	90	17	176
Personality	148	79	5	64
Interest	117	64	7	46
Mechanical ability or aptitude	295	34	157	104

commercially available tests for both white-collar and blue-collar employees. A company employee with training in psychology was found to be in charge of the testing program in more than one half of the firms surveyed. Outside testing services were called upon in only 15 percent of the cases.

GOVERNMENT REGULATIONS AFFECTING THE SELECTION OF OFFICE WORKERS

With the passage of federal legislation requiring that management eliminate racial and age discrimination from all aspects of employment, a brand new era in labor relations has emerged. To comply with the pertinent laws and the requirements of his business, today's administrative manager must be thoroughly conversant with federal, state, and local regulations in order to solve his problems of fair employment and those affecting wages earned, hours worked, and minimum age requirements.

Civil Rights Act of 1964

For the first time, in 1964, a national policy of fair employment practices was expressed by law. Nearly half of the pages contained in the Civil Rights Act of 1964 affect the administrative manager and his responsibility for staffing the office. Although the act contains sections dealing with voting rights; prohibition of discrimination on the basis of race, color, religion, or national origin in hotels, restaurants, and certain other facilities; and the creation of new federal agencies; the present discussion is concerned with Title VII, known as "Equal Employment Opportunity." This section of the act, affecting the hiring practices not only of business firms but also of unions and employment agencies, defines certain actions (or inactions) as unlawful employment practices. For the purposes of the Civil Rights Act, an employer is defined as a person engaged in an industry that affects commerce and having 25 or more workers for each working day in each of 20 or more weeks in the current or preceding calendar year.

If an employer fails or refuses to hire a person because of his race, color, religion, national origin, or sex, the action is looked upon as an unlawful employment practice. It is unlawful for an employer to discharge any individual "or otherwise to discriminate against any individual with respect to his compensation, terms, conditions, or privileges of employment" because of that person's race, color, religion, nationality, or sex. Further, an employer is prohibited from limiting, segregating, or classifying employees for the reasons given above if doing so "would deprive or tend to deprive any individual of employment opportunities, or otherwise adversely affect his status as an employee."

Separate provisions bar similar discriminatory practices by employment agencies and labor organizations. Both employers and unions, or joint labor-management committees, are prohibited from discriminating, on the bases mentioned above, against an individual in apprenticeship or training programs, including on-the-job training.

Employers are still permitted, however, to hire and train persons on the basis of their religion, sex, or national origin when these are bona fide occupational qualifications necessary to the normal operation of the business. Employers may not place help-wanted advertisements that specify any preference, limitation, specification, or discrimination based on sex unless sex is a bona fide occupational qualification. This provision has been interpreted to mean not only that the content of classified ads must be free of such preferences but also that the placement of ads in separate male and female columns, when sex is not an occupational qualification for the advertised job, is in violation of Title VII. Employers may legally refuse to employ members of the Communist Party or Communist-front organizations. If the hiring firm is subject to the government security program, it may refuse employment to or may discharge any worker who does not fulfill the security requirements of the position.

Employers may continue to apply different standards of compensation or different terms and conditions of employment, provided such differences are not the result of an intention to discriminate on account of race, color, religion, national origin, or sex. Thus, an employer may set his hiring and work standards as high as he pleases, but he may not enforce them in a discriminatory manner among racial groups. Concerning the use of tests, employers may administer and act upon the results of any professionally developed ability test, provided the test is not designed or used to discriminate. A "professionally developed ability test" is interpreted to mean a test that fairly measures the knowledge or skills required or which fairly affords the employer a chance to measure the applicant's ability to perform. Regardless of how neutral an employment test may appear on the surface, the Supreme Court has ruled out employment tests and practices that have the effect of discriminating against Negroes.[30] The court declared that employers must be prepared to demonstrate that the tests and testing practices are directly related to the jobs involved and are applied without regard to race.

Under the act, an Equal Employment Opportunity Commission (EEOC) was created to help enforce the law. The EEOC, consisting of five members appointed by the President, can advise, consult, and assist, but is unable to start suit. Enforcement of the law differs as to whether the alleged unlawful employment practice occurs in a state having or not having a fair employment practice statute. Over half the states have passed fair employment practices laws that are characterized by varying degrees of enforcement powers. In some states court orders and criminal penalties are used to enforce the prohibitions against race or religious bias. Normally charges must be filed by individuals, although a member of EEOC can file charges if he has reasonable cause to believe that the law was violated. Also, the Attorney General can sue for a restraining order or injunction if he discerns a pattern or practice of resistance to the full enjoyment of rights under the act.

If the court finds that an employer has *intentionally* engaged in an unlawful employment practice, it can enjoin the employer from engaging in it further, and order "affirmative action" such as hiring back the aggrieved party with or without back pay. If the employer fails to comply with the court order, he risks contempt-of-court proceedings. The employer may, of course, appeal the decision.

Age Discrimination in Employment Act of 1967

The purpose of the Age Discrimination in Employment Act, as declared by Congress, is to promote the employment of older persons

---

[30] "Supreme Court Bars Employment Tests that Result in Anti-Negro Discrimination," *The Wall Street Journal,* March 9, 1971, p. 4.

based on ability rather than age, to prohibit arbitrary age discrimination in employment, and to help employers and workers find ways of meeting problems arising from the impact of age on employment. The law prohibits age discrimination by employers, employment agencies, and labor unions (that are engaged in an industry affecting interstate commerce) against those individuals who are between the ages of 40 and 65 years. No protection is extended directly to individuals outside these age limits. An employer is defined similarly under both the Age Discrimination Act and the Civil Rights Act.

Under the law, employers are forbidden to fail or refuse to hire, or to discharge, any individual, or to otherwise discriminate against any individual with respect to his compensation, terms, conditions, or privileges of employment because the individual's age lies within the specified range of 40 to 65 years. Employers are also barred from using age as a basis for limiting, segregating, or classifying an employee in any way that deprives or tends to deprive him of employment opportunities, or otherwise adversely affects his status as an employee. The law is enforced in accordance with the powers, remedies, and procedures provided in the Fair Labor Standards Act, which provides for enforcement through suits by individual employees, collective actions by employees, and wage collection suits and injunction suits by the Secretary of Labor.

Since the age discrimination law imposes retention requirements for many personnel records not heretofore required, the administrative office manager should be familiar with the specific record-keeping requirements of the law.[31] For example, a covered firm must create and maintain the following records for at least two years: job descriptions, occupational qualifications, collective bargaining agreements, details concerning such employee benefit or pension plans, insurance programs, retirement benefits, help-wanted ads, and job orders and requisitions.

In many cities a concerted drive is being made to find jobs for those over 40 who are unable to obtain work, primarily because of their age. The usual reasons given for not hiring older workers show that they are too slow, too set in their ways, less creative than younger workers, more difficult to train, more prone to absenteeism, and not in so good a physical condition as younger workers. With the exception of the last reason, which is applicable only to heavy physical work, the reasons are mostly myths.

---

[31] Joseph L. Kish, Jr., "Records Required for 40-65 Workers," *The Office* (December, 1969), p. 30.

Usefulness is not determined by age. The National Association of Manufacturers surveyed more than three million workers and found that 93 percent of the older workers were equal or superior to the younger workers. A survey by the University of Illinois revealed that absenteeism and tardiness were less among the older employees; their loyalty, sense of responsibility, and morale were higher; and they were less prone to accidents. In a study by the Department of Labor in which the job performance of production employees in 26 plants was analyzed, it was disclosed that the difference in output between various age groups was very small. Similar results were obtained in another study of office employees in five government agencies and 21 private companies.[32] Both studies found that, on the average, a large proportion of the older employees exceeded the performance of the younger workers; those between the ages of 55 and 64 were more consistent in their work performances and attitudes than younger employees; and the older employees tended to be absent from work less than younger employees.

In spite of these findings and the fact that it is now illegal to discriminate because of age, a syndicated columnist observes:

> A disproportionate 20 percent of the nation's unemployed and a disgraceful 40 percent of our long-term unemployed (27 weeks or more) are aged 45 or over. By one estimate, one in four private job openings is now closed to a worker if he is over 45, and one half of these job openings are not open to those over 55.[33]

The preceding comments prove rather strongly that many businesses are failing to make use of the reservoir of talent available through the hiring of older workers. Many older persons find themselves in a position to take seasonal and part-time work, and the administrative manager should avail himself of this labor supply in filling those jobs not requiring the services of full-time employees.

Very often a firm is reluctant to hire older workers because of the effect upon its company pension plan and the increase in other costs. However, many pension plans can be modified and adapted to the hiring of older men and women. True, the costs of providing insurance and benefits increase when a man over 35 is hired. However, one insurance expert states that premiums for group life

---

[32] Allen K. Trueman, "Hiring Older Employees," *Administrative Management* (February, 1965), p. 14.

[33] As quoted by Sylvia Porter in "The Older Employee—A Neglected Manpower Resource," *Personnel* (January-February, 1969), p. 32.

insurance and medical coverage are likely to be higher for a group of 25-year-old workers than for a group of 45-year-olds, since the rates of insurance firms are based upon the claims experience of different age brackets. Although life insurance rates increase with age, the heavy maternity benefits paid many young workers cause their medical claims to rise above those of workers in their midforties. It is estimated that for a group of workers 55 years old, premium costs for life insurance and medical coverage run 20 percent or so above those for a work force of 25-year-olds.[34]

The problem of hiring older workers is one of how the increased costs may be removed or absorbed by the employer, for this country cannot afford to discard unemployed enthusiasm and energy merely because they happen to be possessed by a worker over 40 years of age.

Wages and Hours

The wages to be paid and the hours to be worked by newly employed persons and those presently employed are regulated under federal law by a number of statutes. Those having broadest application to the administrative manager are the Fair Labor Standards Act and the Walsh-Healey Act. The former, commonly known as the Federal Wage-Hour Law, applies to employment in private industry; the latter imposes additional regulations for employers who are government contractors. Under the Equal Pay Act of 1963, an amendment to the Fair Labor Standards Act, an employer is forbidden to discriminate solely on the basis of sex in the wage rates of men and women doing equal work under similar working conditions. States have clearly defined laws regarding the employment of minors, and the Federal Wage-Hour Law imposes similar restrictions on the employment of minors under 18 years of age. These regulations, and others affecting the compensation practices of office managers, are described further in Chapter 20, "Office Salary Administration."

EMPLOYING THE DISADVANTAGED

Virtually every major company in the country is involved or has plans to become involved in training and employing the disadvantaged, often with financial assistance from the government under

[34] Condensed from *The Wall Street Journal,* January 7, 1963, and reported in *Management Review* (February, 1963), p. 43.

both the Manpower Development and Training Act and the Economic Opportunities Act. In the BNA survey on recruiting practices, it was found that 69 percent of the large firms (more than 1,000 employees) conduct programs to recruit disadvantaged persons; 27 percent of the smaller firms (less than 1,000 employees) have such programs.[35] A few other companies, although they have no formal program, indicated interest in hiring the disadvantaged. Many of the companies with programs for the disadvantaged recruit their workers by contacting the offices of the United States Training and Employment Service, while others contact various federal, state, and local government agencies. Some of the firms surveyed have programs that participate in the National Alliance of Businessmen's efforts to hire and train the hard-core unemployed. Of the firms taking part in the survey, 66 percent indicated that their programs to recruit disadvantaged persons have been successful.[36] Those who have had unsuccessful experiences with the programs mentioned the following reasons for their lack of success: the hard-core unemployed are usually not conveniently located to the jobs; few of the unemployed are willing to relocate to the areas wherein labor is needed; those that do relocate to areas of labor shortage soon tire of the hard work and leave to return to their home areas.

Another study, conducted several months later by the American Society for Personnel Administration and The Bureau of National Affairs, concentrated upon the hiring of disadvantaged persons by over 200 companies representing a cross-section of business by size, industry, and location. This survey indicated that 86 percent of the companies make a special effort to recruit the disadvantaged.[37] Most of the firms use the United States Training and Employment Service as the main recruiting source, followed by agencies such as NAACP, CORE, and Urban League. In selecting the workers, about one half use written achievement or intelligence tests; 25 percent use written psychological tests; and 35 percent administer work sample tests.[38] Seventy percent of those firms that used written psychological, achievement, or intelligence tests validate the test results against job performance, with the firm's own personnel research unit doing the validation in most cases. Eighty percent of the firms give special orientation programs before a disadvantaged or minority employee begins work.[39] About three fourths of the firms conduct orientation

[35] *Recruiting Practices, op. cit.*, p. 13.
[36] *Ibid.*, p. 14.
[37] "Hiring the Disadvantaged," *The Office* (December, 1969), p. 24.
[38] *Ibid.*, p. 26.
[39] *Ibid.*, p. 28.

or sensitivity training sessions for the supervisors involved, and many make a special effort to assign the disadvantaged workers to "sympathetic" supervisors. Of the firms surveyed, 70 percent feel that the time, expense, and effort involved in hiring the disadvantaged are worthwhile. In over half of the firms, the turnover rate among the disadvantaged is above average; 35 percent report that the turnover rate is average.[40] The following problems attached to the employment of disadvantaged persons were mentioned: stereotyped views held by coworkers and supervisors of minority group and individual abilities; resentment by other workers of a presumed "special treatment" of the disadvantaged persons hired; inexperience of staff managers in recruiting, selecting, and instructing disadvantaged workers; reluctance of hard-core workers to bid for new jobs and training; the formation of cliques; and exaggerated fears regarding the reactions of workers and customers to minority group personnel.[41]

Some guidelines to be considered by the administrative office manager for implementing a program of employing and retaining the disadvantaged include:

1. Supervisors and other management levels must be sold on the program so that they see it is to their direct benefit to bring the new workers into the labor force. They, in turn, should be trained in selling other workers on the importance of the program.
2. Supervisors should be taught to be patient and understanding, but not paternalistic, for the newly hired workers have outlooks and cultural experiences different from those of the supervisors. The supervisors should be encouraged to view matters as the disadvantaged do and to tailor their approaches accordingly by taking a genuine interest in the worker as a person. Sufficient incentive should be provided to the supervisory staff to motivate them toward successful training and retention of the workers, for one of the major problems is keeping the worker on the job once he has been trained.
3. During the training and indoctrination period, a gradual introduction to the work station should be provided, making allowances for temporarily poorer performance and accepting different standards of efficiency within a department so that the talents within the group will be balanced. The training and orientation program may have to be modified so that less dependence is placed on traditional instructional methods such

---

[40] *Ibid.*, p. 30.
[41] *Ibid.*

as self-study from highly technical procedures manuals. The training should be simplified with more use being made of visual aids such as slides and filmstrips. Much repetition, but with variation in presenting the same ideas, is needed.

4. Through extensive counseling, the newly employed must be made to understand all company rules and routines and the reasons therefor. Rules, especially those pertaining to absence, tardiness, rest periods, safety, and discipline, should be enforced firmly and fairly.
5. Supervisors should strive to develop the worker's pride in himself as a good workman and insist on a high level of performance that will be recognized and rewarded concretely.

The training of minority groups and other disadvantaged persons is discussed in further detail in Chapter 14.

QUESTIONS FOR REVIEW

1. What services do public employment agencies offer the employer who is recruiting office personnel?

2. What steps should the administrative office manager take to make sure he is selecting a private employment agency that is professionally qualified?

3. In what ways does the use of temporary office help effect significant savings for employers?

4. Briefly describe the main types of employment forms used in the offices of large firms.

5. What are the advantages and disadvantages of using the direct interview when compared with the indirect interview?

6. Why do many managers place little confidence in references or in letters of recommendation?

7. Cite several charges that have been leveled against employment tests and for each indicate by what means these charges may be alleviated or overcome.

8. What two basic principles should guide the administrative manager in using tests as an aid in selecting office workers?

9. A test that has proven to be reliable and valid when used in Company A will be equally effective when used in Company B. Evaluate the validity of this statement.

10. Explain the procedure followed in validating an employment test.

11. Into what four classes may personnel tests be grouped? How do these four types of tests rank in their use as a means of selecting white-collar workers?

12. What provisions contained in the Civil Rights Act of 1964 have most relevance for the administrative manager?
13. For what reasons was the Age Discrimination in Employment Act of 1967 enacted?
14. Most of the reasons for not hiring older workers are, in reality, myths. What evidence can you cite to support this statement?
15. What are some of the most pressing problems facing the administrative office manager who is hiring disadvantaged persons?

QUESTIONS FOR DISCUSSION

1. In selecting a supervisor of the office services department, in what order of importance would you rank the use of the following tests: aptitude, psychological, and intelligence? Would your answer differ if you were selecting a legal secretary? If so, how?
2. On some application blanks there is an essay-type question that often begins, "I would like to work for this company because. . . ." What does the job applicant's answer to this question tell the office administrator in charge of employment?
3. What are the benefits or the dangers in trying to match a job applicant to a predetermined company image?
4. Some companies prefer to hire only inexperienced office workers so that they may train them in how the work is to be done in their organization. Do you think this is a good approach to staffing an office?
5. Doris and Julia bid for two job openings in the Huston Company that always had been filled by men. With seniority as well as the law on their side, the girls got the jobs; and during the 30-day probationary period, they performed well. Shortly thereafter, however, their production began to fall off, and after three months their output was only 45 percent of the established standard. Thus, the girls were demoted.

   Doris and Julia have come to you with comments such as: "It is unfair. Those jobs were just a little too much for us. You should simplify the jobs a little so we can keep up with the men. We need a little more help and a little more time to meet the standard." What would your reply be to the girls?
6. In staffing their offices, some firms encourage in-house referrals (recommendations of their present employees). What are some possible objections to this source of job applicants?
7. Some companies have every applicant for a job fill out an application blank, even though he is obviously not fitted for the position. Why is this done?

8. The main office of the Western National Bank, located in San Francisco, has an annual turnover of 600 office workers. As office manager of this bank, discuss in the order of preference the sources you would use in obtaining replacement employees. Would your sources be different if the main office were located in a small community of 35,000?

9. Your firm has just created a new order processing clerical section that will process incoming order information as part of the new computer installation. Along with the other supervisors working in the area of information services, you have decided that all present workers who wish to work in the new section shall have to pass a standard clerical aptitude test. Ted Keel, one of the old-timers who has worked with you for years, has come to your office this morning with the following grievance: "Along with four other old-timers, I feel that taking such a test is unfair. We want to work in this new section and we have been with the company long enough for you to know how well we perform. Also, since all of us are older, we know we shall not do as well in the tests as the younger workers." Would you waive the tests in the case of Ted and the other old-timers? Explain.

10. Two years ago you employed Dick Jarvis, a 38-year old veteran, as a junior accountant. On his application blank, Jarvis indicated that he was a college graduate, with a minor in accounting. Jarvis has been an outstanding worker, and you have prided yourself on having selected him from among several well-qualified applicants. Two days ago, as part of a security clearance check, you find that Jarvis shaved five years off his age when he applied and that he was never graduated from any college. For two days his lying has been gnawing away at you; in spite of his exceptional performance, it is his lying that grates on you and you are seriously considering his dismissal. Explore the pro's and con's of retaining Jarvis and anticipate the decision you shall make.

11. Gladys Downs, in applying for a secretarial position with a chemical firm, was instructed on the application form: "Complete this form in your natural handwriting; DO NOT PRINT." In filling out the form, however, she paid no particular attention to these instructions and proceeded to print neatly the answers to all questions. Her application was rejected for "graphological reasons." Gladys exploded in front of the personnel manager: "This is not fair at all! I can take shorthand at 100 words a minute and type 90 words a minute. I feel I have a pleasing personality and dress very well. Why should I be turned down because I don't cross my t's to suit you?" As the personnel manager for this firm which relies heavily upon handwriting analysis in its personnel selection, how would you explain the rejection of Gladys's application?

PRACTICAL OFFICE CASES

Case 10-1 Discriminating in Departmental Transfers

Prior to the passage of the Civil Rights Act, it was the policy of the Romo Company to employ minority group workers solely for menial jobs such as sweepers, maintenance men, and messengers. Following passage of the act, however, the company abandoned its discriminatory practices and recruited Negroes for good jobs with better pay. Such changes in company attitude were readily noted by Bill Horn, a Negro who had been with the company for over ten years as a messenger in the mailroom. Via the grapevine one day Horn learned that a vacancy would soon exist for the job of duplicating machine operator. Immediately Horn contacted the personnel manager, Hank Boyle, and placed his bid for the job opening to guarantee that he would be among the first applicants interviewed.

Boyle was impressed with Horn's qualifications at the time of the interview. It was discovered that Horn had already learned just about all there was to the job of duplicating machine operator, for he often served as "fill-in" when emergencies arose. Horn was hired on the spot at a salary higher than he was receiving in the mailroom and transferred to the new department—the reproduction department. A few weeks later, Horn came into Boyle's office with the following question: "While I was in the mailroom for more than ten years, I had more seniority than almost anyone else there. Since I am now in a new department, I still have that ten years' seniority, don't I?"

Boyle replied, "No, Bill, you no longer have your seniority, for it is our policy for each department to have its own seniority roster. Thus, when you transferred out of the mailroom, you lost your seniority. Now you will have to start at the bottom of the ladder in the reproduction department."

Horn, taken aback, retorted: "You know that all those years I was in the mailroom I could have handled the duplicator and have been in the repro department. But because of the color bar, I was stuck on the job as messenger. Now, since I am starting as a newcomer in repro, I may be the first one fired if work slows up. You mean when I accepted this transfer, I lost all my seniority?"

Boyle agreed, "Yes, that's right—company policy, you know. I wish I could help you, Bill, but . . ."

After telling his story to the civil rights organization to which he belonged, Horn found that the group would hire a lawyer to bring suit against Romo and force the company to restore Horn's seniority. The group's lawyer maintained in court that Horn would have been in the reproduction department for years if it had not been for the company's discriminatory practices. In conclusion, the lawyer stated that the only fair thing for the company to do would be to grant Horn equivalent seniority.

■ As a representative of the Romo Company, answer the following questions:

1. What arguments can you advance in defense of your firm's practice of not transferring a worker's seniority when that worker is transferred from one department to another?
2. In view of current civil rights legislation, how would you expect the lawsuit to be decided?

Case 10-2 Installing a Testing Program

The Midwest Insurance Company employs an office staff of 3,000. The annual turnover for this firm is about 650, or 21⅔ percent, which seems rather high. It has occurred to you that economies would result if job applicants were screened more carefully by means of a testing program.

■ Prepare a report in which you discuss the following topics with reference to the development of such a testing program:

1. Research work that you, as office manager, would undertake in order to have a reasonable basis on which to install a testing program.
2. The extent to which intelligence tests should be used.
3. The types of other tests to be used.
4. The content of the aptitude and the achievement tests for each of the following positions: (See page 577 for a description of these job titles.)

   (a) Mail Clerk-File Clerk
   (b) Accounting Clerk A
   (c) Typist-Clerk
   (d) Key-Punch Operator B
   (e) Stenographer
   (f) Telephone Switchboard Operator
   (g) Programmer A

Case 10-3 Developing an Interview Routine

As administrative manager, you are responsible for staffing the office of the Paschall Farm Implement Company, a firm that has been in business for more than 50 years. Many of the employees, fortunate enough to be selected for work with this firm, find sufficient opportunities for advancement to enable them to stay with the firm during their lifetime. To be sure that each applicant is given a complete and fair interview, you have been trying to develop a planned routine to follow in each instance.

■ If you were interviewing a key-punch operator, discuss how you would proceed with each of the following phases of the interview:

1. Opening questions that you would pose.
2. Key questions to which you would expect answers.
3. Coverage of these subjects:
   (a) Experience.
   (b) Health.
   (c) Education.
   (d) Interests and hobbies.
   (e) Financial problems.
4. During the interview, when you would use:
   (a) An application blank.
   (b) Tests and what kind.

11

Effective Supervision of Office Activities

Lawrence A. Appley, former president of the American Management Association, observed that, "The function of *supervision* is to close the gaps between desired performance and actual human performance. If the mere issuance of policies and instructions would induce people to do what they are supposed to do, supervision would not be necessary." [1] Administrative office management concerns itself to a large extent with supervision, which includes the planning and organizing of work. Supervision also involves control—securing actual performance that approximates, as closely as possible, desired performance. Planning includes setting up the best methods to produce an acceptable quality of office work in a standard quantity so that production may be measured in terms of these criteria. Maintaining such standards, with due consideration of the human relationships existing in office work and supervision, should make it possible to reduce the cost of production.

The practical aspects of management involve the performance of a certain job by the one *best method* and by the one *best person* in order to accomplish the *best results*. A trained executive and supervisor is therefore needed to assure the accomplishment of these three

[1] Arnold E. Keller, "L. A. Appley—America's Mr. Management," *Business Automation* (January, 1969), p. 41.

aspects of carrying out a job. The supervisor attempts to effect these best results through the media of careful planning and scheduling, and through effective leadership arising from cooperation; for, wherever more than one person is involved in any job, the best results can be obtained only by the utmost cooperation.

DUTIES OF THE SUPERVISOR

In the small office, an office manager directs all the office work. As the office work expands, a centralized transcription department may be developed under a trained supervisor. Further expansion may necessitate supervisors for a centralized filing department, a centralized correspondence department, a mailing department, and a personnel department. Whatever the organization or the number of supervisors, the jobs of supervision are essentially the same. The jobs require dealing with human beings—superiors, associates, and subordinates—in developing and carrying out the plans of office work, in establishing systems and procedures and improving them wherever possible, and in measuring the quality and quantity of work.

The jobs of the office manager and his assistants are usually not on the top-management level. If the office is large enough, the office manager often is on the middle management level, with his assistants on a subordinate level. However, in all of these supervisory positions, there is a certain amount of responsibility. This responsibility has direction; that is, there is responsibility *upward* to higher management, *parallel* to supervisors of equal rank, and *downward* to subordinates. There are also *coordinating* or *interrelating* responsibilities for the work to be done, and *self-development* responsibilities as the supervisor prepares for growth and promotion in the business organization.

An analysis of the supervisor's duties and responsibilities is given below and on the next two pages under appropriate headings. The list is not complete and in certain groups the duties tend to overlap.

Supervisor's Responsibilities to Others in the Business Organization:

A. Upward responsibilities to higher management:

1. Ascertain and carry out what management wants done.
2. Keep superiors informed of what his department is doing. Pass on ideas for improvements.
3. Accept full responsibility for the work in the department without "passing the buck."

4. Refer matters requiring superior's attention promptly; do not bother superiors unnecessarily.
5. Interpret the employees' needs to management, and vice versa.
6. Maintain contacts at executive level with dignity and appropriate diplomacy.

B. Parallel responsibilities to supervisors of equal rank:

1. Cooperate with associates in the same manner that he expects his employees to cooperate with each other.
2. Help coordinate the work of his department with that of others for the good of the firm.
3. Permit interchange and promotion of good workers.
4. Accept full responsibility for work in his department.
5. Try to understand problems of colleagues.

C. Downward responsibilities to subordinates:

1. Aid in selection of new employees.
2. Help new workers get started correctly.
3. Train subordinates to assume greater responsibilities.
4. Assist each employee to know what to do, how to do it, and check the results.
5. Evaluate employees periodically and recommend promotions, transfers, dismissals, and salary adjustments.
6. Commend, encourage, and give credit for work well done.
7. Delegate authority and responsibility in order to develop understudies.
8. Develop harmony, cooperation, and teamwork.
9. Build and maintain employee morale, handling grievances promptly and fairly.
10. Maintain discipline, control absenteeism, and develop punctuality.
11. Take a personal interest in employees without partiality.
12. Use such supervisory characteristics as courtesy, tact, leadership, and consideration of employees as human beings.

Supervisor's Responsibilities in Relation to Office Work:

1. Plan the systems and procedures for each job.
2. Distribute the work fairly.
3. Coordinate the work of different units if this is necessary.
4. See that the work is done correctly, efficiently, and on time.
5. Maintain the quantity and quality of the work to be done by setting standards.

6. Anticipate difficulties and peak loads in the work.
7. Study, develop, and use new methods, equipment, and systems to reduce costs.
8. Train and develop a number of understudies and substitutes so that the absences, overloads, and other interferences with the flow of work may be handled efficiently.

Supervisor's Responsibilities for Self-Development:

1. Constantly analyze and attempt to improve personality traits such as self-control, careful analytical ability, personal appearance, confidence of subordinates and others, initiative, punctuality, courtesy, leadership, and fair play.
2. Thoroughly master all the work in his department and attempt to reduce costs.
3. Study the organization and personnel of the entire firm to develop the maximum of departmental cooperation, train understudies for his job, and study the requirements for the next supervisory job in the line of promotion.
4. Assume membership and active participation in professional organizations.
5. Study up-to-date books, magazines, bulletins, and other literature that will aid in improving the work in his present and future positions.
6. Where possible, continue his formal education in those areas that will aid him in his daily work.

THE SUPERVISOR'S PLACE IN OFFICE ORGANIZATIONS

The type of managerial organization in a business determines somewhat the place of the supervisor. In a line organization, as shown in Figure 3-2, page 66, the duties of the supervisor are limited. All plans, decisions, and methods are mapped out by the head of the firm. In a one-man concern of limited size, such an arrangement may be satisfactory. In a larger firm its use is almost prohibitive because of the mental and physical limitations of one individual.

The functional type of business organization stresses individual expert ability, with little or no control from the head of the organization. A supervisor has control of the activities in which he is most expert, as shown in Figure 3-3, page 68. As the office grows in size, it becomes necessary to add specialists in areas such as employment, payroll, training, health and welfare, and employee counseling. With the increased number of independent specialists, however, there is an overlapping of authority and an absence of fixed lines of responsibility. Because of all its disadvantages, as pointed out in Chapter 3, the purely functional form of organization is seldom found in business offices.

In a line-and-staff organization, the office manager may supervise the head of the records management department, the director of correspondence, and those in charge of other office services. The office manager assumes the chief executive or the line position, and the assistants in charge of the different office services become his staff. In the line-and-staff organization chart illustrated in Figure 3-4, page 69, the controller is at the line position of intermediate management, with a staff consisting of an internal auditor, a systems and methods engineer, a personnel director, a budget director, and the head of the reports department. Reporting directly to the controller is the assistant controller, at the supervisory level, who in turn directs the work of employees in the areas of general accounting, sales accounting, factory accounting, and office services.

In some businesses the managerial organization may function on a committee basis, with a chairman elected by each committee. In the committee form of organization, the supervisors of the different office services work together as a group in planning and executing the office work. This type of organization presumably tends toward the utmost cooperation among supervisors in matters affecting the work of the office in general.

HUMAN RELATIONS IN SUPERVISION

No longer does a person become a supervisor because he is the best worker and because he knows intimately the workings of his department. The supervisor today must use the human approach. He must be a specialist in dealing with human beings, in addition to being familiar with the technical aspects of his job. In dealing with human beings, the supervisor is continually being tested as to his genuine value as an executive. Determining the work to be done and how to do it is the easiest task of supervision since it deals with the objective phase of the work. Most important, however, is the human phase of supervision. Herein lies the secret of motivating and leading employees to perform the maximum quantity of quality work, and to have them happy and satisfied while so doing.

The successful supervisor must possess certain personal qualities if he is to command that respect and loyalty from workers which insure the maximum efficiency in a department. Foremost among these attributes, perhaps, is the ability to treat subordinates as human beings, to be one of the employees without losing the dignity of his executive position. He cannot be too intimate because with intimacy often comes leniency, and with leniency comes the loss of respect and confidence. Yet, aloofness and a policy of strict discipline are equally poor; the supervisor commands obedience at the cost of cooperation. Between these extremes lies an attitude, a personality, that makes a supervisor a leader rather than a boss; this is the attitude that wins the utmost cooperation.

Impartiality, open-mindedness, and fairness are required of the supervisor in dealing with the everyday problems that at times threaten to disrupt the efficient functioning of the department. He must be ready and willing to see both sides of problems and to solve them fairly and reasonably so that no bitter resentment remains in those against whom the decision goes. He must be available for advice when approached by subordinates, and he must be patient and understanding in dealing with their individual and personal problems. Finally, a good supervisor will keep all promises and "stick up" for cooperative workers in his dealings with other departments and with top management.

Personal Characteristics of Supervisors

The Research Committee of the Knoxville Chapter of the Administrative Management Society made a survey of the favorable and unfavorable characteristics of supervisors, with the intention of using it for improving employee-management relations. The results of this survey indicated the following characteristics:

What I Like about My Supervisor

1. He controls his temper.
2. He has a good sense of humor.
3. He is a leader rather than a driver.
4. He treats me as a human being and is interested in my welfare.
5. He does all that he can to assure my health and safety on the job.
6. He is straightforward, honest, and loyal to me.
7. He doesn't ask nosy questions about my private life.
8. He gives me credit for work done.
9. He permits me to use my initiative as much as possible.
10. He is sincere and objective in appraising my work and never criticizes my intentions but only my methods.

11. He doesn't ask me to do things that he would not do.
12. He doesn't play favorites and is fair in dealing with subordinates.
13. He hears both sides before passing judgment or making a decision.
14. He has the courage to admit his errors of decision.
15. He asks my opinion on matters that affect my work and keeps me informed of policies and plans.
16. He makes clear delegations of authority commensurate with responsibility.
17. He gives definite and clear instructions.
18. He is competent in his job, having adequate experience and professional knowledge.

What I Don't Like about My Supervisor

1. He is unkempt and lacks the common social graces.
2. He does not have sufficient professional knowledge to meet the requirements of his job.
3. He gives arbitrary orders without explaining reasons.
4. He uses threats rather than persuasion.
5. He is afraid of criticism.
6. He expects me to be a "yes-man" even as he is to his superior.
7. He does not back up his subordinates.
8. He straddles the fence and gives ambiguous answers.
9. He is "so big" that I have to make an appointment to see him.
10. He bawls me out before others.
11. He asks personal favors of me.
12. He snoops.
13. He takes special privileges.
14. He reprimands all the employees for what one employee does or does not do.
15. He never talks to me about my work or interests.
16. He thinks comfortable working conditions are an unnecessary pampering of employees.

A Human Relations Checklist for Supervisors

It is the job of the supervisor to create the enthusiasm and desire to work and this is best accomplished by treating workers as human beings, not automations. These humanizing incentives help to create this desire: steady work, good hours, comfortable working conditions, good pay, congenial working companions, opportunity for advancement, opportunity to use own ideas, and opportunity to learn the job.

A firm of personnel development specialists has published a human relations checklist to enable management men and supervisors to make a self-analysis of their understanding of the human relations involved in supervision, and the creation of a "desire to work" on the part of employees. This checklist and scoring device is given in Figure 11-1.

In addition to possessing desirable personal qualities, the supervisor must see that certain psychological conditions as well as material satisfactions exist in his department. Several of these conditions and satisfactions are discussed below; others will be treated throughout the later chapters of this section of the book.

Delegating

Delegation has been defined as:

> . . . the process of establishing and maintaining effective working arrangements between a manager and the people who report to him. Delegation results when the performance of specific work is entrusted to another, and the expected results are mutually understood.[2]

The office supervisor has a responsibility to himself and to his subordinates to delegate effectively the work to be done. As a true leader, the supervisor plans for a more efficient operation of his department by strengthening the confidence of his subordinates and developing their initiative and capability. The supervisor has a moral responsibility to his company to inspire his workers by giving them a chance to assume new responsibilities and to explore new methods on their own. The supervisor must realize that, to a great extent, the future of his company lies in the hands of the men who report to him. By effectively delegating the work, the supervisor can guide his subordinates so that they will be well prepared to undertake the future responsibilities for the successful operation of the firm.

Unfortunately, however, too many supervisors are unable to delegate, either because they do not know how to go about it or else

---

[2] Raymond Dreyfack, "How to Delegate—Effectively," from the series *What a Supervisor Should Know About . . .*" (Chicago: The Dartnell Corporation, 1964), p. 7.

	Yes	No
1. Do you know the first names of your employees?		
2. Do you feel your employees confide in you?		
3. Do you have a below-average absentee rate in your group?		
4. Have you had employees promoted from your group?		
5. Do you try quickly to solve causes of potential grievances?		
6. Do you ever visit a sick employee at his home?		
7. Do you try to handle your employees as individuals?		
8. Do you consider it more important to save an employee than to "scrap" him?		
9. Do you try to sell your people new methods instead of "shoving them down their throats"?		
10. Do you call employees in for face-to-face private discussions when problems arise?		
11. Do you try to understand the employee's point of view when problems arise?		
12. Do you give quick straight answers to employees for their questions?		
13. Do you try to get both sides of an argument before attempting to reach any decision?		
14. Can you discipline an employee and still hold his sincere respect?		
15. Do you treat all your people fairly—without playing favorites?		
16. Are your employees loyal to you—and do they speak well of you?		
17. Do you make yourself clearly understood to your employees at all times?		
18. Do your employees put in a full day's work—no loafing, no too-long coffee breaks, etc.?		
19. Do you have a good safety record in your group?		
20. Do you believe people work for more than money alone?		

HOW TO SCORE

"Yes" to all 20 questions....................Tops
"Yes" to 18 questions....................Excellent
"Yes" to 15 questions....................Good
"Yes" to 13 questions....................Acceptable
"Yes" to 11 questions....................Fair
"Yes" to 9 questions....................N.G.

Kelly-Read & Company, Rochester, New York

Fig. 11-1 **Human Relations Quotient (HRQ) Checklist for Supervisors**

they are jealous and mistrusting of their subordinates' abilities to do the job. In addition to feeling that a subordinate cannot handle an assignment or that time is not available to train him to do so, supervisors fail to delegate because of several psychological motives—the fear of competition, the fear of losing credit and recognition, and the fear that their own shortcomings and weaknesses will be exposed. Each of these motives is prefaced by the basic psychological feelings of fear and insecurity by the supervisor, and many times that fear is the cause of low-quality work, low-quantity production, and a complete breakdown in morale among the workers in a department.

The supervisor must be willing to share his knowledge and experience with his subordinates. In fact, he must train them, through delegation of his work, to be ready to step into his job. As he frees himself of work as the result of delegation, the supervisor becomes available for assuming new higher level responsibilities, all of which may lead to new job opportunities for him. When a subordinate accomplishes a task and receives credit for doing so, his recognition is also recognition of the supervisor who has enabled him to perform effectively as a result of skillful delegation. If a supervisor—often the newly appointed young executive—refrains from delegating because he fears that to do so would expose his own shortcomings, he must look within himself and solve the problem by overcoming his own weaknesses. To avoid delegating in order to camouflage his own guilty conscience, the supervisor compounds the problem—his own problem of weakness and the problem of hindering the progress and efficiency of the company for which he works.

Discipline

The words *discipline* and *disciple* can be traced back to the same root, meaning "to teach so as to mold." Most people, however, think of discipline as reprimanding or punishing, rather than teaching or molding. If it is to be effective, however, true discipline should *teach* while at the same time it *corrects*. Discipline should be preventative, not punitive, and should teach employees not to make the same mistake twice.

The supervisor should look upon discipline as a means whereby he can assist, guide, and train his subordinates so that they do become molded into loyal, devoted employees. Discipline should be looked upon as a means of offering constructive, rather than destructive, criticism; for, if properly exercised, discipline can be a profitable experience for both the supervisor who is taking the action and the employee who is being reprimanded.

True discipline should strive to mold the employee so that through self-discipline, he will learn how to subjugate his own personal desires and motives during the working day in order to contribute toward the accomplishment of the objectives of the firm. The development of self-discipline causes the employee to accept as a matter of course the company policies, rules, and regulations, all of which have been designed to provide for the efficient operation of his department. To minimize the resistance to rules—for all employees (including supervisors) at some time resist such barriers—the supervisor should periodically evaluate the rules to make sure that they are reasonable. Employees, especially those newly hired, should be informed in written form, such as a policy handbook or manual, of all company policies and rules. The rules should relate solely to the worker while he is at his place of employment during his working hours. The rules should not attempt to invade the employee's privacy while away from the office unless, of course, his off-job activities prove detrimental to the company business, its reputation, or the employee's performance on the job.

When it is necessary to reprimand an employee, he should be taken aside and talked to privately rather than disciplined in front of his coworkers. Although punitive action is not the goal of disciplinary action, any program of discipline must be tied in with penalties that are uniformly and impartially enforced. Some companies make use of the *demerit system,* under which a certain number of demerits is assigned for each infraction of a rule. Employees' penalties are based on the accumulated number of demerits over a given period of time. Penalties may include a written reprimand that is made part of the worker's personnel file, loss of special privileges, reduced vacation time, time off without pay, a pass over at the scheduled time of promotion, and dismissal.

According to one vice president in charge of personnel, poor supervision accounts for 80 to 90 percent of the disciplinary problems that arise. "Too many supervisors and managers are afraid to discipline, and when they do, they either apologize for it or bellow and rage. A sincere, temperate interview with a supervisor is punishment enough for many employees when they break a rule. Most people want to be good employees and they're more than a little ashamed when they're reminded that they don't always act the way they should." [3]

---

[3] Warren C. Stevens, "What Do You Do When They're Too Old to Spank?" *Modern Office Procedures* (April, 1964), p. 19.

Impartiality

The supervisor must be careful not only to avoid playing favorites among employees but also to avoid giving the appearance of doing so. The characteristic of fair play is one of the most important qualities to be developed by a supervisor for, if once established, it will go far toward overcoming other weaknesses in the supervisor's ability and character.

One of the most effective means of eliminating partiality or favoritism lies in taking from the supervisor the final right of discharging an employee and in placing this right in a group that is personally disinterested. Such a considerate dismissal policy takes away the chances of arbitrary exercise of power by minor executives. It assures fair consideration to each employee, since the usual procedure is to require the supervisor to submit written charges against the employee whose dismissal he is seeking. The employee must be given a hearing, and the final decision is left with the committee, not with the supervisor. Ordinarily, such a committee is composed of executives of higher rank than the supervisor. The committee may or may not have employee representation.

Among other means of avoiding favoritism are an equitable distribution of the quantity of work that each employee must complete, efficient records of work actually performed, and a periodic evaluation of each employee with a subsequent conference and a report to the employee evaluated.

Counseling

It is estimated that 70 percent of all workers dismissed for inefficiency or inability to get along with others are suffering from an emotional disorder. It is also reported that one of every four workers has an emotional disturbance of some severity.[4] Since a worker's personal problems may affect his efficiency, a supervisor should be available for talking with workers as the need arises or be able to refer a troubled worker to the appropriate person either within or outside the company for help. Some firms that are unable to support a staff psychiatrist or psychologist maintain contact with a specialist in industrial counseling and call upon his services as needed. Some

[4] Sara Roche, "Does Your Company Need a Psychiatrist?" *Modern Office Procedures* (July, 1964), p. 13. See, also, James M. Black, "Developing Competent Subordinates," *The Manager As a Counselor* (New York: American Management Association, 1961), Ch. V, pp. 103-126.

smaller companies have set up pools to share the services and the cost of a consultant. Also, industrial psychiatrists can be called upon to conduct group discussions that aid supervisors in recognizing, anticipating, and understanding the needs of their workers.

The supervisor should be on guard to note any emotional disturbances that may creep into his department, and, if they do, he should know how to react to them. The supervisor should watch for symptoms of emotional difficulties such as a marked change in a worker's behavior patterns, as when a worker shifts to an entirely new pattern; for example, when his absenteeism increases sharply. A worker that persistently complains of headaches, hives, and stomach troubles may be exhibiting the beginnings of a psychosomatic illness. When a worker commences to have a series of minor accidents, something is probably bothering him; for such accidents are usually the result of inattention, and inattention is a sign of preoccupation. The biggest problem of all, however, is alcoholism, which may indicate a deeply rooted emotional problem that the worker is unable to handle by himself. Here, the job of the supervisor is to help the worker recognize his weakness and urge him to seek proper professional help before he is dismissed from the company.[5]

How far a supervisor should go in talking with an employee about his job or home difficulties depends upon the perception, sympathy, judgment, and experience of the supervisor himself. In his counseling, the supervisor should listen sympathetically, for it is only through listening that he can come to understand the worker's problems and learn why these problems are affecting his efficiency. The supervisor should pay special attention to the feelings and attitudes exhibited by the worker rather than concentrate solely on the contents of his comments. There may be occasions when the supervisor can help the disturbed worker by granting him a leave of absence or suggesting where he may find the assistance he seeks. But by all means the supervisor should avoid assuming the role of psychologist or human relations counselor in off-job problems and recommending specific courses of action. Not only do most supervisors not have the time available to render in-plant counseling services, but also the emotional problems of workers are not the concern of supervisors, except as those problems affect job performance.

When an employee seeks help on matters that relate to his job, such as how to improve his performance or how to prepare for promotional opportunities, the supervisor should feel free to pass along

---

[5] The topic of alcoholism is discussed in further detail in Chapter 13.

his opinions and recommendations. The supervisor has a responsibility to provide his workers with guidance not only on how they can best prepare themselves to meet performance standards but also on how they can acquire the skills and knowledge needed for advancement.

Much of the supervisor's counseling is concerned with the *performance appraisal* of his workers, wherein the work of the employee is evaluated and constructively criticized. In appraising the performance of his subordinates, the supervisor must measure how well the employee has done the work assigned him, how well the employee can do work that may be more demanding, and to what extent the employee can be depended upon to carry out orders if no one is available to provide close supervision. Such constructive appraisal of employee performance is a valuable tool that can be used by the supervisor to strengthen the superior-subordinate relationship. The performance appraisal program at General Telephone & Electronics Corporation centers around the accomplishment of five major work-oriented goals each year. Using the "management by objectives" approach, management employees and their supervisors mutually agree upon the goals to be achieved, which may range from improving attendance in a specific department to overhauling an outmoded records system. Each goal is evaluated by the supervisor during his yearly performance review, and managers are given the opportunity to discuss any problems they might have encountered. At the time of the performance review, new goals are mutually set for the next period. Thus, the personnel evaluation program emphasizes concrete, measurable goals rather than the traditional, intangible personality traits such as "attitude."[6]

Morale

Morale is the mental state that causes employees to perform their work with a feeling of satisfaction and enjoyment. It is the attitude that creates a feeling of enthusiasm and happiness during and after working hours. The desires, interests, and feelings of most human beings are somewhat alike, and, when the office manager helps to satisfy them for the employee, he aids in improving the morale of the worker. Improved morale will result in the employees doing more and better work and enjoying life at the same time.

---

[6] "The Manager's Letter," American Management Association (September, 1969), p. 3. Employee evaluation is analyzed in detail as part of the office salary administration program in Chapter 20.

In large organizations, unless a proper level of morale is built up and maintained, there will be growing distrust and dissatisfaction with the company and a greater willingness to have labor unions take over the task of obtaining what the workers need or want. The company and its interest in its workers must be "sold" to the workers by a sincere and continuous effort that takes into consideration the four basic wants of human beings: *security, recognition, importance,* and *self-expression.*

Security. Security takes many forms, of which job security and personal security are fundamental.

Job Security. The employee should know that his job is necessary and permanent and that it will provide a basic salary with increments based on performance, promotional opportunities, and a certain amount of seniority. There should be a certain degree of permanence in the fundamental plans of the company with which the employees should be familiar. No changes in these plans should be made without giving the employee advance information and an explanation, especially if the plans may affect his job.

One of the most effective means of improving employee morale is to make the company's intentions and motives clear to employees and to keep them informed as to conditions that affect the firm for which they are working. One means of accomplishing this is to issue special financial reports that show where income is derived and how it is divided among owners, management, and workers. The financial reports, or similar bulletins issued somewhat more frequently, should outline the progress of sales policies, enumerate expenses, and discuss the business outlook for the future. All of these matters affect the stability of employment and salary trends, and therefore are of vital interest to employees. Thus, the employees should be informed of such matters regularly; management should not conceal the true facts until it is time to reduce salaries or to discharge employees. Manuals, house organs, and other literature descriptive of the company and its processes are effective aids in such a program of enlightenment.

The significant factor in the present-day treatment of wages and salary is the application of scientific principles to the problem. The various types of work in a given department are first defined, classified, and ranked; then, by time studies or other means, certain standards are established upon which a fair basic rate of pay is determined for each classification. The standards should be attainable by the average worker. In making the preliminary surveys, due consideration is given to the education and experience required for each task, the physical conditions of the office, the skill or effort necessary to perform the task efficiently, the responsibility of the job, and other considerations needed to evaluate every occupation. The various phases of job analysis, work measurement, and determination of work standards are discussed in Chapters 18 and 19.

Of prime importance is the necessity of establishing uniform wage rates. Studies have indicated that workers are not fundamentally interested so much in their rates of pay as they are in what wages are being received by workers doing similar work in other offices or by employees doing the same kind of work in their own departments. The rates for each classification should be put into written or printed form so that each employee will know how far he can rise within any given classification. Workers should be informed as to how standards were developed; nothing is so demoralizing in a department as a belief that rates of pay are determined arbitrarily, that employees doing similar work are being paid more, and that the rates are not commensurate with the earnings of the company.

Personal Security. There are certain contingencies in life for which everyone tries to prepare. These contingencies affect the health, employment, retirement, and death of the employee. Business firms, either by choice or through the stimulation of union efforts and contracts, have tried to recognize these contingencies and do what they can to ameliorate their effects. Many firms have tried to improve the morale of the worker by providing certain employee benefits such as hospitalization for the employee and his family; medical service; life and health insurance; pension plans; unemployment compensation; and guidance and counseling. The current status of employee benefits is analyzed in detail in Chapter 13.

Recognition. Exceptional work and length of service must be recognized by the supervisor and management if favorable employee attitudes are to be cultivated. So far as exceptional work is concerned, some companies prefer to pay bonuses established on one of many bases, such as units produced or time saved. Other firms use merit rating, whereby outstanding performance is rewarded either by a pay increase within a given classification or by promotion to a higher job classification. Other companies favor incentive wage systems, of which there are scores of basic types and numerous variations, such as piecework payments, differential piece rates, and flat weekly sums plus piece rates. Regardless of the system, the bonus or the incentive plan must be fairly established and administered. It should not be changed unless conditions warrant, and then not until the workers have been acquainted with the facts and shown why a change is necessitated.

Length of service is usually recognized by an annual increment in salary or an annual bonus graduated with the length of employment, or by a combination of the two. Either in connection with annual increments or bonuses or separately, some businesses reward long and faithful service by distribution of company stock or by giving employees a share in the profits.

Importance. Recognition of the importance of the individual is a variation of recognition of work well done. When the element of wanting to feel important and of being needed is recognized, a high level of morale is established. The employee should know and feel the importance of his job and his work to the firm. Explaining the "why of the job" and showing the employee how his efforts contribute to the attainment of the company goals are also helpful in creating a feeling of importance. Recognition should be constantly stressed, and, if possible, should be emphasized by developing group or team work.

Poor supervision causes an employee to lose his identity and creates a feeling of lack of importance. Poor supervision becomes evident in public criticism of the employee, playing favorites, lack of friendliness, unfair treatment, and lack of understanding the basic human relationships.

Finally, an employee feels his lack of importance by his inability to express himself in connection with his work. The need for self-expression is the fourth important factor to be considered in developing employee morale.

Self-Expression. The opportunity for expression is not only part of the element of feeling important in the job and in the firm but also part of the personal development of the worker. The satisfaction of psychological desires is often as important to employee morale as is the satisfaction of material wants. A common concept is that employees are motivated only by a concern for what is in the pay envelope. Although money is the oldest motivator and most companies still rely heavily on salaries and fringe benefits, modern thinkers on the subject of motivation compare the giving of more and more money with heroin—it takes more and more to produce less and less effect.[7] New ideas on motivation include the assumption that man wants to do a good job, but he needs to be challenged. Dr. Frederick Herzberg, who has written and lectured widely on the subject of motivation, believes that the only way to motivate the employee is to give him challenging work in which he can assume responsibility. By means of "job enrichment," as this approach is named by Herzberg, the individual's accountability for his own work is increased; he is given a complete natural unit of work and is granted additional authority in his activity; new and more difficult tasks not previously handled are introduced to the job; and the worker is assigned specific or specialized tasks, thus enabling him to become expert.[8]

Surveys, too, indicate that workers accord great significance to factors other than pay. For example, in a study of 7,000 workers who were asked to rate the importance of various job factors, 61.9 percent included "a steady job" among the first five important factors; the "pay rate" was included in the first five factors by 52.6 percent of the workers; 41.9 percent of the workers included "a chance to get ahead"; 39.6 percent, "a square boss"; and 35.3 percent, "working on the job you prefer." As their first choice, 36.1 percent indicated "a steady job," while only 7.2 percent indicated "pay rate" as their first choice.[9] Other factors important to the job include an opportunity to express oneself by offering suggestions and by presenting grievances, with the knowledge that any grievance submitted will be dealt with fairly and impartially.

Suggestions. The functioning of an office becomes more efficient when management provides an opportunity for employees to make suggestions for improving or expanding the business. Recognition for worthwhile suggestions may be given in several ways. Some companies reward worthy suggestions by means of promotions, others increase salaries, some give a cash bonus, while others use certificates of merit. Employee suggestion systems are discussed fully in the following chapter.

Grievances. The handling of grievances may be considered from two points of view: (1) where the firm has a union contract, and (2) where there is no union of office workers. When the firm

---

[7] Lewis E. Lachter, "Motivation: Old Problem, New Ideas," *Administrative Management* (February, 1969), pp. 22-23.

[8] *Ibid.*

[9] Morton D. Siegel, President of Management Directed Services, Inc., New York, in the seminar, "Employee Motivation—the *Plus* Factor," 1968.

has a union contract, specific rules for handling grievances are provided within the contract. For those firms that do not have a formal procedure for handling employee grievances, some definite arrangement should be provided for their settlement. A simple outline for a grievance-handling plan might include:

1. An executive or a committee should be selected to handle employee grievances.
2. Grievances should be taken up by the committee with the employee and his immediate superior.
3. If negotiations are unsuccessful, the grievance should be referred to the department head or supervisor, who may be able to settle it.
4. Provision should always be made for a *conciliator,* perhaps an industrial relations executive whose aim is to bring both parties together. The conciliator does not make decisions, but works with both parties with the objective of reaching mutual agreement.
5. Final reference must be to an *arbitrator* or umpire who must be authorized to make final decisions if the two parties—company and employee—cannot agree. This decision must be binding on all parties.

The development and maintenance of morale should be a sincere and continuing aim of management. Many firms have recognized this and are trying to do something about it, primarily because it is good business, which means greater profits and lower costs.

DEVELOPING AND MAINTAINING LEADERSHIP ABILITY

Small businesses have difficulty in training and attracting capable middle managers and supervisors. In small firms most promotions come from within unless the position requires a special skill. The relatively low turnover among supervisory personnel may discourage promising young employees. In a study of 437 small businesses located in the western United States, it was found that three fourths of the firms had no organized training program for developing managerial employees.[10] The absence of formal training programs was attributed to either a lack of awareness of the need for such training or the inability or unwillingness to develop the programs. A few firms, however, had good informal training programs in which most commonly the new employees were assigned to experienced workers

---

[10] "Maintaining the Management Staff in Small Businesses," Management Research Summary (Washington, D.C.: Small Business Administration, 1964).

or were rotated from job to job. In another study of 604 small companies in Minnesota, it was found that only about ten percent of the companies had formal programs for developing executives.[11] In most of these firms, the middle management positions and a majority of the top-management positions were filled by promotion within the company. This study concluded that small firms seldom have formal techniques or programs for developing executives, partly due to the tendency for most small businessmen to solve their problems from day to day instead of thinking ahead. Also, many executives of small businesses seem to feel confident that they will be able to find management personnel when they need it.

In a study conducted by Western Michigan University of 75 companies in 14 states (larger firms than those noted above), it was found that 45 percent of the respondents use a formal type of management training program, 33 percent use an informal type, and 22 percent use a combination of both.[12] In spite of the increased frequency of planned training programs, one of the greatest personnel shortages of the larger businesses is that of qualified executives and supervisors. Of course, the supervisory positions have to be filled, but many supervisors are really not qualified for the positions they hold. They are holding their positions for want of better qualified executives. In a survey of 10,000 employees in one organization that was experiencing a turnover of 58 percent, it was found that the real reasons for leaving were poor supervision, depressing working conditions, and lack of future. Of those who quit after 11 months of service, 75 percent indicated that they would like to return under better supervisory programs. The conclusions of the study revealed that inadequate supervision may cost a firm many worthwhile employees and inflate the entire personnel expense, and that a good supervisory training program could reduce terminations and costs.[13] The larger business organizations have come to recognize such deficiencies in supervisory personnel and have attempted to overcome them by encouraging training activities to develop better leaders.

Supervisory Training

There are three principles of supervisory training that must be emphasized:

[11] "Development of Executive Resources in Small Companies," Management Research Summary (Washington, D.C.: Small Business Administration, 1964).

[12] "Trends in Management Training," *Management Overview for Administrative Managers,* Manual 1M-108 (New York: Geyer-McAllister Publications, 1968).

[13] *Cost Reduction Newsletter,* Volume 5, No. 9, as reported in *Management Review* (January, 1965), p. 53.

1. Promotional and executive training should be continuous or periodically repeated at all levels of management.
2. Supervisory training involves knowledge of the work and of the responsibilities of the position to be supervised.
3. Supervisory training involves the human relationships and personal traits evident in skillful instructing, skillful planning, and skillful leadership.

Supervisory training should be offered, or participated in, at all levels of management. The further up the management scale the executive is located, the less necessary it is for him to have training in the knowledge of the work and the responsibility of the position. However, certain phases of executive training should be reviewed, revised, and given periodically.

Promotional Training. Having a definite plan for promoting and transferring supervisors improves the morale in all departments. Nothing is more discouraging to a conscientious supervisor, who has worked many years for a company, than to learn that persons outside the organization are given preferential consideration when promotions are to be made or higher positions filled. He feels, and justly so, that he should be considered first. Forward-looking employers believe that, if a supervisor is worth his salary, he is also worthy of some form of training for higher positions.

Promotional training may take many forms. It may be carried out entirely by the company, or the company may cooperate with nearby junior colleges, business colleges, and universities in providing adult evening classes in areas such as salesmanship, credit management, business English, and data processing applications. Supervisors may take advantage of home-study courses and executive development programs offered by the American Management Association, which sponsors special courses for small businessmen, and the Administrative Management Society, which offers a series of advanced management training courses. The training may be given for a short, intensive period during each year, such as an annual two-week seminar. Some firms engage management consultants to conduct such intensive courses. Others conduct courses in supervision in company-supervised schools and in group conferences.

Whether the training programs should be given on company time or on personal time is a debatable point. Courses in company-supervised schools or during luncheon or dinner meetings will probably be on the employees' time. Otherwise, the training program can become part of the regular job of the employee who is being developed for promotion.

Many methods and techniques of group instruction are used in the promotional training and executive development of supervisors. Most of these methods have been used for many years in universities, in management education centers, and by professional organizations such as the Administrative Management Society, the American Management Association, and the American Institute of Certified Public Accountants. The methods and techniques of group supervisory training used most frequently are briefly described below: [14]

1. *Conference method:* The head of the group leads the discussion by employees. The discussion leader may instruct the trainees who are present to learn, or the leader may guide the trainees to reach a decision partially or entirely by themselves. The conference method is effectively employed in training supervisors in human relations by making use of case histories, followed by on-the-job coaching and understudying a leader skilled in human relations.
2. *Lecture method:* In this nonparticipative technique, the head of the group, instructor, or training specialist is able to impart much information to large groups in a relatively short period of time. Of all the various teaching methods, the lecture method is probably the least expensive, easiest to use, and most universally understood.
3. *Role playing:* This training technique, also known as "play acting," "reality practice," and "psychodrama," calls upon the supervisor to act out his own role or those of others under simulated conditions. The supervisor may assume the role of an executive one or two rungs higher on the ladder of promotion and then "act out" his solution to problems that would face him on that level. Other trainees act as observers, and afterward the supervisor's performance is evaluated by his immediate superior or a training specialist.
4. *Decision simulation:* Originally designed for use by top and middle management, this method, commonly known as "management games," is based on a model of actual business conditions. Competing groups of supervisors are given a description of a mythical business firm and then asked to make decisions on improving the company's position by taking such

---

[14] For a complete description of the training process, see John H. Proctor and William M. Thornton, *Training: A Handbook for Line Managers* (New York: American Management Association, 1961).

actions as cutting costs, improving production, and increasing sales.

5. *In-basket training:* The supervisor is given a brief description of a higher ranking position, after which the supervisor is "promoted" to that job and given a representative sample of the problems as they might arrive in the mail. Within a specified period of time, the supervisor must make all decisions and solve all problems, ranging from taking action on reports and letters to settling conflicts between coworkers.
6. *Case studies:* Prior to the meeting of the training class, the supervisor is given a written case history of a problem or situation that exists or has existed in the business firm. After he has studied the background information available for decision making, the supervisor presents his solution to the problem in class. The trainees then evaluate the decisions reached by each other. After having evaluated their own decisions, the trainees may be told what actually took place in the business firm.
7. *Incident process:* The group of supervisors is given a series of problems about a mythical company, but only a minimum of related information is supplied. The supervisors themselves must obtain all additional data needed and then make the decisions. The objective of this training technique is to teach the supervisor how to examine all facets of a problem and to engage in research by gathering data from many sources.
8. *Sensitivity training:* This method, also known as *laboratory training,* places the supervisor in a controlled environment with a small group of men much like himself, but who are strangers to each other. A psychologist sets the stage for the unstructured group discussion and interaction during which the men talk about the behavior of the group as a group and the behavior of individuals as they relate to the group. Each individual is judged by the group for his strengths and weaknesses, as a personality, as a manager, as a leader, as a speaker, and as someone who is attempting to get a job.[15] An atmosphere of mutual confidence and respect must be established at the beginning, for the criticism may often be bitter when prejudices and shortcomings are laid bare.

Most of the training in industry—perhaps 80 percent of the total—is on a man-to-man basis. At the supervisory level, the major forms of man-to-man training are job rotation and understudy. The

[15] "How AMA Trains Managers," *The Office* (March, 1970), p. 62.

job rotation method exposes the trainee to a number of functions in a relatively short period of time by rotating him through the various departments of the company. The trainee may be assigned to each job solely as an observer or he may be assigned a specific responsibility at each job so that he becomes personally involved in the operations as he moves from one job to the next. In the *understudy method,* a senior executive uses one or more employees as his assistants, discusses with them the problems of the department, and from time to time delegates certain advanced executive responsibilities to them. The employees taking part in either of these programs must be made to realize that the program is a form of supervisory training for their future promotion.

Along with man-to-man and group training methods, supervisory training programs may make use of programmed instructional materials, teaching machines, educational television, and computer-aided instruction (CAI). *Programmed instruction (PI)* is a method of self-instruction in which the training material is presented in small bits of information that are logically structured so that the learner proceeds in a step-by-step sequence from the basic elements of a skill or concept to more progressively difficult material. Since many principles of decision making and exercising good judgment do not lend themselves to a programming approach, the value of this technique for teaching supervisors, middle managers, and top executives is yet to be proven. Programmed instruction materials can be most effectively used at lower levels where specific skills and knowledges, such as how to fill in sales report forms properly and uniformly or how to understand the technical processes of photocopying equipment, are to be taught. By means of a *teaching machine,* the learner progresses step by step through carefully programmed material, proceeding to an advanced concept or aspect of a skill only after each preceding step has been thoroughly mastered. The teaching machine, an electromechanical tabletop device, allows the trainee to read the programmed material, requires him to answer questions at various intervals, scores his response to questions, and instructs him in further completion of the program. *Educational television* offers many potential advantages in the development of supervisory training programs. Films can be easily used, and a training session can be repeated on kinescope at another time during the day or evening. Several companies may share the costs of producing a training program that meets their common needs and thus be able to obtain outstanding instructors, who otherwise would be unable to come into the firms one at a time to participate in a training session. By means of *time-shared computer-aided instruction,* trainees have access to a computer simultaneously, usually through telephones or teletypewriters. Lessons consist of explanations or lectures with questions and quizzes programmed on the computer so that immediate response is available by communicating with the computer. The trainee is informed by the computer of the accuracy of his answer, told where and how to proceed next, and informed of how well he is doing.

Executive Training. Most firms need replacements or additional executives for their expanding businesses. Executive training may take the same general means of instruction as described previously. In the Western Michigan University study referred to earlier, it was found that the management training techniques, classified according to frequency of use, were: on the job, 96 percent of respondents; conference and discussion, 93 percent; job rotation, 76 percent; special projects, 71 percent; case studies, 49 percent; problem solving, 49 percent; management games, 18 percent; role playing, 18 percent; programmed instruction, 16 percent; sensitivity training, 9 percent; brainstorming, 7 percent; and other methods such as instrumented laboratory training and lecture discussions, 7 percent.[16]

One of the most effective methods of establishing confidence, building up a cooperative morale, and stimulating interest in work, is to have some form of executive training that is coordinated with the personnel promotion plan. By such a plan, qualities other than those previously mentioned must be sought when the objective is to locate and to train future executives. One firm lists such qualifications as: (1) the ability to cooperate; (2) the promise of ability to lead and influence; (3) the ability to learn; (4) the ability to study and a habit of study. Here, the emphasis is not so much upon training for specific jobs as it is upon the fundamentals of the business, although some concerns do conduct executive training classes for specific positions. In some firms such a program is carried out on a large scale. Men are sent to a training plant and put to work in every department of the business and allowed to sit in on executive conferences. Smaller firms, however, follow plans similar to those for promotional training.

A training program, regardless of the method adopted and the objectives sought, must be carefully planned and organized before it is put into operation. Particular attention must be paid to the

---

[16] "Trends in Management Training," *loc. cit.*

questions of compulsory attendance, the nature of the courses to be given, whether company executives or outside instructors should conduct the classes, and the content of each course. Training, orientation, and promotion of office personnel are discussed further in Chapter 14.

Knowledge of the Work. Line management, assisted where necessary by staff personnel, should be in charge of the training program. The training program should be carefully organized and planned so that supervisors obtain full knowledge of the work to be done and its place in the total organization. A knowledge of what work is to be done and how it is to be done can be obtained by experience in the department, by a study of the operations manuals that many firms have developed, or by working on studies with a systems, methods, and procedures department, if the firm has one. Working with the systems department will help supervisors accomplish the following:

1. Determine what work should be routinized and standardized.
2. Determine if any of this work can be eliminated.
3. Develop flow charts to check on the smoothness and efficiency of the work.
4. Develop standards of output for each employee or group.
5. Develop manuals for recording standards and procedures.
6. Measure the output and develop records or reports to indicate the efficiency of the plan, the standards, and the flow charts.
7. Periodically make a thorough recheck of the steps above because new business methods, machines, and developments may have made present office procedures obsolete.

Information relating to company policies, rules, regulations, authority, and responsibility may be obtained from company manuals, organization charts, and personal consultations with senior executives.

Human Relationships and Personal Traits. Many lists have been prepared to indicate the personal traits that must be developed by study or by experience. Such lists form an excellent basis for discussion in all training programs, and can be reviewed from year to year without impairing their effectiveness. One such list of executive traits, given below, includes many of the items that appeared previously in the tabulation of the responsibilities of a supervisor:

1. Be a believer in the ability of others.
2. Analyze true conditions beyond criticism and complaints.

3. Respect the rights and the aspirations of others.
4. Know the strong and the weak points of each person working under his direction.
5. Understand the potential and the limitations of associates and superiors.
6. Give credit where it is due.
7. Be a believer in teamwork.
8. Inspire people; build confidence in their ability.
9. Remember that management must exercise all four of its functions—organizing, planning, controlling, and leading.

Illustrative Examples of Formal Supervisory Training Programs

Supplementing the personal guidance and coaching offered supervisors by senior executives, the more formal training programs make use of manuals, bulletins, instruction sheets, and various audio-visual aids such as films and filmstrips. The use of these aids is decribed in the following illustrative examples of supervisory training programs.

One large firm having branch offices throughout the United States has developed a comprehensive manual covering company organization, policies, and branch office management. A thorough study of this manual may take as long as two years. Assistant office managers having managerial potential and candidates for promotion to the position of branch office manager must study this manual. When positions are available and the assistant feels that he is prepared, he is given a comprehensive examination to ascertain his rating. Those ranking the highest are given first choice of positions available. The others may be required to take a second examination if the time interval between the first examination and the filling of a manager's position is too long.

A mail-order firm maintains a Supervisory Personnel Department that conducts courses for the training and improvement of supervisory personnel. Through its Supervisory Personnel Department, the firm made a study of desirable traits of supervisors and from this study developed a training course. The course consisted of a series of mimeographed bulletins that constantly keep before the supervisors the common errors made in their work. The following list gives the titles of the bulletins issued in one of their series:

1. Don't Try to Do Everything Yourself.
2. Build a Winning Team.
3. Build Morale and Loyalty.
4. How to Train People.

5. Plan Ahead.
6. Don't Try to Act Like a Big Shot.
7. How to Handle "Heat."
8. Put Your Best Foot Forward.
9. Get New Employees Off to a Good Start.
10. Watch Your Health.
11. Develop Assistants.
12. Lay the Cards on the Table.
13. Give a Pat on the Back for Work Well Done.
14. Set a Good Example.

Another very fine example of a program for the development of executives and supervisors is that given by the training director for Johnson & Johnson. This program is organized on two levels—supervisory and executive. The supervisory training covers such group topics as human relations skills, administrative skills, company information, and technical skills. The training tools used in this work include the management or supervisory letters and bulletins, a large technical library, job rotation, staff meetings, individual assignments, problem-solving meetings, lectures, conferences, practice-management in which the supervisor discusses what he is doing and what he plans to do, and case studies on the Harvard Business School plan. The company also at times pays part or all of the tuition for special technical courses given at nearby universities. This program may seem to be rather comprehensive, but the firm has more than ten thousand employees and five hundred supervisory managers and executives. Each of its plants uses its own personnel and training staff, with assistance and service from the parent organization.

In the Kimberly-Clark Corporation, a firm with approximately 25,000 employees of whom about ten percent have supervisory responsibilities, a supervisory training film is used in the training program. The classes, limited to 15 or 20 persons, are scheduled as needed, with an instructor from the company's Supervisory Development Group always in attendance. The training film is part of a program that may last the entire day.

In another company with 1,700 employees, the training supervisor schedules annual sessions for his company's 30 clerical supervisors, all of whom are women. Each year one week is devoted to training or refresher training in the area of improved supervisory performance. The one-week sessions are devoted to discussing the most pressing problems that line management will have to handle during the coming year, and a training film is used to bridge the gap between the discussion of the problem and its solution.

Key executives in 40 of the nation's largest industrial corporations (including General Motors, American Can, Radio Corporation of America, International Business Machines, and Continental Oil) participate in home-study accounting courses offered by a correspondence school. One correspondence school has offered a new group training plan that combines the home-study approach and the conference method. Under this plan a group of executives from within the same company meet in a series of weekly conferences held after business hours. Each executive takes turn in leading the group as they work through the home-study course. Thus, the executives have an opportunity to discuss the problems of the course as they relate to their own company operations. Among the firms taking part in this training plan are Caterpillar Tractor, General Aniline, Texas Instruments, and Brunswick Pulp & Paper.[17]

Through its Regional Management Center in Chicago, the American Management Association provides guidance to company representatives for the establishment of in-company training programs. The in-company training program, known as IMPACT IV (Improved Managerial Performance Through Action Training) is designed for first-line supervisors and uses such participating training techniques as role playing, team simulation exercises, filmed case studies, programmed instruction, and audio and video tapes. The program, "Improving Supervisory Planning and Organizing Skills," includes the following topics: Using the Planning Process to Manage Effectively, Scheduling Work to Optimize Results, Using and Interpreting Network Scheduling Techniques, Managing Within the Organizational Framework, and Dealing with the Problems of Change.[18]

Although the number of subjects that can be covered in a supervisor's or executive's training program is large, the important fact to be kept in mind is that a program must be developed and used continuously. Many executives, as well as employees, get "in a rut." The executive or the supervisor is an extension of the arm of management to the worker. It is a sound investment to train for and improve this phase of the work.

---

[17] "A New Trend in Training?" *Administrative Management* (January, 1963), p. 84.

[18] "Management News" (New York: American Management Association, 1970), p. 3.

RECOGNITION OF THE SUPERVISOR

Most of the preceding discussion of effective supervision and human relations has concerned itself with the duties of the supervisor and not with the recognition that the supervisor should receive from his superiors. For success in his job, the supervisor, too, must receive recognition. Some of the factors that should receive attention from top management are:

1. There should be an organization chart showing the supervisor where he "fits into the picture." This chart should be supplemented by a definite statement of his duties and responsibilities. The chart should, if possible, indicate possible lines of promotion.
2. Every assistance should be given the supervisor to help him improve his work and grow in his job—that is, *training for supervision.*
3. The supervisor should not be held responsible for delays or increased costs if he does not have control over the situations that caused them.
4. The supervisor should be able to see his superiors as often as necessary.
5. The supervisor needs recognition and credit for a job well done, just as often as do other employees.
6. Top management should make every effort to develop and maintain close cooperation and assistance among coworkers—meaning, in this instance, among supervisors. This spirit of cooperation should result in a coordination of supervision so that there may be no weak links in this chain of work.
7. The supervisor should be paid a salary commensurate with his responsibilities.
8. There should be some form of supervisory rating system.

In return for obtaining this cooperation from top management, the supervisor must know how, must learn, or must be taught to display proper leadership in his work. Proper leadership refers to organizing his department so that he will command the respect of his subordinates and coworkers by making proper decisions and by delegating work wherever practical.

QUESTIONS FOR REVIEW

1. What types of responsibility does the supervisor have? In what directions do these responsibilities flow?

2. Contrast the duties of the supervisor in a line organization with those in a line-and-staff organization.
3. "The supervisor today must use the *human* approach." Carefully explain the meaning of this statement and indicate its relevance for the administrative office manager.
4. What is delegation? What are the underlying reasons why many supervisors do not delegate?
5. Is it possible for a supervisor to teach while at the same time he is disciplining a worker? Explain.
6. How far should a supervisor go in counseling an employee about his personal problems, such as alcoholism?
7. What is morale? How is morale related to the four basic wants of human beings?
8. What action (or lack of action) taken by a supervisor may cause an employee to feel that he is not important to the organization? How can the supervisor improve himself and his actions so that the employee properly identifies himself as part of the firm?
9. Why, in most small businesses, are there no formal programs for developing and maintaining leadership ability?
10. Describe briefly the several methods and techniques of group supervisory training. Which of these methods is the least expensive and easiest to use?
11. Contrast the job rotation and the understudy methods of training.
12. The supervisor has a duty and a responsibility to recognize the contributions of his subordinates. The contributions of the supervisor must be recognized also, if he is to be successful. Explain.

QUESTIONS FOR DISCUSSION

1. The supervisor is usually looked upon as "the man in the middle." What is the meaning of this statement? Do the definitions of "supervisor" contained in the National Labor Management Relations Act and the Fair Labor Standards Act bear out this characterization of the supervisor?
2. What factors do you believe contribute most to the influence of a supervisor? Which do you believe is the most important?
3. Why is there need for providing a method of handling employee grievances? What is to be gained by having a procedure for handling employee grievances when no labor union is involved?
4. Why are studies of employee attitudes toward office supervisors an important phase of office administration?
5. What authority, if any, should a departmental supervisor have in the selection of employees who are to work in his department?

6. A weakness of many promotional training programs is that employees are often trained for advanced positions which are not available when the training courses are completed. Do you agree with this statement? Explain.
7. Evaluate the following statement: "You could dispose of almost all of the leadership training courses for supervision in American industry today without anyone knowing the difference."
8. If a company is interested in furthering the education of its employees and is willing to pay part of the costs, the firm must supervise their employees' study. How can such supervision be accomplished?
9. A former high-ranking military officer was recently employed to head a business organization whose morale had slipped considerably in recent years. The Board of Directors became aware of the morale problem and informed the new president accordingly. At the first board meeting, the president indicated that the strength and the success of a business depends 25 percent on the number of employees and 75 percent upon its morale. Furthermore, the president stated that the essentials of morale in a business organization are the same as those in the army: (1) respect for the officers or supervisors, (2) discipline, and (3) training.

   Do you agree with the statements made by the president? Discuss the various methods by which morale may be developed in a business organization on the basis of these facts.
10. The office manager of a small company is so anxious to do a good job that he always comes to the president before making a decision affecting policy. In the past two months, the office manager has called upon the president no less than ten times for advice. In nine of these instances, whatever the president recommended seems to have been what the office manager would have done himself. This was found out by a series of questions asked whenever the problem of making a decision arose. What would you do in this instance if you were the president, assuming that the office manager is otherwise doing a good job?
11. Norman Schneider is president and office manager of the Steel Cutlery Company. He has grown up with the business and has become successful through his own efforts—the hard way. He has an assistant, Paul Crabbe, who is really the operating office manager. Crabbe has taken a course in office management, has had considerable experience outside the firm, and therefore his ideas seem more progressive than those of Schneider. In the past, whenever Crabbe suggested improvements that could have saved the company money, Schneider resented the suggestions. He seemed to feel they were a reflection on his lack of training and education. Crabbe is anxious to do a good job, does not want to make a change in position, and would like to save the company money if he will not cause himself undue discomfort and embarrassment. Crabbe comes to you for advice in

handling the situation. Explain what you would do if you were in his position.

12. Jenny Maxon, recently appointed supervisor of the office services department, has in the past few months found her job very demanding, with the result that she seems to have no time to do anything. It seems as if she is always attending meetings from which she exits with more projects to complete. Jenny has begun to hand more and more responsibilities to other members of her department, often giving a task to a worker with no more directions than "See so-and-so for more information. She'll give you the details." At times, Jenny even delegates the assignment of the projects themselves.

Jenny has given more and more freedom to her secretary, Arlene Haines, who now issues verbal instructions instead of Jenny. Often Arlene makes decisions on her own when questions arise that Jenny is not prepared to answer. Many of the workers in the department, old enough to be Arlene's mother, resent taking orders from Arlene, who is young and has had only a few years of work experience.

During the past week Jenny has found she is so rushed that she must assign various employees to attend project planning meetings in her place. Since these people have no authority, they are at quite a disadvantage and can only listen and make recommendations. The result has been that the meetings are a waste of time and have to be rescheduled when Jenny has more time.

What is the real problem here? As Jenny's supervisor, what steps should you take to remedy the situation?

PRACTICAL OFFICE CASES

Case 11-1 Hiring Supervisory Personnel from the Outside

Bunn Abrasive Products has in its inventory more than 200,000 different items, of which many are produced according to the special formulas of its customers. In the past, the handling of sales orders and inventory records has been slow and cumbersome, causing much customer dissatisfaction and, at times, loss of sales.

For the past year the company has engaged in a feasibility study in which a computer, coupled with the present punched-card equipment, would be used for the sales orders and inventory procedures. The new computer and auxiliary equipment will be delivered in about three months, but the firm is now faced with the problem of obtaining proper supervision for this work.

The present punched-card installation is handled by an expert who is approaching 63 years of age. He has not been too anxious to cooperate in the adaptation of the work to the computer system because he feels that he has only a few more years to go before retirement. Most of the other employees in the data processing department are more or less routine clerical workers, none of whom are qualified for supervisory work on the new equipment. However, several of these workers are anxious for promotion in this department.

Faced with the problem of obtaining suitable supervisory help for the new installation, the firm has decided to go outside the organization to fill the position. The starting salary will be $15,000 a year. The man now in charge of the punched-card installation is earning $12,500 a year.

▪ Discuss:

1. The qualifications the new supervisor should possess.
2. The employment sources you would contact to secure the supervisory help for the new installation.
3. How the firm might handle this situation without creating a morale problem in the data processing department.
4. The type of training program the firm might develop to provide for future supervisory needs in the computer field.

Case 11-2 Analyzing a Supervisory Technique

Geneva Clifford, formerly an officer in the WAVES, has been employed as supervisor of the stenographic and transcription department of the Robertson Advertising Agency. In this department there are 30 girls whose work consists of taking dictation, transcribing, and typing various kinds of statistical reports. Because of a scarcity of qualified office help and a lack of adequate supervision in the past, the girls have been coming in at various times in the morning—from 8:35 to 9:15.

Geneva decided to "take the bull by the horns" and called the girls together on her first day in the office. Her opening remarks were: "I am Geneva Clifford, your new supervisor. I have just been released from the WAVES, where I was a lieutenant in charge of 65 girls. I hope we get along together; but before you forget, you are supposed to be at your desks each morning at 8:30." The girls smiled. The next day they came in as tardy and as indifferent as before.

▪ If you were the supervisor:

1. Would you have used the same approach as Geneva Clifford? If so, what course of action would you take now?
2. If you would not have taken this approach, how would you have handled the situation?

Case 11-3 Working with Supervisors on a Feasibility Study

Linn's Toys, a manufacturer of children's toys, has its main offices in San Diego, California. In the San Diego offices there are 250 office employees and 440 workers in the manufacturing, assembly, and shipping departments. Each of the branch offices in Albany, Chicago, and Houston has a staff of 12 to 18 office employees and 15 to 20 workers in the shipping department. In charge of each branch office is a branch sales manager, who has jurisdiction over eight to ten sales representatives who call upon wholesalers and retail outlets. Toy shipments are made, on a geographic basis, from each of the branch offices and the home office. Each branch office handles its own processing of orders. Copies of all shipping orders are sent daily by airmail to the home office, where all billing is done.

In addition to approximately 200 orders that are processed daily in San Diego, 600 to 750 copies of shipping orders are received from the branch offices. Thus, on the average, about 800 shipping orders are verified for stock number, description, and unit price daily in the home office. At the present time all invoices are completed on electric typewriters by a crew of ten clerk-typists. The completion and mailing of invoices may lag as much as four days behind the shipping date and on some occasions, such as during the Christmas rush, the lag between shipping date and invoice preparation may exceed one work week.

The order processing and billing is under the supervision of Helen Meyer, a conscientious, faithful employee who has been with the company 30 years. Helen is often looked upon by the clerk-typists as a tough supervisor, but one whom they all respect and admire for her loyalty and drive. She prides herself on the meticulous care with which each order is processed and each invoice is typed, and has often told the typists, "We may not get too many orders out today, but we know they will be correct in all respects. Right?"

In addition to handling all the billing operations, the San Diego office prepares the semimonthly payroll for all employees in the home office and the branch offices, answers all correspondence from customers in the several western states serviced by the home office, and follows up on all correspondence and salesmen's contacts forwarded from the branch offices. Also, all requests for credit approval from the branch offices are handled by the credit manager, Paul T. Cutter, in the home office.

Linn's Toys has a modest card-punch installation—three key-punch machines, a sorter, and a tabulator, all of which are used on a rental basis. The punched-card system of data processing is used primarily for stock control and inventory purposes. For each item listed on a sales invoice, a card is punched to record the customer's account number, date of sale, stock number, units sold, and amount of sale. From these cards, various reports are prepared to analyze sales by branch office, by stock number, and by sales representative.

All sales promotion literature—brochures, flyers, catalogs, price lists, broadsides—is mailed from the San Diego office. The number of direct-mail pieces may amount to as many as 20,000 each month. The names and addresses of all customers—past, present, and prospective—are recorded on metal plates that are used to address the mailing pieces. The plates are filed alphabetically by branch office and home office territory so that, as needed, specialized geographic mailings may be made. At the present time, five persons are employed in the mailing room, with the job of keeping the plates up-to-date, addressing the mailing pieces, and sorting the bulk mailings by ZIP code numbers. The department is supervised by Mary Davis, age 60, who has established a warm "mother-daughter" relationship with her coworkers. Due to her failing eyesight, many errors creep past Mary, but management is reluctant to dismiss her because of her long and faithful service to the company—one of the few workers who has been with the firm since its establishment. The mailings are characterized by numerous errors such as wrong street addresses, incorrect spellings, and incorrect ZIP code numbers. Speaking of the latter, on many occasions she has been heard to say, "What is this world coming to? Pretty soon I'll have to apply six months in advance for a number on my casket. Why all these numbers, I don't know. . . ."

The growth in toy sales has increased ten to fifteen percent each year and the company president, Peter G. Linn, looks to an exceedingly bright future, at least for the next ten to twelve years. However, Linn and the four vice presidents who make up the board of directors are well aware of several internal problems that they feel must be overcome if the future goals are to be achieved. In fact, at a recent meeting of the board, Harvey T. Kyle, vice president in charge of sales, stated very emphatically, "Sales would have been up at least another one percent during the past six months if the order department could have kept up with the pace. What are you going to do about that slow poke, Helen Meyer?" William L. Carter, the executive vice president, broke into Kyle's comments by saying, "I'm not so much worried about the order department as I am about the fouled-up situation in the mailing room. Those girls, including Mary Davis, can't seem to get anything straight. There are too many customers complaining about our direct-mail service and I'm afraid we have been creating a lot of hard feelings."

Toward the end of the board meeting, Kyle remarked, "I think we should be getting a computer in here. That will speed up things. Then, Carter, you'll have no errors in those mailings and the stuff will get out on time." Peter Linn said that he had been thinking about a computer, too, for he had seen one in operation recently when he visited the offices of a competing manufacturer. As he commented, "That ATC computer over at Beck's is sure doing the job. Maybe that accounts for the pickup in their sales lately. Why, I hear that their sales are up 12 percent this period." Linn went on by telling Carter that he should get started in undertaking a feasibility study.

■ As chairman of the feasibility study, answer the following questions:

1. How can you best work with Helen Meyer and Mary Davis? If you appoint these two supervisors to your committee, how will you go about "winning them over" to the computer age?
2. If these two supervisors are not appointed to your committee, how will you plan to educate them to the electronics era? Should these two women be dismissed or retired earlier than planned so that new "computerized blood" can be brought into the firm?

12

Human Relations and Office Personnel Policies

A planned program of personnel policies guides a business firm in handling its employees' needs most effectively in the interests of a smoothly functioning organization. To obtain maximum productivity, workers must be satisfied and content, not only with their physical environment, but also with their working conditions. In its broadest aspects, a planned personnel program encompasses the entire field of human relations in the office. Some of these activities were discussed in the preceding chapter that dealt with the supervision of office activities. In this chapter attention will be focused upon labor relations, communications, and ethics. The personnel policies, rules, and regulations relating to these three areas can best be explained to new as well as older employees by means of the policy manual or the employee handbook.[1] The use of manuals helps both management and the workers to eliminate the friction and misunderstanding that arise when policies and practices are not put in writing.

LABOR RELATIONS IN THE OFFICE

If the business office is unionized, the personnel policies developed by management and the ease with which these policies can be administered may hinge upon the degree of acceptance and cooperation

[1] See Chapter 23 for an explanation of each of the major types of office manuals.

forthcoming from the union and its representatives. If the office is not unionized, management must be prepared to deal with any union that may seek to represent the employees in the company. To do so intelligently and to maintain a fair but firm relationship with a union, management must have some knowledge about the objectives and the problems of the unions. Before examining the extent of unionization among office workers, a brief history of the labor movement and the major pieces of legislation affecting workers is presented. This very short excursion into the past will help set the stage for a description of union activities that are taking place in business offices today and of those that may occur tomorrow.

A Brief History of the Labor Movement

In the late 1700's long before the mass-producing, assembly-line factories came upon the scene in the United States, workers were grouping themselves together to meet an urgent human need—protection from low wages and long workdays. The labor philosophies of the first organized societies exerted a strong influence on the craft unions and other labor groups that formed later during the early part of the nineteenth century. Following a long period of unemployment and inactivity on the part of labor groups, as a result of the financial panic of 1837, trade unionism revived with the discovery of gold in California in the 1850's. Workers' demands still lay in the areas of increased wages and shorter workdays. With the Civil War came the need to increase the output of plants; the period was marked by the building of railroads and the establishment of modern factories in the Midwest. In 1869, the Noble Order of the Knights of Labor was formed, uniting mining and railroad men with all the craftsmen and clerks to combat the employers' opposition to unionization by means of lockouts and blacklists. However, in spite of the craft and railroad strikes, the unified opposition of employers led to the defeat and dissolution of most organized groups.

In 1886 the American Federation of Labor (AFL) was formed under the leadership of Samuel Gompers. Gompers' goals, applicable to all workers in their particular crafts, included bringing about economic changes by: abolishing child labor, shortening the workdays, improving working conditions, and providing collective bargaining for workers. In 1938, led by John L. Lewis, the Congress of Industrial Organization (CIO) was founded, with the aim of unionizing all workers in mass-production industries, and with no restriction as to trade or craft. The growth of the CIO membership and the development of new local unions came into direct competition with the AFL unions; as a result, jurisdictional disputes broke out, with violence between both unions, and costly, prolonged strikes forced upon employers. The early disputes between the AFL and the CIO unions were characterized by the presence of radical elements that began to bore from within the labor movement. Along with other disruptive conditions, the desire to purge their ranks of these extremist elements led to the merging of the two unions in 1955 under the name of AFL-CIO.

Labor Legislation

By 1920 most states had adopted workmen's compensation laws that provided for the payment of benefits to employees injured while on the job or to the dependents of those workers who are killed on the job. The Railway Labor Act of 1926, amended several times since, provides for mediation, voluntary arbitration of wage disputes, and compulsory investigation by the National Railroad Adjustment Board before a strike can be called. If the Mediation Board cannot settle a dispute, the matter is referred to the President of the United States, who appoints a fact-finding committee. The Davis-Bacon Act of 1931 specifies the payment of certain prevailing wages, as determined by the Secretary of Labor, on federal construction projects. The Norris-LaGuardia Anti-Injunction Act of 1932 defines and limits the powers of federal courts that issue injunctions in labor disputes by explaining when and under what circumstances injunctions may be issued. This act made unenforceable in federal courts the so-called "yellow-dog contracts" in which a worker agrees not to join a union as a condition of his employment.

To put people back to work at a decent living wage following the depression years, the National Industrial Recovery Act (NIRA) was passed in 1933. The NIRA attempted to equalize wage differentials geographically and to prescribe equal wages and salaries for the same work in all areas. All attempts failed, however, and in 1935, the United States Supreme Court ruled that the NIRA was unconstitutional since it was based upon an unconstitutional delegation of legislative power. Until the passage of the National Labor Relations Act (Wagner Act) in 1935, union organization was at a standstill. This act gave to employees "the right to self-organization, to form, join, or assist labor organizations to bargain collectively through representatives of their own choosing." Employers were prohibited from interfering with the formation or administration of any labor organization. Collective bargaining was made an instrument of national policy, and the way was paved for labor to organize and to bargain collectively without interference from employers.

The Social Security Act of 1935, amended many times since its passage, is one of the most important laws that protects the worker who is out of a job through no fault of his own. In addition to providing assistance to unemployed workers qualifying under the act, insurance is provided for old age, survivors, and disability benefits, and health insurance for the aged (popularly known as Medicare). The Walsh-Healey Public Contracts Act of 1936 establishes minimum wages and maximum hours for work done on government contracts amounting to $10,000 or more, with the Secretary of Labor deciding the minimum wages that contractors are to pay. The Fair Labor Standards Act of 1938, commonly called the Wage and Hour Law, provides a 40-hour workweek for employees in firms engaged in interstate commerce. Covered employees receive a minimum wage and payment of time and one half for all hours worked over 40 in one week. The act also prohibits, with certain exceptions, the employment of children under 18 years of age in order to protect their health and safety.

The most far-reaching piece of labor legislation in the United States was marked by the passage of the Labor-Management Relations Act (Taft-Hartley Law) of 1947. During World War II, employers and unions cooperated with governmental agencies in carrying out the war in accordance with the National Labor Relations Act. After the war, however, there was strong public agitation to amend or change the act because it prohibited employers from performing certain labor practices and did not provide for unfair union practices. As a result, the National Labor Relations Act was amended by the Taft-Hartley Law. Some of the important provisions of this law with which the office manager should be familiar are given below:

1. The National Labor Relations Board is the quasi-judicial agency that hears testimony, renders decisions, determines the collective bargaining unit or agency, and prosecutes unfair labor practices.

2. Unfair labor practices on the part of the employer and the union are enumerated in Figure 12-1.

3. A 60-day notice must be given to either party before the normal termination of a labor contract, and the Federal Mediation and Conciliation Service must be notified within 30 days after the 60-day notice if no agreement is reached.

By the Employer	*By the Union*
(a) Cannot interfere with or restrain employees from joining a union.	(a) Cannot coerce or restrain an employee who does not want to join a union.
(b) Cannot dominate or influence a labor organization.	(b) Cannot coerce or restrain an employer in his selection of the parties to bargain in his behalf.
(c) Cannot discriminate against employees because of union membership.	(c) Cannot charge excessive or discriminatory union initiation fees.
(d) Cannot terminate employment or discriminate against employee for testifying before National Labor Relations Board or other agency in connection with Taft-Hartley Law.	(d) Cannot refuse to bargain collectively with an employer.
(e) Cannot refuse to bargain collectively with duly chosen representatives of his employees.	(e) Cannot participate in secondary boycotts and jurisdictional strikes.
	(f) Cannot practice "featherbedding"—making employer pay for services not rendered.
	(g) Cannot persuade an employer to discriminate against any of his employees.
	(h) Cannot attempt to force recognition from an employer when another union is already the certified representative.

Fig. 12-1

Unfair Labor Praitices

4. Union shop agreements must be in accordance with prevailing state laws and are void where prohibited by state laws.
5. Nonpayment of dues under an authorized union-shop contract is the only cause for loss of good standing with the union for which the employer can be compelled to discharge an employee.
6. Union dues check-off (deducting of union dues from paychecks by the employer and remitting of collections to the union) requires the written consent of the employee.
7. An individual employee can present grievances directly to his supervisor, but the union representative must be informed and be given an opportunity to be present.
8. Foremen and supervisors may be unionized, but the employer does not have to bargain with them, since they are presumed to represent management.
9. Both unions and employers can be sued for violation of the contract.

After the Taft-Hartley Law had been in operation, the need for certain changes in its provisions became apparent. As the result of the investigations into corrupt practices occurring within the field of union-management relations, the Labor-Management Reporting and Disclosure Act was passed in 1959 to: protect the rights of individual union members, protect the equities of members in union welfare funds, and prevent racketeering or unscrupulous practices from being committed by certain employers and union officers. One of the most important provisions of this act, also known as the Landrum-Griffin Act, is the Bill of Rights of Union Members, which requires that every union member be given the right to: (1) nominate candidates for union office, (2) vote in union elections or referendums, (3) attend union meetings, and (4) participate in union meetings and vote on union business. Under the act unions are required to file a financial report with the Secretary of Labor each year and employers must report any expenditures that are made in attempting to persuade employees to exercise their bargaining rights.

In Chapter 10 several pieces of legislation were described as marking the beginning of a new era in labor relations. In 1963 the Equal Pay Act, an amendment to the Fair Labor Standards Act, provided that no employer may discriminate solely on the basis of sex in determining the wage rates of men and women who are doing equal work under similar working conditions. In the following year a national policy of fair employment practices was set forth in the Civil Rights Act. Of major concern to the administrative office manager is the section of this act known as Title VII, Equal Employment Opportunity. This act provides that, in their hiring and training practices, employers, unions, and employment agencies may not discriminate on the bases of race, color, religion, national origin, or sex. The Age Discrimination in Employment Act of 1967 prohibits age discrimination by employers, employment agencies, and labor unions against those individuals who are between the ages of 40 and 65 years. The purpose of this act is to promote the employment of older persons based on their ability rather than age, to prohibit arbitrary age discrimination in employment, and to help employers and workers find ways of meeting problems arising from the impact of age on employment.[2]

Trends in Labor-Management Relations

As the result of the introduction of automated methods and equipment in factories and offices, labor agreements now include

[2] See Chapter 10 for a complete discussion of governmental regulations affecting the selection of office workers.

provisions aimed at protecting the worker against technological unemployment. Some of the efforts that have been made to insure jobs and income and to maintain fringe benefits include: (1) guarantee against job or income loss, and in some cases, against loss of supplementary benefits for varying periods, (2) compensation for employees who lose their jobs, (3) guarantee of income for workers required to take lower paying jobs, (4) provision for retraining, (5) provision for transfer to other plants and payment of relocation expenses, and (6) agreements to provide workers with notice of plant closing or other major changes.[3] There appears to be growing acceptance of the philosophy that layoffs resulting from automation and other forms of technological innovation should be handled exclusively through attrition, as evidenced in the labor agreements of the railroads, among West Coast longshoremen, and at Kaiser Steel Company.

Use has been made of *joint labor-management committees* in a wide variety of industries in an attempt to ease collective bargaining and to find solutions to many labor problems ranging from minor grievances to automation. Several years ago the steel industry and the United Steelworkers of America set up the *Human Relations Committee,* composed of labor and management representatives, whose job was to meet regularly in an endeavor to solve as many problems as possible in advance of normal bargaining. The newly formed committees differ in one major respect from the Human Relations Committee, for the former are company-union committees rather than industry-union committees. By means of exploring mutually the changing industrial trends in manufacturing processes, working conditions, or employee benefits, such committees are able to lay the groundwork for early settlement of labor-management difficulties rather than waiting until time of contract expiration and its period of crisis bargaining.[4]

The concept of total job security is emerging, with stress being placed on incorporating into the labor agreement provisions for more generous pensions and early retirement. Probably many unions will forge ahead to obtain a sabbatical plan for their employees, similar to that introduced by the United Steelworkers in 1962 under which

---

[3] *Automation: Impact and Implications, Focus on Developments in the Communications Industry,* prepared by The Diebold Group, Inc., for Communications Workers of America, AFL-CIO (April, 1965), p. 165. Several selected agreements are summarized to show specifically how labor and management have attempted to solve the problems created as the result of automating the production processes.

[4] For an excellent discussion of labor-management committees, see "Emerging Idea No. 6, Labor-Management Committees," *Business Management* (January, 1965), pp. 58-60, and "What's Ahead in Collective Bargaining?" *Management Review* (May, 1964), pp. 4-15.

13-week paid vacations are given every five years to about one half of the work force.

Another potential bargaining issue with the unions is the shortened workweek. In 1969, the president of the United Steelworkers reported to the convention of the AFL-CIO Industrial Union Department that his target for getting his whole union onto the four-day week is 1974.[5] Four years earlier at the meeting of the Office & Professional Employees International Union in San Francisco, the union had urged that locals press for a 32-hour, four-day week under a three-shift arrangement that would keep office operations staffed Monday through a full day Saturday. Kenneth E. Wheeler, president of the consulting firm, Wheeler Associates, Inc., strongly predicts that the four-day workweek is most definitely coming—sooner than most people expect.[6] The success of the short week, according to Wheeler, will be directly proportionate to the sustained increase in productivity that is initiated before implementation of the shorter work schedule. Howard Coughlin, president of the Office & Professional Employees International Union, anticipates a four-day week in the 1970's, as the result of social forces that have been in motion for many years.[7] Coughlin notes that the workweek for white-collar workers is constantly changing, having declined three hours each decade since 1900 until it has recently reached 37½ hours in the eastern United States. The workweek plan of Coughlin would embrace one shift of persons working Monday through Thursday, others Tuesday through Friday, and a third group Wednesday through Saturday.[8] In this manner, a business firm would have the advantage of six days work at straight-time rates. Taking an opposite stand, the editors of *Administrative Management* magazine cite the foreseeable shortage of competent workers and the added element of cost and disagree that the anticipated four-day workweek will be widely observed within this decade.[9] Other authorities, such as Riva Poor in her book *4 Days, 40 Hours,*[10] say that the four-day week will become widespread before too long. As a result of her extensive study of firms in the United States, she predicts that the four-day week will sweep the country—and much

[5] Kenneth E. Wheeler, "Small Business Eyes the Four-Day Workweek," *Harvard Business Review* (May-June, 1970), p. 143.

[6] *Ibid.*, p. 147.

[7] "A 4-Day Work Week Is Inevitable," *Administrative Management* (May, 1970), p. 22.

[8] *Ibid.*, p. 23.

[9] "4-Day Week Soon? We Doubt It," *Administrative Management* (May, 1970), p. 17.

[10] *4 Days, 40 Hours,* copyright 1970 by Bursk & Poor Publishing, 66 Martin Street, Cambridge, Massachusetts.

faster than the five-day week replaced the six-day week, a move that spanned some four decades between 1908 and the end of World War II.[11] Throughout the country a number of firms are modifying the traditional five-day, 35- to 40-hour workweek with other ideas and practices such as spring and summertime four-day weeks, five-hour days, and cutbacks of not only the day but the pay.[12] If the administrative office manager considers that his workers are, on the average, only 50 percent productive during the 37½ hours of each workweek, he finds that his firm is now operating under a 20-hour workweek (or less)—far exceeding the projected four-day workweek!

Each of the developments in the labor movement and the anticipated trends in labor-management relations are of prime concern to the administrative manager. The labor movement is now reaching out into an area that has been relatively untouched—the white-collar workers in government, trade, transportation, public utilities, finance, insurance, real estate, and other services.

Labor Unions for White-Collar Workers

The trend toward unionization of all workers during the past four decades could not help but affect office employees. The increased activity of unions during the period of labor legislation, as described earlier, has helped to swell union membership to approximately 18 million workers. This trend has tended to emphasize the problem of organizing office and clerical workers, and probably this tendency may increase more and more in the future. However, it should be noted that, according to the Bureau of National Affairs, unionization of white-collar employees in the private sector continued to decline in 1969 from the nine-year peak that had been reached in 1967.[13] Governmental employees, numbering about three million federal workers and more than nine million persons on various state and local government payrolls, are a huge organizing target for the unions. The unions feel that if they can successfully organize public employees, resistance on the part of office workers in the private sector will be substantially lessened.

In many firms having manufacturing operations that have been unionized, the office workers have also shared in the privileges and

[11] "The Leisure Class—Firms, Workers Cheer as the Four-Day Week Makes Some Inroads," *The Wall Street Journal,* October 15, 1970, p. 1.

[12] For illustrations of the various practices related to shortening the workday and workweek, see "The New Hours," *Administrative Management* (March, 1971), pp. 18-20.

[13] *The Wall Street Journal,* May 26, 1970, p. 1.

benefits that the factory workers receive through union activities and contracts. Where the firm is primarily staffed by office and clerical workers, as in the finance, insurance, and real estate industries, the trend toward unionism has been less successful. However, strong unions do exist among telephone operators, telegraphers, letter carriers, railway clerks, restaurant cashiers, and factory and warehouse clerical workers. These groups account for about two thirds of all clerical union members.

Some of the reasons advanced for the slowness in unionizing office workers are:

1. Many female office workers deem their jobs temporary, until they can get married.
2. The total office work force is characterized by a high percentage of women workers and part-time clerks, many of whom work for reasons other than individual or family support.
3. Many office workers aspire to future executive jobs, in which case they must represent management, not the workers. Thus, white-collar workers feel the need for identification with management and for recognition of their individuality.
4. Many office workers object to the methods used by unions in organizing industrial workers.
5. Many office workers resent the leveling process of membership in unions and feel that there is a loss of status.
6. A vast number of white-collar employees work in comparatively small offices, which are expensive and difficult to organize.

On the other hand, the greater routinization of office work because of computer systems and company growth, which tends to make certain jobs akin to factory production work, may stimulate the further unionizing of office workers. Also, the shortsightedness of management at times in its failure to establish satisfactory working conditions and to provide satisfactory employee benefits may stimulate the further formation of white-collar unions. The main reasons white-collar workers have joined unions, according to authoritative studies, are: [14]

1. Discontentment over earnings and their economic position in relation to that of blue-collar workers.
2. Lack of a sense of job security in that they felt there was no guarantee they would not be laid off arbitrarily.
3. Poor handling of day-to-day grievances by management.
4. Importance of employees' work not recognized by the company.

---

[14] Robert L. Caleo, "Can the Unions Take Your Office?" *Administrative Management* (February, 1963), pp. 37-38.

5. Inadequate channels of communications between employees and management.

The Opinion Research Corporation, in its study of the attitudes of clerical employees toward management during the past 15 years, has found evidence that the traditional clerical loyalty to management is breaking down.[15] Results of the studies show that there has been a marked and growing dissatisfaction among clerical workers in the following three areas, which indicates that some fundamental union arguments should have increasing receptivity among clerical workers: (1) basic employment conditions (pay, benefits, job security, and working conditions); (2) personnel practices; and (3) communication.[16] The conclusion is reached that unless management commences to act now, clerical discontent will increase in the future and possibly history will repeat itself, with management losing out to the unions, a situation that occurred when the discontent of factory workers emerged in the 1930's.

Status of White-Collar Unions

The nearly 21 million white-collar workers (5.5 million professional and technical employees and 15.3 million clerical and sales employees) in the United States offer a fertile field for unionization, especially since only slightly more than 2.7 million of them were white-collar union members in 1966.[17] Of the total white-collar union membership, about 62 percent of those unionized were in nonmanufacturing industries (transportation and public utilities, wholesale and retail trade, service, finance, insurance, and real estate); 27 percent were in government service; and 11 percent were in manufacturing industries.[18] In recent years most of the gain in white-collar unionization (almost 80 percent of all new white-collar union members) was made in government service. During this same period the number of white-collar workers in manufacturing experienced a decline.[19]

In the 1971-72 Salary Survey conducted by the Administrative Management Society among 5,411 companies in the United States representing about 2 million employees, 1.9 percent of the firms

---

[15] Alfred Vogel, "Your Clerical Workers Are Ripe for Unionism," *Harvard Business Review* (March-April, 1971), p. 48.

[16] *Ibid.*, p. 50.

[17] From *The Conference Board Record,* June, 1969, as quoted in *Personnel* (July-August, 1969), p. 6.

[18] *Ibid.*

[19] *Ibid.*

reported that all their office employees were unionized; 5.7 percent of the firms reported that part of their office employees were unionized; 92.3 percent indicated no office unionization.[20] The geographic area of the United States that reported the highest concentration of unionization was in the western United States, where 10.7 percent of the companies' offices are all or partly unionized. In the remaining geographic areas, the percentage of all or partly unionized offices ranged from 8.6 percent in the East Central United States to 5 percent in the southern United States.[21] Similar findings were found in the 1970 Union Survey undertaken by the Administrative Management Society. Of the 481 firms completing the survey forms, 93 percent of the firms in the United States answered that the firm had no office union. Total unionization of office personnel stood at 3 percent; partial unionization was reported by 4 percent of the companies.[22] Of those firms not having a union, 97 percent indicated that no overtures were then being made to office personnel; 99 percent indicated that there did not seem to be any desire among the office employees to organize a union.[23] Based upon these and other findings of the survey, the Administrative Management Society confirms that unions have made very little headway toward organizing white-collar office employees and there seems to be no indication that the number of office unions will increase substantially in the near future.[24]

About 40 unions, such as the Office & Professional Employees International Union,[25] the United Office and Professional Workers of America, and the Retail Clerks International Association, are predominantly or wholly white-collar unions. Several blue-collar unions have white-collar members; for example, the United Steelworkers of America counts approximately 45,000 office and technical workers in its membership. In 1969, the Teamsters union remained the most active white-collar organizer, although the International Union of Electrical Workers was the most successful.[26] It is felt by some that the smaller independent unions offer the best chances for long-range growth among office workers, for the smaller unions are generally more informal and office oriented than the larger organizations.

---

[20] *Directory of Office Salaries, 1971-72* (Willow Grove, Pa.: Administrative Management Society), p. 9.

[21] *Ibid.*

[22] *AMS NEWS* (Willow Grove, Pa.: Administrative Management Society, February, 1970), p. 1.

[23] *Ibid.*, p. 2.

[24] *Ibid.*

[25] This union was formerly known as the Office Employees International Union, but in 1965 the name was changed as the first step in its campaign to recruit white-collar workers in a variety of professional fields.

[26] *The Wall Street Journal,* May 26, 1970, p. 1.

The Role of the Office Manager in Relation to Office Unions

What should the office manager do about office unions? The answer to this question involves the time factor. What should be done before union activity starts? What should be done while attempts are being made to organize the workers? What should be done after the workers become organized? There are many arguments both for and against unions, none of which seems absolutely unbiased. However, it is no longer a question of being for or against a union for office workers. Rather, it is a question of what the office manager will do about the creation of office workers' unions or attempts to unionize office workers.

Before Union Activity. Long before union activity starts among a group of office workers the office manager should have studied the working conditions in his office and compared them with those of unionized offices. Probably by now it is far too late to initiate programs that are specifically designed to avoid unionization. However, wherever possible, conditions should be improved to equal or surpass those that prevail in unionized offices. But these conditions and the attempts of management must be properly communicated to the workers. In one instance, a firm was paying higher salaries than those offered by unionized shops in the area, but still dissatisfaction with salaries existed among the employees. This dissatisfaction was not due so much to the company's salary structure as to the employee's lack of reliable information from management about its wage and salary program.

Among the questions to which the administrative office manager must have answers are the following:

1. Are the working conditions good in the office? If not, how can they be improved?
2. How can the work be made more challenging by means of enriching the jobs?
3. How can the company become more responsive to the underlying needs of its workers—to be heard by management, to count in the scheme of things, and to be treated fairly?
4. How can the company become more responsive to complaints about tangible matters—grievances, salary increments, vacations, suggestion plans, recreational programs, and other employee benefits in order to create better human relations between management and employees?

5. Are the office workers at too great a disadvantage over their fellow workers in the unionized offices and plants?
6. How can the personnel program and its policies be improved to place it on a more impersonal and meritorious basis?
7. If the union is the choice of the employees, what can be done to make the relationship between management and the union most cooperative?
8. If the union is not the choice of the employees, how can the employees be organized so that management and workers can work together more closely and with better understanding?

While Attempts Are Being Made to Organize. If a firm is not able to provide its office workers with benefits equal or superior to those offered by the unions, then it must expect that in many cases the workers will seek the benefits of unions. Thus, the office manager becomes faced with the problem of how to deal with the unions. In some cases, a worker may contact a union itself, but ordinarily a union will seek out and approach the dissatisfied worker, evaluate the situation, and where the opportunity presents itself, ask management to accept voluntarily the jurisdiction of the union.[27] If the firm does not voluntarily accept the union, the National Labor Relations Board is petitioned to call for an election, which must be held within 30 days if 30 percent of the employees have so petitioned.

At the time of the election, workers vote for or against unionization and a simple majority vote determines the decision. If the vote is against unionization, the election procedure can be undertaken again at a later date. If the vote is for unionization, the employees are first classified by salary and job and then a list of specific proposals is prepared. After the proposals are approved by the workers, management is presented with the suggested changes. At this stage of the unionization process, a bargaining committee made up of employee representatives and a business agent from the union meet with management to draw up the contract. After the contract has been approved, shop stewards are appointed for the various office departments and a grievance procedure is established.[28]

In most cases, because of the contracts involved, a business firm will need legal help in the acceptance and preparation of agreements. Supplementing such legal help, the office manager must be familiar with labor legislation and current labor relations practices.

---

[27] For an exceptionally fine description of a typical union campaign, see James O. Dunn, "Union Campaign—Organizer vs. Supervisor," *Personnel* (August, 1970), pp. 15-24, and (January, 1971), pp. 8-15.

[28] See page 345 for an outline of a typical grievance-handling plan.

After the Workers Become Organized. Once the union has been established, management should work toward realizing its objectives and those of the union. The objectives of management and the union, which will be attained only through harmonious labor relations, and for which the office manager may be called upon to do his part, are listed in Figure 12-2.

Fig. 12-2

Objectives of Management	*Objectives of the Union*
(a) Profit for the owners of the business.	(a) Reasonable wages to maintain a decent standard of living.
(b) Reasonable retention of part of the earnings for contingencies, expansion, and improvements.	(b) Security of employment and promotional opportunities.
(c) Reputable products and services, based upon good workmanship of employees.	(c) Good or improved working conditions, and protection against economic catastrophies of old age and illness.
(d) Favorable public relations.	(d) Opportunities to contribute to the growth and development of the company and its products.

Union-Management Objectives

The apparent conflict of objectives can be reconciled by means of across-the-table *bargaining;* by *mediation* of a third party; by *conciliation,* which is more aggressive than mediation; or by *arbitration,* which provides a binding, impartial umpire of the dispute. Both parties must realize that the interests of the employer and the union are mutual and that "everyone loses by a strike."

Provisions Contained in the White-Collar Union Contract

The main differences between union contracts covering production workers and those covering office workers relate to vacations, holidays, severance pay, and other employee benefits. The outline of the contents of the union contract will usually include:

1. Objective of the agreement.
2. Duration of contract.
3. The bargaining unit to be represented by the union.
4. Whether check-off is included and whether solicitation of new members is to be permitted on company time.
5. Pledge of no strike and no lockout during contract period.

6. A clear statement of management's right to arrange work schedules, make temporary transfers, increase or decrease the working force, maintain right to hire, fire, promote, and discipline.
7. Methods of job classification.
8. Method of establishing new rates for existing and new jobs.
9. Payment for overtime, vacations, and sick leaves.
10. Seniority rules.
11. Handling of grievances.
12. Merit rating program and practices.

Provisions found in many of the union contracts covering office workers are as follows:

1. Layoff of workers is governed by seniority.
2. Promotion is governed by seniority. If it is a question of seniority versus ability, the senior employee is frequently given a trial period of employment in the higher position.
3. Most contracts provide a trial period during which the employee has no seniority rights.
4. Most grievance procedure clauses provide ultimately for arbitration. Most grievances on the part of white-collar workers follow three stages: (a) the employee takes his grievance to the division head; (b) if not settled, the grievance is submitted to the bargaining committee of the union for discussion with management; (c) if still not settled, the grievance is submitted to arbitration.
5. Most white-collar workers come under a 40-hour week, with time and one half for overtime, and overtime or double time pay for Saturday or Sunday or the sixth and seventh days of any week.
6. Most contracts provide for pay increases either automatically or at the time of an agreed-upon merit rating.
7. Most office workers get six or more paid holidays during the year, of which the most common are Christmas Day, Thanksgiving Day, New Year's Day, Independence Day, Labor Day, and Memorial Day. When other paid holidays are granted, they are usually Election Day, Washington's Birthday, Veteran's Day, Columbus Day, and Lincoln's Birthday.
8. Most contracts provide one week's vacation after six months and two weeks' after twelve months of employment.
9. Employee benefits usually provide for sick leave with pay; group insurance on life, accident, and health; and hospitalization.

10. Some contracts provide for ten- or fifteen-minute rest periods, for supper money in case of overtime, and for personal leaves in case of death.
11. Severance pay is provided in about one third of the contracts, unless the employee is discharged because of strike or for another cause.
12. About two thirds of the contracts provide for company check-off of dues.
13. The majority of contracts include no-strike or restricted-strike clauses.
14. Management usually reserves the right to hire, discharge, lay off, transfer, and direct the employees.

EMPLOYER-EMPLOYEE COMMUNICATIONS

Communications aid in motivating people to perform their jobs in the most efficient and productive manner possible. The establishment of effective communications between management and employees is one of the most important and demanding problems of human relations that face business organizations today. Communication is not a one-way matter—from management to the employees. To be successful, communications must be two-way —*up and down* between management and its employees; and *sideways* between management, and between employees. This two-way communication is often a major factor in the success of many business firms. As the firm, and in this instance the office, becomes larger, the problem of maintaining adequate communications becomes more difficult. In some of the largest firms, the problem of keeping the communication lines open and operating is so important that the employee relations, or labor relations, division conducts periodic personnel surveys of what the worker thinks of his firm. its products, and its management.

The kind of information contained in an effective program of communications from management to the employees is indicated below:

1. *The company:* its history, products, or services; its organization and lines of responsibility; its future plans, and so on.
2. *Company policies:* in relation to the employees and customers, and the reasons therefor.
3. *Special events:* relating to the company, its products, or employees.
4. *New methods, products, or plans:* how they will affect employees, the community, and the company.

In each instance, it is necessary for management to determine what information the employees want or need in order to develop human relations of mutual trust and understanding. Employees like to be informed about events before they happen, not after everyone else has learned about them.

Management, on the other hand, wants to learn just exactly what the employees think of the company. By means of an effective communications and employee relations program, the following kinds of information should flow freely from the employees to management:

1. The needs and aspirations of employees.
2. The employees' attitudes toward their working conditions, their work, and their work place.
3. The employees' complaints and grievances.

It should be borne in mind that communication is a highly personal and emotional process. Business offices, like the individuals working therein, have their own individual personalities and what works in one office to improve communications may be only slightly effective or may fail in another office. In many instances it is probable that the lack of good communications lies not in the media or mechanisms of communications but in the communicator himself. The communicator must concern himself not only with the methods of communication but also, and perhaps more importantly, with the emotional reactions, attitudes, and feelings of employees, which play a vital role in any program of communications improvement.[29]

Providing for Two-Way Communications

Several procedures and methods, each designed to keep the communications lines open between management and employees in order to promote effective human relations, are described below.

Meetings. Meetings with middle management personnel should be regularly scheduled to convey to them the importance of keeping open the lines of communication between top management and the workers. Without this emphasis, the second-echelon management personnel may attempt to exert its imaginary authority by preventing this communication from taking place. The managers should be

[29] For a report of a two-year study that challenges some of the basic beliefs about the way that people learn to communicate, see A. W. Lindh, EBS Management Consultants, Inc., "Plain Talk About Communicating in Business," *Business Management* (April, 1964), pp. 91-95.

urged to make frequent trips into the office to talk with the workers. One official of a bank regularly walks through the bank offices and talks to junior executives and other personnel. It is surprising how much effect this practice has on the morale of the employees, and at the same time the executive learns what the workers think and how they feel.

Another technique for maintaining workable relationships between employer and employees is the *personnel council,* made up of employee representatives of various departments who meet regularly with executives. Such a council can anticipate and prevent many complex problems before they emerge. In one company a council of personnel relations holds monthly meetings on four different levels: departmental, sectional, divisional, and main council. Employee representatives at the various levels are elected every two years.[30]

Publications. House organs or company publications may be used to keep employees informed of the operations, plans, and changes in the firm. The communications should be carefully selected and timely. Very often the employees must be subtly "sold" on what the firm is doing or planning to do. For example, a firm planning to install automated equipment in the office can disrupt its entire personnel by not preparing them for the change, indicating the future effects, and reassuring them of their security. In one large bank, forced by competition to convert its paper-work operations to automated data processing, the officers realized that their employees were afraid of automation because they thought of it as a job stealer and because it was new and unknown. As a result of an automation information program, the employees became informed on automation as it applied to their operations and were assured that the automated installation would not put them out of work. In turn, the employees themselves, through an organized public relations program, helped management sell the new and expanded services to the bank's customers.

Special pamphlets, booklets, and manuals, for all levels of employment, may be utilized to cover company policies, new methods, products, or plans. Special or regular letters to all employees from the president or other officials of the company are especially effective when a new procedure, product, or equipment is to be used or installed. One aircraft company uses a "wired newscast" technique to

[30] "Employee Council Can Prevent Problems," *Administrative Management* (September, 1966), p. 14.

communicate management messages to its 7,000 employees. By means of telephones that are in reasonable proximity to its employees, the company is able to communicate *orally* such matters as why a new building is being erected, who were the visitors touring the plant yesterday, the name and background of new employees, and why the firm is emphasizing a cost-cutting program. The company reports that the wired newscast has won 90 percent acceptance by the employees, that a 60 percent coverage is obtained, and that the technique is particularly effective in killing rumors.[31] In another company, employees learn the latest news via dialing a three-digit telephone number that gives them taped announcements on topics ranging from company progress reports to scores in the latest employee ball games.

Employee-association publications may be produced to indicate the off-work experiences of the workers and to announce company cultural and recreational activities. Motion pictures and radio or television programs are useful in training employees and explaining company history or new products.

Bulletin Boards. Many firms consider the bulletin board as the best means of keeping employees informed. Bulletin boards may be used by firms for posting rules and regulations, recreation activities, safety records, employee illness, job openings, attendance records, new product announcements, vacation schedules, lost and found notices, personal announcements of births and weddings, educational opportunities, and press releases. To be a most effective means of communication, there should be a sufficient number of boards to attract the attention of all employees. One person should be responsible for the upkeep of the boards so that outdated material is removed promptly.

Many companies use an information rack with a variety of bulletins to inform employees of the details of company operations and the underlying philosophies and economics of the business. By giving employees the free choice of selecting the information they want from the rack, these firms eliminate the "propaganda" accusation of some employees when the material is given to all workers.

Finally, a well-organized employee suggestion system is an excellent type of employee-to-management communication. The suggestion system is singled out for further discussion in the section that follows.

---

[31] Robert E. Perry, Hughes Aircraft Company, "Spoken Words Versus Writing in Employee Communications," *Administrative Management* (December, 1963), pp. 62-65.

Employee Suggestion Systems

As indicated in the preceding chapter, the efficient functioning of an office requires that management provide an opportunity for employees to make suggestions for improving or expanding the business. Employee suggestion systems are used in both business and governmental offices as a means of building better morale among office workers, getting workers to think more seriously about their jobs, and as a means of communication between employees and top management. The reasoning that underlies the use of employee suggestion systems is: (1) those closest to the work being done are probably best able to understand the inefficiencies and to recommend changes, and (2) it is wasteful not to use the abilities of all workers to the fullest extent by permitting them to make suggestions and to pay for these ideas on the basis of their value.

The employee suggestion plan is a tool that can be used by the office manager to increase the volume and the quality of the work, at the same or less cost than if the plan were not in effect. Such a plan enables the worker to feel that his knowledge and ability are worth something to the company and that the company appreciates his ideas enough to want to pay him. In theory, suggestion systems are excellent. In practice, however, the results have not been so successful. Management has not always appreciated the full value of such systems, perhaps as the result of poor planning and organization of the suggestion system.

The outline of an effective suggestion system covers the following steps:

1. Appointing a suggestion committee.
2. Establishing rules for submitting suggestions.
3. Developing a procedure for processing the suggestions and making the awards.

Appointing a Suggestion Committee. The suggestion committee has the responsibility for reviewing and evaluating all incoming suggestions. Those persons named to this committee should be competent, responsible, and ineligible to participate in the suggestion program. In one bank, the suggestion committee was composed of the officer in charge of operations, the personnel manager, the auditor, and representatives of various operating divisions who would be interested in the awards in their divisions.

Establishing Rules for Submitting Suggestions. The rules for submitting suggestions vary from firm to firm. However, all rules should consider the two major factors of eligibility and identity.

Eligibility. Generally, all employees are eligible to participate in the suggestion system, with the exception of salaried supervisory employees (excluding officials and heads of major departments) who receive awards only for ideas not connected directly with their own departments or fields of activity. It is claimed by some that supervisory employees submit a better quality of suggestions than those of the rank and file. This argument seems to have little validity, however. The disadvantage of having both workers and supervisors submit suggestions is that the workers and the supervisors come into competition with one another and as a result, conflicts may arise. The workers may also think that their ideas are being taken by the supervisors.

Identity. Identifying the person who makes a suggestion may follow one of three plans:

1. The suggester does not sign his name, but is identified by the number shown on the suggestion form used, with the stub being retained by the employee.
2. The suggester is required to sign his name.
3. The suggester has the option of either signing his name or being identified by number.

The plan used is dependent to a large extent upon whether or not employee relations are good and whether employees have confidence in management. If so, signing the suggestion form may be acceptable; if not, the anonymous procedure may be more successful. However, the optional plan seems to be best for employee morale, since it leaves it up to the employee to decide which plan of identification he prefers.

Processing the Suggestions and Making the Awards. The routine for handling and investigating the suggestions submitted varies with different concerns. Whatever plan is followed, it must be fair and prompt; otherwise, it will fail because of lack of interest. Many firms have found the unsigned, numbered suggestion blank, with a detachable receipt, most desirable. On the suggestion form shown in Figure 12-3, no signature appears on the blank; the detachable numbered

Fig. 12-3

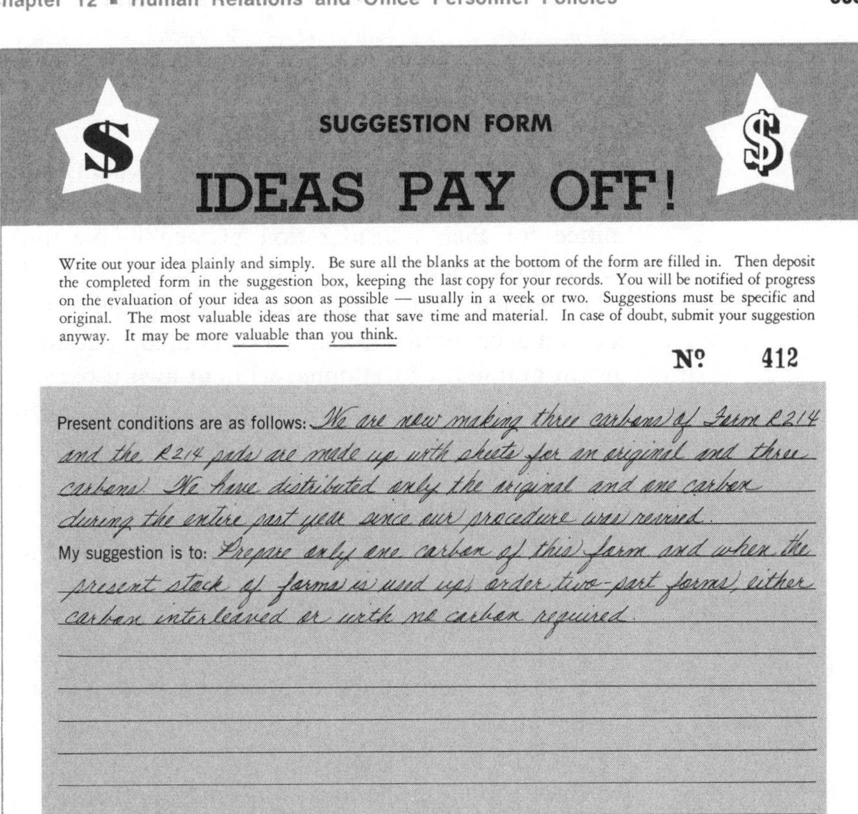

SUGGESTION FORM

IDEAS PAY OFF!

Write out your idea plainly and simply. Be sure all the blanks at the bottom of the form are filled in. Then deposit the completed form in the suggestion box, keeping the last copy for your records. You will be notified of progress on the evaluation of your idea as soon as possible — usually in a week or two. Suggestions must be specific and original. The most valuable ideas are those that save time and material. In case of doubt, submit your suggestion anyway. It may be more valuable than you think.

No. 412

Present conditions are as follows: We are now making three carbons of Form R214 and the R214 pads are made up with sheets for an original and three carbons. We have distributed only the original and one carbon during the entire past year since our procedure was revised.

My suggestion is to: Prepare only one carbon of this form and when the present stock of forms is used up, order two-part forms, either carbon interleaved or with no carbon required.

I submit the foregoing suggestion for consideration under the rules of our suggestion system. I understand and agree that if my idea is found to be original and valuable, the company shall have the right to make full use of my suggestion and I will be paid in cash according to its estimated worth.

DATE August 1, 19— EMPLOYEE'S SIGNATURE Ruth E. Hardy

NAME Ruth E. Hardy CLOCK NO. 39

JOB TITLE Clerk-Typist DEPARTMENT Order Processing & Billing

PLANT BADGE NO.

HOME ADDRESS 507 Jefferson Road CITY Easton, Pennsylvania

No. 412

Personnel Materials Company

Suggestion Blank

receipt serves as identification. In this particular plan, a signature on the form itself would disqualify the person making the suggestion. The suggestion must be placed in a sealed envelope addressed to the suggestion committee and placed in a suggestion box or mailed to the committee. The receipt numbers of the accepted suggestions are posted on the bulletin board, and claims for awards are made on a special award claim form.

Suggestions may be collected daily or at less frequent intervals if the number received is not large. In many firms, the suggestions are copied and distributed to the members of the suggestion committee for their consideration at weekly meetings. The variety of recognitions that can be given include: (1) adopted with award; (2) adopted with shared award, where someone else may have had the same or similar idea; (3) adopted, but not as suggested, and award granted; (4) adopted without award because it did not pertain to a field in which awards are given; (5) adopted without award to managers, officers, etc.; (6) already under consideration; (7) rejected; and (8) additional award when it is learned that the idea is more valuable than originally anticipated.

The basis of the awards is usually a point of much confusion and perhaps dissatisfaction. Some concerns, particularly in connection with office work, pay a flat amount such as $2, $5, $10, and up for each suggestion accepted. Others—and this plan seems more desirable—pay a percentage of the savings that result from the implementation of the award. At United States Steel, suggestors are given 20 percent of the company's first-year savings after deducting the expense of putting the idea to use.[32] Another firm pays from 5 to 15 percent of the increase in profits during the first year. One bank pays both an initial award and an additional award if the savings exceed the estimate. Some companies give merchandise awards, such as Ford automobiles given by the Ford Motor Company as a bonus to the employees who earn the maximum suggestion awards.[33] In an attempt to elicit suggestions from their employees, firms have also given as an award the right to use special reserved parking places for a month, trading stamps in addition to cash bonuses, and shares of company stock. When determining the amount of the awards, consideration should be given to whether the idea involves recurring or nonrecurring savings and to the possibility that the idea itself may be superseded later.

Characteristics of a Successful Employee Suggestion System. Three "musts" are essential if a suggestion system is to work satisfactorily and achieve its purpose of improving employee attitudes:

---

[32] Joseph A. Montana, "Managing an Effective Suggestion System," *Administrative Management* (October, 1966), p. 38.

[33] *Ibid.*, p. 41.

1. The suggestions must be acted upon promptly so that employees are informed of what happens to their suggestions once they have been submitted.
2. If the suggestions are accepted, immediate recognition must be given to the employees making them.
3. If the suggestion is rejected, a full explanation must be given to the employee.

At General Motors, the following information is placed on the back of the suggestion form:

> When your suggestion is received, it is date stamped, assigned a suggestion number, and acknowledged by card to you. Your suggestion will be investigated as quickly as possible. This may involve consulting many people, making and trying out tools, and other things that all take time—so please be patient. You will be contacted as soon as possible and given an answer. If any questions arise concerning your idea after you have submitted it, have your foreman call the Suggestion Office for an explanation.

The suggestions should be considered fairly and promptly. Too often suggestions are evaluated hastily and haphazardly. If the suggestion offers possibilities but is incomplete, the suggester can be asked to give additional information. If a suggestion is rejected, the reason must be a good one, not an evasion nor an avoidance of proper credit, nor because it is too much trouble to put the idea into effect.

The suggestion system should be used by the majority of employees; otherwise, there is something wrong and the system should be investigated. Enthusiasm for suggestions on the part of management will stimulate employee interest. This enthusiasm can be highlighted by distributing the blanks often; placing suggestion boxes where they will not be missed (one firm places them at the entrance to the lunchroom); developing competition between departments or branches; and giving clues of suggestions needed, such as "need for billing cost reduction" or "how to speed up monthly statements." Another approach is to hold a "suggestion of the month" contest in which each winner receives a bonus prize. Enthusiasm for the suggestion plan can also be stimulated by implementing the suggestions that have been accepted. When suggesters see their ideas put into action, they receive an additional incentive to seek new and improved ideas. Some workers may be reluctant to submit a timesaving idea because of the fear that the suggestion, if accepted, would eliminate their own jobs. Thus, there is need to establish a policy that if a suggestion derives its full value as the result of a reduction in the work force, the suggestion will not be adopted until such time as it will not adversely affect current company personnel.

The awards must be fair. How much satisfaction can an employee get out of a $5 or $10 award if his suggestion saves the company thousands of dollars a year? Large awards in the hundreds or thousands of dollars are warranted when the ideas save the company this much or more each year. During the three years following the mechanization of the Treasurer's Department at Esso Standard, the receipt of ideas increased 110 percent and the awards granted increased 850 percent. Of the office ideas submitted, 24 percent earned awards, for which employees received $18,000. At the same time, management realized net savings during the first year of more than $156,000.[34] In 1969, 30,000 ideas were submitted by the employees of United Airlines, Inc., with 7,500 suggestions being eventually accepted for a distribution of $326,000 in awards. The airlines firm estimates that the suggestion program saves the company about $3.3 million each year.[35] In 1970 the federal government paid out $5.3 million for the 81,070 suggestions received from its workers, which led to increased efficiency and improved operations worth $176 million. The average award was $65.[36] Several years ago the National Association of Suggestion Systems reported that the average cash award per suggestion paid by its member companies was $35.85.[37] During the same year firms belonging to the Association reported that they received, on the average, 40 suggestions for every 100 eligible employees.

Management should attempt to show its appreciation of what the suggestions accomplish by giving a certain amount of publicity and recognition for all ideas accepted. Merely sending the employee a check or noting on his personnel record that he has made an acceptable suggestion causes the system to lose much of its morale-building effect. The names of the suggestion award winners, as well as the amounts of their awards, can be publicized in local newspapers and company publications. A well-operated suggestion

---

[34] William C. Whitwell, "Administration of an Office Suggestion System," *Personnel* (January, 1961), p. 30.

[35] "Power of Suggestion Lifts Airline's Savings," *Management in Practice,* American Management Association (July, 1970), p. 1.

[36] *The Wall Street Journal,* November 3, 1970, p. 1.

[37] Robert L. Caleo, "Motivating Employees to Think," *Administrative Management* (July, 1963), p. 25. The National Association of Suggestion Systems is a nonprofit organization concerned with encouraging the use of company suggestion systems.

system, although one of the most valuable management tools, is too often neglected or overlooked entirely.

ETHICS IN THE OFFICE

Ethics is the systematic study of that part of science and philosophy which deals with moral conduct, duty, and judgment. A person's concept of what is ethically and morally right and what is not stems from deep religious convictions, personal philosophy, and motives. Thus, as individuals differ, so do their ethical concepts vary. Personal guidelines or policies for everyday ethical conduct, like policies for labor relations and communications, are needed in the office. Like all policies, a code of ethics must be capable of enforcement.

The inspiration for ethical behavior must originate at the top level of management, filter down through middle management, and permeate the business organization. The best guarantee of high standards of morality in business is that subordinates work under the direction of men who themselves have high standards. For at least one third of each working day, the office manager is entering into social relationships with his subordinates. During the remaining two thirds of each day the attitudes, ideals, and beliefs that the employees have formed while at work in the office are being carried back and relayed to society—the families and friends of the employees. Thus, the office manager has a social responsibility to set a good example for his employees. As a leader, the ethical and moral conduct of the office manager must rise above his own personal and individual motives and needs.

In communicating with his superiors, the office manager should strive to report all the facts honestly, accurately, and objectively. He must train himself and his workers to avoid distorting the facts in order to fill a psychological need, for all too often the communications lines become warped by the personality, prejudices, and embellishments of the sender. In reaching decisions, the goal of the office manager should be to discipline his thinking into a logical, orderly inductive process, rather than impulsively jump to conclusions. In working with subordinates, it becomes easy for the office manager to abuse his authority and prerogative, with the result that employees feel "let down" and unsupported in their actions. To gain employees who will *work with him,* the office manager must *work with them*; be kind, fair, and just; and sincerely praise the satisfactory performance of his workers.

Basic to an ethical and moral conduct is loyalty. Without this fundamental quality, no office manager, no office, and no business firm can perform at its top peak of potential capability. When the office manager is unable to bear allegiance to the authority of his firm, he finds himself in a position of conflict and mental torment, which in turn hinders him from being loyal to either himself or his company. The only workable solution to the problem of an office manager who cannot abide by the policies and principles set forth by his firm is to search out another firm to which he can give his loyalty.

In a series of interviews, office and business executives were asked to judge the ethics and morality of several questionable office practices, some of which are described below.[38] How does your evaluation compare with that of the executives, which is given in parentheses following each of the practices?

1. "The employee who punches in another's time card." (Definitely unethical.)
2. "The executive who doesn't want to be bothered and tells his secretary to inform callers that he's not in." (Questionable, but not really immoral. The best solution is to be truthful; have her tell callers that he's too busy to be disturbed.)
3. "Pirating an employee from another company." (It's part of the free enterprise system. If a man wants to work for you, that is his business. However, the company that hires a man away from a competitor solely to hurt the other company is being unethical.)
4. "Taking credit for another employee's idea." (Definitely immoral, unless the idea has been substantially improved upon.)
5. "Padding an expense account." (Very bad. However, some companies with unrealistic rules force their employees into the practice. In that case, it's their own fault.)
6. "Undermining another employee in an effort to get ahead." (When it exceeds the bounds of good clean competition, it's unethical and should be stamped out before it infects the entire organization.)

QUESTIONS FOR REVIEW

1. What are the major provisions of the National Labor Relations Act of 1935?

---

[38] With permission of Warren C. Stevens, Editor, "What's Happened to Morality in the Office?" *Modern Office Procedures* (February, 1964), pp. 19-22. Copyright by the Industrial Publishing Co., Division of Pittsburgh Railways Company.

2. The Labor-Management Relations Act of 1947 enumerates certain unfair labor practices. What are the unfair labor practices (a) on the part of the employer and (b) on the part of the union?
3. For what purposes are joint labor-management committees formed?
4. Why have unions progressed relatively slowly in unionizing office workers?
5. What are the main reasons advanced for white-collar workers joining unions?
6. Compare the role of the office manager in relation to office unions under each of the following situations: (a) before union activity, (b) while attempts are being made to organize, and (c) after the workers become organized.
7. Contrast the objectives of management with those of the union. Are the objectives compatible?
8. In a typical union contract covering office workers, what are the usual stages in the handling of grievances?
9. "To be successful, communications must be two-way." Explain.
10. Describe several procedures and methods by means of which the communication lines between management and employees may be kept open.
11. What benefits may management realize from the use of an employee suggestion system? What benefits may the worker receive?
12. List several characteristics of a successful employee suggestion system.
13. What is the best guarantee of high standards of morality in business?

QUESTIONS FOR DISCUSSION

1. The Vearling Company has just won a union representation election by a very small margin. Management now intends to increase wages and salaries, to improve certain employee benefits, and to accomplish the other aims listed by the union in its leaflets distributed prior to the election. Evaluate the wisdom of such a move by management at this time.
2. Grievances are as much a part of our life as the human race itself and to expect to eliminate grievances is to wish for a Utopia. Although grievances will never be eliminated, there are steps that the office manager can take, especially in nonunion offices, to reduce and prevent the number of gripes and grievances. Prepare a list of these steps.
3. By means of an employee opinion survey, a company surveyed its workers and found that there were two major areas of unrest—the matter of pay and benefits. After a study was made of the pay and

benefits in neighboring business firms, the company found that its pay rates were close to the means of the area and that its benefits were better than average in most respects. Management now wants to explain all these facts to its employees. Discuss the various techniques and methods that management may use to communicate the results of the community survey and the company's relative standing.

4. The Tanenbaum Supply Company has been having a regular coffee break in its offices both in the morning and in the afternoon. Recently there seems to be some unionizing activity that has concerned the office manager. In an effort to discourage the unionizing activities, he has told his employees that if they join a union, the coffee breaks will be discontinued. This did not deter their efforts nor the formation of an office workers' union. Discuss the actions of the office manager in light of modern administrative office management.

5. Why is conversation not necessarily communication?

6. Why do superior-subordinate communications probably create more types of communication problems than communications between two persons on the same organizational level?

7. Ed Boyle, after scanning the list of this month's suggestion awards, remarks to you, supervisor of the records management department: "What good is our suggestion plan? None of the awards ever equal the amount of the savings that the company surely realizes. No wonder so few of our workers take part in the plan." Are Ed's comments legitimate? How would you reply to Ed?

8. React to the following Principle of Ethics: The ethical standards of any industry are determined by the ethical standards of the individual executives of each member company in that industry.

9. During the past few months Bill Robinson, office manager of the Greenfield Steel Company, has noticed that his boss, E. G. Rutherford, works so many more hours than he. On many occasions Rutherford is at the office an hour or more before the others report in and often he works on Saturdays, in addition to taking work home at night. Bill realizes that his boss is a thoroughly devoted, loyal "company man." Bill, however, is a thoroughly devoted, loyal "family man."

Rutherford is well aware of Bill's devotion to the family and on several occasions has told Bill that as long as he is a "family man," Bill will never get to the top in the company. Although this statement has been made jokingly, Bill suspects that his boss is serious. Discuss how Bill should go about convincing his boss that he, too, is concerned about the company and that he is loyal, but, on the other hand, that he is married to his family and not to the business.

10. What is an office grapevine? Discuss the pros and cons of attempting to eliminate the grapevine.

PRACTICAL OFFICE CASES

Case 12-1 Installing an Employee Suggestion System

You have recently been appointed office and personnel manager of the Schearer Data Processing Center. There are 300 persons in the offices. Their morale is at a low ebb because your predecessor was a hard taskmaster who always felt that he knew it all. Further, he never gave a salary increase until forced to do so. Since his resignation, the jobs have been classified and a salary program with regular increments has been installed. You now feel it would be a good time to develop a suggestion plan. Recently you read in a magazine that one firm paid an employee $2,500 for one idea, and another firm paid $1,350 for an idea. These figures scare you because you do not think that your company can pay any such amounts. Yet you feel that if the amounts are not large enough, the workers will lose interest and will not cooperate.

▪ With these facts in mind, outline the approach you would use to develop a workable suggestion plan for your office workers. This plan should cover:

1. Who would be eligible.
2. How the person who makes the suggestion will be identified.
3. The nature and the amount of awards.
4. Frequency of review of suggestions and making of awards.
5. Publicity for awards.
6. Recommendations to help make the suggestion plan function successfully.

Case 12-2 Overcoming a Communications Breakdown

Hank VanKoski, supervisor of the information services department of a very large automobile manufacturer, was asked to attend a planning meeting to discuss the development of a new, expanded office services department. Hank had been aware for the past four months that shortly planning would have to begin on the project, and he had become uneasy because he had heard nothing about it from his boss, Herb Witzky.

All the management team who were requested to sit in on the planning session arrived in the board room, and Herb opened the meeting by announcing the names of the manager and the staff for the new department. Hank just sat there, utterly amazed, and never said a word. He was taken completely by surprise because he was expecting the discussion to center around who the management team of the new department *should* be, not who it *would* be. Hank's mind was closed to the remainder of the discussion that took place, for he felt all respect for his judgment was lost and that Herb had bypassed him prior to making a decision on this important personnel appointment.

When Hank returned to his department, his assistant, Pat Skea, knew at a glance that something was bothering Hank and asked if he could help in some way. Hank told Pat about the meeting and explained that he just could not understand why he had not been informed prior to the meeting of the selection of the new management team and also why he had not been asked for his recommendations. Pat started to apologize by stating that two weeks earlier while Hank was out of the city, Herb had called to ask Hank for his recommendations on the matter. Pat said that immediately after the call, an emergency had developed in the computer room and he had rushed out, forgetting to make a note of the matter.

▪ Answer the following questions:

1. What mistakes were made in this situation and which individuals were at fault?
2. Explain how each of the mistakes might have been overcome originally by applying workable principles of communications.
3. If you were Hank, what steps would you now take?

13

Current Office Personnel Practices

Along with the basic principles of effectively supervising an efficient work force, the administrative office manager should be familiar with the current practices regarding personnel problems that occur in the office. A knowledge of how other managers solve their problems will aid the office manager in improving the quality and quantity of his work and at the same time motivate his subordinates to create a better environment in which to work. The office personnel practices discussed in this chapter are grouped under the following headings: practices relating to fringe benefits; practices affecting the physical and mental well-being of employees; and practices relating to special personnel problems.

PRACTICES RELATING TO FRINGE BENEFITS

Office practices relating to fringe benefits are designed to attract and to maintain a stable, happy, and productive work force. Several current practices, each of which is aimed at achieving this goal, are discussed in this section.

Coffee Breaks and Rest Periods

The purpose of providing coffee breaks and rest periods is to increase the productivity and efficiency of workers. Coffee breaks and rest periods should be so explained to the workers and so understood by management. They are not a charitable contribution to paternalism. The coffee breaks and rest periods should be scheduled at such intervals and for such length of time as seem most successful. They should be administered with the same regularity and control as arrival in the morning and departure at night. Otherwise, their purpose is defeated by creating more wasted time and decreased production in the office than if they were never provided.

Underlying the provision for coffee breaks and rest periods is the principle that certain types of work, being repetitive, soon become monotonous. This monotony increases fatigue, which in turn slows down production. The work output of employees performing motor-skill tasks such as typewriting varies at different times throughout the day. After a worker starts in the morning, he tends to increase his productivity. Physiologically the ability of the worker's muscles to function increases as the body adjusts to the activity. Psychologically warming up involves a change in attitude and attention. As the worker becomes more absorbed in his work, an increase in productivity results. There is a similar warm-up period following the lunch break. The initial warm-up period is followed by a period of high productivity; but as work continues, the performance begins to fall off and continues to decrease to the end of the work period. As shown in Figure 13-1,[1] the morning's maximum productivity is usually higher than that reached in the afternoon; and the afternoon warm-up period starts at a higher performance level than the worker's initial efforts in the morning. Also, in the afternoon the downward trend often begins earlier and the productivity usually falls to a much lower level by the end of the afternoon.

To be most effective, rest periods should be introduced just before performance begins to drop from its maximum. The typical work curve shown in Figure 13-2[2] indicates that most motor-skill tasks require only two official work breaks each day to maintain high-level performance. Most office activities have natural breaks, and many tasks require only intermittent attention of the worker. It is recommended for an eight-hour day that the breaks be placed between the second and third hours in the morning and between the sixth and seventh hours in the afternoon. For a limited number of activities, such as visual inspection of punched cards, that require a high degree of concentration, two work breaks each day may not be

[1] I. L. Bosticco and Robert B. Andrews, "Is Worker Fatigue Costing You Dollars?" Technical Aids for Small Manufacturers (Washington, D.C.: Small Business Administration, January-February, 1960).

[2] *Ibid.*

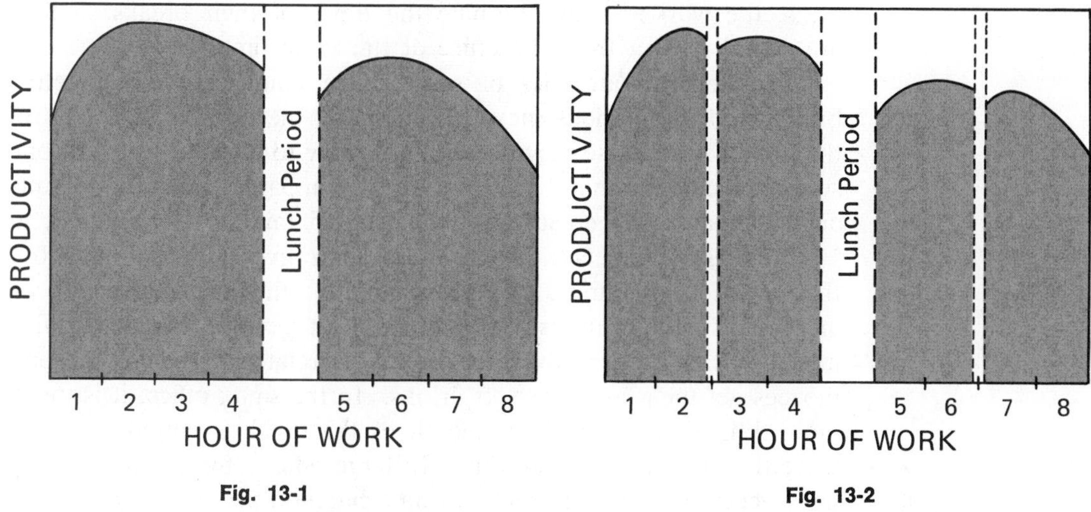

Fig. 13-1

Typical Work Curve for a Motor-Skill Task

Fig. 13-2

Typical Work Curve for a Motor-Skill Task with Rest Pauses

sufficient to maintain an acceptable level of performance. Whether or not coffee breaks and rest periods are the answer to the problems of fatigue and slowdown of production is not conclusive. The fact that in this way management shows concern for the well-being of its employees may be the most important aspect of the coffee break.

If an office worker earns \$120 during a 40-hour week and spends 20 minutes a day on coffee breaks, he is away from his desk about 83 hours—more than two workweeks—during the year; and the cost of this lost time is about \$250! When long lunches, leaving work early, lateness, sick days for nonsickness, extensive socializing with coworkers, and inattention to the job at hand are added to coffee breaks, the costs to businesses are about \$33.7 billion each year, according to the Robert Half Personnel Agency of New York.[3] The average worker is guilty of "stealing" three and one-half hours each week at a total cost of \$11.78.[4]

According to a survey of companies in a wide cross-section of different types of businesses, conducted by the National Industrial Conference Board, up to 97 percent of the companies questioned provide coffee breaks and many of the firms are paying at least part of the beverage cost.[5] In many small offices, the workers are permitted to take their breaks whenever they have a chance. In larger

[3] AMemo, *Administrative Management* (March, 1971), p. 96.
[4] *Ibid.*
[5] AMemo, *Administrative Management* (September, 1965), p. 96.

firms, the workers may alternate the times of their breaks so they are not all absent from the office at the same time.

The negative attitudes of some office managers toward coffee breaks and rest periods may be caused by their inability to control the breaks or because they do not know how to control them. In one study it was found that 42 percent of the companies set no time limits on the breaks; 36 percent limit them to 15 minutes; 20 percent, to 10 minutes; 2 percent, to no more than five minutes. Of those that have set time limits, 31 percent admitted they are unable to keep the breaks within limits.[6] The amount of control that the office manager can exercise over the breaks is related to where the employees get their coffee or soft drinks. In the small office, it is much more difficult to control the length of the break if employees must leave the premises at break time. In large offices, the employees may have access to vending machines and cafeteria services. Some firms are able to control the coffee break problem by permitting their employees to eat and drink at their desks because it is felt that if the coffee is drunk while the employees are at their desks, the workers will lose less time.

Although most office managers feel that coffee breaks and rest periods are desirable, they object to the abuse of the privilege. Some office managers excuse the lack of coffee breaks and rest periods by stating that the freedom enjoyed by most office workers makes such breaks unnecessary.

The following guidelines should govern the use of coffee breaks and rest periods:

1. For some types of office work, rest periods are absolutely necessary.
2. Rest periods should be scheduled when they will be most helpful—not too early in the morning and not too late in the afternoon. The coffee breaks should be scheduled so that not all employees are absent from their desks at the same time. Such an approach tends to discourage the overly long "talk" sessions that commonly characterize many coffee breaks.
3. Definite time limits should be set for the length of the breaks and these limits should be observed. Habitual offenders should be reprimanded and, if necessary, discharged. The inability of a few to abide by the rules only sets a poor example for the others.

---

[6] Warren G. Stevens, "The Great American Coffee Break," *Modern Office Procedures* (October, 1960), p. 15.

4. Supervisors should be held responsible for the abuse of the coffee break and rest period privileges.
5. If possible, facilities should be provided for getting coffee and snacks in the office so the employees do not have to leave the premises. In some offices, vending machines are located throughout the office area or in the cafeteria so that at a convenient time the employee can go to the nearest machine and obtain the coffee or food. No breaks are formally scheduled; each employee leaves his desk for ten or 15 minutes whenever convenient. In other firms, caterers or deliverymen are hired to provide coffee, soft drinks, and snacks at break time.

Cafeteria Services

In large offices, providing cafeteria services is becoming an important part of office administration. In some of the larger banks and industrial firms, company-operated lunchrooms supply either free or low-cost lunches to their employees. The Metropolitan Life Insurance Company estimates that it spends about $7.5 million each year feeding 18,000 employees at its New York City headquarters.[7] Many lunchrooms are serviced by catering companies, with the employee securing his meals at a lower cost and the company paying the difference. Such a service is a supplemental and indirect wage benefit. It is particularly applicable in large cities, where a deluge of 3,000 or more employees from one building seeking meals in a variety of restaurants is not conducive to the best physical and mental conditions of the employees. Also, in the suburbs where the office building may be located far away from restaurants, lunchroom facilities have become a necessity.

Music in the Office

Music in the office is designed to reduce fatigue due to strain, monotony, or just plain tiredness from long periods of work. Music *in itself* does not increase efficiency, reduce errors, or keep employees from leaving their jobs. Music helps relieve the boredom and mental strains that lead to poor productivity and dissatisfaction. The amount of benefit to be received from music in the office is related to the type of work being performed. The more tedious, monotonous, or

[7] Reported in "Hidden Paychecks: Where Fringe Benefits Stand Today," *Management Review* (June, 1963), p. 13.

routine the work, the greater the soothing effect that background music may have on mental fatigue.

A number of firms that specialize in furnishing music to offices and factories have made careful studies of what kind of music to use and when to use it. One large supplier of music to offices has found that music for offices must be more subdued than music for factories. Distracting influences in the music, such as vocals, loud brasses, or changes in tempo, are usually avoided; strings and woodwinds in orchestras predominate. A good music program incorporates all types—classical, semiclassical, show tunes, and popular music. The music should be so unobtrusive that it can be absorbed without mental distraction. Furthermore, the music should not be continuous. It should be turned on and off for brief periods, totaling about one to two and one-half hours a day.

Some companies keep the cost of their music programs at a minimum by installing their own music system, using an FM radio or their own collection of records. Other companies make use of one or several commercial background music services that administer the music program by playing specially recorded music that is carefully controlled in volume, range, and sound effects.

Muzak, a "functionally programmed" music service, has achieved a high degree of satisfaction among all employees who were surveyed at the Radio Corporation of America plant and offices in Moorestown, New Jersey.[8] About 90 percent of the respondents to a follow-up questionnaire liked Muzak and voted to continue the service. Supervisors in all departments tended to notice both socio-emotional and functional output changes that they ascribed to the introduction of the programmed music. Of all workers in the firm, the programmed music was liked most by the office workers, who found their work more enjoyable. Analysis of the different kinds of satisfactions received by varying percentages of the office workers revealed the following:

Satisfaction	*Percent of Office Workers Surveyed*
Helps me in my work	69.4%
Makes time go faster	63.8
Makes me feel more relaxed	86.0
Tends to reduce fatigue	69.7
Concentration is easier	56.6

[8] Information supplied the authors by N. H. Patterson, Director of Public Relations, Bulletin Company, Muzak Division, Philadelphia, 1970.

Tends to create more friendly atmosphere	90.3
Fellow employees are less tense	66.2
Helps counteract irritating noises	83.9
Work is less monotonous	77.8

An AMS survey of 336 member companies of varying types and sizes in the United States and Canada showed that 254 firms provide music for their employees; 70 percent of the firms polled use piped-in music; 63.8 percent use wire and 36.2 percent use radio; 75 percent have the music professionally programmed, while only 25 percent prepare the programs themselves.[9] Most respondents felt that music can improve employee morale, relieve job monotony, and help to level out disturbing noise peaks. Although the majority of respondents felt that music helps "cool down" temperamental workers, that same majority stated that music does not help to reduce turnover or help in recruiting.

The cost of music per employee each month was estimated by 50 of the respondents as shown below.[10] These costs do not include installation or equipment—only month-to-month rental or service fees.

Size of Firm	*Cost per Employee*
Over 1,000 employees	23 cents
501-1,000 employees	21 cents
101-500 employees	30 cents
Under 100 employees	81 cents

Recreational Programs

The recreational program in many companies consists mostly of employee parties, picnics, bowling, softball, and dances. With the additional leisure time resulting from a shorter workweek, there is a trend toward providing programs in adult education, and sports and hobbies for the entire family. Some of the types of activities that have become a part of company recreational programs are: chess, music concerts, horseback riding, swimming, fishing, foreign language study groups, guided tours, theater parties, hunting, and sports car racing clubs. The scope is almost limitless. Good recreation planning should provide organized activities for those employees who prefer to spend their leisure time in individual or small-group pursuits.

---

[9] "Piped-In Music Is Money to Employers," *Administrative Management* (March, 1971), p. 66.

[10] *Ibid.*

Most firms feel that the improvement in employee morale is worth whatever it costs to achieve. In many companies, the employees themselves bear some of the expenses of the recreational program, while in other firms the costs of recreation are partially defrayed by income from vending machines located throughout the offices and plant. In an insurance company in Columbus, Ohio, the organizing agency for recreation is the Activities Association, which consists of representatives from each of the company's departments and from each of the more than 50 activities that it sponsors. Employees become eligible to participate in all events by joining the Association and paying a fee of $2. More than 97 percent of the employees in this firm are members of the Association. The Association rents all its recreational facilities, and this expense, which may amount to as much as $12,800 a year, is underwritten by the company. In addition, the company pays the salaries of a five-man professional staff to administer the recreational activities.

Vacations

A study made by a management services organization shows that virtually all white-collar workers surveyed receive two weeks' vacation with pay after one year of service. Most white-collar workers get three weeks' vacation after ten years, and more than two thirds of the firms give their white-collar workers four weeks' paid leave after 20 years of service.[11] The study brings out that distinctions between office and factory workers are becoming fewer and that there is a tendency to reduce the service time requirements.

The traditional vacation shutdown, once very common in so many companies, is also seen less frequently, with less than one third of the firms closing for an official vacation.[12] In periods of economic slowdown, however, the trend seems to reverse itself; for in 1970, one study of 15,000 employees showed that there was an increase in the number of companies planning summer shutdowns.[13] Few employers allow their workers to carry over vacation time from one year to the next. Also, most employers stipulate that the vacation time actually be taken away from work rather than the employee requesting extra pay in lieu of the time off.[14]

---

[11] "Vacations Getting Longer," *Administrative Management* (November, 1968), pp. 80-81.

[12] *Ibid.*

[13] "Labor Letter," *The Wall Street Journal,* June 9, 1970, p. 1.

[14] "Vacations Getting Longer," *op. cit.,* p. 81.

Holidays with Pay

More liberal holiday policies are being found in today's offices. Along with the usual six holidays (New Year's Day, Independence Day, Labor Day, Thanksgiving, Memorial Day, and Christmas), others such as Washington's Birthday, Good Friday, Friday after Thanksgiving, a half-day on Christmas Eve, and a half-day on New Year's Eve are becoming recognized more frequently as paid holidays. According to a study by The Bureau of National Affairs, Inc., of 400 collective bargaining contracts during the past several years, the number of contracts granting 9 or 9½ holidays have tripled, while those contracts granting 10 holidays have doubled.[15]

Effective January 1, 1971, the dates of four legal holidays were changed for all federal government employees and for observance in the District of Columbia so that five three-day holiday weekends would result. Under the new law, Washington's Birthday will be observed on the third Monday in February; Memorial Day on the last Monday in May; Columbus Day to become a national holiday observed on the second Monday in October; and Veteran's Day on the fourth Monday in October. The fifth weekend results from Labor Day, which is the only regular Monday holiday.

Monday holiday laws have been enacted by 45 states for their employees, with the legislatures of Louisiana, Oklahoma, South Dakota, West Virginia, and Wisconsin not yet having acted as of June, 1971. In adopting the Monday holiday idea, however, the states have added some variations. For example, only 41 states have adopted Columbus Day as a new holiday. Although private business firms make their own decisions regarding holidays, it is expected they will follow suit and grant the same holidays as those received by public employees. Many observers foresee a growing trend over the next several years toward creating more three-day weekends.

Insurance

Group life insurance is designed to provide benefits should the worker die or become totally disabled. The benefits range from modest burial funds to amounts equal to two or three times the employee's annual salary. The morale-building effect of a group life insurance plan cannot be overestimated, for this benefit relieves the

[15] AMemo, *Administrative Management* (July, 1969), p. 80.

employee of a certain amount of worry and insecurity. In many cases the group life insurance plan provides for total and permanent disability benefits, accidental death and dismemberment coverage, as well as modest amounts of life insurance for the employee's surviving spouse and children. Companies usually provide reduced amounts of life insurance for retired employees, especially after they reach age 65 or 70.

Group medical insurance affords the employee protection by covering all or the major part of the hospital, surgical, and medical expenses for the employee and his dependents. This type of benefit is so common that almost all firms have established group medical plans for their workers, either paying the costs entirely or having the employee contribute part or all of the costs at reduced rates. Retired workers and their dependents are usually covered under such plans, at least until they reach age 65 when they are eligible for Medicare.

Many companies have expanded their group medical insurance coverage by providing *major medical insurance*, which protects employees against catastrophic medical bills resulting from serious accidents or prolonged illness. In one type of plan, after the employee has paid $100 toward his own annual medical bills (or that of any member of his family), 80 percent of the remaining charges are covered by the major medical insurer. A few companies are also experimenting with dental protection for their employees.

Practically all firms have a company-paid *sick leave plan* that provides the worker with continuing income during short periods of illness. Usually the benefit period increases with the length of employee service and may have a period of full pay followed by a period of half pay. The *short-term weekly indemnity plan* provides continuing income for the worker who is unable to return to his job after he has exhausted his sickness and accident benefits. The period of payment may range from six months to two years, with the benefit level usually at 50 to 70 percent of his pay. *Long-term disability income insurance*, often an extension of the short-term program, usually provides a benefit equal to 50 or 60 percent of the pay for the worker who is medically determined to be totally disabled. The period of payment may range from a few years to age 65, or for life, depending upon the design of the plan. The benefits paid under the plan are usually reduced by any social security benefits or other statutory disability benefits received by the worker.

By 1980 it is estimated that the total United States health care costs will reach $180 billion; employers are now paying about five percent of their payroll costs in the form of health insurance premiums.[16] To minimize this outlay, preventive medicine is the answer. Many firms supplement their insurance benefits programs by providing health services for their employees. This is done under a variety of conditions that range from providing first-aid stations to complete medical departments staffed by doctors and nurses. Yearly physical examinations are also provided free or at a low cost for the employees of some companies.

Retirement and Pension Benefits

Since in many instances social security benefits are inadequate for the retired employee and his dependents, many firms modify their retirement and pension plans to supplement the government benefits, thus maintaining the interest of their employees in long-term employment with the firm. Findings of a survey conducted by The Bureau of National Affairs, Inc., show that over 80 percent of the firms questioned have pension plans.[17] Although benefit formulas and eligibility rules vary, the coverage is about the same for production, office-clerical, and managerial workers. Voluntary early retirement prior to age 65 is permitted in about three fourths of the larger companies, but in only one fourth of the smaller firms.[18]

Many retirement plans require that eligible employees contribute toward the cost of their benefits, with the contributions usually being expressed as a percentage of earnings, such as two percent of the first $5,000, and four percent of the excess. Ordinarily, the employee is guaranteed the return of his contribution with interest either in cash when he terminates his employment, as a death benefit should he die before retirement, or in the form of retirement income. A number of plans also provide a variable annuity, which serves as a hedge against inflation.

Banks manage nearly 50 percent of all pension funds, while companies with their own investment management staffs handle nearly a quarter of the funds. Insurance companies, once dominant in the field, manage nearly one eighth of pension fund receipts. Economic forecasters believe that the private pension plans of the future—if the system continues to grow parallel to the social security program—

---

[16] AMemo, *Administrative Management* (April, 1971), p. 84.

[17] "290 Managers View Fringe Benefits," *Administrative Management* (October, 1969), p. 59.

[18] *Ibid.*

will provide complete portability (transfer of pension fund accumulations from company to company), inflation compensation, lower retirement age, and more sizable benefits.[19]

Educational Assistance

Many firms provide some sort of educational assistance to their employees, with the result that office workers can continue to grow professionally and to prepare themselves for maximum flexibility of career pursuit and for future promotion to supervisory and middle management positions. In a study of 620 firms in the United States and Canada, the Administrative Management Society found that 96 percent of the companies provide educational assistance and 73 percent support studies that are job related, either directly or indirectly.[20] Less than 10 percent of the firms permitted employees to enroll in courses nonrelated to their present jobs.

For courses that qualify for assistance, over 50 percent of the firms reimburse the employee 100 percent for tuition costs; nearly 15 percent of the companies pay 75 percent or 50 percent of the tuition costs; a little more than one percent of the companies pay less than 50 percent of the tuition. When assistance is related to the grade obtained in the courses, much variation in reimbursement practice is noted. For example, 12 firms indicated 100 percent tuition reimbursement for an A grade; 75 percent reimbursement for a B; and 50 percent reimbursement for a C. Slightly less than 50 percent of the respondents did not pay for books, but here again considerable variation in practice exists. One firm paid a maximum of $10 toward books, while another paid up to $20 for the textbooks for each course.[21]

Some companies provide for furthering the education of their employees within the firm's own classrooms. For example, one utility company in Florida has established its own "college" which is taught by employees for employees. The "college" grants credits and "degrees" in much the same fashion as a university. The company offers 40 courses on all educational levels, ranging from advanced physics to speed reading. Further discussion of company schools as

---

[19] "Pensions: 100% Vesting after 10 Years on Job?" *Administrative Management* (April, 1971), p. 46.

[20] "Going Back Means Moving Up," *Administrative Management* (May, 1971), pp. 61-63. In addition to giving results of the survey, this article describes the tuition policies of three firms wherein (a) an "A" merits a refund of 90 percent, (b) full tuition is paid for a degree, and (c) the job and school must be related.

[21] *Ibid.*, p. 62.

a means of training and of upgrading skills is presented in the next chapter.

PRACTICES AFFECTING THE PHYSICAL AND MENTAL WELL-BEING OF EMPLOYEES

The office manager and his supervisors and department heads are faced daily with a multitude of employees' problems that affect their physical and mental well-being. Each problem requires a fair and equitable hearing and a decision that will be satisfactory to both the manager and the worker. Many of these problems are quickly disposed of by reference to the employee handbook or the company's policy manual. Other problems may require further study and consultation with the employee before a decision can be made.

Smoking in the Office

The problem of smoking in the office and its effect upon worker productivity must receive the attention of the office manager because it affects the morale and efficiency of those whom he supervises.

The arguments against smoking in the office include:

1. Smoking is unhealthy.
2. It looks unbusinesslike and makes a poor impression on the public.
3. Smoking is a fire hazard.
4. The lack of adequate ventilating conditions makes smoking undesirable.
5. It is unfair to coworkers who do not smoke.
6. It impairs the efficiency of the worker.

The arguments against smoking have been answered as follows:

1. There is some disagreement about the unhealthiness of smoking, and many smokers will smoke anyway. Despite the reports on the relationship of smoking to health, few businesses have changed their smoking rules. In fact, some firms have increased their smoking privileges in order to improve production by permitting employees to smoke while working, to reduce the time wasted for smoking breaks, and to abolish smoking rules that discriminated against women. Some companies have tried by means of films, posters, literature, and financial incentives to encourage employees to stop or to reduce their smoking.

For example, office workers in a Cleveland department store are barred from smoking in areas with several desks; a Philadelphia clothier has sent all workers a memo urging them to forego smoking; workers in a Rhode Island company can win up to $43 in bonuses if they do not smoke for 26 weeks; and one company puts up posters showing what one employee calls "an icky picture of the lungs of someone who smoked" on each floor of its headquarters building.[22]

2. Few office workers come directly in contact with the public and, furthermore, many visitors smoke when they come into the office. Many office workers object to the fact that executives in their private offices can smoke but the office worker cannot. If smoking makes an unfavorable impression on the public in the general offices, why not in the private offices?
3. There is only a very small fire hazard in most offices and smoking can be prohibited in hazardous areas.
4. If ventilating conditions are poor, most office workers would not mind refraining from smoking; but doing so means that more time out will be taken to smoke in the lounges.
5. If some of the workers do not smoke, it might be wise to determine whether the smokers or the nonsmokers are in the majority and to adjust the program accordingly. Nonsmokers are exposed to smoke in many other places besides the office.
6. Many office workers find that their efficiency improves, rather than decreases, with smoking.

If smoking in the office is prohibited, some workers will leave the office and go to the lounges to smoke. Where this is not permitted, the workers may become nervous and fidgety, and their efficiency decreases. If the attitude of the office manager is based upon increasing the efficiency of the work, he must either accept the situation or tend to improve it by making rules relating to smoking. In some of the larger offices, the employee manual states that smoking is permitted before 10:00 a.m. and after 3:00 p.m. each day. This plan is a sort of compromise. Other offices permit smoking anywhere and at any time, except where the hazard of fire is an important consideration.

Safety in the Office

Office hazards cause accidents which are costly both to management and to employees due to loss of time, loss of production, and

[22] "Labor Letter," *The Wall Street Journal,* January 26, 1971, p. 1.

loss of income. It has been estimated that the calculable costs of accidents in industry average about $70 for each worker. When the hidden costs connected with accidents are included, their cost may be nearer $300 for each worker.[23] The National Safety Council has estimated that the annual cost of on-the-job employee accidents is $4.6 billion.[24] In 1969 there were 10,200 fires in offices and banks, with a loss of $27.1 million.[25]

To reduce the number of deaths and disabling injuries that occur on the job each year, the Occupational Safety and Health Act of 1970 was enacted. Effective in April, 1971, this act imposes safety and health standards upon any business involved in interstate commerce. Employers must comply with the specific occupational and health standards and must furnish each of their employees "a place of employment free from recognized hazards that are causing or are likely to cause death or serious physical harm." Under the act employers are required to keep records of work-related deaths, illnesses, and injuries; maintain records of employee exposure to materials that are potentially toxic; and notify employees of their exposure to such materials when the toxic effects exceed the standards set. Each worker has the right to report any safety and health hazard to the Secretary of Labor, and employers may not discriminate against any employee who exerts his right to file such a complaint.

Every accident has a cause, and since it is the problem of management (long recognized by state compensation laws) to furnish a safe place in which to work, managers should attempt to reduce office hazards. To provide a scientific plan of safety administration in the office requires, first, a recognition on the part of management that potential hazards may lurk in the office. Then, someone, perhaps the office manager or an assistant, should be given the responsibility for conducting a safety campaign in the office. However, an effective safety plan must be company wide. There should be a coordinated system of establishing and enforcing safety rules, of recording and analyzing accident data, and of using the results to track down unsafe employee practices as well as potential hazards.

Employees should be informed of the types of accidents that may occur. For example, very often in offices an employee may open two or more drawers of a file cabinet at the same time, forgetting that such an action may cause the file to topple over. As the result

---

[23] Robert L. Caleo, "The Scientific Approach to Safety Administration," *Administrative Management* (October, 1963), p. 50.

[24] AMemo, *Administrative Management* (May, 1963), p. 92.

[25] "Fire Hazards in New Buildings," *The Office* (October, 1970), p. 40.

of investigating such an accident and determining its causes, the office manager may decide to tape a warning sign on top each file cabinet or line the cabinets back to back and bolt them together, thus preventing their toppling over.

Each department supervisor should be required to complete a written report at the time of each accident so that the person in charge of safety administration will be able to analyze the causes and to improve the safety conditions. To aid the proper reporting of data pertaining to accidents, a standard reporting form known as the "American Standard Method of Reporting Basic Facts Relating to the Nature and Occurrence of Work Injuries" is available.[26] By means of a standard reporting system, the safety administrator can compare the effectiveness of the safety program in his firm with that of other companies in the same industry.

The elimination of office hazards should start with a study of the causes of office accidents. The National Safety Council cites the following causes of office accidents:

1. Crowding on stairs, at elevators, and at entrance doorways. High heels are especially dangerous on stairs and escalators.
2. Walking without looking—around corners, into open doors, while reading correspondence, etc.
3. Climbing on chairs, boxes, and other makeshift supports.
4. Leaving desk drawers or file drawers open to be stumbled over.
5. Tipping back too far in a chair.
6. Straining at tight windows, lifting improperly, or lifting too heavy a load.
7. Piling objects insecurely on shelves or elsewhere.
8. Failing to cover the points of pins used in fastening papers.
9. Using knives, scissors, or shears carelessly.
10. Tossing matches, cigarette and cigar stubs, and broken glass into wastebaskets.
11. Throwing objects out of windows.

All the hazards that cause office accidents are too numerous to list. There are, however, a few simple basic precautions that every office manager should insist upon in order to reduce the number of accidents:

---

[26] Approved and published by American Standards Association, 10 East 40th Street, New York, New York 10016.

1. Treat floor surfaces with a nonslip finish.
2. Adjust springs on doors to prevent them from banging into persons, and avoid having employees go through swinging or revolving doors too quickly.
3. Instruct workers in proper use of desk drawers to avoid banging into open drawers.
4. Instruct workers in proper use of filing cabinets to prevent a cabinet from tipping or falling on a person because more than one drawer is open at a time.
5. Place pencil sharpeners so that they do not injure persons passing by.
6. Check the surfaces of all desks and chairs to prevent injuries from splinters or rough edges.
7. Check electrical cords and connections for machines and equipment to eliminate fire and shock hazards.
8. Check the spring adjustments of swivel chairs to avoid accidents of upsetting and injuring employees.
9. Avoid placing loose or movable materials on top filing cabinets or lockers so that the objects cannot fall on employees.
10. Check the level of illumination along stairways and consider the painting of walls in a bright color to make the stairways more visible.
11. Where smoking at the desk is permitted, be aware of the possibility of fire resulting from hot ashes being dumped into a wastebasket. Should a fire start in a wastebasket, an effective method of containing the fire is to place another wastebasket over the top of the first.

Receiving Personal Mail at the Office

This problem, like most of those mentioned in this chapter, is influenced by the size and the location of the office, and sometimes by general working conditions. In the small office, greater freedom is allowed in receiving personal mail at the office. In larger offices, however, it is necessary to impose rules because the volume of personal mail may interfere seriously with efficiency of work in the mailing department.

Some firms state as a policy that personal mail should not be sent to the office. Some firms reserve the right to open all mail sent to the firm, even though addressed to a particular individual, unless marked "Personal." This is done on the assumption that any mail sent to the office is business mail. Although the propriety of this action may be questioned, it can readily be appreciated that where there is a large number of office employees, the receipt of a large volume of personal mail seriously interferes with and delays the work of the mailing department. Some office managers claim that employees waste too much time in the office or in the lounges in reading personal mail that is received at the office.

Many office managers prefer to ignore the problem of employees receiving personal mail at the office until such a time as it seems to become annoying or interferes with the work. The problem may then be handled in one of several ways:

1. If the firm has an employee handbook, a paragraph may be inserted to the effect that the firm does not approve of having personal mail sent to the office.
2. All personally addressed mail may be opened but not read.
3. On all incoming personal mail, small stickers stating "Personal mail should not be sent to the office" may be attached.
4. A notice may be posted on the bulletin boards to the effect that personal mail should not be sent to the office.

Personal Use of the Telephone

Personal telephone calls prevent the firm from receiving its business calls and actually obstruct the business of the firm. At the outset it should be stated that no firm would object to receiving urgent or emergency telephone calls for any employee, but it is the other personal calls that pose the problem.

One bank urges its employees to have personal calls come through either before 9:30 a.m. or after 4:00 p.m. Another way in which the problem of personal telephone calls may be handled is to have the number or the nature of the incoming call noted by the switchboard operator on a specially printed form. When the employee goes to lunch or takes his coffee break, the notation is given to him so that he can return the call. In this way the office work is not interrupted.

The office manager or the department supervisor should talk with those who persistently abuse the privilege to the extent that the work flow is interrupted. The offenders should be told that all personal calls should be made before or after office hours or during the breaks. If these efforts do not succeed in solving the problem, the switchboard operator may be asked to supply a list of those employees who make personal calls on company time. Such a list can be used by the office manager or the supervisor to justify a probation period or a termination, depending upon the circumstances.

The mildest way of handling the personal telephone problem is, as in the case of personal mail, to have it noted in the employee handbook or posted on the bulletin boards, thus attempting to discourage the use of the telephone for personal matters. If the office staff is large enough, public telephones may be installed in several locations for employee use.

Alcoholism

Alcoholism is not only a social and physical problem, but also it is generally considered to be a psychiatric one. It ranks behind heart disease and cancer as America's top three killer diseases. The National Council on Alcoholism estimates that untreated problem drinkers cost employers over $4 billion a year in absenteeism, accidents, sickness benefits, lowered morale, and damaged customer and public relations.[27] An estimate by *Dun's Review* places the national annual cost figure higher at $7.5 billion and asserts that an alcoholic employee costs his firm at least 50 percent of his annual wage.[28] Of the more than 58 million industry and civilian government workers in this country, the National Council on Alcoholism estimates that 5.3 percent are alcoholics, with 70 percent of all alcoholics holding white-collar, professional, or managerial jobs, and 50 percent having attended or graduated from college.[29]

Companies should develop a straightforward policy regarding alcoholism with the aim of correcting behavior problems in their employees before they become unemployable. The company should look upon alcoholism the same as it would any other disease that affects an employee's output or behavior while at work. In those firms that have instituted some kind of rehabilitation program,[30] the plans usually operate along the lines of the three-step process advocated by the Council: (1) education, (2) early detection of the alcoholic by his supervisor, and (3) referral to a treatment center.

Education. The firm must get across to its workers the fact that alcoholism is a disease and will be treated as such. As the past president of the National Council on Alcoholism, Merle Gulick,

---

[27] Anthony D. K. Carding, "Booze and Business: Can Your Employees Mix Them?" *Administrative Management* (December, 1969), p. 20.

[28] Susan Margetts, "The Staggering Cost of the Alcoholic Executive," *Management Review* (July, 1968), p. 31.

[29] Carding, *loc. cit.*

[30] For a complete description of a modern approach to the treatment of alcoholics in the business firm, see "How Boeing Handles Alcoholism" *Industrial Medicine* (October, 1969), pp. 37-44.

emphatically stated: "The biggest thing about alcoholism is to get it out in the open. Everyone in the company must be convinced it is a disease." [31]

At Union Carbide, which follows the Council's recommended rehabilitation program, all supervisors are given a statement that reads in part:

> Alcoholism is a disease in which alcoholic consumption is interfering with an individual's normal process of behavior and living. The supervisor must be alert to the earliest signs that alcoholism is interfering with work performance and insist that immediate corrective action should be taken.[32]

Early Detection. The responsibility for detecting an alcoholism problem lies with the immediate superior, usually the supervisor. Supervisors should be aware of what signs may denote a case of alcoholism and be alert as to how the effects of alcohol cause an employee to behave. A close study and understanding of the employee's behavioral patterns and visible signs of alcoholism during its several phases, as shown in Figure 13-3, must be undertaken by the supervisor.

The supervisor should not try to make a medical diagnosis of his alcoholic employee's problems nor delve into the employee's private affairs unless invited to do so. The supervisor should, however, discuss with the employee his poor performance on the job and make it clear that unless his performance improves, or unless the employee tries to solve his problem by treatment, his job is in jeopardy.

Referral. If the company retains a counselor or a physician either on a full-time or a part-time basis, the alcoholic worker can be referred to the counselor by the supervisor. Often the company counselor is a recovered alcoholic himself, and his function is to persuade the employee to accept suitable treatment, which may be through a lay group such as Alcoholics Anonymous, a professional agency, or a hospital detoxification center.[33] The task of the counselor is to impress upon the worker that his undergoing and responding to treatment is the only way to avoid endangering his job. In companies where there is a treatment policy in force, about two out of three problem drinkers who accept treatment recover.[34]

---

[31] Margetts, *op. cit.*, p. 33.
[32] *Ibid.*, p. 34.
[33] Carding, *op. cit.*, p. 21.
[34] *Ibid.*, p. 22.

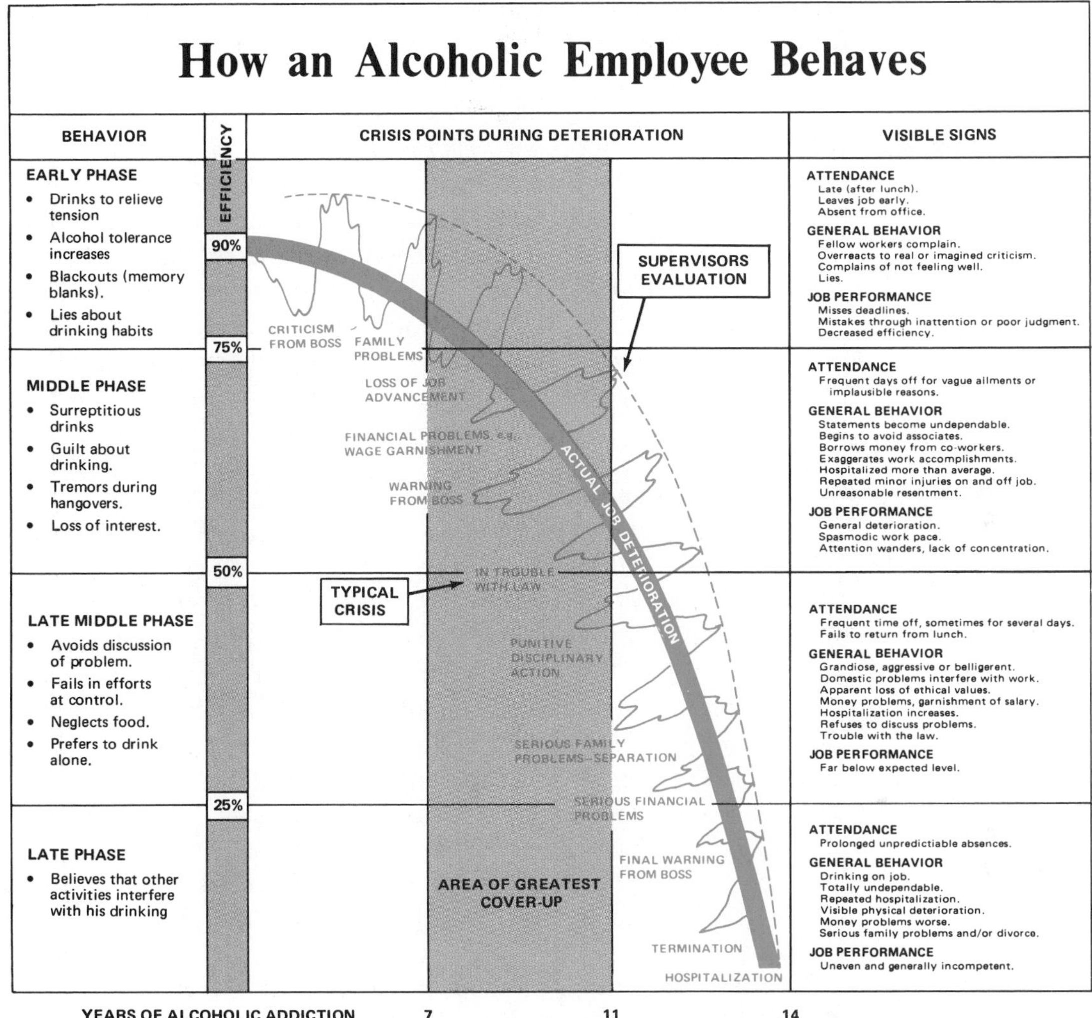

How an Alcoholic Employee Behaves
BEHAVIOR
EFFICIENCY
CRISIS POINTS DURING DETERIORATION
VISIBLE SIGNS
EARLY PHASE
• Drinks to relieve tension
• Alcohol tolerance increases
• Blackouts (memory blanks).
• Lies about drinking habits
90%
75%
CRITICISM FROM BOSS
FAMILY PROBLEMS
SUPERVISORS EVALUATION
ATTENDANCE
Late (after lunch).
Leaves job early.
Absent from office.
GENERAL BEHAVIOR
Fellow workers complain.
Overreacts to real or imagined criticism.
Complains of not feeling well.
Lies.
JOB PERFORMANCE
Misses deadlines.
Mistakes through inattention or poor judgment.
Decreased efficiency.
MIDDLE PHASE
• Surreptitious drinks
• Guilt about drinking.
• Tremors during hangovers.
• Loss of interest.
LOSS OF JOB ADVANCEMENT
FINANCIAL PROBLEMS, e.g., WAGE GARNISHMENT
WARNING FROM BOSS
ACTUAL JOB DETERIORATION
ATTENDANCE
Frequent days off for vague ailments or implausible reasons.
GENERAL BEHAVIOR
Statements become undependable.
Begins to avoid associates.
Borrows money from co-workers.
Exaggerates work accomplishments.
Hospitalized more than average.
Repeated minor injuries on and off job.
Unreasonable resentment.
JOB PERFORMANCE
General deterioration.
Spasmodic work pace.
Attention wanders, lack of concentration.
50%
TYPICAL CRISIS
IN TROUBLE WITH LAW
LATE MIDDLE PHASE
• Avoids discussion of problem.
• Fails in efforts at control.
• Neglects food.
• Prefers to drink alone.
PUNITIVE DISCIPLINARY ACTION
SERIOUS FAMILY PROBLEMS—SEPARATION
ATTENDANCE
Frequent time off, sometimes for several days.
Fails to return from lunch.
GENERAL BEHAVIOR
Grandiose, aggressive or belligerent.
Domestic problems interfere with work.
Apparent loss of ethical values.
Money problems, garnishment of salary.
Hospitalization increases.
Refuses to discuss problems.
Trouble with the law.
JOB PERFORMANCE
Far below expected level.
25%
SERIOUS FINANCIAL PROBLEMS
LATE PHASE
• Believes that other activities interfere with his drinking
AREA OF GREATEST COVER-UP
FINAL WARNING FROM BOSS
TERMINATION
HOSPITALIZATION
ATTENDANCE
Prolonged unpredictiable absences.
GENERAL BEHAVIOR
Drinking on job.
Totally undependable.
Repeated hospitalization.
Visible physical deterioration.
Money problems worse.
Serious family problems and/or divorce.
JOB PERFORMANCE
Uneven and generally incompetent.
YEARS OF ALCOHOLIC ADDICTION
7
11
14

Reprinted from Administrative Management, Geyer-McAllister Publications, Inc.

Fig. 13-3
How an Alcoholic Employee Behaves

A study by the National Industrial Conference Board, in which it was emphasized by authorities that alcoholism is never cured but only arrested, showed that some 60 percent of those who accepted treatment were helped and were able to hold their jobs.[35]

If the firm does not retain a company doctor or counselor, the supervisor can obtain help and information from the following sources: Alcoholism Information Center; Alcoholics Anonymous;

[35] AMemo, *Administrative Management* (April, 1970), p. 96.

out-patient alcoholism clinics, which are listed in the telephone directory; and the National Council on Alcoholism, Industrial Services Department, New York.

Drugs and Narcotics

At the present time no one has adequate information to determine just how much a problem drug usage presents in the business office. Dr. David H. Goldstein, professor of environmental medicine at New York University Medical Center, in an interview reported by *The New York Times*, stated that: ". . . drug addiction is a problem of great gravity to industry. It robs an employee of the motivation to do his job, makes a thief of him because his salary is too small to pay for increasing drug needs, and turns him into a security risk." [36]

Some findings support the relatively widespread illegal use of drugs and narcotics in business and industry. For example, Attorney General John Mitchell has estimated that one out of every 40 workers in this country uses drugs illegally.[37] In a survey by Chicago's Industrial Relations Newsletter, the conclusion was reached that three out of every four plants with 50 or more workers have a serious drug problem.[38] Newspaper columnist Sylvia Porter has written that one out of eight employees has had a drug experience and one out of four job applicants has experimented with drugs.[39] Most studies reveal that the hardened drug users in business are usually in their early 20's and have low-echelon jobs. Most activity seems to be centered on campuses, the major employment market for business offices, and in commune-oriented neighborhoods of the nation's largest cities.

Other findings tend to support the conclusion that presently no real drug abuse problem exists in the business office. In an AMS survey of 140 firms in the United States and Canada, it was reported that in only 15 companies was there any evidence of drug abuse problems.[40] In most instances, the problems were single cases and not necessarily confined to large urban centers. A national survey undertaken by the AFL-CIO Department of Community Services found that there is no major problem of drug abuse among union

---

[36] David Sohn, M.D., "Screening for Drug Addiction," *Personnel* (July-Aug., 1970), p. 22.

[37] "The Rising Problem of Drugs on the Job," *Time* (June 29, 1970), p. 70.

[38] *Ibid.*

[39] Joseph G. Zalkind, "Is Your Office Part of the Drug Scene?" *Administrative Management* (October, 1970), p. 41.

[40] "Drug Abuse Survey Reveals No Problem—Yet," *AMS News* (June, 1970), p. 1.

men and women in most cities and that where the problem exists, it is minimal.[41] Where the problem did exist, it was concentrated largely on the east and west coasts, with most users of drugs being under the age of 20. To determine how much of a recognized drug usage problem there is and in what sort of industry the problem exists, the Management Counselors Associates of Los Angeles undertook a survey study of 11 of its client firms. Nine of the companies indicated that drugs represent no problem to their firms both in terms of the number of users and in reduction of company efficiency.[42] The same number of firms stated that they had no specific personnel policies related to drug usage and that it has not been necessary to initiate any sort of special steps to screen out potential drug users among applicants. A survey by the Life Extension Institute of New York in its examination of 1,000 men and women, aged 18-30, applying for work at 84 client companies revealed that only 0.7 percent showed evidence of using hard drugs (heroin and morphine).[43] This study concluded that alcoholism remains the greater industrial threat.

A knowledge of these facts alone should motivate the administrative office manager to realize and to understand the potential threat of the use of drugs to the employee and to his continuing employability. In dealing with drugs in the office it is suggested that the office manager follow a three-step program similar to that described in the preceding section dealing with alcoholism.

Education. Cooperative education efforts with the community and its social agencies possibly represent to business the one major means of halting the spread of drug usage. Some firms have undertaken broad educational programs aimed at initially preventing the use of drugs or narcotics, supporting the principle that the only real cure for an addict—one who is physically dependent on drugs—is never to start using drugs. In its drug-prevention program the New York Telephone Company runs a question-and-answer column on drugs, written by the company doctor, in its employee newspaper.[44] Other companies conduct special drug seminars for their supervisors and set up programs for spotting drug-using personnel. Information that can be distributed in the office about drugs and narcotics may

---

[41] "The Drug Addiction of Business Personnel," *The Office* (December, 1970), p. 49.

[42] "Finds Drugs Use Small," in Letters to the Editor, *Administrative Management* (February, 1971), p. 6.

[43] AMemo, *Administrative Management* (May, 1971), p. 96.

[44] "Drugs on the Job," *The Wall Street Journal,* May 7, 1970, p. 1.

be obtained from the following sources: a city, state, or national Bureau of Narcotics and Dangerous Drugs; National Clearinghouse on Drug Abuse Information; and the United States Public Health Service.

Detection. Detecting the on-the-job user and addict, again the major responsibility of the supervisor who is closest to the worker, is a much more difficult task than spotting the alcoholic. The addict's symptoms are not always apparent, even to the trained observer. The chart in Figure 13-4 shows the most common symptoms of drug abuse. However, not all the signs are always evident, nor are they the only signs that may occur. The reaction of a drug usually depends on the person, his mood, his environment, and the dosage taken.

Company officials should be very cautious about accusing an employee of drug usage or addiction or even searching his locker and personal belongings, for an error in judgment can lead to a costly lawsuit including both the supervisor and the employer. Those in charge of interviewing should be alerted to the telltale signs that may indicate a drug problem. In the case of a suspicious situation, the application form should be carefully scrutinized and searching questions asked about gaps in employment history, frequent job changes, and reasons for leaving former jobs. Previous employers and references also should be contacted directly. In the screening process some firms demand that the applicant submit to a special urinalysis in which for drug users, the test results will show traces of barbiturates, amphetamines, and morphine (which the body metabolizes out of heroin). However, such urinalyses are not foolproof, for the appearance of quinine (often used to cut heroin) may indicate that the applicant recently had a few gin and tonics, which also contain quinine. Further, such tests cannot detect heavy users of marijuana because its use leaves no noticeable aftertrace.

Referral. A modern, enlightened approach in the referral of drug users and addicts appears in the Statement on Company Position on Narcotics and Dangerous Drugs of one of the country's major mutual life insurance companies.[45] A portion of this statement appears below:

> Persons in management and supervisory positions are expected to, and all other employees are urged to, bring immediately

[45] Company name withheld by request.

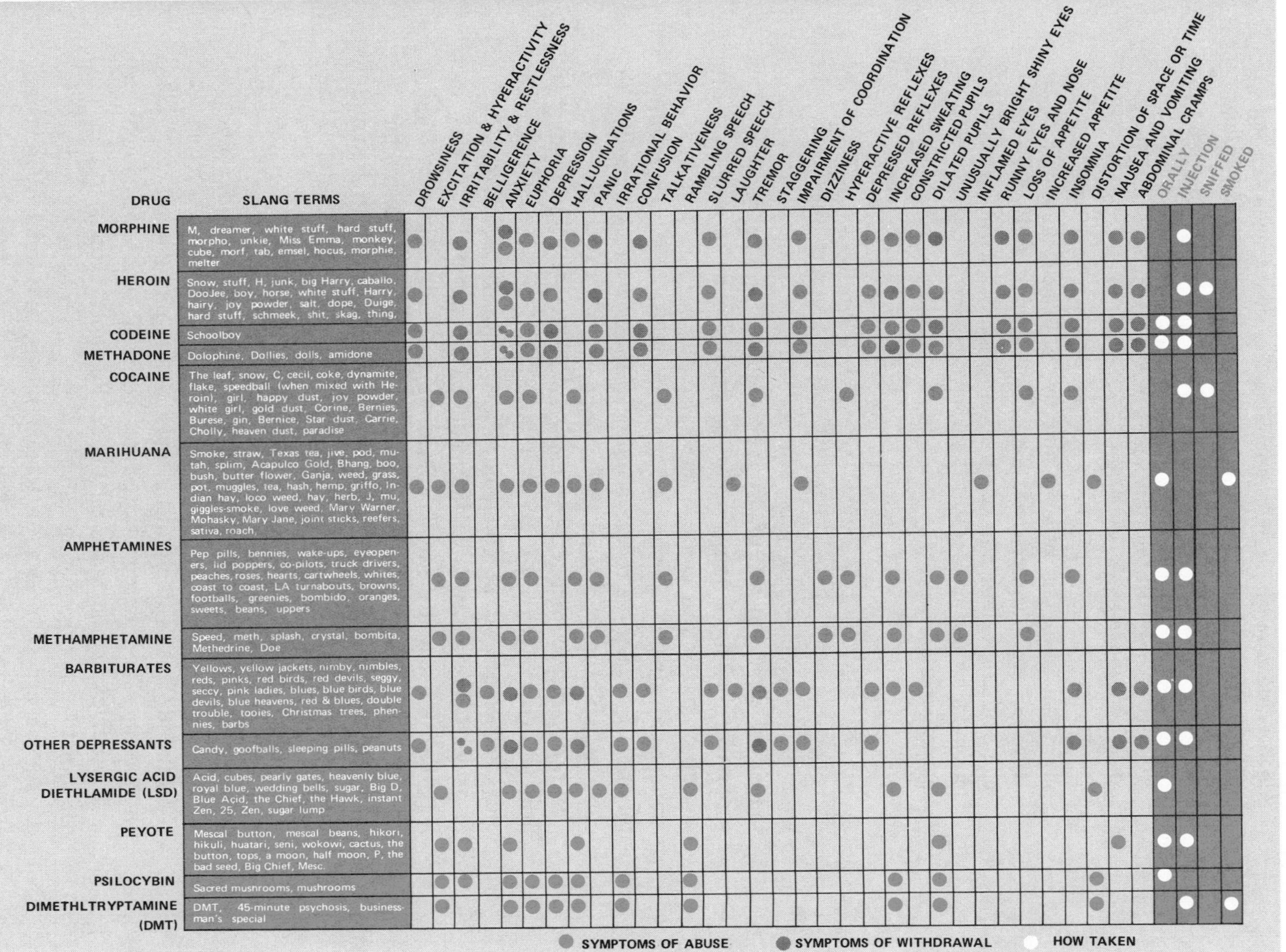

DROWSINESS
EXCITATION & HYPERACTIVITY
IRRITABILITY & RESTLESSNESS
BELLIGERENCE
ANXIETY
EUPHORIA
DEPRESSION
HALLUCINATIONS
PANIC
IRRATIONAL BEHAVIOR
CONFUSION
TALKATIVENESS
RAMBLING SPEECH
SLURRED SPEECH
LAUGHTER
TREMOR
STAGGERING
IMPAIRMENT OF COORDINATION
DIZZINESS
HYPERACTIVE REFLEXES
DEPRESSED REFLEXES
INCREASED SWEATING
CONSTRICTED PUPILS
DILATED PUPILS
UNUSUALLY BRIGHT SHINY EYES
INFLAMED EYES
RUNNY EYES AND NOSE
LOSS OF APPETITE
INCREASED APPETITE
INSOMNIA
DISTORTION OF SPACE OR TIME
NAUSEA AND VOMITING
ABDOMINAL CRAMPS
ORALLY
INJECTION
SNIFFED
SMOKED
DRUG
SLANG TERMS
MORPHINE
M, dreamer, white stuff, hard stuff, morpho, unkie, Miss Emma, monkey, cube, morf, tab, emsel, hocus, morphie, melter
HEROIN
Snow, stuff, H, junk, big Harry, caballo, DooJee, boy, horse, white stuff, Harry, hairy, joy powder, salt, dope, Duige, hard stuff, schmeek, shit, skag, thing,
CODEINE
Schoolboy
METHADONE
Dolophine, Dollies, dolls, amidone
COCAINE
The leaf, snow, C, cecil, coke, dynamite, flake, speedball (when mixed with Heroin), girl, happy dust, joy powder, white girl, gold dust, Corine, Bernies, Burese, gin, Bernice, Star dust, Carrie, Cholly, heaven dust, paradise
MARIHUANA
Smoke, straw, Texas tea, jive, pod, mutah, splim, Acapulco Gold, Bhang, boo, bush, butter flower, Ganja, weed, grass, pot, muggles, tea, hash, hemp, griffo, Indian hay, loco weed, hay, herb, J, mu, giggles-smoke, love weed, Mary Warner, Mohasky, Mary Jane, joint sticks, reefers, sativa, roach,
AMPHETAMINES
Pep pills, bennies, wake-ups, eyeopeners, lid poppers, co-pilots, truck drivers, peaches, roses, hearts, cartwheels, whites, coast to coast, LA turnabouts, browns, footballs, greenies, bombido, oranges, sweets, beans, uppers
METHAMPHETAMINE
Speed, meth, splash, crystal, bombita, Methedrine, Doe
BARBITURATES
Yellows, yellow jackets, nimby, nimbles, reds, pinks, red birds, red devils, seggy, seccy, pink ladies, blues, blue birds, blue devils, blue heavens, red & blues, double trouble, tooies, Christmas trees, phennies, barbs
OTHER DEPRESSANTS
Candy, goofballs, sleeping pills, peanuts
LYSERGIC ACID DIETHLAMIDE (LSD)
Acid, cubes, pearly gates, heavenly blue, royal blue, wedding bells, sugar, Big D, Blue Acid, the Chief, the Hawk, instant Zen, 25, Zen, sugar lump
PEYOTE
Mescal button, mescal beans, hikori, hikuli, huatari, seni, wokowi, cactus, the button, tops, a moon, half moon, P, the bad seed, Big Chief, Mesc.
PSILOCYBIN
Sacred mushrooms, mushrooms
DIMETHLTRYPTAMINE (DMT)
DMT, 45-minute psychosis, businessman's special
SYMPTOMS OF ABUSE
SYMPTOMS OF WITHDRAWAL
HOW TAKEN

U.S. Bureau of Narcotics and Dangerous Drugs

Fig. 13-4
Common Symptoms of Drug Abuse

to the attention of the Personnel Department the names of employees known to be or believed to be actively and illegally using, transporting, selling, or promoting the use of narcotics or dangerous drugs on company premises; or where apparent use of narcotics or dangerous drugs outside of working hours have a direct effect on the employee's performance on the job.

Such referrals will be discussed and handled on a confidential individual basis. Our primary objective is to help the employee. However, we must recognize the serious nature of the problem, and at times it may be necessary to provide corrective measures, discipline or termination of the employee(s) involved as the facts may warrant.

In its "Guidelines for Supervisors" this insurance company advises its supervisors not to become involved in a counseling relationship with any suspect employees; for as the law stands, accusing an individual of illegal use of drugs is a cause for libel, and both the supervisor and the employer may be sued. Trying to counsel a drug abuser probably will cause a supervisor to become involved in the abuser's personal problems and certainly will make it more difficult for the supervisor to reflect accurately the facts in succeeding discussions with the Personnel Department.

In a survey conducted by *Industrial Relations News* among 108 firms employing from 275 to over 80,000 workers it was found that only 34 percent of the companies have a formal policy on the use of drugs.[46] In slightly more than half of the companies having such a policy, the penalty for those violating the organization code on drugs is immediate dismissal. In a few other companies the firm takes an additional step of referring the employee to a rehabilitation agency. These firms do not dismiss the worker unless rehabilitation efforts fail.

Some of the treatment techniques available to the drug abuser include: the Methadone Maintenance program under which controlled doses of Methadone are given to the addict under a doctor's care (Methadone is a synthetic drug that helps to end an addict's craving for heroin); the Therapeutic Center concept, whereby addicts help each other overcome the habit under the supervision of professional personnel by living together and through a series of reinforced job stages, prepare to return to normal living; and suicide prevention programs where addicts can call and receive a sympathetic hearing from trained personnel.

---

[46] Sohn, *op. cit.*, p. 26.

Nepotism

Nepotism is the showing of favoritism in the employment of relatives. Many critics of management look upon nepotism as unprofessional and feel that an intellectual, analytical approach to management spells the decline and ultimate extinction of nepotism. However, the actual practices of business executives appear to contradict the beliefs of many students of management. In a study of more than 2,700 executives undertaken by the *Harvard Business Review*,[47] it was shown that, generally, businessmen look upon nepotism as undesirable. This attitude changes, however, when the businessman looks at a specific case and makes his decision. The study revealed that although more than 60 percent of the executives professed an unfavorable attitude toward nepotism in general, 85 percent justified it on special occasions in the normal course of business. In another national survey of office executives,[48] it was found that 48 percent of the companies interviewed permit close relatives to work in the same office; 36 percent do not permit their employment; and 16 percent have no policy in the employment of relatives. In the majority of the companies surveyed, the same rules apply to both management and clerical employees.

Firms that practice nepotism believe that the employment of a relative, compared with a nonrelative, gives them an employee who is more loyal and dependable. At the top managerial level, especially in close corporations, the employment of a relative may assure continuity of the business and an effective perpetuation of the corporate policies. The relative placed in a junior executive position need not be concerned with "making points with the boss" and can thus concentrate on developing his potentialities to the utmost. Some employers feel that relatives working in the same office share a strong sense of responsibility in their work, take more interest in the company operations, and are likely to "fit in" better—all of which contribute to an improved level of morale.

In other companies the practice of nepotism brings about problems. Often, the hiring of relatives creates jealousy and resentment among the employees. Employees ask themselves, "What's the use of trying?" and as a result the level of morale sinks. The hiring of relatives may also tend to discourage outsiders from seeking employment in a "family-togetherness" company. Then, too, some firms

[47] David W. Ewing, "Is Nepotism So Bad?" *Harvard Business Review* (January-February, 1965), p. 23.

[48] "Should Husbands and Wives Walk Down the Office Aisle?" *Modern Office Procedures* (July, 1965), p. 25.

have found that if a relative is employed and later proves to be unqualified for the job, he cannot be discharged or demoted as readily as nonrelatives.

In some offices the employment of husband and wife makes for a close-knit, harmonious working group, while in other offices the employment of a married couple may bring about marked personality conflicts, especially when both the husband and wife work in the same department or are in direct supervisory relationships. According to a national survey conducted by *Modern Office Procedures*,[49] 43 percent of the companies surveyed do not permit husbands and wives to work in the same office; 30 percent permit their employment; the remaining firms indicated that they have no policy in this area. Most of the companies take no action to discourage office romances and if marriage results, about one half of the companies permit both parties to continue working. Although no action is taken to discourage office romances, the respondents to the survey recognized the following problems that do occur: office gossip, reduced efficiency for one or both persons involved, and more sensitive discipline problems.

In connection with the employment of relatives and married women, the provisions of the Civil Rights Act of 1964 must be kept in mind. It has been ruled by the Equal Employment Opportunity Commission that it is legal for a company to have a policy against hiring a person whose husband or wife already is on the company's payroll. However, this rule must apply to male and female workers alike. It is illegal for a company to have a policy against hiring married women unless the same rule is applied to the employment of married men. Also, to discharge women when they get married is illegal unless there is a similar rule for male workers.

PRACTICES RELATING TO SPECIAL PERSONNEL PROBLEMS

In this section several practices pertaining to special personnel problems arising in the office are investigated. These problems, more so than any of those discussed previously in this chapter, are directly tied in to the element of cost and their effective solution requires expert leadership by the office manager and his first-line supervisors.

Tardiness and Absenteeism

Tardiness and absenteeism are serious problems for the office manager, particularly in times when there are many jobs available. In

[49] *Ibid.*

some firms the workers do not even bother to notify the company when they are to be absent. Such conditions seriously impair the efficiency and morale of the office.

Tardiness. Tardiness, which is really a form of absenteeism, is usually handled by a written or an oral reprimand, pay deductions, temporary layoff, or discharge, if habitual; postponement of scheduled salary increases until improvement is shown; loss of coffee break privileges; and a deduction of points in the merit rating of the employee. One of the simplest methods of controlling tardiness is not to tolerate it. In many instances this will work, but there may be extenuating circumstances, such as transportation delays, automobile breakdowns, and strikes, that mean breaking the rule. A better approach is to place tardiness on a cooperative basis so that all departments work together and perhaps compete for the best record of punctuality. Usually there are a few chronic offenders, and these can be dealt with accordingly. Most workers try to be punctual, but their efforts are nullified by the few who arrive late because of indifference or lack of effort.

Tardiness in the office is traceable more often to laxness in discipline than to any other cause. Of course, supervisors themselves must set the proper tone by arriving promptly for work. The practice of many companies in not tolerating tardiness except under emergency conditions proves that it can be controlled.

Absenteeism. The absence of certain key workers may interfere seriously with the work of others in the office unless there are "floating" replacements. Some offices have all their employees indexed so that their capabilities for performing other jobs are known; thus, employees can readily be transferred to take over the jobs of the absentees. But the problem is one of management and must be studied more carefully. The office manager should analyze the problem of absenteeism by finding out:

1. The extent of absenteeism.
2. The causes of absenteeism.
3. The cost of absenteeism.
4. The action to be taken to reduce and to control absenteeism.

Extent of Absenteeism. To obtain the facts on absenteeism may be very simple. When a person has been absent from his job for one full day or longer, he should be required to report to the office manager or the personnel office before returning to work. Thus, a record may be kept of the absentee time and the reasons for it. Such a record should be placed in the personnel files of the employees affected so that it may be considered when opportunities for promotion and salary increases arise. The individual absentee records can be combined to give an absentee record for the entire company, or for each department, that will show the total days of absence during the year, a classification of the reasons for absences, and the frequency of times absent by each employee. Determining the frequency of times absent for each employee aids in locating and controlling chronic absentees who exhibit a pattern of being ill or having a headache on Friday afternoons or Monday mornings. Some firms define a chronic absentee as one who is away from his job four days or more each month, without excuse, for two successive months.

Causes of Absenteeism. Sickness and on-the-job accidents are the most common causes for absenteeism, and the theory has been advanced that perhaps 80 to 90 percent of all accidents are psychological in origin. Some employees seem to avoid working on the slightest pretext of illness; others work when they are so ill that they should stay at home. It is estimated that alcoholism causes an average of three percent of all industrial absenteeism.[50] Sometimes economic conditions and age are factors in absenteeism. Studies indicate that those who save more, own their own homes, and live in better locations have fewer absences than those who do not. Similarily, the chronic absentees tend to be younger than those workers who are regular in their attendance.

New employees are often found among the most chronic absentees, perhaps because of dissatisfaction with their jobs. This points up the need for careful selection of employees, proper assignment to jobs, the enrichment of jobs, and effective supervision that pays more attention to the psychic satisfactions of work. If management were to realize how much it costs to hire and train each office worker and how much the company loses if a worker leaves and must be replaced, perhaps a more careful matching of workers with the job openings, together with appropriate supervision, might result.

In the University of Michigan survey of "Absences and Employee Attitudes" at the Detroit Edison Company, a definite correlation was found between the absence rate of an employee and the employee's satisfaction with his supervisor.[51] For the supervisor, the results of

---

[50] Charles J. Sternhagen, M.D., "Medicine's Role in Reducing Absenteeism," *Personnel* (November-December, 1969), p. 32.

[51] Robert L. Caleo, "Absenteeism," *Administrative Management* (June, 1963), p. 24.

this study mean that, prior to taking disciplinary action, he should freely talk over job problems with his workers to discover why they are remaining away from their jobs. The supervisor should not be permitted to overstaff his department, for eventually this may increase absenteeism, as the result of less being demanded of each employee. The supervisor must be trained in techniques of absence control, checked on his performance, and helped in his efforts to keep employees satisfied.

Cost of Absenteeism. Statistics from the Public Health Service's National Center for Health show that in 1969 absenteeism by employees due to illness or injury averaged 5.8 work days per man. The Center estimated the annual cost of absenteeism to industry to be in excess of $10 billion.[52] In 1970 the Bureau of National Affairs' survey showed that 62 percent of the small firms and 28 percent of the large companies were reporting higher absenteeism than in prior years.[53]

Absenteeism costs for the individual firm can be computed as shown below. In this example for an assumed 400-employee firm, the annual cost of absenteeism is $96,000.[54] This amount does not include lost production, overtime costs, etc., which could easily double the final expense.

Total sick days paid previous 12 months	3,200	Based on 400-employee firm with average of 8 days' absence per employee
Average daily pay multiplied by total sick days	x $30	Based on average daily pay of $30
Annual cost of absenteeism to firm	$96,000	
Total accrued 5-year expense	$480,000	

Action to Be Taken. What can be done about the absenteeism problem? Penalties, fines, and incentive bonuses have not produced

[52] AMemo, *Administrative Management* (November, 1970), p. 84.

[53] "What Ails the Absentees?" *Administrative Management* (September, 1970), p. 19.

[54] "How to Cut Absenteeism and Turnover," *Administrative Management* (March, 1971), p. 65.

the desired effects. Penalties and fines with their demoralizing effects create hard feelings and dissatisfaction; incentive bonuses are usually only temporary in effect. But most of all, it should be remembered that only a small number of workers are chronic offenders, and each of these individual cases should be studied in solving the problem. In the case of chronic absenteeism, surveys by the Bureau of National Affairs indicate that the traditional three-step disciplinary technique—warning, layoff without pay, and finally discharge—is still enforced by many companies.[55]

Reference to the causes of absenteeism may indicate the cure. Every effort should be made to reduce the absences caused by illness and on-the-job accidents. A good medical department available to the office may help. An educational campaign to maintain the health and safety of employees may be undertaken. For example, serving vitamins and providing free influenza shots have been successful in some offices in reducing substantially the absences caused by illness during winter and spring months. Rest periods, good lighting, air conditioning, music, and noise control may also be effective in reducing absenteeism.

Standards can be established for the amount of absenteeism that will be tolerated, under normal circumstances, as the result of various kinds of illnesses. In establishing its standards, one company looks upon eight or more *absence periods a year* for an employee as excessive and classifies any such worker as a chronic absentee. In this same firm, after installing its absentee-control program, the percentage of chronic absentees was reduced during a three-year period from 12.5 to 2.[56]

Each departmental supervisor should be held accountable for the attendance record in his department. To do so, however, the supervisor must be provided with guidelines for disciplinary action to impress upon employees the need for good attendance. When it comes to taking disciplinary action, decisions are often made on the merits of each case—the employee's seniority, his work record, and the recommendations of his supervisor. In a survey of 190 medium-size and large companies undertaken by the research staff of *Business Management*,[57] it was found that 80 percent of the firms interviewed penalize employees for excessive absenteeism, with over 2/3 of the

[55] Caleo, *op. cit.*, p. 23.

[56] For a detailed explanation of how this company established its standards, see Henry Dawes and Donald D. Illig, "Absenteeism," *Administrative Management Society Personnel Management Bulletin* (March, 1965), p. 3.

[57] "How 190 Companies Handle Absenteeism and Tardiness," *Business Management* (February, 1964), pp. 14-18.

firms deducting pay for excessive days absent. Over one half of the companies follow through by investigating all absences. Some conduct their investigations in subtle ways, while others ask the office workers to bring in proof of legitimate absence, such as a physician's statement. Others telephone employees who are absent and inquire as to their state of health. In the case of chronic tardiness in about 90 percent of the firms, the supervisor warns the offender, eventually resorting to reducing the offender's paycheck. If the offender ignores the counseling, 34 percent of the firms state that they will discharge the employee. The researchers conducting this study noted a correlation between those firms having tough attendance rules and those firms that did not have serious attendance problems.

Turnover

Unless there is some strong reason to the contrary, personnel turnover is a measure of the success of personnel policies and practices. If the wrong person is hired, he will either leave or be discharged. If working conditions are unsatisfactory, they may be the result of the personnel practices of the company. But above all, it should be remembered that excessive turnover is expensive and represents a measure of inefficiency. As indicated in Chapter 10, recruiting, interviewing, testing, placing, orienting, training, and supervising a newly hired clerical worker may cost from $700 to $1,325. When a company loses a supervisor, the cost of replacement may be as great as $3,000; and for a middle manager, it may be $10,000 to $15,000. Since some firms experience turnover rates as high as 35 percent among office workers, a strong influence is exerted upon the profit picture of the firm.

Turnover Rate. According to a study made by the Dartnell Corporation, almost 80 percent of the turnover falls in the "controllable" category, with the remaining 20 percent being caused by death, accident, retirement, sickness, military service, or pregnancy.[58] Experts in the area of turnover studies estimate that an annual turnover rate of 10 to 15 percent among male office workers and of 20 to 30 percent among female office workers is normal.

In 1969, the Administrative Management Society conducted a very comprehensive turnover study among business firms, educational

---

[58] Peter R. Weill, "Your Firm Can Be 'Good to Work In'," *Administrative Management* (February, 1963), p. 23.

institutions, and government offices in the United States and Canada.[59] The findings of this survey that have significant implications for the administrative office manager are listed below:

1. The annual turnover rate for 1969 was 26 percent, which means that for every 100 office workers in the firms surveyed, 26 left their employment during the year. In the AMS survey the 1969 turnover rate was calculated as follows:

$$\frac{105{,}535 \text{ (total number of separations from the payroll)}}{399{,}484 \text{ (average annual employment)}} \times 100 = 26 \text{ percent}$$

2. The highest rate of turnover (35 percent) was in the "retail sales and distribution" classification, while the lowest rate (14 percent) was in the "transportation" grouping.
3. The turnover rate was little affected by the size of office and geographical location. The highest turnover rate, about 29 percent, occurred in offices with 251-500 employees. The lowest turnover rate, 23 percent, occurred in offices with over 5,000 employees. The highest rate was found in the West Central United States, while the lowest rate was in the East Central and the South.
4. For female workers, the turnover rate of 35 percent was almost twice that of male workers, 18 percent.
5. The major reasons for separations were: finding another job (40 percent), dismissal (12 percent), and leaving the city (11 percent).

Reasons for Turnover. Among male workers, the strongest reason for terminating their jobs was to find another job; the second major reason for separation was dismissal from the job. Those areas of business that were most affected by male terminations were the service industries, educational institutions, and wholesale and advertising. Among female employees, the major reasons for separation include finding another job, leaving the city, staying home, dismissal, and pregnancy. The Equal Employment Opportunity Commission (EEOC) believes that women returning from maternity leave should be reinstated. To provide substantial equality of treatment of both sexes, there must be special recognition of absence due to pregnancy, according to the government agency. Absence due to illness or injury should not be equated with absence due to maternity,

[59] Conducted by the AMS Personnel Research Committee and summarized in "Turnover Drops 25% for Large Offices," *Administrative Management* (September, 1970), pp. 63 and 64.

for maternity is a temporary disability unique to the female sex, which should be anticipated by the manager. According to a 1968 EEOC decision a leave of absence should be granted for pregnancy whether or not it is granted for illness.

In an AMS survey of 219 companies responding to policy in regard to pregnancy, 67 firms (the largest group) said that pregnant workers were required to leave before they reached their sixth month; however, 45 replies listed no set time for women to leave. The worker is paid under the company's sick leave plan in 165 companies. Re-employment is guaranteed in 105 firms, but there is no guarantee that the worker will be placed on the same job when she returns to work.[60]

Analysis of the major reason for separation—to find another job—would show that the two main causal factors are the desire for better salaries and for better jobs. This would seem to indicate that if higher salaries were paid and workers were promoted, there would be about 40 percent less turnover. Thus, there is need to examine and to evaluate the present salary structure and promotional opportunities in the firm. Opposing this reason for separation is the large number of employees who are discharged for incompetency during the first year of their employment, which may be due to faulty selection, improper job training, and unsatisfactory working conditions. If job dissatisfaction and personality conflict account for a large number of separations, attention should be paid to the function of counseling, and consideration should be given to the possibility of transferring desirable employees to other departments.

Reducing Turnover Expense. The turnover expense may be calculated for an individual company as shown in the following example, which assumes a 400-employee firm:[61]

Total number of employees separated in past 12 months	104	based on 400-employee firm with 26 percent turnover (1969 rate)
Average cost of employee separation	x $750	national average
Annual cost of turnover .	$78,000	
Total accrued 5-year turnover expense	$390,000	

[60] "Most Firms Limit Work of Expectant Mothers," *Administrative Management* (March, 1971), p. 50.

[61] "How to Cut Absenteeism and Turnover," *loc. cit.*

To reduce excessive turnover expense or to control a presently satisfactory turnover rate, the office manager should make sure that in the selection process, the nature and the responsibilities of the job are carefully explained to each job applicant. The job should not be "oversold," nor should it be "undersold." The job applicant should be presented a realistic picture of the job at the time of interview so that if he has any reservations about the work to be done, he and the company can fully investigate them prior to his accepting employment. The employee must be carefully matched to the job by following the workable employment procedures outlined in Chapter 10. After the employee has been carefully evaluated and selected, provisions must be made for his training and orienting as described in the following chapter.

At the time of terminating an employee's services, an *exit interview* may be conducted to make sure that the real reasons for termination are known. During such an interview, there should be a warm, permissive atmosphere in which the interviewer refrains from criticizing or arguing as the employee gives his reasons for leaving. Copies of the exit interview should be made available to interested executives so they may be kept informed of the reasons for separation.

Some companies make use of a *post-exit interview* in which a written questionnaire and a letter are sent to former employees asking their opinions of the company and their reasons for selecting work elsewhere. The former employee is asked to be frank in his reply, and if he wishes he may omit his signature on the questionnaire form.

Collections, Gifts, and Parties

A practice found in many offices is the collection of money to provide gifts for office employees or members of their families. Many firms feel that this is not a problem of management. Others feel that such collections interfere with the morale and efficiency of office work because collections are made too often, the amounts collected are too large, and the funds collected are used for purposes that are too partial. The purposes for which collections are made include: marriage of an employee, departure of an employee, death of an employee, death in the family, illness of an employee, birth in the family, illness in the family, employee birthday, service anniversary, and military service.

A number of companies have developed rather detailed gift collection plans, such as the following plan used by a western light and power company. This firm has a gift collection committee of three persons—two women and one man. Each member serves for three years, one being elected each year, and acting as chairman during his last year on the committee. Membership on the committee presupposes one year's service with the firm and a paid membership in the fund. Contributions are purely voluntary and cannot exceed 25 cents each month for employees and 50 cents each month for supervisors. A workable fund is estimated at not less than $20 nor more than $50. Certain general policies have been adopted to make this plan workable:

1. An employee must have worked for the company at least a year in order to receive a gift when leaving.
2. A person getting married will receive a gift no matter how long he has been with the firm, so long as he continues to work for the company after marriage.
3. No gifts may cost more than $10, but the committee considers length of service and other factors when making a purchase.

In the offices of a printing company in the Midwest, an envelope is routed to all office workers, supervisors, and executives at the time of an employee's illness or his death. Each person voluntarily contributes the amount he wishes. If the amount collected should be insufficient to purchase the desired gift or floral arrangement, the deficit is made up by the company. Any amounts collected in excess of that required to purchase a gift are retained in the collection fund by the office manager and are used at the time of the next collection.

Another type of office collection is that which is taken for donations to charitable organizations. Rather than permit numerous charity drives to be undertaken throughout the year, many firms limit their office collections to one or two voluntary drives each year and select as the recipient of the funds a combined-type charity such as the Community Chest or the United Fund, each of which helps as many worthwhile causes as possible.

Many charitable organizations provide individual collection envelopes. Some organizations provide punched-card forms upon which the employee records his pledge and indicates whether he wishes to pay the donation in full at the present time, whether he prefers to be billed at home in installments, or whether he prefers to have his contribution deducted periodically from his payroll check.

At Christmas time, companies are faced with the problem of giving and receiving gifts. More and more firms have established the policy of accepting no gifts that are likely to obligate the employee or the company, and to give only nominal or token presents that are not likely to embarrass the recipient. One company advises its employees not to accept any monetary gifts or bonds and urges them to exercise "prudent judgment" in turning down nonmonetary gifts that exceed the "bounds of propriety." Another firm handles the problem of Christmas gifts by including the following statement of policy in its employee handbook:

> Christmas gifts are wonderful gestures, but they sometimes can become embarrassing. Certainly no supervisor or officer expects any gifts from employees. The practice is unnecessary, and it can cause embarrassment to other employees when there is a public display of gifts.

Some firms donate to charities the money that would have been spent on Christmas gifts for their customers and clients. The charitable organizations then send notices to the donor firm's clients, advising them that gifts have been made in their name and by whom. Rather than exchange Christmas cards among the workers, supervisors, and officers, some offices ask each employee to contribute to a charitable organization the amount that he ordinarily spends on Christmas cards and postage. In one office a gaily decorated container is made available in which employees place an amount representing what they would have spent for cards. Each year several local charities are named by the office manager and from this listing the employees select the one organization to which the contribution will be made in their name.

Closely related to the practice of giving and receiving gifts at Christmas is the policy to be established with regard to Christmas parties in the office. In a study of 183 companies, the Management Information Center of Deerfield, Illinois, found a strong trend away from employee Christmas parties and the giving of gifts by suppliers to customers. Instead, more companies are granting extra time off to their employees rather than sponsoring a company party. Some companies take the money they would ordinarily spend on a party and donate it to a charitable organization.[62] Like other companies that found the annual Christmas party to be an unhealthful influence upon employee morale and company relations, one firm abandoned its long-time practice of sponsoring an annual Christmas party and placed the following statements in its policy manual:

---

[62] AMemo, *Administrative Management* (October, 1964), p. 96.

> We do not wish to interfere in the normal social life of employees. Individuals and groups may do as they wish. However, we do have a definite policy on office Christmas parties. Much has been said and written on this subject. Most companies have given up their large Christmas parties and so has your company. We do not permit office-wide Christmas parties at which liquor is served. In the home office at Christmas, each department gets together at the close of the office just before Christmas for a brief period of exchanging presents. This plan has worked out quite satisfactorily.

Although the annual office party, picnic, or outing is still fairly popular, only 39 percent of the 107 companies participating in a survey conducted by *Administrative Management* regularly organize such an outing.[63] The strongest element that supports continuance of annual outings is tradition.

Employee Dishonesty

In spite of precautionary procedures in internal control, including the principle that one employee should check the work of another, business is losing some $8.5 billion in cash and goods annually because of employee dishonesty.[64] It is estimated that clerical employees steal more than $125 million each year by taking advantage of their companies' indifference to the pens, pencils, stationery, staplers, and typewriter ribbons that find their way into the employees' homes and into the classrooms of the employees' children. Control over theft and fraud is a problem in human relations, and the attitude and policies of management contribute to the problem. If managers and supervisors are indifferent toward the rules that have been established and the atmosphere is one of "Who cares?" the office can become a school for dishonesty.

Some guidelines that the administrative office manager should follow in developing an effective control system to insure employee honesty are listed below:

1. Department heads should be assigned the responsibility for developing and enforcing a program of control over the purchase and issuance of supplies. The supplies needed by

---

[63] "Today's Office Outing: Inexpensive, Traditional," *Administrative Management* (April, 1968), p. 38.

[64] "Are Your Employees More Dishonest Than You Think?" *Business Management* (September, 1968), p. 12.

each department should be estimated and planned for in preparing the annual budget for each department. Budgeting a dollar estimate will impress upon workers the cost of the supplies and create greater respect for usage. Supplies should be ordered in bulk only a few times during the year in order to reduce the number of orders and the opportunities for employees to "pad" the orders. Requisitions for supplies should be signed by a department head or someone so authorized. When delivered, the supplies should be turned over to the department head so that he may acknowledge their receipt and safeguard them by placing the items in a department storage cabinet.

2. All job applicants should be screened by investigating their references and any gaps in their employment history. If applicants for positions of trust and those who are promoted to such positions are required to fill out bonding questionnaires, the bonding company will investigate the person's character references. Psychological as well as financial benefits will be realized from bonding employees, for experience shows that employees who know they are bonded are far less likely to steal than those who are not bonded or do not know they are covered by a fidelity bond. For the relatively inexpensive premiums, the psychological benefits are enormous.
3. Any employee leaving the firm should be required to report to an executive outside the former employee's department to make sure that the employee's name is removed from the payroll. Otherwise, an unscrupulous person might continue to issue checks in the name of the former employee and cash them with a forged signature.
4. Realistic performance standards should be set. If the standards are not realistic, and the employee cannot achieve the goal, quota, or benefit, he is faced with two alternatives—to fail or to be dishonest. Periodic unannounced spot checks should be taken upon employee performance at all levels in the office. Employees should be informed that such checks are a normal part of internal control. Spot checks may be made more effective by introducing deliberate errors as a means of detecting indifference and inefficient performance. All critical areas of office operations—cash handling, disbursements, and safeguarding of important records—should be inspected and reviewed periodically.
5. The enforcement of policies should be uniformly fair and firm at all levels. Double standards of enforcement and a vacillating approach on the part of the office manager will break down

the discipline and morale quickly and lessen the employees' respect for management and company procedures.

QUESTIONS FOR REVIEW

1. If providing coffee breaks and rest periods is not a charitable contribution to paternalism, what are the reasons for providing them?
2. How common is the practice of providing coffee breaks? What principles should be followed in scheduling coffee breaks?
3. What is meant by the statement that "Music *in itself* does not increase efficiency"?
4. Briefly describe the current practices in providing insurance benefits to employees.
5. What are the nature and extent of educational assistance provided by many business firms?
6. In view of the government reports that link smoking with unhealthful effects upon the body, how can the office manager defend smoking in the office?
7. What steps should be taken in developing a scientific plan of safety administration? What role should the office manager play in such a program?
8. In what ways can the office manager handle the problem of the employee who receives a great deal of personal mail at the office?
9. Describe the three-step process recommended by the National Council on Alcoholism in working with the alcoholic in the office.
10. What steps should a first-line supervisor take in dealing with one of his workers who is suspected of being a drug addict?
11. What is nepotism? How is nepotism affected by the provisions of the Civil Rights Act of 1964?
12. Tardiness more often is traceable to laxness in discipline in the office than to any other cause. Explain. What steps can the administrative office manager take to reduce or, better yet, to eliminate tardiness?
13. What should be the role of the department supervisor in controlling absenteeism in his department?
14. Explain how personnel turnover is calculated. What is the average annual turnover rate for male and for female office employees?
15. What steps should the office manager take to reduce excessive turnover in his company?
16. Should management be concerned with the practice of collecting money to provide gifts for employees? Why?
17. Describe an effective control system aimed at insuring honesty among office employees.

QUESTIONS FOR DISCUSSION

1. The management of a company has decided to authorize a charity contribution and is considering the use of a "Buck of the Month Club" to obtain the funds voluntarily through payroll deductions. Each employee who cares to contribute will grant management the right to deduct $1 from his paycheck each month. What is your reaction to the use of the "Buck of the Month Club" plan? If you react negatively to this proposal, what other approach would you recommend management take to obtain the funds?

2. One writer states that American management generally clings to the pessimistic view that people will take days off no matter what management does. Management cannot stop them, short of firing, and this would mean increased turnover. Management just pays them for so many sick days a year and hopes for the best.

In your opinion, do these statements accurately portray American management? What evidence can you cite to the contrary?

3. Personality disturbances, ranging from anxiety and psychosomatic illnesses to severe mental disorders such as schizophrenia are common causes of absenteeism. Emotional sickness is believed to provoke more absences than any other illness except the common cold. One large insurance company reports that out of the 120,000 employee visits made to its medical department each year, 200 or 300 result in recommended psychiatric treatment.

What steps should the office manager take in dealing with the psychoneurotic or maladjusted employee, who as a result of his absenteeism, is really costly to the organization?

4. A midwestern newspaper reported that a 22-year-old secretary in charge of a $300 petty cash box secretly withdraws $100 every Friday to bet on horses, ball games, and fights. The secretary feels that she is doing nothing wrong, for she reasons that the petty cash fund is her responsibility and that eventually she returns all she takes. Do you agree that the secretary is "doing nothing wrong"? How can management anticipate and prevent such a practice?

5. In the offices of the Thornton Tax Service, there had been an increasing amount of smoking on the part of secretaries and stenographers during working hours. The office manager felt this was unbusinesslike and decided to curtail all smoking in the offices. Following his announcement regarding nonsmoking, production in the secretarial and transcription departments fell about 50 percent. Discuss the office manager's method of handling the smoking problem.

6. In the Sterling Tie Corporation, there are several employees who frequently make local outgoing personal calls on office time. Since they can dial outgoing numbers directly from their desks, the situation is rather difficult to control, especially since personal calls cannot be distinguished from business calls without listening in. As office manager, discuss how you would solve this problem.

7. The Egnew Textile Company has recently tried to improve its office personnel relations. First, it improved the appearance and comfort of the employees' lounges by installing new furniture; one of the office employees was delegated to make the purchases. Then it was decided to provide 15-minute rest periods twice a day. Soon the employees had burned cigarette holes in the cushions of the new furniture and otherwise damaged it. Furthermore, shortly after the rest periods were started, many employees persisted in returning to their desks 20 minutes after they had left, instead of at the end of 15 minutes.

Discuss the weaknesses of management in planning and implementing its personnel procedures.

8. Gerald Roberts, executive vice president of the Shelby Company of New York City, is becoming concerned about the increasing number of his middle managers who are having a cocktail or two during their lunch. He is also aware that a couple of his men must have a "fortifier" before coming to work in the morning. Although Roberts has never seen any of his men "tipsy," he firmly believes that drinking during lunch (or the first thing in the morning) causes a man to slow down mentally. Roberts feels that drinking during the workday is totally undesirable and he wants his men to discontinue the practice.

Is Roberts justified in telling his men not to drink during the day? If so, how do you recommend that he proceed in telling them? Do you believe that Roberts will be able to abolish his men's custom of having a cocktail or two at lunch?

9. At the Bux Data Processing Center, food services are provided under a contractual arrangement with a coffee cart vendor. During the past six months the cost of coffee and doughnuts has increased to such an extent that the workers have commenced to complain. The company does not want to give up its practice of granting coffee breaks to its workers, but at the same time the firm is financially unable to subsidize the food service. What suggestions do you have for the company whereby the employees can retain their coffee breaks without the firm becoming financially involved?

10. During his two weeks' vacation Tony DiDonato was forced to leave the motel at the seashore and undergo an appendectomy at a nearby hospital. Upon returning to work, DiDonato indicated to the office manager that, in view of his hospitalization, the company should reschedule his vacation date and treat his former two weeks' vacation as sick leave. As office manager, how would you answer DiDonato?

11. George Koch, office manager of Santo Industries, Inc., is aware of the company policy that forbids any form of gambling on the company premises. However, each year Koch sees (and occasionally participates in) World Series and football pools being organized by the office workers. As Koch, how would you defend such pools in view of the company's policy against gambling? Is it unethical for Koch, as a manager, to participate in any of the pools?

PRACTICAL OFFICE CASES

Case 13-1 Employing a Vice President's Son-in-Law

The Griffith Credit Corporation is considering hiring the son-in-law of one of the vice presidents for the position of administrative office manager. The son-in-law, Robert W. Carr, is as well qualified for the position as any other person who has been interviewed. The position involves planning and control responsibilities in areas where services and technology are undergoing great change.

Management wants an executive who can "grow with the job," for the position is expected to increase rapidly in scope and status. There is a chance, however, that any man employed will not be the right man for the job tomorrow because of changing trends and problems. Although the company has employed relatives of executives for other managerial posts in the company, there is no consensus that employing a relative for the administrative management job will work equally well.

The four executives who have the responsibility for making the final decision have evaluated the situation as follows:

1. H. J. Cole, the father-in-law of Carr, feels that since his son-in-law is well qualified for the position, he should be hired.
2. Lee Adams, the vice president in charge of personnel, also feels that Carr should be hired. But Adams is aware that the position is subject to much stress and change. Therefore, he feels that special measures must be taken to see that Carr's performance is evaluated objectively and impartially. Adams firmly believes that if and when Carr should fail to measure up to the job, he should be replaced immediately.
3. Walter Fox, the vice president in charge of finance, feels that nepotism in a situation such as this is too much of a gamble. He sees that the son-in-law may not measure up and, as a result, the company will be faced with a messy and extremely unpleasant decision.
4. You, as the president of the company, are trying to reconcile the different points of view and reach a decision.

   You hold a great deal of admiration and respect for the ability of Cole, but you know that this is no guarantee that his son-in-law will perform equally well. Still, as you realize, there is a family tie here. And if you vote against Carr, what will be the effect upon Cole?

You appreciate Adams' point of view and agree wholeheartedly that if Carr is employed, his performance must be evaluated objectively and his rating must not be influenced by the position of his father-in-law. But, you ask yourself, how can a *relative's* performance be evaluated *objectively*?

Fox has made a good point, too, for you recall that ten years ago the former president's son-in-law was hired and he turned out to be a misfit. It was a sticky situation and the company had no alternative but to let the son-in-law "gracefully resign." After that, things were never the same with the former president, up until the day he retired.

■ After listening to Cole, Adams, and Fox evaluate the capabilities of Carr and express their viewpoints on nepotism, you realize that the next step is up to you—to cast your vote. What will your vote be? How would you justify your position to each of the three vice presidents if you were asked to do so? How would you proceed to evaluate objectively the performance of an executive's relative?

Case 13-2 Solving the Sweet Smell Problem [65]

Harold London found a note on his desk Monday morning that had curtly ominous overtones: "See me in my office as soon as possible. T.C." It was from Ted Curry, the executive vice president, a man with whom Harold had a stable, amicable relationship. But he was not used to getting abrupt notes from Ted, so he went to see him immediately.

"What's up?" asked Harold, trying to keep from sounding apprehensive.

"Something important, Hal. Sit down." Ted was troubled. "You've been in charge of the mailroom operations for five years now, and I've never had any reason to fault your decisions seriously. But this new development troubles me."

"I don't understand," said Hal, though he was beginning to suspect the problem.

"I've heard, and occasionally seen, that a group of your boys, a clique, seems to take their breaks surreptitiously, and in out-of-the-way places, like distant closets. I've also heard that the reason is because they're smoking marijuana. How about it, Hal?"

"You may be right, Ted. I can't honestly say I'm their confidante."

"But have you confronted them with the idea? Have you asked them outright?"

---

[65] AMS News (Willow Grove, Pa.: Administrative Management Society), April, 1971, p. 6.

"No," Hal answered directly, "and I'm not sure it's a good tactic."

"Why not? And what would you suggest in lieu of it?"

"To answer the first question, there are several reasons we can't ask them outright if they're smoking grass. One is that they probably would lie, for fear of being fired. Another is that I'm not eager to be guardian of their morals, especially since break time is strictly their own. Oh, I know that it's illegal, and the company could get into trouble even though we don't control their breaks, but still, we would be discriminating against them because of their more vulnerable positions."

"What does that mean?" Ted wanted to know.

"You know as well as I do," said Hal, "that there are a couple of younger men under you who have spoken openly about the effects of pot, and who may have tried it themselves. Do I have to name names?"

Ted looked thoughtful. "I know," he said finally, "but if they've stepped out of line, they haven't done it in here. And I wouldn't say that they condoned its use, just discussed it. You're right that we can't be everyone's guardian, but you're also right that the weed is illegal. We just can't take the risk that it is being used on company property, even if not on company time."

■ What would be your approach to finding a solution to this problem?

14

Training, Orienting, and Promoting Office Personnel

> The increasing pace of technological change and economic growth in modern industry daily create new challenges and opportunities for American business. Each of these challenges and opportunities brings with it heavy demands on a company's resources, especially its most essential resource—people. For it is the people of a company who must solve today's problems, cope with tomorrow's concepts, and anticipate the trends of the day after tomorrow. To do this, they must be well-educated people with the skills and energies needed to meet these demands. But more is required. If a company is to prosper, its people must be creative, they must be flexible; otherwise, they will be unable to function in the modern industrial world.[1]

To have people who can function in an environment such as that described above, companies expend a great deal of time, energy, and money annually. High standards and well-defined recruiting and hiring procedures may be established, but the process cannot end there, for even the best people can grow stale. Thus, each worker must be provided with opportunities for continuous growth and development. To accomplish this goal of learning and improved

[1] From the training manual of Johnson & Johnson, with the permission of Richard P. Rooney, February, 1970.

performance, companies, looking upon themselves as educational institutions as well as producers of goods and services, maintain formal training and development programs as tools to equip their personnel with the knowledges and skills they need to grow. As indicated in the preceding chapter, more and more companies, by means of company-financed tuition plans, acknowledge the importance of continuous education by permitting, encouraging, and guiding their workers in furthering their education and training.

TRAINING

Training is the process of exposing the trainee in a systematic way to a series of events, experiences, and materials that, in themselves, comprise opportunities to learn.[2] What takes place within the trainee, what changes in his behavioral patterns and attitudes, is known as *learning*. Training not only increases the self-confidence and improves the morale of workers but also increases production, reduces initial errors, and improves the quality of the employees' work. Training lessens the amount of supervision necessary, reduces turnover caused by unsatisfactory adjustment to jobs, corrects mistaken judgments as a result of the interview process, and increases interest in the job because of a more thorough understanding of the work and its relation to that of other employees.

The money spent for training must pay dividends as a result of fewer errors, greater production, and smaller turnover. Eastman Kodak Company estimates that perhaps ten percent of a person's time over the years is spent learning about his job and keeping abreast of new developments. For this firm this means an annual payroll investment of more than $30 million. Kodak believes that it should earn as good a return on its training investment as it does on any other investment it makes.[3] The key to profitable investment in training is the assurance that the process accomplishes something, for employees who are well adjusted to their working conditions usually are happy and efficient workers.

Objectives of Training

Before any training can commence, the question to be answered is: "What are the goals of the training to be given?" The objectives

[2] "Examine Both Hardware and Software You Need," *Administrative Management* (March, 1970), p. 86.

[3] From information supplied the authors by Robert M. Jacobs, Company Training Development, Eastman Kodak Company, March, 1970.

of the entire training program, its courses, and its instructional content must be clearly and precisely identified. Some programs that provide merely an acquaintance with the organization structure and the policies and practices of the firm are orientation programs, not training programs. Included among the goals of training programs are the following: to provide initial training, to provide for upgrading present workers, and to retrain for changing job assignments.

After setting the objectives for training, general rules of procedure may be stated. Of course, the objectives must be derived from what is actually required for performance of the jobs to be filled. The objectives must be communicated to the trainees and each unit of instruction must be based on the knowledges and skills already within the repertoire of trainees before training commences so that the new material is reasonably within the achievement level of the trainees.[4]

Principles of Training

Each of the following principles of effective training is directly related to the objectives of the training program—trainees who have learned to work differently through improved performance and who are actually using the new learning on the job:

1. By having participated in training and development, employees contribute to the profit motive of the firm. As a result of their more accurate, rapid, and improved performance, the firm is able to realize additional economies in the production of its goods or services. Closely allied to this principle are the cost-reducing factors of standardization and uniformity of output, both of which characterize the end results of effective training.
2. With an up-to-date training program that utilizes the best available equipment and information, employees are prepared for promotion when there is a change in business conditions, such as expansion. Also, if employees are trained for promotion, the illness, death, reassignment, or resignation of other workers will have little effect upon the smooth operation of the business.
3. Effective training of office employees, often a prime responsibility of the first-line supervisor, lessens the need for close supervision. A well-trained employee asks fewer questions and cooperates more readily with his coworkers, all of which reduces the burden placed upon his supervisor.

[4] Blair J. Kolasa, *Introduction to Behavioral Science for Business* (New York: John Wiley & Sons, Inc., 1969), pp. 192-198.

4. By providing training that is relevant to the real world and geared to individual needs, a more accurate evaluation can be made of the employee's capabilities, thus insuring his proper placement in the organization.

In order to meet the specific objectives of its training program, a company must determine the types of training that will be utilized, assign the responsibility for the training function, select the training techniques and methods, and set measurable criteria that can be used to evaluate the effectiveness of the training program.[5]

Types of Training

Training, as a form of practical education, is essentially of two types: (1) basic training for new employees and (2) promotional and executive training. Promotional and executive training was discussed in Chapter 11 as part of the supervisory training process. There it was pointed out that promotional and executive training should be a continuous process at all levels of management. In this chapter attention will be focused upon the basic training for new office employees.

Basic training for new office employees may be given in the office by coworkers, department heads, or first-line supervisors; in the facilities of the training department; in a company school that cooperates closely with the firm's offices; in conjunction with public institutions such as high schools, trade and vocational schools, junior and community colleges, and four-year colleges and universities; and in cooperation with private institutions such as business colleges.

From a survey of 930 companies of all sizes and kinds from coast to coast, conducted by the American Society for Personnel Administration and the Manpower Research Council, the following findings have significance in determining the types of training to be made available:

1. About 92 percent of the firms surveyed offer some kind of in-plant training to one or more levels of their employees. The

[5] As an aid to the small businessman who needs to set up a systematic program for training his employees, Leonard J. Smith, Executive Director, Training Services, Inc., Rutherford, New Jersey, has prepared a "Checklist for Developing a Training Program." The checklist, titled Management Aids No. 186 for Small Manufacturers, is available from the Small Business Administration, Washington, D.C. 20416.

nature of the training varies from training designed to fit employees to existing jobs to that designed to fit them for better jobs. In some instances, the training may be merely orientation, which is discussed later in this chapter.

2. Nearly 51 percent of the companies offer courses specifically designed to train their workers for jobs that require greater skills. However, it is interesting to note that over a period of 21 months, less than one percent of the total number of employees in these companies took any of the courses. It appears as if many firms are offering courses to upgrade their workers, but the courses are benefiting only very few employees.
3. Over half of the firms feel that their own in-plant training programs or those offered by public institutions, or both, fall short of meeting their needs. Some of the factors that account for the discontent include public institutions that do not provide any training at all, lack of training on a regular basis, poor quality of instruction, and nonexistent or antiquated equipment.
4. Over half of the companies feel that their communities lack a sufficient number of vocational training facilities. Of the surveyed firms, 85 percent favor the development of vocationally oriented two-year public colleges to aid them in filling their training gap.

From these survey findings it can be concluded that most of the firms are doing something to train at least some of their employees on a formal basis, but many companies believe they can do much more and that more could be done by public institutions such as high schools and colleges.[6]

Responsibility for Training

For companies planning to provide basic training for their new office employees, a number of questions designed to establish the responsibility for training, such as the following, must be answered: Should basic training be on the job or away from the job (vestibular training)? Should company executives, training department specialists, or trained educators be selected as instructors? Should funds from the federal government be used to subsidize in-plant training? What kind of training should be made available to attract minority-group workers?

---

[6] "How 930 Companies Tackle Training Today," *Business Management* (February, 1968) pp. 35-38.

Illustrative On-the-Job and Vestibular Training Programs. In an Administrative Management Society survey of 141 administrative managers,[7] it was found that most managers feel that the following subject areas are best learned in a formal company training program or through on-the-job training: human relations, oral communications, supervision, and office organization and planning. Skills such as accounting, business law, and business mathematics are best taught in the university. Generally the survey noted that those skills and knowledges which were thought of as best being presented in formal college programs were least likely to be selected as being best taught in an on-the-job training program, and vice versa. Areas such as economics were generally considered to be in the college domain, while other topics such as duplicating equipment and office machines were overwhelmingly favored to be in the on-the-job training realm.

The following descriptions of training programs offered by several firms show but a sampling of the wide variety of ways in which training can be provided either on the job or away from the job.

At Eastman Kodak Company, on-the-job training is used since it is felt that only at the work station does the employee receive coaching and counseling that are directly relevant to the tasks that are performed. When factors prevent training from occurring at a specific work place, the firm tries to keep the training site as close as possible to the work station. If the supervisor is unable to conduct the training, the department training specialists do so. The firm feels very strongly that training is a supervisor's responsibility and for that reason requires line superiors of the trainees to discuss the training courses and their relevance with the trainees.

Newly hired secretaries at the New York headquarters of International Paper Corporation are trained in an intensive two-week program under the direction of the supervisor of administrative and clerical training. The newly employed persons meet in a lecture room for ten days from 9 a.m. to 5 p.m. At the end of this period the secretaries are assigned temporarily to various departments for on-the-job training until there is an appropriate opening. In the lecture room, which is equipped with movie, slide, and filmstrip equipment and in another room housing electric typewriters, the employees use programmed learning materials to upgrade their typing and stenographic skills. Although the girls produce no actual work during the two-week period, they do handle company forms and become familiar with company terminology. The girls also attend

[7] Harold T. Smith, "Favor On-Job Supervisory Training," *Administrative Management* (August, 1970), p. 53.

special seminars in the proper use of the telephone, in improvement of their typing proficiency on electric machines, and in proper filing methods and filing system techniques.[8]

Manpower, Inc., a supplier of temporary office help, provides a series of nine training manuals for self-study by each of its temporary office workers. The objectives of the training course are to offer knowledge of a lasting value; to "sharpen" the techniques and abilities of the workers by presenting hints, shortcuts, and new procedures that will make the temporary worker a better office employee; to learn about new office equipment and supplies; to learn how to adapt quickly to new office routines; to understand advanced telephone techniques; and to gain a clearer understanding of human relations in the office. Upon completion of the training course, the temporary office worker receives a certificate that recognizes her as a well-informed business woman.

Throughout the training manuals, case studies and office situations are used as teaching techniques. Upon completion of the training manuals, the worker is quizzed on her understanding of the concepts and principles presented. The titles of the manuals that make up this training program are: (1) An Introduction to Manpower and Temporary Office Work, (2) Adapting Quickly to New Office Routine and Advanced Telephone Technique, (3) Tips and Shortcuts in Typing, Dictation, Filing, and Office Procedure, (4) The White Glove Girl's Book of Beauty, Wardrobe, and Personal Grooming, (5) How to Be an Effective Vacation Replacement, (6) Office Work in the Field of Banking, (7) Office Work in the Field of Insurance, (8) The Legal Secretary, and (9) The Medical Transcriber.[9]

At Micro Switch, a division of Honeywell, Inc., interested personnel within the firm as well as those outside the company are encouraged to attend the firm's Voluntary Employee Education Program (VEEP). The purpose of the courses provided by the company is to further the career development of its employees by bettering their current job knowledge and skills and aiding them in accomplishing long-term career goals. The courses, taught after working hours in conjunction with a nearby college, are available free of charge each semester to the company employees.[10]

---

[8] Lewis E. Lachter, "How Seven Firms Educate Their In-Office Personnel," *Administrative Management* (August, 1967), p. 26.

[9] Information supplied the authors by the Cincinnati Office of Manpower, Inc.

[10] From information supplied the authors by R. E. Silver, Training Director, Micro Switch, Freeport, Illinois, February, 1970.

The New York investment firm, Hayden, Stone Inc., provides training for high school graduates who are preparing for a variety of clerical positions in the credit department. A four-week course is offered in which classes meet from 9 a.m. to 5 p.m. daily. In addition to attending lectures that are presented by staff and management personnel, the trainees visit the credit department both to observe and to participate in clerical duties.[11]

A ten-hour course in adding machine operation is open to any employee at the Memphis Methodist Hospital, Memphis, Tennessee. The classes, designed for beginners as well as for those wishing to become more proficient, meet one hour each day for ten consecutive workdays. Instruction is given in one of the hospital's classrooms which is used for other types of training. After the local representative of the adding machine manufacturer taught the hospital's training staff how to conduct classes, the staff took full charge of instruction.[12]

A manufacturer of building materials, finding it difficult to obtain a sufficient number of trained secretaries, went to an outstanding secretarial school in the city where one of its main offices was located and made the following arrangements:

1. The firm advertises in the city newspapers indicating that it will pay for secretarial training for future employees.
2. The secretarial school offers an intensive course for those applicants accepted by the company.
3. The firm pays the applicant for the course on the following basis: 50 percent when the course is completed and the applicant accepted for the job, and 50 percent after one year's service with the firm.

A chemical manufacturing company, suffering a shortage of applicants for clerical and office jobs, approached a local business college and made arrangements whereby the college furnished an instructor who, in cooperation with the personnel director of the chemical firm, outlined a special intensive course for training the applicants for future employment with this firm. The firm advertises for the students and interviews them, and then hires them upon completion of the training course. Upon employment the firm pays the employee for part of the cost of training, and after one year's employment the firm reimburses the employee for the entire cost of the training program.

---

[11] Lewis E. Lachter, "Ten Case Histories: Designed to Educate," *Administrative Management* (August, 1968), p. 28.

[12] *Ibid.*, p. 30.

Instructional Staff for the Training Program. The training staff of a firm should possess the following: (1) human relations ability, (2) leadership ability, and (3) technical ability.[13] Those in charge of training, whether it is a company executive or a trained educator, must know enough about human nature and behavioral patterns and attitudes to realize that the trainees should be accepted as they are. In trying to adapt new employees to work situations, the trainer, even if a most skilled teacher, cannot completely remold their personalities or alter significantly their behavioral patterns. The teacher himself should have had experience in exercising the managerial functions of organizing, planning, controlling, and leading in order to develop the skills, attitudes, and work habits of his trainees. The instructor in a training program must be technically competent, through appropriate education and experience, in order to command the respect of his trainees and to impart to them the knowledge and skills required to qualify them to produce a quality product or service.

Possibly the most important part of the overall training picture is the supervisor and the manner in which he handles his responsibility. He must permit his subordinates to use their knowledge and to be more independent and professional; otherwise, he will be an obstacle to their effectiveness as well as to his own.[14] What is called for is employee-centered supervision, or self-supervision. The role of the supervisor must be redefined, and he himself must be trained for his new and different duties. At the Eastman Kodak Company where many training specialists are employed at various points in the organization, the company is adamant on the principle that the responsibility for training rests with the line superior.[15] This responsibility cannot be delegated to any other person, regardless of the specialized skills he may have. The training department has the task of providing staff assistance to the supervisor, who conducts the training rather than personnel in the training department. The responsibility of the supervisor goes beyond conducting courses, however. It is his job to be alert to the training needs of his workers and to the opportunities for meeting these needs. His job is to see to it that training which cannot be provided personally is provided from some other source and to follow up on the training when it has been completed.

---

[13] F. Arnold McDermott, "Office Training Returns More Than It Costs," *Administrative Management* (March, 1964), p. 53.

[14] Bernard J. Bienvenu, "Changing Concepts in Training," *Personnel* (January-February, 1969), p. 59.

[15] From information supplied the authors by Robert M. Jacobs, Company Training Development, Eastman Kodak Company, March, 1970.

Subsidization of the Training Program. Under the Manpower Development and Training Act (MDTA) of 1962, individual companies are enabled to use federal funds to provide basic training of persons, who because of changing technology and the obsolescence of their job skills, are unable to obtain gainful employment. Firms are helped to set up and administer on-the-job training programs and to make changes in their existing training programs. The act provides funds for the training of new personnel for unfilled jobs, initial job training for present personnel, and training for part-time employees who want to work full time. The financial provisions of the MDTA are applicable, among others, to the training of skilled and semiskilled workers, clerical and sales personnel, nonprofessional scientific and technical personnel, and semiprofessional personnel.[16]

In 1963 the Vocational Education Act, which placed emphasis on the needs of the people, was enacted. The following year the Opportunities Industrialization Center (OIC), a federally funded program, was founded in Philadelphia. The OIC, which has more than 25 centers in the country, offers training programs spanning some 40 different vocational areas, including business machines, key punch, computer maintenance, and office machines repair. In 1965 the MDTA was amended to reach the disadvantaged, unemployed, and underemployed. Three years later the Vocational Education Act and the MDTA were further improved, and the National Alliance of Businessmen (NAB) emerged. NAB is a cooperative government-business program designed to find jobs in the private sector of the economy for the hardcore unemployed. NAB was founded on the principle of hire first and then follow through with on-the-job training and remedial counseling.[17] Government funds to offset the costs of training are obtained through a Labor Department program called Job Opportunities in the Business Sector (JOBS), which is sponsored by NAB. In 1969 the Job Corps, a voluntary program designed to provide basic education and job-skill training to youths 16 to 21, was integrated into the Labor Department's comprehensive manpower program under the Office of Economic Opportunity (OEO), which operates a number of antipoverty programs. Additional government subsidy programs include proposed legislation that would assure an employment opportunity

[16] Those interested in more details about the Manpower Development and Training Act should contact the nearest office of the Bureau of Apprenticeship and Training or write the Director, On-the-Job Training, Bureau of Apprenticeship and Training, U.S. Department of Labor, Washington, D.C. 20210.

[17] Lawrence A. Johnson, *Employing the Hard-Core Unemployed,* AMA Research Study 98 (New York: American Management Association, 1969), p. 69.

for every American seeking work and would make available the education and training needed by any person to qualify for employment consistent with his highest potential and capability. Such legislation contemplates that companies would be permitted to deduct a certain percentage of the cost of their approved training programs toward corporate income taxes.

In the survey cited earlier in this chapter,[18] it was found that the majority of the firms questioned have not been aided by government-supported employee training. Only 19 percent of the firms have employed persons trained in Job Corps centers and only 20 percent have been helped by programs sponsored by the MDTA. The largest proportion of the firms that report they have not been helped by the MDTA programs, some 32 percent of the companies, state that these programs are not producing workers with skills that are useful to their businesses. In that part of the survey designed to discover what businesses are thinking about in relation to their training needs, it was found that some 70 percent of the firms oppose government subsidies for their in-plant training programs. Such opposition is to be expected, for historically business has opposed government subsidies, especially those subsidies that might entail a certain amount of government regulation and control. Although all the ways have not been explored in which business and industry might contribute to training and to making use of the services of many types of individuals unable to meet market tests of employment, if business takes on in any extensive way the work of the educational system, then business should be compensated or reimbursed through some form of tax incentive or allowance.[19]

Training Minority-Group and Other Disadvantaged Workers. In Chapter 10 it was brought out that in the employment of the disadvantaged, the objective is to place these persons in jobs where they can be productive, gain self-respect, and have hope for advancement. For many firms this is a new experience since the disadvantaged have been long thought of as unemployable. Typically these men and women are poorly educated and without skills. Their attitude, characterized by tardiness and absenteeism, betrays a great lack of understanding of what is expected of them in the world of work.[20]

[18] "How 930 Companies Tackle Training Today," *loc. cit.*

[19] Robert N. Hilkert, "A Humanist's View: The Art of Management and Other Talks," (Philadelphia: Federal Reserve Bank of Philadelphia, 1970), pp. 30-31.

[20] Leonard Nadler, "Helping the Hard-Core Adjust to the World of Work," *Harvard Business Review* (March-April, 1970), p. 117.

Similarly many business firms do not know what is expected of them nor how to proceed in helping the disadvantaged and minority groups, but they do want to help, as evidenced by survey results cited in this chapter and Chapter 10.

Most attempts by business to provide jobs and training for the poor and for minority group members have foundered, and the business firms are now frustrated and disappointed.[21] Jules Cohn, formerly a consultant for McKinsey & Company and now directing research for the Economic and Manpower Corporation, states: "The JOBS program—sponsored by the Labor Department and the National Alliance of Businessmen—has fallen far short of its goals, and a host of other, less well-publicized training programs set up by some of the nation's largest companies have either completely folded or been drastically curtailed." [22] The major mistake made by business firms in devising and setting up special training programs for the disadvantaged was to allow themselves to be persuaded that entirely new—and costlier—methods were needed rather than believing in their time-tested techniques for training new employees.[23] Companies found themselves also providing a host of "supportive services," which, according to Leonard Nadler, an original member of the President's Task Force on the War Against Poverty (1964), are needed. Nadler has written: ". . . what is necessary is not only training that gives the person skills, but company procedures that help produce new behavior patterns and 'support' those patterns while he is undergoing training and also later while he is becoming adjusted to his job." [24] However, Cohn finds that the armada of new supportive services (programs of advice and counsel on a wide variety of subjects from how to use deodorants and comb the hair to how to shop for frozen foods, day-care centers, transportation of trainees to and from work, and legal services) has created no jobs for the disadvantaged nor has it improved society's ability to provide them with marketable skills.[25] From Cohn's study of job training, he asserts that the disadvantaged workers want jobs, job training, and the opportunity to advance; they, therefore, resent patronizing lectures and intrusive advice. Cohn points to a few companies that have shown that vocational training alone can succeed with the disadvantaged, and he advocates sensibly conceived job training that is geared to real jobs.

---

[21] Jules Cohn, "Job Training Should Stick to Basics," *The New York Times,* June 20, 1971, p. 14.

[22] *Ibid.*

[23] *Ibid.*

[24] Nadler, *loc. cit.*

[25] Cohn, *loc. cit.*

Nadler, on the other hand, describes in detail the successful training programs and support systems of five companies [26] to back up his conviction that "merely hiring and training these 'unemployable' men and women is not enough. These suspicious, nearly defeated persons must be helped to achieve a significant change in attitude before they can take their places as self-respecting, full-fledged members of the work force." [27]

Most training programs for the minority groups and disadvantaged are characterized by at least three identifiable components:

1. *Attitude changing or social skills.* Many minority-group and disadvantaged workers have never known regular employment nor have they lived in areas where steady employment was part of the usual situation. Programs in social skills development are aimed at ridding the fear of failure and developing within the trainees an image as regular members of the work force.
2. *Remedial education.* Being literate enough to function in our society as an economic unit is generally considered to have been achieved upon completion of the fifth grade. However, many of the urban poor have not attained this level. Thus, remedial education, especially in arithmetic and English skills, is needed.
3. *Job skills development.* Here the training is directly related to the kind of entry-level position for which the trainee is being prepared.[28]

The following brief descriptions of several training programs designed for minority-group workers in office and clerical positions show the extent to which the three kinds of training elements are found.

At Western Electric in New York new employees are actively recruited from minority groups, and all upgrading in the firm is done without bias. The company has devoted itself to providing marketable skills to minority-group people who do not have them. The Skills Level Improvement Program makes the company office facilities available to people who want to develop office skills. The

---

[26] Boeing Company, Renton, Washington; Eastman Kodak Company, Kodak Park Division, Rochester, and General Office, Rochester; Westinghouse Electric Corporation, East Pittsburgh and Bloomfield, New Jersey; UAL, Inc.; and Bankers Trust Company, New York City.

[27] Nadler, *op. cit.,* p. 126.

[28] Johnson, *op. cit.,* pp. 99-163, and Nadler, *op. cit.,* p. 118.

12-week program of instruction is held after hours by company instructors who work closely with the local Urban League offices.[29]

The Employment Qualification Program is designed to qualify disadvantaged young people for opening positions in the home office of Metropolitan Life Insurance Company, New York City. The program is geared to 18-22 year-olds who have been out of school for some time and can be described as typical high school dropouts. Because of their backgrounds, none of the students are able to qualify for regular employment. The program is a combination of work-study experience and part-time on-the-job training. The trainees are paid the minimum hourly rate for a six-hour day. They spend four hours on a regular basis learning and doing beginning level clerical work; the other two hours each day are spent in self-development activities to improve their basic skills of reading and arithmetic. The program is designed to cover a period of 13 weeks but can be extended for some trainees to provide further opportunity to show improvement.[30]

The Continental American Insurance Company of Chicago recruits juniors from a high school that is a predominantly black ghetto school with a 70 percent dropout rate. Students are provided with additional course work, part-time jobs, and assistance in getting into college. The program is designed to give young black students a sense of identity, responsibility, and the basic skills needed to succeed in business occupations. The assistant to the personnel director at the company has stated: "We're helping ourselves, too, because there is always a scarcity of good employees, which we hope these boys will become."[31] The students attend classes in the company's headquarters. When they return to high school for their senior year, the students work about 20 hours each week in one of the firm's departments at $2 an hour. When the students obtain their diplomas, they are aided in obtaining scholarships to colleges of their choice or they may attend a ten-week business orientation course at the company, followed by a 16-week schedule of half-time work and half-time academic instruction. At the end of this intensive preparation, students are given the option of going to work full time for the company or not. If they wish to work for the firm after

---

[29] Lachter, "How Seven Firms Educate Their In-Office Personnel," *op. cit.*, p. 29.

[30] John G. Reiners, "Personnel Training and Upgrading Programs," Personnel Management Bulletin (Willow Grove: Administrative Management Society, October, 1969), p. 11. Also, see E. G. Burnap, "75% Qualify in 'Real-Life' Work-Study Plan," *Administrative Management* (March, 1970), pp. 60-62.

[31] "Blacks Learn New Skills," *Administrative Management* (November, 1970), p. 34.

graduation from college, the company will have jobs for them, but working for the firm upon graduation is not obligatory.[32]

Avco Corporation, matching a $1.1 million federal grant with $1.2 million of its own funds, provides black residents of Boston ghettos with job training that pays them a decent wage and provides them with requisite printing skills for employment elsewhere. According to the president of the firm, "Our success here will demonstrate to the nation that private industry and government, working together, can create profitable businesses staffed and run by people who could not qualify for employment under normal industry standards."[33] The trainees serve a five-year apprenticeship, working up to full journeyman status. To qualify for training, the workers are required to show manual dexterity, common sense, and a desire to succeed on the job. Since a high school diploma is not required for admission into the training program, the enrollment is open to a greater number of deserving applicants.[34]

Training Methods and Techniques

Each of the man-to-man training methods discussed on pages 349-351 of Chapter 11 (job rotation, understudy, programmed instruction, teaching machines, TV, and computer-aided instruction) is used in the training and retraining of office employees. The following three examples illustrate only a few of the many applications of training methods and techniques used in today's training of office workers.

Training manuals have been replaced by videotape at American Security & Trust Company, Washington, D.C., with the result that the training time has been reduced by more than 50 percent. The bank's training supervisor found that trainees using the manuals of programmed instruction materials were spending about 40 minutes to read the first 13 pages; the same material on videotape takes only 13 to 15 minutes to present. Since the bank's materials change so frequently, the company is able to capitalize upon one of the major advantages of video tape recording (VTR): easy updating and instant replay of materials. Six 40-minute tapes covering subjects such as check cashing, savings accounts, and miscellaneous transactions are shown to trainees during a period of two and one-half days. Role-playing sessions are also held and played back for criticism

---

[32] *Ibid.*

[33] "Avco Teaches Printing in a Boston Ghetto," *The Office* (December, 1970), p. 22.

[34] *Ibid.*, pp. 22-28.

and evaluation. Since all the information is contained on tapes, the instructor, who is present in the classroom, need not be a professionally trained person.[35]

In the Employment Qualification Program at the Metropolitan Life Insurance Company, described earlier in the chapter, heavy reliance is placed upon programmed materials in the teaching of arithmetic and grammar. For those having very low achievement levels, special taped presentations to be used in stimulating reading, improving diction, and providing arithmetic drill have been developed by the training staff.[36]

An automated instructional system for the teaching of typewriting with materials programmed to the individual's ability and absorption rate is used in the Blue Cross-Blue Shield training programs in Newark, New York, and Boston. In the initial class using the automated instruction system, six disadvantaged trainees accomplished the following results: one student already familiar with the keyboard and typing about 14 to 20 words per minute (wpm), passed the 35 wpm test for job placement after one hour of learning each day for three weeks; the other five students reached 7 to 8 wpm in six hours, one hour each week. After six weeks, four girls were typing 35 wpm and one 30 wpm. Following this level of accomplishment, the girls were trained on the job where they applied their typing skills to actual office work.[37]

Evaluating the Training Program

The results of the training program must be evaluated in order to determine the extent to which the original objectives of the training function were achieved. For certain clerical tasks such as keypunching, billing, and filing, direct measures of output can serve as a measurement of the skill level attained. Or production figures based on the percentage of workers that meet standards or accomplish the task within the time required to do the job may be used. In Chapter 19 it is pointed out that the development of performance standards, created through a work measurement program,

---

[35] "Bank Cashes in on Videotape Program," *Administrative Management* (June, 1970), p. 40. For a comprehensive discussion of videotape recording, see Thomas F. Stroh, "The Uses of Video Tape in Training & Development," AMA Research Study 93 (New York: American Management Association, 1969).

[36] Reiners, *loc. cit.*

[37] "Typewriter Training System for Personnel on the Job," *The Office* (October, 1970), p. 211.

is one means by which the effectiveness of a new employee and his rate of learning may be measured. By means of standards it is possible to determine at what point in the training process a trainee should be able to handle a normal workload on a full-time basis. Indirect measures of the effectiveness of training include the savings realized as a result of error reduction, lessened absenteeism, and decreased turnover. More difficulty in evaluating the effectiveness of training occurs in the human relations or social skills training, for the outcomes of desirable attitude development and modification of behavioral patterns are less amenable to review and measurement.

A seven-step plan for evaluating the effectiveness of training is given below:

1. Check the results of the training against the goal or objective of the program.
2. Establish standards of learning time against which the progress of trainees may be checked.
3. Develop data on trainee performance before, during, and after training.
4. Keep records on the progress of each trainee.
5. Test trainees on the knowledge and skills acquired.
6. Provide for the instructor to rate each trainee during and at the end of the training program.
7. Follow up on the trainee periodically to determine the long-range effects of his training.

ORIENTING

In the field of administrative office management, *orientation* refers to a carefully planned, scientific, and effective introduction of the new worker to his job so that he may start working with a minimum of delay, misunderstanding, and error. Orientation covers many topics, such as: (1) company history and organization, including that of the department in which the new employee is working; (2) products manufactured or services rendered; (3) kinds of customers and services rendered them; (4) compensation plans and pay periods, including overtime arrangements; (5) payroll deductions; (6) employee benefits such as group life insurance, hospitalization, cafeteria services, and recreational programs; (7) vacation schedules, holidays, and rules of conduct; (8) suggestion plans; and (9) promotion plans.

Sometimes orientation is provided as part of the new worker's vestibular training. The objective of vestibule training is to provide the trainee with the basic information necessary for a complete knowledge and understanding of the practices and procedures of the firm before the worker enters on the job. In their vestibule training, most firms use an employee handbook that contains general company policies and information. Supplementing the employee handbook is the *induction checklist,* which contains items that the supervisor should cover when introducing a new employee to his job. The induction checklist is one of the most effective means of making sure that a new employee is properly introduced to the firm and to his job.

The illustration of the sample induction checklist used by one large corporation (Figure 14-1), shows that the orientation program extends over a period of about two weeks. This carefully planned program leaves a more lasting impression than merely reading a handbook and thus is more effective in "breaking in" the new employee. Furthermore, using this checklist insures a complete orientation in all the details of the firm's policies and procedures. Sometimes the checklist is followed up by a formal induction class in which company-wide information such as company history, products and services, systems of evaluating employees, salary increases, promotion plans, and social activities, are discussed.

Many companies have found the *sponsor system* to be an effective technique for orienting new employees. Under the sponsor system, each new employee is assigned to a present employee who takes care of the new employee, acquaints him with his duties, and answers his questions. Not only does the sponsor system relieve a supervisor or department head of part of the orientation procedure, but it also gives the sponsors an added sense of responsibility and aids in their self-improvement. The sponsor selected to orient a new employee should have a job similar to that which will be assumed by the new worker, a complete knowledge of company policies and department operations, a pleasant outgoing personality, and an interest in people and their problems.

PROMOTING

To be successful, a promotion plan must be definite, systematic, fair, and adhered to rigidly. The basis of promotion is the functional organization chart, developed after a systematic job analysis. Each employee should understand his position, his line of promotion, the requirements for the next job, and the salary. A promotion plan must have the confidence of the employees. To provide for promotions that are based upon objective data and not solely upon personal opinion and assessment, the personnel department should keep complete files of personal data on each employee—his age, marital status, education, experience, special abilities, and physical condition. The personal data sheet should be supplemented by the history of employment record. Regular entries should be made on the personal data sheets—not too much to make the work cumbersome but sufficient to present an unbiased, factual basis for promotion. Such personal data cover absences from work, tardiness, suggestions offered by the employee to the firm, disciplinary action taken, and most important, periodic evaluations of the worker.

Some firms have adopted the civil service idea of *promotion trials* for positions frequently vacated. Any promotion in position or in responsibility is made with the consent of the person being transferred and with the privilege of returning to his present job and salary if he desires, after a probationary period. A promotion should always carry with it an adjustment of compensation, which should never be less than the present pay and at least the minimum for the position in the new classification or rank.

Some firms look to the outside for professional help in obtaining an objective evaluation of their employees' potential for promotion. Management consulting firms may be called upon to give general intelligence and personality tests to employees and to conduct interviews in an attempt to determine which employees possess the abilities and characteristics for promotion. In addition to the use of these tests and interviews, one management consulting firm gives a personality index test that enables the consultant who is evaluating the test results to obtain a better understanding of the employee's attitudes and opinions and whether or not they will be of benefit to the company. The consulting firm looks upon the personality index as a means of validating the findings it has obtained by use of other appraisal techniques.

In some large companies, psychological tests are used to observe and to evaluate rank-and-file workers in order to locate future managerial ability. Other criteria, such as recommendations of supervisors, seniority, and excellence of technical skills are also given appropriate weight in locating supervisory and managerial ability among nonsupervisory workers.

Seniority is frequently a basis of promotion and probably should be since it is based upon the principle that those who have served

Sample Induction Checklist

FOR USE BY SUPERVISORS AS A GUIDE IN INDUCTING NEW EMPLOYEES

One of the most effective tools which can be used in inducting new workers is the induction checklist. Its primary value lies in the fact that it spreads induction over a number of days, giving the new employee a chance to absorb and digest the various facts and figures, rules and policies he should know. With the use of a checklist like this one, the employer can be certain that the new worker is getting all the information about the company he needs in order to do a good job. And it helps the supervisor present the information in a logical, orderly manner.

Supervisor__________ Date__________

For Employee__________ Dept.__________

BEFORE WORKER ARRIVES

Check when completed

____ **1. Prepare Future Associates** (by individual or group conference) **If**
- a. The job is different
- b. The person is different
- c. If someone could have been promoted from within

____ **2. Have Desk and Supplies Ready**
- a. Have workplace arranged as you want it kept (inspect personally)

____ **3. Alert Job Instructor**

____ **4. Arrange for Luncheon Escort**
- a. Escort will explain location of rest room and other facilities (show him)

FIRST DAY

____ **1. Review the Job**
- a. Confidential aspects
- b. Stimulate job enthusiasm and satisfaction in a job well done
- c. Explain work to other sections (give copy of job description and organization manual)
  1. The way his work originates
  2. Where it goes
  3. Relation of his job to other jobs in section
  4. Relation of his section to division
  5. Relation of his division to company
  6. Let him know you are depending on him
  7. Give assurance he will learn quickly

____ **2. Explain Hours of Work** (give copy of company manual of personnel policies)
- a. Starting and quitting time
- b. Hours per week
- c. Rest periods
- d. Lunch period
- e. Not to leave desk or put away work until bell rings

____ **3. Review Compensation**
- a. Amount
- b. When paid
- c. Cost of living allowance
- d. Mention deductions
  1. Income tax
  2. Social Security
  3. Retirement (if applicable)
- e. If applicable, review company's retirement plan (give copy of retirement plan)
- f. Emphasize value of fringe benefits paid by company (give copy of Group and U.C.D. cost to company)
- g. Salaries must be kept confidential
- h. Cashier not permitted to cash checks
- i. Right reserved to deduct for absence

Check when completed

____ **4. Discuss Attendance Requirements and Records**
- a. Filling out time card (show card and demonstrate)
- b. Method of reporting tardiness (stress honor system)
- c. How and to whom absence is reported
- d. Stress punctuality
- e. Explain effect of good attendance and punctuality on employee's record

____ **5. Has the Employee Any Questions?** (ask him)

____ **6. Explain Induction Quiz**
- a. Voluntary; will be given if he chooses at end of first 10 days

____ **7. Introduce to Immediate Associates**
- a. In department and supervisors and others in related departments

____ **8. Introduce to Workplace**
- a. Workplace to be in order as employee expects to keep it
- b. Stress good housekeeping

____ **9. Have Chair Adjusted**

____ **10. Give Job Instruction** (use job breakdowns or manuals if available)
- a. Prepare
- b. Tell
- c. Show
- d. Practice
- e. Check
- f. Explain what to do about any idle time
  1. Report to supervisor for more work
  2. Emphasize this is not a reflection on employee, but responsibility of management

(Have a trainer well prepared and temperamentally suited to teach)

____ **11. Discuss Work Instructions**
- a. Majority will come from supervisor
- b. Occasionally from department head
- c. Question any orders received from fellow-workers—check with supervisor
- d. Stress that all instructions should be clearly understood

____ **12. Explain Learning Aids**
- a. Examples of work (show him)
- b. Job instruction breakdown, if available
- c. Special terms used, including abbreviations

____ **13. Encourage Him to Ask Questions**
- a. They aid in learning
- b. They help develop judgment

____ **14. Explain Where to Store Work Overnight** (show him)

Fig. 14-1

Sample Induction Checklist (page 1)

SECOND DAY

Check when completed

____ 1. **Explain Performance Review** (show the form and illustrate with examples)
   a. Important to him
   b. Raises depend upon work, attitude, length of service

____ 2. **Explain Quality and Quantity of Work**
   a. Production standards, if any
   b. Importance of accuracy
   c. Quality before quantity
   d. Speed will come with experience

THIRD DAY

____ 1. **Explain Telephone Technique, if Employee Conducts Company Business on Telephone** (give copy of telephone company booklet)
   a. Speak clearly
   b. Give your name when answering
   c. Take messages in writing for those not present
   d. Deliver messages before you forget
   e. Find numbers in company directory

____ 2. **Give Reasons for Rules, Policies and Plans**
   a. To make cooperation easier
   b. To result in greater efficiency
   c. To avoid duplication of effort

____ 3. **Explain Voluntary Disability Plan and Company's Group Insurance Plan** (give copy, if not already included in company manual)
   a. Sign up employee for group insurance

____ 4. **Has Employee Any Questions?** (ask him)

FOURTH DAY

____ 1. **Give Employee Opportunity to Say How He Is Getting Along**

____ 2. **Explain Use of Medical Facilities**
   a. Reason for compulsory physical examination
   b. Report to company doctor at any time ill—with knowledge of supervisor

____ 3. **Discuss Suggestion System** (show current scoreboard on bulletin board)
   a. How it encourages initiative and ideas
   b. How awards are made
   c. How to submit
   d. Should be well thought out ideas
   e. Must sign suggestion form
   f. All suggestions are thoroughly considered

____ 4. **Explain Messenger Service**
   a. Messengers work on regular schedule (show message carrier envelope and illustrate how to fill out)
   b. Don't expect special service
   c. Don't make a messenger of yourself

FIFTH DAY

____ 1. **Discuss Personal Telephone Calls**
   a. Can be made during working hours if urgent
   b. Incoming calls only when urgent

____ 2. **Explain Policy on Donations**
   a. No solicitors allowed in building
   b. Start no subscriptions without approval

____ 3. **Discuss Departmental Policies Which Are in Addition To (But Not in Conflict with) Overall Company Policy**

____ 4. **Has the Employee Any Questions?** (ask him)

SIXTH DAY

Check when completed

____ 1. **Explain How to Get Additional Supplies**
   a. On requisition, on approval of department head
   b. Don't visit supply department
   c. Explain conservation of supplies

____ 2. **Discuss Personal Mail**
   a. Best to have sent to home
   b. Deposit outgoing letter in box outside of building (or in lobby)
   c. Company does not pay postage
   d. Can get stamps from cashier
   e. Do not write personal letters on company time

SEVENTH DAY

____ 1. **Explain Change of Address**
   a. Company must have complete record
   b. Notify personnel department of changes
   c. Same for telephone number

____ 2. **Explain Company Educational Program** (give copy of plan)
   a. Tuition, if any

EIGHTH DAY

____ 1. **Explain the Employee's Association**
   a. Membership advantages
   b. Dues
   c. How collected

____ 2. **Explain Company Library**
   a. Free to use it
   b. Where located

____ 3. **Describe Company Magazine** (give copy of latest issue)

NINTH DAY

____ 1. **Describe Vacation Plan** (show copy of schedules)
   a. Explain vacation system
   b. How length of vacation is determined
   c. The part seniority plays
   d. The part convenience to section plays
   e. Time selected must be approved by department head
   f. Subject to change for good of company

____ 2. **Explain Company's Bulletin Boards**
   a. Do not post anything on it without approval
   b. Watch it for current announcements

TENTH DAY

____ 1. **Explain that Patience and Understanding are Important Qualities to Develop** (give examples)
   a. He will work with all types of persons as to age training, education, experience, background

____ 2. **Encourage Him to Talk Things Over with Immediate Supervisor**

____ 3. **Department Manager is Glad to Talk Things Over When Necessary and with Knowledge of Immediate Supervisor**

____ 4. **Administer Quiz** (get written answers)

____ 5. **Review Employee's Public Relations Influence**

ELEVENTH DAY

____ 1. **Review Quiz Results**

Employee's Induction Completed: ....
Department Manager Signature

Instructions: Upon completion of this checklist, return it to Personnel Department for inclusion in employee's personnel file.

California-Western States Life Insurance Company

Fig. 14-1

Sample Induction Checklist (page 2)

loyally for a long period merit recognition. The idea itself tends to stabilize employment and to reduce turnover. Seniority must not, however, be adhered to rigidly because it is an arbitrary check on the younger worker and, if continued, may result in a somewhat stagnant staff. New ideas and ability must be given recognition, even at the expense of seniority. Otherwise, the younger and perhaps more original and aggressive employee will seek work with a competitor or perhaps start in business for himself, with either action possibly being detrimental to the firm.

In a study of 200 companies to determine the most commonly used techniques for promoting employees,[38] the New York Chapter of the Administrative Management Society found that management judgment ranked first, overwhelmingly, as the prime consideration in selecting people for promotion. The second-ranking technique was formal appraisal of the individual's performance on the job. Other high-ranking techniques used by more than half of the companies surveyed included: personal characteristics of the employee; formal training, including that given to him on the job to help him qualify for the work; understudy system; observation; and skills inventory (a formal record of skills, prior experience, hobbies, etc.). Techniques used by fewer than one half of the companies surveyed included: tests; seniority; family factors; posting job openings; management committee; promotion lists; and three-position plan (organization chart showing the three best qualified persons for each position, including a code number indicating readiness of each employee).

One type of promotion, the potential of which is often overlooked, is known as *horizontal* promotion. An employee may have reached a certain level in his department at which the future is not too promising because there is little turnover and his department is not expanding. It would therefore be wise to transfer such a capable worker to another department where promotional opportunities are greater. This type of transfer is really in the form of a promotion, though there may not be any increase in salary or rank. It is a promotion because in the new position there will be an earlier chance for advancement. Such horizontal promotion should be recognized and given emphasis among the employees so that it is fully appreciated.

Transfers and promotions are closely related, although not all transfers are promotions. For instance, transfers may be necessary because an employee has been improperly matched to the job. In

[38] W. R. Noe, Jr., "Selecting the Right Employees for Promotion," *Administrative Management* (October, 1963), pp. 74-76.

some firms an employee misfit would be discharged. The more intelligent way of handling such a situation, however, is to transfer the employee to a position for which he is better suited. This can be done only where the firm has a staff sufficiently large to absorb the transferee.

There are a number of sound reasons for transfers. The one indicated above stresses the policy of the firm by which the constant fear of being "fired" is removed from the mind of the new employee. Such a policy creates in the worker a more wholesome attitude toward the firm and toward his work. Moreover, the company does not incur the expense of hiring workers who later turn out to be unsatisfactory.

The fundamental purpose of transferring regular employees is to stimulate them out of the monotony, and perhaps inefficiency, in which their long service may have placed them. Some firms believe in the practice of developing understudies and therefore have a regular schedule of transfers so that resignations, promotions, reassignments, deaths, and illnesses of employees do not seriously affect the office work. There is always someone who can step in and do the work. This policy also stimulates the worker. Few workers will feel that their services are indispensable or that "the firm cannot get along without them."

Other firms have rush and slack periods either during the month or during certain periods of the year. By having a series of employee transfers, experience is secured in a variety of positions, thus enabling the office manager to shift workers during the busy seasons.

QUESTIONS FOR REVIEW

1. Distinguish between the concepts of *training* and *learning*. What is the relevance of this distinction for the office manager who may be in charge of training?
2. As the result of effective training and development of its office workers, what benefits may a company receive?
3. What do you consider the major objectives of training? Why do you rank these objectives as most important?
4. What advantages can be cited for on-the-job training as contrasted to vestibular training?
5. Of the three abilities that should be possessed by the person in charge of training, which do you look upon as being most vital? Why have you assigned this ability number one ranking?

6. Define the role of the supervisor in an effective training and development program.
7. For what reasons have many firms not availed themselves of government funds to subsidize their training programs? Do you believe the availability of a tax-reduction incentive would spur these firms on to applying for government subsidies for their training programs?
8. Two points of view (Nadler and Cohn) are presented in this chapter as to the nature of the training for minority-group and disadvantaged workers. Which viewpoint best parallels your philosophy of training such workers? Why?
9. Describe how the administrative office manager might proceed in evaluating the effectiveness of his training program.
10. What is orientation? How is the use of an induction checklist related to the orientation process?
11. Explain how a sponsor system operates.
12. Enumerate the characteristics of a successful promotion plan.
13. To what extent should seniority be considered in the promotion of office personnel?
14. A horizontal transfer may, in effect, be a promotion. Explain.

QUESTIONS FOR DISCUSSION

1. In the offices of Barnett Supply Company all new employees are placed on an official three-month trial basis. Is the company able to discharge a worker after one month if that person proves to be unsatisfactory by the end of that time?
2. Should a training and development program be continued during a recession when few or no employees are being added to the working force and when few promotional opportunities are available?
3. In a firm having 40 first-line supervisors, one fourth of them feel that they have been working for the company for such a long period of time that a training course for supervisors will not benefit them now. Do you agree? Explain.
4. What may be some shortcomings of having a training program conducted at a nearby community college? Under what conditions do you think a cooperative program of training between a business firm and a community college would be desirable?
5. The Hall Insurance Company includes as part of its employment procedure the giving of tests to determine whether or not an applicant will be hired and also to determine his potential for promotion. No employee is considered for promotion unless he attains a stipulated score on the tests. What is your reaction to using test scores as the major determinant of an employee's promotion potential?

6. Some firms encourage their executives and supervisors to teach courses in nearby colleges and universities, especially in the evening. Do you consider this a desirable practice? Explain. Other companies prohibit their employees from engaging in any kind of "moonlighting," including teaching. Do you consider such a restriction to be in the best interests of the firm? Explain.
7. Barbara McGinnity has just accepted the job of file clerk in the home office of the Mabry Transport Company. This is her first job and she has had no business experience other than a short period of cooperative work experience as part of her course requirements at college. It is your plan, as manager of office services, to have each new worker such as Barbara properly oriented and trained before actual employment begins. Your budget allows you to pay all new workers the minimum hourly wage during the initial training period. The home office, with its 400 office workers, has an annual turnover rate of 24 percent. Outline a complete plan for orienting and training all new employees.
8. In the Gleim Tool Company, the assistant to the president is also the administrative office manager. The firm gives an orientation booklet to all new employees in the office as well as in the plant. The booklet covers all the points the firm wishes to communicate to new employees, but the workers tend to forget or to ignore some of the items that management considers very important. Discuss the procedures that you as the administrative office manager might follow to impress upon all employees the importance of remembering the contents of the orientation booklet.

PRACTICAL OFFICE CASES

Case 14-1 Developing a Remedial Training Program

Edward Kohlhepp has been employed for six months in the accounts payable department of an office machines manufacturing firm. During the past three weeks you, as supervisor, have been conducting a random sampling check of the quantity and quality of output in the accounts payable department. With the exception of Kohlhepp, all workers are producing at or close to the standards set earlier in the year by the firm. Along with numerous errors, Kohlhepp's work is characterized by low output, often 25 percent less than that of other accounts payable clerks in the department.

Today, as you examine a sampling of Kohlhepp's work for the past week, you begin to think about the need for installing some sort of remedial training for persons such as Kohlhepp, whom you wish to retain in your employ.

■ Determine the need for a remedial training program by answering the following questions:

1. How can I as Kohlhepp's supervisor check his work to determine if the poor performance is due to inadequate training or to some other cause?
2. If my checking should indicate that Kohlhepp has been inadequately trained, how do I go about introducing a remedial training program?
3. If my investigation indicates that Kohlhepp has been adequately trained, what do I do next?

Case 14-2 Improving the Orientation Procedure

The headquarters office of the Witzky Manufacturing Company, located in a suburb of Seattle, employs 800 office workers. Although the company pays above-average salaries, the turnover of office workers has been very high, often reaching 32 percent among the newly employed. In four of the departments, the turnover has been greater than in others. Management has assumed that the high turnover rates have been due to faulty supervision and improper selection procedures.

Recently an investigation has indicated, however, that those hired were properly qualified for the work for which they were selected. Exit interviews with a number of those who had left resulted in the discovery that they felt lost in the company and did not know too much about what they were to do nor whether their work was satisfactory.

A management consulting firm which was called in suggested that perhaps the orientation procedures were faulty and that the supervision of the new employees was inadequate, especially in the four departments mentioned. It was recommended that an orientation checklist be used. When this recommendation was passed along to the supervisors, they objected vigorously. They said that the checklist would not help and, besides, they did not have time to do the additional clerical work.

■ Prepare a report to the president of the company in which you, as administrative manager, answer the following questions:

1. How would you handle this situation from the viewpoint of top management?
2. What would you do about implementing the consulting firm's recommendation that a checklist be used?
3. Assuming that the checklist is an effective tool, how will you go about "selling" its use to the supervisors? Does the use of the checklist need your selling?

15

Systems and Procedures Analysis

Control, the underlying theme of Part 4, is that managerial function concerned with seeing that operating results conform as closely as possible to the plans made for the business. In the process of control, the principal steps are to establish standards, to measure performance, to evaluate performance, to take corrective action, and to render long-term appraisals. Throughout this part each of these steps will be described in relation to the role that it plays in controlling office costs. The functions of planning and controlling are closely related in that both functions directly influence the attainment of the organization's objectives. Activities in a firm are set into motion as a result of managerial planning; the activities are kept "on the right track" by means of the control processes.

In the past twenty years office costs have been steadily increasing. Office costs arise primarily as a result of: (1) the payroll for office personnel; (2) the cost of office supplies and printing; (3) the large investment in office machines, equipment, and furniture that must be depreciated over a period of years; and (4) the fixed and semifixed costs of electricity, heat, rent, taxes, insurance, and other similar items. During the last two decades the ratio of office workers to factory workers has increased from one to nine to one to four;

wages have increased for office workers; and requirements of governmental agencies have placed additional burdens on the information-gathering and data-reporting systems in the office. Interwoven throughout every office organization is a network of systems, procedures, and methods which, if efficient and effective, is beneficial to the organization and helps to control costs. Office costs have many ramifications, extending to the most minute office activity. Sometimes the very fact that the cost of some phase of office work is very small means that the cost is ignored. This is a mistake, especially if this relatively minor task occurs many times each day.

Top management no longer looks upon the management of office systems as merely a form of overhead that is necessary but undesirable. Top management realizes that administrative management and the office manager are part of that integrated managerial plan which is considered the "brain" of a business organization. Thus, the office manager is increasingly being given opportunity and recognition in the form of higher pay and increased authority so that the profit realization becomes more interesting and more favorable. Such opportunity and recognition create a cost consciousness in the office manager and in all his subordinates.

THE NATURE OF SYSTEMS, PROCEDURES, AND METHODS

Most office work is composed of a pattern of office systems, procedures, and methods. The term *system* refers to the framework of personnel, forms, records, machines, and equipment involved in completing a major phase of office work. For example, there is the sales system that involves the forms, personnel, equipment, and records necessary to complete a sale from the time an order is received until the goods are shipped and payment is received. A similar system is developed for handling purchases. Sometimes the system, such as the cost accounting system, may be an auxiliary control function of the business.

Each system is composed of a number of procedures. A *procedure*—sometimes called a subsystem—is a planned sequence of operations for handling recurring business transactions uniformly and consistently. For example, in the sales system there are procedures for processing an order, shipping the goods, accounting for the shipment, receiving payment for the sale, handling claims and adjustments, and analyzing the sales.

For each operation within a procedure, there is a method for accomplishing that phase of the work. A *method* is the manual or mechanical means by which each operation is performed. Thus, in an order-processing procedure there are methods for acknowledging the incoming order, checking the credit status of the customer, preparing the sales invoice, and distributing the copies of the invoice.

Effective management requires the office executive to understand that his work is made up of various systems, all of which integrate into a *total system*—the company-wide information network. The office manager must know which systems are the framework of his office organization, and what procedures make up each of these systems. He is in much the same position as a physician who must know that the human body (the total system) is made up of a large number of systems such as the circulatory system, the nervous system, the respiratory system, and the reproductive system, and that each of these is composed of a large number of subsystems.

With the advent of electronic data processing and its application to the functional aspects of business operations, the total systems concept has taken on increasing importance. Under this concept the necessary operating documents, records, and reports are linked together and presented simultaneously as part of the company-wide information network, as discussed in Chapter 1. At the same time management is provided with control information that permits the making of timely decisions. The total systems concept results in more effective management since it not only takes into consideration the present operating procedures and methods but also projects the probable effect of expanded and modified operations. Furthermore, in place of a number of independent operating systems, the total systems concept stresses the interrelationships of all business operations, all of which are made possible by the use and application of electronic data processing. If developed and used properly, the total systems approach to managerial planning, organizing, controlling, and leading should result in great economies.

Common Office Systems and Procedures

Most firms have certain basic systems, each made up of a number of procedures, which form the routines of business operation. These in themselves provide a summary of the office activities. Sometimes the systems or procedures overlap each other. The major systems of business concerns involve purchasing, sales, financial accounting, cost accounting, employee relationships (employment), and certain corporate relationships such as borrowing money or paying dividends. Figure 15-1 illustrates some of these systems and their procedures.

Throughout all these office systems and procedures there are a large number of clerical, or office, services. These services may affect the various systems or procedures independently of each other, or they may be centralized in such a manner that they are considered as separate minor procedures. Office services, such as dictation and transcription, duplicating and reproduction services, and incoming and outgoing mail, can thus be analyzed independently of the major office systems and procedures.

Objectives of Systems and Procedures Analysis

Systems and procedures analysis, lying at the heart of scientific office management, is designed to reduce the cost of office work without impairing its effectiveness and to help management achieve its objectives. Systems and procedures analysis is also referred to as *methods analysis, procedural analysis*, and *work simplification*. The objectives of systems and procedures analysis center around business information and forms, the flow of work, and the use of machines and personnel. These objectives may be listed as follows:

1. *Eliminate* as much unneeded information and as many unessential business forms and records as feasible.
2. *Combine* as many of the business forms as possible.
3. *Simplify* the forms both in content and in method of preparation.
4. *Mechanize* the repetitive, routine tasks where possible when automatic equipment will do the work more quickly, more accurately, and at a reduction in cost that will pay for the equipment in a year or two.

The first three of these objectives are discussed in the following chapter, "Forms Design and Control." The fourth objective pertaining to mechanization is analyzed in Chapter 17 through the illustration of several basic accounting procedures.

Importance of Systems and Procedures Analysis

The importance of systems and procedures analysis is indicated by the following advantages that management obtains by constantly analyzing the office work:

Fig. 15-1

MAJOR SYSTEMS OF BUSINESS	PROCEDURES
Purchasing	Requisitioning the purchase Requesting quotations from suppliers Placing the order Receiving the goods Accounting for purchase and payment of goods Return of unsatisfactory goods
Sales	Receipt of order Processing the order Shipment of goods Accounting for sale Accounting for receipt of payment Sales returns and allowances
Financial Accounting	Purchases Sales Cash receipts Cash payments Payrolls Financial reports
Cost Accounting	Material costs Labor costs Manufacturing overhead costs Completed work Inventory procedures
Employee Relationships	Hiring procedure Training procedure Payroll procedure (see Financial Accounting) Evaluating and follow-up procedure Operating a suggestion system
Corporate Relationships	Borrowing money from banks Sale of additional stock or bonds Payment of dividends Preparation of tax reports

The Major Systems and Procedures of Business

1. *A uniform procedure is followed for each similar transaction.* The uniform procedure, based upon a standard time allowance for identical manual and machine operations, reduces or

eliminates waste motion, delays, and errors in the smooth flow of work.

2. *The cost of performing routine office work is reduced.* Waste motion is eliminated, and automatic equipment is installed, simplified, and standardized.
3. *Responsibility is more easily fixed for satisfactory performance.* Delays, errors, and unsatisfactory results are eliminated.
4. *Training of personnel is simplified and becomes more effective.* The result is *one best way* to perform each office job.
5. *Improvements are constantly made.* Systems and procedures analysis becomes part of a continuous phase of scientific office management. It eliminates the weakness found in so many offices, namely, the idea that because a job was always done this way before it must still be satisfactory. Systems and procedures analysis stresses the statement, "When something has been done in a particular way for 15 to 20 years, it is a pretty good sign in these changing times that it can be done in a better way."

ORGANIZING FOR SYSTEMS AND PROCEDURES ANALYSIS

The most common means of organizing for systems and procedures analysis are:

1. Employing a firm of management consultants or systems engineers to make special or overall surveys of office systems and procedures.
2. Developing an internal staff organization of systems and procedures analysts.
3. Assigning systems and procedures analysis to the office manager.

The organizational approach used for systems and procedures analysis will be determined by the size of the office and the attitude of management toward this phase of the work. Whatever the subdivision of office work may be, the office manager must realize that the analysis of office systems and procedures requires the support and approval of top management if the procedures are to be successfully installed and operated. Thus, before a program of systems and procedures analysis can be undertaken, top management must be sold on the merits of such a program. The entire program must have the backing of the highest ranking officers of the company if it is to grow and assume its potential position. Management must be convinced that the objective of systems and procedures analysis is to actively seek change, to discover ways to profitably change any operation, even those operations where change may seem unnecessary or impossible. Not only must the program of systems and procedures analysis be recognized by top management, it must also be recognized by the company as a whole. The entire company must participate in recognizing, defining, analyzing, and solving problems, and in implementing the recommended changes that are aimed at increasing company profits. Through the issuance of company regulations or instructions, systems and procedures analysis must be sold to the employees so that they will realize that in most instances they can do more work with less effort, that they will not lose their jobs, that their skills and abilities will be used more effectively, and that they will not receive less pay.

Employing a Firm of Management Consultants or Engineers

There is an ever-increasing number of firms engaged in systems and procedures analysis. Many of them are industrial engineering firms that specialize in factory layout, machines, and methods, but with a separate department for office systems. Others specialize solely in office functions, such as office personnel. The management consulting firm is hired by a company in much the same way it would hire an auditor or a lawyer to render his special services and to give his expert advice.[1]

The advantage of employing a management consulting firm is that the recommendations are made by a very expert group of men who, because of their experience with other firms, can bring in many new ideas. Because the consulting firm is an outsider, it is able to study the systems and procedures with an objectivity that the management does not possess. However, management, as the client, does not give up its responsibility for final acceptance, modification, or rejection of the recommendations made by the consulting firm. Management must, on the other hand, be prepared to cooperate to the fullest extent with the consulting firm by giving it total access to company data and policies that are needed to arrive at sound conclusions.

---

[1] For an interesting discussion of how to select the best consultant for the firm's needs and the kinds of help that can be expected from the consultant, see Robert I. Weil, "How To Select a Management Consultant," *Administrative Management* (November, 1966), pp. 59-60.

The main disadvantage of hiring a consulting firm is that this approach may be costly (daily rates may range from $75 to $500) and sporadic. It is ordinarily used only when conditions are very poor. The study of systems and procedures should be a continuous job, for methods are changing continuously. Making periodic improvements does not produce the highest degree of efficiency, nor does it make supervisory management or the employees conscious of the fact that systems and procedures can be improved constantly.

One large office employed an outside engineering firm to study its methods. One of the first defects discovered was the absolutely unnecessary duplicate filing of three million records. The result was that 30 clerical employees were absorbed elsewhere in the office. When this was pointed out to management, the somewhat traditional reply was, "We always did it that way, and no one told us to change it."

Developing an Internal Staff of Systems and Procedures Analysts

Developing a staff organization of systems and procedures analysts may be expensive, but it should be done in a large firm. Firms having many branches or plants, such as Sears, Roebuck & Company, find the creation and use of an internal staff of systems analysts a worthwhile business investment. There is no set rule as to the optimum number of systems people that should make up the staff unit. In a small company there may be no one who acts as a systems specialist; yet the work of systems and procedures analysis must be carried on. Where a staff unit is created, it is often estimated that an acceptable number of systems people is one percent of the clerical personnel employed by the firm. Other estimates indicate that there should be one analyst for every 100 to 300 office workers. The number of systems people required should be determined by the results that the unit can produce. Along with its major aim of supplying management with better information, the systems staff must produce tangible savings in order to justify its existence.

For an effective systems and procedures program in the firm, a definite organizational responsibility must be established for the staff. If the systems staff is to represent the corporate viewpoint and interpret top-level directives, it should report to a person in the upper management echelon. Studies of firms, such as insurance, banking, and public utilities, that employ a large number of office workers indicate that the head of the systems department reports to top management as follows:

To the president of the firm ...... in 25 to 50% of the firms
To the controller (chief accounting officer) .... in 20 to 28% of the firms
To the department heads .... in 8 to 10% of the firms
To the treasurer of the firm ...... in 4 to 13% of the firms

The management line of reporting usually indicates the recognition and importance given to the systems analysis work. Most commonly the systems staff is centralized and serves the entire organization. As the organization becomes larger and more complex, however, there may be a need to decentralize the staff so that its numbers may more effectively deal with each of the divisions of the company.

The staff organization should be available to all departments of the firm that have need for the service. This method permits the development of experts for various types of work and is an excellent training ground for future executives. Because of the specialized nature of its work, such a staff unit will strive constantly to seek out and recommend areas where improvements in systems and procedures can be made. The disadvantages are that there may not be enough work to keep the staff busy and that some executives may look upon staff analysis as a reflection on the work of the executive whose department is being studied. Then, too, top management sometimes feels that the intermediate or supervisory managers are being paid to do the work that such a staff organization would be called upon to do.

Assigning Systems and Procedures Analysis to the Office Manager

In considering the assignment of systems and procedures analysis to the office manager, top management will want to make sure that the office manager possesses the attributes that characterize the analyst—a logical, analytical, perceptive mind; imagination; and ingenuity. The office manager, of course, must have a thorough understanding of diversified business practices and possess balanced judgment.

The office manager must realize that office systems and procedures involve employees, forms, records, machines, and equipment. He must understand that in progressive administrative management the systems and procedures can always be improved to increase the volume of work, to expedite the performance of work, and thus to reduce the cost of office operations. The increasing use of automated systems in office work amply supports this statement.

The advantages of selecting the office manager to assume the full-time job of analyst are that it is a less expensive method, that it can be used by small as well as by large offices, and that the office manager is closer to the work than anyone else. The disadvantage is that the office manager may be so busy with other work that he may neglect this important phase of administration. Another disadvantage is that the employees working under the direction of the office manager may resent his efforts more than those of a staff group or an independent management firm. Then, too, the office manager may not be so aware of modern methods as he should be and therefore may follow an established routine rather than to inaugurate changes.

The office manager who is charged with responsibilities for systems and procedures analysis may obtain much help from membership in the Association for Systems Management, a professional organization of systems people, by attending its meetings and by studying its publications. There are many firms, such as Moore Business Forms, UARCO, Inc., Standard Register Company, and Shaw-Walker, which specialize in the design and preparation of forms to be used with certain systems or procedures. There are other companies manufacturing office machines and equipment that will aid in the design or adaptation of a standard system to their equipment. Among these are International Business Machines Corporation, Burroughs Corporation, National Cash Register Company, Sperry Rand Corporation, and A. B. Dick Company. Through contact with such firms, many office managers are able to study and improve their present systems or procedures, oftentimes adapting a procedure used by some other firm.

ANALYZING OFFICE SYSTEMS AND PROCEDURES

The analysis of office systems and procedures refers basically to the *flow of work* through the office. The objective of studying the flow of work is to reduce the time required to complete the work so that a greater volume of work can be done by the same personnel without increasing costs. In other words, an analysis of office procedures should result in *cost reduction*.

Analyzing office systems and procedures may involve motion and time studies of the various repetitive clerical jobs. (Motion and time studies in relation to an analysis of office jobs are described in detail in Chapter 18.) This presumes that the forms used are efficient, that the internal movement or flow of the forms or records is satisfactory, and that the best equipment that can economically be installed is being used. Since these assumptions are not always valid, analyzing office procedures may also involve the following three phases:

1. *Studying the forms used*—eliminating those not required and simplifying or combining those that are usable.

2. *Mechanizing the use, preparation, and movement of the forms.* This may involve installing new office machines, changing the rules for record keeping or filing, and changing the internal flow of forms.

3. *Analyzing the flow of work* by means of office layout charts or flow process charts.

Studying the Forms Used

In many offices the number of forms and the number of copies of each form used require constant study. Some forms can be eliminated entirely; others may be simplified or changed so that they will require fewer clerical operations; or they may be combined with other forms and thus eliminate the duplication of effort required in preparing two or more forms. The number of copies of each form prepared may also be reduced. For example, a manufacturer working on government contracts at one time prepared sixteen copies of each receiving report. When he was told that he did not need that many copies, he replied, "We always did use them." Without too much discussion, the manufacturer was told to think it over. After several weeks he reported that the number of copies had been reduced to thirteen. Again he was told that he did not need that many. Again he returned with the statement that ten copies were needed. The same approach was repeated until finally the firm realized that only six copies were actually needed. This may seem a little fantastic, yet it actually happened in the offices of one of our largest corporations. It is not the cost of printing the extra copies of a form that is so important, but the cost of handling, transporting, and filing the extra copies that is so expensive. It has been estimated that it costs about $20 to prepare and handle a form that costs $1 to print.

Analyzing office systems and procedures through the study of forms involves a study of the number of copies that are made, the route taken by business forms, and the final disposition of each copy. This analysis may be accomplished by one or more of the following tools:

1. A *descriptive outline* of the procedures.
2. A *diagram* showing the number of copies of a form and their disposition.
3. *Specialized flow charts* that provide a medium of effective communication between management and the operating personnel with reference to forms, procedures, and methods. These charts may be classified as:
   (a) *Management-type charts* of the flow of office work. These are read either horizontally or vertically and do not require any specialized symbols for understanding or interpreting.
   (b) *Symbol-type charts* developed and used originally by professional industrial engineers and since adopted by other management engineering firms and by firms manufacturing automated data processing equipment.
   (c) *Office layout charts* showing the flow of the office work on the basis of the location of the various employees or departments.
   (d) *Work simplification flow process charts* showing either the present or suggested flow of the work; or both the present and the improved suggested flow of work.

Each of these tools used to study forms is discussed in the following paragraphs.

Analysis by Descriptive Outline. The outline is a simple tool of forms analysis since it describes verbally the number of copies of the forms used and their disposition, all presented in outline form. Figure 15-2 outlines the processing of a sales order by a wholesaler's office staff.

Analysis by Diagram. To illustrate the diagram method of studying forms, the purchasing system of a business firm is shown in Figure 15-3. The diagram shows the number of copies prepared of a purchase requisition, a purchase order, and a receiving report; their movement throughout the business firm; and the final disposition of each copy.

Analysis by Specialized Flow Charts. Many varieties of specialized charts have been developed to present the flow of office work. Some of the charts use descriptive titles and illustrations that are readily understood; others are more technical and use symbols that must be studied at length in order to be understood by the reader.

Fig. 15-2

PROCESSING A SALES ORDER

I. The order clerk receives the order by mail, telephone, telegraph, or in person.
   A. Two copies of the order are prepared on regular order blanks.
   B. The original copy goes to the credit manager.
   C. The duplicate copy is filed.

II. The credit manager checks the credit rating of the customer.
   A. In the case of an old account:
      1. He notes on the back of the sales order the information needed to show the condition of the account.
      2. He inquires of the cashier whether a payment has been received for the account in question.
   B. If the account is in satisfactory condition, he approves the sales order by:
      1. Signing his name on the sales order.
      2. Sending the approved sales order to the billers.
   C. In the case of an account that is past due:
      1. He writes a letter to the customer, carefully stating the condition of the account. In the letter he may ask the customer if orders may be sent C.O.D. until the account is brought to a satisfactory credit standing.
      2. He files the sales order for which payment has not been received in the unfilled sales order folder. The original letter is mailed while the duplicate letter is filed.
   D. In the case of a new account, the credit manager:
      1. Refers to the credit rating manual of Dun & Bradstreet or some other agency.
      2. Refers to companies giving credit information service.
      3. Sends the customer a letter stating that the order is receiving prompt attention but that further information is being requested as part of the customary routine of opening an account.
      4. May analyze the financial statements of the new customer and may establish a credit limit.
      5. May refuse to extend credit based on his findings from various sources.
      6. If the credit rating is O.K., he sends the order to the biller.
      7. If the credit rating is not acceptable, a letter is sent asking the customer whether a C.O.D. shipment is acceptable.

Analysis of Processing a Sales Order by Means of a Descriptive Outline

Management-Type Flow Chart. The management-type flow chart is easily understood since it does not use any specialized symbols. The chart may be read from left to right or from top to bottom.

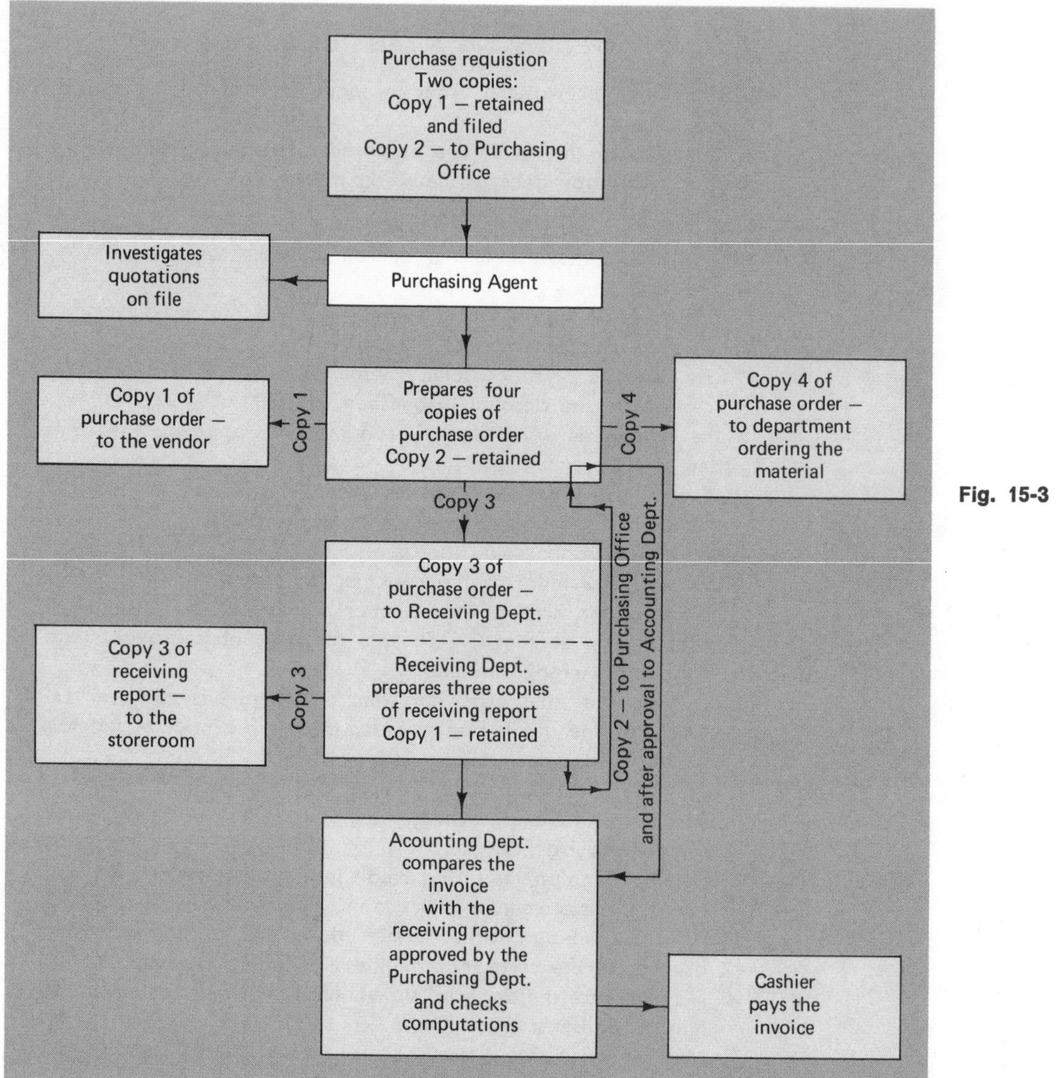

Fig. 15-3

Analysis of a Purchasing System by Means of a Diagram

This type of chart has been used and promoted by such outstanding business firms as Moore Business Forms, Inc., because of its simplicity in sales promotion. Simple line drawings or photographs of the equipment used in the procedure studied may be used to complete the picture of the flow of office work. The management-type flow chart follows the trail of the data used in the procedure whether the data are on printed forms, tabulating cards, punched paper tapes, or magnetic tapes. The simplicity and the clearness of the steps in the procedure make the chart easy to use as compared with the more formal, technical charts that employ specialized symbols to indicate the operations. The management-type flow chart in Figure 15-4 illustrates the steps involved in an order processing procedure.

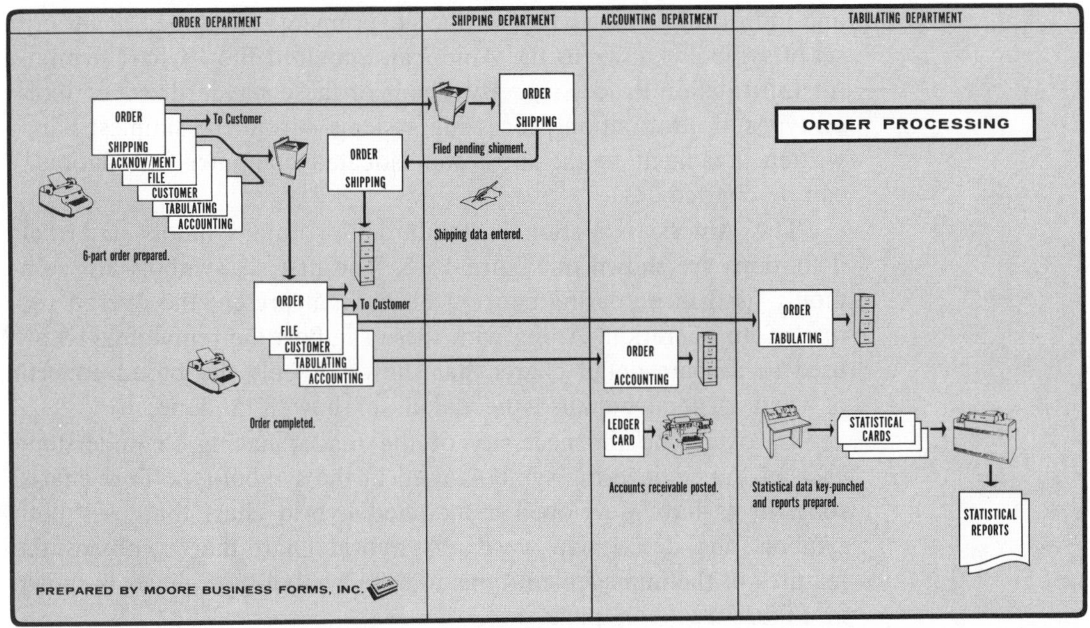

Fig. 15-4

Management-Type Flow Chart of an Order Processing Procedure

Symbol-Type Flow Chart. Many systems analysts develop flow charts using special symbols to indicate the origin of a clerical operation, the different copies of the form used, the flow of the form or the work, and the disposition of each copy of the form. The use of the various symbols provides a standardized method of communication but requires the reader to be familiar with the symbols. Symbol-type flow charts are used by some office machine manufacturers, by some special office forms manufacturers, and especially by office management consultants and manufacturers of automated data processing equipment.

In the past the manufacturers of office machines and forms and other firms involved in systems and procedures work have used different types of symbols for preparing their flow charts. This lack of uniformity often resulted in confusion and misinterpretation when persons attempted to read the charts. Also, with the advent of automated data processing, many of the symbols formerly used proved inadequate for a clear understanding. To overcome this condition, a committee composed of representatives from commercial and industrial firms, as well as the government, developed a uniform set of symbols known as the American Standard Flow Chart Symbols for Information Processing. By means of these standardized symbols, all types of information processing systems—from the simplest handwritten document to the most sophisticated computer installation—can be charted.

The American National Standards Institute symbols and their definitions are shown in Figure 15-5. The first six symbols are commonly used in preparing concept charts that present the overall picture of an operation. Along with these symbols the remaining 13 are used to prepare detail charts that show not only the broad concept of what is done but also the details of how it is done.

To overcome the necessity of the reader having to understand each of the engineering symbols used in the symbol-type flow charts, some firms have developed a modified hybrid chart that uses both symbols and descriptive words. A hybrid chart that combines the features of the management-type and the symbol-type charts is shown in Figure 15-6 on page 484.

Office Layout Chart. If the number of forms and the number of copies of each form prepared have been carefully studied so that these are reduced to a minimum consistent with efficiency, it is possible to give attention to the flow or movement of each form throughout the office. This may be accomplished by studying the office layout, preparing a separate before-and-after layout chart for each important office system or procedure, and drawing lines to indicate the movement of the various business papers throughout the organization. Office layout charts should be prepared for those transactions that occur most frequently. The direction and distance of the movement in the office will point out waste motion and backtracking. Measuring the distance traveled before and after the changes in office procedures are made will indicate the distance and time saved in performing certain office activities.

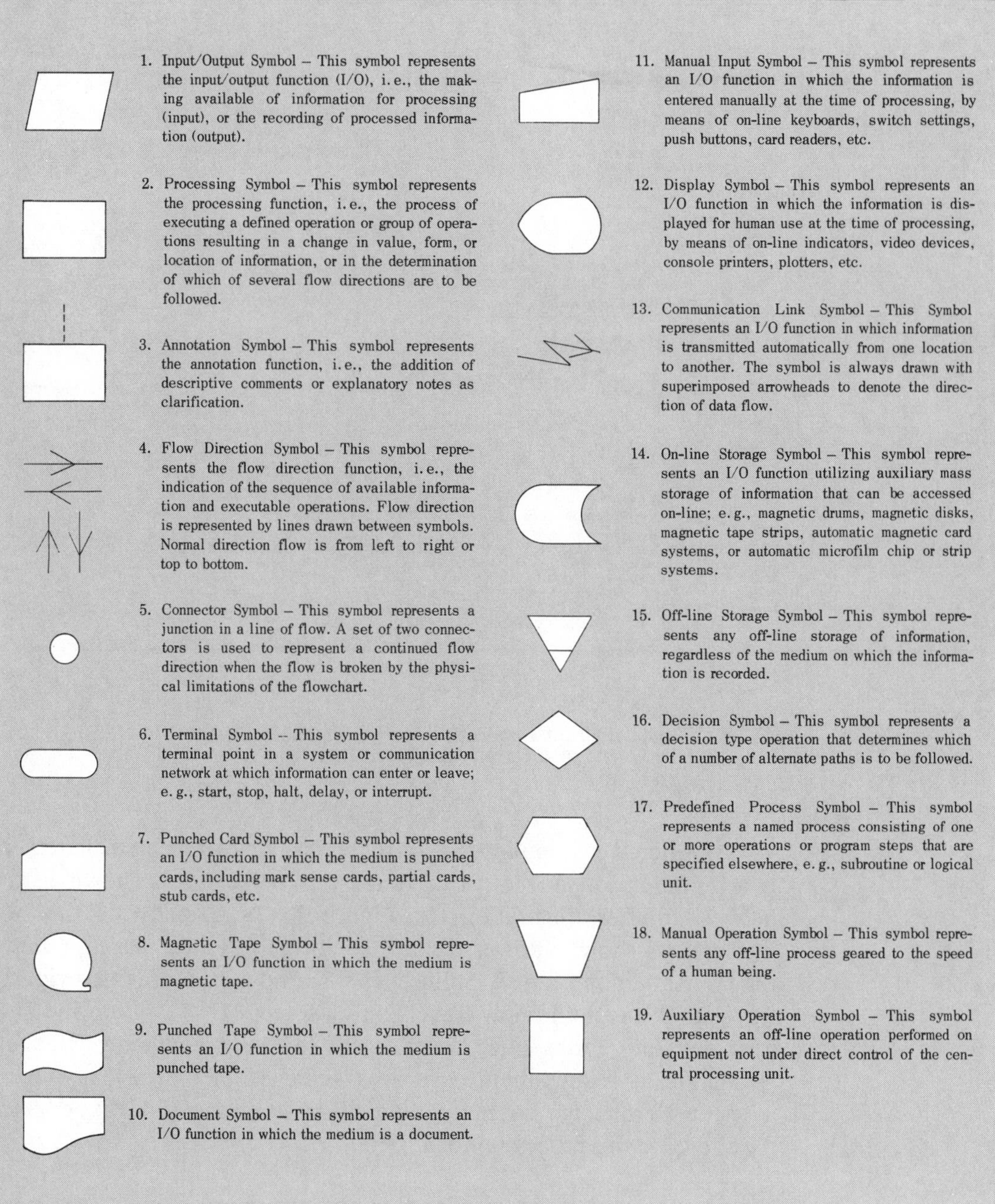

1. Input/Output Symbol – This symbol represents the input/output function (I/O), i. e., the making available of information for processing (input), or the recording of processed information (output).
2. Processing Symbol – This symbol represents the processing function, i. e., the process of executing a defined operation or group of operations resulting in a change in value, form, or location of information, or in the determination of which of several flow directions are to be followed.
3. Annotation Symbol – This symbol represents the annotation function, i. e., the addition of descriptive comments or explanatory notes as clarification.
4. Flow Direction Symbol – This symbol represents the flow direction function, i. e., the indication of the sequence of available information and executable operations. Flow direction is represented by lines drawn between symbols. Normal direction flow is from left to right or top to bottom.
5. Connector Symbol – This symbol represents a junction in a line of flow. A set of two connectors is used to represent a continued flow direction when the flow is broken by the physical limitations of the flowchart.
6. Terminal Symbol – This symbol represents a terminal point in a system or communication network at which information can enter or leave; e. g., start, stop, halt, delay, or interrupt.
7. Punched Card Symbol – This symbol represents an I/O function in which the medium is punched cards, including mark sense cards, partial cards, stub cards, etc.
8. Magnetic Tape Symbol – This symbol represents an I/O function in which the medium is magnetic tape.
9. Punched Tape Symbol – This symbol represents an I/O function in which the medium is punched tape.
10. Document Symbol – This symbol represents an I/O function in which the medium is a document.
11. Manual Input Symbol – This symbol represents an I/O function in which the information is entered manually at the time of processing, by means of on-line keyboards, switch settings, push buttons, card readers, etc.
12. Display Symbol – This symbol represents an I/O function in which the information is displayed for human use at the time of processing, by means of on-line indicators, video devices, console printers, plotters, etc.
13. Communication Link Symbol – This Symbol represents an I/O function in which information is transmitted automatically from one location to another. The symbol is always drawn with superimposed arrowheads to denote the direction of data flow.
14. On-line Storage Symbol – This symbol represents an I/O function utilizing auxiliary mass storage of information that can be accessed on-line; e. g., magnetic drums, magnetic disks, magnetic tape strips, automatic magnetic card systems, or automatic microfilm chip or strip systems.
15. Off-line Storage Symbol – This symbol represents any off-line storage of information, regardless of the medium on which the information is recorded.
16. Decision Symbol – This symbol represents a decision type operation that determines which of a number of alternate paths is to be followed.
17. Predefined Process Symbol – This symbol represents a named process consisting of one or more operations or program steps that are specified elsewhere, e. g., subroutine or logical unit.
18. Manual Operation Symbol – This symbol represents any off-line process geared to the speed of a human being.
19. Auxiliary Operation Symbol – This symbol represents an off-line operation performed on equipment not under direct control of the central processing unit.

Fig. 15-5

American Standard Flow Chart Symbols for Information Processing

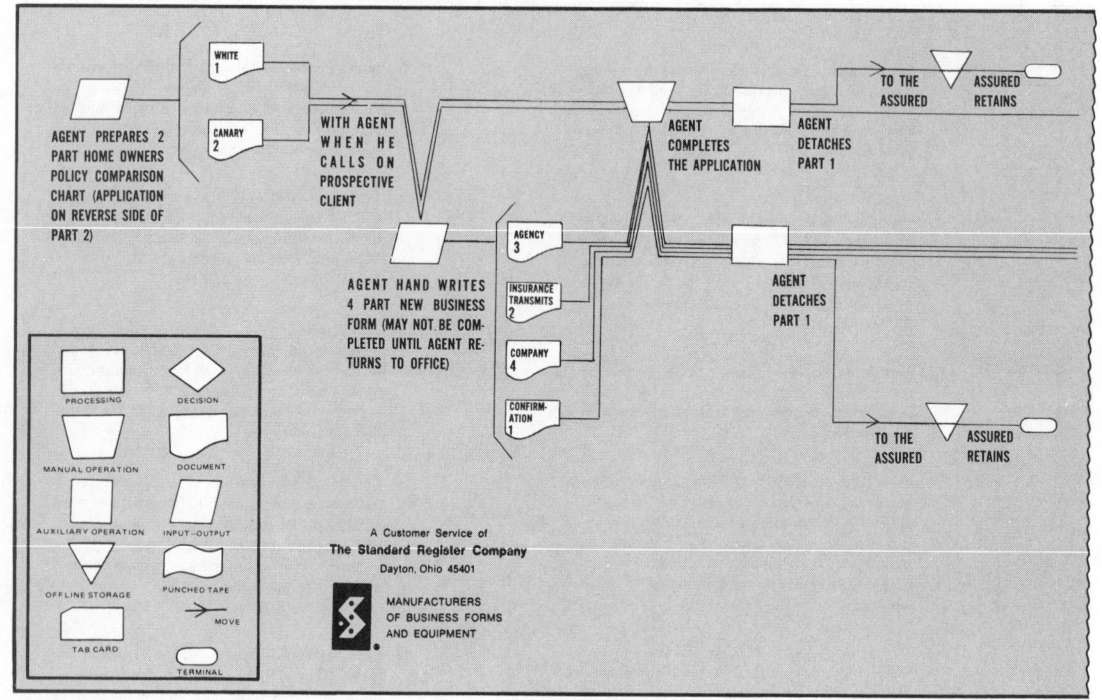

Fig. 15-6

Analysis of Completing an Application for an Insurance Policy, by Means of a Specialized Flow Chart

An effective example of how to rearrange an office so that there is a minimum of movement of forms and personnel is shown in the before-and-after illustrations in Figure 15-7. A study of the two illustrations shows the waste that had formerly taken place in steps, time, energy, and money. Solid lines show how each order previously traveled 162 feet and now travels only 35 feet. Broken lines indicate how auxiliary forms once traveled 80 feet and now only 35 feet. A significant reduction in costs was achieved in the new layout as a result of reducing by more than 50 percent the total floor space required for the processing of orders.

Flow Process Chart. The flow process chart is one of the most widely used tools for studying office work. Through its use, it is possible to analyze graphically office systems and procedures by using certain standardized symbols that make the presentation and reading of charts easier and more effective. Since the flow process chart aims

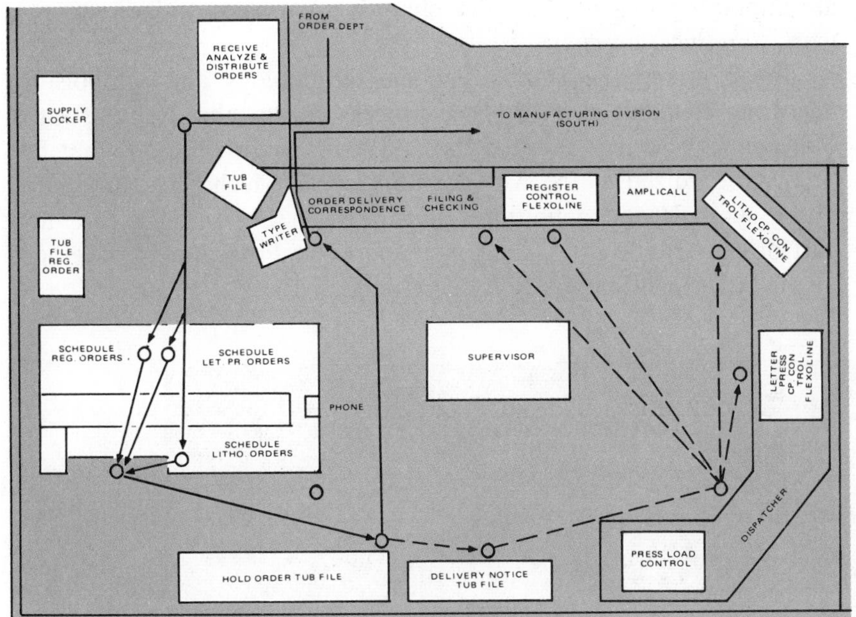

Office Layout Chart *before* Study

The proper arrangement of desks in sequence, consistent with the flow of paper work, corrected the "before" situation. Total floor space was reduced from 960 to 460 square feet.

Office Layout Chart *after* Study and Changes

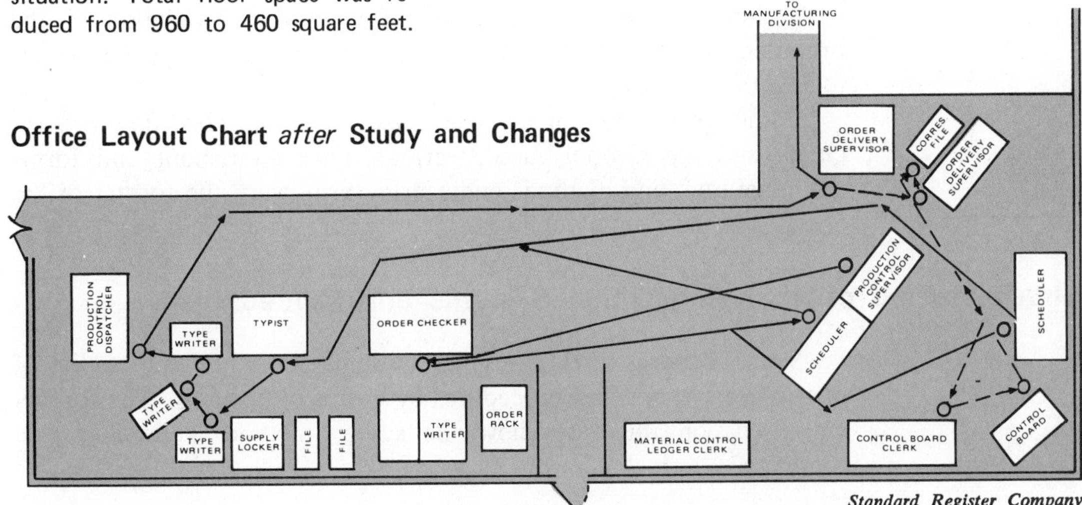

Standard Register Company

Fig. 15-7

at simplifying office work, the chart is sometimes spoken of as a *work simplification chart*.

In an attempt to standardize the terminology and symbols for the work elements used in flow process charts, the Administrative Management Society adopted those symbols and definitions that had been standardized by the American Society of Mechanical Engineers. These symbols and definitions, illustrated in Figure 15-8, are now part of the "Method of Charting Paperwork Procedures" developed by the American Standards Association.[2]

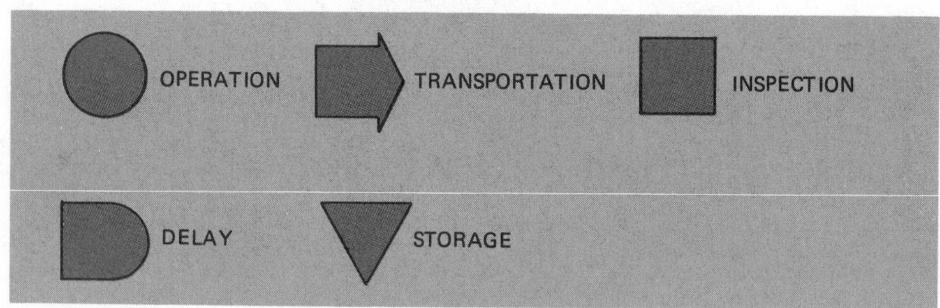

Fig. 15-8

Standardized Flow Process Chart Symbols Developed by the American Standards Association

Figure 15-9 shows a flow process chart of the present and the proposed methods of handling an incoming check in a branch bank. Note that with an investment of $100 in the installation of the proposed method, the estimated net saving for the first year amounts to $9,900.

Although an attempt has been made to standardize flow process charts and the symbols used, various office equipment and forms manufacturers and methods engineering firms vary the format of the charts and the symbols they use.

Survey Method of Analyzing Office Systems and Procedures

Some concerns having large office staffs make periodic studies of their office systems and procedures by means of a survey. The following discussion illustrates how the survey method is used in one company.

---

[2] The Administrative Management Society is no longer actively engaged in the development of standards. Standards developed in the past by AMS are now referred to as ASA Standards and are available through the American Standards Association, 10 E. 40th Street, New York, New York 10016.

FLOW PROCESS CHART

IDENTIFICATION

SUBJECT CHARTED: Check in branch bank	CHART NO. 0000
DRAWING NO. ____ PART NO. ____	TYPE OF CHART: Material
POINT AT WHICH CHART BEGINS: Receipt of batch from main office	SHEET NO. 1 OF 1 SHEETS
LOCATION: Rack Dept.	CHARTED BY: John Spear
POINT AT WHICH CHART ENDS: Filing of checks	DATE: 8-18-
LOCATION: Bookkeeping Dept.	APPROVED BY: S. Brown
	DATE: 8-19-
QUANTITY INFORMATION: 100 checks make one block.	YEARLY PRODUCTION: 3,600,000 checks
	COST UNIT: 1 check

SUMMARY

TOTAL YEARLY SAVING—DIRECT LABOR	$10,000.00
INSTALLATION COST OF PROPOSED METHOD	$ 100.00
ESTIMATED NET SAVING—FIRST YEAR	$ 9,900.00

	PRESENT METHOD		PROPOSED METHOD		DIFFERENCE	
UNIT COST-DIRECT LABOR & INSP.	.545		.425		.120	
DISTANCE TRAVELED IN FEET	321		155		166	
	NO.	TIME IN hrs.	NO.	TIME IN hrs.	NO.	TIME IN hrs.
○ OPERATIONS	10	.4355	7	.3220	3	.1135
⇨ TRANSPORTATIONS	8	.0120	4	.0055	4	.0065
□ INSPECTIONS	4	.0975	4	.0975	0	.0000
D DELAYS	5	.2250	4	.1750	1	.0500
▽ STORAGES	1	.0000	1	.0000	0	.0000

PRESENT METHOD

QUANTITY UNIT CHARTED	SYMBOLS	DESCRIPTION OF EVENT	DIST. MOVED IN FEET	UNIT OPER. TIME IN hrs.	UNIT TRANSP. TIME IN hrs.	UNIT INSPECT TIME IN hrs.	DELAY TIME IN hrs.	STORAGE TIME IN
1 block	⇨ 1	to Rack Dept. by messenger	36		.0014			
	○ 1 □ 1	Blocks proved on hand adding machine. Corrections made on form.		0850				
	⇨ 2	to "coop" sorting rack by "proofing check"	33		.0012			
	D 1	await sorting					.0050	
	○ 2	sorted by ledger		0205				
	D 2	await proofing					.0250	
	⇨ 3	to proofing desks	33		.0012			
	○ 3 □ 2	ledger totals run on hand adding machine and compared with block total		0800				
	⇨ 4	to storage table by "proofing clerk"	18		.0007			
	○ 4	placed on storage table by ledger breakdown		0050				
	D 3	await pickup by bookkeepers					.0500	
	⇨ 5	to bookkeeper's work station	75		.0028			
	○ 5	sorted by account name		.0350				
	□ 3	sight pays ledger file				.0975		
	○ 6	balances prelisted on extended sheets		0400				
	○ 7 □ 4	machine post amounts and prove total		0750				
	D 4	await microfilming					.0500	
	⇨ 6	to microfilm machine by operator	63		.0024			
	○ 8	microfilm		0300				
	⇨ 7	to cancelling machine by micro.op.	6		.0002			
	○ 9	perforate to cancel		0080				
	⇨ 8	to bookkeeper by micro.op.	57		.0021			
	D 5	await filing					.0500	
	○ 10	filed by account name by bookkeeper		0570				
	▽ 1	in file.						

PROPOSED METHOD

QUANTITY UNIT CHARTED	SYMBOLS	DESCRIPTION OF EVENT	DIST. MOVED IN FEET	UNIT OPER. TIME IN hrs	UNIT TRANSP TIME IN hrs.	UNIT INSPECT TIME IN hrs.	DELAY TIME IN hrs.	STORAGE TIME IN
1 block	⇨ 1	to Rack Dept. by messenger	20		.0007			
	○ 1 □ 1	blocks proved on automatic adding machine. Corrections made on form. Sorted by ledger		.0425				
	D 1	await proof					.0250	
	○ 2 □ 2	ledger totals run on automatic adding machine and compared with block total.		.0345				
	D 2	await pickup by messenger					.0500	
	⇨ 2	to bookkeeper	75		.0028			
	○ 3	sort by account name		.0350				
	□ 3	sight pays ledger file				.0975		
	○ 4	balances prelisted on extended sheets		.0400				
	○ 5 □ 4	machine post amounts and prove total		.0750				
	D 3	await pickup by messenger					.0500	
	⇨ 3	to microfilm operator	30		.0010			
	○ 6	microfilm and perforate to cancel		.0380				
	⇨ 4	to bookkeeper by messenger	30		.0010			
	D 4	await filing					.0500	
	○ 7	filed by account name by bookkeeper		.0570				
	▽ 1	in file						

Fig. 15-9

Flow Process Charts of Present and Proposed Methods for Handling an Incoming Check in a Branch Bank

The services of five regular office employees with previous experience in analysis work were required to carry out the survey shown in Figure 15-10. Data were collected from three sources—from the worker, from the supervisor, and from an observation of the physical aspects of the department. To secure working knowledge of each job, a questionnaire supplemented by a personal interview was used. All departments were studied simultaneously. It was felt that the members of the organization, if approached in the right manner, could contribute from their own observation and experience many of the facts that would otherwise be discovered only by a very detailed analysis.

From this survey it was possible to prove (1) that the department was doing its work efficiently, or (2) that a detailed analysis could be profitably made, or (3) that certain changes might be desirable.

JOB SURVEY

Department____________________ Your Name____________________

Division or Group____________________ Date____________________

Name of Desk or Job____

Purpose

The purpose of this set of questions is to aid you in writing a description of what you do. The collection of this information into a permanent form will not only be helpful to you but will aid your department head and the personnel department. Your department head will be able to plan better the future work of the department, while the personnel department will obtain information of value to it in future selection as well as in training and promotion throughout the company.

General Directions

Answer all questions in detail. When you have finished the description, ask yourself this additional question, "If I knew nothing about this particular job, but were given this survey to read, would I get an accurate picture of the work?" If there is any additional information, it should be given in answer to Question 13. In case sufficient space has not been allowed, please use a regular 8½ × 11 inch sheet, marking it so that the information can be readily identified, and attach the sheet to the survey forms.

1. Who is your immediate supervisor?____________________________

2. List your regular duties in the order of their importance and show approximately how much time is spent on each one. An easy way would be to make a brief statement starting with a verb in the present tense, such as "Type daily sales reports," "Clear orders," etc. The time element is an important one and should be based upon what you consider as an average. The time unit for daily duties can probably be best expressed in "minutes a day," while the less frequent work might be expressed in "hours each month." List the various parts of your job under the following headings and show the time required for each item at the right-hand side of the sheet.

   a. *Daily.* Those which occur regularly every day.

   Minutes a Day

   b. *Periodic.* Those which occur regularly at longer intervals, say weekly, monthly, etc. State the number of times the work is done during an average month.

   Total Hours a Month | Approx. Times a Month

   c. *Special.* Work done in spare time, of an unusual nature, or not provided for in advance.

   Total Hours a Month | Approx. Times a Month

   d. *Recurrent.* Those which are not regular and which occur less frequently than daily but cannot be listed under the other headings.

   Total Hours a Month | Approx. Times a Month

Fig. 15-10

Survey Undertaken to Analyze Office Systems and Procedures (page 1)

3. What duties shown under the last question come directly to your desk, are handled on your own initiative, and leave your desk without being checked by some other member of your department, thus making you responsible for the entire job while it is in your department?________
4. Are you held responsible for supervising the work of others?
____
   a. If so, of how many?________
   b. List the names of their jobs.________
5. List all machines you are required to operate, such as a typewriter, a calculator, etc., and estimate the amount of training or speed required to do your work.________
6. Where does your work come from?________
7. Where does it go after it has been handled?________
8. Is there anything about your job which requires special physical qualifications? For example, are you required to stand, walk, or operate some machine all day?________
9. Do you have business contact (daily, weekly, etc.) with

Employees________	By phone________
Customers________	Telegraph________
Executives________	Correspondence________
General Public________	Personal________

Fig. 15-10

10. What is the minimum amount of education (in years, months, etc.) and kind of experience, whether obtained here or elsewhere, necessary to start on your job?
   Education________
   Experience________
11. With the proper qualifications, what is the minimum time (in days, weeks, etc.) it would take for a new worker to become sufficiently acquainted with the duties of your present job to handle the work alone?
____
12. Peculiarities of the job.
   a. Is accuracy or speed the more important?________
   b. Are there periods when your work is increased beyond the usual amount?________
   c. Is your work checked before leaving the department?
   ____
   d. Are there written instructions for this job?________
   e. Would it be helpful to have written instructions?
   ____
   f. What would be the result of errors in your work?
   ____
   g. What specialized abilities or knowledge are required?
   ____

Survey Undertaken to Analyze Office Systems and Procedures (page 2)

The results of one survey were surprising. The employees felt for the first time that their ideas or suggestions for improvement in systems were worthy of consideration. Consequently, the morale of the workers was improved. The department heads felt a greater spirit of cooperation between themselves and the workers. In addition, specific changes were made as follows:

1. The elimination of many useless forms.
2. The simplification of a number of forms without reducing the efficiency of the work but reducing the cost of forms.
3. The installation of timesaving machines and office equipment.
4. Standard methods of doing certain routine jobs.
5. Standard and reasonable production schedules.
6. Incentive wage payment systems in a few departments.

Each one believed that his job was more secure because inefficiency was eliminated and office costs were reduced. Moreover, everyone asked that the survey be repeated annually.

QUESTIONS FOR REVIEW

1. Define the function of control. What are the main steps taken in the process of control?
2. Explain the interrelationship that exists among a system, a procedure, and a method.
3. Why is it necessary for the administrative office manager to understand fully the analysis of office systems and procedures?
4. What are the objectives of systems and procedures analysis?
5. What advantages accrue to management as the result of constantly studying and analyzing office work?
6. Compare the use of a management consulting firm with the development of an internal staff of systems analysts as a means of studying the systems and procedures of a firm.
7. What are the advantages and disadvantages in assigning the sole responsibility for systems and procedures analysis to the office manager?
8. What are the basic principles of analysis with which the office manager must be familiar if he is to perform his duties efficiently?
9. Describe briefly the tools employed in analyzing the systems and procedures involved in the use of office forms.
10. What are the different methods of charting business systems and procedures?

QUESTIONS FOR DISCUSSION

1. An office administrator believes that work simplification can be improved by means of brainstorming. Discuss how the technique of brainstorming might be used in conjunction with work simplification.
2. People with new ideas for modern office procedures have difficulty putting their ideas into effect because many of the present complex

procedures have been built up over a period of years. Explain how this situation can be remedied.

3. Discuss the office inefficiencies that occur as a result of having all employees start working at the same hour in the morning and stop at the same hours for lunch and for closing.

4. The main purpose of a new office system is not necessarily the reduction of operating costs but a strengthening of the office's role as a nerve center of business through which management coordinates corporate activities. Explain your reaction to this statement.

5. The president of the Carmichael Glass Company agreed to employ a procedures analyst on a full-time basis with the understanding that each year the firm must save twice the man's salary of $15,000 a year. During the first three years the savings amounted to $30,000, $33,000, and $35,000, respectively. During the fourth year the savings fell to $12,000. The analyst was then dropped from the staff since the annual savings did not exceed his salary.

   Discuss this procedure of employing an analyst and the discontinuance of his services from a managerial point of view.

6. The controller of the Acme Supply Company wants to have the accounts receivable system of his firm studied with the view of improving the work. What facts would you want to study in an attempt to improve this system?

7. The Cooper Manufacturing Company has on its staff a methods man who has already saved the firm $15,000 through his methods program and who is interested in expanding the program to save even more money. Before agreeing to an expanded methods program, the firm is interested in the answers to two questions:

   a. How many people can be placed on a methods staff before the point of diminishing returns is reached?

   b. If the methods department is enlarged, should an expert from the outside be employed, or can the same results be obtained by training or teaching the line people in the organization?

   Discuss your answers to these questions.

PRACTICAL OFFICE CASES

Case 15-1 Functionalizing the Systems Department To Aid in Reorganizing Office Services

Office operations in the Bordwell Company, a service business with about 500 office employees, have become unworkable. This situation is due to the fact that the office services have become highly centralized over the past ten years, during which the company has grown from an office force of 20 workers to its present size. The company plans to decentralize its office services, but the president wants to precede the decentralization by setting up a systems department to advise in the reorganization.

■ On the basis of these data, prepare a report indicating:

a. Who should be in charge of the systems department.
b. To whom the head of the department should report.
c. Who and how many should staff the department.
d. The sequence of system analyses to be undertaken.
e. The method of initiating the analyses.
f. The method of effecting the results of the analyses.
g. The method of obtaining acceptance and development of the systems program.

Case 15-2 Preparing an Office Layout Chart and a Flow Process Chart

The office of the Yelland Gates Company is small. The office manager is progressive, however, and is constantly studying the systems, procedures, and layout in order to seek improvement. A recent study of the procedure involved in processing an incoming order indicated the following methods and personnel involved:

Method	*Personnel Involved*
1. Order received by telephone recorded on formal order blank.	1. Receptionist-Clerk.
2. Credit standing of customer is checked.	2. Bookkeeper (Accounts Receivable) and Receptionist-Clerk.
3. If credit is satisfactory, order is priced and given to Shipping Department.	3. Receptionist-Clerk.
4. Notification of shipment is received from Shipping Department, and invoice is computed and checked.	4. Calculating Machine Operator.
5. Invoice is billed.	5. Billing Clerk.
6. Invoice is compared with original copy of order for verification.	6. Receptionist-Clerk.
7. Copies of invoice:	7. Copies of invoice to:
a. Mailed to customer.	a. Mail Clerk.
b. Sent to Bookkeeper (Accounts Receivable) for posting.	b. Bookkeeper (Accounts Receivable).
c. Sent to files.	c. Receptionist-Clerk.

The present layout of the office is illustrated at the top of page 493.

■ As office manager of the Yelland Gates Company, do the following things:

a. Analyze the present office layout in relation to the flow of paper work and personnel involved, with the objective of improving the

Fig. A

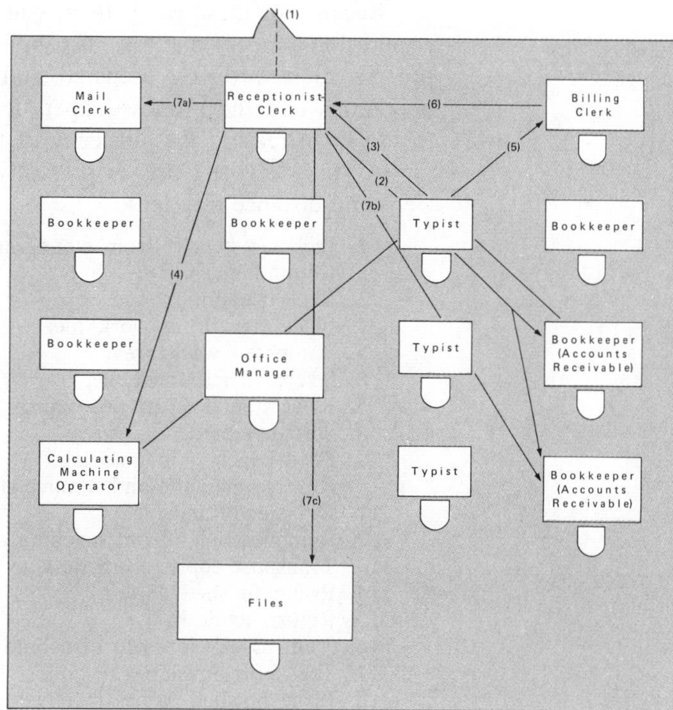

Layout of Office in Yelland Gates Company

flow of work. Construct an office layout chart similar to that illustrated in Figure 15-7 in which you incorporate your recommended changes.

b. Prepare a flow process chart, similar to that illustrated in Figure 15-9, which will show the effect of the office layout on the flow of work. In preparing your chart, use the ASA standardized flow process chart symbols illustrated in Figure 15-8.

Case 15-3 Preparing a Flow Process Chart of Present and Proposed Procedures

As office manager for McKissick Electronics, you have been using an informal work simplification program for the past few years. Reproduction services, done primarily by the stencil method, have been centralized because of the tremendous volume of work. Lately there have been many complaints about the work in this department. Those requesting materials to be duplicated complain that they cannot get their work done promptly. The girls in the reproduction department feel that they are overworked and rushed too much.

Because of these complaints, you have decided to analyze the stencil duplication process and the distribution of work. You feel that a flow process chart, properly prepared and summarized, both for the present operations and the proposed operations, might be an effective approach to use in increasing the efficiency of this department.

A study of the work as presently performed indicates the following steps and distance traveled:

1.	Pick up stencils from stenographers.	200 feet
2.	Count stencils.	
3.	Record count.	
4.	Place stencils in work file.	
5.	Straighten work area.	
6.	Select stencil from file.	
7.	Place stencil on mimeograph.	
8.	Start machine.	
9.	Feed papers into machine.	
10.	Reverse machine and remove stencil.	
11.	Dry stencil and file.	
12.	Remove copies from machine and stack on desk.	2 feet
13.	Transport copies from desk to table.	5 feet
14.	Route finished copies.	
15.	Return to desk.	5 feet
16.	Address envelopes to distribute finished copies.	2 feet
17.	Transport envelopes to table.	5 feet
18.	Place finished copies in envelopes.	
19.	Return to desk.	5 feet
20.	Stack envelopes on desk.	
21.	Pick up all operation and finished sheets.	
22.	Distribute finished copies.	100 feet

As a result of studying these operations, you revise the procedure as follows:

1.	Select stencils from rack placed in duplicating room.	2 feet
2.	Count stencils.	
3.	Record count.	
4.	Place stencils in basket file near "feed" end of mimeograph.	2 feet
5.	Select stencil from basket file.	1 foot
6.	Place stencil on mimeograph.	1 foot
7.	Place supply of paper in machine.	
8.	Start machine.	
9.	Set count indicator for number of copies desired.	
10.	Stop machine, remove stencil.	
11.	Dry stencil.	2 feet
12.	File stencil.	
13.	Remove finished copies from machine.	2 feet
14.	Place copies in distribution rack for delivery.	2 feet

■ Prepare a flow process chart of the present and the proposed procedures, similar to that illustrated in Figure 15-9. In preparing your chart, use the ASA standardized symbols.

16

Forms Design and Control

In every business organization there is an intangible force that holds men and machines together and enables them to function as a coordinated unit. No business can exist for any great length of time without the assistance of this force. This system is the combination of forms, records, and reports that are necessary to transmit information or instructions for work or to record data. For example, thousands of invoices are used daily merely to transmit to customers a charge for goods or services purchased. Duplicate copies of these invoices become the source documents for recording the accounting data. Other copies of the invoices may be used for sales analyses, inventory entries, packing slips, or salesmen's commission copies. Each copy is a form of record or a means of transmitting business information.

The first three objectives of systems and procedures analysis as presented in Chapter 15 relate to business information and forms because they are such an important and costly phase of office work. These objectives are: (1) to *eliminate* as much unneeded information and as many business forms and records as feasible; (2) to *combine* as many of the business forms as possible; and (3) to *simplify* the forms in content, arrangement sequence, and method of preparation.

Each of these objectives is emphasized in this chapter in its relation to the design and control of office forms.

NATURE OF OFFICE FORMS

Forms are carefully designed papers used to perform, simplify, and standardize office work and to accumulate and transmit information for historical or reference purposes. Forms may be classified according to the office functions for which they are used, such as purchase forms, sales forms, correspondence forms, and accounting forms. A second classification of business forms is that of outside contact forms and internal office forms. *Outside contact forms* are those sent to customers, creditors, or persons outside the organization with whom a firm does business. Such forms include sales invoices, statements, checks, vouchers, and purchase orders. *Internal office forms,* those received or used by employees of the business, may be subdivided into memorandum forms, such as requisitions and time tickets used for conveying instructions or information to other employees; accounting records, such as journals and registers; and report forms used for presenting data gathered from other records.

A simpler and perhaps more basic analysis categorizes the forms as single copy or multiple copy. *Single-copy* forms are complete in themselves and usually become the source documents. *Multiple-copy* forms, on the other hand, either with or without carbon paper, are made up of an original and one or more duplicates. The duplicate copies are used to transmit information or serve the function of providing additional records. Multiple-copy forms may be issued in pad form, in loose forms banded together, or in continuous form.

PRINCIPLES OF FORMS DESIGN AND CONTROL

The three principles of forms design and control with which the administrative manager should be familiar pertain to the use, the standardization, and the centralized control of office forms.

Principle of Use

A form should come into existence only when there is a purposeful need for the use of that form.

This principle is basic. The job to be accomplished must first be planned and then the form can be developed. A form should be used:

1. Whenever something must be recorded as a matter of necessity, such as orders, requests, records, and instructions.
2. When certain data must be recorded repeatedly. These data can be preprinted on each copy of the form, thus saving time in forms preparation.
3. When it is necessary to have all information recorded in the same place on each copy of the form. This arrangement serves as a check on the completeness of the record.
4. When it is desirable to fix responsibility for work done by providing spaces for signatures or notations of who did the work.

Principle of Standardization

The size, quality, and color of paper used in all forms should be standardized to reduce costs and confusion.

Standardization of forms affects primarily their physical arrangement—size, quality of paper stock, color, and printing styles.

Size of Forms. Standards should first be set for the size of office forms. Odd-size forms increase printing costs because of the waste incurred in having to print such forms on standard-size sheets of paper stock that do not lend themselves to an economical layout of the forms. Thus, waste is entailed in the surplus paper trimmed off the standard-size printing sheet. The number of approved sizes of forms used by a business firm should be kept at a minimum. The individual or committee in charge of forms control should be familiar with the data in Table 16-1, which shows the sizes of forms that can be cut without waste from standard sheets of paper stock used by printers.

Table 16-1 shows 25 different sizes of forms, some of which are not practical for office use. For example, the smallest sizes are odd sizes that do not lend themselves to index card files in common use. In determining the size of a form, consideration must be given to the size that can be cut, without waste, from the standard-size printing sheet—17″ x 22″ or 17″ x 28″. Odd-size forms also contribute to increased office costs in that such forms make the tasks of filing and handling more difficult, often requiring the purchase of odd-size envelopes or containers for transmittal through the mail. Before the form size is selected, a study should be made of the envelopes and the mechanical equipment to be used with each respective form.

Quality of Paper Stock. A second factor affecting standardization of office forms pertains to the quality of paper. Quality of paper

STANDARD FORM SIZES

Size of Form	* Cuts Without Waste from Standard Sheet Measuring:	Number Obtained from Single Standard-Size Sheet	Number of Single Forms Obtained from One Ream of Paper
2¾ x 4¼	8½ x 11	8	4M
2¾ x 4¼	17 x 22	32	16M
2¾ x 8½	8½ x 11	4	2M
2¾ x 8½	17 x 22	16	8M
3½ x 4¼	17 x 28	32	16M
3½ x 8½	17 x 28	16	8M
4¼ x 5½	8½ x 11	4	2M
4¼ x 5½	17 x 22	16	8M
4¼ x 7	17 x 28	16	8M
4¼ x 11	8½ x 11	2	1M
4¼ x 11	17 x 22	8	4M
4¼ x 14	17 x 28	8	4M
5½ x 8½	8½ x 11	2	1M
5½ x 8½	17 x 22	8	4M
5½ x 17	17 x 22	4	2M
6 x 9	19 x 24	8	4M
7 x 17	17 x 28	4	2M
7¼ x 10½	22 x 34	9	4½M
8½ x 11	17 x 22	4	2M
8½ x 11	22 x 25½	6	3M
8½ x 14	17 x 28	4	2M
8½ x 22	17 x 22	2	1M
8½ x 28	17 x 28	2	1M
11 x 17	17 x 22	2	1M
14 x 17	17 x 28	2	1M

Hammermill Paper Company

Table 16-1

* In some sizes a small "trim" may be allowed, and a form may be permitted to be a small fraction of an inch under the "stated dimensions."

stock affects its durability and ease of handling, as well as the length of time that the form may be kept. Paper stock is sold by the ream and in multiple packages of reams by the carton. The weight is figured by the ream in 17″ x 22″ size. For example, a ream (usually 500 sheets) of 17″ x 22″ paper which weighs approximately 20 pounds is called substance 20, or 20 lb. stock. Commonly used weights for three kinds of office paper stock are shown in Table 16-2.

For multiple-copy forms, weight is particularly important because it determines the number of copies that can be made in one writing. The weight of paper stock used also affects the mailing costs.

GUIDE TO OFFICE PAPER WEIGHT

Table 16-2

TYPE	BOND					LEDGER			COPY		
Weight *	24	20	16	13	9	32	28	24	11	9	7
Letterhead	x	x							x	x	x**
General Typing		x	x							x	x
Interoffice		x	x	x	x					x	x
Legal Documents	x										x
General Ledgers						x	x				
Bookkeeping Machines						x	x	x			
Data Processing Continuous Forms											
1st sheet			x	x							
2d-4th copy										x	x
5th-7th copy											x
Form Sets											
3-part form 1st sheet		x				x					
2d and 3d sheets			x					x			
5-part form 1st sheet			x				x				
2d-5th sheets				x	x					x	x

Adapted from *Modern Office Procedures*

* Weights are for average office requirements.
** Depending on number of carbon copies.

The physical handling that a form will receive must also be considered in deciding upon the quality of stock to be used. Normal treatment, such as that given an invoice form, can be provided for by using an all-sulphite paper. Extremely hard treatment received by some factory orders requires a tough sheet with great tensile strength so that the paper will not crack after many foldings. Some forms, such as shipping tags, are printed on cloth. It is sometimes advisable to provide a strong, compact case with celluloid facing to protect such forms.

The manner in which the form is filled in determines the finish of the paper to be used. Forms completed in ink must be of nonabsorbent paper that will withstand erasures and will prevent the ink from "bleeding." Forms filled in by means of spirit duplicators and other reproducing equipment must be sufficiently absorbent so that the inks will dry quickly and not offset on each succeeding sheet being duplicated. Continuous multiple-copy forms are usually printed on a lighter weight of paper with a medium finish to secure copying legibility. If the finish is too high, however, the fibers will be so flattened that they will not readily receive the carbon image. If the finish is too soft, the surface of the paper will be rough, which results in poor copying qualities with part of the copy being clear and other parts indistinct.

Most business forms are printed on the *commercial writing class* of papers, a group of writing papers commonly used in ordinary business transactions and for advertising purposes. The types of paper falling under this heading are bond, copy or onionskin, ledger, and index, each of which is described in the following paragraphs.

Bond. Bond paper is the traditional paper used for letterheads, office forms, and certificates where fine appearance and durability are essential. Bond paper stands up better than other commercial writing papers under handling because its fibers are stronger. Bond paper usually has definite writing and erasing qualities, cleanliness, uniformity of finish and color, and freedom from fuzz. Thus, bond papers are more expensive than other commonly used papers.

For many years it was felt that a sufficient rag content was required for high-grade business papers. Today, however, many papers made without a rag construction possess all the necessary qualities for normal office use, including letterhead stationery. Sulphite and sulphate papers, for example, are made entirely of wood dissolved into pulp by chemical processes. Sulphite bonds are available in a variety of colors and finishes, and today these bonds represent the standard office papers for typewriting and writing. Where durability and permanence are important factors, cotton fiber bonds should be used. For example, in the manufacture of insurance policies, legal forms, and other permanent records, a long-life paper is generally required. Thus, a 100 percent cotton fiber bond is commonly specified. Since the life of paper is a function of its use, it is difficult to estimate how long paper will last. However, it is maintained by papermaking authorities that 50 percent cotton fiber paper should have a life of 35 to 50 years.

Erasable bond is a special type of paper that permits errors in typing to be corrected quickly and cleanly with an ordinary pencil eraser. Erasable bonds are manufactured like ordinary bond papers, but before the last process a special solution is applied to the surface of the paper which permits freshly typed letters to be removed easily. Once the typing has "set," however, it stays on the paper for good.

Copy. Copy paper is a general term that describes a group of lightweight writing papers such as onionskin and manifold papers that are used for making carbon copies. Onionskin paper is a lightweight writing paper that is thin, partly transparent, and highly glazed. It is very durable and may be used for permanent records where a minimum of bulk is desirable. Generally 9 lb. and 11 lb. tissue are used for carbon copies. If the number of carbon copies required is 5, 7, or up to 10, the tissue weight may be reduced to 7 lb. stock in order to give good reproduction on all copies. Manifold paper is a lightweight writing paper which, when used alternately with carbon papers, produces multiple copies of written or typewritten work with either an unglazed or glazed finish.

Ledger. Ledger paper is commonly used for systems work since it has a good writing surface for any type of ink or pencil and a card-like finish that stands a lot of abuse. Ledger paper withstands erasing and creasing, and both sides may be ruled clearly and distinctly. Loose-leaf records should be printed on heavier ledger paper than the bound-book type. Generally the most used type of ledger paper is a hard-surface stock in weights from 24 to 40 lbs.

Index. Index papers, the "heavyweights" of office papers, are used for machine-posting records, punched-card systems, index files, and library files. Index papers have the same smooth finish as ledger stock, but are tougher and more rigid. Common weights of index papers are 43, 53, 67, and 82 lbs.

Color. Colors used on office forms should be standardized. The use of carefully selected colors expedites the routing, sorting, and filing of forms. Forms may be color coded to indicate departments, branches, or other divisions to which copies are to be sent or in which they are to be used.

Printing Styles. Printing styles should be standardized since a uniform typography improves the appearance and legibility of forms, thus reducing the possibility of error.

Principle of Centralized Control

The design, use, and replacement of office forms should be centrally controlled.

Too many offices create a new form for every conceivable record and perpetuate all the old forms. This problem can be avoided or solved by providing a system of forms control under the direction of one office executive, such as the records management supervisor, or a committee of individuals closely concerned with the objectives of forms control. Various aspects of centralized forms control will be discussed later in this chapter.

DESIGNING OFFICE FORMS

The widespread use of automated data processing and standard filing equipment no longer permits spur-of-the-moment forms design. To speed up manual record keeping and to obtain efficient machine operation, forms must be carefully planned and designed. In the designing of office forms, there are a number of factors in addition to those previously described that must be considered in order to secure the maximum efficiency from the use of forms.

The capabilities and limitations of existing and planned record-keeping procedures and filing equipment should be studied by taking inventory of all equipment that will be used with the forms. All equipment and devices that perform a function in the procedure—typewriters, accounting machines, file drawers, collators, etc.—must be included in the inventory so that no item possibly overlooked may create a bottleneck that will slow down the operation of a fast-moving, efficient system. For each manual procedure and piece of equipment, the following information should be listed in the inventory:

1. The maximum and minimum dimensions of paper stock that the equipment will handle.
2. The maximum and minimum stock weight and/or thickness that the equipment will handle.
3. The direction of feed into the equipment. In the manufacture of paper, the fibers tend to line up with the direction in which the paper machine moves. Thus, the paper is said to have a *grain direction.* Grain direction is highly important where automatic office equipment is concerned. In specifying the paper stock to be used for forms, a grain direction should be selected to parallel the direction of feed into the equipment. If the grain direction runs at a right angle to the feed, the stock will curl and snag, thus slowing down or stopping operations. In some cases very sensitive equipment may be damaged.

   If a form is to be stored in a stand-up file, the grain direction should be on the vertical in order to give support. If, however, such a form is to be used on automatic equipment, the feed direction should take priority. When a binder is used in manual posting, the grain direction should parallel the binding edge.

Paper makers usually indicate the grain direction by underscoring the dimension that runs the same way as the grain. For example, 25 x 38 means that the grain runs parallel to the longer edge. The terms "grain long" or "grain short" are also used to indicate that the grain runs parallel to the long or the short edge of the sheet.

4. The method of feed into the equipment. Office or accounting equipment that prints on a cylindrical surface will usually handle up to 36 lb. ledger paper. Sample stock should be checked to make sure that the printing is legible and that the machine does not jam. Equipment that prints on a flat surface will print on most all weights of ledger paper stock.
5. The amount of margin to be provided at the top, bottom, and sides of the form.
6. The space required for printing each digit or letter. For manual entries, usually ⅛″ is allowed for each character. For automatic equipment, the number of characters printed per inch should be measured in relation to each piece of equipment. For the recording of numbers, vertical columns should be used for easy tabulation. The width of vertical columns must be designed to match machine requirements.
7. The space required for printing digits and letters on each horizontal line. For manual entries, ¼″ space is usually allowed. Automated equipment may print 6 to 10 lines for each vertical inch. On some equipment the vertical and horizontal spaces can be easily adjusted by the manufacturer's representative to increase or decrease the number of lines or spaces per inch in order to permit more working space on each form.

Attention should also be given to the arrangement and sequence of the items to be recorded on the form. A logical sequence should be followed so that each item can be entered with a minimum of delay and without constantly zigzagging up and down or back and forth on the form. If several departments use similar information on the forms, all sequences should be identical so that comparisons and use will be facilitated. Information should be grouped wherever possible by use of ruled lines and white space between the groups.

To facilitate sorting, every form should have a number and/or a name, as shown in Figure 16-1. In this illustration of a combined purchase order and vendor's check, the distribution of each copy is indicated at the bottom of the form as follows:

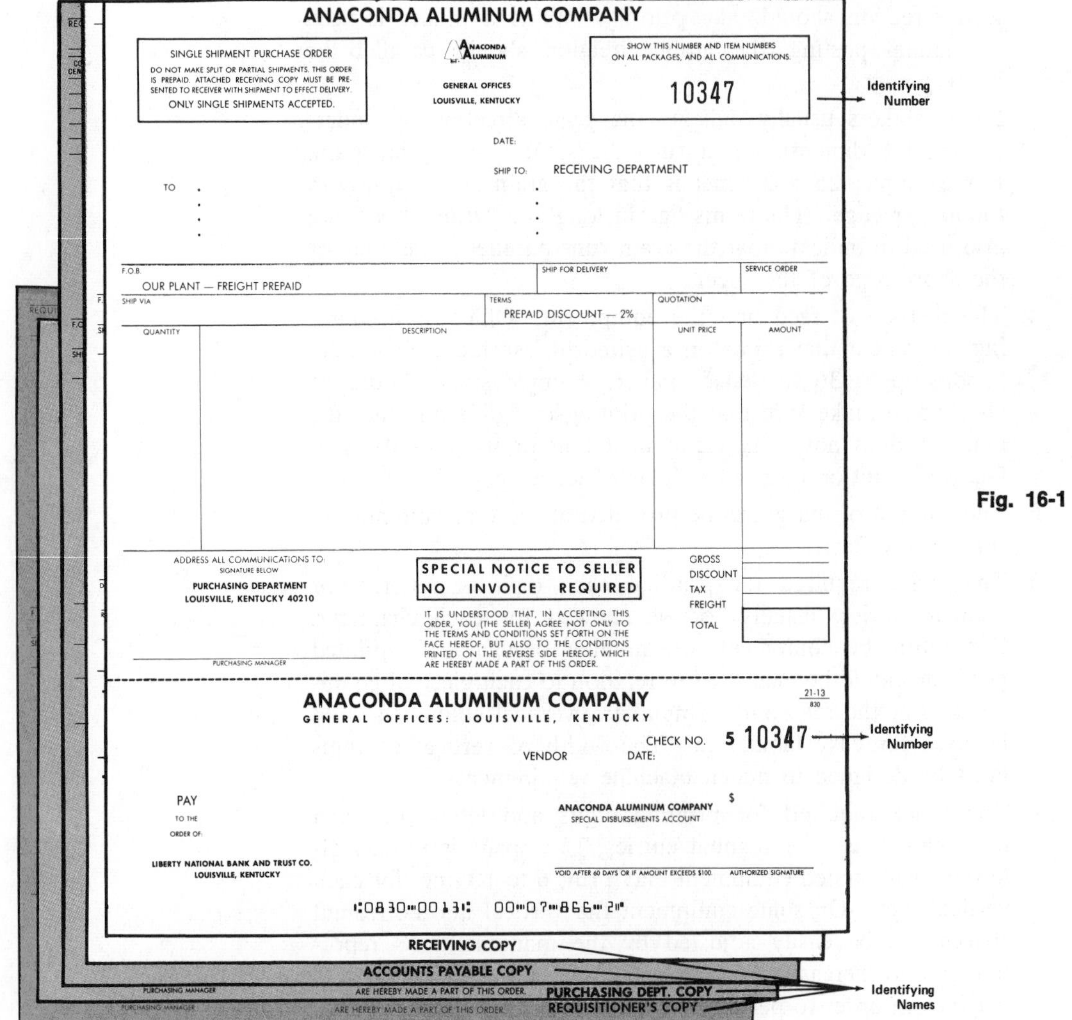

ANACONDA ALUMINUM COMPANY

SINGLE SHIPMENT PURCHASE ORDER
DO NOT MAKE SPLIT OR PARTIAL SHIPMENTS. THIS ORDER IS PREPAID. ATTACHED RECEIVING COPY MUST BE PRESENTED TO RECEIVER WITH SHIPMENT TO EFFECT DELIVERY.
ONLY SINGLE SHIPMENTS ACCEPTED.

ANACONDA ALUMINUM
GENERAL OFFICES
LOUISVILLE, KENTUCKY

SHOW THIS NUMBER AND ITEM NUMBERS ON ALL PACKAGES, AND ALL COMMUNICATIONS.
10347 → Identifying Number

DATE:
SHIP TO: RECEIVING DEPARTMENT
TO

F.O.B. OUR PLANT — FREIGHT PREPAID		SHIP FOR DELIVERY	SERVICE ORDER
SHIP VIA	TERMS PREPAID DISCOUNT — 2%	QUOTATION	

QUANTITY	DESCRIPTION	UNIT PRICE	AMOUNT

ADDRESS ALL COMMUNICATIONS TO:
SIGNATURE BELOW
PURCHASING DEPARTMENT
LOUISVILLE, KENTUCKY 40210
PURCHASING MANAGER

SPECIAL NOTICE TO SELLER
NO INVOICE REQUIRED

IT IS UNDERSTOOD THAT, IN ACCEPTING THIS ORDER, YOU (THE SELLER) AGREE NOT ONLY TO THE TERMS AND CONDITIONS SET FORTH ON THE FACE HEREOF, BUT ALSO TO THE CONDITIONS PRINTED ON THE REVERSE SIDE HEREOF, WHICH ARE HEREBY MADE A PART OF THIS ORDER.

GROSS
DISCOUNT
TAX
FREIGHT
TOTAL

ANACONDA ALUMINUM COMPANY
GENERAL OFFICES: LOUISVILLE, KENTUCKY
21-13
830
CHECK NO. 5 10347 → Identifying Number
VENDOR DATE:

PAY
TO THE
ORDER OF:
$
ANACONDA ALUMINUM COMPANY
SPECIAL DISBURSEMENTS ACCOUNT

LIBERTY NATIONAL BANK AND TRUST CO.
LOUISVILLE, KENTUCKY
VOID AFTER 60 DAYS OR IF AMOUNT EXCEEDS $100. AUTHORIZED SIGNATURE

⑆0830⑈0013⑆ 00⑈07⑈866⑈2⑈

RECEIVING COPY
ACCOUNTS PAYABLE COPY
PURCHASING DEPT. COPY
REQUISITIONER'S COPY
→ Identifying Names

Fig. 16-1

Identifying Names and Number of Copies to Facilitate Sorting

Original purchase order and check. Note that the purchase order and check bear the same preprinted number, 10347.

Receiving Copy, sent with original purchase order and check to vendor, who returns receiving copy with shipment. Receiving Copy is then referred to accounting department to match and file with Accounts Payable Copy.

Accounts Payable Copy, referred to accounting department for accounts payable record keeping and control.

Purchasing Department Copy, retained as a follow-up and file copy.

Requisitioner's Copy, returned to department that initiated request for goods.

Some firms use a letter to identify each department and a number for each form originating within that department. For example, *A* may be used for the Accounting Department, *P* for Production, *S* for Sales, and *O* for Order. As a further aid in identifying and distributing copies of forms, manufacturers of forms make available a wide variety of colors of paper stock.

Adequate instructions for using the form should be provided. When instructions are lengthy, the reverse side of the form may be used; but the stock selected must be sufficiently heavy to avoid show-through which reduces legibility. The instructions should be clearly worded, keeping in mind the people who will have to use and work with the forms.

To avoid needless expense, the person in charge of forms control must be certain that the copy is correctly composed and laid out and that the printer has clear and complete instructions of what is to be done. It should be noted that the pricing structure in the paper industry is based on standard units such as reams, cartons, cases, 5,000 and 10,000 lb. lots, and carloads. Fractional quantities will cost extra as will several small orders rather than one large order.

A Check Sheet for Forms Design

The Hawthorne Paper Company has contributed to the intelligent use and control of business forms by making scientific studies for business firms. One of these studies resulted in the preparation of the check sheet shown in Figure 16-2. By means of this check sheet the person in charge of forms control may either survey the present forms used and make such changes as might be suggested from the preceding discussion, or may study new forms recommended for use within the organization. The use of such a check sheet simplifies and standardizes the matter of forms control with its resulting efficiency and economy.

The Hammermill Paper Company provides a Form Planning Checklist that can be used before placing a printing order for a new or an old form. This checklist is illustrated in Figure 16-3.

An Illustration of Good Forms Design

The cash report form shown in Figure 16-4 was designed for use within a banking organization. The supervisor of forms control

FORMS SURVEY

Form Title .... Dept. .... Form No. ....

Original date of form .... Survey date .... Survey by ....

Where explanations are necessary, use reverse side of this form. Indicate item number.

1. General purpose of form? ....

....

2. Is this form absolutely necessary? Yes ☐ No ☐
3. Can some other form be used? Yes ☐ No ☐
4. Can this form be combined with another? Yes ☐ No ☐ If so, Form No. ....
5. What other forms are used in conjunction with it? Form Nos. ....

   Information taken from Nos. .... Transcribed to Nos. ....
6. Has this form been checked by actual users of it in all departments on following points? Yes ☐ No ☐

TEXT

7. Does title clearly indicate purpose? Yes ☐ No ☐
8. Are instructions and text clear? Yes ☐ No ☐
9. Are all included items necessary? Yes ☐ No ☐
10. Are all necessary items included? Yes ☐ No ☐
11. Is arrangement in sequence with operations? Yes ☐ No ☐
12. With related forms? Yes ☐ No ☐
13. Are all recurring items printed with variables only to be filled in? Yes ☐ No ☐

DESIGN

14. Are spaces ample for entries? Yes ☐ No ☐
15. Are adequate margins provided? Yes ☐ No ☐
16. Lines properly spaced for typing? Yes ☐ No ☐
17. For other office machine use? Yes ☐ No ☐
18. Is appearance pleasing and orderly? Yes ☐ No ☐
19. Consistent with standard styles? Yes ☐ No ☐
20. Can multiple copies of this form be printed from same type or plate without charge? Yes ☐ No ☐

PAPER STOCK

21. Is grade right for the life of form? Yes ☐ No ☐
    Folding? Yes ☐ No ☐
    Handling? Yes ☐ No ☐
22. Is weight right for handling? Yes ☐ No ☐
    No. of copies? Yes ☐ No ☐
    Machines? Yes ☐ No ☐
23. Is size right for cutting without waste? Yes ☐ No ☐
    Fitting standard office equipment? Yes ☐ No ☐
    Fitting standard envelope? Yes ☐ No ☐
    Proper information? Yes ☐ No ☐
    Appearance? Yes ☐ No ☐

PRODUCTION

24. What quantity is used? Monthly.......... Quarterly.......... Annually...........
25. Where is this form stocked?...........What quantity should be maintained?..........
26. Who should be contacted for reorder or revision? ....

CONCLUSION:................. APPROVED BY................. DATE................

Hawthorne Paper Company

Fig. 16-2

Forms Design Check Sheet

Fig. 16-3

HAMMERMILL FORM ORDER SHEET • PART 1

FORM PLANNING CHECK LIST

A quick and easy method of checking the efficiency and economy of any form — new or old — before placing your printing order. Read the text at the bottom of this sheet.

NECESSITY	OK	?
1 Has the entire system been checked and would a written procedure for the use of this form help put it into more efficient operation?		
2 Are all copies of the form or report necessary?		
3 Have the actual users of this form been consulted for suggested improvements, additional requirements and possible eliminations?		
4 Can the data furnished by this form be combined with some other form or can some other form be eliminated or consolidated with it?		
5 Has everyone responsible for the form or the form system approved it?		

PURPOSE	OK	?
6 If form is to be sent from one person to another, are proper spaces for "to" and "from" provided?		
7 Will routing or handling instructions printed on each copy be helpful?		
8 Should this form be consecutively numbered, or have a place for inserting a number?		
9 If this is an Outside Contact Form, should it be designed to mail in a window envelope?		
10 If this form is to take information from, or pass information to, another form, do both have the same sequence of items?		
11 Have we taken into consideration the number of forms which will be used in a given time (4 to 12 months) — the possibility of changes, and how long the form will remain in use?		

SIZE AND ARRANGEMENT	OK	?
12 Is the size right for filing, attention value, ample room for information and to cut without waste?		
13 Is all recurring information being printed so that only variable items need be filled in?		
14 Has space been provided for a signature?		
15 Is spacing correct for handwriting or typewriting? (The Hammermill Form Layout Sheet will help check this.)		
16 Are the most important items, which should be seen first, prominently placed? (Near the top, if practicable.)		

WORDING	OK	?
17 Does the form, by title and arrangement, clearly indicate its purpose?		
18 Is there a proper space for the date?		
19 Is the form identified by company name and firm name or code number to aid reordering?		
20 If this is a revised form, can it be distinguished from the previous form?		

PAPER AND PRINTING (*Specifications*)	OK	?
21 Should the form be on colored paper to speed up writing, distribution, sorting and filing; to designate departments or branch offices; to indicate days, months or years; to distinguish manifold copies; to identify rush orders?		
22 Have we specified paper which will be thoroughly satisfactory, economical enough for form use, consistent in performance and surely available for later reorders?		
23 Is proper weight of paper used for original and each carbon copy? (Bond Substances 13, 16 and 20. Ledger Substances 24, 28 and 32. Mimeo-Bond Substances 16 and 20. Spirit and Gelatin Duplicator Substances 16 and 20.)		
24 Are detailed specifications complete? (Paper, type, ink, rules, punch, perforate, score, fold, gather, pad, carbon sheet, stitch, etc.)		
25 Can other forms, printed on the same paper as this one, be ordered now to reduce production costs?		
26 Have requirements been estimated correctly and is the quantity to be ordered most economical? (Consider probability of revision and rate of use.)		

Pt. #	REMARKS *ON POINTS QUESTIONED (?)*

Date________________19____ Signed____________________

HOW TO USE THIS FORM

Run through this list and appraise a new or revamped form point by point with an initial (rather than a check mark) either in the column headed "OK" or "?." This will help in working out the most efficient form size and specifications and the best working arrangement of items and copy.

Points marked (?) for further study can then be appraised systematically and discussed with those who will regularly use the form. Findings and further details can be elaborated upon in the column for "Remarks" at bottom of the second column.

To pin down responsibility, the person or persons giving the final OK should place their initials opposite the remarks. The whole Check List should be filed with a copy of the form for future reference.

Hammermill Paper Company

Hammermill Form Planning Checklist

studied and revised this form extensively so that in its final form it illustrates the essentials of good forms design. Because of this fact, the form promotes economy, efficiency, and convenience. By studying this form carefully, many points of good design can be noted. Here, 15 items that make this form a good one are discussed: [1]

1. The size 5½" x 8½" cuts without waste from standard-size printing sheets. (The illustration in Figure 16-4 has been

COPY FOR
President
Sec.-Treas.
Comptroller
Cashier
Chief Acct.

DATE

REPORT OF CASH

CASH	TO-DAY	MONTH TO DATE
Received		
Disbursed		

LOCATION OF FUNDS

CITY	BANK	AMOUNT ON DEPOSIT
Chicago	First National Bank Harris Trust & Savings Bank Northern Trust Company	
Evansville	Citizens National Bank National City Bank Old National Bank	
Los Angeles	National Bank of Commerce	
New York	Bank of Manhattan Company Central Hanover Bank Chase National Bank First National Bank National City Bank	
St. Louis	Central Union Bank First National Bank	
	TOTAL—CASH IN BANKS TOTAL—CASH ON HAND PETTY CASH FUNDS GRAND TOTAL CASH	

MEMO

AC-1246 ACCOUNTING DEPARTMENT

BY____________________

Hammermill Paper Company

Fig. 16-4

An Example of Good Forms Design

[1] With permission of the Hammermill Paper Company.

reduced to fit the textbook page; thus, this point cannot be observed on the reproduced form.)

2. An original and four copies of this form are prepared. Therefore, substance 16 bond is used to permit legibly typed carbon copies. (This point cannot be observed in Figure 16-4.)
3. The firm name and address do not appear on the form. For internal forms such as this, such company information is unnecessary and space consuming.
4. The titles of all executives who may receive a copy of the form are printed in the upper left corner. The distribution of each copy is indicated by placing a check mark in the appropriate box alongside the executive's title. An alternate plan would be to print on each copy the title of the executive to receive a copy. Also, by using a different color paper for each copy, the forms can be identified and distributed promptly.
5. Double horizontal rules are used at the top and bottom of each box section. The vertical rules are of a different weight so that the form is divided into logical sections. This makes for easier reading and rapid comprehension of the facts presented.
6. The type selected is easy to read but is not so large as to draw attention from the more important typewritten or handwritten information.
7. All rules are unbroken and clean. Careful craftsmanship makes the form neat and easy to read. Neat forms encourage neatness by the users.
8. The horizontal lines are spaced six to the inch, vertically, to match typewriter requirements, thus saving typing time. Otherwise, the typewriter would have to be adjusted for each line.
9. No horizontal rules are used for recording amounts, since such lines are confusing on most typewritten forms. In order to make reading easier on very wide forms, faint horizontal rules may be used as a guide for the eye.
10. The banks are grouped by cities and the cities are listed alphabetically. This permits a quick analysis of the funds in each location.
11. The side margins have been kept narrow to provide all available space for actual use.
12. Additional spaces are provided for extra bank names, when needed.
13. Space for writing memos by the executives concerned is provided. The bank officers frequently make such notes; if a

place is provided for this writing, illegible scribbling is reduced.

14. The form bears a proper and readable number to facilitate reordering, handling, and storage.
15. Ample space has been provided for the signature of the officer issuing the form.

KINDS OF OFFICE FORMS

The most commonly used type of office form is the printed single sheet of paper. This form is usually designed by the user and printed by the company's printing department or by a local printer or purchased in ready-made form from a stationery dealer. In addition to this type of form, several other kinds have been developed for processing data by hand and by means of automated equipment. In the design of each kind of form, one of the major aims is to plan for one initial recording of all the data that will be used repeatedly in later data processing operations.

Carbonless and Carbon-Coated Forms

The type of form used and the equipment with which it is used determine the method of obtaining copies. Modern technology has developed many and varied paper treatments that permit impressions from copy to copy without the use of carbon. The image is made when special coatings on the back of one sheet and the face of the following sheet are brought together under pressure. Carbonless paper can be used in business machines to obtain up to eight legible copies; by hand, up to five copies may be produced.

Developments in "clean-image" materials and carbons make possible the coating of the entire back of each copy with a substance that will transfer the image to the face of the subsequent copy. Thus, by eliminating the bulk of the carbon paper tissue, it is possible to obtain more copies in one writing. By carbon coating only certain areas or spots on each copy, confidential or unneeded information will not be readable on each subsequent copy of the form.

Practically every kind of business form—from a simple bank deposit slip to highly complex continuous forms—can be manufactured without the use of carbon paper or by "spot" carbon coating as desired by the forms designer. One manufacturer of carbonless business forms offers the following advantages to the user:

1. No smearing or smudging of copies.
2. No soiling of hands or clothing.
3. No time-consuming fussing with insertion or removal of carbons.
4. No need to dispose of used carbon sheets.
5. Erasures are easily detected.

Each of these advantages is of major importance to the business forms user. Smearing and smudging, for example, become a serious problem when forms are handled many times, as in certain accounting procedures. Shuffling flimsy carbon paper is not only hand-soiling but time-consuming as well. With today's high clerical costs, lost time is the same as lost money. In many government offices, security requires the burning of used carbon paper. Since carbonless forms use no carbon of any kind, this problem is eliminated. Finally, because of its chemical coatings, carbonless paper cannot be erased without detection. Improper or excessive erasures that tend to remove the chemical coatings prevent retyping of information in this area because of the absence of the chemical coating. In many business firms this may be an important safety feature.

Two costs often overlooked in planning the purchase of forms are the transportation cost from the forms manufacturer's plant and the cost of storing the forms. Since carbonless papers weigh less and bulk less, some economy is to be realized from their use, as shown in Table 16-3. In this table the differences between a 4-part carbon interleaved form and a 4-part carbonless form are compared. This comparison is based upon a 14⅞″ x 11″ form, a standard arrangement of 15 lb. papers with lightweight 7 lb. carbons, and a popularly used type of carbonless paper.

SAVINGS IN WEIGHT AND VOLUME REALIZED FROM USE OF CARBONLESS FORMS

Table 16-3

Weight and Volume	4-Part Forms—Size 14⅞ x 11		
	Carbon Interleaved	Carbonless Paper	Saving
Weight per M	69 lbs.	63 lbs.	**6 lbs.**
Weight—10M forms	690 lbs.	630 lbs.	**60 lbs.**
Weight—100M forms	6900 lbs.	6300 lbs.	**600 lbs.**
Volume per M	1.68 cu. ft.	1.47 cu. ft.	**.21 cu. ft.**
Volume—10M forms	16.8 cu. ft.	14.7 cu. ft.	**2.1 cu. ft.**
Volume—100M forms	168.0 cu. ft.	147.0 cu. ft.	**21.0 cu. ft.**

Autographic Business Forms, Inc.

Continuous Forms

Printed forms, such as invoices and special accounting forms, are sometimes printed and supplied in multiple strips; that is, the forms make up a series that comes in multiple-copy sets arranged in proper numeric order. The principle underlying the use of such continuous forms is based upon the automatic feeding of prearranged sheets. The greater the number of copies to be made of a business transaction at any one time, the greater the advantage and economy of using forms in a prearranged series.

Two kinds of continuous forms are in use—the fanfold and the separate strip form. The *fanfold form* has alternate edges that are held together, without pasting or stapling, for subsequent handling. The *separate strip form* is composed of sheets that are printed and arranged separately in long strips, but the multicopies are not attached to each other.

The use of continuous forms saves the time of employees concerned with their completion. The greater the number of copies to be made at any one given time, the greater the savings in the worker's time. Any comparison must therefore consider the usual manual operations of collecting, inserting, removing, and separating the sheets when a noncontinuous form is used as compared with the continuous feed forms. This savings in operations is then multiplied by the number of copies to be made.

The manufacturers of continuous forms have had time-study engineers make stopwatch studies comparing the time used for completing loose, unassembled forms with the time required for using continuous forms with loose carbons. As shown in Table 16-4, their results point up the wasted time caused by inserting carbons between sheets, jogging into alignment, inserting in the typewriters, straightening in the machines, removing from the machines, and taking out the carbons.

WASTE SECONDS AND UNPRODUCTIVE SALARY COSTS FOR EACH SET OF FORMS

Number of Parts to Each Set	Seconds Wasted	Weekly Salary—40 Hours		
		$120	$140	$144
2	14	10.56	12.16	12.72
4	32	24.24	28.12	29.04
6	50	37.84	44.16	45.44
10	85	64.32	75.08	77.20
12	102.5	77.60	90.56	93.20

Table 16-4

The wasted time can be translated into the dollars and cents cost of unproductive labor as shown in Table 16-4. Based upon a 40-hour week, with allowance for small waste from the use of fanfold forms, the cost is given at three salary levels for every 1,000 forms, under the assumption that 1,000 sets of forms are prepared during the week.

Against the savings to be realized from the use of continuous forms must be charged the cost of a continuous forms machine and the higher cost of forms printed in continuous sets. For some types of continuous forms work, a simple $25 attachment to the typewriter can be used. In other types of continuous forms work, a special fanfold arrangement must be purchased and attached to the machine. This device may cost at least $200. If the cost is prorated over the life of the machine, however, the machine cost is negligible. Therefore, the savings effected through decreasing the time spent by employees in preparing the form must be compared with the higher cost of the continuous forms used, before arriving at a decision as to which kind of office forms should be used.

Comparatively speaking, for forms having the same printed matter, the continuous forms are slightly more costly than those that come unassembled. However, use of continuous multiple forms frequently brings about an improved system so that more copies of a form may be prepared and used, thus avoiding the necessity of having several persons prepare closely allied forms. For example, before one firm installed its punched-card accounting system, an order clerk prepared an acknowledgment of each order. Subsequently, the shipping department prepared the original bills of lading, the memorandum copy of the bill of lading, and the shipping order. Finally, the invoicing department prepared a series of four invoices. After a study of the system and slight modification of the forms, it was possible to prepare in one writing all nine copies, thus saving the time of the order clerk and the shipping department clerk. As emphasized before, the more copies that can be made in one writing, the greater the savings to be realized from the use of continuous forms.

Unit-Set Snap-Out Forms

Many firms use unit-set forms instead of continuous forms because more copies can be made simultaneously and some of the copies may be longer or shorter than others. Using longer and shorter copies permits the deletion of material from some of the copies. Unit-set forms, such as those shown in Figure 16-5, may

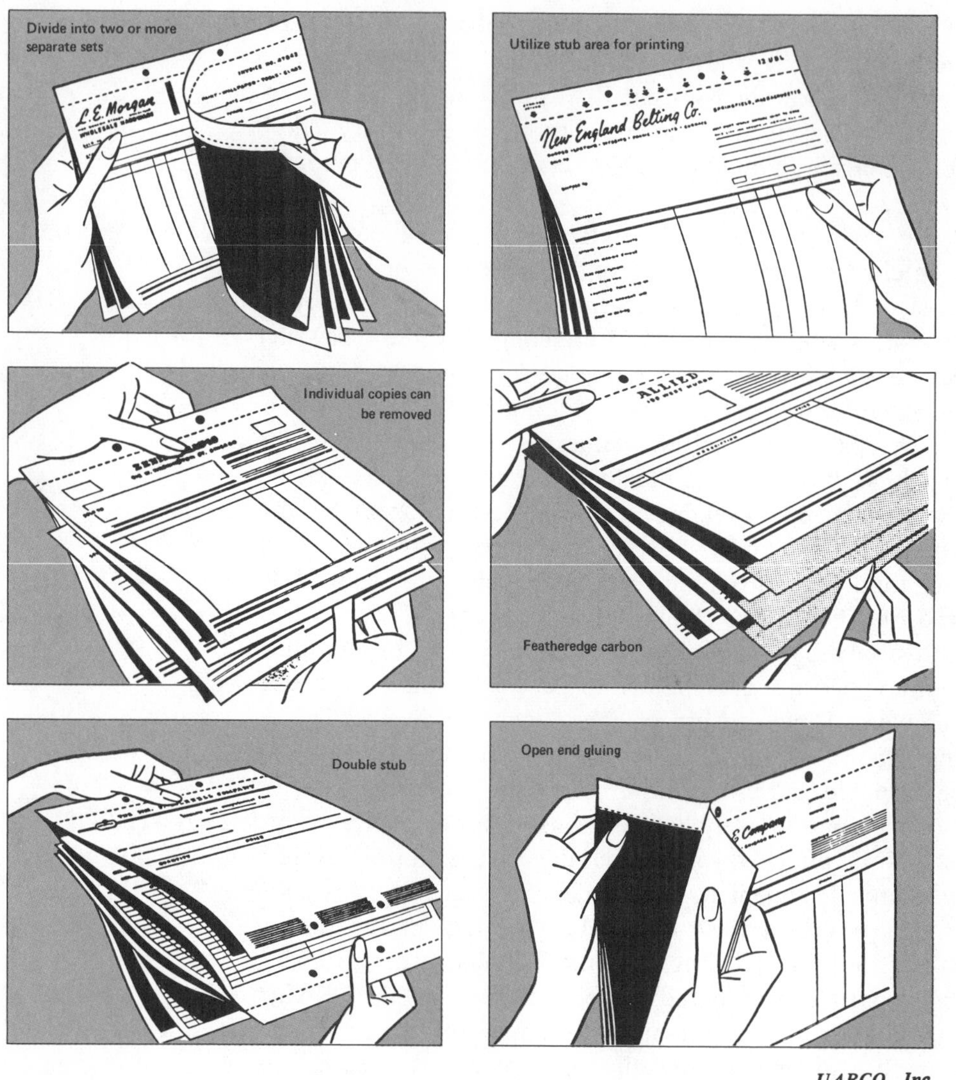

Fig. 16-5

UARCO, Inc.

Unit-Set Snap-Out Forms

be assembled with one-time carbon and a snap-out margin that permits easy removal of the carbons. Or the unit sets may be constructed using carbonless or carbon-coated papers. The forms are specialized and expensive to print, but are justified by the tremendous savings effected in the typist's time. An illustration of the percent of time saved from the use of snap-out forms is indicated in Table 16-5.

TIME SAVED USING SNAP-OUT FORMS

Table 16-5

Number of Parts in the Form	For Average of Five Lines of Typing	For Average of Ten Lines of Typing	For Average of Fifteen Lines of Typing
2	38%	23%	17%
4	55%	38%	30%
6	64%	47%	37%
8	70%	54%	45%
10	74%	59%	50%

UARCO, Inc.

Two-Wide Forms

The technique of printing two-wide forms has been used for many years. By means of this technique, a form, such as the statement of account shown in Figure 16-6, can be printed for each of two different customers or individuals at the same time. It was not until the introduction of the computer-controlled output printer that flexibility was provided in the printing of data at great speeds on

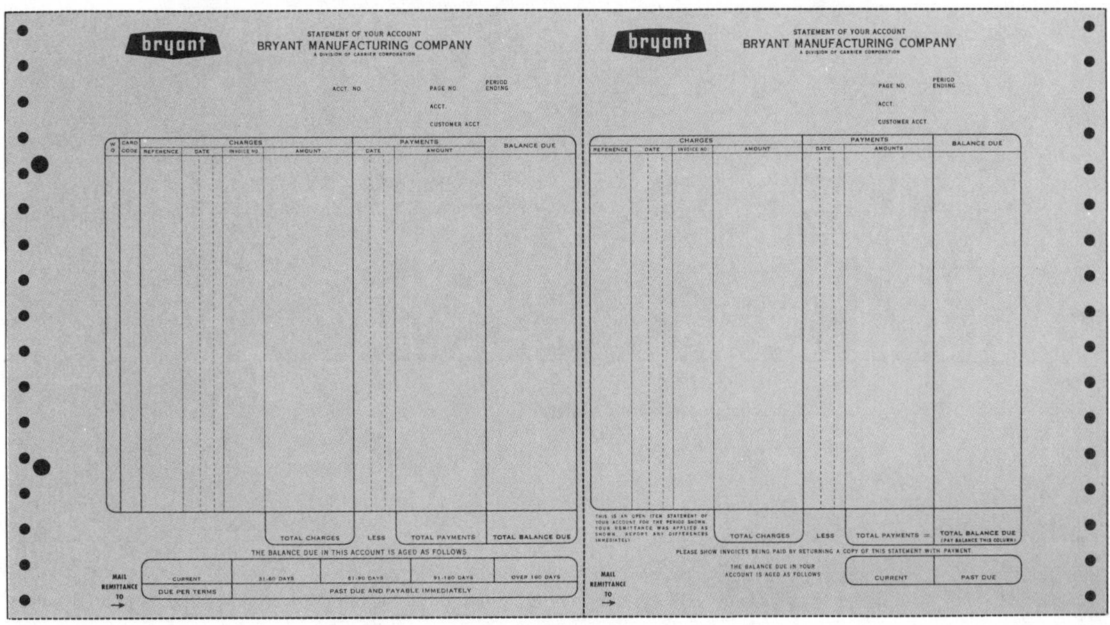

bryant
STATEMENT OF YOUR ACCOUNT
BRYANT MANUFACTURING COMPANY
A DIVISION OF CARRIER CORPORATION
ACCT. NO. PAGE NO. PERIOD ENDING
ACCT.
CUSTOMER ACCT.

W O	CARD CODE	CHARGES REFERENCE	DATE	INVOICE NO.	AMOUNT	PAYMENTS DATE	AMOUNT	BALANCE DUE

TOTAL CHARGES LESS TOTAL PAYMENTS TOTAL BALANCE DUE
THE BALANCE DUE IN THIS ACCOUNT IS AGED AS FOLLOWS
MAIL REMITTANCE TO →

CURRENT	31-60 DAYS	61-90 DAYS	91-180 DAYS	OVER 180 DAYS
DUE PER TERMS	PAST DUE AND PAYABLE IMMEDIATELY			

bryant
STATEMENT OF YOUR ACCOUNT
BRYANT MANUFACTURING COMPANY
A DIVISION OF CARRIER CORPORATION
PAGE NO. PERIOD ENDING
ACCT.
CUSTOMER ACCT.

CHARGES REFERENCE	DATE	INVOICE NO.	AMOUNT	PAYMENTS DATE	AMOUNTS	BALANCE DUE

THIS IS AN OPEN ITEM STATEMENT OF YOUR ACCOUNT FOR THE PERIOD SHOWN. YOUR REMITTANCE WAS APPLIED AS SHOWN. REPORT ANY DIFFERENCES IMMEDIATELY
TOTAL CHARGES LESS TOTAL PAYMENTS = TOTAL BALANCE DUE (PAY BALANCE THIS COLUMN)
PLEASE SHOW INVOICES BEING PAID BY RETURNING A COPY OF THIS STATEMENT WITH PAYMENT
THE BALANCE DUE IN YOUR ACCOUNT IS AGED AS FOLLOWS
MAIL REMITTANCE TO →

CURRENT	PAST DUE

Fig. 16-6

Two-Wide Forms

two-wide forms, however. With a computer-programmed output printer, two-wide forms can be printed for many different types of data processing applications. The simultaneous printing of two-wide forms, such as the payroll check and the employee's earnings statement, has greatly increased printer output and resulted in significant forms economies. In addition to printing economy, the forms handling costs after machine processing are significantly reduced.

Tab Card Forms

As shown in Figure 16-7, tab card (punched card) forms are available (a) in continuous form (one- or two-wide) for high-speed continuous writing in single or multiple copy, (b) in tab card sets with a side stub, (c) in single tab card form, and (d) in piggyback form which provides a means for automating those applications requiring added form space for recording supporting data.

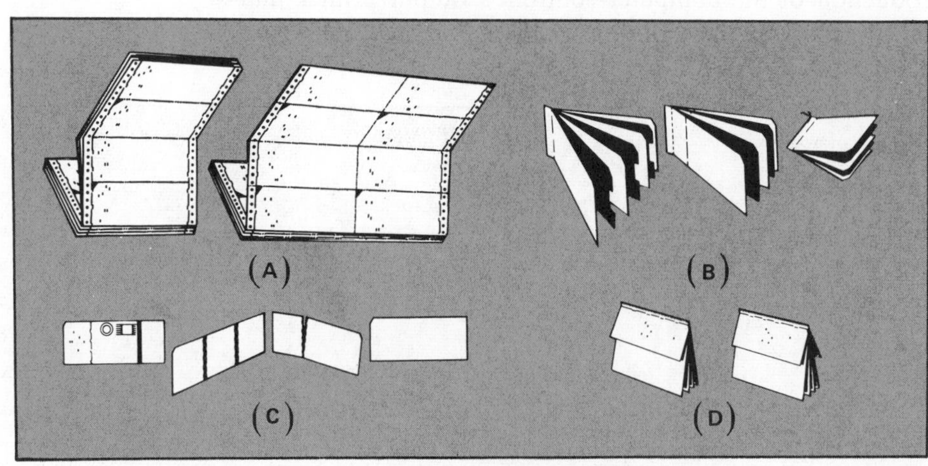

Fig. 16-7

Tab Card Forms

MICR and OCR Forms

MICR (Magnetic Ink Character Recognition) is a system used by banks to sort and process numeric data that have been recorded in special magnetic ink characters on checks and other business papers. Automatic equipment is used to sort, read, and transmit to a computer the data printed on the business forms. *OCR (Optical*

Character Recognition) is a system of reading numeric and alphabetic data that have been printed in a distinctive type style on business forms and records. As each character is read from the business document, it is translated into electrical impulses that are transmitted to the computer for processing. The development of MICR and OCR equipment was dependent upon the ability of the forms industry to provide printed forms that the machines could read. The printing of such forms requires precision manufacturing equipment and quality papers and inks. Sample forms upon which magnetic and optical characters appear are illustrated in Figure 16-8.

Optical readers have been developed that can also scan and read handwritten data to a limited degree. One type of optical scanner can read handwritten numbers and pencil-written marks in predefined areas on business forms for direct feeding into and processing of the data by a computer.

Fig. 16-8

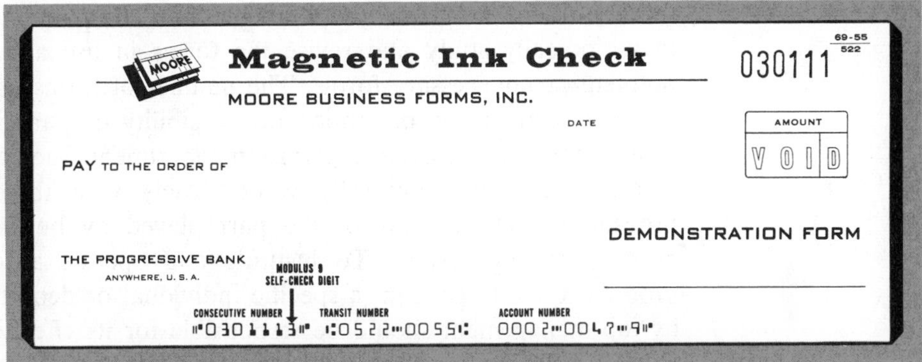

MOORE

Magnetic Ink Check

030111

69-55
522

MOORE BUSINESS FORMS, INC.

DATE

AMOUNT

VOID

PAY TO THE ORDER OF

DEMONSTRATION FORM

THE PROGRESSIVE BANK
ANYWHERE, U. S. A.

MODULUS 9
SELF-CHECK DIGIT

CONSECUTIVE NUMBER TRANSIT NUMBER ACCOUNT NUMBER

⑈0301113⑈ ⑆0522⑉0055⑆ 0002⑉0047⑉9⑈

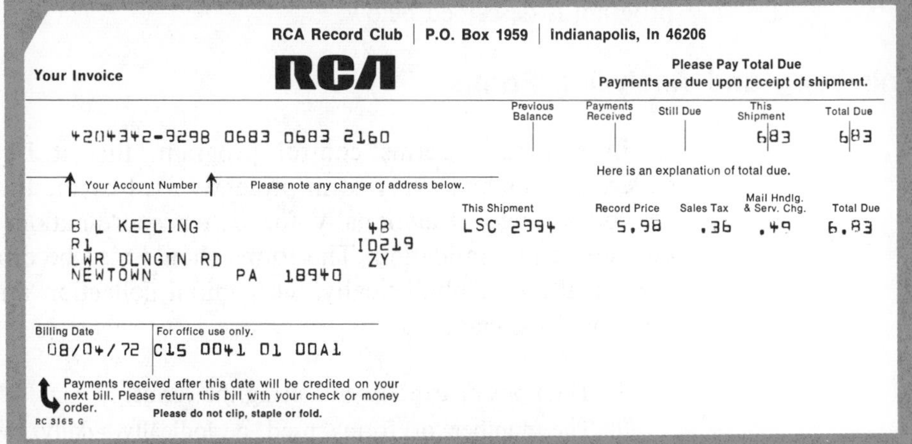

RCA Record Club | P.O. Box 1959 | Indianapolis, In 46206

Your Invoice

RCA

Please Pay Total Due
Payments are due upon receipt of shipment.

	Previous Balance	Payments Received	Still Due	This Shipment	Total Due
4204342-9298 0683 0683 2160				6 83	6 83

Your Account Number

Please note any change of address below.

Here is an explanation of total due.

This Shipment	Record Price	Sales Tax	Mail Hndlg. & Serv. Chg.	Total Due
LSC 2994	5.98	.36	.49	6.83

B L KEELING 4B
R1 10219
LWR DLNGTN RD ZY
NEWTOWN PA 18940

Billing Date: 08/04/72

For office use only: C15 0041 01 00A1

Payments received after this date will be credited on your next bill. Please return this bill with your check or money order.

Please do not clip, staple or fold.

RC 3165 G

MICR and OCR Forms

THE FORMS CONTROL PROGRAM

Since business forms are an important phase of record keeping and communication and since the proliferation of forms has increased the operating costs of office work, it is the duty of the office administrator to establish a practical control system over the use of forms. A forms control program results in the elimination of unneeded forms, the design of forms for their most efficient use, the most economical distribution of the forms to avoid needless waste and expense, and an organized and continuous review of all forms. For forms control to be effective, top management must know what forms are used, the costs involved, and the inefficiencies of overlapping and duplication. Finally, top management must give its continuing support to the control program.

The nature and scope of the forms control program are influenced by the nature of the business organization and its operations, the size of the firm, and the willingness on the part of management to periodically study and revise the forms in use and to eliminate obsolete or unnecessary forms. The number of forms used daily and the cost of their use determine the feasibility of establishing a centralized forms control and supervision department. Such a department, if organized, must naturally work closely with the systems and procedures staff because of the part played by business forms in every operating system. To institute and operate a forms control program for a large firm, a specific individual or department backed by top management should be responsible for its effective operation. Each of the steps to be taken in implementing a forms control program is described below.

Collecting and Analyzing Forms

In starting a forms control program, first it is necessary to collect and analyze every form presently used by the firm. The forms can be arranged functionally for better coordination, study, combination, and elimination. The forms should also be cross-referenced numerically or alphabetically. This initial collection and analysis of forms will indicate:

1. The units or departments using the forms.
2. The number of forms used periodically—daily, weekly, or monthly.
3. The method of issuance or distribution of the forms to the users.

4. The method of preparation (machine or handwritten), the number of copies, and the routing of the copies.
5. The equipment required in preparing the forms.
6. The relationship to other forms in use.

Eliminating, Consolidating, and Standardizing Forms

The second step in a forms control program is to eliminate all nonessential forms or nonessential parts of forms, to consolidate forms where feasible, and, finally, to standardize forms. The elimination of forms requires tact by the individual responsible for forms control. By questioning individuals using the forms, it will be found that some forms should be eliminated, some redesigned, and others kept. By the use or lack of use of forms and their cost of printing and preparation, a department head will readily understand why a form should or should not be eliminated. Sometimes by slightly changing an existing form it is possible to use one form to replace several others. Such consolidation decreases the number of forms and reduces the printing costs.

The adoption of standards will systematize the work and simplify the supervision and control of the use of forms. Among the recognized standards are: (a) use of identifying numbers where sequential control is necessary as in the case of vouchers, invoices, and checks; (b) use of appropriate descriptive titles, such as acknowledgment of order, invoice, and routing slip, to avoid misuse and to facilitate operating use; (c) uniform placement of items that occur consistently on a large number of forms; (d) arrangement of items in order of preparation and in order of observation or reading; and (e) footnote dates and quantities of original printing or revisions.

Initiating and Revising Forms

The third step in forms control requires a definite procedure for initiating all new forms and for the revision of presently used forms that are about to be reprinted. As indicated previously, such a procedure must take into consideration the systems department, the department requiring the form, and the forms control administrator. A procedure sometimes followed by a large company for achieving the efficient operation of this phase of control includes (a) a formal written request for a new form or a revised form, (b) a central control log showing the date and nature of the request and its ultimate disposition, and (c) the preparation and issuance of the accepted form.

Printing the Forms

The fourth step in an effective forms control program requires a constant study of the most economic quantity of the form to be printed and stocked at any given time. This decision is influenced by the rate of use and the possibility of future revisions, as offset by the fact that the larger the quantity printed, the lower the cost.

APPLIED FORMS CONTROL

Forms control may or may not be combined with office systems and procedures analysis, as explained in the preceding chapter. Usually, however, the two go together, for a change in forms may involve a change in procedure. It all adds up to the same thing—less cost for doing the work more accurately and more quickly. The following illustrations are but a few examples of the potential savings to be realized by firms having an effective forms control program.

In a study of its purchasing procedures, a university in New York City found that more than 75,000 purchase orders were issued each year and that approximately 80 percent of these involved amounts of $100 or less. It became apparent that the clerical effort expended was definitely out of proportion to the amount of money being controlled. It was decided to combine a check and a purchase order into one form so that the supplier could be paid at the same time the order was placed. The new purchase order form which is used for all purchases of $100 or less enables the university to reduce its key-punching time and the use of tabulating cards by 75 percent, to eliminate checkwriting through the combined writing of the check and the purchase order, to reduce the overall accounting time, and to receive additional discounts given by suppliers who are, in effect, receiving cash often before the merchandise is shipped.

One large airline, by studying the forms and the procedure followed in issuing passenger tickets, was able to save $60,000. This saving was brought about by abolishing 78 ticket forms and reducing the time for issuing tickets from five to fifteen minutes to one minute or less.

One corporation redesigned four sets of forms, each previously written separately, into a single form which in one writing produced a label, an invoice, an acknowledgment, and production records. The savings in dollars was tremendous, even though the newly designed forms cost more for each set. This change also involved a slight modification in office procedures and the elimination of three workers.

A manufacturer of archery supplies, by using a seven-copy, snap-out form with one-time carbon, was able to send out invoices to customers one day earlier. Here, forms were combined for completion in one writing, thus further simplifying the office routine.

One large textile manufacturer, by continuously studying its sales and shipping forms over a period of more than 12 years, was able to develop and use a form that consolidated into a single writing all the forms and records that formerly required 16 separate operations. The form was almost too cumbersome to be used efficiently, but with electric typewriters it proved very worthwhile and economical.

By having a specialist in charge of all forms design and analysis, one firm was able to reduce by 35 percent the cost of the printing and the use of 750,000 tags. Similarly, the incorrect specification of 20 lb. paper for a form that was to be prepared in seven copies almost caused an expensive mistake in this office.

One manufacturer formerly prepared 16 different forms before starting any factory production orders. A redesign of the entire system enabled the company to concentrate into three forms all the information needed for complete control of production processes. This revision and reduction in costs was possible only after management realized that the number of its forms had grown without plan or control.

Another firm that felt the debilitating effects of "formitis" examined its entire array of 3,000 forms and was able to eliminate more than 1,500 of them because of unnecessary duplication, obsolescence, and even lack of use or purpose. The saving in filing space and personnel costs and the expediting of office work were tremendous.

In a case study of "There's Money in Forms Control," the vice president in charge of finance of a large manufacturing concern, realizing that the cost of processing a form is 20 to 30 times the cost of the form itself, issued this communication before starting a forms control program: [2]

> The cost of forms used in administering, recording, and reporting company affairs amounts to several million dollars annually. The intangible costs of using or processing forms . . . adds many times the initial cost.

---

[2] Ford Motor Company, as reported in *American Business* by D. W. Baird.

It is believed that considerable savings and increased efficiency of our operations can be accomplished with company-wide forms control.

The results of this control program in the 12-month period of its use were:

325 company-wide forms were revised and improved.
165 company-wide forms were added, and 144 were discontinued.
1,661 division-wide forms were revised and improved; 3,112 were added and 4,020 were discontinued.

QUESTIONS FOR REVIEW

1. What are the three principles of forms design and control with which the administrative manager should be familiar?
2. Explain what is meant by standardization of business forms.
3. What factors should be studied before the *size* of a form is determined?
4. Describe briefly the main types of paper that make up the commercial writing class.
5. Why is grain direction important in the design of office forms to be used on automatic machines?
6. In what ways may copies of forms be identified for the purposes of sorting and distributing to the proper departments?
7. What is a *carbonless* business form? What are the advantages of its use?
8. What are continuous forms? For what kinds of work can the use of continuous forms be justified?
9. What steps should be taken in implementing a forms control program?

QUESTIONS FOR DISCUSSION

1. What qualifications would you look for in selecting a supervisor for the forms control program?
2. If you were appointed supervisor of a forms control program, what preliminary and operating prerequisites would you plan? What basic questions would you ask in making a functional analysis of the business forms in your firm?
3. It has been stated that the chief savings in the use of multicopy forms is not in the cost of the paper or the forms, but in other kinds of savings. Explain.

4. Should the development of a new office form begin with the *author* of the form or with the *designer* of the form? Why?

5. Even though reports are necessary, there is a tendency for many managers to request more reports than necessary in their decision-making processes. Some of the reports are marginal and constitute a wasteful burden on business operations. Discuss how the administrative office manager can improve the reporting phase of his firm's operations.

6. The Elgin Clothing Company, manufacturers of men's wearing apparel, is presently using four forms to complete an order. Each form is prepared separately. These forms are:

   a. Shipping Label—one copy to be attached to express package or parcel post package.
   b. Invoice—prepared in quadruplicate in billing department.
   c. Packing Slip and Shipping Memo—numbered consecutively and prepared in triplicate by the shipping department.
   d. Receiving Memo—made out in duplicate in the invoice department.

   After considerable discussion with manufacturers of business forms, the office manager feels that all four forms can be prepared in continuous fanfold form and numbered consecutively so that they can be completed in one single writing. You are asked to discuss the design of such a form and to prepare a rough sketch of a suitable form which will then be turned over to the drafting department for final preparation.

7. The invoice form shown in Figure A on page 524 has been handed to you for criticism and suggestions for improvement. The actual size of the form is 7 x 9 inches. Using the principles of forms design that are presented in this chapter, indicate the good and poor features of this form.

8. A forms manufacturer has given you completed artwork for the invoice form illustrated in Figure B, page 525. Prior to releasing the form for printing, you want to give the layout a critical inspection. The actual size of the invoice is 7¼ x 10½ inches. Five copies of the form are to be completed in one writing for each shipment. The copies are to be identified by means of red type at the bottom of the form as follows: (1) Original Copy, (2) Duplicate Invoice, (3) Remittance Copy, (4) Numerical File Copy, and (5) Alphabetical File Copy. Each copy is to be printed on a different color of paper stock. Invoice numbers beginning with 0001 will be preprinted in red at the time of printing.

   Examine the form carefully and indicate whether or not there are any last-minute changes that should be made before the artwork is released for printing.

Jongeward Presentation Company

13 Walnut Avenue, Grand Rapids, Michigan 49502

ORDER NO. DATE

SHIP TO

REMIT TO:
JONGEWARD PRESENTATION COMPANY
P.O. BOX 13
GRAND RAPIDS, MICHIGAN 49502

"SOLD TO" SAME AS "SHIP TO" UNLESS OTHERWISE SPECIFIED

SOLD TO

CUSTOMER NUMBER

INVOICE NO.

F.O.B. FACTORY

S/M NO.	SALESMAN'S NAME	ZONE	CODES	PAGE NO.

SHIP VIA	TERMS

STYLE NO.	QUANITY	DESCRIPTION	UNIT PRICE	AMOUNT
		ORDER COMPLETED ☐ BALANCE TO FOLLOW ☐		

IMPORTANT: PURCHASER REPRESENTS THAT THE MERCHANDISE DESCRIBED HEREIN IS BEING PURCHASED FOR RESALE ONLY AND THAT ANY FEDERAL, STATE OR LOCAL TAXES ARE THE OBLIGATION OF THE PURCHASER.

ORIGINAL INVOICE

Fig. A

PRACTICAL OFFICE CASES

Case 16-1 Using Business Forms Efficiently

The B & G Company is one of the largest stock brokerage firms in the East. The firm has developed so many forms that it feels must be used in the efficient operation of its business that it has prepared a catalog of some 30 pages, listing alphabetically all the forms. The catalogs are used in preemployment training and are issued to employees for their guidance on the job.

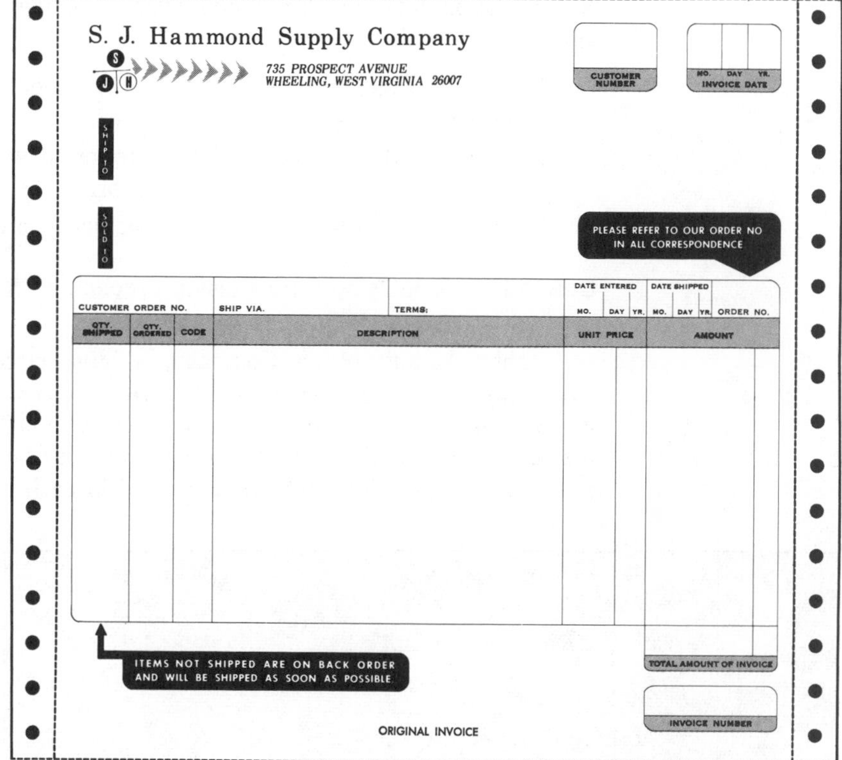

S. J. Hammond Supply Company

735 PROSPECT AVENUE
WHEELING, WEST VIRGINIA 26007

CUSTOMER NUMBER

MO. DAY YR. INVOICE DATE

SHIP TO

SOLD TO

PLEASE REFER TO OUR ORDER NO IN ALL CORRESPONDENCE

CUSTOMER ORDER NO.	SHIP VIA.	TERMS:	DATE ENTERED MO. DAY YR.	DATE SHIPPED MO. DAY YR.	ORDER NO.

QTY. SHIPPED	QTY. ORDERED	CODE	DESCRIPTION	UNIT PRICE	AMOUNT

ITEMS NOT SHIPPED ARE ON BACK ORDER AND WILL BE SHIPPED AS SOON AS POSSIBLE

TOTAL AMOUNT OF INVOICE

INVOICE NUMBER

ORIGINAL INVOICE

Fig. B

In spite of this apparently excellent training and orientation plan, numerous errors occur in the operations, with the resultant costs of expensive corrections and loss of customer goodwill. The employees complain that there are so many forms that they get confused and sometimes use the wrong form or no form at all.

■ You, as supervisor of the forms department, are asked to develop a workable plan of forms control for remedying this situation.

Case 16-2 Correcting a Faulty Forms Procedure

The Harris Company prepares 15 copies of its receiving reports. Since this seemed like an extraordinarily large number to the newly employed office administrator, he asked, "Why so many copies?" The reply was, "We always did it this way, and it seems to work even though there are extra copies. We do not want to change for fear that the extra copies will be needed."

A subsequent study made by the office administrator indicated that only six copies of the receiving report were needed, but that seven copies could be prepared in one typing.

■ On the basis of the office administrator's finding, prepare a brief report indicating:

1. The possible reasons for the initial adoption of the inefficient procedure.
2. The plan that should have been followed when first installing the procedure using the receiving report.
3. How to avoid repetition of this inefficient procedure in the future.

Case 16-3 Simplifying a Purchasing Procedure Through Forms Analysis and Design

Ashby Manufacturing Company, a large electrical hardware company, has been using the following form, prepared in triplicate, for all its purchases. Because the purchasing agent thought it was economical, a stock form carried by all stationery stores has been used. Thirty-three sets of forms (in triplicate) are contained in each pad.

FROM Ashby Manufacturing Co.
77 Wilson Boulevard
Dayton, Ohio 45429

PURCHASE ORDER
NO. 1001

CONDITIONS
1. PLACE ABOVE NUMBER ON INVOICE PACKAGES AND CORRESPONDENCE.
2. ACKNOWLEDGE ORDER AND STATE WHEN YOU WILL SHIP.
3. NO CHARGE ALLOWED FOR PACKING OR CARTAGE.

DATE 5/10 19

TO Carter Paint Co.
624 Western Avenue
Denver, Colorado 80234

PLEASE ENTER OUR ORDER AS FOLLOWS: SHIP VIA Best

QUANTITY	DESCRIPTION	PRICE	PER	AMOUNT
5	Gals. Ivory #191	2 95	gal.	14 75
1	Qt. Sample Ivory #2101	60	qt.	60
				15 35

By Victor Luce

Fig. C

Under the method used by the company, whenever a purchase order is placed, the following steps are taken:

1. **Fill in purchaser's name and address, purchase order number, and date.**
2. **Fill in the supplier's name and address and complete the purchase order.**

3. Remove 1st carbon from pad.
4. Remove 2d carbon from pad.
5. Tear off forms.
6. Replace 1st carbon in pad.
7. Replace 2d carbon in pad.
8. Enter next order number.
9. Tear stub from original copy.
10. Address envelope and insert original copy.
11. File 2d and 3d copies of purchase order until goods are received.

After a careful study of the present procedure, it has been recommended that an autographic register system be installed in which the following type of form would be used.

Fig. D

ORIGINAL

ASHBY MANUFACTURING CO.

Manufacturers

GENERAL OFFICES AND FACTORY
77 WILSON BOULEVARD DAYTON, OHIO 45429

QUALITY ELECTRICAL PRODUCTS SINCE 1903

CONDITIONS

No. 1001

1. Above order number must appear on all invoices and packages.
2. Memorandum of goods and bill of lading must be mailed to us on date of shipment.
3. This order must be acknowledged at once and a definite date of shipment stated.

PURCHASE ORDER

TO Carter Paint Co.
624 Western Avenue
Denver, Colorado 80234

DATE 5/10 19

F.O.B.

TERMS: 2% 10 DAYS NET 30 DAYS

SHIP VIA Best

PLEASE ENTER OUR ORDER AS FOLLOWS:

QUANTITY	DESCRIPTION	PRICE	PER	AMOUNT
5	Gals. Ivory #191	2 95	gal.	14 75
1	Qt. Sample Ivory #2101	60	qt.	60
				15 35

ASHBY MANUFACTURING CO. By Victor Luce Purchasing Agent

In the autographic register, continuous forms with interleaved carbon paper are to be used. Five steps are required under the new procedure:

1. Fill in the supplier's name, address, and the date, and complete the purchase order.
2. Turn the handle of the autographic register to eject the three copies of the form. (As the handle is turned, the carbon paper is wound around a roller inside the register.)
3. Tear off the copies.

4. Insert the original copy of the purchase order in a window envelope.
5. File 2d and 3d copies of purchase order until goods are received.

■ After analyzing the present and the proposed procedures and studying both forms, you are asked to:

1. Prepare a flow process chart similar to that shown in Figure 15-9, page 487, in which the present and the proposed procedures are depicted.
2. Prepare a formal report to the owners of the company in which you indicate the improvements that are expected as a result of the new procedure and the newly designed form.

17

The Mechanization of Basic Accounting Procedures

The tremendous impact of the expanded use of simple machines and electronic devices during the past few years has made the office a different kind of place in which to work. In most offices there are certain routine, repetitive operations that are performed satisfactorily through the use of basic machines and mechanical devices such as adding and calculating machines and accounting or bookkeeping machines. However, in many offices the volume of work involved in systems and procedures justifies the use of electromechanical punched-card equipment and electronic data processing equipment. In this chapter some of the more common automatic machines and equipment are described in relation to the roles they play in the simplification and mechanization of basic accounting procedures. Electromechanical machines and electronic data processing equipment will be discussed in Part 5.

Four common accounting procedures found in modern business offices relate to (1) order processing and billing as part of the accounts receivable system, (2) payroll accounting, (3) purchasing and receiving, and (4) processing vendors' invoices for payment as part of the accounts payable system. Each of these procedures may be under the supervision of the administrative office manager. A study of these procedures together with the machines that may be used will acquaint the students of administrative office management with the variety of methods used and may indicate possible changes that can be made to perform the office work more efficiently, accurately, and economically.

THE ADMINISTRATIVE OFFICE MANAGER'S ROLE IN THE MECHANIZATION OF PROCEDURES

The increased volume of office work in modern business and the resultant higher costs require that the successful office administrator become more cost conscious than ever before. He must constantly study the newer methods and equipment available for performing office work. He will probably have in his department one or more persons trained to service, operate, and maintain intricate electro-mechanical and electronic equipment. The office manager need not necessarily be an expert in the operation of these machines, but he should have a working acquaintance with them and know for which applications each kind of machine can be used most effectively and economically. This relationship with the mechanical equipment will involve the office administrator in three decisions: (a) a determination of the need for certain types of mechanical equipment; (b) a comparison of the merits and costs of the various makes of similar equipment; and (c) a determination of the advisability of purchasing or leasing the equipment. This latter decision is one of growing importance that has developed only in recent years when almost any type of equipment may be leased.

In the area of supervision, the personnel problems facing the office manager have become more challenging and varied. The characteristics and attributes of machine operators are not the same as those of other office personnel. The training and background of data-processing personnel present problems unlike those encountered elsewhere. One life insurance company spent a long time learning that the most efficient key-punch operators were girls whose educations did not take them beyond the lower high school grades. In some firms having centralized office management and control in the home office, with merely remote transmission and machine operations in the branch offices, the branch office supervisors have been placed on a higher managerial level and have entirely new responsibilities.

The rapid changes being brought about in the field of administrative office management by the newer methods, equipment, and materials involving automation necessitate that the office manager of the future be a much more responsible executive—one whose duties will require a greater amount of constant study, experimentation, and knowledge. For example, with the use of electronic computers large commercial banks and independent data processing centers will perform some of a firm's information processing at less cost and provide more effective managerial reports than if all the work were performed by the firm itself. To the individual business firm, the advantages of utilizing the services of a commercial bank or a data service center are:

1. No large investment in computers and auxiliary hardware is required by the firm.
2. The work is done accurately and expeditiously by the center.
3. There is a savings in payroll taxes and fringe benefit costs because the office staff is reduced.
4. The work can be done more economically by the center or the bank because of their skilled technical personnel who have been trained to operate the equipment.

ORDER PROCESSING AND BILLING PROCEDURES

The departments and forms used in order processing and billing procedures are determined by the nature of the business, whether it be retailing, wholesaling, or manufacturing either for direct-to-consumer sales or for sales to wholesalers. The departments usually involved are: (1) the sales order department, existing either as two separate divisions or as a single combined unit; (2) the warehouse and shipping department; and (3) the accounting and control departments. Commonly used forms are: (1) the sales order, (2) the shipping forms, (3) the sales invoice, and (4) accounting records. The forms may be prepared separately in the various departments or they may be prepared as a part of *prebilling*, whereby the customer's invoice and its copies, together with the shipping order forms, are prepared simultaneously; or there may be a combination of these two methods. The forms may be handwritten or prepared on mechanical devices, but in every instance the objective must be directed toward elimination, combination, and simplification of forms—the first three objectives of systems and procedures analysis.

Separate Order Processing and Billing Procedures

A customer may send his order to the firm on a preprinted form, the order form may be prepared by a salesman who sends the form to the office, or the order may be given by telephone to a clerk in the order department. In most firms the customer's order must be approved by the credit department, after which the order department reviews the order for completeness and verifies the shipping instructions.

When separate order processing and billing procedures are followed, separate forms are commonly prepared for the shipping order, the shipping report, and the sales invoice, as follows:

1. Shipping orders are prepared in the office and sent to the warehouse or shipping department. The number of copies prepared varies with the type of business organization and its products. As a minimum, three copies are usually prepared: the original copy and the packing slip, which are sent to the shipping department; and a file copy, which is retained in the office.

2. In the shipping department the packer prepares a separate shipping report. Three copies are ordinarily prepared: the original, which is sent to the office for pricing the shipment; the packing slip, which is included with the shipment; and a copy that is filed in the shipping department for future reference.

   Meanwhile the shipping department selects the goods ordered and prepares them for shipment. Where necessary, bills of lading may be prepared in quadruplicate. Two copies, an original and a duplicate, go to the transportation company; one copy is sent to the customer along with his invoice; and one copy is retained in the office.

3. The office (or billing department) receives a copy of the shipping report, together with a copy of the bill of lading.

   If a complete order has been shipped, the shipping order is priced and sent to a billing clerk for extension and the addition of freight and other charges where necessary. If the order was only partially filled, a "back order" or "follow-up" must be prepared to be used with the subsequent shipment, which will follow the same routine outlined above.

   Billing clerks then prepare copies of the invoices. The number of copies again is affected by the type of business and its products. Four copies are usually the minimum number—one sent to the customer, one filed for future reference, one sent to the accounting department, and one retained in the billing department.

   In the accounting department the invoice copies become the source documents for recording the sales and updating the accounts receivable ledger. If necessary, sales analyses by product, by department, by salesman, or by geographical area may be developed from the invoice copies and incorporated into the records.

Figure 17-1 illustrates this separate order processing and billing procedure.

Fig. 17-1

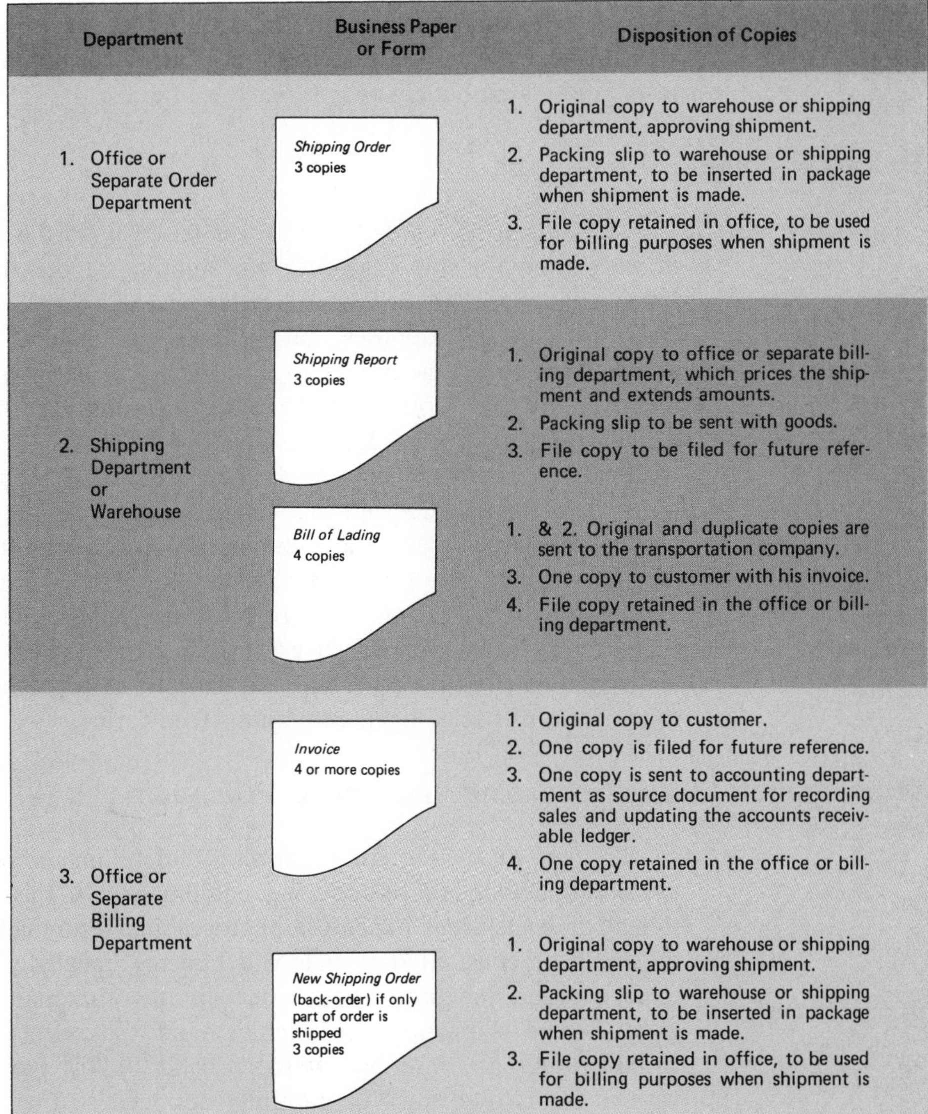

Department
Business Paper or Form
Disposition of Copies
1. Office or Separate Order Department
Shipping Order
3 copies
1. Original copy to warehouse or shipping department, approving shipment.
2. Packing slip to warehouse or shipping department, to be inserted in package when shipment is made.
3. File copy retained in office, to be used for billing purposes when shipment is made.
2. Shipping Department or Warehouse
Shipping Report
3 copies
1. Original copy to office or separate billing department, which prices the shipment and extends amounts.
2. Packing slip to be sent with goods.
3. File copy to be filed for future reference.
Bill of Lading
4 copies
1. & 2. Original and duplicate copies are sent to the transportation company.
3. One copy to customer with his invoice.
4. File copy retained in the office or billing department.
3. Office or Separate Billing Department
Invoice
4 or more copies
1. Original copy to customer.
2. One copy is filed for future reference.
3. One copy is sent to accounting department as source document for recording sales and updating the accounts receivable ledger.
4. One copy retained in the office or billing department.
New Shipping Order
(back-order) if only part of order is shipped
3 copies
1. Original copy to warehouse or shipping department, approving shipment.
2. Packing slip to warehouse or shipping department, to be inserted in package when shipment is made.
3. File copy retained in office, to be used for billing purposes when shipment is made.

Separate Order Processing and Billing Procedure

Separate order processing and billing procedures involve a large amount of duplication of effort, writing, and forms. There may be reasons for requiring such a system, however. The customer's product specifications may be complex and yet not have to be shown on the sales invoice. Many orders may not be shipped complete at one time and therefore require rather involved back-order or follow-up procedures. Sometimes the seller is permitted to substitute other merchandise for that ordered; thus, the customer's order and the sales invoice will not be identical. But a separate order processing and billing procedure must be considered inefficient except where its installation is absolutely necessary.

Unified Prebilling Procedures

The *unified prebilling procedure* is based upon the principle that in *one* writing the shipping order, the shipping report, the customer's invoice, and in some cases, the sales journal entry are prepared. This procedure presupposes that the firm has on hand the required merchandise to fill the orders so that there will be few, if any, back orders. Also, the forms must have been carefully designed so that the information can be recorded on all forms in one writing.

Sometimes the unified prebilling procedure is modified in that only the shipping order and the shipping record are prepared in one writing; the invoice and the sales journal entry are completed in a second writing. To reduce the time required in completing the various forms, most firms use forms that are preassembled with one-time carbon paper. Increased use is also being made of carbonless and carbon-coated paper in the construction of preassembled forms, in the form of packs, or in continuous feed forms.

Write-It-Once Order Processing and Billing Procedure

The *write-it-once* order processing and billing procedure makes use of duplicating or reproducing equipment. In this procedure a stencil or translucent paper for photographic reproduction contains the basic or constant data that will appear repeatedly on the customer's order, the production order (if the firm manufactures the goods before shipment), the invoice, and the sales journal. The variable data are inserted later by hand or by typewriter. The various forms used must be carefully designed so that all the same information will appear in the same location on each form; so that information which must not appear on some forms will be blocked out; and where an order is only partially filled, so that the master stencil can be reused for future completion of the transaction.

Figure 17-2 presents the order processing and billing procedure for a manufacturing concern that uses the Ditto Direct Process method of duplication. In this procedure,

1. A master stencil is prepared from the customer's order.
2. Using the stencil and the appropriate forms with areas properly blocked out so that unwanted data do not appear on certain copies, the following forms are prepared:

   Production order to manufacturing departments
   Order acknowledgment

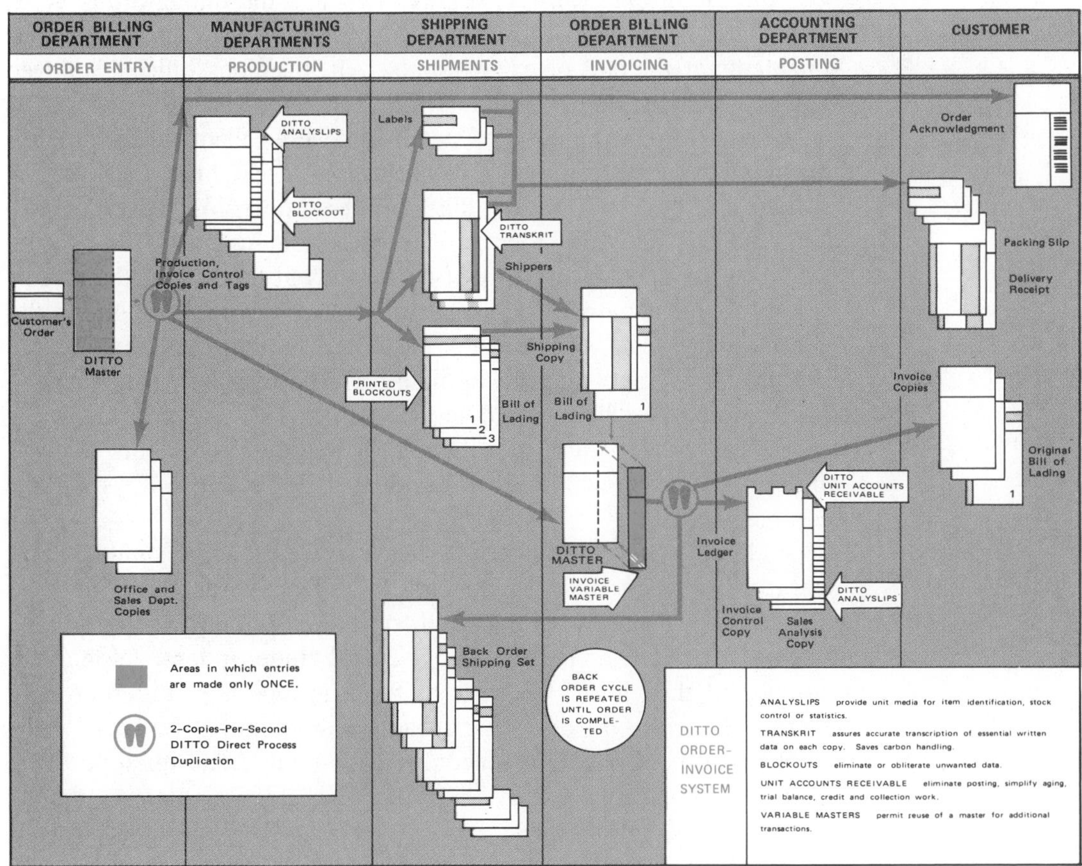

Fig. 17-2

Write-It-Once Order Processing and Billing Procedure Using Ditto Direct Process Method of Duplication

Labels for shipment
Packing slip
Bill of lading
One copy for Accounts Receivable Ledger (invoice copy)
One copy for Sales Analysis (invoice copy)
Invoice for customer

3. In the event of partial shipment, a new master stencil is prepared to cover the back order, and the procedure is repeated until the order is shipped in full.

Cycle Billing

One of the most notable improvements in billing procedures has been the use of *cycle billing*. Many years ago the public utility companies were faced with a tremendous volume of work in sending out statements at the end of each month. An ingenious office employee suggested that it would be much more efficient and also cheaper if the preparation and mailing of statements were scheduled throughout the month. As a result of this suggestion, cycle billing developed and is used today by many public utilities, retail stores, banks, telephone companies, and stock brokerage and industrial firms.

To overcome the difficulty of peak loads at the end of the month and to obtain a more uniform distribution of work throughout the month, many firms divide their customers' accounts alphabetically into groups. There may be as many as 16 or 20 groups, each of which should be about equal in size in order to balance the work among the bookkeeping personnel. Each group represents a cycle and covers certain letters of the alphabet and certain days of the month.

Following the closing day for each cycle group, a single billing operation is performed. Statements for all active accounts may be thus produced in one high-speed run. With the division of the accounts receivable ledger into several independent, alphabetic groups and the closing of each of these groups at a different time during the month, the daily work load is spread more evenly throughout the month. Collection schedules, cash intake, and all supporting operations flow more evenly.

Using an Outside Data Service Center

In small companies an adding or calculating machine is the only equipment needed in order to utilize a customer billing service and to receive an analysis of sales and accounts receivable via the electronic computer of the data service center. The data service center provides weekly or monthly reports to the small business firm and individual statements to be mailed to the company's customers. On these statements the unpaid items are listed by date and invoice number regardless of how old the unpaid items happen to be. The company is also given ledger cards that show all unpaid items by date and invoice number, and the total sales for each of the last 12 months. A weekly or monthly summary report provided by the data service center shows the aged schedule of all the accounts receivable with supplementary information, such as credit limits, and how much of the outstanding account balance is current. Special reports are also prepared that list all customers' names by volume of business with the company, sales and returns for the month and the year, and salesmen's commissions.

For providing a basic reporting system of a monthly ledger statement and an aged schedule of accounts receivable, assuming annual sales of $1 million, 1,000 customers, and 2,000 transactions a month, one data service center charges a minimum fee of $190 a month. For sales of $5 million a year, 2,500 customers, and 6,000 transactions a month, the cost is approximately $450 a month. Each special report costs about $50 extra.

Basic Computing Machines

In order processing and billing procedures, as well as in the payroll accounting procedures to be described later, several kinds of basic computing machines, such as those shown in Figure 17-3, are ordinarily used. Probably the most common type of computing machine found in the office is the *adding machine*. Although there are a number of different makes and models of adding machines on the market, the primary use of each one is for addition. Most adding machines also perform subtraction, and several models can be used for multiplication and division. A *calculating machine* performs each of the four fundamental arithmetic operations, but it is most frequently used for multiplication and division because of the speed with which it performs these operations.[1] Although most types of

[1] In the approved definitions of the American Standards Association, calculating machines are partly defined as "devices having manual means for entering numerical data and are intended primarily for multiplying/dividing; however, they may be used for adding/subtracting. There are two major classifications of these machines: printing calculating machines and nonprinting calculating machines." For further approved definitions and a report on projects in the process of being standardized, see "Office Standards: A Progress Report," *Administrative Management* (January, 1966), pp. 34-40.

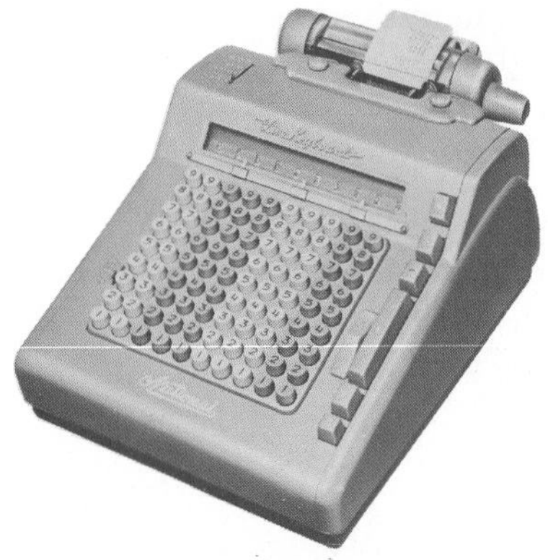

The National Cash Register Company

Full-Key Listing Machine

Victor Adding Machine Co.

Ten-Key Listing Machine

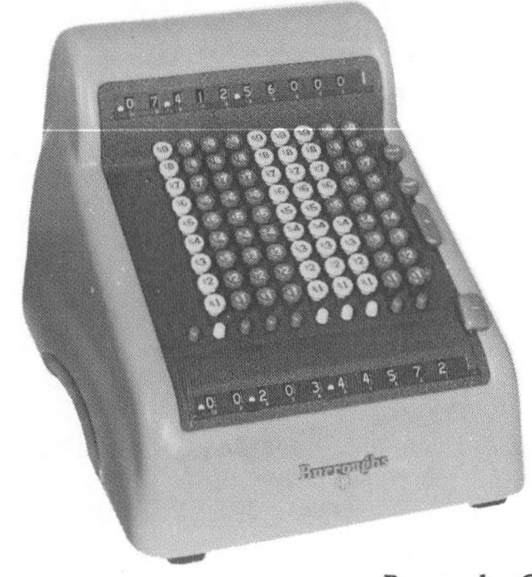

Burroughs Corporation

Key-Driven Calculator

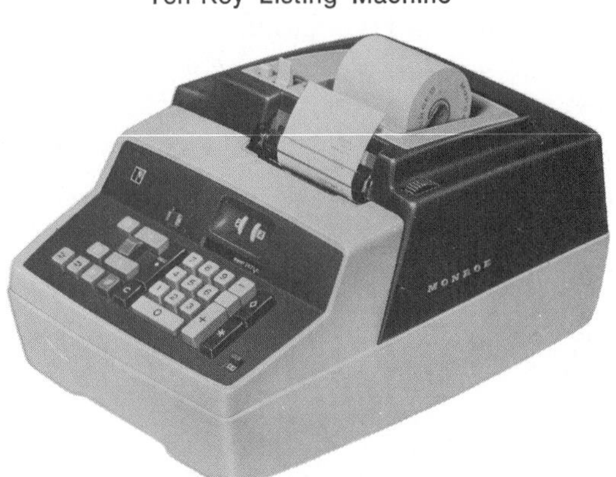

Monroe International, Inc.

Ten-Key Printing Calculator

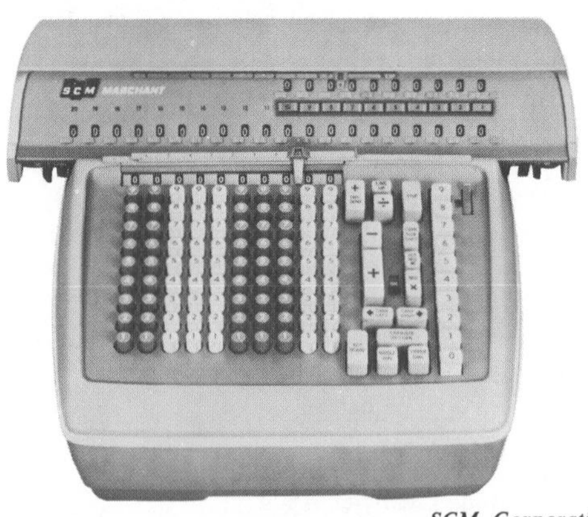

SCM Corporation

Rotary Calculator

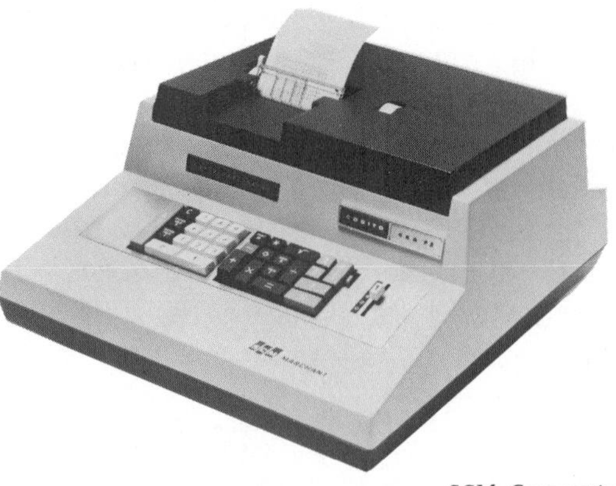

SCM Corporation

Electronic Calculator

Fig. 17-3
Basic Computing Machines

adding and calculating machines can be obtained in hand-operated as well as electrical models, the latter have become increasingly popular because of their greater speed of operation.

With the advent of automated data processing systems in the office, adding machines and calculators have become more important than ever. No matter how sophisticated the data processing system, there is a need for some basic computing machines in every office. Many of these are used to provide the input for computer systems and data processing procedures.

Adding and calculating machines may be classified as follows:

1. Listing and nonlisting.
2. Full-keyboard and ten-key.
3. Key-driven, rotary, and electronic.

Listing and Nonlisting Machines. The *listing* machine not only records the individual numbers of a problem in the register of the machine but also prints these numbers on a paper tape. Checking totals is thus simplified since the individual numbers appear on the tape. Some listing machines such as the printing calculator perform all arithmetic operations and can be used for a wide range of office problems. Many models carry a credit balance, handle fractions, do negative multiplication and automatic squaring, and carry a constant.

The *nonlisting* machine, such as the rotary calculator, records the numbers only in the register of the machine. It is claimed that the operation of such a machine is much faster than a listing machine, thus making it feasible to do the addition a second time for the purpose of checking.

Full-Keyboard and Ten-Key Machines. A *full-keyboard* machine may have from five to twenty columns of numbers, with each column containing keys from 1 to 9. A zero is printed in any column in which no number key is depressed. The machine provides full visibility of the numbers entered on the keyboard.

The *ten-key* model has a keyboard that consists of one set of keys numbered 0 through 9. The digits of a number must be entered in the order of their occurrence. Zeros must be entered whenever they occur, but some ten-key machines have double and triple zero keys that speed the entry of large numbers. The ten-key model is especially adaptable to "touch" operation and has wide application in performing operations containing many digits.

Key-Driven, Rotary, and Electronic Machines. On the *key-driven* machine, calculations are automatically performed by depressing the keys. This type of machine is nonlisting and full-keyboard. Key-driven machines are especially suitable for those problems characterized by the need for fast addition and multiplication. The *rotary* machine requires that a number be entered on the keyboard and then a motor bar or a lever be operated to record the number in the register. This type of machine may be full- or ten-key keyboard. Rotary calculators perform ordinary addition and subtraction, but they are primarily used for complex, high-speed multiplication and division problems.

The newest type of calculating equipment upon the market is the *electronic calculator,* a miniature desk-size computer that performs operations electronically rather than mechanically. The machine operates at the speed of light and is completely silent. One of the major advantages of the electronic calculator is its excellent performance as the result of no moving parts that wear out and cause inaccuracies. The electronic calculator possesses storage memories or registers that afford the ability to hold and store many different totals for continuous use in operation, thus eliminating the possibility of error in manually reentering or transferring amounts. Because of its high cost, the electronic calculator is best suited to the solution of complicated problems that require full-time use of the machine.

Some of the newer electronic machines, in addition to calculating, are capable of being programmed and of printing out the problems along with the answers. One desk-top electronic machine may be operated as an electronic printing calculator or as a completely automatic computer with the ability to follow stored instructions and to make logical decisions such as choosing between alternative courses of action.

PAYROLL ACCOUNTING PROCEDURES

Payroll accounting procedures arise in every office, and in some offices the amount of clerical and accounting effort directed toward this activity is large. With governmental agencies making increasing and more frequent demands on business firms for payroll and tax records, the time and money expended for payroll work is of vital significance to the office manager.

There are many variables in payroll accounting procedures. Some of these arise as a result of the type of business activity, and others as a result of the type of wage-payment plans, incentives, and bonuses. The payroll procedure for a life insurance company or a bank that has mostly clerical workers paid on a weekly or semimonthly basis is much simpler than that of a manufacturing concern paying some of its workers on a piece-rate basis, others on an hourly basis, and office employees on a weekly basis. Furthermore, there are certain legal requirements as to minimum wages and hours, income tax and social security deductions, and unemployment compensation and disability insurance taxes that must be taken into consideration in the preparation of payrolls. It becomes apparent that computing all the deductions and taxes, with different limitations on the amount taxable in any one year, makes the payroll procedure complicated and expensive. It also indicates that in most cases mechanical equipment must be used, for such equipment will permit simultaneous preparation of the forms and will accumulate the various totals from one pay period to the next, all automatically. Procedures such as these are particularly suited to electronic computer operations, as described in Chapter 25.

Because of the mounting costs and requirements of payroll accounting work, it has become increasingly important for the office manager to inaugurate systems and procedures that will do the work more quickly, more accurately, and at less cost. To be able to do this, the office manager should become familiar with various methods and procedures that can be used in payroll accounting.

Outline of Basic Payroll Accounting Procedures

A typical payroll accounting procedure for workers on an hourly basis involves:

1. Obtaining a record of the time worked by employees. Time clocks are the most commonly used method of obtaining a record of the time worked. In some firms office employees are not required to use time clocks, but some form of time record is needed for proof of compliance with federal and state minimum wage and hour laws. In some offices time sheets prepared by the department head are used; in others a time register with employee signatures is kept.

   Two types of time cards are commonly used: one, the *regular time* card with a 12-hour clock; and the other, the *continental time* card used with a 24-hour clock. Figure 17-4 illustrates these two types of time cards and shows how they may be used for computing preliminary data for payroll accounting.

2. Obtaining and recording the rates of pay.
3. Computing and recording the deductions for various taxes, union dues, and other authorized deductions.
4. Preparing the following records: payroll journal, employee's earnings records, and the pay envelopes or paychecks.

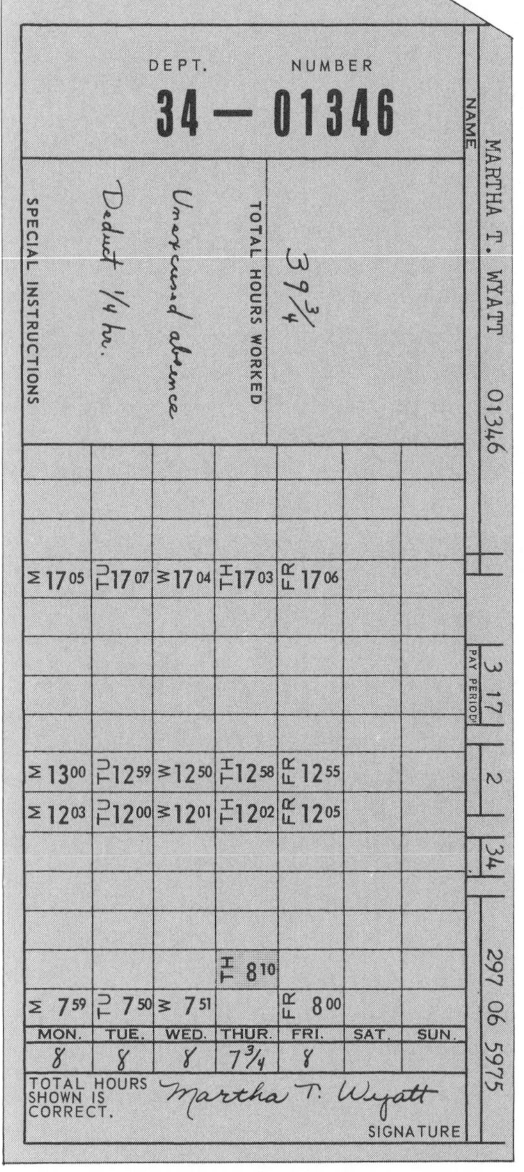

DEPT. NUMBER

34 — 01346

NAME MARTHA T. WYATT 01346

SPECIAL INSTRUCTIONS: Unexcused absence Deduct 1/4 hr.

TOTAL HOURS WORKED: 39 3/4

PAY PERIOD 3 17 2 34 297 06 5975

MON.	TUE.	WED.	THUR.	FRI.	SAT.	SUN.
M 17 05	TU 17 07	W 17 04	TH 17 03	FR 17 06		
M 13 00	TU 12 59	W 12 50	TH 12 58	FR 12 55		
M 12 03	TU 12 00	W 12 01	TH 12 02	FR 12 05		
			TH 8 10			
M 7 59	TU 7 50	W 7 51		FR 8 00		
8	8	8	7 3/4	8		

TOTAL HOURS SHOWN IS CORRECT. *Martha T. Wyatt* SIGNATURE

NO. **44**

NAME Mark Randall PAY END JUL 1 19--

REG. TIME HRS. 40 RATE 1.75 AMT. 70.00
OVERTIME HRS. 6 " 2.63 15.78
TOTAL EARNINGS 85.78

FED. W. T. 9.30
F. I. C. A. 4.46
INS. .85
HOSP. .61
OTHER
TOTAL DEDUCTIONS 15.22
AMOUNT DUE 70.56

Days	MORNING IN	MORNING OUT	AFTERNOON IN	AFTERNOON OUT	OVERTIME IN	OVERTIME OUT	Daily Totals
1	M 7 59	M 12 03	M 1 00	M 5 05			8
2	TU 7 50	TU 12 04	TU 12 59	TU 5 07			8
3	W 7 51	W 12 01	W 12 50	W 5 04	W 5 29	W 7 35	10
4	TH 8 00	TH 12 02	TH 12 58	TH 5 03			8
5	FR 8 00	FR 12 05	FR 1 01	FR 5 06			8
6	SA 7 55	SA 12 04					4
7							

Fig. 17-4
Two Types of Time Cards

Types of Payroll Accounting Procedures

In this section several payroll accounting procedures, which make use of the following mechanical devices and equipment, are described and illustrated:

1. Combination time book and payroll journal.
2. Accounting board.
3. Unit control or ledgerless bookkeeping.
4. Addressograph system.
5. Basic accounting machines.
6. Data service center equipment.

Combination Time Book and Payroll Journal. One of the simplest types of payroll accounting procedures utilizes a combination time book and payroll journal similar to the one illustrated in Figure 17-5. In small firms this payroll record is commonly prepared by hand. The record may be used with or without time cards. Although this procedure is simple, it is laborious; and its use is recommended only where the clerk responsible for its preparation has sufficient time left over to do other work.

Accounting Board. The *accounting board,* or the *pegboard,* relies upon the use of pen and ink, whereby carefully designed forms are prearranged in shingle-like fashion so that it is possible to prepare simultaneously the payroll journal, the individual employee's earnings record, and the pay envelope or the payroll check. This procedure requires that the forms for the payroll journal, the employee's earnings records, and the pay envelope or check be designed so that, in one writing, identical information appears in the same location on each form. Thus, by use of carbon paper, spot-carbonized forms, or carbonless paper, only one writing is necessary to prepare all records simultaneously, as illustrated in Figure 17-6. The accounting board procedure does not require the large investment in accounting machines, and yet by means of pen and ink has the advantages that the machine method gives in simultaneously preparing several records.

The accounting board technique can also be effectively used in the areas of accounts receivable and accounts payable. In one entry the accounts receivable clerk records the transaction in the sales journal, posts to the customer's account, and prepares a statement that is ready for mailing at any time. Similarly, in one manual writing on the accounting board, the accounts payable clerk can record the transaction in the cash payments journal, post to the

PAYROLL JOURNAL

FOR WEEK ENDING *January 17* 19--

	CLOCK No.	NAME OF EMPLOYEE	No. EXEMP.	TIME RECORD						REGULAR EARNINGS	
				MON.	TUE.	WED.	THUR.	FRI.	SAT.	RATE PER HOUR	AMOUNT
1	10	Adams, Ralph C.	3	8	8	8	8	8	4	2 10	84 00
2	12	Archer, Perry R.	4	8	8	8	8	10		2 90	116 00
3	13	Atwater, Betty C.	1	8	8	8	8	8		1 75	70 00
4	22	Baker, Lloyd J.	2	8	8	8	8	8	8	2 60	104 00
5	24	Barrett, Ann P.	1	8	8	8	0	8		1 70	54 40

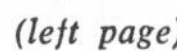
(left page)

Fig. 17-5

Fig. 17-6

Shaw-Walker

Accounting Board

creditor's account, and prepare the check. Thus, in both of these systems, small and medium-size businesses can benefit from the economies and accuracies of mechanized accounting equipment without having to buy posting machines or employ specially trained operators.

PAYROLL JOURNAL

PAGE 27

OVERTIME EARNINGS				DEDUCTIONS					NET PAID		
HOURS	RATE	AMOUNT	TOTAL EARNINGS	F.I.C.A. TAX	GROUP INS.	CITY INCOME TAX	FED. INCOME TAX	OTHER DEDUCT.	CHECK NO.	AMOUNT	F.I.C.A. TAXABLE EARNINGS
4	3 15	12 60	96 60	5 02	90	97	6 00		898	83 71	96 60
2	4 35	8 70	124 70	6 48	90	1 25	8 20		899	107 87	124 70
			70 00	3 64	30	70	6 50		900	58 86	70 00
8	3 90	31 20	135 20	7 03	90	1 35	14 70		901	111 22	135 20
			54 40	2 83	30	54	3 40		902	47 33	54 40

(right page)

Handwritten Time Book and Payroll Journal

Unit Control. Under the *unit control* or *ledgerless accounting* procedure, multiple copies of the paycheck or pay envelope are prepared by pen and ink or on the typewriter. One of the multiple copies is filed by employee name and serves as the record for preparing the employee's annual withholding tax statement. Another copy may be summarized weekly and used as the payroll journal. A third copy may be filed by check number if the employees are paid by check. Because of the number of separate forms that must be used, this procedure has limited application and is usually restricted to firms having few employees.

Addressograph System. The Addressograph system for handling payroll accounting employs the principle of imprinting from raised type. The Addressograph, shown in Figure 17-7, is most commonly associated with the preparation of permanent mailing lists for the repetitive addressing of envelopes and cards. However, this same equipment may be used to print identifying information on time cards, paychecks, and other payroll records and reports. The metal plates used in the Addressograph machine are prepared on a lettering machine called the Graphotype, which embosses the name, address, date, number, or other required data. Information recorded on the metal plates is transcribed through an inked ribbon by means of a rubber-covered platen that exerts pressure on the raised typeface of the plates. Business forms are fed into the writing position of the Addressograph either manually or automatically, depending on the model of machine used and the nature of the work.

At the heart of the Addressograph system is the master record or "memory unit." Information recorded on the master record

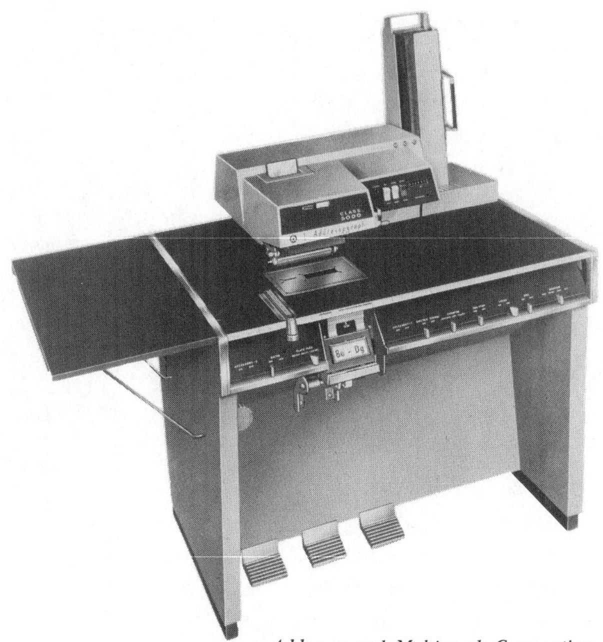

Addressograph-Multigraph Corporation

Fig. 17-7

Addressograph Accounting Machine

can be printed over and over again on many different types of records and forms. In the master record illustrated in Figure 17-8, two metal sections have been prepared. The top section contains constant information that would be repeatedly printed on various payroll forms and records such as the payroll journal, paycheck and earnings statement, earnings record, pay envelope, and on tax reports. On the top section illustrated appear the employee name and clock number, social security number, department, and hourly rate. The information embossed on the bottom section of the master record, although looked upon as constant but subject to more change than that described above, includes the amounts of the various deductible items, such as hospitalization insurance, savings bonds, and pension fund contribution. Thus, such payroll information, once embossed on the master record, becomes an original source record that is authentic and indisputable. Once the data have been embossed and verified, they can be repetitively imprinted on any payroll record or form with complete accuracy.

A further extension of the master record involves the embossing of *all* payroll data, both constant and variable, in the usual manner on the Graphotype. By means of an electric key punch, all variable

Fig. 17-8

Addressograph-Multigraph Corporation

Master Record of the Addressograph System

data are converted to numeric codes and punched into the proper columns or "fields" on one section of the master record. These fields of the coded section are laid out to correspond to columns on the particular payroll forms that are to be printed. As the master records are fed into the printing section of the payroll writer, an electric selector reads the data and transfers them to the tabulator, shown at the extreme right in Figure 17-7. Thus, while the Addressograph is printing all information on the payroll forms, the figure data are sensed and distributed to the appropriate columns on a continuous journal form in the tabulator. These data are automatically stored in accumulating registers so that, as the last step in the printing and tabulating operation, grand totals can be automatically secured for each column and printed out on the journal.

Because of its high operating speed, the Addressograph is adaptable to relatively small as well as large payrolls. In addition, the equipment can be used for many procedures other than payroll accounting—disbursing dividends and tabulating stockholder lists, processing personal and real estate tax bills, collecting insurance premiums and fixed rate bills of many types, writing insurance annuity and installment checks, and compiling statistical reports.

Basic Accounting Machines. *Accounting machines,* also known as *bookkeeping machines,* not only record entries in ledger accounts and journals but also add, subtract, extend balances, and provide direct and indirect methods of proving the amounts recorded. Payroll procedures that involve the use of basic accounting machines provide for the simultaneous preparation of payroll records. In a single operation it is possible to prepare (1) the payroll journal in which are listed all deductions from the employee's wages; (2) the payroll check or envelope upon which all deductions are listed; and (3) the employee's earnings record, which shows the weekly earnings and deductions with cumulative earnings and deductions. With an accounting machine one payroll clerk can do the work that would ordinarily require at least three clerks. The payroll accounting machine pays for itself in a very short time.

Accounting machines are also used in order processing and billing procedures. For example, one firm has eliminated the posting from its accounts receivable ledger by using their accounting machines to prepare the invoice and post to the ledger and prepare the statement in one operation. Proof totals are obtained automatically, and at the end of the month statements are ready for mailing. Through the use of accounting machines, this firm has been able to save 400 clerical hours a month and secure a significant rise in accuracy.

Accounting machines may be programmed so that the operator can switch from one accounting task to another. The machines use changeable program bars, panels, wires, tapes, or combinations of these to guide the posting work. The program controls move the carriage from one column to another, thus "telling" the machine which calculation to make in each column, and when and where to write the totals. The various types of accounting machines may be classified as:

1. *Numeric* or *nondescriptive*—adding machine keyboard with date keys; acts as a horizontal adding-subtracting machine. These machines are used most commonly for posting ledger cards, but since most of them are equipped with front-feed carriages, they can be used for any type of bookkeeping that does not require a completely itemized description.
2. *Alphanumeric* or *descriptive*—typewriter-adding machine with alphabetic and numeric keyboard. This type is universally used in bookkeeping work requiring the typing of names, descriptions, or other pertinent data. Since alphanumeric accounting machines can also be used for nondescriptive work, the field of application for this type of machine is broader than that of the numeric model.

Accounting machines are used to accomplish applications that are uneconomical for a computer, or they may be used along with a computer as part of the information-processing cycle. Extensions of the two basic accounting machines through the use of punched cards, punched tape, and magnetic tape will be discussed in Part 5.

Numeric Accounting Machine. In a payroll accounting procedure using a numeric accounting machine, the data are copied onto a payroll journal sheet. Simultaneously either by means of carbon paper, spot-carbonized forms, or dual-automatic repeating registers, the same information is printed on the employee's earnings record and on the paycheck or pay envelope. The basic record is the time card or time book in which are recorded the hours worked, the deductions for income and social security taxes, and other deductions.

The payroll journal can be prepared by using an addressing machine which, as described earlier, prints either from metal plates prepared on an embossing machine or from fiber stencils. Using the Addressograph machine, the name and the social security account number of each employee are automatically listed on the payroll journal. Using the same plates, the names of payees are recorded in the same sequence on the payroll checks or the pay envelopes.

The payroll journal with all employee names listed is then inserted in the accounting machine. By means of a front feed, it is possible to insert, properly aligned, the employee's payroll check and the employee's earnings record or earnings statement. The name and social security account number have been preprinted by means of the Addressograph plates. The date key is depressed to record the proper date on all forms. The horizontal adding-subtracting mechanism prints the following information on the earnings statement: earnings (regular, overtime, to date, and gross), hours worked, deductions, check number, and net amount. Carbon figures appear on the employee's earnings record. The payroll journal sheet, along with the check register, is prepared as a carbon copy record; or by means of dual registers, the identical information printed on the check and earnings statement is repeated on the payroll journal sheet automatically.

Posting Machines. ***Posting machines,*** which may be classified as a type of numeric accounting machine, are primarily designed for a posting operation, such as updating a customer's account and preparing his statement of account. On the posting machine shown in Figure 17-9, the operator records or "indexes" on the keyboard the account number and pre-audit proof balance from the customer's ledger account and the account balance from the customer's passbook (or receipt). Next, the amount of the transaction and the transaction code are indexed. The transaction amount and the automatically updated account balance are printed on both the passbook and the ledger, as shown in Figure 17-10. By depressing a key and a bar, the posting machine prints the new pre-audit proof on the ledger, thus completing the transaction.

At the end of the day the machine is totaled. As shown in Figure 17-10, the charges are broken down and listed by seven departments plus the total payments on account (credits). The listing of departmental totals is printed on the miscellaneous listing tape located at the left of the carriage of the machine. Before updating the Accounts Receivable Control ledger account, the individual departmental accounts receivable charges are added together to arrive at the Grand Total charges. The Grand Total charges are posted to the Accounts Receivable Control ledger account with the total payments on account, thus indicating at a glance the amount owed the company in the form of accounts receivable.

Alphanumeric Accounting Machine. By using an *alphanumeric accounting machine,* such as that shown in Figure 17-11,

Burroughs Corporation

Fig. 17-9

Posting Machine

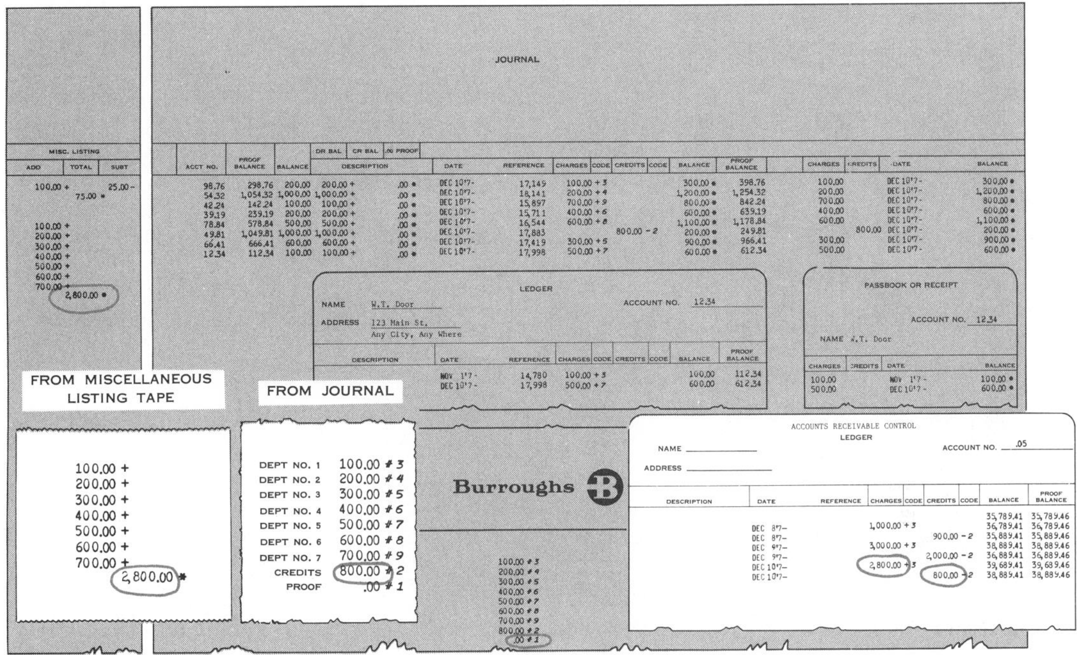

Burroughs Corporation

Fig. 17-10

Journal, Customer's Ledger Account, and Passbook or Receipt Prepared in One Writing on a Posting Machine

more flexibility is permitted in the payroll work and in the use of forms. With this machine it is unnecessary to prerecord the names and the social security account numbers by means of Addressograph plates. On an alphanumeric accounting machine, one operator can prepare simultaneously all the information that must be spelled out on the payroll journal sheet, the employee's earnings record, the pay envelope or check, and the statement of earnings. The machine has the advantage of doing all the work except the multiplication of hours worked by the hourly or piece rate.

Figure 17-12 shows the payroll records for one firm that were prepared simultaneously on an alphanumeric accounting machine. Earnings and taxes paid for the year to date are automatically printed on each employee's earnings record. Totals for hours, earnings, and deductions are automatically accumulated in order to balance against whatever controls are established. Because earnings and tax balances are updated and proved each pay period, government reports, such as those described below, can be prepared with a minimum amount of time and effort.

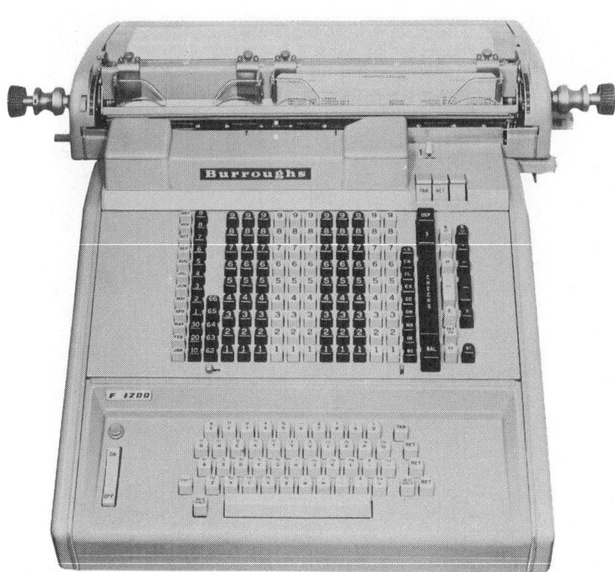

Fig. 17-11

Alphanumeric Accounting Machine

Burroughs Corporation

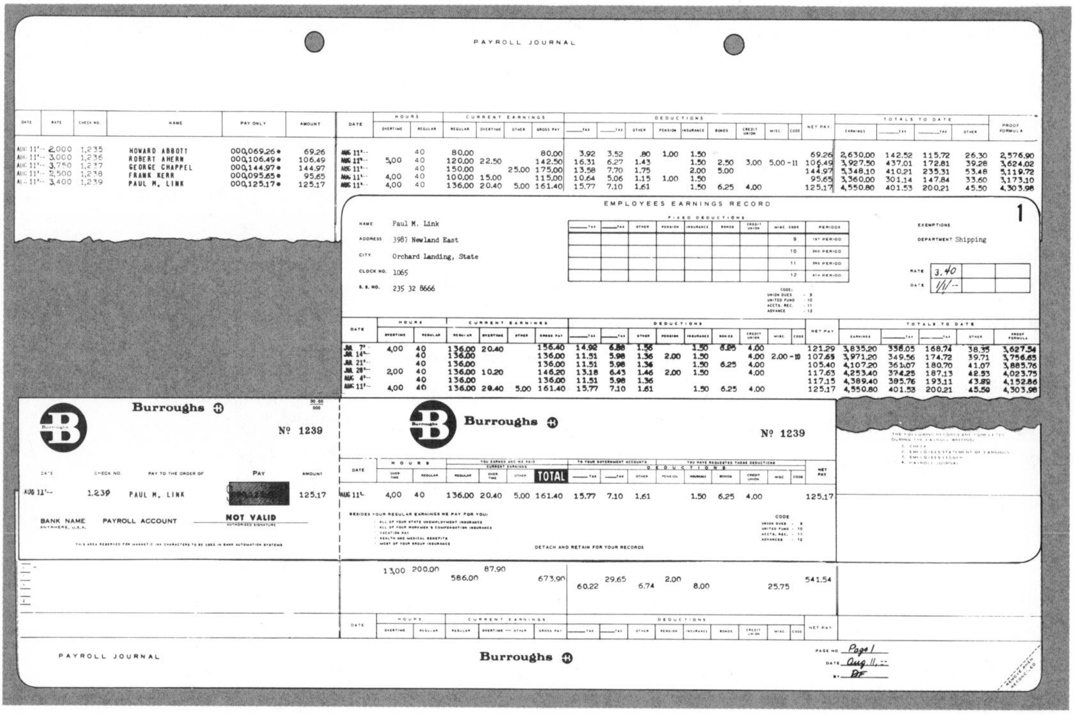

PAYROLL JOURNAL

DATE	RATE	CHECK NO.	NAME	PAY ONLY	AMOUNT	DATE	HOURS OVERTIME	HOURS REGULAR	CURRENT EARNINGS REGULAR	OVERTIME	OTHER	GROSS PAY	DEDUCTIONS ___TAX	___TAX	OTHER	PENSION	INSURANCE	BONDS	CREDIT UNION	MISC.	CODE	NET PAY	TOTALS TO DATE EARNINGS	___TAX	___TAX	OTHER	PROOF FORMULA
AUG 11'--	2,000	1,235	HOWARD ABBOTT	000,069.26•	69.26	AUG 11'--		40	80.00			80.00	3.92	3.52	.80	1.00	1.50					69.26	2,630.00	142.52	115.72	26.30	2,576.90
AUG 11'--	3,000	1,236	ROBERT AHERN	000,106.49•	106.49	AUG 11'--	5,00	40	120.00	22.50		142.50	16.31	6.27	1.43		1.50	2.50	3.00	5.00	11	106.49	3,927.50	437.01	172.81	39.28	3,624.02
AUG 11'--	3,750	1,237	GEORGE CHAPPEL	000,144.97•	144.97	AUG 11'--		40	150.00		25.00	175.00	13.58	7.70	1.75		2.00	5.00				144.97	5,348.10	410.21	235.31	53.48	5,119.72
AUG 11'--	2,500	1,238	FRANK KERR	000,095.65•	95.65	AUG 11'--	4,00	40	100.00	15.00		115.00	10.64	5.06	1.15	1.00	1.50					95.65	3,360.00	301.14	147.84	33.60	3,173.10
AUG 11'--	3,400	1,239	PAUL M. LINK	000,125.17•	125.17	AUG 11'--	4,00	40	136.00	20.40	5.00	161.40	15.77	7.10	1.61		1.50	6.25	4.00			125.17	4,550.80	401.53	200.21	45.50	4,303.98

EMPLOYEES EARNINGS RECORD 1

NAME Paul M. Link
ADDRESS 3987 Newland East
CITY Orchard Landing, State
CLOCK NO. 1065
S. S. NO. 235 32 8666

FIXED DEDUCTIONS

___TAX	___TAX	OTHER	PENSION	INSURANCE	BONDS	CREDIT UNION	MISC. CODE	PERIODS
							9	1ST PERIOD
							10	2ND PERIOD
							11	3RD PERIOD
							12	4TH PERIOD

CODE: UNION DUES - 9; UNITED FUND - 10; ACCTS. REC. - 11; ADVANCE - 12

EXEMPTIONS
DEPARTMENT Shipping
RATE 3.40
DATE 1/1/--

DATE	HOURS OVERTIME	HOURS REGULAR	CURRENT EARNINGS REGULAR	OVERTIME	OTHER	GROSS PAY	DEDUCTIONS ___TAX	___TAX	OTHER	PENSION	INSURANCE	BONDS	CREDIT UNION	MISC.	CODE	NET PAY	TOTALS TO DATE EARNINGS	___TAX	___TAX	OTHER	PROOF FORMULA
JUL 7'--	4,00	40	136.00	20.40		156.40	14.92	6.88	1.56		1.50	6.25	4.00			121.29	3,835.20	338.05	168.74	38.35	3,627.54
JUL 14'--		40	136.00			136.00	11.51	5.98	1.36	2.00	1.50		4.00	2.00	10	107.65	3,971.20	349.56	174.72	39.71	3,756.65
JUL 21'--		40	136.00			136.00	11.51	5.98	1.36		1.50	6.25	4.00			105.40	4,107.20	361.07	180.70	41.07	3,885.76
JUL 28'--	2,00	40	136.00	10.20		146.20	13.18	6.43	1.46	2.00	1.50		4.00			117.63	4,253.40	374.25	187.13	42.53	4,023.75
AUG 4'--		40	136.00			136.00	11.51	5.98	1.36							117.15	4,389.40	385.76	193.11	43.89	4,152.86
AUG 11'--	4,00	40	136.00	20.40	5.00	161.40	15.77	7.10	1.61		1.50	6.25	4.00			125.17	4,550.80	401.53	200.21	45.50	4,303.98

Burroughs

№ 1239

DATE	CHECK NO.	PAY TO THE ORDER OF	PAY	AMOUNT
AUG 11'--	1,239	PAUL M. LINK	[illegible]	125.17

BANK NAME ANYWHERE, U.S.A. PAYROLL ACCOUNT NOT VALID AUTHORIZED SIGNATURE

THIS AREA RESERVED FOR MAGNETIC INK CHARACTERS TO BE USED IN BANK AUTOMATION SYSTEMS

Burroughs

№ 1239

DATE	HOURS OVER-TIME	HOURS REGULAR	YOU EARNED AND WE PAID CURRENT EARNINGS REGULAR	OVER-TIME	OTHER	TOTAL	TO YOUR GOVERNMENT ACCOUNTS ___TAX	___TAX	YOU HAVE REQUESTED THESE DEDUCTIONS OTHER	PENSION	INSURANCE	BONDS	CREDIT UNION	MISC	CODE	NET PAY
AUG 11'--	4,00	40	136.00	20.40	5.00	161.40	15.77	7.10	1.61		1.50	6.25	4.00			125.17

BESIDES YOUR REGULAR EARNINGS WE PAY FOR YOU:
- ALL OF YOUR STATE UNEMPLOYMENT INSURANCE
- ALL OF YOUR WORKMEN'S COMPENSATION INSURANCE
- VACATION PAY
- HEALTH AND MEDICAL BENEFITS
- MOST OF YOUR GROUP INSURANCE

CODE: UNION DUES - 9; UNITED FUND - 10; ACCTS. REC. - 11; ADVANCES - 12

DETACH AND RETAIN FOR YOUR RECORDS

	HOURS OVERTIME	HOURS REGULAR	CURRENT EARNINGS REGULAR	OVERTIME — OTHER	GROSS PAY	DEDUCTIONS ___TAX	___TAX	OTHER	PENSION	INSURANCE	BONDS	CREDIT UNION	MISC	CODE	NET PAY
	13,00	200.00	586.00	87.90	673.90	60.22	29.65	6.74	2.00	8.00		25.75			541.54

PAYROLL JOURNAL   Burroughs

PAGE NO. Page 1
DATE Aug. 11, --
BY BF

REMOVE WHEN RECONCILED

Burroughs Corporation

Fig. 17-12

Payroll Records Prepared Simultaneously on an Alphanumeric Accounting Machine

Employers' Quarterly Federal Tax Return, Form 941. Schedule A of Form 941, the quarterly report of wages taxable under the Federal Insurance Contributions Act, can be prepared in a single operation by copying from the employee's earnings records only the present and previous earnings. Automatically, each employee's federal taxable wages, state taxable wages, and state excess wages, as well as page totals, are computed and printed as shown in Figure 17-13. The totals of federal and state taxable wages; state excess wages; present, previous, and quarterly earnings; and federal excess earnings are accumulated and printed automatically.

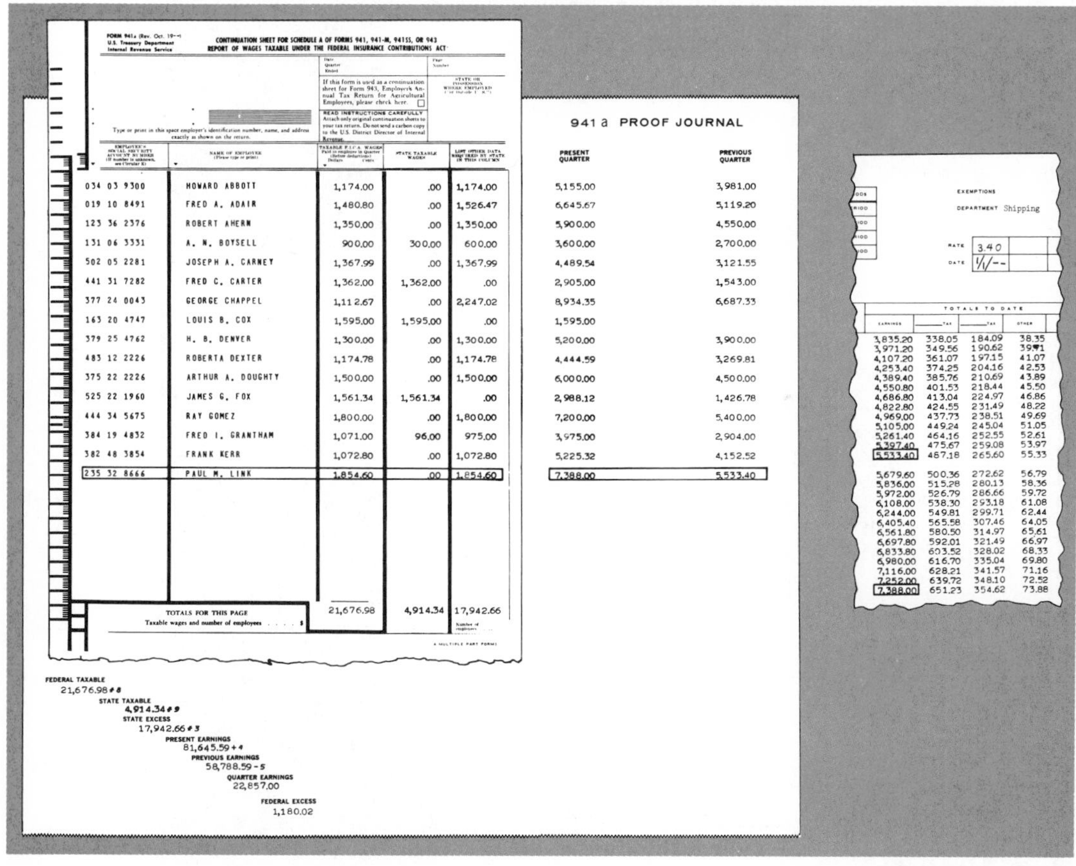
FORM 941a (Rev. Oct. 19--)
U.S. Treasury Department
Internal Revenue Service

CONTINUATION SHEET FOR SCHEDULE A OF FORMS 941, 941-M, 941SS, OR 943
REPORT OF WAGES TAXABLE UNDER THE FEDERAL INSURANCE CONTRIBUTIONS ACT

If this form is used as a continuation sheet for Form 943, Employer's Annual Tax Return for Agricultural Employees, please check here. ☐

READ INSTRUCTIONS CAREFULLY
Attach only original continuation sheets to your tax return. Do not send a carbon copy to the U.S. District Director of Internal Revenue.

Type or print in this space employer's identification number, name, and address exactly as shown on the return.

Employee's Social Security Account Number	Name of Employee	Taxable F.I.C.A. Wages	State Taxable Wages	List Other Data Required by State in This Column
034 03 9300	HOWARD ABBOTT	1,174.00	.00	1,174.00
019 10 8491	FRED A. ADAIR	1,480.80	.00	1,526.47
123 36 2376	ROBERT AHERN	1,350.00	.00	1,350.00
131 06 3331	A. N. BOYSELL	900.00	300.00	600.00
502 05 2281	JOSEPH A. CARNEY	1,367.99	.00	1,367.99
441 31 7282	FRED C. CARTER	1,362.00	1,362.00	.00
377 24 0043	GEORGE CHAPPEL	1,112.67	.00	2,247.02
163 20 4747	LOUIS B. COX	1,595.00	1,595.00	.00
379 25 4762	H. B. DENVER	1,300.00	.00	1,300.00
483 12 2226	ROBERTA DEXTER	1,174.78	.00	1,174.78
375 22 2226	ARTHUR A. DOUGHTY	1,500.00	.00	1,500.00
525 22 1960	JAMES G. FOX	1,561.34	1,561.34	.00
444 34 5675	RAY GOMEZ	1,800.00	.00	1,800.00
384 19 4832	FRED I. GRANTHAM	1,071.00	96.00	975.00
382 48 3854	FRANK KERR	1,072.80	.00	1,072.80
235 32 8666	PAUL M. LINK	1,854.60	.00	1,854.60
TOTALS FOR THIS PAGE — Taxable wages and number of employees		21,676.98	4,914.34	17,942.66

FEDERAL TAXABLE
21,676.98 ♦8
STATE TAXABLE
4,914.34 ♦9
STATE EXCESS
17,942.66 ♦3
PRESENT EARNINGS
81,645.59 +4
PREVIOUS EARNINGS
58,788.59 -5
QUARTER EARNINGS
22,857.00
FEDERAL EXCESS
1,180.02

941 a PROOF JOURNAL

PRESENT QUARTER	PREVIOUS QUARTER
5,155.00	3,981.00
6,645.67	5,119.20
5,900.00	4,550.00
3,600.00	2,700.00
4,489.54	3,121.55
2,905.00	1,543.00
8,934.35	6,687.33
1,595.00	
5,200.00	3,900.00
4,444.59	3,269.81
6,000.00	4,500.00
2,988.12	1,426.78
7,200.00	5,400.00
3,975.00	2,904.00
5,225.32	4,152.52
7,388.00	5,533.40

EXEMPTIONS
DEPARTMENT Shipping
RATE 3.40
DATE 1/1/--

TOTALS TO DATE

EARNINGS	____ TAX	____ TAX	OTHER
3,835.20	338.05	184.09	38.35
3,971.20	349.56	190.62	39.[illegible]1
4,107.20	361.07	197.15	41.07
4,253.40	374.25	204.16	42.53
4,389.40	385.76	210.69	43.89
4,550.80	401.53	218.44	45.50
4,686.80	413.04	224.97	46.86
4,822.80	424.55	231.49	48.22
4,969.00	437.73	238.51	49.69
5,105.00	449.24	245.04	51.05
5,261.40	464.16	252.55	52.61
5,397.40	475.67	259.08	53.97
5,533.40	487.18	265.60	55.33
5,679.60	500.36	272.62	56.79
5,836.00	515.28	280.13	58.36
5,972.00	526.79	286.66	59.72
6,108.00	538.30	293.18	61.08
6,244.00	549.81	299.71	62.44
6,405.40	565.58	307.46	64.05
6,561.80	580.50	314.97	65.61
6,697.80	592.01	321.49	66.97
6,833.80	603.52	328.02	68.33
6,980.00	616.70	335.04	69.80
7,116.00	628.21	341.57	71.16
7,252.00	639.72	348.10	72.52
7,388.00	651.23	354.62	73.88

Burroughs Corporation

Fig. 17-13

Federal and State Quarterly Reports Prepared on an Alphanumeric Accounting Machine

Wage and Tax Statement, Form W-2. Form W-2, which shows the federal taxes withheld from wages, is prepared annually in quadruplicate for each employee. At the close of the year, the employee's earnings record reflects all the information required to complete Form W-2. The earnings and tax balances for each employee are entered into the accounting machine and at the same time the W-2 forms are being prepared a summary journal with accumulated totals of earnings and taxes is created. (See Figure 17-14.) The totals in the summary journal may then be proved against master control totals to insure the accuracy of the tax statements.

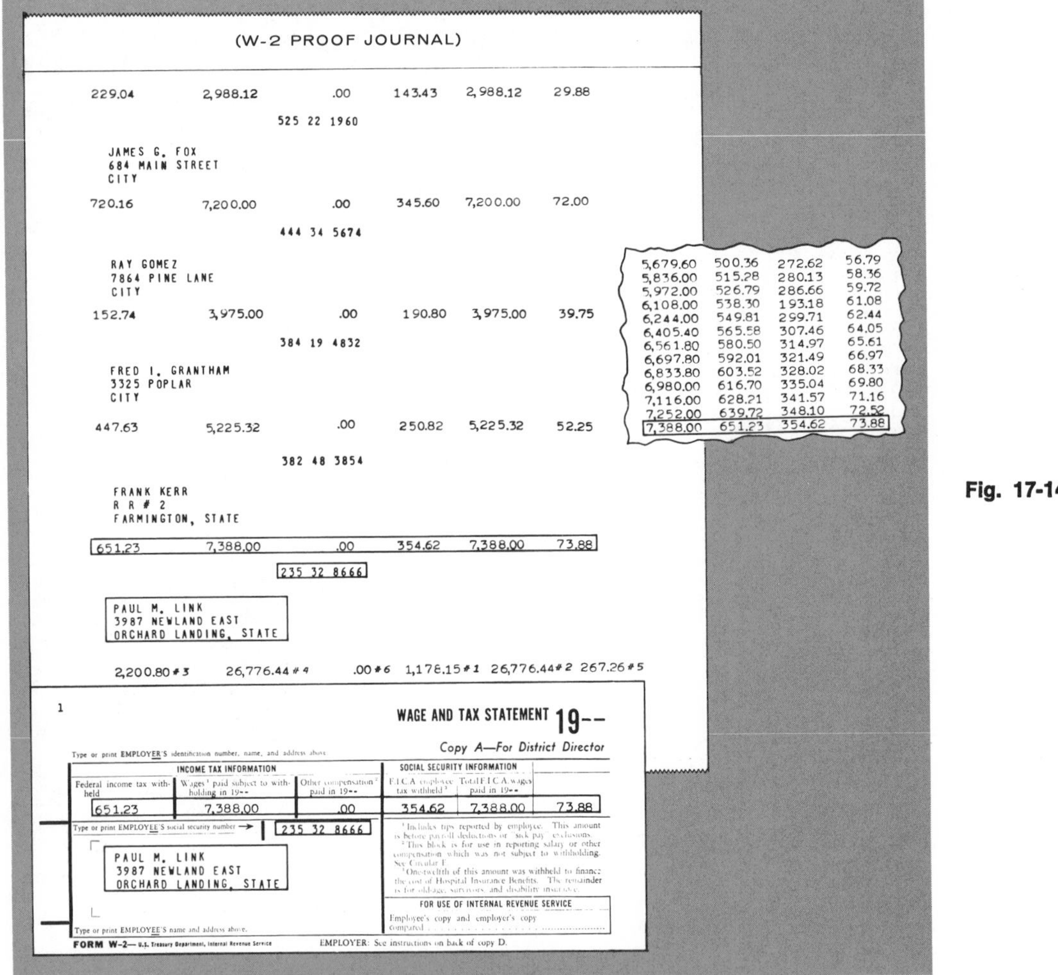

(W-2 PROOF JOURNAL)

229.04	2,988.12	.00	143.43	2,988.12	29.88
		525 22 1960			

JAMES G. FOX
684 MAIN STREET
CITY

720.16	7,200.00	.00	345.60	7,200.00	72.00
		444 34 5674			

RAY GOMEZ
7864 PINE LANE
CITY

152.74	3,975.00	.00	190.80	3,975.00	39.75
		384 19 4832			

FRED I. GRANTHAM
3325 POPLAR
CITY

447.63	5,225.32	.00	250.82	5,225.32	52.25
		382 48 3854			

FRANK KERR
R R # 2
FARMINGTON, STATE

651.23	7,388.00	.00	354.62	7,388.00	73.88
		235 32 8666			

PAUL M. LINK
3987 NEWLAND EAST
ORCHARD LANDING, STATE

2,200.80 #3	26,776.44 #4	.00 #6	1,178.15 #1	26,776.44 #2	267.26 #5

5,679.60	500.36	272.62	56.79
5,836.00	515.28	280.13	58.36
5,972.00	526.79	286.66	59.72
6,108.00	538.30	193.18	61.08
6,244.00	549.81	299.71	62.44
6,405.40	565.58	307.46	64.05
6,561.80	580.50	314.97	65.61
6,697.80	592.01	321.49	66.97
6,833.80	603.52	328.02	68.33
6,980.00	616.70	335.04	69.80
7,116.00	628.21	341.57	71.16
7,252.00	639.72	348.10	72.52
7,388.00	651.23	354.62	73.88

1

WAGE AND TAX STATEMENT 19--

Copy A—For District Director

Type or print EMPLOYER'S identification number, name, and address above

INCOME TAX INFORMATION			SOCIAL SECURITY INFORMATION		
Federal income tax withheld	Wages[1] paid subject to withholding in 19--	Other compensation[2] paid in 19--	F.I.C.A. employee tax withheld[3]	Total F.I.C.A. wages paid in 19--	
651.23	7,388.00	.00	354.62	7,388.00	73.88

Type or print EMPLOYEE'S social security number → 235 32 8666

PAUL M. LINK
3987 NEWLAND EAST
ORCHARD LANDING, STATE

Type or print EMPLOYEE'S name and address above.

[1] Includes tips reported by employee. This amount is before payroll deductions or "sick pay" exclusions.
[2] This block is for use in reporting salary or other compensation which was not subject to withholding. See Circular E.
[3] One-twelfth of this amount was withheld to finance the cost of Hospital Insurance Benefits. The remainder is for old-age, survivors, and disability insurance.

FOR USE OF INTERNAL REVENUE SERVICE

Employee's copy and employer's copy compared . . . .

FORM W-2—U.S. Treasury Department, Internal Revenue Service EMPLOYER: See instructions on back of copy D.

Fig. 17-14

Burroughs Corporation

W-2 Annual Report Prepared on Alphanumeric Accounting Machine

Using an Outside Data Service Center

As in the case of order processing and billing procedures, the services of a large commercial bank or an independent data service center may be used to automate the voluminous clerical work involved in payroll preparation and reporting. Weekly or bimonthly, depending upon the frequency of the pay periods, a firm sends to the bank or to the data service center the following payroll data: (1) the name, address, and social security account number of each employee presently employed, newly hired, or recently discharged; (2) each employee's withholding income tax status (number of exemptions); and (3) the hours of employment during the pay period and the rate of pay for each employee. At the data service center, the following services are performed:

1. Writing and signing the payroll checks.
2. Preparing the payroll register showing gross pay computations, deductions, and net earnings.
3. Reconciling the payroll account with the bank statement.
4. Preparing and filing federal, state, and local payroll tax reports.
5. Preparing, as needed, job or departmental cost reports.

About 95 percent of the clerical work involved in the preparation of the payroll and the reports required by law can be performed by the data service center.

PURCHASING—RECEIVING PROCEDURE

The following description of a purchasing-receiving procedure which makes use of the diazo copying process illustrates the time that can be saved and the economies to be realized as a result of mechanizing the repetitive, routine paper-work operations. By means of the diazo copying process discussed in Chapter 9, anything written, typed, printed, or drawn on *translucent* paper can be reproduced in seconds. Any number of sharp copies can be made from the same original source document. Since most repetitive writing appears on forms created for internal use, the company forms should be initially printed on translucent paper or card stock in order to utilize this particular copying process.

The steps followed in a typical purchasing-receiving procedure that employs the diazo copying process are listed below and illustrated in Figure 17-15.[2]

1. The purchase order is typed on a multiple-copy form, signed, and distributed to the vendor; the purchasing, receiving, and accounts payable departments; the requisitioner; and the numeric file.
2. The Receiving Copy of the purchase order, containing columns for recording multiple receipts, is filed. Each receipt against the original purchase order is recorded successively on this translucent form, thus eliminating a separate receiving report form for each receipt of goods.
3. When the first shipment arrives, the receiving clerk pulls the translucent form out of the file, verifies the contents of each package received, and fills in only the receiving information at the bottom of the form. There is no need to transcribe the vendor's name, descriptions, codes, and other information since it has previously been recorded in the purchase order section of the form.
4. After the receiving data are entered, the form is inserted into the copying machine, and copies are made for distribution to the proper departments and individuals.
5. In the accounts payable department, the reproduced Receiving Copy is matched with a copy of the purchase order and the vendor's invoice. If all items are in agreement, the invoice is approved for payment.
6. For each successive receipt of goods against the same purchase order, the same translucent receiving form is again pulled out of the file and receiving data are added to the previous record. Copies are made and distributed as before, with the latest receiving report representing a complete file in itself, showing all receipts to date.

As a result of employing the diazo copying process as part of the purchasing-receiving procedure, the following advantages are realized:

1. The transcribing of purchase order details by the receiving clerk to a separate receiving report form is eliminated. His writing is reduced to recording the receiving information only.
2. A translucent receiving report form (prepared as part of the purchase order) that can accommodate multiple receipts against a single purchase order is provided. The translucent

[2] Taken from "Bruning for Business, A Guide to Paperwork Simplification," with permission of the Charles Bruning Company, Inc., Mount Prospect, Illinois.

Fig. 17-15

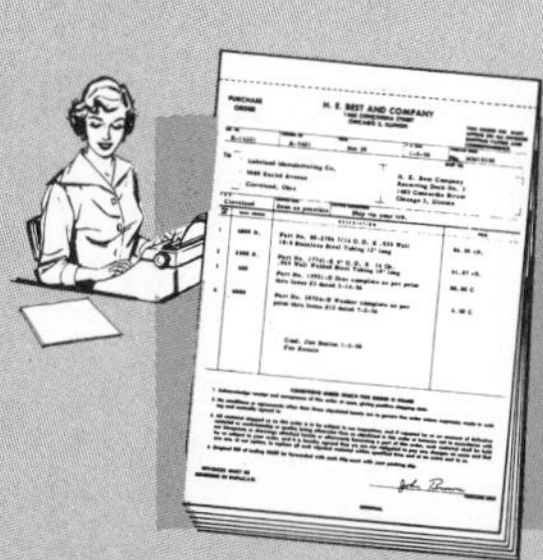

1. Typing Purchase Order

Purchase order is typed on a multiple-part form, then signed and distributed to vendor, purchasing, receiving, accounts payable, requisitioner, expediter, and numerical file.

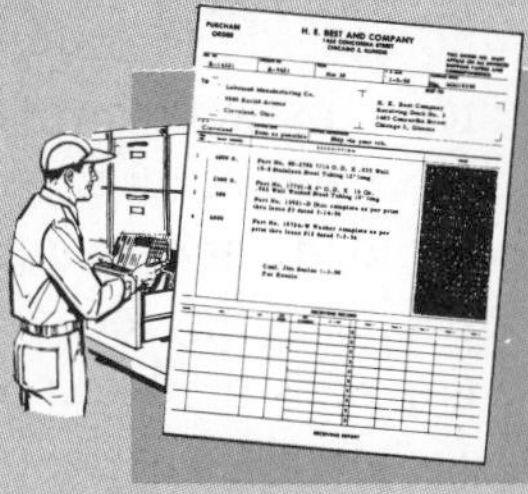

2. Filing Receiving Copy

This copy of the purchase order contains columns for recording multiple receipts, thus eliminating a separate receiving report form for each receipt of goods. Each receipt against the original purchase order is recorded successively on this translucent form.

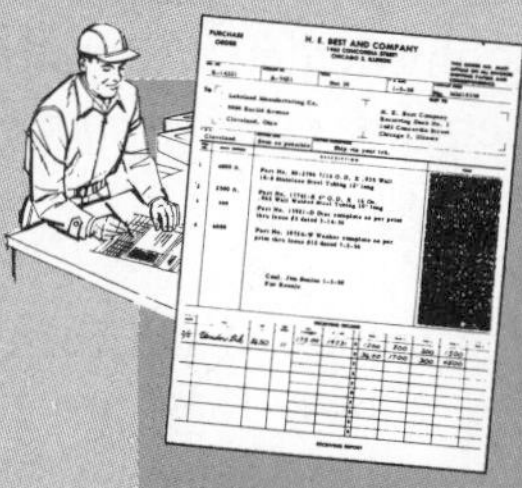

3. Recording First Receipt

Receiving clerk pulls translucent form out of the file. After verifying contents of each package, he fills in only receiving information at the bottom of the form. There is no need to transcribe vendor name, descriptions, codes, and other order information, because it is already in the purchase order section of the form.

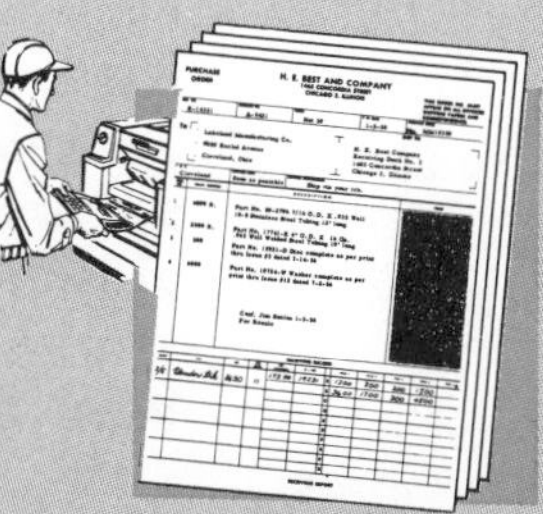

4. Producing Receiving Reports

After receiving data is entered, the form is inserted into a Copyflex machine together with a sheet of Copyflex paper. Copies are made on white and color-tinted paper for material identification, accounts payable, purchasing, and for any other departments or individuals concerned. The flexible Copyflex process permits making additional copies when needed, such as for special purchases involving research personnel.

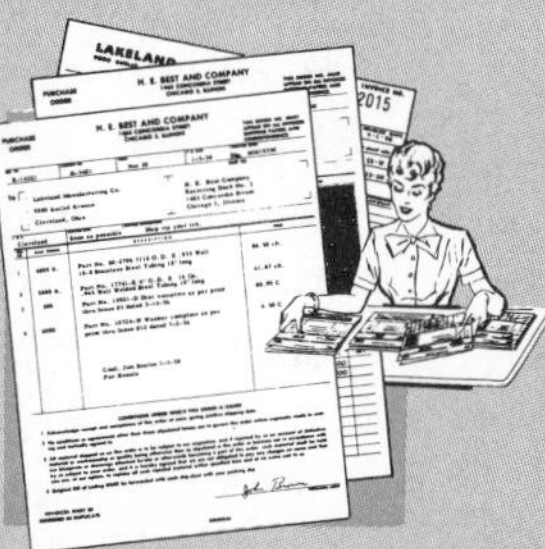

5. Matching, Auditing and Preparing for Payment

In the accounts payable department, the Copyflex receiving copy is matched with a copy of the purchase order and the vendor's invoice. If all items are in agreement, the invoice is OK'd for payment. The job of sorting and matching can be eased by using color-tinted paper (such as green for the original purchase order and pink for the Copyflex receiving copy).

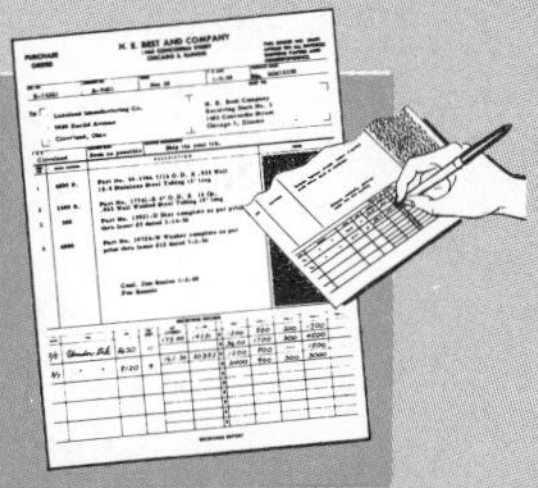

6. Recording Successive Receipts Against Same Purchase Order

For each successive receipt of goods against the same purchase order, the same translucent receiving form is again pulled out of the file and receiving data is added to the previous record. Copyflex copies are made and distributed as before. Latest receiving reports is a complete file in itself, showing all receipts to date.

A Purchasing-Receiving Procedure that Employs the Diazo Copying Process

form can be used for reproducing any number of receiving report copies.

3. Incoming materials are quickly moved to their point of use, and at the same time prompt notification of receipts is given to the purchasing department.
4. Maximum control over all operations—from purchase to payment—is insured.

INVOICE PROCESSING PROCEDURE

As part of the accounts payable operations, the processing of vendors' invoices for payment requires frequent "lookups" of invoices, purchase orders, receiving orders, and other documents. Direct examination of one or more of these source documents is needed to reconcile any discrepancies between what was ordered from the supplier and what was received; to account for differences between prices quoted and prices billed; and to answer questions about the status of open orders, specifications, delivery dates, and transportation charges. In many companies the lookups are time-consuming and require the use of expensive clerical help. To reduce the cost of retrieving accounts payable documents and to expedite the timely processing of invoices for payment, some firms have turned to mechanization of their accounts payable procedures through the installation of a microfilm system. (Microfilming as a medium of records retention was discussed in Chapter 8.) The typical microfilm system is simple, flexible, and readily adaptable either to computerized operations or to less sophisticated accounts payable operations.

The microfilm system of processing vendors' invoices shown in Figure 17-16 operates as follows:

1. After the incoming invoices have been approved for payment and the pay date added, they are microfilmed in random sequence. As the invoice is automatically fed into the microfilmer, an identifying number is first imprinted on each invoice, and then the invoice passes into the microfilmer for photographing. As the document is photographed, a "blip" is simultaneously recorded on the film alongside each document. As many as 3,000 invoices, each sequentially numbered from 1 to 3,000, can be recorded in this manner on a 100-foot roll of 16mm microfilm, with each invoice tied into a "blip" that becomes the key to retrieving a specific image after the film has been processed and loaded into film magazines.

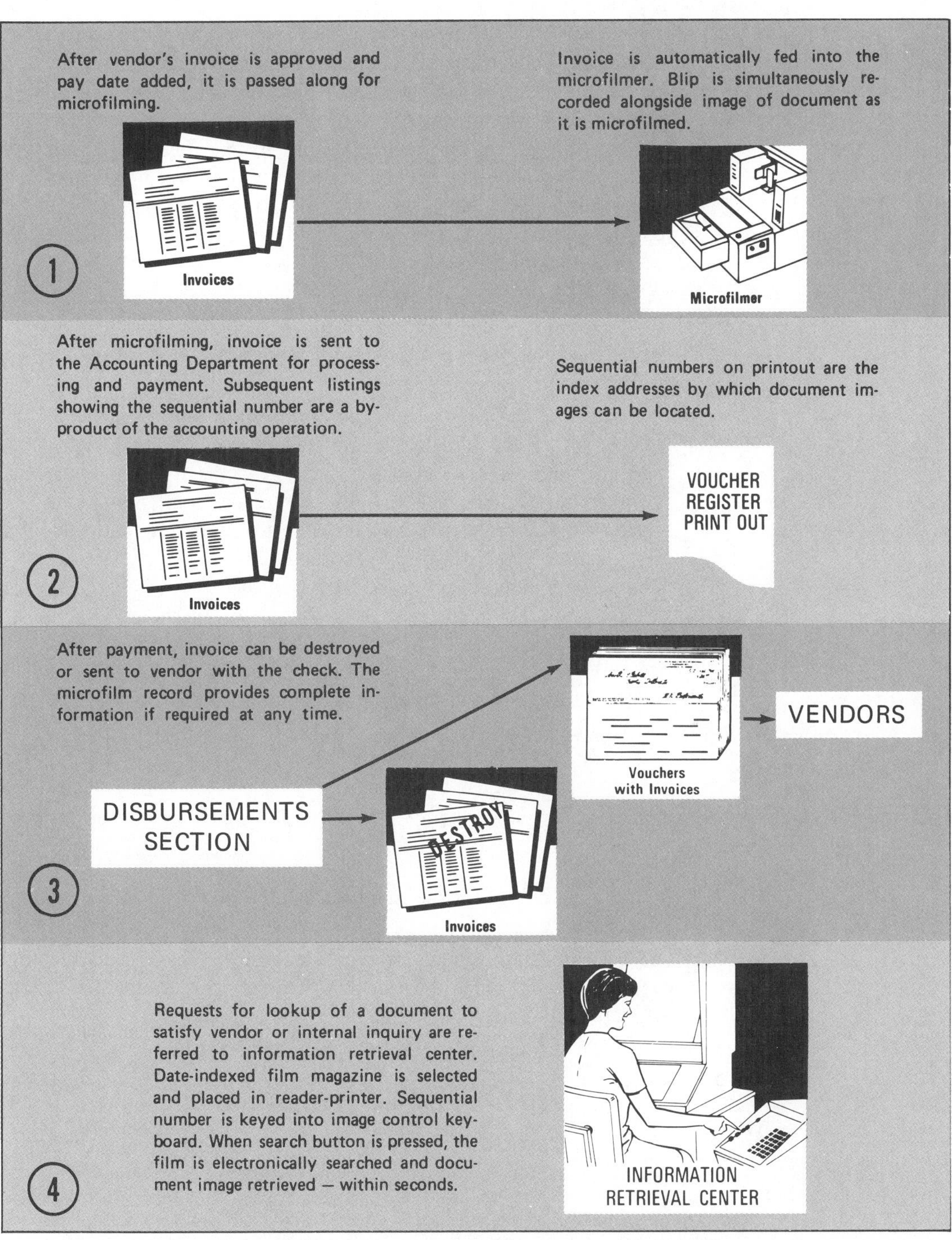

After vendor's invoice is approved and pay date added, it is passed along for microfilming.
Invoice is automatically fed into the microfilmer. Blip is simultaneously recorded alongside image of document as it is microfilmed.
1
Invoices
Microfilmer
After microfilming, invoice is sent to the Accounting Department for processing and payment. Subsequent listings showing the sequential number are a by-product of the accounting operation.
Sequential numbers on printout are the index addresses by which document images can be located.
VOUCHER
REGISTER
PRINT OUT
2
Invoices
After payment, invoice can be destroyed or sent to vendor with the check. The microfilm record provides complete information if required at any time.
VENDORS
Vouchers
with Invoices
DISBURSEMENTS
SECTION
DESTROY
3
Invoices
Requests for lookup of a document to satisfy vendor or internal inquiry are referred to information retrieval center. Date-indexed film magazine is selected and placed in reader-printer. Sequential number is keyed into image control keyboard. When search button is pressed, the film is electronically searched and document image retrieved — within seconds.
INFORMATION
RETRIEVAL CENTER
4

Eastman Kodak Company

Fig. 17-16
An Accounts Payable System Employing Microfilm

2. After each batch of invoices has been microfilmed, the invoices are put through the normal accounting procedures to create payment checks for the vendors. The imprinted numbers on the invoices are entered into the paying process and thus appear on any listings or registers such as the voucher register or the check register. The sequentially imprinted numbers provide the index by means of which any particular invoice can be located on its roll of microfilm which is housed in the information retrieval center.
3. After the invoice has been paid, it may be destroyed or sent to the vendor with the check in payment of the amount due. The microfilm record provides the complete information required at any time.
4. When a lookup is requested, the appropriate film magazine is selected from the film file in the information retrieval center and placed in a reader-printer. The proper sequential index number is push-button keyed into the reader-printer unit, the start button is depressed, and the film advances automatically. By means of the previously recorded "blips," the number of images is counted until the desired invoice number is reached. At this point the film stops and the image of the requested invoice appears on the screen of the reader. The entire retrieval operation takes about five seconds. If needed, a readable-size facsimile print can be made which is delivered in seconds by the reader-printer.[3]

QUESTIONS FOR REVIEW

1. What factors account for the trend toward the increased mechanization of office work?
2. What are the disadvantages of separate order processing and billing procedures for all offices? When may separate order processing and billing procedures be justified?
3. Explain the meaning of a unified prebilling procedure.
4. Why is there need for duplicating or reproducing equipment in write-it-once order processing and billing procedures?
5. Under what circumstances do you feel that a data service center could be used for accounts receivable work?

---

[3] The operation of the microfilm system is adapted from Kodak's Recordak Microfilm System, "Accounts Payable," with permission of Eastman Kodak Company, Business Systems Markets Division.

6. Outline the steps involved in a typical payroll accounting procedure.
7. In recent years the write-it-once principle has been developed by firms manufacturing basic accounting machines. Explain how this principle has been applied to payroll accounting procedures.
8. Under what conditions can the accounting board procedure be effectively used in business?
9. Business firms are making an increased use of data processing service centers to handle their payroll work. What advantages may a business firm gain from the services of such a center?
10. Describe how the diazo copying process can be used to eliminate repetitive paper-work operations in a typical purchasing-receiving procedure.
11. What are the major advantages that characterize the microfilm system for handling accounts payable?

QUESTIONS FOR DISCUSSION

1. Arthur Wilcox, an administrative office manager, is frequently faced with the problem of mechanizing certain phases of his office work. On what considerations should he base his decision to mechanize or not to mechanize?
2. Carlton Davis, the office manager of a large untility company, has encountered a problem in selecting and installing mechanical equipment. In this connection he wants to standardize the solution to his problem by preparing a list of factors to be considered in selecting such equipment. What factors do you feel should be included in such a list?
3. The Southern Oil Company has attempted to simplify its purchasing procedure for those orders whose total does not exceed $200 on any given invoice. The company has been experimenting with the idea of sending the vendor a check in full payment, less the discount if applicable, whenever the company places an order that does not exceed $200. Thus, certain bookkeeping entries are eliminated. Discuss the advantages and disadvantages of such a procedure.
4. The Beeman Trucking Company finds itself in need of additional computing machines. The payroll department wants a rotary calculator such as the Marchant, Friden, or Monroe. Those in the billing department and the accounting department want printing calculators such as the Victor or Olivetti Underwood. A few in this department would also like a full-keyboard adding-listing machine such as the Clary or Burroughs. One of the men in the accounting department recently saw an electronic calculator being demonstrated at a business

equipment show and he is very enthusiastic about its purchase for his department.

Because of the varying requests from the supervisor of each department, the treasurer of the company is a bit confused. He does not want to antagonize any of his supervisors by purchasing machines that they may not consider suitable for their work, yet the budget is limited to the purchase of about five machines.

Discuss how you would handle this situation if you were the treasurer and indicate the type of computing machines you recommend be purchased for each department.

5. Carol Everard is the one-clerk accounting staff of the Langhorne Country Club. Each month she has the job of preparing and mailing the monthly statements to the 2,000 members. During a typical month the club members sign approximately 15,000 credit receipts which must be tabulated and then posted to their accounts. Ordinarily this job requires two weeks' time, along with 60 hours of overtime work each month.

Discuss how cycle billing might be used by the Langhorne Country Club to reduce its work load at the end of each month. What kind of computing machine might best be used in the processing of members' accounts? Is there an application for an accounting machine in this billing procedure? Explain.

6. The Davidson Novelty Company uses a combined order processing and billing procedure whereby the orders are filled directly from a copy of the invoices. When an order is received in the sales department, the clerk prepares an invoice set of five copies which are distributed as shown below. The invoice sets are prenumbered and arranged with one-time carbon paper.

a. Original invoice—held for mailing to customer after goods have been shipped.
b. Acknowledgment of order—sent to customer when invoice is prepared.
c. Duplicate of invoice—held in follow-up file.
d. Packing room copy—routed to storekeeper for entry on inventory records.
e. Shipping room copy—sent to shipping clerk.

Unit prices and extensions are not shown on any copies at time of preparing the invoices but are inserted on all necessary copies after the order has been shipped. Discuss this order processing and billing procedure, indicating its good points and the possibility for improvements.

PRACTICAL OFFICE CASES

Case 17-1 Improving the Payroll Accounting Procedure

The Lee Canning Company has a processing plant in which there are 450 employees, most of whom are paid at the rate of $2.50 an hour for a 37½-hour week, with time and one half for all overtime work. At present a staff of five girls is required to calculate earnings on the time cards, prepare the payroll sheets, post to employee's earnings records, prepare the periodic statements of earnings for the governmental agencies and the statements of earnings given to employees at the end of the year. The average weekly salary of each girl is $120.

The office manager is eager to improve the payroll accounting work in his firm. Presently the girls use payroll tax tables and rotary calculators in their work. It is felt that further mechanization of their payroll work will reduce costs. After giving the matter attention and talking with several systems men, the office manager has concluded that the two best ways in which to improve the present payroll procedure are:

1. Install two alphanumeric accounting machines that will prepare the payroll, the earnings record, and the paycheck in one writing. Each machine will cost approximately $8,000. Two girls, instead of the present five, would be required to handle all payroll work.
2. Install an accounting board system that would not require any investment in machines. Three girls would be required to prepare all payroll records. The investment in forms and three accounting boards would be approximately $600.

■ Discuss the procedure you recommend the office manager install and indicate the approximate savings to be realized in each case.

Case 17-2 Using a Data Processing Billing Service

The Mulvey Corporation, a grocery wholesaler, averages $10 million in sales annually, with 4,000 customers and 7,200 sales per month. The company classifies its sales under six major headings, two of which have their greatest volume in September and October. Presently two girls calculate all invoices from the shipping or delivery slips, and three girls prepare the invoices and the monthly statements as a combined operation. They average 15 invoices an hour in an eight-hour day. The salaries of the girls are $100 each week, a total weekly payroll of $500.

You have been considering having the billing and the sales analysis work performed by an outside data processing bureau. Your studies indicate that you would still need the two girls to do the calculating that precedes the billing, as under the present order processing procedure.

However, only one girl would be required to prepare a specially coded adding machine tape that would be sent to the data processing bureau for their work. An adding machine tape would also be prepared for the daily cash receipts from customers. The initial investment in the adding machine with a special tape attachment would be approximately $800.

The bureau will supply your firm with monthly detailed statements that would be mailed to your customers. The bureau will also supply a monthly ledger card for each customer to show the status of his account (including the previous balance), render monthly sales analysis reports by product line, and prepare customer delinquency reports. For this service the bureau charges $500 a month.

▪ On the basis of this limited information, you are asked to report on the probable savings that may be realized from using the data processing bureau. Your report should also indicate any possible disadvantages in the use of the service.

18

Analyzing Office Jobs

No matter what type of business a company is engaged in, the administrative office manager must know what systems and procedures are carried out, what jobs and personnel are required, what qualifications are necessary to hold the jobs, how much should be paid for the various jobs, and the comparable relationships between the jobs. As a program of personnel administration, the researching of jobs has as its aim the accomplishment of work in the one best way, by the best qualified persons, and at the fairest wage or salary that will produce the largest volume of satisfactory work. The various components of a job study program may be outlined as follows:

1. *Job analysis:* The process of gathering information and determining all the elements involved in performing a specific job.
2. *Job description:* An outline of the informational data compiled from the job analysis, presented in an organized form that identifies and describes the contents and essential requirements of a specific job or position.
3. *Job specification:* A detailed record of the minimum job requirements explained within a uniform framework of job factors (skill, effort, responsibility, and working conditions) so that the job can be easily rated during the job evaluation process.

4. *Job evaluation:* The procedure of classifying, ranking, and grading jobs in order to set a monetary value for each specific job in relation to other jobs.
5. *Work measurement and setting work standards:* The procedure of determining the time required to accomplish each job and of determining criteria by which the degree of performance may be measured.

The first four phases of a job analysis program are explained in this chapter. The measurement of office work and the setting of work standards are described in Chapter 19.

JOB ANALYSIS

As part of a sound administrative management procedure, a program of job analysis may be used for several purposes. In the area of job evaluation, the analysis of jobs is a prerequisite to ascertaining job requirements, working conditions, health and safety requirements, and standardization of job terminology. In the appraisal of employees, job analysis is used to determine the qualifications of employees and to facilitate their promotion, upgrading, counseling, and transferring from one job to another. Job analysis is fundamental to the preparation of specifications for the recruitment, selection, placement, training, and guidance of employees. Job analysis places a firm's personnel practices on a positive antidiscrimination basis and aids in meeting the demands and requirements of the Civil Rights Act of 1964 and the Employment Act of 1967 (see Chapter 10). These acts make it mandatory that all job applicants be accorded equal treatment, regardless of race, color, religion, sex, national origin, and age. The acts place particular emphasis upon an evaluation of the skills required by the job and an upgrading of those persons who merit promotion, free of discrimination.

Through job analysis jobs may be standardized, thus leading to the establishment of performance standards and detailed operation elements of doing work in order to set time-rates for wage and salary plans. Job analysis aids in analyzing work processes to find better methods of doing work in connection with work simplification.

It is necessary not only to know what type of person should be employed in each job, but also to select a worker in terms of the education, experience, age, and other qualifications necessary to perform that job. In job analysis all the elements involved in performing a specific piece of work are determined. The difficulty in analyzing jobs accurately is the problem of defining a "piece of work." Building a 20-story building is a piece of work as is the sharpening of a pencil. The term *job,* as used in this book, means the work performed by an individual and the relationship of that work to the work produced by all other workers in the company.

Job analysis leads to standardization and simplification of jobs and stabilization of office work. As a result, office work is performed according to the instructions of the office manager, who has the facts of job analyses to back up his decisions. The use of job analysis improves the control in an office, for once a job has been standardized, it is easier to measure the output of employees in similar positions. The office manager can follow up the job analysis by testing the basic production for certain kinds of jobs and setting up bonuses or other incentives for increased output.

Job analysis aids in the elimination of waste motion in an office just as in the factory. This waste motion may be found in the operation of a calculating machine, in the filing of correspondence, or in the daily flow of paper work into, within, and out of the office.

Job analysis supplies facts that improve the work of the personnel department. Employers seek the best qualified individuals for their concerns and consider their offices as the training ground for future executives. Should the work of any department lag, it may be because the best qualified employees are not in that department. This, in turn, may be the result of faulty selection of workers. It may be that the department head and therefore the employment department did not have complete, detailed information on the requirements of the position, thus causing a poor selection of workers. To gather information about a job, a job analysis must be made.

METHODS OF GATHERING JOB INFORMATION

The entire study of office jobs rests firmly upon obtaining reliable information. The office manager, or the individual charged with analyzing jobs, must decide which method of gathering job information will be most effective at a minimum cost. These methods of obtaining job information are described on the following pages:

1. Questionnaire.
2. Interview.
3. Observation.
4. Combination of methods.

Questionnaire Method

Office managers, personnel managers, and management consultants have developed and used a variety of questionnaires whereby the employee who is most familiar with the job does most of the clerical work involved in this method of job analysis. Some of the questionnaires consist of only a series of four or five questions; others may use three or four pages of questions. Whatever the form of questionnaire, its results must be organized and interpreted in the form of job descriptions or specifications that provide management with a knowledge of what the job requires of a new employee.

For the simpler form of questionnaire, which may be used in small firms, two groups of questions may be given. In the first group of questions, the employee is required to give information such as the following:

Description of duties.
Special knowledge required for job.
Experience required to qualify for job.
How long a period of time must be spent on the job before the employee considers himself independently proficient.

In the second group of questions the employee is asked to indicate:

Daily routine tasks performed.
Work performed weekly.
Work performed monthly.
Special work performed.
Other comments.

If the office force is made up of a large number of employees, a much more detailed questionnaire may be prepared, such as the prose form of questionnaire, two pages of which are illustrated in Figure 18-1. At Pittsburgh Plate Glass Company the job description form is given to the employee and he is asked to write up his job in accordance with the instructions on the form. The employee's write-up is reviewed and edited by the employee's immediate superior and submitted to a trained job analyst to aid him in preparing a formal job analysis. The analyst obtains any additional information necessary to prepare the job analysis and indicates the presence or absence of, degree of, and frequency of characteristics required by the job if such is not indicated in the job description.

For some jobs it is necessary to analyze not only the operations but also the forms used, handled, and transferred. In Figure 18-1

Fig. 18-1

PITTSBURGH PLATE GLASS COMPANY • • • *Job Description*

DEPARTMENT: ______ SECTION: ______

NAME OF EMPLOYEE: ______ JOB TITLE: ______

ALTERNATE TITLES: ______

IMMEDIATE SUPERIOR: ______ TITLE: ______

LENGTH OF TIME ON THIS JOB: ______ JOB CODE: ______

EXPLANATION

Purpose:

This Job Description form is designed to assist you in describing your job. Such factual information as you furnish concerning the duties, responsibilities, and other requirements of your job will be used in helping to determine its relative value in comparison with other jobs in the Company. You are requested to complete this form since you are most familiar with the details of your work.

Completed Job Descriptions will be verified and other studies made to insure that all of the facts that properly apply have been obtained.

It must be noted that it is the *job* that is being analyzed and not the employee or the employee's ability to prepare the Job Description.

Instructions:

Please fill out the form as carefully and thoroughly as possible. State your duties and responsibilities as you understand them rather than confer with others who perform similar work. Any questions which arise should be discussed with your supervisor.

In describing your job, tell what you do and show the importance of each task as well as how often it is performed. Make the description sufficiently clear and complete to give the uninformed reader a true picture of the work performed and the skills required.

The following suggestions may be helpful in arranging and setting forth your duties in a simple and effective manner:

Describe all of your duties in detail:

1) Divide your job (including special assignments and irregular duties) into separate steps or tasks, devoting one, concise, numbered statement to each;
2) In defining each task, state from whom the work or data is obtained, explain the operation which you perform, and indicate to whom the completed work is given (unless apparent);
3) Separate the tasks according to the frequency of their performance (i.e. daily, weekly, monthly, occasionally, etc.) and, under the appropriate headings on the form, enter the statements which describe them;
4) Show in the columns provided the approximate amount of time devoted to each task;
5) Emphasize the important features of your job.

The attached example illustrates the application of these recommendations.

IF MORE SPACE IS NEEDED USE ADDITIONAL 8½" x 11" SHEETS

Prose-Type Questionnaire (page 1)

note that in Question 4 of Section B, "Supplementary Information," the worker is asked to indicate the reports and forms he personally prepares and to attach sample copies of the forms used. In another

A. DESCRIPTION OF DUTIES (Contd.)

	Hours Per Period
2. Weekly, Semi-Monthly, Monthly, Quarterly, Semi-Annual, Annual Duties:	
3. Occasional Duties:	

B. SUPPLEMENTARY INFORMATION

1. List Machines and Equipment used and show approximate % of time devoted to each:

NAME	MAKE	% OF TIME

2. Proportion of time spent:

Sitting:	____%
Standing:	____%
Walking:	____%
Lifting & Carrying:	____%
________	____%
	100%

3. If Supervisory Duties are performed, list the Names and Job Titles of those supervised:

NAME	JOB TITLE

4. What Reports and Forms do you personally prepare? (If practicable, attach sample copies of forms used)

5. What contacts with other people are you required to make, other than with your immediate superior and those under your supervision? Indicate nature, frequency and method (in person, telephone, correspondence) of contact.

Fig. 18-1

Pittsburgh Plate Glass Company

Prose-Type Questionnaire (page 3)

questionnaire each form handled by the clerk is analyzed. This information supplements the specific operation job analysis and aids in controlling office forms, as explained in Chapter 16. On this questionnaire the following data pertaining to forms are requested:

Received from ______________________________

Copy number ______________ Number per month ______________

Operations performed in connection with form ______________

____

Clock hours for operations ______________________

Transferred to ______________________________

Such an inquiry is necessary only in those cases where the number of forms handled and transferred is so large as to require a major portion of the clerk's time.

The possible disadvantages that characterize the questionnaire method of gathering job information include the difficulty in designing a questionnaire that will bring forth all the data required by the job analyst. There is the temptation to ask for so much information that the questionnaire becomes top-heavy, complex, and often confusing. The data provided may be misleading or incomplete because the employee does not take time to complete the form correctly. Some employees are not necessarily skilled in properly analyzing their jobs and thus may exaggerate the importance of their jobs. On the other hand, employees may underemphasize those phases of their jobs that occupy a fairly large percentage of their total work time. The personal touch, which characterizes the interview method, is entirely lacking since the employee is called upon merely to fill out a questionnaire. Unless the questions are precisely and clearly worded, it may be difficult for the worker to communicate and for the analyst to interpret the information supplied. Finally, the completed questionnaire requires a careful reanalysis and editing, all of which represent a costly means of obtaining job information.

Against all these possible disadvantages must be weighed the major advantage of being able to obtain information rapidly by means of a questionnaire, at least when compared with the time-consuming chore of personally interviewing each worker. The questionnaire method does serve as a starting point in job analysis, however, and can be expanded by means of the interview, the observation method, or a combination of the two methods.

Interview Method

The interview, which requires the job analyst to talk personally with the employee in order to gather information about the job, is costlier than the questionnaire method. For some types of job analyses, the interview may be undertaken at the employee's work station so that at the same time the job may be observed. In other instances the interview may take place in the analyst's office or in a general conference room. Prior to the interview rapport with the worker must be obtained, and he must be put at ease so that there will be little hesitancy in replying to the questions asked. As the worker responds to the questions asked, the analyst may record his findings on a job information sheet such as that illustrated in Figure 18-2. All information thus recorded should be read to the employee to confirm the correctness of the data. Following the interview the employee's supervisor should be consulted to verify the accuracy of the information obtained.

Using the method of interviewing and questioning two or more workers about their jobs and then interviewing their supervisor, the Pacific Gas and Electric Company requires the following job information in its study:

1. The present job name.
2. Division, district, and department in which located.
3. The immediate supervision.
4. Any indirect supervision or division of authority.
5. Regular duties of position.
6. Special or unusual requirements of knowledge, ability, or skill.
7. Degree and type of responsibility.
8. Any unusual or disagreeable working conditions.
9. Minimum requirements of education, training, experience, and any special abilities needed.

This information is gathered by interviewing and observing each man at his job. This is a study of positions, not of persons holding the positions; and, as a result, positions are standardized. Equivalent jobs in each department and throughout the organization are given similar titles and compensation. Maximum and minimum rates of pay are established for each occupational class, together with consistent levels and grades within each class. Finally, motion and time studies, supplemented by motion pictures, are frequently made of the jobs.

JOB INFORMATION SHEET

(Questionnaire for Nonsupervisory Employees)

Date issued ____________

Job Title ____________ Dept. # ____________ Date due ____________

Name of your Supervisor or Foreman ____________

Describe your job fully ____________

____

1. EDUCATION REQUIRED. Indicate schooling required for your JOB by check mark.
   No schooling required____ 4 yrs. high school____ Engineering college____
   Grammar school____ Technical high school____ Special schooling____
   2 yrs. high school____ College________
   Do you make any reports? No____ Yes____ If yes, what are they?____
   ____
2. EXPERIENCE AND TRAINING. Experience and training required for your JOB.
   Months: 1__ 2__ 3__ 4__ 5__ 6__ 7__ 8__ 9__ 10__ 11__ 12__
   Years: 1__ 2__ 3__ 4__ 5__ 6__ 7__ 8__
   Does your job require many skills? No__Yes__ If yes, enumerate and describe briefly. ____________
3. INITIATIVE AND INGENUITY. Do you make your own decisions?
   No__ Yes__
   If yes, what are they? ____________
   Do you inspect someone else's job? No__ Yes__ Who inspects your job? ________ How often does your job repeat itself? Per Hour ________
   Per Day________ Per Week________
4. PHYSICAL DEMAND. What kind of equipment do you use? ________
   What is the maximum weight of your work in pounds? Lifting________
   Pulling______ Pushing______ The heaviest work is done___% of working time. Your work position is Sitting__ Standing__ Walking__ Shoveling__
   Holding steadily__ Lifting overhead__ Bending__
   Worker height must be__ft.. __in. Weight must be __lbs.
5. MENTAL OR VISUAL DEMAND. What accuracy is required on the job? ____
   Are the hands and eyes constantly coordinated? ____________
   Are operations automatic? No__ Partly__ Yes__
6. RESPONSIBILITY FOR EQUIPMENT. What is the cost of possible damage to equipment? No damage__ Minimum $__ Maximum $__ Do you repair equipment? No__ Yes__ If yes, what kind? ____________

Fig. 18-2

Job Information Sheet (Continued)

7. RESPONSIBILITY FOR MATERIAL OR PRODUCT. Are you responsible for any materials? No___ Yes___ If yes, what are they? ____________
How much spoilage may occur? Loss in dollars $___ What is required to avoid spoilage? ____________
Can the spoiled work be repaired? No_____ Partly_____ Completely_____
Enumerate and briefly describe various materials you have to recognize.
____

8. RESPONSIBILITY FOR SAFETY OF OTHERS. How many people may be injured if carelessness would occur?___ Are there hazards which may cause injury? No___ Yes___ If yes, what are they? ____________
____

9. RESPONSIBILITY FOR WORK OF OTHERS. Are you responsible for work of others? No___ Yes___ How many?___ For new employees only______

10. WORKING CONDITIONS. Are the surrounding conditions Agreeable?___ Disagreeable?___ In what way do disagreeable conditions affect your job? Noise___ Fumes___ Cold___ Hot___ Changes in temperature___ Dirt___ Dust___ Oil___ Steam___ Too wet___ Glare___ Somewhat dark___ Drafty___

11. UNAVOIDABLE HAZARDS. Is your health affected? No___ Yes___
If yes, in what way? ____________
Which accidents may occur? Burns___ Shock___ Cuts___ Crushed Fingers___
Injury to ____________ Feet___ Eyes___ Ears___ Lungs___

12. SUPERVISION. Received from ____________
Occasionally___ Daily___ Hourly___
Do you supervise? No___ Yes___ If yes, how many?___ Occasionally___
Daily___ Hourly___

13. Would you prefer to be transferred to another job? No___ Yes___ If yes, which job could you perform? ____________

14. REMARKS. Give additional information which has not been covered, and which may assist in a better description of your job. ____________
____
____
____

Fig. 18-2

Job Information Sheet (Concluded)

Observation Method

In addition to gathering job information by the questionnaire and the interview methods, in some businesses the analyst may be able to obtain job data from the time-study department. The time-study engineer is concerned with observing and studying all aspects of the job, including skill requirements, physical and mental effort required, job environment needs, and information flows—to name several factors—which may not be precisely included in job descriptions. These factors are necessary, however, for the preparation of performance standards as explained in the following chapter. Another approach to analyzing the job is the planning of a conference with the worker and his supervisor during which the analyst records his findings while both the worker and the supervisor participate in clarifying job requirements and in answering detailed questions about the job.

Combination of Methods

The methods described above can be combined to obtain a complete job analysis. Employees may be sent a brief questionnaire with instructions to return it to their supervisors. At the same time a more elaborate questionnaire is sent to the supervisors, who are requested to return it to the analyst about the same time as the employees are returning theirs to the supervisors. The supervisor looks over the employees' forms, makes the necessary corrections and additions, and returns the forms to the analyst. The analyst then interviews employees in order to verify their answers. Later, at a conference of the supervisor and a group of employees' representatives, the job contents are further clarified for final adoption in the form of job descriptions.

JOB DESCRIPTIONS

The results of the job analysis are expressed in the job description, or the position description as it is often called. From the job description a job specification may be developed separately or it may be combined with the job description.

Writing the Job Description

In preparing the job description, clarity and simplicity of expression are prerequisites. The terms used should have universal acceptance or be carefully defined since the descriptions will be used by several persons for many purposes, including wage surveys. Job titles and descriptions should compare as closely as possible with those listed in the *Dictionary of Occupational Titles*,[1] which contains standardized descriptions for almost 22,000 jobs that are

[1] *Dictionary of Occupational Titles* (Washington, D.C.: U.S. Government Printing Office, undated).

known by 36,000 titles. Another valuable source of job information is the *Occupational Outlook Handbook*.[2] The 19 job titles and descriptions used by the Administrative Management Society in conducting its annual survey of office salaries in the United States and Canada are shown in Figure 18-3. The data collected in a recent survey covered more than 620,000 employees in over 7,300 companies of all sizes and types in 132 cities.

A job description usually includes the following information:

Name of job.

Resumé or summary of job.

Description of duties performed.

Equipment, materials, and forms used on job.

Special environmental conditions that facilitate performing the job, such as proper lighting, elimination of noise, and proper air conditioning.

Relation to other jobs:
- Transfer of work.
- Checking of work of other departments, or vice versa.
- Promotional opportunities of this job.

Special qualifications for job:
- Mental.
- Physical.
- Experience.

Prerequisite knowledge for job.

Although there is no prescribed amount of detailed information that should be included in a job description, it should contain enough information to assure that the job can be accurately evaluated and rated. The job is to be described *as it is;* no modifications should be incorporated into the descriptions for what the job *ought to be.*

Typical Job Descriptions

Figure 18-4 represents one complete job description for a shop order clerk in the Clerical and Technical Department of a steel company. Sometimes jobs are grouped and described concisely, as given in the following job descriptions taken from the *Dictionary of Occupational Titles* and the Michigan Civil Service Commission's listings.[3]

[2] *Occupational Outlook Handbook* (Washington, D.C.: U.S. Government Printing Office, undated).

[3] "Clerical Job Evaluation" (Willow Grove, Pennsylvania: Administrative Management Society, 1965).

JOB TITLES AND DESCRIPTIONS

A MAIL CLERK – FILE CLERK
Circulates office mail, delivers messages and supplies. May process incoming or outgoing mail and operate related machines and perform other routine duties.
Performs routine filing and sorting operations according to an established system. Locates and removes material upon requests and keeps records of its disposition. May perform related clerical duties.

B GENERAL CLERK B
Performs clerical duties in accordance with established procedures. Maintains records and may prepare reports from basic data which does not require the development of secondary data. Job requires considerable supervision.

C GENERAL CLERK A
Performs complex and responsible clerical duties requiring independent analysis, exercise of judgement and a detailed knowledge of department or company policies and procedures. Minimum supervision required.

D ACCOUNTING CLERK B
Checks, verifies and posts journal vouchers, accounts payable vouchers or other simple accounting data of a recurring or standard nature.

E ACCOUNTING CLERK A
Keeps a complete set of accounting records in a small office, or handles one phase of accounting in a larger unit which requires the accounting training needed to determine proper accounting entries, prepare accounting reports, analyze accounting records to determine causes of results shown, etc. May direct work of junior clerks or bookkeepers. (Excludes supervisors)

F BOOKKEEPING MACHINE OPERATOR
Operates a bookkeeping machine to record business transactions of a recurring and standardized nature, where proper posting has been indicated or is readily identifiable. May balance to control figures.

G OFFSET DUPLICATING MACHINE OPERATOR
Sets up and operates offset duplicating machines. Cleans and adjusts equipment but does not make repairs. May prepare own plates and operate auxiliary equipment, and may keep records of kind and amount of work done.

H TELEPHONE SWITCHBOARD OPERATOR
Operates a single or multiple position PBX telephone switchboard. May keep records of calls and toll charges, and may operate a paging system and perform duties of receptionist.

I TYPIST – CLERK
Types letter, reports, tabulations, and other material in which setups and terms are generally clear and follow a standard pattern. May prepare stencils or offset masters. Performs clerical duties of moderate difficulty.

J STENOGRAPHER
Transcribes from dictating equipment, or records and transcribes shorthand dictation involving a normal range of business vocabulary. May perform copy typing or clerical work of moderate difficulty incidental to primary stenographic duties. May operate as a member of a centralized stenographic area. May perform the secretarial function for a small group.

K SECRETARY B
Performs secretarial duties for a member of middle management. General requirements are the same as for Secretary A (listed in opposite column), but limited to the area of responsibility of the principal.

L SECRETARY A
Performs secretarial duties for a top level executive or a person responsible for a major functional or geographic operation. Does work of a confidential nature and relieves principal of designated administrative details. Requires initiative, judgment, knowledge of company practices, policy and organization.

M KEY PUNCH OPERATOR B
Operates an alphabetic or numerical key punch machine to record pre-coded or readily usable data following generally standardized procedures. May verify the work of others, using a verifying machine.

N KEY PUNCH OPERATOR A
Operates an alphabetic or numerical key punch or verifier to record or verify complex or uncoded data working from source material which may not be arranged for key punching. Selects appropriate number and kinds of cards. Follows a pattern of operations generally standardized but frequently including rules, exceptions, and special instructions which demand operator's close attention.

O TABULATING MACHINE OPERATOR
Sets up, operates and wires a variety of punched card equipment, including tabulators and multipliers. Wires boards from diagrams prepared by others for routine jobs, uses prewired boards on complex or repetitive jobs. May locate and correct job difficulties and assist in training less experienced operators.

P COMPUTER OPERATOR B
Operates computers utilizing established programs or programs under development. Loads computer and manipulates control switch on console in accordance with programmed instructions. Observes functioning of equipment. Detects nature of errors or equipment failure and makes normal console adjustments. Maintains necessary operating records.

Q COMPUTER OPERATOR A
Operates computer utilizing established programs or programs under development. Oversees loading of computer and manipulation of controls. Detects nature of errors or equipment failure. May instruct or give limited directions to less experienced operators.

R PROGRAMMER A
With general supervision, analyzes and defines programs for electronic data processing equipment. Is generally competent in most phases of programming to work on his own, and only requires general guidance for the balance of the activities. Conducts analyses of sufficient detail of all defined systems specifications and develops block diagrams and machine logic flow charts, codes, prepares test data, tests and debugs programs. Revises and refines programs as required and documents all procedures used throughout the computer program when it is formally established. Evaluates and modifies existing programs to take into account changes in systems requirements. May give technical assistance to lower level classifications. Normally progresses from this classification to a Lead programmer.

S SYSTEMS ANALYST
Under close supervision, assists in devising computer system specifications and record layouts. Is qualified to work on several phases of systems analysis, but requires guidance and direction for other phases. Conducts studies and analyses of existing and proposed operations. Prepares all levels of computer block diagram and may assist in the preparation of machine logic flow charting.

Fig. 18-3

Job Titles and Descriptions Used by the Administrative Management Society

594 **MASTER JOB DESCRIPTION**

Job No. 594

DEPARTMENT CLERICAL AND TECHNICAL
SUBDIVISION MILL RECORDING (MAINTENANCE)
JOB TITLE SHOP ORDER CLERK
DATE 1-1-72

MASTER JOB DESCRIPTION

PRIMARY FUNCTION:
Maintains files of all Shop Orders received.

TOOLS AND EQUIPMENT:
Pencil, various forms, phone, and files.

MATERIALS:
Miscellaneous forms and stationery supplies, etc.

SOURCE OF SUPERVISION:
General and Assistant General Foremen.

DIRECTION EXERCISED:
None.

WORKING PROCEDURE:

1. Receives Shop Order folders from Planning Office and affixes departmental stamp showing date, etc. Stamps receiving, inspecting, and shipping form on Dispatch Cards. Indicates drawing revision number on Shop Order folder from blueprint inside folder.
2. Detaches Material Card and Print Card from Shop Order folder and files according to Shop Order number and print number, respectively. Files Shop Order folders according to Shop Order number or delivers to proper foreman as indicated on folder by Assistant General Foreman.
3. Stamps location on Shop Order folder and Dispatch Card as orders are submitted at beginning of each operation.
4. Posts to dispatch cards material received and dates received, inspected, and shipped from shipping, inspection, and receiving notices received from Shipper and Inspection Department.
5. Files receiving, shipping, and inspection notices according to dates.
6. Refers discrepancies on received and shipped material to others.
7. Stamps Dispatch Cards, Print Cards, and Shop Order folders when work is completed, and files Dispatch Cards and Print Cards in completed files according to Shop Order number.
8. Maintains a constant record of the number of Shop Orders completed, in process, backlog file, and on material not received. Prepares monthly report of same.
9. Receives blueprint revisions from Chief Inspector and Maintenance Planning Office; determines from files the number of Shop Orders requiring revised prints; orders prints; destroys old copies; and inserts new copy in folder. Enters date revision received on Shop Order folder.
10. Locates information of status of Shop Orders requested by foreman, etc. from Dispatch Cards.
11. Maintains Rack-Up Sheet showing current status of large jobs from Dispatch Cards.
12. Periodically bundles up completed records and sends to vault.
13. Files Shop Order folders for castings in "No Casting" file until material is received.

The above statement reflects the general details considered necessary to describe the principal functions of the job identified, and shall not be construed as a detailed description of all of the work requirements that may be inherent in the job.

Fig. 18-4

Job Description for a Shop Order Clerk

In Figure 18-5 the group, Business Machine Operations, consists of five typical office positions and job descriptions.

Fig. 18-5

BUSINESS MACHINE OPERATIONS

1. **Accounting Machine Operator**

   Operates a machine to prepare accounting records on ledger sheets, forms, listing tapes, invoices or similar records such as posting, billing, accounts receivable, accounts payable, accumulating or distributing amounts on tapes or forms by key-depressed operations. (Punched card method excluded.)

   In addition to the operators of the usual bookkeeping machines, include here operators of specially built machines for banking functions.

2. **Calculating Machine Operator**

   Presses proper keys on keyboard of a key-driven machine and presses keys and manipulates certain levers on rotary-type machine to perform automatically the basic arithmetical computations of adding, subtracting, multiplying, and dividing. May also perform other computations, such as taking the root of a number, or raising a number to a power. May calculate or check the figures on such records as inventories, financial accounts, payrolls, balance sheets, invoices, discounts, sales and statistical reports.

3. **Duplicating Machine Operator**

   A. Performs any and all duties involved in making reproductions or preparing for reproduction on such equipment as addressing machines, photographic reproducing machines of all types, blueprint work.

   B. Performs any and all duties involved in making reproductions on machines, using cut stencils, special metal plates, composition gelatin or liquid process.

4. **Key Punch Operator**

   Records accounting and statistical data on tabulating cards by punching a series of holes in the cards in a specified sequence using a numerical key punch machine. Transcribes written information into perforations on the tabulating cards by punching corresponding numbers or symbols on the machine keyboard.

5. **Tabulating Machine Operator**

   Operates a machine that automatically analyzes, makes calculations, and translates or divides information represented by holes punched in groups of tabulating cards, and prints the translated data on form sheets, reports, special cards, or accounting records, sets or adjusts machine to add, subtract, multiply, and make other calculations.

Office Positions and Job Descriptions for the Grouping, Business Machine Operations

JOB SPECIFICATIONS

A *job specification* describes the minimum requirements of the job in relation to the job factors of skill, effort, responsibility, and working conditions. The job specification is used primarily as the basis for rating the job in the process of job evaluation. Job specifications are the natural outcome of job analyses and, as indicated previously, may be combined with job or position descriptions. For example, in Figure 18-6 the specifications for the job of tabulating machine operator are combined with the position description.

Job specifications are often used in the employment, selection, training, and counseling of workers because the education and experience specifications imply what qualifications a person should possess in order to be hired. However, more effective use can be made of the *man specification,* or *employee specification,* which states specifically the minimum qualifications a prospective employee must possess in order to be considered for employment. When the job specification and the employee specification are brought together, the interviewer has accurate data at hand for matching the job applicant to the job opening.

The interviewer or job counselor is assisted by job specifications in that they better enable him to recommend courses of action to inexperienced or handicapped workers. Much information can be obtained from job specifications for rating the job in relation to other jobs in the company, for the development of a training curriculum, for the establishment of physical requirements for workers from the standpoint of safety, for the purpose of conducting salary surveys, and for establishing lines of promotion and demotion.

The job specifications illustrated in Figures 18-6 and 18-7 can be used not only for a promotional program for office workers but also for an employee training program. Every phase of the job is brought to light in the specification after the results of the job analysis are known. An employee specification can be used to assist in the proper selection of office employees, as shown in Table 18-1. This table indicates the education, experience, appearance, and other qualifications required for four selected clerical positions.

JOB EVALUATION

Job analyses and descriptions are prerequisite to management's determination of the relative value of each job. *Job evaluation*

SPECIFICATION

Clerical, Supervisory and Technical Position

Occ. No. 105-11

Class — Division Accounting

Department Tabulating

Position Name TABULATING MACHINE OPERATOR Grade E

Position Description

Under direct supervision of Supervisor--Tabulating, operate various types of electric tabulating machines to analyze, calculate, translate, summarize information represented by punched holes on tabulating cards and print translated data on form sheets, reports or accounting records. Operate machines such as interpreter, multiplier, collator, sorter, tabulator, reproducing summary punch. Compile and print payroll and earnings statements, payroll deductions, accounts payable, sales analyses, billings, miscellaneous reports as requested. Change plug boards; wire up boards. Repunch cards which fail to pass through machines. Keep machines clean and oiled.

Promote From ____________ To ____________

	Analyst		Dept. Head		Revised	Revised	Revised	
Initials								
Date								

THIS JOB DESCRIPTION IS NOT A COMPLETE STATEMENT OF ALL THE DUTIES AND RESPONSIBILITIES WHICH GO WITH THE JOB. IT CONTAINS ONLY THE FACTS NECESSARY TO RATE THE JOB FAIRLY.

National Electrical Manufacturers Association

Fig. 18-6 **Position Description for Tabulating Machine Operator (page 1)**

SPECIFICATION

Clerical, Supervisory and Technical Position

Occ. No. 105-11

Division Accounting

Department Tabulating

Class —— Grade E

Position Name Tabulating Machine Operator Points 255

FACTOR	SPECIFICATION	Rating	
		Deg.	Pts.
EDUCATION	Use arithmetic. Work with punched cards, statements, and reports. Knowledge of operation of electrical tabulating machines equivalent to general academic education plus specialized training up to 1 year.	3	60
EXPERIENCE	Over 1 up to 2 years.	4	100
COMPLEXITY OF DUTIES	Plan and perform a sequence of semiroutine duties working from standard procedures. Make decisions which require some judgment to wire up boards, check form of data, assure all cards are sorted for run, determine action to be taken within limits prescribed.	3	60
MONETARY RESPONSIBILITY	Limited monetary responsibility since the work is usually checked or verified before it leaves the Section.	2	10
RESPONSIBILITY FOR CONTACTS WITH OTHERS	Routine contacts with Accounting, Payroll, Sales, to give or get information requiring only courtesy.	2	10
WORKING CONDITIONS	Somewhat disagreeable due to noise from equipment.	3	15

FACTORS TO BE ADDED FOR SUPERVISORY POSITIONS ONLY

TYPE OF SUPERVISION			
EXTENT OF SUPERVISION			

National Electrical Manufacturers Association

Fig. 18-6

Job Specification for Tabulating Machine Operator (page 2)

Fig. 18-7

JOB SPECIFICATION

Job Title: Senior General Clerk

Qualifications:

Educational: High school graduate.

Experience: Two or more years with company as general clerk and typist-clerk.
Experience in office systems and procedures.

Personal: Speed and efficiency in handling volume of detail.
Ability to instruct others in clerical jobs.
Ability to supervise work of others.

Duties:

1. Handle mail and dictate correspondence.
2. Check, index, and file important records and correspondence.
3. Handle all payroll records and reports.
4. Summarize and tabulate cost information and records.
5. Receive, take care of, and account for petty cash and office funds.
6. Supervise work of general clerks in routine jobs.

Promotional Opportunities:
Advancement to Assistant Chief Clerk after two years

Salary Range:
$430-$475 a month.

Job Specification for Position of Senior General Clerk

Table 18-1

EMPLOYEE SPECIFICATIONS FOR CLERICAL POSITIONS

Job Title	File Clerk	Typist-Clerk	General Clerk	Senior General Clerk
Monthly salary range	**$340-$360**	**$365-$395**	**$370-$420**	**$430-$475**
Section A—to be determined by interview				
1. Education	High school	High school	High school	High school
2. Experience	None	6 months	1 year	2 years
3. Appearance	Average	Average	Average	Average
4. Tact and poise	Average	Average	Average	Average
Section B—to be determined by test				
5. Intelligence	I.Q.—90	I.Q.—95	I.Q.—100	I.Q.—105
6. Arithmetic	80% of test	80% of test	85% of test	90% of test
7. Spelling	80% of test	80% of test	85% of test	90% of test
8. Typing or rotary calculator		50 words or 80% of test	60 words or 90% of test	65 words or 90% of test

Note: Titles and salary ranges are illustrative and for comparison purposes only.

aims at an equitable payroll policy on the basis of the estimated or measured worth of each job in relation to other jobs. The larger the organization, the more necessary it becomes to evaluate office jobs. When jobs are properly evaluated, employees doing similar work are paid approximately the same salary. However, the cost of living, the supply and demand of office workers, and competitive conditions also influence the salaries paid for office jobs.

There are two basic plans of evaluating jobs in order to group those with the same apparent requisites so that salary schedules may be made comparable: (1) *nonquantitative* grouping of jobs according to their relative or estimated difficulty; and (2) *quantitative* grouping of jobs according to mental, physical, skill, and experience requisites. The two basic plans may be subdivided into the following four methods of job evaluation:

A. *Nonquantitative evaluation plans*
   1. Ranking method.
   2. Job classification method.

B. *Quantitative evaluation plans*
   1. Factor-comparison method.
   2. Point method.

In recent years a fifth method of job evaluation known as the *guideline method* of job evaluation has been developed. This method combines the techniques of direct pricing, ranking, and grading of the jobs in the evaluation of the job descriptions. The guideline method is not concerned with the value of a job as related to other jobs within the company but instead reflects the marketplace interpretation of the relative job value.

In this part of the chapter, each of the five methods of job evaluation is described. The pricing of the jobs and the determination of pay ranges are discussed in Chapter 20, "Office Salary Administration."

Ranking Method

The *ranking method,* also known as the "rank order," "order of merit," and "departmental order of importance system," is the simplest and oldest method of determining the economic value of a job. Under the ranking method the individual jobs are analyzed and ranked according to the difficulty and the overall responsibility of each job. Jobs are ranked according to job titles from the most important to the least important in relation to their contribution to the business.

It is assumed that the salary increases as the job becomes more difficult. This is not always true, however, because sometimes a salary is determined by the working conditions, responsibility, or experience involved.

A simple ranking of office jobs is given in Table 18-2.

Table 18-2

SIMPLE RANKING OF OFFICE AND CLERICAL JOBS

Rank Order	Job Title	Monthly Starting Salary
1	Bookkeeper, General Ledger	$480
1	Senior Stenographer	480
2	Cost Accounting Clerk	470
3	Advertising Clerk	460
4	Head File Clerk	440
5	Accounting Clerk	420
5	Cashier	420
5	General Clerk	420
6	Junior Stenographer	410
6	Payroll Clerk	410
7	Purchasing Clerk	400
7	Sales Clerk	400
8	Addressograph-Multigraph Operator	390
9	Billing Clerk	380
9	Order Clerk	380
9	Switchboard Operator-Receptionist	380
9	Typist	380
10	Bookkeeper, Customers' Ledger	370
11	File Clerk	340
12	Messenger	320

Note: Titles and starting salaries are illustrative and for comparison purposes only.

The ranking of jobs is often accomplished by an evaluating committee consisting of supervisors and department heads. The ranking may be done in terms of job titles alone or by combining titles, job content, and compensation rates. The number of ranks will vary with the number of jobs or positions and the type of business organization. In Table 18-2, for example, the 20 jobs making up one activity field—office and clerical jobs—are arranged in rank order from 1 through 12.

Two types of job ranking methods sometimes used are the *card-ranking method* and the *paired-comparison method*. In both methods the supervisors are asked to rank the jobs in the order of their importance from highest to lowest, or vice versa.

Card-Ranking Method. In the card-ranking method each job title is placed on a 3″ x 5″ index card. The job analyst arranges the cards in the order of the relative importance of the jobs to the company, ignoring the present salary of the jobs, the historic position or status of the job in the company, and the performance of any particular employee holding that job. This approach to job evaluation gives a fairly intelligent analysis of the jobs without the influence of established, historical precedents and appears more like an independent survey based upon sound operations. If there are too many jobs to be thus ranked, it may be necessary to rank them first by groups of jobs and then to rank the jobs within each group.

Paired-Comparison Method. In the paired-comparison method each job is ranked against another job of comparable ranking on the basis of the total difficulty of the job. The more times a job is ranked as more difficult, the more important the job becomes. One type of form used in the paired-comparison method is shown in Figure 18-8.

In small offices where comparatively few jobs (less than 25) are to be evaluated and where the employees respect the employer's integrity in ranking the jobs, the ranking method may be used

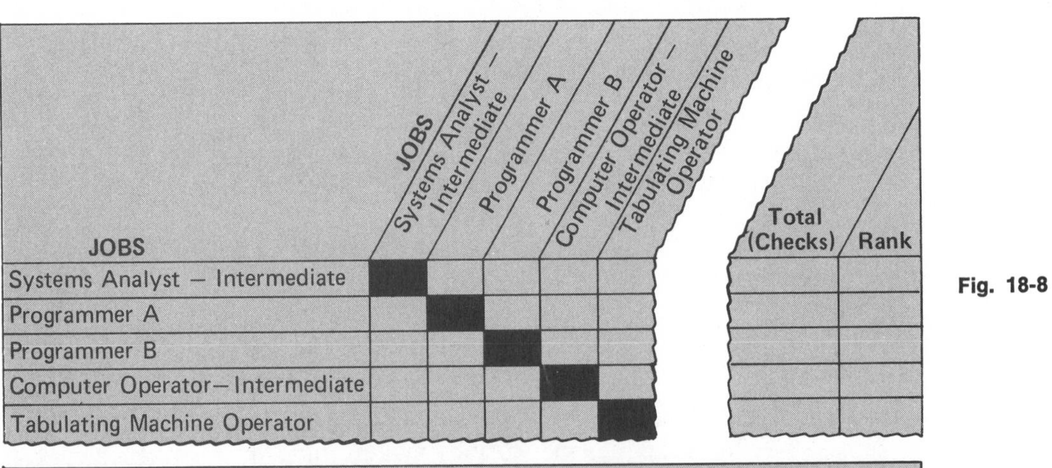

JOBS	Systems Analyst — Intermediate	Programmer A	Programmer B	Computer Operator — Intermediate	Tabulating Machine Operator	Total (Checks)	Rank
Systems Analyst – Intermediate							
Programmer A							
Programmer B							
Computer Operator—Intermediate							
Tabulating Machine Operator							

Directions: Compare the first job in the first column with each job in the slant columns. If the job in the first column is considered to have greater value to the firm than the job in the slant column, place a check mark (✓) in the box below the job in the slant column. Repeat process until all jobs have been compared. Tally check marks to find rank of jobs.

Fig. 18-8

Form Used in Paired-Comparison Method

satisfactorily. One advantage of the method is its simplicity; it is easily understood by all parties concerned. However, the rating is extremely subjective and is often incorrectly based on the employee performing the job rather than on the job itself. Also, the relative ranking of jobs depends greatly on current salary and wage rates which fluctuate upward or downward with economic conditions. The method can be installed without undue expense, but much grievance and loss of time may be caused by the inability to explain the arbitrarily determined salary or wage rates since there are no objective studies to back up the established rates. The evaluation process often becomes unwieldly when there is a large number of jobs, and it is unlikely that there is any one person who knows all the jobs and is thus qualified to evaluate them.

Job Classification Method

The *job classification method,* also known as the *grading method,* is an outgrowth of the ranking method. This method has long been used by civil service authorities in employing office and clerical workers and in granting periodic salary increments. Prior to the actual classification of jobs, a number of predetermined classes or grades are selected on the basis of common denominators such as levels of responsibilities, abilities or skills, knowledge, and duties that run through the jobs. The jobs or positions are then analyzed and grouped into specific classes or grades. The grades are arranged in order of importance according to the job and the work performed. Thus, it is assumed that each job or position involves duties and responsibilities that fit into the respective graded classification.

Two methods of grouping jobs in a classification chart are shown in Tables 18-3 and 18-4. The nature of the work is combined with the salary range to show that there is a direct relationship between the rating of the importance of the job and the salary paid. In Table 18-3, the four family groupings are: clerical, stenographic, accounting, and engineering. Under each of these family groupings, the jobs are ranked according to their importance, which in turn is influenced by the salary range. In Table 18-4 the accounting family is broken down into the following job classifications: junior accountants, accountants, senior accountants, accounting supervisors, and accounting department managers. Below each of these classifications the individual jobs, after being analyzed, are arranged in the order of importance according to the work performed.

Table 18-3

BREAKDOWN OF JOB CLASSIFICATIONS BY JOB LEVELS AND SALARY RANGES

			Family Groupings			
Job Level	Salary Range	Midpoint	Clerical	Stenographic	Accounting	Engineering
1	$375-$ 425	$400	Junior Clerk	....	....	....
2	395- 445	420	Assistant Clerk	Jr. Stenographer	....	....
3	400- 500	450	Clerk	Stenographer	....	....
4	440- 540	490	Senior Clerk	Sr. Stenographer	....	....
5	450- 550	500	Principal Clerk	Jr. Secretary	Jr. Accountant	....
6	470- 570	520	Chief Clerk	Secretary	....	Jr. Engineer
7	525- 675	600	....	Exec. Clerk	Accountant	....
8	575- 725	650	....	....	....	Engineer
9	625- 775	700	....	....	Sr. Accountant	....
10	650- 850	750	....	....	....	Sr. Engineer
11	725- 925	825	....	....	Accounting Supv.	....
12	750- 950	850	....	....	....	Engineering Supv.
13	850- 1,050	950	....	....	Acct. Dept. Mgr.	....

Table 18-4

BREAKDOWN OF THE ACCOUNTING FAMILY BY JOB CLASSIFICATIONS AND INDIVIDUAL JOBS

Job Classifications		$500 Junior Accountants	$600 Accountants	$700 Senior Accountants	$825 Accounting Supervisors	$950 Acct. Dept. Managers
	1	Time Clerks	Sr. Time Clerks	Time Clerk Supv.	....	Mgr. Timekeeping
	2	Payroll Clerks	Sr. Payroll Clerks	....	Asst. Paymaster	Paymaster
	3	....	....	Asst. Cashier	Cashier	....
Individual Jobs	4	Cost Clerks	....	Cost Supv.	....	Mgr. Cost Account.
	5	Accts. Pay. Clerks	....	....	Accts. Pay Supv.	....
	6	Accts. Rec. Clerks	....	Accts. Rec. Supv.	....	....
	7	Etc.	Etc.	Etc.	Etc.	Etc.

Note: In both Tables 18-3 and 18-4, titles and salaries are illustrative and for comparison purposes only.

The most common example of the job classification method is the *General Schedule* used by the federal government, which covers all its jobs and positions (professional, scientific, clerical, administrative, and custodial). The General Schedule is composed of 18 job classes (GS-1 through GS-18) with the job classes differing in the levels of job difficulty, responsibilities, and qualification requirements of the work performed. The lower the job class number, the less difficult the job becomes. The higher the job class number, the greater are the responsibilities and qualifications needed to fill the job.

Like the ranking method the job classification method possesses the advantages of lack of expense in its installation and ease of explanation to employees. Also, like the ranking method the job classification method may be applied in small business firms or offices where employees are hired by supervisors. Since there is usually a hierarchy already present in the office, this informal ranking by employees is easily accepted and serves as a good starting point. The job classification method has the disadvantage of a subjective grading and rating of jobs by total content, which may create distrust among employees. By like token, the very purpose of this method of job evaluation is defeated if outside influences such as the existing wage rates or the present job holders create a biased effect on the job classification rating.

Factor-Comparison Method

The *factor-comparison method,* a quantitative evaluation plan, is also known as the "key-job system," the "job-comparison system," and the "job-to-money method." This method refers to rating the jobs in terms of money. Each job is evaluated in terms of the following five critical factors, based on selected key jobs that are related to a money value, the "going rate":

1. Mental requirements.
2. Skill requirements.
3. Physical requirements.
4. Responsibility.
5. Working conditions.

Installing the Factor-Comparison Method. The first step in using the factor-comparison method is to select 10 to 20 key jobs that represent a cross section of all the jobs that will be evaluated. In selecting the key jobs, the committee representing the workers and management should select jobs that range from the lowest to the highest paid jobs. The key jobs are next analyzed by each member of the committee. At this time the committee must also agree on the definition of each of the five basic factors so that each person will be interpreting each factor alike.

The key jobs are next ranked according to the five basic factors, one factor at a time, in the order of their relative importance. The ranking should first be arranged numerically, as shown in Table 18-5. Note that in the factor column "Mental Requirements," the highest rank (1) is given to the job of Senior Accounting Clerk while the lowest rank (10) is assigned to the Messenger. In the factor column "Physical Requirements," the job of Senior Accounting Clerk is assigned the next to lowest rank (9) while the job of Messenger is assigned the next to the highest rank (2). The jobs of Senior Accounting Clerk and Messenger are ranked in the same relative position in the factor column "Working Conditions."

Table 18-5

SIMPLE RANKING OF KEY JOBS IN FACTOR-COMPARISON METHOD

RANK	MENTAL REQUIREMENTS	SKILL REQUIREMENTS	PHYSICAL REQUIREMENTS	RESPONSIBILITY	WORKING CONDITIONS
1	Sr. Accounting Clerk	Private Secretary	Tabulating Machine Oper.	Sr. Accounting Clerk	Key Punch Operator
2	Private Secretary	Tabulating Machine Oper.	Messenger	Private Secretary	Messenger
3	Tabulating Machine Oper.	Sr. Accounting Clerk	File Clerk	Tabulating Machine Oper.	Tabulating Machine Oper.
4	Senior Stenographer	Senior Stenographer	Private Secretary	Telephone Operator	File Clerk
5	Senior Typist	Key Punch Operator	Key Punch Operator	Key Punch Operator	Telephone Operator
6	Telephone Operator	Senior Typist	Senior Stenographer	Jr. General Clerk	Senior Typist
7	Key Punch Operator	Telephone Operator	Telephone Operator	Senior Stenographer	Jr. General Clerk
8	Jr. General Clerk	Jr. General Clerk	Senior Typist	Senior Typist	Senior Stenographer
9	File Clerk	File Clerk	Sr. Accounting Clerk	Messenger	Sr. Accounting Clerk
10	Messenger	Messenger	Jr. General Clerk	File Clerk	Private Secretary

The average salary is next established for all ranked key jobs and the money value for each job is divided among the five factors according to the importance of the respective factor to the key job. Table 18-6 shows the average monthly salary apportioned to the five basic factors for three of the key jobs ranked in Table 18-5. The assumed monthly salaries are distributed for each factor of the three jobs.

Table 18-6

AVERAGE MONTHLY SALARY APPORTIONED TO FIVE FACTORS FOR THREE KEY JOBS

Factor	Key Jobs and Graded Salaries		
	Private Secretary	Key Punch Operator	Messenger
Mental requirements	$150	$ 55	$ 30
Skill requirements	180	90	30
Physical requirements	90	85	120
Responsibility	150	90	60
Working conditions	30	125	100
Total monthly salary ...	$600	$445	$340

Note: Job titles and rate ranges are illustrative and for comparison purposes only.

After the monthly salaries have been distributed to the key jobs according to the ranked and evaluated factors, the rankings are pooled in a master reference table such as Table 18-7. The titles of the key jobs are listed in the first column from the highest to the lowest paid job. The average monthly salaries are entered in the next column. The monetary rates, representing the factor rankings for each key job as well as the rank numbers, are recorded under the five major factors. The total distributed money values for each factor are then added horizontally to determine the established average monthly salary.

The final step in the installation of the factor-comparison method is to study all jobs that can be compared with the key jobs listed in Table 18-7. For evaluating clerical jobs in life insurance companies, the Life Office Management Association (LOMA) has developed a Key Job Comparison System. In this system the five job families of clerical workers—processing, accounting, secretarial, operating, and supervisory—are broken down into 23 key jobs.

Advantages and Disadvantages of the Factor-Comparison Method. The major advantage of the factor-comparison method in relation to the ranking and the job classification methods is that each job is evaluated on the basis of five factors basic to the job. Since each job is compared against a key job, and factor against factor, it is possible to obtain a fair degree of accuracy. Thus, the method

Table 18-7

RANKINGS AND MONEY VALUES IN THE FACTOR-COMPARISON METHOD

Key Job	Average Monthly Salary	Factor Rankings and Rates									
		Mental Requirements		Skill Requirements		Physical Requirements		Responsibility		Working Conditions	
		Rank	Rate	Rank	Rate	Rank	Rate	Rank	Rate	Rank	Rate
Sr. Accounting Clerk	$640	1	$180	3	$150	9	$ 70	1	$170	9	$ 70
Private Secretary	600	2	150	1	180	4	90	2	150	10	30
Tabulating Machine Operator	580	3	120	2	150	1	125	3	90	3	95
Senior Stenographer	530	4	120	4	150	6	85	7	85	8	90
Key Punch Operator	445	7	55	5	90	5	85	5	90	1	125
Telephone Operator	425	6	85	7	80	7	75	4	90	5	95
Senior Typist	425	5	115	6	90	8	70	8	60	6	90
Jr. General Clerk	380	8	55	8	80	10	70	6	85	7	90
File Clerk	365	9	50	9	60	3	120	10	40	4	95
Messenger	340	10	30	10	30	2	120	9	60	2	100

Note: Job titles and rate ranges are illustrative and for comparison purposes only.

provides each firm with a tailor-made plan of job evaluation that meets its own needs. The main disadvantage of using this method lies in the application of "going rates" as standards. It becomes very difficult to assign more than arbitrary monetary or wage values to the following set of questions which must be answered about each job before attempting to classify and evaluate that job:

1. How difficult is the work that is to be performed?
2. Does the worker do one kind of work, or has he a multiplicity of duties?
3. Is the volume of work to be done on the job large?
4. Is the finished work checked, either partially or totally?
5. Would the company suffer a serious or a minor loss in case of error?
6. What responsibility is assumed on the job?
7. Does the job require much supervision?
8. Is the work of a confidential nature?
9. Does the job call for supervision of others?
10. How much previous training or experience is required for the work?
11. How long does it take to learn to do the work properly?
12. How much contact both within and outside the office with fellow employees, executives, and customers is involved in the job?

As salaries are adjusted because of economic conditions, it is claimed that inequities creep into the operation of the factor-comparison method. Management and labor are faced with considerable difficulties because of the fluctuation of the dollar, a situation that is especially noticeable when employers and unions enter into collective bargaining over wages and salaries. Also, employee morale tends to decline when supervisors are unable to explain how wages have been established in view of fluctuating wage levels.

Point Method

In the point method of job evaluation, each of the basic factors is divided into degrees, and points are assigned to each factor and its degrees. No wage or salary rates are taken into consideration. In evaluating most jobs, the four widely accepted factors used in the point method are: skill, effort, responsibility, and job conditions. Since these factors are broad and may be interpreted differently in different situations, each factor is subdivided into subfactors such as the following:

Skill:

1. Education and Job Knowledge.
2. Experience and Training.
3. Initiative and Ingenuity.

Effort:

4. Physical Demand.
5. Mental and/or Visual Demand.

Responsibility:

6. For Equipment or Tools.
7. For Material or Product.
8. For Safety of Others.
9. For Work of Others.

Job Conditions:

10. Working Conditions.
11. Unavoidable Hazards.

Each of the subfactors is divided into a number of *degrees* which serve as a scale for measuring the distinct levels of each factor. The degrees, in turn, are evaluated separately by a number of *points*. The sum of all the points for all subfactors represents the total score for the job. In the job specification sheet for a tabulating machine operator, shown in Figure 18-6 on page 581, the total number of points is 255. Thus, in a firm using this point method, jobs with similar point values would be paid the same salary even though the points are related to different factors.

The point method is probably less subjective in its approach and provides more consistency of results than any of the other job evaluation methods since each subfactor is clearly defined in terms of degrees. With each subfactor divided into five to eight degrees, the rater is enabled to judge quickly and at the same time to minimize discriminations and inequities. Since the rater evaluates the job independently of wage and salary rates, he is not influenced by pressure from unions, workers, or management. The number of points assigned to a job as the result of an equitable rating remains the same until the job is changed. Thus, bargaining for wage and salary rates can be easily accomplished since the job evaluation continues to serve its purpose as a measuring stick.

Some critics of the point method feel that it is inflexible because of the limited number of degrees and the fact that the largest number of points depends on, and is assigned to, the highest factor degree. Also, some feel that the point system, with its elements of factors, degrees, and weighting, requires personnel trained for administering the plan and for explaining it to employees. Thus, it is imperative that the rater educate employees about the nature of the job evaluation program, perhaps by means of preparing an employee information sheet that describes the method. In one company the job evaluation supervisor visits each plant at the request of the union or of management and conducts discussion sessions with the employees wherein the evaluation method is fully explained. Thus, a great deal of time is needed to install the method, and a large amount of clerical detail is required.

A company that uses the point method in evaluating its jobs must make sure that the plan complies with the Equal Pay for Equal Work provisions of the Fair Labor Standards Act, which cautions the user of point plans. For example, the application of the equal pay standard is not dependent on job classifications or titles but on actual job requirements and performance. The fact that jobs performed by male and female employees may have the same total point value under an evaluation system in use by the employer does not in itself mean that the jobs concerned are equal according to the terms of the statute. Conversely, although the point values allocated to jobs may add up to unequal totals, it does not necessarily follow that the work being performed in such jobs is unequal when the statutory tests of the equal pay standard are applied.[4]

Guideline Method

In this relatively recent method of job evaluation,[5] the techniques of direct pricing, ranking, and grading are employed. In contrast to the four methods of job evaluation described previously, the guideline method is little concerned with the relative values of jobs within the firm. Instead, the method concentrates upon an interpretation of the relative value of jobs in the marketplace. Thus, in the final analysis the ruling factor in establishing workable salary grades is the market price of the job.

The guideline method uses a standard scale of salary ranges or grades that serves as a common scale for all jobs to be evaluated. Each salary grade consists of a minimum, a midpoint, and a

---

[4] See "Equal Pay for Equal Work" under the Fair Labor Standards Act Interpretative Bulletin, Title 29, Part 800 (Washington, D.C.: United States Department of Labor, undated).

[5] Reprinted by permission of the publisher from *Management Bulletin No. 128,* "A New Dimension to Job Evaluation," by Anthony M. Pasquale © 1969 by the American Management Association, Inc.

maximum salary, as shown in Table 18-8. Typically the grade spread starts at 30 percent in the lower grades and gradually increases to 60 percent in the higher grades, following the fact that there is progressively less room open for promotion as employees move up the scalar chain. Thus, the salary ranges for higher levels must be wider in order to provide room for recognition of meritorious performance on the same job over considerable lengths of time.

THE GUIDELINE WAGE SCALE

Grade	Minimum	Midpoint	Maximum
1	$ 4,900	$ 5,775	$ 6,650
2	5,150	6,075	7,000
3	5,400	6,400	7,400
4	5,650	6,725	7,800
5	5,900	7,050	8,200
6	6,200	7,400	8,600
7	6,500	7,750	9,000
70	118,300	153,600	188,900
71	124,100	161,300	198,500
72	130,300	169,300	208,300
73	136,800	177,800	218,800
74	143,700	186,700	229,700
75	150,900	196,000	241,100
76	158,500	205,800	253,100

Table 18-8

Table 18-8 indicates that the midpoint of each preceding salary grade provides a definite overlapping of the successive ranges. Thus, it is possible to move jobs up or down one or even two grades in order to adjust internal relationships without fear of creating gross inequities.

To evaluate jobs using the guideline method, the following steps are taken:

1. A substantial number of key jobs, or bench-mark jobs, are selected. The key jobs are those that are easily identified in the marketplace by other firms through salary surveys—the direct pricing feature of the plan. The greater the number of key jobs, the more effective the evaluation process.
2. Each job is evaluated by matching the average salary for the job with the nearest midpoint on the wage scale. At this point the manager in charge of the department being evaluated can

use his judgment in changing relationships that appear to be inequitable from the standpoint of the inside labor market. Disparities between the company's present rate of pay and the outside labor market prices are then adjusted.

3. All key jobs are reviewed in relation to one another and necessary changes made as desired. The remaining jobs in the company for which no outside comparability can be established are now evaluated. This process is nothing more than the ranking method and is based solely on the evaluator's judgment by comparing each job with the key jobs already assigned grades. Thus, the key jobs have been evaluated on the basis of factual salary data and now become the guidelines for the remainder of the evaluation.
4. The complex array of jobs listed in each evaluated grade are now reviewed within each department and among the various other departments. The evaluators can correct any inequities existing as a result of this inspection.

The success of the guideline method of job evaluation, performed without the use of a job evaluation committee, is dependent upon the availability of factual salary survey data. The method is simple to use, for no lengthy, time-consuming evaluations are necessary. The evaluation of 40 to 50 jobs can be done in less than one hour. The method is objective since bias and errors in human judgment are significantly reduced. The cost of the method is less than that of other methods, for savings arise in reduced staff requirements, fewer record-keeping procedures, and elimination of consulting fees. An experienced wage and salary administrator should be able to analyze, install, and keep the method current. Finally, there is no need to develop two or more salary structures to satisfy different geographic areas, for the guideline covers all employees and all locations in one integrated structure.

In developing its proposed salary administration manual, the Administrative Management Society has utilized a modified form of the guideline method. That part of the overall salary administration program which deals with position evaluation and the use of the modified guideline method is described below.[6]

Before the positions in a company are evaluated, the following steps must be completed:

[6] From the proposed Salary Administration Manual being prepared by the International Salary Administration Committee, with the permission of the Administrative Management Society, November 1, 1971.

1. Position descriptions must be written.
2. Outside labor market information must be obtained.
3. A salary schedule must be established.

After these steps have been completed, the positions are ready to be evaluated by means of the following step-by-step guides:

1. Select approximately 50 percent of the positions to be compared with outside sources. The positions selected should be easily identifiable in the market place by other firms through salary surveys.
2. Match the average salary for each position surveyed with the nearest midpoint on the wage scale. This is done for each division or each department. To aid in the visualization, a visual display board with the salary midpoint along one side may be constructed.
3. The jobs that are unique to the organization are slotted into the visual array, using the key jobs as "guidelines." The process is really nothing more than the ranking of jobs and is based solely on the evaluator's judgment by comparing each job with the key jobs that have already been assigned grades.
4. The salary administrator and the divisional and department managers meet to review the visual display of ranked jobs, along with the job descriptions of all the jobs in the division or department. A manager will seldom want to move a particular job up or down more than one or two grades. This allows the individual manager the flexibility of placing the job, while at the time not upsetting the balance of the system because there is a $\pm$ 5 percent margin of error built into the evaluation system.
5. After the vertical pay relationships have been resolved within a division, all the panels on the visual display board are reviewed by a committee of divisional managers or executive officers who will make the necessary horizontal adjustments to provide for equity.

The end result is that the jobs are now properly lined up both in relation to the labor market in the judgment of the supervisors and in relation to each other within departments and between departments.

The evaluation of new jobs takes place when a job description for the job is written and submitted for approval. After the job description is approved, the job is priced according to the market survey and ranked by comparing it with other existing jobs. The salary range is thus established and in turn a value is placed on how much the job is worth to the company and to other companies having the same type of job. Finally, the ranking is approved by division managers and becomes a regular part of the salary program.

Relative Use of the Job Evaluation Methods

Although many trade and professional associations have developed job evaluation plans to meet the needs of their own members, as pointed out earlier in this chapter, most job evaluation experts recommend that a company not adopt *in toto* the method currently used by another firm. Any plan established and installed by another company or association should be modified to meet the individual peculiarities of the firm involved. Some companies have installed the ranking, job classification, and factor-comparison methods but have discarded them in favor of the point system, especially when the method is used as the basis for compensating the rank-and-file workers. In other companies two methods of job evaluation may be used concurrently, and each method may be keyed to different types of jobs.

The trend is toward the disappearance of the ranking and the job classification methods and the conversion of other plans to the point method. In a study made at the University of Texas covering companies surveyed in 1947, 1953, and 1957, it was reported that:

> Of the four major types of job evaluation systems, the point method continues to be the most widely used, followed by the factor-comparison method and the classification system in that order. The ranking system is currently used to a very limited extent.[7]

Others, from their practical experience and the numerous opinions received and surveys conducted, substantiate the popularity of the point method and claim that it is the most logical and satisfactory method, which renders it worthy of acceptance. One writer, noting that the point method is the most widely used method of job evaluation in industry, states that the method conveys an impression of being accurate, utilizes the most detailed analysis of all plans, and has the greatest reliance on quantitative measurement.[8]

---

[7] William R. Spriegel, John Robert Beishline, and Alfred G. Dale, "Personnel Practice in Industry," *Personnel Studies,* No. 8 (The University of Texas Bureau of Business Research, 1958), p. 48.

[8] Richard P. Calhoon, *Personnel Management and Supervision* (New York: Appleton-Century-Crofts, Inc., 1967), p. 292.

The guideline method, designed to meet contemporary business challenges and to bring together job pricing and job evaluation, has gained increasing acceptance over the past few years among corporate wage and salary administrators.[9] One of the contemporary business challenges to the evaluation of jobs is the increasing application of automated systems and procedures, which makes necessary a thorough reexamination of the firm's present job evaluation method. With physical effort being practically eliminated on a particular job, it would no longer be valid in evaluating that job to employ a method that places great weight on the factor of physical effort. With the advent of many new office jobs that require different skills and abilities and increased responsibilities to work under different processes, the evaluator will need more technical knowledge in order to evaluate the jobs accurately.

QUESTIONS FOR REVIEW

1. Explain the managerial significance of a program of office job analysis.
2. Which method of gathering job information seems most satisfactory? Why?
3. Distinguish between a job description and a job specification, indicating the purposes of each.
4. What basic information should be included in a job description?
5. Indicate some of the principal uses of a job specification.
6. What is the difference between a quantitative and a nonquantitative plan of job evaluation?
7. Why is the selection of key jobs essential in the operation of the factor-comparison method of job evaluation?
8. Should the office manager devise his own method of job evaluation to fit his firm's needs, or should he adopt a standard plan that has proven satisfactory for other companies?
9. Why is the point method of job evaluation more commonly used than the factor-comparison method?
10. Explain briefly each of the five basic methods of job evaluation, indicating under what conditions each method might be used most satisfactorily.

QUESTIONS FOR DISCUSSION

1. It has been claimed that an efficient job analysis program improves the working relations between workers and management. Evaluate the validity of this statement.

[9] Pasquale, *ibid.,* p. 10.

2. An employee in the office feels that his job should be ranked higher than it is under the company's ranking and evaluation system. How would you justify to the employee your ranking of the job he holds?
3. Some firms "glamorize" or "dress up" their job titles. Why is this done? Do you favor this practice?
4. Should management lower job ratings while a union contract is in effect? Explain.
5. Since most office employees today have had at least a high school education and in many instances a college education, they are qualified to write a satisfactory description of their jobs. Discuss the relevancy of this statement.
6. Job evaluation is subjective no matter which method is used. How can the evaluation of jobs be made more objective?
7. What are the advantages and disadvantages to both management and the union of having a union participate in job evaluation?
8. What qualifications should a job evaluator possess? Why?

PRACTICAL OFFICE CASES

Case 18-1 Reanalyzing Office Jobs

Hughes Sports Equipment, manufacturers of a wide line of sporting goods, athletic supplies, and games, employs 270 office workers. Although a job evaluation point plan has been in operation for more than a year, there is some discontent among the office workers arising from so-called salary inequities.

A job analysis was performed on each office job, and job descriptions and specifications were prepared on the basis of the data gathered in the analyses. In preparing each analysis, the office manager interviewed a typical worker in each department, chosen by the supervisor in whose department the work was performed. The analysis was verified by interviewing the worker's immediate supervisor. Later, the job descriptions and specifications for each job were verified by the appropriate supervisor.

Three or four of the supervisors have been with the company for many years and have received their promotions for performing outstanding work as accountants. The remaining supervisors have been promoted directly from clerical positions or have been recruited from outside the company.

Although the work performed in several of the departments tends to fall in similar labor grades (mostly skilled machine operators), the wages in those departments tend to be dissimilar. The wages in the departments headed by the former accountants tend to be higher than those in the other departments.

■ Prepare a concisely written report in which you answer the following questions:

1. What are some possible explanations for the differences in wages among departments?
2. Should the company require another analysis of the jobs? If not, why not? If yes, should the analysis be undertaken for all jobs, for those paying the lowest salaries, or for those paying the highest salaries? Why?
3. What can the office manager do to increase the accuracy of his analyses?

Case 18-2 Recommending the Installation of a Job Evaluation Method

The Bolden Oil Company, a distributor of fuel oil for a major oil producer, is located in eastern Pennsylvania. Cyrus Bolden, the president of the company, is fourth in the line of family presidents that the company has had. His great grandfather founded the business, and most of his policies have been perpetuated over the years. The company employs 42 men in its distributor operations (drivers and maintenance men). All of these workers are unionized, and their hourly wages are determined through union-management collective bargaining. In the office there are 11 women, an office manager, and his assistant. The office staff, non-unionized, is paid on a monthly salary basis.

Hank Beeman, the assistant office manager, was graduated two years ago from a nearby community college. When employed by the company last year, Hank was assigned the handling of all personnel functions. Last week he received a complaint from Peggy Trevor, the switchboard operator, who is dissatisfied with her salary. Peggy has heard via the grapevine that Diane Clark, a filing clerk, is earning more than she and thinks this is unfair since Peggy has more seniority than Diane. Art Brogan, supervisor of the drivers, has remarked to Hank about a similar dissatisfaction among the drivers. Two of the drivers are being paid less than the maintenance men, and the drivers feel that this is unfair since their jobs require more skills and responsibilities than those of the maintenance men.

Hank believes that a job evaluation system should be installed in the office and in the yard in order to minimize the complaints about inequitable wages and salaries. Hank has spoken to Bill Keller, the office manager, who agrees with Hank but believes that Mr. Bolden would never agree to such an evaluation system. Bill feels that any job evaluation method should be limited to the office workers since the drivers and the maintenance men are unionized.

■ Hank has been instructed by Bill to write a report to Mr. Bolden on the situation in the office and in the yard. Assuming that you are the assistant office manager, write the report in which you make recommendations for a course of action to be taken in the Bolden Oil Company.

19

Work Measurement and Work Standards

With the increased employment of clerical personnel, a critical test of the administrative office manager is his ability to control the increases in administrative costs. Salaries and employee benefits may represent as much as 60 to 75 percent of the cost of operating an office. Management can control this expense only to a limited extent, for the salary structure that prevails in the community must be matched. But management can control the use made of the office force and effect increased productivity by measuring the work done during working hours. A program of work measurement and the development of work standards are two extremely valuable approaches that the office manager should investigate to achieve additional control over rising office costs.

NATURE OF WORK MEASUREMENT AND WORK STANDARDS

Work measurement is a tool of cost control for determining how much work is completed and how effectively it is completed. Usually this suggests a measurement of the volume of work and the amount of time required (quantitative measurements) as well as the accuracy and appearance of the work (qualitative measurements). A *work standard* is a guideline or a yardstick of performance indicating what is expected of the office worker and by which his work can be evaluated. Work standards are tools of managerial control that are best applied to routine and repetitive operations such as typing, transcribing, calculating, filing, billing, and posting. By means of work standards the administrative manager can determine what should be the quantity and quality of work produced and can compare this with the actual quantity and quality of work produced, thus establishing managerial control. All work standards are aimed at obtaining 100 percent efficiency, which is defined as the rate of production at which the average well-trained employee can work all day without undue fatigue, or simply stated, "a fair day's work."

To be most effective and satisfactory, standards must be set up in such a way that they are reliable. They must be realistic and capable of achievement under normal, reasonable working conditions. They should not have to be changed too often or confusion will result. They must be understood both by employees and by management. Standards must also be flexible in order to meet the variations in working conditions. For example, a standard for typing a one-page, 100-word letter of straight-copy matter is not the same as a standard for typing a one-page, 100-word letter involving technical material and tabular data. Similarly, setting standards for the number of invoices to be filed under an alphabetic filing system and those under a numeric filing system will not result in the same quantitative figure.

Benefits to Be Realized from Work Standards

By providing data on the two elements of *volume* and *time*, a program of work measurement and work standards offers the administrative office manager many benefits. Standards aid in determining the number of employees required to perform various office activities. By means of measuring the work and setting standards, the office manager is able to determine the volume of work that each employee should complete and to indicate the meaning of "a fair day's work." As a result of the work measurement program at the Behr-Manning Division of Norton Company, Troy, New York, the office manager was able to reduce the number of employees in the stenographic pool from 20 to 7 and to reassign the 13 stenographers to much needed secretarial jobs.[1] Following a work measurement program at

[1] Richard Martin, "How Companies Are Using Office Work Measurement," condensed from *The Wall Street Journal,* June 2, 1966, in *Management Review* (July, 1966), p. 69.

Minnesota Mutual Life Insurance Company, St. Paul, the firm was able to reduce its clerical staff by 26 percent, to make use of temporary employees during frequent peak periods, to raise salaries and give its clerks more responsible jobs, and to realize recurring annual savings of $450,000.[2] At the Aerospace Corporation in El Segundo, California, during 1964-69, the work measurement program, costing $614,000, resulted in a net savings of $1.8 million. The program came into existence in order to determine how many administrative workers were needed to support the technical organization. Today the program concentrates upon maintaining standards, gaining coverage of groups that were not studied earlier, and developing and installing standards for plant maintenance.[3]

Standards are basic in planning, scheduling, and routing the work through the office. The office manager is enabled to determine when a certain volume of work or a special job should be scheduled for completion. Prior to their time-standards program, the Behr-Manning Division considered as satisfactory performance a clerk who was able to fill 259 supply orders from branch offices each week; but following the program, it was found that the average clerk could fill 418 orders weekly.[4] Standards also let the employees know when their work is to be completed on the basis of normal production.

Standards are helpful in determining the cost of the work performed, a hitherto unanswered question in many offices. Thus, management is aided in preparing budgets and in measuring the effectiveness of forecasts. For example, at the Equitable Life Assurance Society of the United States, the annual time studies of employees are converted into performance standards as part of the computerized cost management system. For one month each year, employees keep detailed records of the time spent on activities such as typing and filing during that month. The time figures, combined with time-study results from the Life Office Management Association study to determine accurate standards of time and cost performance for each activity, are used by cost center managers in planning their quarterly budgets. After budgeted cost figures are fed into the computer, the cost center manager is provided with up-to-date comparisons between his own operating costs and predetermined standards of what these costs should be. The computer output figures do not reveal individual performance, but supervisors are encouraged to identify any workers

---

[2] "Temporaries Follow Workflow Pattern," *Administrative Management* (February, 1968), p. 40.

[3] Arnold E. Nelson, "This Work Measurement Program Is Self-Simplifying," *Administrative Management* (September, 1969), pp. 44-49.

[4] Martin, *loc. cit.*

who may be throwing off the group's records when anticipated performances do not materialize.[5]

Standards aid in performance evaluation and should result in improved morale. Employees know what the performance goals are that are expected of them in terms of volume and quality, and they know that these are objective figures based upon reasonable working conditions. The superior worker receives recognition for a job well done, and the poorer worker is rated accordingly. With the installation of its program of work measurement Liberty Life Insurance Company of Greenville, South Carolina, estimated potential savings of $230,000 in payroll costs each year. Several years after the program was initiated, actual savings were totaling more than $190,000 each year.[6] The savings were achieved without terminating the services of any employees as the result of work measurement. In addition to the savings in payroll costs the company cites as a tremendous success the morale of its employees, which is better than ever before.

Standards are helpful in installing incentive wage systems where management deems these desirable. During one year the weekly bonuses paid employees at the Aetna Life Insurance Company, Hartford, Connecticut, amounted to $1 million, with key-punch operators regularly receiving $40 a week in bonuses, transcribing secretaries making $30 extra each week, and file clerks receiving $20 to $25 each week.[7]

Standards may be used as guides in suggesting the need for newer or more efficient office systems and procedures. Knowing what volume of production should be maintained and the cost of the salaries necessary to maintain this volume, the office manager is able to study and to lower the costs of office systems, such as those involving automated data processing. The manager is better able to answer questions pertaining to the installation of new equipment, since the cost of proposed mechanized systems can be realistically compared with present clerical costs and volume of output to ascertain improvement or loss from the method or system change.

Standards serve as a basis for measuring the effectiveness of any department in the office by indicating the achievements as compared with the standards. Consistently lower performance by a department or a wide disparity of performance levels among several departments

---

[5] "The Manager's Letter" (New York: American Management Association, September, 1969), p. 2.

[6] Joseph J. Gilstrap, "Work Measurement," *Systems Management Bulletin* (Willow Grove: Administrative Management Society, April, 1965), p. 6.

[7] Martin, *op. cit.*, p. 70.

indicates that something is wrong, and the supervisor is prompted to learn the causes and to correct them. Outdated work measurement standards may be the cause, in which case remeasurement is required. On the other hand, the problem may lie in the caliber of managerial skill that is directing the activity. The problem may lie in such areas as overstaffing, motivation, employee selection, training, and work scheduling. Each of these areas has an effect on the performance of a department and each is largely the responsibility of the first-line supervisor. (Quality control, as a vital phase of the work measurement and standards program, is discussed in Chapter 21).

A standard of performance which was created through a work measurement program for a particular job enables the immediate supervisor to measure the effectiveness of a new employee and the rate of learning that has taken place. At what point should a specific worker on a specific job be able to handle a normal workload? This is the type of question that the supervisor must be able to answer for himself so that he may follow up on employees and determine if they have received the necessary training in the learning aspects of their work performance.

In spite of the potential benefits to be realized from work standards, work measurement is still a very young science. A formal program of clerical work measurement is not commonly found in offices, as is noted in the following section.

Reasons for Failure to Apply Work Measurement

The AMS Office Fringe Benefit Survey Summary No. 19 indicated that for the United States as a whole, three fourths of the companies do not measure their clerical output in any manner whatsoever. In a survey of 46 companies representing over 30,000 employees in a wide variety of industries, it was reported that only 15 firms had a program of clerical work standards. The employees for whom standards had been developed represented about 21 percent of the total number of workers in all the firms.[8] In a similar study made for *Dun's Review and Modern Industry*, it was revealed that only 29 of the 191 companies surveyed, or approximately 15 percent, had any form of work measurement covering clerical employees.[9] A significantly small percentage is reported by one management

[8] P. M. Grieve, "Can You Profit from Clerical Work Standards?" *Management Review* (March, 1956), p. 195.

[9] Thomas Kenny, "Office Productivity—New Path to Profits," *Dun's Review and Modern Industry* (September, 1960), p. 44.

consultant who found that less than five percent of the total clerical work force is measured against accurate standards of "a fair day's work," while over 80 percent of the blue-collar workers are working under some form of work measurement system.[10]

In view of the rapid rate with which the size and cost of office staffs have grown during the past 50 years, it would be expected that the measurement of clerical work would have been utilized to a much greater extent. Several reasons are commonly advanced, however, to explain the failure to apply the principles of work measurement to office operations.

Perhaps the major reason for the lack of interest in office work measurement is the widespread opinion that office work is either impossible of measurement or the measurement is too difficult and costly to prove practicable. Proponents of this point of view feel that clerical work is so varied, so complex, and so nebulous that it does not lend itself to measurement. Repetitiveness does not exist in most office work to the same extent as it does in manufacturing operations. Often an office employee may process several kinds of work units—orders, invoices, vouchers—in a single day. Even though the work may be repetitive, there are phases of the job, such as answering and placing telephone calls and looking up information, that prove difficult, if not impossible, to measure. Others advance the argument that since in many offices the number of employees is small, there is no need for measurement. Some feel that clerical workers are so closely related to management that they should be exempt from a formal program of measurement. Traditionally work measurement has been associated with the blue-collar worker. Since many white-collar office workers do not wish to be considered on the same level as the blue-collar worker, there has been a negative reaction to work measurement. In other instances there is a lack of desire on the part of top management to engage in any work measurement program, for it is felt that the office work is going along well enough and there is no need to disturb the tranquility of the workers by attempting to measure their work load.

Many management consultants contend that most of the reasons offered for the failure to establish a work measurement program in the office are more imaginary than real. It is claimed that most of the routine and semiroutine office activities can be measured quantitatively and qualitatively.

---

[10] Bruce Payne, "Office Efficiency Rated at 60 Percent," *Administrative Management* (June, 1967), p. 102.

Office Operations That Can Be Measured

Estimates of the amount of office work lending itself to measurement range from two thirds to three fourths of all work done in the office. If this major portion of work were measured and work standards prepared, the office manager would possess another tool of clerical cost control that would improve his office operations. To be capable of measurement, office activities must meet certain criteria: [11]

1. The work must be done in a repetitive, reasonably uniform manner.
2. The content of the work must be consistently the same from one period to another.
3. The work must be countable (that is, discernible in precise quantitative terms, such as a case, a form, or a letter).
4. The volume of work must be sufficient to be worthwhile for counting and recording.

The types of office activities described above are commonly found in those cost centers or groups that have the largest number of employees performing routine clerical tasks. Some of the office tasks that can be measured include: filing, typing, transcribing, addressographing, opening mail, stuffing and sealing envelopes, posting, billing, keypunching, and calculating. Each of these tasks is characterized as highly routine and repetitive. For a job such as that of a layout artist or an editor, where the work is essentially creative, it would be somewhat impractical to attempt its measurement. Likewise, if an office worker, such as a receptionist or a switchboard operator, is kept at her work station regardless of the volume of work, there is no advantage in trying to determine the work load.

When work measurement methods are applied to certain types of office operations, experience shows that efficiency and output have increased. According to the management consulting firm, Serge A. Birn Company, output in offices using clerical work measurement rose from 59 to 83 percent.[12] The Administrative Management Society has conducted surveys which show that in offices without standardized activities, transcription from shorthand notes produces only 50 to 60 percent of typing efficiency. In offices where all the

---

[11] Lionel J. Deschamps, Systems Engineer, Albany Felt Company, Albany, New York, in a paper given before the Charleston Chapter of AMS.

[12] AMemo, *Administrative Management* (February, 1970), p. 96.

activities are standardized, however, typing efficiency almost doubles. Another study demonstrated that work measurement programs usually increase clerical productivity by about one third. Although the reductions in office costs reported resulted from a wide variety of techniques, it is significant that the companies with work measurement programs reported an average cost reduction that was nearly twice as large as that of companies without such programs.[13] It has been estimated that about 80 percent of all office work is direct productive effort. The additional 20 percent of the work is made up of variables such as telephone calls, personal time, interruptions by supervisors, and cleanup time. Although an evaluation of the variables may not be scientific, it is offset by the accurate measurement of the remaining 80 percent.[14]

PREPARING FOR THE WORK MEASUREMENT PROGRAM

For a work measurement program to be effective, management must fully support the program and its objectives and make active use of the information obtained. The nature of the program and its aims must be communicated to employees so that they fully understand the program. A supervisor must administer the program at each level of office operations. Analysts who have some college training or equivalent work experience and a "feel" for paper work should be properly selected. Finally, there must be a realization and acceptance of the fact that the clerical work standards developed are feasible and accurate.

Gaining Management's Support

Work measurement as a modern management tool must receive complete and unqualified endorsement by those for whose use the tool has been designed; otherwise there is little point in installing the program. Management must understand the objectives of the program and how it will work, take an active interest in the program, be willing to make the decisions needed to implement the program, and demonstrate in a tangible way that the managers stand behind the program. Involved in management's support is an effective control over the replacement of personnel who have left the firm so that an adequate work load is assured each employee. Top management must

---

[13] Kenny, *loc. cit.*

[14] Adolph Langsner and Herbert G. Zollitsch, *Wage and Salary Administration* (Cincinnati: South-Western Publishing Co., 1961), p. 557.

convey to middle and first-line management the idea that the program is permanent and that acceptance on their part is mandatory.[15]

Communicating the Program to Employees

Since the work measurement program affects the employees, they are naturally interested in the program; and consideration must be given to their feelings. Before the installation of the program the administrative office manager must provide the worker with a complete, honest, and satisfactory answer to the question: "How is this program going to affect me?" Although a satisfactory answer to the question may not be liked by all the workers, the answer is usually welcomed by the more capable, conscientious employee. What is important is that the workers understand the techniques to be used in the program and how the results of the program will be applied to them. Thus, employee fears and natural resistance to change will be lessened.

Each employee must be convinced that in no way will he lose his job as a result of work measurement. In developing work measurement programs one group of specialists states that no one ever need lose his job as a result of the program, for high turnover rates are invariably more than adequate to adjust staff and to absorb expected increases in productivity.[16]

When informing the workers of the program, the timing and the nature of the communication medium are very important. Rather than have knowledge about the program circulate via the grapevine, it is recommended that a letter announcing and fully explaining the program be sent to all employees at the same time and from the same source. Thus, any suspicions and questions on the part of employees may be anticipated before the first phase of the program gets underway.

Administering the Program

The backbone of a work measurement program is the first-line supervisor and much is required of him, for ultimately it is he who determines the success of the program. If the workers are given adequate supervision and leadership, most of them can meet the performance standards and will do so willingly. The supervisor must

[15] David V. Swett, Executive Vice President, Bruce Payne & Associates, Inc., "Work Measurement v. Unionization," *The Office* (November, 1970), p. 28.

[16] *Ibid.*

be able and willing to review his operations and to weed out the inefficiencies that can cause the failure of his department or cost center to meet standards. The work of his unit must be planned and scheduled, and work loads shifted in order to maintain a balance of work among his employees. To coordinate the work flow and keep peak loads at tolerable minimums, the supervisor has to plan and consult with other supervisors. Adequate records must be kept to provide a sound basis for performance reports. Importantly, there is the need to evaluate individual productivity and to use the results of the program to determine training needs, to ready people for promotion, and to justify salary increases. Thus, the program takes on meaning in the eyes of the workers and management is enabled to identify and to reward outstanding workers. Through the effective accomplishment of these activities, the supervisor at each level is discharging his responsibilities for processing the work in the most economical manner.

In the training sessions where first-line supervisors are introduced to the program and to the roles they will play, it must be made clear that the results of the program will not dictate how the supervisor's department is to be operated, nor will his ability to operate the department be restricted. The program should be introduced to the supervisor as a managerial tool that will aid him in doing a better job.

Selection of Analysts

Often as a means of reducing employee fears about the work measurement program and to prevent any undue resentment, employees from within the firm are selected and trained as work analysts. Acceptability of the program as a whole is better assured when the work analysts are known to their fellow employees. In addition, analysts who have been recruited from within the ranks, such as from the systems and procedures division, are familiar with company routines, methods, and procedures, which is a valuable contribution when defining methods and setting standards. Although an analyst selected from within the firm must be trained in work measurement, an outsider must also be retrained in the special techniques used by the company. One important qualification needed by the employees selected from within the firm is the ability to sell their ideas to others. The TTC (Total Training Concept) approach to training used by the Serge A. Birn Company, a leading consulting firm, consists of three-week classroom sessions in which analysts learn how to interview employees, analyze procedures, improve the procedures, and measure the work.[17]

The Serge A. Birn Company recommends for the actual installation that a team of three to five men or women, including the team leader, be used in a medium-size office (200 employees). In very large offices with as many as 10,000 clerical workers, 30 or more analysts may be involved. However, once the program is underway, no more than one third of the original team is needed to maintain lower office costs.[18]

Feasibility and Accuracy of the Standards

Regardless of the office task, some mental and physical effort is required to complete a unit of work, and the amount of the productive activity to accomplish the job can be measured. As noted earlier, there is a natural reluctance by many firms to establish clerical work standards, a fact that must be accepted at the outset when installing a work measurement program. Thus, the administrative manager should resign himself to obtaining something less than perfection in his program. When he has done this, he will be pleasantly surprised at how much can actually be accomplished through work measurement.

To encourage employee confidence in the standards, the worker must understand how the standards have been developed, what is included in each standard, and how he is to proceed if unforeseen conditions, such as a machine breakdown, should occur. Standards must be accurate and consistent, for approximate standards will not gain the confidence of employees. It is recommended that management take the time and effort to insure that the standards are accurate to a minimum of ± 5 percent over the period for which performances will be calculated.[19]

METHODS OF MEASURING WORK AND SETTING STANDARDS

The earliest methods of measuring office work and setting standards were the same as those used in the factory to measure the

[17] Robert E. Nolan, Manager, Office Services Division, Serge A. Birn Company, Louisville, Kentucky, "How to Prepare Clerical Employees for a Cost Improvement Program," *The Office* (October, 1970). See pages 20 and 22 for a detailed presentation of the program used for training work analysts.

[18] *Ibid.*, p. 15.

[19] Swett, *loc. cit.*

output of blue-collar workers. Many of the attempts to measure office work were clumsy in their application of techniques that were designed to measure the output of workers in machine shops and foundries. With managers utilizing work measurement techniques that paid little attention to the feelings of the individuals being measured, many of the programs failed and in some cases the discontent among office workers paved the way for unionization activities. In the last decade, however, new techniques centering around a consideration for human values have been utilized.

Past Performance Method

Under the *past performance method*, one of the easiest and simplest to use, past records of various office activities such as transcribing, typing, filing, and billing are studied. Production records are maintained and analyzed to measure the increase or decrease in the productivity of groups of employees doing similar repetitive work. For example, the output of workers in a stenographic pool or a typing center may be measured by using one of the following bases:

1. *By the page, letter, belt, or disc.* Measurement according to this base is probably the simplest plan to undertake. Simply counting the number of pages, letters, belts, etc., is too inaccurate to be of much value, for letters vary in length, and belts and discs hold varying amounts of dictated matter. However, additional accuracy can be obtained as in the Transcribing Department of The Procter & Gamble Company, where a "stat letter" has been developed as a standard unit of production.[20] A "stat letter" is a measurement of the length of a letter from the top to the bottom of the text, with six inches being used as a full letter. Typists are supplied with a graduated six-inch cardboard scale so that they can easily measure their daily output. The volume of "stat letters" produced serves as an accurate measurement of departmental and individual employee productivity.
2. *By standard lines.* Some companies count the number of standard typewritten lines produced. A standard line is usually 60 spaces—6 inches for pica type and 5 inches for elite type. The number of lines may be counted either by hand or by use of a line counter, which is a cardboard or plastic scale graduated

---

[20] From a letter written to the authors by Bruce P. Coffin, Manager, Buildings & Services—General Offices, The Procter & Gamble Company, Cincinnati, Ohio, March 4, 1970.

for pica and elite type. Such a base cannot easily be used for tabulated or statistical matter. The standard-line base is particularly useful, however, where workers are compensated on a piece-rate basis.

3. *By square inches.* Some companies use the square-inch base in place of the standard line base. The production of typists may be measured by use of the Leffingwell-Ream or the Sherwin-Cody scales, which are transparent celluloid sheets blocked off in square inches. When the scale is placed over a letter or a report, the number of square inches of typewritten material may be read at a glance. This base is especially satisfactory in the measurement of tabulated material.
4. *By key strokes or taps.* A commonly used base is the number of key strokes or taps made on the typewriter. A meter, called a *cyclometer,* is attached to the typewriter to record either the individual key strokes or groups of key strokes. In the Central Stenographic section of Armstrong Cork Company, the daily output of stenographers is measured by means of cyclometers. The variety of work is factored by a formula so that a uniform unit of measurement can be applied to the mixture of tasks performed, such as transcribing from a machine, copy typing, and proofreading. The daily and monthly results are charted for each worker, and this information becomes a valuable supervisory tool in determining who needs help, in making work assignments, in determining eligibility for promotion, and in providing other operating information.[21]

In each of the bases described above, the *best performance* is used as standard on the theory that "we did it before; we should be able to do it again." The worst past performance may also be used, but this is not helpful except from a morale viewpoint. In this instance, the least that can be expected of any worker is the poorest performance of the past. Or the average work of the best and of the poorest may be used as a standard. Although the average may be more reasonable than the best or the worst performance, this method is little better than having no standards at all. By means of the method, management is informed of simply how long a certain job would take rather than the amount of time the job should have taken. Built into the performance reporting system are all the inefficiencies present during the period from which the data are drawn.

[21] From a letter written to the authors by J. Richard Bauman, General Manager, Administrative Services, Armstrong Cork Company, Lancaster, Pennsylvania, February 5, 1970.

Use of the past performance method may cause difficulty if management becomes accustomed to it and a decision is later made to install a more precise method of measurement. On the other hand, the past performance method can be easily installed at a very low cost, and there is no need for highly trained personnel to administer the program.

Time Analysis Method

One of the simplest methods of measuring office work and establishing work standards is the *time analysis*, or *time log, method*. First, it is necessary to identify the work activity being performed during the day. For each of the various office activities, a simple code number is established. On a special time analysis recording sheet, such as the activity log shown in Figure 19-1, the employee participates in the measurement of his output by recording the actual time spent and the units of work produced for a period of a week or a month. At the end of the time period, the forms prepared by the various employees are summarized, reviewed, and edited to isolate any unusual patterns. A time analysis list for the entire department is prepared, upon which each activity is summarized by code number. This report provides the total time spent on each activity in a particular department. Dividing the total hours into the quantity produced converts the data into a rate-per-hour figure and places all the performances on a comparable basis. From these figures it is possible to establish a standard time for each item being processed.

The major advantage of the time analysis method is that it can be used with little additional cost. Permanent control over activities can be maintained by continuing to record work assignments on the

ACTIVITY LOG

Date *April 15, 19--* Employee *Betty Barnett*

Activity Code	Units Produced	Time			Remarks
		Start	Finish	Elapsed	
43	*10*	*8:20*	*9:10*	*50 min.*	
38	*176*	*9:15*	*12:30*	*3 hrs.*	*15 min. break*
33	*52*	*1:30*	*2:45*	*1 hr. 15 min.*	
38	*91*	*2:50*	*4:30*	*1 hr. 25 min.*	*15 min. break*

Fig. 19-1

Time Analysis Recording Sheet

activity log. The time analysis method becomes unreliable, however, to the extent that personal time allowances and absences from the work station are not recorded by the individual employees. Also, the selection of a standard time from the array of data involves a great deal of subjectivity.

Work Sampling Method

The *work sampling method* of measuring work is based on the fundamental laws of probability. If a sufficient number of valid random samples of the work are taken, the findings can be relied upon to represent the results that would have been obtained if the whole universe had been observed in a continuous 100 percent time study.

How Work Sampling Works. In a work sampling study a trained observer makes a number of observations of the work being performed by a clerk or clerks. The time of each observation and the clerk to be observed have been statistically predetermined for the observer. When the sample has been completed, the percentage of total observations recorded for each activity observed is determined. The total clerk time available for work during the study is calculated. This time, expressed in clerk minutes and multiplied by each of the observation percentages developed above, equals the time spent on each activity observed. This activity time, divided by the corresponding volume count, produces the unit time or standard.

For example, suppose the observer wants to find out how much time a team of clerks spends on the various tasks that make up their day. Assume that he also wants to determine how long it takes to accomplish one unit of each of these tasks. Using work sampling, he would make a number of quick observations of one or another of the clerks. After each observation, he would immediately record what the clerk was doing at the instant he observed her. When he has completed the sample and tallied his observations, the results might look like this:

Activity	Observations	Ratio	Percent of Total
Filing	100	100/1,000	10
Typing	300	300/1,000	30
Sorting	150	150/1,000	15
Merging	200	200/1,000	20
Personal	250	250/1,000	25
Total Observations	1,000		100

During the study the observer maintained the following record of the time that each clerk involved in the study was available for work:

Name	Minutes
Mary	429
Janet	429
Linda	324 (part-time employee, 9:30-3:30)
Helen	Absent
Betty	254 (key-punch school, 8:45-11:55)
Total available minutes	1,436

Having the total number of clerk minutes available for work, the observer can readily determine the time consumed by each activity:

Activity	Percent of Total Observations	×	Minutes Available for Work	=	Minutes Spent on Each Activity
Filing	10		1,436		143.6
Typing	30		1,436		430.8
Sorting	15		1,436		215.4
Merging	20		1,436		287.2
Personal	25		1,436		359.0
Total	100				1,436.0

In addition to maintaining a record of the work time available, the production counts for each activity were recorded. With this information the unit time or standard for each activity can be determined as follows:

Activity	Minutes Spent	÷	Work Counts	=	Unit Time or Standard
Filing	143.6		450 cards		.32 min.
Typing	430.8		110 policies		3.92 min.
Sorting	215.4		600 pieces of mail		.36 min.
Merging	287.2		150 applications		1.91 min.
Personal	359.0				
Total	1,436.0				

These unit times have been based on the premise that the percentage distribution of the various activities as they occurred during the random observation period tends to equal the exact percentage distribution that would be found by continuous observation. The accuracy and validity of the study depend upon the care with which each step is performed.

Determining Proper Sample Size. The number of observations to be made in any work sampling study depends upon the following three factors: (1) how much tolerance will be accepted, (2) what portion of time is expected to be consumed by the smallest activity to be measured, and (3) how reliable the results have to be.

Tolerance refers to the degree of accuracy. Suppose it is specified that a tolerance of 10 percent will be acceptable. If the study results show that an activity consumed 5 percent of the available time, the analyst can be certain that the actual time consumed was within 10 percent of that 5 percent; that is, it was not less than 4.5 percent nor more than 5.5 percent. The larger the tolerance one is willing to accept, the smaller the number of observations that must be made.

Besides specifying an acceptable tolerance, an estimate must be made of the percentage of time consumed by the least time-consuming activity for which reliable results are required. This is an educated guess made after the observer has familiarized himself with the operations of the unit to be studied. The smaller this estimated critical percentage becomes, the larger the sample must be. For this reason, observation codes are often set up so that the smallest activity will account for at least 5 percent of the total number of observations. Whenever possible, separate observation codes are eliminated for those activities that are estimated to consume less than 5 percent of the available time. These activities can be combined with related work codes or grouped under a miscellaneous observation code.

As the size of a sample is increased, the reliability of the results also increases. However, nearly every sampling application reaches a point of diminishing returns—a point beyond which the increased reliability achieved does not justify the additional time, effort, and expense required. A sample size that produces a reliability of 80 percent is generally considered to be sufficient for work sampling purposes.

Suppose a work sampling study is planned and:

1. An acceptable tolerance of 10 percent is specified.
2. The critical percentage is estimated to be 5 percent.
3. 80 percent reliability has been determined to be adequate.

The table of sample sizes shown in Table 19-1 indicates that 3,210 observations must be made.[22]

---

[22] For those interested in learning how the sample size is derived by statistical formula, consult any basic textbook in statistics.

Table 19-1

SAMPLE SIZES COMPUTED FOR 80 PERCENT RELIABILITY

	Net Number of Observations When:			
P is	*T* is ± 5% (of *P*)	*T* is ± 10% (of *P*)	*T* is ± 15% (of *P*)	*T* is ± 20% (of *P*)
1%	66,920	16,730	7,440	4,180
2	33,120	8,280	3,680	2,070
3	21,860	5,460	2,430	1,370
4	16,220	4,060	1,800	1,010
5	12,840	3,210	1,430	800
6	10,590	2,650	1,180	660
7	8,980	2,250	1,000	560
8	7,770	1,940	860	490
9	6,840	1,710	760	430
10	6,080	1,520	680	380
15	3,830	960	430	240
20	2,700	680	300	170
25	2,030	510	230	130
30	1,580	390	180	100
35	1,260	315	140	80
40	1,020	260	110	60
45	830	210	90	50
50	680	170	80	40

P = Estimated Critical Percentage
T = Tolerance Factor

Suppose it had been decided that greater reliability, say 90 percent, were needed. In that case the number of observations for 80 percent reliability shown in Table 19-1 would be multiplied by the appropriate factor given in Table 19-2.

To find the net number of observations required for $P = .05$, $T = .10$, with a reliability of 90 percent:

From Table 19-1:

When $P = .05$ and $T = .10$, $N = 3{,}210$

Using Table 19-2 for reliability of 90 percent:

$$N = 3{,}210 \times 1.601$$
$$N = 5{,}139$$

Table 19-2

RELIABILITY FACTORS *

Reliability	Factor	Reliability	Factor
50%	.269	85%	1.227
55	.337	90	1.601
60	.420	95	2.273
65	.517	96	2.496
70	.637	97	2.786
75	.783	98	3.204
80	1.000	99	3.926

* Factors to be applied to sample sizes in Figure 19-1 to provide indicated degrees of reliability.

Pro's and Con's of Work Sampling Method. If there are enough random samples taken over a long enough period of time to make the samples representative and valid, the data obtained under the work sampling method are considerably more reliable than those secured from the time analysis method. The major disadvantage of the work sampling method is the need for trained analysts to set up the study and to perform the required observations. In some cases the method may prove to be uneconomical if the sample size required to produce valid results is too great. Also, some employees may not fully understand the sampling technique employed and may be wary of statistical arguments to the extent that they will alter their performance, such as slowing down, so that the sample being taken will produce a performance standard on the low side. Of course, such a sample would not be a valid one, nor would the performance standard derived from it. Thus, when introducing the work sampling method, employees must be thoroughly informed about the nature and objectives of the measurement program.

Motion Study and Time Study

In most office systems and procedures, there is usually one best way in which to perform each operation. By observing and timing the worker at his job, much waste motion and effort can be eliminated. The purposes of motion study and time study are not synonymous, for *motion study* is used primarily to improve work methods, while *time study* is used to determine time standards. However, in relation to measuring work performance and setting standards, motion study and time study are inseparable. To improve an old work method or to introduce a new job, it would be difficult to determine the most desirable procedure without utilizing *motion economy*. Similarly, the gains brought through the new method could not be measured without *time values* for comparison.

Motion Study. The detailed motion study was originated by Frank B. Gilbreth at the end of the nineteenth century. Motion study is a recognized fundamental of obtaining "the one best way to do work," a phrase coined by Frank B. Gilbreth and his wife Lillian M. Gilbreth, who specialized in industrial psychology and industrial management engineering. The Gilbreths considered motion study a scientific method of waste elimination. According to their definition: "Motion study consists of dividing work into the most fundamental elements possible; studying these elements separately and in relation to one another; and from these studied elements, when timed, building methods of least waste." [23]

In a simple motion study, a single operation or a series of operations is studied visually by means of a stopwatch. However, if management can justify the cost of installation and the time required for analysis, the precise micromotion study is preferred. The Gilbreths originated the term *micromotion study* when they began to use motion pictures for studying the component parts of an operation. In a micromotion study, the human and mechanical movements are observed and analyzed in order to reduce a given operation to the fewest component parts in their logical sequence. Instead of relying upon the uncertain eye of an observer, a motion picture camera is used. On each picture frame appears the face of a specially prepared clock called a *microchronometer*, which is divided into 100 sections. Since the clock revolves 20 times each minute, it is possible to obtain 2,000 pictures per minute. The 1/2,000 of the minute time division, shown on each picture frame, is the unit of measurement in a micromotion study.

Micromotion techniques are ordinarily used for studying office work of a repetitive and costly nature. Although the micromotion technique involves time-consuming methods and expensive motion pictures, the study is worth the expenditure since simultaneously the entire office operation is being analyzed and recorded.

Following either a motion study or a micromotion study, a standard time can be determined. The standard time becomes the basis

---

[23] Frank B. Gilbreth and L. M. Gilbreth, *Applied Motion Study* (New York: Sturgis & Walton Company, now the Macmillan Company, 1917), p. 43.

for the most efficient method of doing a particular type of office work. It must be remembered, however, that this time allows for the natural fatigue of the worker as well as for delays due to machine difficulties. As in most factory operations, the actual working hour in the office is usually 50 to 54 minutes.

Figure 19-2 illustrates a job analysis for Addressograph operators based upon a micromotion study. The analysis represents the type of instruction sheet that is prepared for each job after a motion and time study has been completed. The purpose of this sheet is to outline the most efficient method for performing a job. For the job described in Figure 19-2, a study made of the average Addressograph machine operator indicated that 20 pieces per minute could be addressed on a straight run, but that for every 150 pieces addressed there was one job change requiring 2½ minutes. Thus, in one hour six jobs of 150 pieces each could be completed. After making an allowance for contingencies such as delay, fatigue, and personal needs, however, the standard was reduced from 900 to 800 pieces per hour.

Fig. 19-2

JOB ANALYSIS FOR ADDRESSOGRAPH OPERATORS

The cycle of work at the Addressograph machine consists of **seven elements:**

1. The operator receives the job ticket, material to address, and a time ticket—"rung in."
2. The plates specified are taken from the file.
3. The plates are placed in the machine.
4. The operator takes a working supply of the material to be addressed and places it face down on the left side of the machine table.
5. The operator feeds the machine with the left hand, material face down, and removes and turns it over with the right hand. A foot lever is used to regulate the speed of the machine.

   Note: A helper inspects the work for defects. If necessary, it is immediately returned to the operator who adjusts the machine and reruns defective work, or the helper makes the corrections by hand.
6. If other trays of plates are to be used for the same job, the operator returns the used plates to the filing cabinet and repeats operations No. 2 and No. 4.
7. When the job is completed, the time ticket is rung out.

Instruction Sheet for Job Performance

Time Study. The main purpose of time study is to measure job performance to establish the time required for performing each operation at an average pace. Another aim of time study is to develop standard time data that can be used as synthetic times for performance rating of similar operations without making further time studies. (The development of synthetic times is explained later in this chapter.) Time studies are also helpful in comparing relative wage rates, as well as aiding in the control of production.

Generally workers accept standard operation times if they are assured that the time studies have been made under the best standardized conditions. Management, in turn, expects the operator to perform the job in the established time. Of course, adherence to a time standard requires that all standardized conditions and job specifications be described in detail, as discussed in Chapter 18.

Unless the time study analyst has the confidence of the office personnel, his efforts will be ineffective. The analyst must be capable of dealing with people honestly, tactfully, and sympathetically. He must maintain a reputation for making fair and accurate studies by using a systematic and exacting procedure when analyzing operations.

One limitation of the time study method is that a degree of subjectivity is involved in the initial selection of people who will be studied to determine a standard time value. In selecting from several employees doing the same work that employee who is to be observed, it is probably best to select the most skilled operator because ordinarily he is respected by his coworkers. The operator should be chosen for his consistency in using the most efficient movements. Of course, the time taken by the most skilled operator must be adjusted, as explained below, to obtain the average time for the average operator.

On a time study sheet the analyst describes each element in the operation according to the sequence in which it occurs. Extreme care must be exercised to see that all operations are covered and that none are left out of consideration. The analyst must also decide on the number of work cycles to be studied. It is generally recognized that the more observations made and the more accurate the basic time, the greater the assurance that unnecessary delays and inconsistencies will be eliminated.

The stopwatch studies cover only the actual time that it takes the operator to perform the operational element. Thus, adjustments must be made to determine the time for an average operator. The technique of adjusting individual differences is called *performance rating* or *leveling*. The goal of leveling is to obtain a theoretical "normal" time—neither slow nor fast—that the average worker requires to complete the job under standardized conditions.

Since a worker cannot produce steadily and uninterruptedly throughout the day, allowances must be made for the extra time that may not be consumed in actual job performance. Therefore, in addition to the normal working time, proper time allowances must be determined for delays, fatigue, and personal needs such as walking to the drinking fountain, washing face and hands, and obtaining refreshments from the automatic vending machines. At the Albany Felt Company, the following allowances were made for jobs being measured.[24]

1. *Relief and reporting:* A daily allowance of 10 minutes per day for determining the volumes and times recorded on the accumulation sheet. In addition, normal daily allowance for two 10-minute breaks per day.
2. *Other time:* A daily allowance of 18 minutes for those conditions that are inherent in any average work day. This allowance was developed as a result of a time study of 12 different employees who performed more than 100 different jobs.

William H. Brush, a pioneer in the field of clerical work measurement, states that the extent to which delays affect the work cycle is expressed in terms of the percentage of time they represent in relation to the total time of the cycle. Under normal conditions this percentage will range from 5 to 8 percent.[25] For example, if the elemental times of a particular work cycle add up to a total standard time of 2 minutes, a minimum allowance of 5 percent for delays would increase the standard to 2 minutes and 6 seconds.

After all the allowances have been determined, the time study is complete. The necessary entries are made on a time study observation sheet for a permanent record. An instruction card similar to the one in Figure 19-2 or a list of work standards, such as that shown in Figure 19-3, is prepared for everyone interested in the standard time. The yardsticks for measuring the production of clerical workers presented in Figure 19-3 were compiled in cooperation with some 50 business executives. The standards represent the average output of first-class workers in the offices of cooperating companies. In making the time study each operation was divided into its elements, and the elements were timed. Then allowances were made for personal

---

[24] Deschamps, *op. cit.*

[25] Robert L. Caleo, "Measuring Repetitive Office Work," *Administrative Management* (August, 1964), p. 22.

OFFICE WORK STANDARDS

FILING

To file correspondence alphabetically including inspection for file authorization stamp, and place in security type folders which must be removed from and returned to the cabinet.
100 pieces an hour

To read and code correspondence according to Library Bureau plan, to sort and tray correspondence according to code number, and to file correspondence alphabetically in folders and at the same time check by the code number.
105 pieces an hour

To inspect, sort, and file invoices alphabetically.
200 pieces an hour

To find correspondence in an alphabetical file.
22 pieces an hour

To search in several possible places in file for a particular piece of information.
6 to 8 pieces an hour

To sort in distributor, remove, and resort in alphabetical main file.
275 pieces an hour

To look up references in alphabetical file.
50 pieces an hour

To file 8½- by 11-inch letters in alphabetical file.
300 pieces an hour

To file account cards in alphabetical file.
225 pieces an hour

To mark 8½- by 11-inch letters for alphabetical filing and to rough sort.
250 pieces an hour

ADDRESSING

To place blank alloy stencils in machine, to place list of names in holder on machine, to emboss stencils, and to place finished stencils in empty tray.
118 stencils an hour

To Addressograph regular sized tabulation cards.
25 minutes a job
.0324 minute a card

To make Addressograph plate showing name, address, and other information.
90 plates an hour

To wet manila stencils, insert, and cut on typewriter; 3-line address and 4-digit number.
.55 minute a stencil

To address 6- by 9-inch envelopes on Elliott hand-fed machines.
2.53 minutes a job, and
.0383 minute an envelope

To address 3- by 5-inch slips (three in a group) on Elliott machine.
2.53 minutes a job, and
.0498 minute a slip

TABULATING

To punch payroll distribution cards, including getting work ready, punching 30 to 40 holes, inserting space cards between cards for different employees, telephone for corrections where necessary, and put work away, using key punch.
.480 minute a card

To punch sales statistical cards, including getting work ready, figuring split credits where necessary, punching 40 to 45 holes, placing cards with corresponding invoices for proving, and putting work away, using key punch.
.520 minute a card

To punch master control card with salesmen's territory numbers, salesmen's numbers, and other information.
.1468 minute a card

To sort tabulating cards on sorting machine —less than 1,000 sorted.
.21 minute a card

To tabulate sales and cost of sales by account numbers including getting work ready, setting up machines, selecting proper report sheet, needle select cards, running through machine, entering total of sales and cost of sales for each account, and putting work away using nonlisting tabulator.
6 minutes a job, and .01 minute a card, and .310 minute a tabulator stop

Used with permission of the Dartnell Corporation, Chicago, Illinois

Fig. 19-3

Office Work Standards

needs, fatigue, and unavoidable delays. Conditions under which these operations must be performed vary greatly in each office. The operation is affected not only by the equipment provided but also by such environmental factors as lighting, noise, and air conditioning.

Standard Time Data

Gilbreth's basic divisions of work into its fundamental motions were the forerunners of *predetermined time values*, which are also known as *synthetic basic motion times* and *systems of motion time data*. When predetermined time values are grouped into motion patterns, accurate time standards can be obtained for the fundamental manual motions. The use of standard time data for the setting of wage rates is explained in Chapter 20.

The development of standard time data is based on the assumption that if the same motions are used in all situations and under the same conditions, the time values are constant and may be used to reduce subjective judgment. In all predetermined motion time methods, the elements of the operation are described according to various physical or mental factors. Thus, by analyzing a job and dividing it into its basic motions, each motion receives a time value. The time value for each motion is obtained from a table, and the total time for all motions involved in performing the element becomes the time standard for the job. Standard time data are usually developed from engineered stopwatch studies or micromotion studies. Many of the standard time tables have been developed by management consulting firms and may be obtained for a fee.

Advantages of Using Standard Time Data. The advantages ascribed to the use of standard time data include:

1. Micromotion or stopwatch time study can be eliminated on many job studies, thus conserving time in establishing time values and wage rates.
2. The time standards are more consistent than those obtained under time study because the standards do not vary as does the daily efficiency of the time-study man.
3. Use of synthetic time values may settle labor disputes more effectively. Predetermined time data are more realistic in settling grievances since the standard time values for each motion have been empirically established and are not based upon a small sample or a possibly faulty time study.
4. Workers are usually convinced that wage rates based upon the use of standard data are equitable.

Methods Time Measurement (MTM). There are more than a dozen methods available for determining standard time data, but the basic techniques of each method are essentially the same. Among these methods are: Motion-Time Analysis (MTA), Universal Maintenance Standards (UMS), Work-Factor (W-F), Master Clerical Data (MCD),[26] Methods Time Measurement—General Purpose Data (MTM-GPD), and Methods Time Measurement (MTM). The latter method is briefly described below to indicate the basic techniques that are common to each method.

The Methods Time Measurement system originated at Westinghouse Electric Company and later was fully developed by the Methods Engineering Council at Pittsburgh and the MTM Association for Standards and Research. MTM is built around basic motions developed from motion picture analysis in shops and offices as well as from laboratory experiments covering a variety of work. The motions required to complete a given activity are analyzed and by applying standard time values for each motion, a theoretical standard is derived for each element of the operation. Thus, the emphasis is placed on the method and the job content rather than on the time the operator actually takes to do the job. Standard times are expressed as *time measurement units* (TMU's), each of which represents .00001 of an hour, or .0006 of a minute. According to the MTM table of standard times, a "reach" to an object in a fixed location about nine inches away should take 8.3 TMU's.

The advantages of using the MTM method in establishing time values include:

1. MTM is faster than time study since the need for making stopwatch studies is eliminated.
2. Standards are consistently applied since there is less chance for the analyst's personal judgment to enter into the study as it does in stopwatch analyses. Thus, employees readily accept the standards and recognize them for their fair and consistent application.
3. Because of the techniques involved in MTM, the analyst becomes more methods conscious, and the worker feels he has participated in developing the standard since his ideas for job improvement have been sought and given careful consideration by the analyst.

---

[26] For a detailed presentation of the installation of the MCD method at the Northwestern National Life Insurance Company, Minneapolis, see "We Let Supervisors Set Our Clerical Norms," *Administrative Management* (October, 1970), pp. 30-32. Also, see "How To Prepare Clerical Employees for a Cost Improvement Program," *The Office* (October, 1970), pp. 14-28, in which the MCD tables, copyrighted by the Serge A. Birn Company, are illustrated.

4. The findings and the standard data obtained from MTM help in training new employees.
5. MTM aids in planning for new work by providing elemental times for all phases of the job being constructed, thus in advance providing the total time required for its completion.

On the other hand, after the time standards have been established through use of the MTM method, there are several disadvantages:

1. There is less personal contact with employees. Standards set from actual observation, where the people who have to live with the standards can actually see time study going on, tend to create greater confidence.
2. MTM requires data regarding the frequency of the work, which are often difficult to obtain.
3. A higher caliber of staff is usually needed where standards are being synthesized than under other methods where a lower grade staff can be quickly taught the measurement techniques.

QUESTIONS FOR REVIEW

1. How can the administrative office manager utilize work standards as tools of managerial control?

2. In addition to aiding in evaluating labor costs and measuring production, there are a number of other benefits to be derived from the development of sound work standards. What are these benefits?

3. Why are formal programs of clerical work measurement not commonly found in today's offices?

4. To be capable of measurement, office activities must possess certain characteristics. What are these characteristics?

5. What are the major points to be kept in mind when the administrative office manager communicates to the firm's employees the planned work measurement program?

6. What is the nature of the role played by the first-line supervisor in a work measurement program?

7. What are the limitations of the past performance method when used to measure work and to set standards?

8. Explain how the employee participates in the measurement of his work when the time analysis method is used.

9. Upon what underlying premise is the work sampling method based? In determining the proper sample size to be used in the work sampling method, what factors must be taken into consideration?

10. A work sampling study is planned for which a 15 percent tolerance factor is specified, the critical percentage is estimated at 6 percent, and 95 percent reliability has been determined. Determine the net number of observations to be made in the proposed study.

11. What are the disadvantages of the work sampling method of setting standards?
12. What is the essential difference between motion study and time study?
13. For your subject in a time study, would you select an "average" or "above-average" worker? Explain.
14. Compare the advantages and disadvantages of using standard time data in the setting of standards for office work.

QUESTIONS FOR DISCUSSION

1. According to a management consultant, clerical efficiency today is about 60 percent. In view of this level of productivity, what are the implications for the administrative office manager as he contemplates a work measurement and standards program?
2. "A methods or procedures improvement program might be called a war against habit." Explain the significance of this statement.
3. Explain why you agree or disagree with this statement: "Once job performance standards have been determined, they should never be changed."
4. For your work measurement and standards program, you have adopted the following definition of a fair day's work: "A fair day's work is that amount of work that can be produced by a qualified employee when working at a normal pace and effectively utilizing the employer's time." One of your coworkers has asked what you mean by "normal pace." How will you answer him?
5. "Some psychologists believe that individual differences prevent certain workers from accepting improved methods." Do you agree or disagree with this statement? Explain.
6. A unionized company uses micromotion study in measuring work and setting standards. Should the union be given access to the files of micromotion films for which the company has paid? Why or why not?
7. How would you go about convincing "the most efficient worker" that he should agree to be the subject of a micromotion study?
8. It is said that a time study is used to establish a time standard for performing a specific task by an average qualified worker. How does one recognize a worker as being "average" and "qualified"?
9. Do not time allowances for fatigue and personal reasons defeat the very purpose of time study? Cite an example to justify your answer.
10. How precisely can standards be set for indirect labor, such as office and clerical workers, through motion and time study? Do you think that

standards for indirect labor will become as widespread as those for direct labor? Why?

11. The Dale Department Store has made a procedural analysis of the posting work in its accounts receivable department and has arrived at the standard figure of 100 postings per hour. When this standard was announced to the supervisor of the accounts receivable department and later to the employees doing the work, a confused and panicky situation arose, which resulted in more errors and less work than before.

Assuming that the production of 100 postings per hour is feasible and accurate, discuss the use of this standard and the method of presenting it to the supervisor and employees.

PRACTICAL OFFICE CASES

Case 19-1 Overcoming Resistance to Time and Motion Study

In your unionized offices the workers in the data processing department have just learned via the grapevine that the company is planning to undertake a time and motion study to aid in developing an equitable clerical salary plan. The union business agent, who respects your abilities as Manager of Office Services, has asked you for information on what effect the proposed time and motion study will have on salaries. In talking with the agent you sense that he is firmly opposed to any time study being made.

Several of the key-punch and console operators have told you that they are not in accord with the firm's plan to conduct a time and motion study in their department. They claim that by establishing standards in the department, a number of workers will lose their jobs or employment will be shortened throughout the year. In the billing department you have overheard a heated discussion by several workers who feel that the time study is nothing more than a management trick to "speed up" the workers.

▪ Prepare a report in which you:

1. Outline the approach you would follow in working with the union business agent.
2. Include all possible points and factors that will convince your workers that the time and motion study will bring favorable results.

Case 19-2 Measuring Typewritten Work and Setting Standards

The Northern Insurance Company, which employs 860 clerical workers, has for the past several years been considering the use of work standards in the centralized typewriting service center. The objective of the proposed program of work measurement is to obtain additional managerial control over the work being done. In the typewriting service center, there are 60 employees who perform a variety of work. Many of the typists transcribe from plastic belts, using transcribing machine equipment. Some do straight-copy typing and fill-in of insurance forms. A few typists specialize in preparing statistical copy and tabulated reports.

▪ As supervisor of the centralized typewriting service center, prepare a formal report to the administrative manager in which you discuss each of the following:

1. The appropriate method or combination of methods to be used in measuring each different kind of work.
2. The bases to be used in determining the time standards in view of the different kinds of work performed.
3. What use the company may make of the results of the work measurement program.

20

Office Salary Administration

The goal of office salary administration is to provide an effective compensation plan that will attract people to the organization and then motivate them to stay with the firm and devote their best interests to accomplishing the objectives of the company. Such a compensation plan aims to satisfy the following three basic desires of all workers:

1. A fair and reasonable compensation for the work done.
2. Recognition for work well done—through employee evaluation, by which the firm takes note of the quality and the quantity of work, and in some instances, through the use of incentive pay systems, in which additional rewards are given for an exceptional quantity of work.
3. Promotion from within the business firm, not on the basis of seniority alone, but also on the basis of merit.

These three desires form the need for a unified compensation plan, and they must be considered with all their interrelationships. But the desires must be analyzed in relation to a foundation built on job analysis and job evaluation, which were fully discussed in Chapter 18. The importance of job analysis is indicated by its use in establishing levels or grades for office positions. Establishing these grades or levels is a form of job evaluation. To make the job classifications most satisfactory, there should not be too many levels or grades. Furthermore, within each grade or group of jobs, there must be a maximum and a minimum salary range, with periodic increments based upon successful performance of work as indicated by some form of employee rating. If a company is to realize the full value from its compensation plan, the company must communicate to its employees the nature of the compensation plan, that its basis is an objective evaluation of each job and an analysis of salaries paid by other firms, and that each worker has an opportunity to earn more as the result of his good job performance.

Much has been written and spoken about placing office workers on an incentive pay basis, but little has been done. Previous to installing an incentive pay system, the work must be measured and standards set, as explained in Chapter 19. In measuring work and setting standards, office managers have seemed interested but have done little about it. In order to set standards, the work must be carefully analyzed, all unnecessary motions and waste of time must be eliminated, and then a number of studies of the output must be made in order to obtain an average performance figure. This average can be used as the basis for setting incentive wage payments.

One very significant phase of compensation plans for office employees relates to the various fringe benefits or nonsalary payments that are made. Office workers obtain these benefits from time to time through management's attempt to put the office workers on a par with the workers in the plant, to build morale, and to retain good workers. Office workers and workers in the plant usually receive equal pension, profit-sharing, and insurance benefits, but the office employee ordinarily receives more lenient sick-leave privileges and longer paid vacations for a given period of service.[1] While these benefits are often paternalistic in nature, some are given in lieu of wage increases since they are not taxable to employees and are deductible as a business expense by the company. Many of the fringe benefits, particularly those in factories, were first instituted in Europe by such firms as the Carl Zeiss Optical Works and by many industries in Switzerland, where the employer was held responsible for his employees in times of illness and unemployment. In this country, strong union activity and high income taxes have been major stimulants to the increasing number of fringe benefits offered.

---

[1] From the Bureau of National Affairs survey, reported in "Compensation: Office v. Factory," *Administrative Management* (August, 1963), p. 78.

DETERMINING COMPENSATION FOR OFFICE PERSONNEL

Once the jobs have been standardized and grouped and their relative importance to one another has been established, the important problem to solve is: How much should the workers be paid?

In the discussion of the *ranking method* of job evaluation in Chapter 18, it was pointed out that the jobs are ranked according to job titles from the most important to the least important, in relation to their contribution to the business. In determining salaries under the ranking method, setting salaries for the highest rated and the lowest rated jobs is all that is necessary because all other jobs must bear a direct or a relative ratio to the two extremes. (See Table 18-2, page 585.) In the *job classification method,* a number of predetermined classes or grades of jobs are selected on the basis of varying levels and responsibilities, and all other jobs or positions are analyzed and grouped into specific classes or grades in relation to the predetermined categories. For each job classification or family grouping of jobs, a salary range is established that bears a relationship between the importance of jobs in that group to all other groups of jobs. (See Tables 18-3 and 18-4, page 588.) In the *factor-comparison method,* each job is evaluated in terms of five critical factors based on selected key jobs that are related to a money rate. (See Tables 18-5, 18-6, and 18-7, pages 590-592.) In each of these three methods of job evaluation, provision must be made for annual increments so that the employee can progress from the lowest to the highest level of his particular job and then be promoted to the next grade of work.

In Chapter 18 it was noted that the *point method* of job evaluation probably provides more consistency of results than any of the other job evaluation schemes. In the point method, each factor common to a job is divided into subfactors, which are clearly defined in terms of point values. Independently of wage and salary rates, the job evaluator looks at the factors and subfactors that are characteristic of each job. After the total number of points has been determined for each job, the points are equated to a table of salary ranges from which the salary may be ascertained. Table 20-1 shows how five job levels or grades might be developed from use of the point method of job evaluation, the salary range for each job level, and the annual increment associated with each job.

In the *guideline method* of job evaluation, all jobs are evaluated against a standard scale of salary ranges or grades. As shown in Table 18-8, page 596, the higher salary ranges are wider; for at these levels

SALARY RANGE AND ANNUAL INCREMENT FOR FIVE JOB LEVELS DETERMINED UNDER THE POINT METHOD OF JOB EVALUATION

Job Level	Salary Range	Annual Increment
1. 400 to 500 points . .	$ 7,700—$ 8,300	$425
2. 501 to 600 points . .	8,300— 9,050	450
3. 601 to 700 points . .	9,050— 9,950	500
4. 701 to 800 points . .	9,950— 11,050	550
5. 801 to 1,000 points .	11,050— 12,400	600

Table 20-1

there is progressively less room open for promotion and the wider ranges permit the evaluating committee to recognize meritorious performance on the same job over a considerable period of time.

In the establishment of each salary range in any job evaluation method, a number of factors must be considered. Basic, of course, is that the salary must not exceed the ability of the firm to pay and still make a profit on its efforts. However, there are other factors, such as the wages and salaries paid by other companies in the same area and governmental regulations, that must be analyzed.

Wages and Salaries Paid by Other Companies

In developing a salary structure for office employees, as shown in Table 20-1, the company may first prepare an *external average pay curve* that shows the salaries being received by employees in other companies in the community. To obtain data on salaries being paid for comparable jobs in similar industries within the community or in surrounding areas, a wage and salary survey may be undertaken. The individual or committee in charge of preparing the wage survey questionnaire should make sure that information is asked about a number of stable key jobs, such as those for job evaluation and rating purposes. Standard job titles should be listed on the survey form for the lowest and the highest paid key jobs. Since the terminology of job content may differ from company to company, a brief summary of each job title should accompany the questionnaire form so that all respondents are providing data about like jobs.[2] One form of wage and salary survey data sheet is illustrated in Figure 20-1.

[2] The gradual change in job content and titles and the disappearance of some jobs as a result of administrative employees being retrained for newly created data processing jobs necessitate a description of each job on the questionnaire form. For example, at Lever Bros., a former clerk-typist is now a console operator. At the Singer Company, personnel records clerks have been transformed into records specialists. "The Manager's Letter" (New York: American Management Association, November, 1969), p. 2.

Fig. 20-1

WAGE AND SALARY SURVEY DATA SHEET

Name of participating company____________________Code________

Address____________________Business____________________

Survey No.________Data furnished by________Title________Date________

	SHOP	OFFICE	SALARY	INCENTIVE
1. Number of employees in your company				
2. Minimum hiring rates				
3. Do you use training rates for new employees?				
4. Number of hours worked.				
Per week				
Per year				
5. What method of progression do you use?				
Within the range				
Automatic Increase				
Merit Increase				
Part Automatic — Part Merit				
6. Are you granting rest periods				
With pay				
Without pay				
7. Do employees working on holidays receive				
Straight hourly rate				
Time and one-half				
Double time				
Other compensation				
8. What is the average percentage of base rate paid as supplemental wages?				
Afternoon shift	%	%	%	%
Night shift	%	%	%	%
Saturday	%	%	%	%
Sunday	%	%	%	%
Holiday	%	%	%	%
9. Do you supply work clothes and laundry?				
10. Do you use a single rate (SR) or a rate range (RR) for each job? SR				
RR				

11. If you use an incentive plan, briefly explain the incentive method used__________

____

____

General Wage and Salary Survey Form (Continued)

WAGE AND SALARY SURVEY DATA SHEET (continued)

	Shop	**Office**	**Salary**	**Incentive**
12. What are the average incentive earnings per hour as a percentage of base rate?	___%	___%	___%	___%

13. Do you pay supplemental wages (Fringe Benefits)?
Annual Bonus___ Attendance Bonus___ Christmas Bonus___ Profit Sharing___ Stock Purchase Plan___ Seniority Bonus___ Vacation with Pay___ Paid Holiday___ Other Payments___

	Shop	**Office**	**Salary**	**Incentive**
14. Are you guaranteeing an annual wage? Yes	___	___	___	___
No	___	___	___	___

If "yes," please explain amount and number of weeks per year, etc. ___

15. Which of the following holidays do you grant with pay?

	Jan. 1	Feb. 12	Feb. 22	May 30	July 4	Labor Day	Thanksgiving	Dec. 25
Shop	___	___	___	___	___	___	___	___
Office	___	___	___	___	___	___	___	___
Salary	___	___	___	___	___	___	___	___
Incentive	___	___	___	___	___	___	___	___

16. Are vacations granted with pay	**Shop**	**Office**	**Salary**	**Incentive**
After 1 year employment	___wks.	___wks.	___wks.	___wks.
" 2 " "	___ "	___ "	___ "	___ "
" 3 " "	___ "	___ "	___ "	___ "
" 4 " "	___ "	___ "	___ "	___ "
" 5 " "	___ "	___ "	___ "	___ "

17. If you have employee benefit plans, excluding social security and workman's compensation, who contributes—

	Company only	**Employee only**	**Both**	
			Company	**Employee**
Accident Insurance	___	___	___%	___%
Life Insurance	___	___	___%	___%
Hospitalization Insurance	___	___	___%	___%
Pension	___	___	___%	___%
Savings	___	___	___%	___%

18. If sick leave is granted with pay, how is it paid?	**Shop**	**Office**	**Salary**	**Incentive**
Full Pay	___	___	___	___
% of Base Rate	___%	___%	___%	___%

19. Attached are condensed descriptions of key jobs designated by our job numbers as indicated below. These jobs will also be used in repetitive surveys. Please fill in correct current data.

Job Code No.	Job Code No.	Job Code No.	Job Code No.
___	___	___	___
___	___	___	___
___	___	___	___
___	___	___	___

Fig. 20-1

General Wage and Salary Survey Form (Concluded)

Since many companies provide supplemental compensation in the form of fringe benefits or nonsalary payments, the questionnaire should solicit data on the status of supplementary compensation such as paid vacations, group insurance, and pensions. Data pertaining to the nature and extent of incentive wage payments may also be obtained from firms in the community by including questions about the incentive method used and the amount of average incentive earnings expressed as a percentage of basic salary.

Additional comparative salary data that may be helpful in establishing the external average pay curve mav be obtained from the Bureau of Labor Statistics, which conducts an annual National Survey of Professional, Administrative, Technical, and Clerical Pay for 81 occupational work levels. Other sources of data on salaries paid clerical workers include the annual Directory of Office Salaries prepared by the Administrative Management Society and the Annual Survey of Data Processing Salaries compiled by *Business Automation* magazine in cooperation with the Administrative Management Society. In the AMS office salaries survey, data are provided on a national and regional basis for 19 job titles (see Figure 18-3, page 577). In the data processing salary survey, national and metropolitan area data are supplied for some 50 job titles. The 1971 Office Personnel Survey conducted by the Executive Compensation Service of the American Management Association includes detailed data on salaries (with weighted averages) for 49 office and clerical positions in all fields, including government, hospitals, and schools.

Of special help to the salary administrator in relating the average salaries paid by other companies in his community to the salary structure of his firm are the results of the salary survey conducted annually by many of the local chapters of the Administrative Management Society. For example, in its annual survey of companies in the county, covering more than 9,000 employees, the Montgomery Chapter (Pennsylvania) of AMS makes available to all participating firms the following salary data:

1. Number of office employees employed, by 19 job titles—monthly, semimonthly, and weekly salary rates.
2. Average weekly rates by type of business.
3. Average weekly rates by size of office.

In addition, the following corollary information is contained in the annual report:

1. Number and classification of businesses participating in the survey.

2. Extent of unionization among office workers.
3. Number of employees represented by participating companies.
4. Size range of offices.
5. Membership in AMS.
6. Paid vacations (minimum length of service required).
7. Basic workweek in hours.
8. When overtime is paid.
9. Paid holidays granted employees.
10. General information such as extent of job evaluation plans, merit rating systems, wage incentive plans, suggestion plans, group participation in company earnings, bonus payments to individuals, pension plans, group life insurance, hospitalization, medical surgical benefits, and sickness benefits insurance.

At the middle management level, annual salary data may be obtained from surveys such as those conducted by the Administrative Management Society. In its 1971 pilot study of 482 companies in the United States and Canada, which covered the salaries of 3,584 middle managers, the average annual income of an administrative services manager was found to be $13,500.[3] For purposes of the survey the job description of the administrative services manager included the following responsibilities: supervising such services as typing, stenography, reception, duplicating, filing, mail and messenger, switchboard, supply, and similar units; negotiating the purchase of supplies and supervision of receiving; controlling interoffice communications; and conducting comparative cost investigations of supplies. For comparative purposes, other average annual income figures obtained from the survey were: Shift Foreman, $10,400; General Accounting Executive, $16,100; Personnel Manager or Director, $16,100; and Plant Manager, $20,700.[4]

After having prepared an external average pay curve by means of one or more of the sources of data described above, the company can relate the external pay curve to the salary being paid within the office and decide to match, to pay more, or to pay less than the salaries shown on the external pay curve. Some companies build their salary standard around the competition in their area for employees performing similar types of work. Other firms prefer to tie their standard more closely to salaries paid to employees within the same industry. A few companies follow the principle of paying a higher

---

[3] "Salaries Average $10,400 to $20,700," *Administrative Management* (April, 1971), pp. 49 and 50. It is planned by AMS to conduct future surveys of managers' salaries every two years.

[4] *Ibid.*

than average pay for better than average work and thus pay salaries that are higher than those paid by other companies. In companies that provide a wide program of fringe benefits or supplemental pay, the decision may be to pay a smaller base salary than that received by other workers in the general market. After the *internal pay curve* has been determined for the range of jobs within the company, a salary range is calculated for each job level, as previously established under the point method. As shown in Table 20-1, the company may set a flat percentage spread, such as a 10 percent spread around the midpoint of each range on the salary curve. Or it may be decided to apply a percentage increase that becomes progressively greater, such as 10 percent for the lowest job level up through 40 to 50 percent for the highest level.[5] If the money ranges have been developed accurately and are kept current, the minimum rate at each level should be sufficient to attract new employees to the company.

Governmental Regulations

The two federal statutes that are of most significance to the office salary administrator are the Fair Labor Standards Act (commonly known as the Federal Wage and Hour Law) and the Walsh-Healey Act. The Fair Labor Standards Act (FLSA) pertains to the employment of workers in private and public industry, while the Walsh-Healey Act imposes additional restrictions upon an employer who is a government contractor. Both of these laws are concerned with the payment of minimum wages, the payment of overtime for hours in excess of a fixed number of hours, the payment of equal pay for equal work regardless of sex, and the regulation of child labor.

Fair Labor Standards Act. Whether a company is covered by the provisions of this act and is thus subject to minimum wages, overtime payments, and equal pay depends upon the nature of its employees' activities and on the annual gross sales. If a business is not specifically named in the statute to meet conditions other than those listed below, the business is covered if:

1. Two of its employees are personally engaged in interstate commerce, produce goods for commerce, or handle goods that have already been produced by someone else for commerce.
2. The yearly gross sales (exclusive of certain excise taxes) amount to $250,000.

---

[5] See the guideline wage scale, Table 18-8, page 596, which shows a grade spread starting at 30 percent in the lower grades and gradually increasing to 60 percent in the higher grades.

Some enterprises such as those in the construction industry; laundries and dry cleaners; and schools, hospitals, and nursing institutions are covered under FLSA provided they meet only the two-employee commerce condition. Other enterprises such as hotels, motels, and restaurants; food services; automobile, aircraft, and farm implement dealers; and agriculture are exempted from the statute for overtime pay only.

If the employees of a firm are covered by the FLSA, they must be paid a certain minimum rate, equal pay for equal work, and an overtime premium for all hours worked beyond a certain number. The FLSA also places certain restrictions upon the employment of children and requires the employer to keep certain information in his payroll records.

Minimum Wages. Unless specifically exempt from the provisions of the FLSA, all covered employees must be paid at least the applicable minimum wage, whether the employees are paid by the hour, by salary, by piece work, or by any other method. Under the 1971 amendments to the FLSA, the minimum wage for covered employees (other than agricultural workers, certain federal employees, and certain employees under federal contracts) was established at $2 an hour. Under certain conditions, an employer may apply a special minimum rate for learners, apprentices, messengers, handicapped workers, and full-time students. In order to use such rates a special certificate that authorizes a lower than minimum rate must be obtained from the Wage and Hour and Public Contracts Division of the U.S. Department of Labor.

Equal Pay for Equal Work. The Equal Pay Act of 1963, an amendment to the FLSA, prohibits an employer from setting wage differentials that are based solely on the sex of workers who are entitled to the minimum wage and who are doing "equal work on jobs the performance of which requires equal skill, effort, and responsibility, and which are performed under similar working conditions." Wage differentials between sexes are allowable if the differences are based on a seniority system, a merit system, a payment plan that measures earnings by quantity or quality of production, or any factor other than sex. If there is an unlawful pay differential between men and women, the employer is required to raise the lower rate to equal the higher rate.

Maximum Hours. The FLSA requires that overtime be paid at the rate of at least one and one-half times the regular rate of pay for a workweek greater than 40 hours. The law does not require extra pay for Saturday, Sunday, or holiday work as such. It does not require vacation pay, holiday pay or severance pay, or a discharge notice. Nor does the act set any limit on the number of hours that may be worked by persons 16 years of age or over. If, however, such types of pay and working conditions are agreed upon in union contracts or are imposed by state regulations, the employer cannot use the FLSA as an excuse for their nonpayment or nonfulfillment. Under the FLSA employers are not required to give rest periods to their employees. If, however, rest periods are given, either voluntarily by the employer or in keeping with the terms of a union contract, the rest periods must be counted as hours worked if they last 20 minutes or less. Likewise, coffee and snack breaks are compensable rest periods and cannot be excluded from hours worked.

Child-Labor Restrictions. The FLSA restricts the employment of children by stipulating that children below certain ages may not be employed in interstate activities. A business is prohibited from the interstate shipment of its goods if the manufacture of those goods involved unlawful child labor. Generally, the regulations prohibit the employment of a child under 14 years of age. Within certain limits in retail, food service, and gasoline service establishments, children 14 and 15 years old may be employed. To be employed in manufacturing, mining, and certain other businesses and occupations, however, the child must be at least 16 years old. No child below the age of 18 may be employed in any occupation that is classified as hazardous by the Secretary of Labor.

In agricultural employment different rules apply, for children of any age may be employed outside their school hours. However, children under 16 years of age may not be employed in hazardous jobs except by their parents on their parents' farms.

Under the act, in most states a state employment or age certificate is accepted as a child's proof of age. The employer cannot be charged with having violated the child-labor restrictions of the law if he has on file an officially executed certificate of age which shows that the child-employee has reached the stipulated minimum age.

Employer's Payroll Records. The FLSA requires that records of wages, hours, and other terms and practices of employment be kept by the employer, but most of this information is the same that the employer would normally keep in operating his business and in complying with other laws. Although the records need not be kept in any particular form,[6] they should be retained for seven years. Supporting payroll data such as time cards, piece-work tickets, and order and shipping records should be kept three years. Microfilm copies of such documents are generally acceptable.

Exempt Employees. Certain types of employees such as executives and administrative employees are exempt from the minimum wage, equal pay, and overtime pay requirements of the FLSA. For purposes of the executive exemption, the executive must possess discretionary powers and exercise managerial functions. His primary duty must be to manage the enterprise in which he is employed, or at least manage some customarily recognized department or subdivision of the firm. Generally, "primary duty" is defined to mean that he must spend the major part or over 50 percent of his time in managerial duties. However, an employee who may spend less than 50 percent of his time in managerial duties may be classed as exempt if he customarily and regularly directs the work of two or more other employees; if he can hire or fire employees or make suggestions and recommendations that will be given weight in deciding upon hiring or firing or promoting the workers; or if he customarily and regularly exercises discretionary powers. In addition, the employee must be paid on a salary basis at a rate of not less than $125 per week. For highly paid executives there is a short test to determine exemption. If the employee is compensated on a salary basis of at least $200 per week, he usually qualifies as an exempt executive provided his primary duty consists of the management of an enterprise or of a recognized department or subdivision thereof and if he regularly directs the work of two or more other employees.

Administrative employees who are exempt from minimum wages, equal pay, and overtime pay requirements of the act include the following:

1. The employee who assists an executive or administrative official in the performance of his duties without himself having such duties to perform; e.g., an executive secretary.
2. A staff or functional employee who is not a department head but whose duties are usually advisory and specialized; e.g., a tax expert or a personnel director.
3. One who performs special assignments, often away from the employer's place of business; e.g., a traveling auditor.

[6] See "The New Minimum Wage Law," *Modern Office Procedures* (September, 1961), p. 25, for the layout of a Salary Adjustment Record in which all basic information required by the FLSA is compiled on a single form.

4. A person employed in the capacity of academic administrative personnel in elementary or secondary schools.

The primary duty of employees such as those described above is to perform office or nonmanual work directly related to the management's policies for a major part or over 50 percent of the employee's time. In addition, the work customarily requires the exercising of discretion and independent judgment. Administrative workers, like executive employees, may perform a limited amount of work that is not directly and closely related to the employee's administrative work. Generally a 20 percent limitation is placed on the performance of such nonexempt work by exempt administrative workers. The administrative employee is generally compensated on a salary or fee basis at a rate of not less than $125 a week. As for the executive employee, there is a short exemption test for higher salaried administrative employees. If the administrative employee is paid $200 or more a week and if his primary duty requires the exercise of discretion and independent judgment in the performance of his office or nonmanual work, he falls within the definition of administrative employee.

Some employees such as apprentices, handicapped workers, students in retail or service establishments and in agriculture, and messengers are partially exempt from the minimum-wage requirement. Other employees are completely exempt from the overtime payment requirements. Among these are: hotel, motel, and restaurant employees; food service employees of retail or service establishments; salesmen, partsmen, and mechanics employed by automotive, farm implement or aircraft dealers; drivers and drivers' helpers making local deliveries and paid on a government-approved trip rate basis; and airline employees. Workers partially exempt from the overtime pay requirements include employees working under certain collective bargaining agreements containing semiannual or annual guarantees; bowling establishment employees; and nursing home and hospital employees.

Walsh-Healey Act. Under the Walsh-Healey Act, employers must pay the minimum wage and overtime to employees who are working on government contracts for the purchases of supplies exceeding $10,000 unless the employees are otherwise exempt. The minimum hourly rates are fixed by the Secretary of Labor on an industry basis, and an overtime payment of one and one-half times those rates must be paid for hours worked in excess of eight each day or 40 during the workweek, whichever is more beneficial to the employee. The act also prohibits the employment of boys and girls under 16 years of age on production work.

Other Laws. The Davis-Bacon Act requires the payment of minimum wages to laborers and mechanics who are employed on federal public works contracts that exceed $2,000. The minimum wage rates are determined by the Secretary of Labor after a study has been made of those rates that prevail in the area for similar work. The Work Hours and Safety Act and the Eight-Hour Law require that laborers and mechanics covered by the Davis-Bacon Act must be paid time and one half for hours worked in excess of eight daily or 40 weekly.

INCENTIVE WAGE SYSTEMS

The rationale underlying incentive wage systems is that the better workers should be rewarded for their extra effort and production. As pointed out in earlier chapters, *nonfinancial incentives,* such as recognition for a job well done, opportunities for advancement, better human relations, and effective leadership, are also important in bringing about higher individual effort among workers. Some office managers feel that the reward for increased production and outstanding work should be given in the nature of promotions when opportunities arise. But for many employees the time of promotion is too far away, especially if they lack the necessary supervisory qualities. For these workers, an immediate financial reward is much more effective.

In the office, incentive wage systems can be used where: (1) the work to be done is routine and repetitive, (2) the workers are centralized and properly supervised, (3) the workers are not called on to perform a variety of different kinds of tasks, and (4) the work can be measured and standards developed. As noted in Chapter 19, the measurement of work and the development of standards are not commonly found in the office, although it is estimated that two thirds to three fourths of all the work done in offices lends itself to measurement.[7] Where standards have been developed, they vary with each company. The office manager should consider the development

[7] For a detailed study in the area of incentives for clerical personnel, see J. J. Jehring and K. E. Voelker, "Office Incentives," a research report based on a cooperative study of clerical incentives conducted by the Administrative Management Society and the Center for Productivity Management of the University of Wisconsin (Willow Grove, Pennsylvania: Administrative Management Society, 1964). Although Mr. Jehring, Codirector of the Center for Productivity Management, states that the number of questionnaires completed and returned was a poor return for this type of survey, it was felt that a good cross section as to types of firms reporting and as to sizes of companies and office staffs was obtained.

of standards, if not for the purpose of installing an incentive wage system, at least for supervisory control. Many concerns maintain records of production for the psychological effect of using them when making recommendations for promotions and transfers. Thus, these companies achieve partially the effects of an incentive system of wage payment.

Incentive wage systems for office workers fall into two major categories: (1) individual incentives and (2) group incentives.

Individual Incentives

In an *individual incentive plan,* the office worker is paid according to his own production or effort. An example of an individual incentive plan is the *piece-rate system.* For a piece-rate system to be successful, the following principles should be recognized in its development:

1. The incentive pay system should be characterized by a basic pay that is given to all workers doing a certain kind of work. This takes care of holidays when the workers would not be paid if they were on a straight incentive or piece-rate pay basis.
2. The incentive rates should be set so that 5 to 10 percent of the workers will earn more than the usual pay, 80 percent will just about make the standard set, and 5 to 10 percent will not quite make the grade. This last group should be given every opportunity to make the grade, but sooner or later these workers should be placed in other positions or discharged.
3. The incentive rates must be fairly set and carried out in the spirit of fairness.

Underlying the practice of an individual incentive wage system is the problem of measuring the work of employees. The more routine the work and the smaller the number of different kinds of work, the easier the job of measuring the work. An example of work that lends itself to measurement under the individual incentive system is that of typing. The various methods of measuring the work produced by typists were described in Chapter 19.

Group Incentives

In a *group incentive plan,* the office worker shares in the achievement of a small group of workers or of a total group, such as the entire company. Included in total group incentives are cash profit sharing, deferred profit sharing, and employee stock ownership. In theory, since all employees reap the benefits of reduced costs of production through the payment of cash bonuses, employees will constantly be in search of new cost-cutting methods.

More than 90,000 companies, or one out of every six firms with 20 or more employees, have some type of profit-sharing plan.[8] Companies that make use of profit-sharing plans cite that employee teamwork is stimulated, labor turnover is reduced, production is increased, the quality of product is improved, and costs are lowered. Profits may be shared by paying cash to employees at a stipulated period during the year; by paying the share of profits into a trust fund for distribution at a later date, such as at time of retirement, death, or severance; or by paying part of the profits directly in the form of cash and placing the remainder in a trust fund under a deferred-payment plan. A company may benefit from a deferred profit-sharing plan since a portion of its contribution to the plan can be deducted as a business operating expense for income tax purposes. For the employee, the receipt of a part of his currently earned income is postponed, thus enabling him to spread his income from years of high earnings to years of lower earnings such as at time of retirement.

In the profit-sharing plans of some companies, a predetermined percentage of profits is set aside each year, while other firms use a sliding scale for determining the amount of profit to be shared. To guarantee the stockholders a return on their investment or to retain funds for company growth, some firms may first deduct from their annual profits a basic minimum return on the invested capital before calculating the share to be distributed among the employees. To provide a real incentive for employees, the profit-sharing plan must provide a sufficiently large payment to the workers but still permit the retention of reserves by the company for future growth. The most successful *deferred* profit-sharing plans produce, on the average, 8 to 15 percent or more of the employee's annual pay. For employees to respond to *cash* profit-sharing plans as a substitute for individual production incentives, they should receive 15 percent or more of their annual pay.[9]

In one firm that has been paying a profit-sharing bonus to its employees for a number of years, the amount of the annual bonus varies each year according to the profits earned. The amount of

---

[8] "Sharing Profits in Small Firms," *Administrative Management* (March, 1964), p. 64.

[9] *Ibid.*, p. 66.

bonus is calculated as a percentage of each eligible employee's straight-time salary at the rate in effect on the last pay period in June of the year in which the bonus is paid. In computing the amount on which the bonus is paid to an employee, deductions are made for nonpaid absences, regardless of their nature, during the year. A person must work three years on a permanent basis before he can participate in the profit-sharing bonus. As stated in this company's policy manual:

> Our bonus plan is based on teamwork. If everybody does his work well and we have a successful year, all eligible employees will share in the bonus. In this respect, each one of us depends upon the other to do his job well.

Many companies issue shares of stock to their employees, primarily the executives and managerial personnel,[10] as a formal wage payment in the form of a deferred bonus or profit sharing. During periods of rising prosperity, the stock ownership plan may also be extended to the rank-and-file workers. In a *stock option plan,* with participation commonly based on job function, job performance, and length of service, the employee is permitted to purchase company stock at book value, which is usually below the market value. In the office, the stock option plan is limited to those workers who are willing and financially able to make such investments. Most firms limit their stock options to a stipulated percentage, such as 10 percent, of the employee's annual salary. Thus, an office manager earning $18,000 a year would be given an annual option to purchase 60 shares at a book value of $30 each, while a secretary earning $7,500 would be given the right to buy 25 shares.

Illustrative Office Incentive Standards

For the firms that have used incentive wage systems to compensate their office employees, the following represent a few of the standards used:

1. One firm with a centralized machine transcription department pays a basic wage of $70 a week, plus a bonus per line (60 strokes a line) for all production over 4,000 lines a week.

[10] In a survey of the 100 leading industrial companies conducted by Towers, Perrin, Forster & Crosby of Philadelphia, it was found that 93 of the companies use some form of incentive awards or stock options in their executive compensation program. Reported in "People at Work," *Personnel* (November-December, 1968), p. 5.

Other standards have been set for output, but have not yet become the basis for incentive pay plans. Such standards are:

a. Filing: 100 to 125 pieces an hour in alphabetic filing.
b. Preparing an Addressograph stencil: 125 an hour.
c. Mimeograph: Putting stencil on machine, proofing, and running copies—2,500 to 3,000 copies an hour.
d. Preparing Mimeograph stencils: 200 lines an hour.
e. Calculating machine operators: 140 items an hour in checking invoices.
f. Burroughs calculating billing machine: 5,000 key strokes an hour.

2. A firm that has used an incentive wage system for many years pays its employees a basic wage depending upon the length of service, plus a bonus per point for all production over 600 points a week. Each point is 240 strokes, or the equivalent of four lines of 60 strokes each.
3. One of the most comprehensive and successful wage incentive programs for office workers has been inaugurated by Pitney-Bowes, Inc., manufacturers of mailing equipment. Those office activities that have been placed on a workable and practicable incentive system are listed in Figure 20-2.
4. In a large department store, an incentive plan was established for the opening of incoming mail, a job consisting of removing the contents of envelopes and sorting the material. The proper time for completing the task and the bonus percentage were determined after a careful time study. In the incentive wage payment plan used, the bonus is calculated on the percentage of efficiency that is attained each week. The standard time allowance for opening each letter and placing the material in classified stacks was established at 0.17 minutes per letter. For a clerk who has an efficiency rating of 89 percent for the week, the bonus is calculated as follows: [11]

$$\frac{\text{Standard minutes allowed}}{\text{Actual minutes on operation}} = \%\text{ of Efficiency}$$

a. Number of letters opened during the week 11,280
b. Standard minute allowance per letter .... 0.17 Min.
c. Actual minutes on operation .. 2,160
   11,280 × 0.17 = ... 1,918 Std. Min.
   1,918 ÷ 2,160 = ... 89% Efficiency Rating

[11] Herbert G. Zollitsch and Adolph Langsner, *Wage and Salary Administration* (Cincinnati: South-Western Publishing Co., 1970), p. 544.

Fig. 20-2

In the Order and Traffic Department, all typing work, calculation, and preparation of order forms, all filing, and the composing for postmark ads are worked against incentive rates.

In the Duplicating Section, we have measured all the typing and preparing of forms to be duplicated, all the printing of forms on the Multilith and Xerox machines and all the collating, stapling, binding, and padding operations.

In the Addressograph Section, the maintenance and the running of lists for various purposes are on incentives.

In the Mail Section, employees work on incentive while sorting, distributing, and delivering incoming and outgoing mail; also while running the inserting, folding, letter-opening, and our own postage meter machines.

In the Payroll Department, we have rated the complete process of computing and preparing the payroll for the factory, home office, and all our branch offices, as well as the keeping of all records pertaining to payroll accounts. Also on rates is the computation of bonuses and salesmen's commissions.

In the Field Consignment Section, the maintenance of records indicating the location by serial number of all machines and meters in our branch offices and in service is performed on incentive rate.

In the Distributing Section, we have measured the work of those who receive, open, and sort customers' checks for forwarding to Accounts Receivable; also those who receive invoices from the Billing Section and who separate, prepare tapes, and forward various copies.

In Accounts Receivable, we have rated those using the Remington Rand "Bookless Bookkeeping" system of Accounts Receivable, and those receiving open invoices, setting up new accounts, application of payments, sending of statements, auditing for collection, and even the taking of periodic trial balances.

In the Billing Section, the typing of those invoices not prepared by the Data Processing Section is performed on incentive.

In the Sales Records Section, we have measured the typing of quota and commission statements as well as the use of bookkeeping machines to analyze and tabulate sales.

In the Branch Accounts Section, the auditing, checking, summarizing, and preparing of statements relative to the financial operations of our branch offices are all done on direct incentive rates.

In the Advertising Department, we have incentive rates on typing advertising leads and filing requests from prospects for sales literature.

In the Data Processing Section, all key-punch operations are performed on incentive.

In the Central Files Section, we have rated the filing of all correspondence relating to customer accounts, sales, etc.

Office Operations on Incentive Plan

Bonus rate paid at 89% efficiency is $7.17. (In this system a bonus payment commences at 66 2/3 percent of efficiency.)

EMPLOYEE EVALUATION AS PART OF THE OFFICE SALARY ADMINISTRATION PROGRAM

The larger the organization, the greater the tendency for an impersonal relationship to develop between the workers and management. This is discouraging to the employees, especially if a company implies that salary increments and promotion are the result of satisfactory or exceptional work. When an impersonal relationship exists, the employee feels like a small, inconsequential unit in a large organization, with a feeling of insecurity and a lack of recognition of his efforts and achievements. In many cases, such situations have encouraged workers to seek help and greater security through some form of employee organization such as a labor union. Many large offices have tried to overcome this failing in human relations by instituting some form of merit rating, or employee evaluation. In an *employee evaluation plan*, the relative value of an employee's traits, personal qualifications, attitudes, and behavior is appraised in order to rate his ability, performance, and aptitude. Thus, employee evaluation is an overall study and analysis of the services and characteristics of the *employee*, not the job that he performs. Such a study results in an equitable compensation plan that rewards each employee according to his true worth.

Employee evaluation may be used in office administration for one or more of the following purposes:

1. To enhance the worker's morale, to contribute directly and indirectly to his self-improvement, and to stimulate his confidence in management's fairness.
2. To stimulate employees to improve their work.
3. To help in deciding who should be promoted, transferred, demoted, or given a salary increase.
4. To discover workers' weaknesses as a basis for planning training programs.
5. To uncover exceptional talents among employees.
6. To furnish a basis for the discharge of totally unfit employees.
7. To help in assigning work in accordance with the worker's ability by furnishing information for the proper placement, counseling, and guidance of the worker.
8. To serve as a check on employment procedures generally, and interviews and tests specifically.
9. To aid in settling disputes in arbitration cases.

From this list it becomes apparent that employee evaluation should provide a more uniform treatment of all employees, a more objective rating, and a feeling by the employee that he is not ignored or overlooked. A regular and consistent evaluation of employees will make each one feel that his work will be taken into consideration when salary increases are due and promotions are available. An employee evaluation plan frequently can be used in developing sound human relations by using it as a basis of employee guidance and counseling.

Factors to Rate

Business executives, personnel managers, and industrial psychologists are not agreed upon what factors should be rated, or how the characteristics should be graded when finally agreed upon. A rating form should present a minimum number of factors that will give a fair and accurate picture of the employee in his relations to the firm. Table 20-2 shows the factors that are evaluated by the supervisors in three firms.

FACTORS USED TO EVALUATE EMPLOYEES

Table 20-2

Company A	Company B	Company C
1. Physical appearance and health 2. Intelligence—judgment and accuracy 3. Character—integrity and dependability 4. Personality—enthusiasm, self-control, initiative 5. Knowledge of job 6. Experience before and since joining company 7. Performance on job 8. Value to company	1. Quality of work 2. Quantity of work 3. Initiative 4. Cooperation 5. Personality 6. Supervisory ability	1. General suitability 2. Quality of work 3. Regularity of attendance 4. Personal appearance 5. Interest in work 6. Quality of work 7. Knowledge of job 8. Personality—including cooperation, initiative, etc.

Methods of Employee Evaluation

The several most commonly used methods of appraising employees may be briefly described as follows:

1. *Simple ranking method,* or *grading method,* wherein all employees are classified by rank as best, second best, third best, and so on throughout the entire employee group. Employees are evaluated on their overall usefulness and value to the firm and no attempt is made to describe and evaluate their performances, traits, qualifications, or characteristics. The simple

ranking method is useful only in very small companies of less than 25 employees where a suitable criterion has been established as the basis for the rating.

2. *Rank-order method,* or *order of merit method,* in which the evaluator ranks all employees in order, from the best to the poorest, on the merits of performance and specific factors such as value and quality of work. This method, which takes considerable time and is very subjective, is successful to the extent that employees accept the criteria used for the rankings and respect their rater's honesty.
3. *Forced-distribution method,* in which employees are rated on only two characteristics—job performance and promotability. A five-point job performance scale is used and the supervisor is asked to allocate 10 percent of his people to the best rating, 20 percent to the next best, 40 percent to the middle group, 20 percent to the group next to the lowest, and 10 percent to the lowest group. The method forces the supervisor or rater not to rank too many on the highest or the middle scale. Also, the rater will not appraise his poorest workers as medium or fair since he is forced to place them among the lowest 10 percent.
4. *Paired comparison method,* in which each employee is paired with every other employee in the group. By means of comparing each pair of workers, the supervisor or rater decides which of the two workers is more valuable. When making each comparison, the supervisor underlines the name of the preferred worker on a specially prepared form. The employee's score is obtained by counting the number of times his name is underlined. After all workers in the group have been thus compared, a list is prepared to show the rank of each employee in order of merit, according to the number of times his name was underlined. The paired comparison method is workable only in very small groups of 10 to 12 employees, for in larger groups the job of rating becomes overly burdensome and time consuming.
5. *Goal-setting method,* or *management by objectives,* in which a number of short-range goals or objectives are established that appear to be within the capabilities of the worker. The goals, which may be established by the employee, the supervisor, or both, become the job performance standards upon which the employee is evaluated for the period of time for which the goals were established. The method rests on the premise that the only real measure of how an individual performs is whether he achieves specific results. Thus, the goal-setting method is results-oriented rather than trait-oriented. Although not practical for use at all levels and for all kinds

of work, the method provides for systematic goal-setting and performance reviews that concentrate upon the work accomplished rather than upon problems exemplified by personality traits and characteristics.

6. *Checklist method,* or *factor-comparison rating plan,* in which numerous phrases or questions referring to a specific factor are listed, as shown in Figure 20-3. The rater checks the statement or answers the questions "yes" or "no" to describe the appropriate characteristic of the worker being appraised. A numerical value is provided for each statement or question, and the complete rating is obtained by totaling all statement values. Using this method, the rater thinks critically about the employee's performance in terms of each important factor and is able to make a study of the worker's specific strengths and weaknesses. The specific statements provide a concrete basis for follow-up discussion with the subordinate and give useful data to check the employee's progress.

Factor	Question	Check Answer	
		Yes	No
A. Dependability	1. When you give him a job to do, are you confident that you will get what you want when you want it?	____	____
	2. Does he follow instructions on routine jobs with a minimum of supervision and follow-up?	____	____
	3. Does he frequently need follow-up on the most routine duties?	____	____
	4. Can you depend on him to try out new ideas?	____	____
B. Attitude	1. Is he a good team worker?	____	____
	2. Is he receptive to change and new duties?	____	____
	3. Does he go out of his way to cooperate with his fellow workers?	____	____
	4. Does he have a constructive attitude toward the company?	____	____
	5. Does he have a constructive attitude toward his coworkers?	____	____

Fig. 20-3

A Partial Form Illustrating the Checklist Method of Employee Appraisal

7. *Rating-scale method,* in which a number of traits or characteristics are listed and rated. The number of factors varies from three on some rating forms to 35 or more on others. A numeric value is assigned to each factor, and an effort is made to weight the factors in the order of their relative importance.

Illustrative Employee Evaluation Forms

The most commonly used evaluation form is a single sheet for each employee covering all the factors to be rated. Should promotional opportunities arise in the firm, the use of this form requires a reclassification of the workers in each department on some graduated basis. Otherwise, the employees in a department need only be rated as satisfactory or unsatisfactory. One type of annual rating plan is illustrated in Figure 20-4. This is an excellent form because it stresses both performance and personality factors.

Fig. 20-4

ANNUAL PERFORMANCE AND PERSONALITY REVIEW
COMPANY A—YEAR 19--

NAME ....

PRESENT JOB CLASSIFICATION ....

A. Performance Factors					
1. Quantity or Volume	Very low output ☐	Below standard ☐	Required amount ☐	Higher than average ☐	Very high output ☐
2. Quality of Work ..	Very careless—slovenly ☐	Many errors—untidy ☐	Normal mistakes ☐	Neat—usually accurate ☐	Very exact ☐
3. Knowledge of Job .	Needs training badly ☐	Weak on fundamentals ☐	Enough for job ☐	Well informed ☐	Accurately informed ☐
4. Attendance	Often late or absent ☐	Irregular ☐	Occasionally late or absent ☐	Seldom out or late ☐	Never late or absent ☐
B. Personality Factors					
5. Job Interest	Can't start any job ☐	Slow to get under way ☐	Satisfactory ☐	Eager to start jobs ☐	Initiates and starts jobs ☐
6. Intelligence	Sees and hears little ☐	Misses details ☐	Average analysis ☐	Good reasoning ☐	Genius ☐
7. Leadership	Always follows others ☐	Indifferent—can't lead ☐	Average—gets along ☐	Satisfactory leader ☐	Willingly followed ☐
8. Planning	Can't find answers ☐	Flounders—copies only ☐	Average for job ☐	Usually sound ☐	Always finds solution ☐
9. Drive	Can't decide or organize ☐	Faulty—too late ☐	Adequate ☐	Sound and deliberate ☐	Accurate and fast ☐
10. Follow-Through .	Needs constant prodding ☐	Leaves loose ends ☐	Average—requires check ☐	Concludes without help ☐	Completes thoroughly ☐

Graded by ....

Approved by .... Date ....

(Use reverse side for comments)

Annual Employee Evaluation Sheet

The grading report shown in Figure 20-5 requires the rater to indicate a numeric or percentage rating for each of the five factors being evaluated, and to compute a composite or general rating average, thus facilitating a determination of the relative standing of each employee within a given department. The rater, in this case the supervisor, also aids the personnel department by indicating the promotional possibilities and the corrective measures that would help make the employee a more satisfactory worker. This seems to be an excellent form for evaluating office employees.

Fig. 20-5

BRANCH OR PLANT ....

PERSONNEL DEPARTMENT

OFFICE EMPLOYEES' GRADING REPORT .... **DEPARTMENT**

Name .... Position .... Date of Birth .... Years in present position ....

Years with Company .... Married ☐ Single ☐ Number of dependents .... Owns or buying home: Yes ☐ No ☐

Self and family willing to move from present location: Yes ☐ No ☐

	OUTSTANDING Possesses Specified Qualities in the Higher Degree	GOOD Possesses Specified Qualities to an Unusual Degree	SATISFACTORY Is Satisfactory in Specified Qualities	FAIR Not Entirely Satisfactory in Specified Qualities	UNSATISFACTORY This Rating Requires Explanation
* AVERAGE	100-91	90-81	80-71	70-61	60 AND UNDER
1. PERSONAL QUALITIES INITIATIVE .... APPEARANCE .... ADAPTABILITY .... IMPRESSIVENESS .... SELF CONTROL .... ENTHUSIASM .... INDUSTRY .... TACT .... CO-OPERATIVENESS .... LOYALTY					
2. WORKING QUALITIES QUALITY OF WORK .... QUANTITY OF WORK					
3. PHYSICAL QUALITIES GENERAL HEALTH .... VOICE .... EYESIGHT .... ENUNCIATION .... HEARING .... IF ANY DEFECTS EXPLAIN UNDER "REMARKS					
4. INTELLIGENCE KNOWLEDGE OF OWN WORK .... KNOWLEDGE OF DEPARTMENT .... KNOWLEDGE OF COMPANY'S BUSINESS .... JUDGMENT					
5. LEADERSHIP PLANNING WORK .... ASSUMING RESPONSIBILITY .... TRAINING OTHERS .... LEADING OTHERS					

* GENERAL AVERAGE ....

PROMOTIONAL POSSIBILITIES (SUMMARY OF ABOVE POINTS)

☐ Class A Has Capacity for Advancement Positions to which he can advance ....
Ready now ☐ Needs more experience ☐ If so, specify ....
Ready about (time) .... Needs special training ☐ (specify) ....

☐ Class B Satisfactory for Present Work only
Chief limitations ....
Special training which would be valuable ....

☐ Class C Unsatisfactory in Present Work Chief defect ....
How can it be remedied? ....
What work might he be fitted for? .... What action is planned? ....

EFFORT TOWARD SELF-DEVELOPMENT:

What is he doing to fit himself for a more responsible position? (Home study, special courses, etc.) ....

Is he learning the duties of the positions above him? .... To what position or type of work does he aspire? ....

REMARKS: ....

Date .... Signed .... Approved ....
Position .... Position ....

* The average number of points for each of the five groups should be obtained. Add together the ratings of the group and divide by the number of qualities rated. The general average will be the average of the ratings shown in the five columns.

NOTE: USE REVERSE SIDE FOR ADDITIONAL REMARKS.

Office Employees' Grading Report

Should it be desirable to rate each member of a department on a single trait on one form and then to prepare a recapitulation to obtain a composite rating for each employee, the form in Figure 20-5 may be redesigned as shown in Figure 20-6.

The rating form illustrated in Figure 20-7 was designed for use in rating nonexempt and supervisory employees. Note that the rater is asked to use the reverse side of the form to explain any rating that is abnormally low or exceptionally high. This form is especially well designed, for five degrees are contained in the range of each factor to be evaluated. The rater is further aided by a brief but clear definition of each of the five degrees.

DEPARTMENT________ DIVISION________ SECTION________

RATING ON WORKING QUALITIES DATE________ RATER________
(Quality and Quantity of Work Produced)

AVERAGE RATING → / EMPLOYEE'S NAME ↓	OUTSTAND-ING 100–91	GOOD 90–81	SATIS-FACTORY 80–71	FAIR 70-61	UNSATIS-FACTORY 60 and under

Fig. 20-6

Form for Rating a Single Factor

A fourth illustration of a rating sheet, which is supplemented by a general rating, is shown in Figure 20-8. To many, the general rating sheet may be even more important than the individual characteristic ratings. In this company the ratings are discussed with the employees, signed by the rater, and reviewed also.

Weaknesses of Employee Evaluation Forms

An examination of employee evaluation forms indicates that some contain certain weaknesses that should be avoided. Some of the common weaknesses are:

1. Too many questions or characteristics to answer, check, or rate. Only enough factors should be rated to give a fair and reasonable picture of the work that is being done and of the

Fig. 20-7

EMPLOYEE EVALUATION FORM RATING FOR________

DEPT. CLOCK NO.

INSTRUCTIONS

1. Disregard your personal feelings. Judge this employee on the qualities listed below.
2. Study the definitions of each factor, and the various phases of each before rating.
3. Call to mind instances that are typical of employee's work and actions.
4. Using your own careful judgment — check the phrase in each factor that is typical.
5. If employee performs no supervision — do not rate additional factor for supervisory ability.
6. Explain on reverse side any unusual characteristic not covered in regular factors.

	FACTOR	RANGE					RATING
1	**QUALITY** Performance in meeting quality standards	Careless 4	Just gets by 8	Does a good job 12	Rejects and errors rare 16	Exceptionally high quality 20	
2	**JOB KNOWLEDGE** Understanding in all phases of his work	Expert in own job and several others 25	Expert but limited to own job 20	Knows job fairly well 15	Improvement necessary — just gets by 10	Inadequate knowledge 5	
3	**QUANTITY** Output of satisfactory work	Turns out required amount but seldom more 8	Frequently turns out more than required amount 12	Slow — output is seldom required amount 4	Exceptionally fast; output high 20	Usually does more than expected 16	
4	**DEPENDABILITY** Works conscientiously according to instructions	Dependable; no checking necessary 20	Very little checking 16	Follows instructions 12	Frequent checking 8	Continuous checking and follow-up 4	
5	**INITIATIVE** Thinks constructively and originates action	Good decisions and actions but requires some supervision 9	Minimum of supervision 12	Thinks and acts constructively; no supervision required 15	Requires constant supervision 3	Fair decisions — routine worker 6	
6	**ADAPTABILITY** Ability to learn and meet changed conditions	Prefers old methods; does not remember instructions 3	Learns slowly; reluctant to change 6	Normal ability; routine worker 9	Short period for mental adjustment; willing to change 12	Learns rapidly — adjusts and grasps changes quickly 15	
7	**ATTITUDE** Willingness to cooperate and carry out demands	Good team worker 10	Cooperative 8	Limited cooperation 6	Passive resistance 4	Poor cooperation; argumentative 2	
8	**ATTENDANCE** Amount of excessive absenteeism	2 to 3 days normal or 2 days own accord 6	1 to 2 days normal or 1 day own accord 8	No days lost 10	3 to 4 days normal or 3 days own accord 4	More than 4 days absence 2	
9	**SAFETY AND HOUSEKEEPING** Compliance with safety and housekeeping rules	Safe and orderly worker; equipment well cared for 10	Workplace clean and safe 8	Occasional warning about safety and orderliness 6	Warned repeatedly about safety and cleanliness 4	Area dirty; safety rules ignored 2	
10	**POTENTIALITY** Potential ability to lead and teach others	Has no more growth 2	Future growth doubtful 4	Slow development ahead 6	Bright future growth 8	Exceptional possibilities 10	
11	**PERSONALITY** Ability to get along with associates	Disagreeable 2	Difficult to get along with 4	Average or reasonable 6	Well liked and respected 8	Winning personality 10	
12	**SUPERVISORY ABILITY** Additional rating for supervisors only	Poor organization and planning 7	Inadequate supervision 14	Nothing outstanding 21	Good planning and effective organization 28	Outstanding leadership 35	

Date rated________ Signed________ TOTAL________

USE SPACE ON REVERSE SIDE FOR REMARKS. EXPLAIN ANY RATING THAT IS ABNORMALLY LOW OR EXCEPTIONALLY HIGH

Factory Management and Maintenance

Employee Evaluation Form Used for Rating Nonexempt and Supervisory Employees

employee who is doing it. Too many questions take too much time and may cause careless rating. Most office and personnel managers feel that six or eight factors are sufficient in most instances.

JOHNSON & JOHNSON
CONTROLLER'S DIVISION
EMPLOYEE RATING SCALE

NAME__________ POSITION__________ PRESENT LEVEL__________ DEPARTMENT__________

BASED ON PERFORMANCE DURING PERIOD FROM__________ TO__________ DATE OF RATING__________

SECTION I

FACTOR OR QUALITY TO BE RATED	RATING							
	SUPERIOR		ABOVE AVERAGE		AVERAGE		BELOW AVERAGE	
JOB KNOWLEDGE: TECHNICAL KNOWLEDGE OF JOB AND RELATED WORK.	Has excellent knowledge of job. Is very well informed on related work.	+ —	Has very good knowledge of job. Is well informed on related work. Seldom needs help.	+ —	Has good knowledge of job and acceptable knowledge of related work.	+ —	Has fair knowledge of job and related work.	+ —
QUALITY: ACCURACY & NEATNESS IN WORK.	Highest degree of accuracy and neatness.	+ —	Does high-grade work.	+ —	Does good work.	+ —	Meets minimum requirements for job as to accuracy and neatness.	+ —
QUANTITY: OUTPUT OF SATISFACTORY WORK.	Exceptionally fast output; considerably above average.	+ —	Is fast; usually does more than average amount of work.	+ —	Output is good; regularly meets standard.	+ —	Output barely meets standard and at times is unsatisfactory.	+ —
COOPERATION: CONSIDER COURTEOUS, HELPFUL ATTITUDE AND COMPLIANCE WITH RULES AND ORDERS.	Always very courteous; goes out of the way to be helpful in the department; cheerfully follows rules and orders; is well-liked by all his associates.	+ —	Always courteous; complies readily with rules and orders; shows a good attitude; is liked by associates.	+ —	Usually courteous; complies with orders, at times not too promptly; is fairly well-liked by his associates.	+ —	Often disagreeable; occasionally is not willing to follow orders without grumbling; slow to help others.	+ —
INITIATIVE: INTEREST IN JOB; SEEKING ADDITIONAL WORK AND RESPONSIBILITY, INTEREST IN IMPROVING THE JOB.	Enthusiastic interest in job, constantly seeks additional work and responsibility. Quick to make suggestions.	+ —	Good interest in job, asks for additional work without urging, voluntarily suggests improvements in job.	+ —	Satisfactory interest in job, willingly accepts additional work when requested, suggests improvements in job when asked.	+ —	Perfunctory interest in job, accepts additional work only upon urging, no interest in improving the job.	+ —
PERSONAL APPEARANCE CLEANLINESS, NEATNESS OF DRESS.			Is well groomed and neat in dress.		Fair in grooming and clothing.		Careless in personal appearance.	

Johnson & Johnson, New Brunswick, N. J.

Fig. 20-8

Part I of Employee Rating Scale

JOHNSON & JOHNSON
GENERAL RATING

1. Consider all the qualities you have rated on this form and any other qualities the employee may possess which affect his value to the Company and check one of the statements below.

A. ☐ THIS EMPLOYEE IS A SUPERIOR EMPLOYEE AT HIS JOB LEVEL.
B. ☐ THIS EMPLOYEE IS ABOVE AVERAGE AT HIS JOB LEVEL.
C. ☐ THIS EMPLOYEE IS AN AVERAGE EMPLOYEE AT HIS JOB LEVEL.
D. ☐ THIS EMPLOYEE IS BELOW AVERAGE AT HIS JOB LEVEL.

2. Consider the following questions from the viewpoint of improving or developing the employee.

A. ☐ IS EMPLOYEE IN THE RIGHT JOB? ____________
B. ☐ IS EMPLOYEE INTERESTED IN ADVANCEMENT? YES______NO______(If not, explain)
C. ☐ WHAT IS EMPLOYEE'S POTENTIAL FOR PROMOTION? CHECK APPROPRIATE BLOCK AND EXPLAIN:
1. ☐ IMMEDIATELY PROMOTABLE.
2. ☐ PROMOTABLE AFTER FURTHER TRAINING.
3. ☐ NOT SUITABLE FOR PROMOTION.

D. WHAT HAS EMPLOYEE DONE TO PREPARE FOR FUTURE PROMOTION? ____________

E. WHAT SPECIFIC SUGGESTIONS DO YOU HAVE FOR SELF-IMPROVEMENT OR DEVELOPMENT? ____________

Discussed with Employee______**Check Employees' reaction — Excellent**______ **Satisfactory**______ **Poor**______
Notes on Discussion ____________

Rating by ____________**Reviewed by** ____________

Fig. 20-8

Part II of Employee Rating Scale

2. Poor phraseology of the questions used in rating. Using detailed and descriptive phrases motivates the rater to use more careful judgment than if he has only to check general terms. Instead of using such words as Very Good, Good, Fair, or Poor to describe a factor, phrases such as the following may be used: (1) Little comprehension of work, needs constant instruction; (2) Understands simple routines and follows instructions; (3) Shows some intelligence and initiative in performing work; (4) Shows extreme intelligence in doing work.
3. Too few or too many degrees. There should not be less than three nor more than five degrees for any factor to be rated.
4. A pattern in the arrangement of the descriptive factors for each item. To prevent the rater from doing too routine a job, it is suggested that the form be arranged so that, for some factors, the highest rating appears first, and, for others, the highest rating appears last. Alternating or otherwise differentiating the order of the ratings requires the evaluater to do an individual job for each employee. The reversal of the descriptive phrases on the merit rating form may also minimize or possibly avoid evaluation errors such as the halo effect, the horns effect, and the central tendency. The *halo effect* is the tendency of the rater to evaluate an employee too high either because of a general impression or because of some outstanding characteristic that influences the rater's judgment. The *horns effect* is the tendency for the rater to evaluate the worker lower than the circumstances justify possibly because the rater lacks training in rating or because of his bias. In the *central tendency* type of error, the rater tends to rate or classify all his subordinates in the same category, which is usually average. When the descriptive phrases are presented in a mixed order, as shown in Figure 20-1 on page 659, the evaluator is alerted and must proceed cautiously.

Too lengthy a rating form and too frequent ratings may defeat the objective of employee evaluation by increasing costs and taking too much of the supervisor's time, resulting in perfunctory execution. Ratings may be completed all at one time or they may be staggered over a quarter or a six-month or a one-year period. If the rating system is to be part of the office salary administration plan, the time of rating should coincide with the time that increments are due.

Who Should Do the Evaluating?

In answering the question, who should appraise employees, it seems logical that the evaluation should be done by those who come in direct contact with the workers. Commonly the rating is done by the immediate supervisor under one of the following plans:

1. Rating by the immediate supervisor and a verification review by the department head.
2. Rating by the immediate supervisor and one or two of his assistants.
3. Rating by the immediate supervisor. If the evaluation is unfavorable, a second rating is made by one or two of the employee's coworkers.

Whatever evaluation system is used, the raters (usually the supervisors) must be given comprehensive training in why the rating system is used, how it should be used, and the nature and interpretation of the questions used on the rating scale. Furthermore, more than one evaluator should be used, especially when adverse ratings are obtained. In some concerns the supervisors are required to appraise each employee on the same factor before proceeding to appraise him on a second factor. This plan has the same efficient and fair effect as when an instructor grades examination papers by rating the same question on all papers before proceeding to another question. The rating system should be carefully planned and controlled by the personnel department. Rating is part of the personnel work of the organization, although it is often performed by persons in a supervisory capacity who are not in the personnel department.

The value of a sound employee evaluation program cannot be emphasized too strongly. In addition to building confidence and higher morale in the office worker, it helps management by placing employee discharges on a tangible basis. In some firms employee evaluation serves as a basis for recommending employee training for improvement in the work or for promotion; in others, the rating may suggest how the employee might be transferred to a department where his abilities will be used to greater advantage. Finally, promotions based upon merit rating systems are excellent stimulants for greater interest and effort on the part of the workers.

FRINGE BENEFITS IN THE OFFICE

The term *fringe benefits* describes any benefits or compensation that employees receive over and above their regular wage or salary. Because of their increased use and variety during recent years, not only in improving the well-being of office employees but also in increasing the costs of doing business, fringe benefits must be considered as part of the office salary administration program. Today the term fringe benefits is a misnomer, for supplementary compensation to workers that amounts to more than 30 percent of the total payroll can scarcely be called a "fringe" or a peripheral item. Although "supplementary compensation" more precisely describes these additional amounts received by the worker, the term fringe benefits persists and will be used throughout this discussion.

Of all fringe benefits, vacations are the most expensive item. Nationally, vacations cost an average of $271 a year per employee, followed by pensions costing $261 per employee and insurance costing $209 per employee. Surveys show that banks and finance and trust companies are most liberal with benefits, which account for nearly one third of their payroll costs; textile and apparel concerns have the smallest fringe benefit ratio, 20.6 percent.[12] In 1966 the U.S. Chamber of Commerce estimated that fringe benefits cost employers about 71.5 cents an hour, on the average, for each employee, or a total of about $1,502 a year for each worker.[13] Five years later the U.S. Chamber of Commerce calculated that fringe benefits cost the employer, on the average, nearly one third of what the staff is normally paid. Thus, if an employee's weekly wage is $100, the true cost to the firm is nearly $132 each week. The one third increase in fringe benefits breaks down as follows: legal costs, 5 percent; pensions, 11 percent; nonproductive time, 3 percent; vacation and sick leave, 11 percent; and profit-sharing, 2 percent.[14] Almost one half of the total fringe benefits made available to workers consists of payments for vacations, holidays, rest periods, etc.[15] These payments must be included in government wage reports as a portion of employee wages and salaries since these benefits represent increased compensation for each hour spent on the job. Other employee benefits such as pensions and social security, although not reflected in the current income or wages of employees, greatly improve the security and well-being of workers and increase operating costs.

Fringe benefits may be extended to office employees for a number of reasons. Management generally looks upon the cost of fringe benefits as an investment in attracting and holding desirable

---

[12] "What Workers Don't Know about Employee Benefits" from *The Wall Street Journal,* reprinted in *Personnel* (November-December, 1968), p. 34.

[13] "Survey: Fringe Benefits Dip," *Administrative Management* (January, 1967), p. 12.

[14] "The New Fringe Benefits," *Administrative Management* (September, 1971), p. 25.

[15] Office personnel practices with respect to these and other fringe benefits are summarized in Chapter 13.

workers. The success of this investment depends, to a great extent, on whether there is a need and desire for the fringe and whether the employees understand and appreciate the value of the benefits provided. Employees must be given the facts about the benefits that are available, especially those that pertain to their hospitalization, disability, and retirement. For the employees to understand fully the efforts made by the company on their behalf, they must be able to evaluate precisely what the benefits mean to them as individuals. The availability of fringe benefits aids management in partially meeting their workers' basic needs of job security and job satisfaction. However, not all fringe benefits are positive motivators. The addition of a new benefit to the company's benefit program does not necessarily bring forth a corresponding increase in productivity; or if any increase can be detected as the result of the newly added fringe benefit, it is doubtful that the increase will be apparent for any prolonged period of time. Benefits may be negative motivators, for if the workers believe that their benefits are inferior to those enjoyed by workers in other firms, productivity may be affected adversely. Fringe benefits are also extended by companies in an attempt to prevent union organization, as the result of labor-management bargaining sessions, or because the pressure of another business firm may have forced the granting of the supplementary payments.

QUESTIONS FOR REVIEW

1. A compensation plan has the objective of satisfying three basic desires of all workers. What are these desires?
2. Compare the determination of compensation under the ranking method of job evaluation with the determination of compensation under the point method.
3. From what sources may data be obtained for preparing the external average pay curve?
4. What are the major provisions of the Fair Labor Standards Act that are of significance to the office salary administrator?
5. Under what conditions are wage differentials between sexes allowable?
6. Distinguish between nonfinancial incentives and financial incentives by giving several examples of each.
7. Under what conditions can incentive wage systems be used in the office?
8. Describe the group incentive plan. What are the various forms that this plan of compensation may assume?
9. For what purposes may employee evaluation be used in office administration?

10. Contrast each of the following methods of employee evaluation: (a) simple ranking, (b) forced distribution, (c) goal-setting, and (d) rating scale.
11. What reasons does management advance for extending fringe benefits to office employees?

QUESTIONS FOR DISCUSSION

1. Regarding the use of money as a motivator, the following statements have been made: "Money isn't everything in life," "The meaning of money is conditioned by its value and importance to each worker," and "Money functions only as a symbol that represents more important psychological factors in the work situation." In view of these statements, why do many managers see money as a prime motivator?
2. Dick Bullock, the supervisor of a three-man data processing department, earns $150 a week. Very little of Bullock's time is required for supervising the workers, and most of the time he operates the data processing equipment with the rest of the workers. Under the FLSA, would Bullock be classified as an exempt employee? Why?
3. Do you feel that key-punch operators should work under an efficiency system of wage payment? As a key-punch operator, would you be content to work for a firm that uses an incentive wage system?
4. It has been stated that, theoretically, management and the workers are always in conflict with each other's interests. Management aims to get as much work as possible accomplished efficiently at the lowest possible unit cost, while the workers strive to obtain as much income and security as possible from their employment. Do you agree that there is such a conflict of interests? How can the theoretical conflict of interests of management and office workers be overcome in part, if not entirely? Explain.
5. Many companies do not agree on what to rate in employees. In view of this, do you feel that employee evaluation is worth very much? Explain.
6. Several of the common weaknesses of employee evaluation forms are listed on pages 658, 659, and 662. Using this list, evaluate the annual merit rating sheet illustrated in Figure 20-4.
7. In order for a firm to get a fair return on the dollars expended in its benefits program, the administrative office manager, along with other managers, must be sure that each worker understands the benefit program and is often reminded of the value he is receiving in addition to his direct compensation. Develop a program of educating employees on the benefits received, indicating the various media of communications that you might utilize.
8. As a company continues to prosper, is it better to (a) expand the amount of fringe benefits that employees are presently receiving, (b)

offer additional benefits, or (c) plow the money back into the company on the grounds that the firm is already providing reasonable benefits?

9. Do you believe that fringe benefits motivate employees to higher productivity?

10. An electronics company has grown during the past several years from its two-man beginning to a firm now employing 150 people. The company is not security-minded and in the early years offered only those fringe benefits required by law. Today many outsiders are amazed that the firm has been able to hold its employees and to avoid unionization, since no benefits other than the usual paid vacations, holidays, and group life insurance have been provided. The company now wants to provide some additional benefits, but it does not wish to appear too paternalistic and alter the enterprise-oriented atmosphere of the firm. What are the most useful or most popular benefits that the company can now offer?

PRACTICAL OFFICE CASES

Case 20-1 Granting a Merit Raise Based upon Tenure

Ken Morneau, a clerk-typist in the Traffic Control department of Acme Trucks, has been with the firm 11 years and is now one step away from the top of his pay range. During his tenure with the firm, Morneau feels that he has been doing as well on the job as anyone else. He has violated no company practices, with the exception of one occasion upon which he received a warning for lateness in reporting to work. One morning Morneau approached his supervisor and asked for a raise, for he felt that after 11 years' tenure, he should be at the top of his pay scale. The supervisor indicated that he would discuss the matter with the manager. About a week later Morneau was told that no raise would be forthcoming. Morneau next filed a grievance on the grounds that he was entitled to the raise in view of his tenure and clean work record. During the grievance procedure, the manager stated that to get a merit raise at Acme, a person must do more than an ordinary job—it must be extraordinary.

▪ As a member of the board of arbitration, how would you rule in this case?

Case 20-2 Preparing an Employee Evaluation Form

In the Williams Manufacturing Company, you are supervisor of the data processing department in which there are 40 employees whom you must evaluate once a year. In this firm the plan is to rate employees on the basis of job performance (75 percent) and on the basis of personality (25 percent). The ratings are reviewed and checked by the office manager and then recorded on the personnel records of each employee.

▪ Prepare an employee evaluation form with five factors in the job performance section weighted 15 percent each, and five factors in the personality section weighted five percent each. Using your form, evaluate the three employees described below.

Betty Crawford

Produces an average quantity of work.
Always willing to help others in the department, even if it slows down her production.
Is well dressed and well mannered.
Plans to get married, but expects to work after marriage, at least for four or five years.
Quits promptly at 4:30 p.m. to meet boyfriend who works in the shipping department.
Tries to find out why she or others have made errors.
Always seeks to improve methods of doing work.
Goes to college at night, studying toward her degree in business administration.
Comes to work on time or a few minutes early.
Commences to work as soon as she arrives, even though the starting bell does not ring until 8:15 a.m.
Very popular with most of her coworkers.

Marlene Miller

Dresses very economically and very conservatively.
Very punctual in attendance.
Volume of work just below average, but very accurate.
Wants to get married.
Quits promptly at 4:30 p.m.
Considers the job very boring but a good source of income.
Doesn't help anyone in the department except when the supervisor asks her to do so.
Does not commence work until the bell rings at 8:15 a.m.
Not very popular with her coworkers.
Minds her own business and gives little information about herself.
Information about her outside activities or interests is not known.

Lois Smith

Volume of production above the average.
Dresses carelessly, occasionally in soiled clothing; careless about cleanliness to a point of offending.
Comes in a few minutes late about once a week.
Makes quite a few errors and has to do her work over.
Satisfied to stay in present job—not ambitious.
Bothers others often to help her find her errors. Doesn't understand why she made the errors.
Is in no hurry to go home at 4:30 p.m. Usually last one out of office.
Frequently borrows items from others but forgets to return them.
Likes to gossip about other people, including those in office.
About one half of the office force do not like her; most of the others tolerate her but regard her as a unique and quaint character.
Is anxious to meet boyfriends.

21

Cost Control of Administrative Office Services

The main objective of modern business is to maximize its profits. Profits may be increased (1) by expanding the volume of sales or income without a corresponding increase in operating costs, (2) by lowering the operating costs and expenses while maintaining the same level of sales or income volume, or (3) through a favorable combination of both of these approaches.

One of the major cost factors in operating a modern business is the cost of the office services. In companies with 25 employees or less it has been found that the cost of office operations is $5,540 per office worker each year; and in firms with as many as 1,000 employees, the average annual cost is estimated to be $12,600 per office worker.[1] In recent years these costs have increased at least 20 percent. General office costs in 1969 consumed 71 percent of the average corporate dollar, compared with only 16 percent for direct labor production costs and only five percent for sales costs.[2] In this connection the administrative office manager must realize that organizing, supervising, and directing the office services is but one phase of his job. He must also coordinate them into an efficient service unit for the entire

[1] "The Costs of Running an Office," *Administrative Management* (November, 1963), p. 53.

[2] AMemo, *Administrative Management* (October, 1969), p. 112.

business establishment. Although the problem of cost control occurs on a reduced scale in small offices, the subject matter and suggestions in this chapter are equally applicable to the small and to the large office.

The administrative office manager must be familiar with the nature and importance of office services, the current practices used in performing them, and the methods of controlling and reducing the costs of their performance. Administrative office management demands a scientific analysis and control of office procedures and jobs, simplification of office forms and reduction in their cost, and specific analysis and control of all office operating costs. These various phases of cost control have been discussed in preceding chapters. In this chapter several additional approaches to the reduction and control of costs will be explored.

DEVELOPING COST CONSCIOUSNESS

Underlying all the approaches that a firm might pursue toward the objective of cost control is the need for developing cost consciousness among its employees. This can be accomplished by a better selection of office workers, by effective training of all new personnel, and by retraining and upgrading of skills for those who have been on the job for long periods of time. In addition, every effort should be made to improve office systems and procedures with the active participation of all office employees. Cost consciousness can be further developed by constantly striving to increase efficiency and, hence, the output of each office worker. This goal may be achieved through the use of financial incentives for various kinds of office work, departmental bonuses for cost reduction, nonfinancial incentives, and greater use of automated systems in office work. All of this adds up to the fact that each employee must be made to realize that he is a part of the cost of the office work.

Cost consciousness may be further emphasized by pointing out to employees cost comparisons such as the sales volume required to cover the cost of office services. For example, if the gross profit on sales is 20 percent and the average cost of office operations is $7,000 per employee each year, the firm must produce at least $35,000 in sales income to break even on the employment of one office worker. But the firm should not be expected to hire an employee just to break even. A more realistic attitude would be to expect the firm to obtain a profit contribution from each worker at least equal to the break-even pay the employee is receiving. Thus, in the example above, an annual sales income of $70,000 per employee would be required to justify his job.

COST ANALYSIS OF OFFICE PLANT AND EQUIPMENT POLICIES

Although there is not too much that can be changed in the office plant once it has been established or leased, there are some factors applicable to the plant and the equipment devoted to office work that may be considered for the purpose of reducing costs. Among these are:

1. A careful study of light, air, and noise conditions in the office.
2. A careful study of the amount of space required by each worker, the width of the aisles, and the location of the desks to expedite the passage and delivery of work within the department and to and from other departments.
3. The use of office machines and equipment when their use can be established as a more economical method than that presently used. The purchase of any new equipment should provide savings in at least one of the following three areas so that the company can recover its costs in a relatively short time: (a) reduction in payroll costs; (b) increased accuracy; or (c) freeing of workers from boring, repetitive jobs so that better use may be made of their time and skills. For example, one firm, faced with difficulty in obtaining replacements for its industrial engineering staff and with personnel shortage resulting in long hours for the remaining staff, especially during peak work-load assignments, invested less than $1,500 in an electronic calculator. The firm was able to achieve a savings of 22.5 manhours each week, or $6,300 a year. The cost of the calculator was recovered in less than three months, and the firm foresees greater savings as the staff becomes more proficient in using the equipment.[3]
4. Use of a depreciation method that will enable the firm to write off the maximum amount of depreciation as soon as possible, thus permitting the firm to purchase newer and more efficient equipment frequently.
5. Standardization of equipment. In the purchase of office equipment, standardization of make and kind of equipment

[3] "Three Ways We Cut Administrative Costs," *Administrative Management* (February, 1968), pp. 72-74.

reduces the need for training of employees who are transferred from department to department, simplifies the maintenance and repair service, and may permit a quantity discount from some vendors. Standardization in office equipment should be flexible enough, however, to permit a company to plan for the future.

6. Making comparative studies of possible use of company service units for repair and maintenance of machines instead of service agreements with manufacturers of the equipment.
7. Making job analyses and developing a program of work measurement and standards so that better methods will be used with the machines, thus increasing office production.
8. Studying the possibility of work simplification through the use or development of special-purpose equipment, such as collators, sorting racks, and modular office furniture.
9. Development and use of an inventory method by which frequent reports will be made of the needed equipment in each department, as well as reports of unused equipment in each department.
10. Locating certain office equipment that must be used by several departments where it will be most accessible to all concerned.
11. Realization by the office manager that scientific management techniques which have improved factory methods in the past several decades can be applied in office planning and layout and in the use of office machines and equipment.

To summarize the factors above, it might be stated that one of the principal items of expense deals not with the initial cost of furniture, fixtures, and equipment, but with their cost over the expected life of each item, considered jointly with what the purchase of each item will mean to the work in a particular office. For example, in some offices where the volume of outgoing mail is large, the use of a small hand-affixing stamp machine would be relatively expensive and probably one of the larger automatic stamping and sealing machines should be installed. However, in a smaller office the purchase of an expensive and complex machine might actually be an unfavorable factor. Before a new office tool or machine is purchased, it must be proven that the economies effected through its purchase will pay for the cost within a relatively short time, the exact period to be determined by the office manager or by the planning division.

COST ANALYSIS OF OFFICE SYSTEMS AND PROCEDURES

A management consultant, in commenting about the inefficiency in white-collar work, stated, "There is little scheduling in the typical office, practically no planning, and little real supervision of clerical work. Like Topsy, the office force just grows." [4] Increased efficiency and cost reduction result from simplification of office systems and procedures, as stressed in Chapter 15. A cost analysis of systems and procedures may be accomplished in several ways:

1. By undertaking a general survey of the office information system, it can be decided whether the system should be redesigned or whether the methods should be improved. In this survey analysis is made of such factors as: (a) the data generated by the office force—its quality and usability; cost of producing, storing, moving, and manipulating the data; (b) the clerical force—its increase over the past few years; number of clerical groups; number of persons in typical clerical groups; overstaffing; (c) character of work performed by the office force—definite assignments given and written procedures followed; interruptions in flow of work; number of reports prepared and their purposes.
2. By studying the forms and establishing forms control, unnecessary forms will be eliminated. Other forms will be combined, and still others will be simplified so that less time will be required in their preparation.
3. By studying the flow of work through the office, shorter routes can be established so that less time will be required for completing the work, thus saving many dollars in office costs.
4. By using a suggestion system, many of the workers may recommend changes that will simplify office systems and procedures. Much waste occurs in the office by failing to use the workers' ideas for making improvements.

One large organization employed a systems analyst to study the actual distance traveled by each letter entering the office. It was found that at the time this study of "letter-traveling" was made, the total distance traveled was about three miles—from the time the letter entered the office to the time that action on the letter was completed and it was placed in the file. It was also found that the number of

[4] "How to Reduce Office Costs," *Business Management* (March, 1967), p. 65.

clerks who processed the incoming letters could not be reduced, but the location of their desks in relation to one another could be vastly improved. Upon completion of the study changes were made in the various steps involved and then the distance traveled was charted again, from the standpoint of continuity in moving forward and in actual distance both between desks and in total distance. It was discovered that the traveling distance of each letter could be reduced from three miles to approximately 1/5 of a mile. When this reduction is multiplied thousands of times each month, the ultimate results in increased production and efficiency are tremendous.

ANALYZING THE COSTS OF FORMS AND SUPPLIES

To some extent the cost reduction that can be achieved in the use of office supplies and forms overlaps the suggestions for improvement of office systems and procedures. Nevertheless, the following factors may be considered as means of reducing the cost of forms and supplies:

1. Centralize the responsibility for the creation of new forms as well as for the improvement of old forms and for the elimination of unnecessary forms.
2. Establish a standard procedure for developing a new form, the guidelines for which must be a need for the form and its cost of preparation.
3. Centralize the issuance of office supplies and develop a requisitioning procedure that will promote the economical use of supplies. As a result of its cost-improvement program, one firm realized savings of about $20,000 in the stationery used at corporate headquarters. Rather than ordering stationery sporadically from two or three vendors with intermittent deliveries, the company found that all stationery needs could be projected for the entire year with orders placed on an annual basis. The entire year's order was placed with one supplier who granted a substantial quantity discount for the year's purchases. Requisitions from headquarters are filed weekly with the vendor, who ships within three business days. By eliminating sporadic deliveries of supplies, secretaries no longer tend to hoard supplies, thus unnecessarily tying up capital inventory.
4. Maintain the supplies stockroom or cabinets in orderly and efficient fashion.

5. Do not use envelopes for interoffice mail unless necessary. If envelopes must be used, do not seal them unless the enclosures are confidential. Unsealed envelopes may be used repeatedly.
6. Use the reverse side of an incoming letter for the carbon copy of the reply. This saves the cost of second sheets and reduces the number of items that must be filed. Also, use the carbon paper thoroughly.
7. Use an all-black typewriter ribbon instead of a two-colored ribbon unless there is special need for a second color.
8. Clean and check the desk drawers often to avoid accumulation of unused or unnecessary supplies.
9. Prepare departmental supplies budgets and compare with actual costs of supplies used.

Because the individual office form and supply item costs so little, many office employees and office managers are prone to overlook the total amount involved over the period of a month or a year. This means that much wastefulness occurs because of lack of supervision or control. Unless the supervisor is interested in economy and cost control, the employees in his department will not pay much attention to better ways of doing the work.

REDUCING CORRESPONDENCE COSTS

When one considers that about one third of the volume of business activity is devoted to letter writing, its cost analysis and control become very crucial. The cost factors that make up letter writing vary from day to day, from office to office, and even from department to department in the same firm. Nevertheless, many executives and supervisors do not realize what factors must be considered in letter-writing costs and therefore are unable to analyze and to control them. The basic factors that must be considered by firms when analyzing their correspondence costs are:

1. *Preparation and dictation,* which cover the time required for jotting down notes, consulting records, and conferring with others, as well as actual dictation. For the average letter of 175 words, it is estimated that ten minutes are required for preparation, and five to ten minutes for actual dictation.
2. *Shorthand and typing,* which cover the work of the stenographer or the machine transcriber. The actual typing takes seven or eight minutes.

3. *Reviewing and signing the letter* takes another two minutes of the dictator's time.

In addition to these basic costs, there are the costs of stationery and supplies, the cost of mailing, the filing expense incurred, and the general office overhead.

In 1971 the estimated cost of dictating, typing, mailing, and filing an average business letter was about $3.19, according to the Dartnell Office Administration Service.[5] The largest cost factor ($1 per letter) involved in this analysis is the salaries paid the dictator of the letter and the secretary who types it. The Management Information Center, Inc., a business research organization, calculates that an executive earning $25,000 a year is being paid at a rate exceeding 21 cents a minute; his secretary's salary amounts to slightly more than 4 cents a minute.[6] Together they are worth more than 26 cents a minute in direct labor costs. When allowance is made for fringe benefits, a more realistic labor cost for the team would be 33 cents a minute.

The costs of writing a letter in terms of salary alone, as estimated by Leahy and Company, management consultants, are shown in Table 21-1.[7]

TIME AND COST FACTORS IN CREATING A TYPICAL 175-WORD LETTER

Action	Minutes Required		
	Steno Dictation	Machine Dictation	Form Letters
Planning what to say.	10	10	0
Dictation	10	5	0
Looking up a letter ..	0	0	1
Transcribing—typing .	7	8	1.5
Reviewing—signing ..	2	2	.5
Total minutes	29	25	3
Costs in terms of salary	$.70 to $2.45	$.60 to $2.25	$.08 to $.15

Table 21-1

With mounting administrative office costs such as those cited above, office managers anticipate future application of a new concept called *word processing*. Going beyond the traditional dictating machine and automatic typewriter, one predicts that inexpensive electronic display editing devices will be used in conjunction with

[5] AMemo, *Administrative Management* (March, 1971), p. 96.

[6] E. M. Ryan and C. M. Weld, "Cutting the Costs of Correspondence," *Administrative Management* (October, 1963), pp. 42-44.

[7] Leahy and Company, Management Consultants, as adapted from *Guide Letters,* publication of the United States Government Printing Office.

high-speed printers to create hard copies. With such an operation set up on a remote basis, an executive can dictate his messages by phone from his office, home, or motel room to a recorder in a word processing center, where all the work is accomplished except for his signature.[8]

In controlling correspondence costs, the objectives are to reduce the time necessary to produce each letter and to reduce the length of the letter without impairing its effectiveness. The following list of suggestions for reducing correspondence costs should be carefully investigated by the office manager:

1. *Learn to write short letters* since they are more effective and take less of the stenographer's time. By frequently issuing bulletins showing the excess wordage carried by the firm's letters, this interest in short letters may be accelerated.
2. *Teach executives how to prepare for dictation.* All dictation should be done at one time, as early in the day as possible. All necessary information should be on hand so that uninterrupted dictation may be completed. Time wasted here is a dual loss—the cost of the executive's time and that of the stenographer.
3. *Eliminate unnecessary dictation* by having the stenographer compose her own replies to routine correspondence. By having the executive place on the letter to be answered a notation indicating the nature of the reply, much executive time can be saved.
4. *Use form letters where applicable.* Form letters play an important part in reducing the cost of office correspondence if they are carefully prepared and intelligently used. See Table 21-1 for a comparison of the time and cost factors in creating a form letter and a letter dictated to a stenographer or a dictating machine.

   With form letters, the use of automatic typewriters is especially recommended. Consider that the average typist can type 30 repetitive letters a day on a standard electric typewriter. However, because of errors and erasures, some of these letters may have to be retyped. With one automatic typewriter, the typist can produce 24 repetitive 200-word letters (5 characters per word) each hour. If additional automatic typewriters are added, the output increases proportionately, but allowance must be made for the manual

[8] "1971: Year of the 'Administrative Profit,'" *Administrative Management* (January, 1971), p. 21. Also, see "A Special Report: Word Processing," *Administrative Management* (June, 1971), pp. 19-50.

insertion of variable data and for paper loading unless continuous forms are used. Automatically produced form letters are error free, exact reproductions of the original and are characterized by the prestige appearance of a custom-typed letter.

5. *Use printed or mimeographed postal cards or form letters* as acknowledgments of incoming letters when no answer is required.
6. *Eliminate all overtime and peak loads* by scheduling letter writing in accordance with its importance and urgency. All mail should be answered the same day as received, if possible, but this should not become a fetish and be overdone, resulting in overtime costs.
7. *Conduct letter clinics.* Having a letter adviser in the organization peruse all carbon copies of letters and prepare suggestions for reducing their length and improving their tone will do much to improve and to expedite the letter-writing function.
8. *Use standardized printed forms for correspondence instructions* such as those shown in Figure 21-1.

CORRESPONDENCE INSTRUCTIONS

Date________________19____

To____________________ ____________________

From____________________________________

- ☐ Investigate and report to me.
- ☐ Advise what to do.
- ☐ For you to handle.
- ☐ See me personally before replying.
- ☐ For your information, please return.
- ☐ Make corrections.
- ☐ Confidential.
- ☐ Read and file.
- ☐ Have you done this? When?
- ☐ Take up with __________.
- ☐ Sent me in error.
- ☐ Returned as requested.

Miscellaneous

Fig. 21-1

Printed Form for Quick Checkoff of Correspondence Instructions

9. *Reduce the length of interoffice communications wherever possible.* This saves time not only for the dictator and the transcriber, but also for the recipient who must read the communication.

10. *Use simplified or streamlined letters.* To help reduce correspondence costs, the Administrative Management Society and certain management engineers have recommended the use of the simplified letter. This letter is characterized by: (a) extreme block form with date at the top at the extreme left-hand margin, (b) name and address in block form for use with window envelope, (c) omission of formal salutation and complimentary close, and (d) simplified language and content of letter. See Figure 21-2 on page 680.

11. *Answer letters by telephone* whenever possible, especially when no written record of the reply need be kept.

12. *Record answers to incoming queries on the bottom of the incoming documents* and make copies of these documents to send out as answers. The originals are then filed. The Federal Housing Administration estimates that by following this approach to answering incoming correspondence, it has been able to realize a gross savings equivalent to 6,000 man-hours each year.[9]

Some suggestions for reducing correspondence costs pertain more particularly to the dictator, the transcriber, and the supervisors than those given in the preceding list. The volume of dictation and transcription work is so great that any small economies will be translated into large sums of money each year. A few of the potential economies for many offices are given below:

1. The dictator should learn how to operate the dictation machine properly, use clear enunciation, carefully select words and thoughts, observe brevity, and supply the transcriber with the necessary reference material to facilitate transcription.
2. The transcriber should learn how to use the machine properly.
3. The transcriber should not be called upon to do a lot of menial office jobs in addition to transcribing. The other assignments can be handled more economically by someone else being paid a smaller salary.
4. The dictator's office and the transcription area should have soundproof ceilings so that a minimum of noise will be picked

[9] Ryan and Weld, *op. cit.*, p. 44.

AMS
ADMINISTRATIVE MANAGEMENT SOCIETY
215 OL 9-4300 WILLOW GROVE, PENNSYLVANIA 19090

Dated Today

Mr. Administrative Manager
Progressive Company
1 Main Street
Anytown, Your Country

SIMPLIFIED LETTER

Since 1947, Mr. Manager, AMS has sponsored the Simplified Letter as a more effective format for business correspondence.

What is it? You're reading a sample.

Notice the left block format and the general positioning of the letter. We didn't write "Dear Mr. ---," nor will we write "Yours truly" or "Sincerely yours." Are they really important? We feel just as friendly toward you without them.

We typed the full address at the left--ready for a window envelope and as permanent reference on the letter itself. We added a subject line at the left--a provocative opening and filing clue. We started each paragraph without indentation and tabular delay. And we typed the signature, again at the left, so that the reader knows who wrote it regardless of signature legibility.

What does all this add up to? A more readable document and, for the typist, a reduction in keystrokes meaning more production.

Try the Simplified Letter. Your correspondence will have greater impact and, at the same time, you will realize savings in both time and money.

Doris M. Graff

(MRS.) DORIS M. GRAFF, STAFF DIRECTOR, PERSONNEL & EDUCATION DIVISION

cc: Messrs. Kostenbader, Walter

Fig. 21-2

The AMS Simplified Letter

up on the recording equipment and so that listening to the material recorded will be easier.

5. The transcribers should be supplied with desks of proper height and with posture chairs to relieve the strain of work.

6. The work should be centralized to improve supervision and to obtain better control and instruction. Where possible, the dictating machines can be concentrated in one centralized transcription center with satellite microphones or telephones spotted throughout the office. In such a remote dictating system, however, productivity tends to fall off when a center houses more than about 20 typists. As the unit expands, it becomes progressively more difficult to preserve the sense of personal responsibility for good work. For a given workload, two units of ten each are usually more productive than one unit of 20 typists.[10]
7. The supervisor should attempt to install incentive systems to control costs. If this cannot be done, the supervisor should develop records showing the production of each operator; analyze the causes of low production; and stimulate increased production by improving the methods.

REDUCING MAILING COSTS

In 1970 about 84 billion pieces of mail were processed, with business mail addressed to individuals comprising almost 80 percent of this volume[11] and postage costs to business firms amounting to about $4 billion. With this tremendous sum of money spent on mail, it is surprising how little attention is given by the average business firm to its mailing function. However, undertakings such as that conducted by the Western Union Telegraph Company and the United States Postal Service may greatly alter future letter writing and mailing and reduce costs accordingly. In this program the facilities of both Western Union and the Postal Service are combined in the form of a *mailgram*. With TWX machines set up in post offices in 24 major cities throughout the country, a firm having TWX equipment in its office can teletype a letter instantly to the destination post office, from which delivery will be made the next business day by the postal authorities. This experiment is merely one of several that may revolutionize the transmission and delivery of mail.

The first requisite for reducing the cost of mailing, whether in the office or in the mailroom, is a thorough knowledge of the postal rules and regulations. Other mailing practices and rules of business procedure that can result in savings are:

---

[10] William E. Perry, Jr., "The Benefits of Dictating Machines," *Administrative Management* (December, 1963), p. 52.

[11] *Management News* (New York: American Management Association, December, 1969), p. 7.

1. Use airmail postage only for important long-distance mail. In most cities served by commercial airlines and in all cities with a population of over 300,000, virtually all first-class mail destined to cities more than 250 miles away goes by air.
2. Deposit as much first-class long-distance mail as possible in the post office by 11 a.m. each business day. If both the sender's and addressee's cities are served by commercial airlines, the mail will usually be delivered the next day.
3. Analyze carefully the delivery of special-delivery mail against that of first-class mail or airmail to make sure that its use results in prompter delivery to the addressee.
4. Do not overinsure packages, since reimbursement for their loss is determined according to their actual value, not their declared value.
5. Do not use registered mail unless the item has insurable value. Certified mail provides the same service but at a lower cost.
6. Eliminate all unnecessary letters. It is surprising what can be done in this respect, with the result that the cost of the letter as well as the postage will be saved.
7. Answer all letters promptly, thus avoiding the necessity for sending follow-up letters that merely add to the volume of mail handled. Do not press for replies to letters except when desirable.
8. Review the advertising materials sent out. The weight of paper stock on which they are printed may be reduced if this will lower the postage rate. Also, the frequency of their distribution may be reduced. Often it is possible to include the advertising flyers with monthly statements, thus avoiding additional postage costs.
9. Require an advance mailing analysis on all printed material. If much circular mail is sent out, the company should have a checkup system for the names on its mailing lists in order to remove duplicates and to eliminate those whose letters have been returned as undeliverable.
10. Analyze the stationery with the objective of reducing the weight or size of the paper in order to place the mailing in a lower weight class, thus reducing costs considerably where the volume of mail is great.
11. In small offices the mail clerk may be given a working fund similar to the petty cash fund. Each morning the clerk makes out a requisition listing the previous day's postage outlay and is reimbursed for this expenditure. A week-to-week study of

postage costs should be made to see that discrepancies are accounted for. This procedure supplements the initial weekly checking of the postal charges, the purpose of which is to be sure that all possible economies have been effected as to proper classification of mail, size and weight of paper and enclosures, and control of stamps by the use of postage meters.

12. Combine the activities of the mailing department with those of some of the other service departments such as filing, messenger service, or duplicating. Some of the employees of these departments can be assigned to the mailing department during rush periods.

13. Use adequate equipment, such as collators, tying machines, sorting racks, and date-time recorders, to expedite the work, even though this equipment will not be in continuous use throughout the day.

    Automatic mail openers feed, open, and stack more than 500 envelopes a minute. Postage meters stamp, seal, and postmark the mail in one operation. The bookkeeping for postage is done in visible registers that show the postage used and that on hand. Postage meters also protect from waste and from "borrowing." Any "spoiled" meter mail will be redeemed by the post office at 90 percent of its face value by submitting the metered envelope or wrapper and a claim form to the post office. Since metered mail is not cancelled by the post office, much of the processing time that holds up stamped mail is avoided.

    The use of mailing scales, periodically checked, eliminates the insufficient-postage error and the expensive over-postage problem.

14. Use envelopes with distinctively colored borders for first-class and airmail material.

15. Use business reply envelopes wherever possible instead of pursuing the wasteful practice of enclosing stamped return envelopes. One central permit number allows the use of business reply envelopes by branch offices. When the business reply envelope is returned by the addressee, the post office of the sender collects the regular postage plus a small fee for the reply privilege. On this basis, it seems that the only time it is more economical to enclose stamped envelopes in place of the business reply envelopes is when a very large percentage of returns is expected.

16. Print in advance the envelopes for branch mail, thus saving the cost of typing addresses each day. Further economies

result by holding all but the most urgent branch mail and enclosing it in one envelope at the close of the day.

17. Use duplex or combination envelopes for sending first- or third-class mail as an enclosure with second-, third-, and fourth-class parcels.

REDUCING THE COSTS OF RECORDS MANAGEMENT

In many offices the management of records is an expensive luxury. It is estimated that business firms allocate from 15 to 40 percent of their sales and administrative expenses to creating and keeping records. According to the National Records Management Council, it costs $250 a year to maintain one five-drawer file cabinet and $8,000 a year to create and to file its contents.[12] One management consulting firm estimates that in the average firm there is a separate operating file location for every two to four employees.[13] Of the more than 1.25 trillion pieces of paper on file, about half are being held in office space renting for $8 per square foot or more. And yet in the average company only four percent of the records by volume have permanent value or historical interest.

The Cost of Records Management

There are many different ways in which to compute the costs of records management, but the important fact is that each firm should have definite cost figures for its filing operations. In computing the cost of filing consideration must be given to the rental value of the space occupied by the files, the depreciation of the filing equipment, and the cost of supplies used.

Table 21-2 shows the cost of operating a records center for firms having centralized and decentralized control programs. It is interesting to note that firms having a centrally controlled program generally spend more for records management than those companies with decentralized control. In small firms (1 to 100 office employees) with decentralized control programs, 100 percent of the firms spend less than $5,000 each year for operating their records centers. Only 63 percent of the small firms with centralized programs spend less than $5,000 each year. Of the medium-size firms (101 to 500 employees), 54 percent spend less than $5,000 to operate their decentralized programs, but the majority of large companies, 32

[12] "Your Copying Costs: Facts or Fantasies?" *Administrative Management* (March, 1967), p. 23.

[13] Leahy & Company and its affiliate Leahy Archives, Inc., as reported in *Administrative Management* (July, 1963), p. 23.

percent, report their costs as being between $15,000 and $30,000 each year.

COST OF OPERATING A RECORDS CENTER
(Including salaries, space, and equipment)

Table 21-2

Cost	Firms with Centralized Control Program			Firms with Decentralized Control Program		
	1-100*	101-500	Over 500	1-100	101-500	Over 500
Under $5,000	63%	36%	29%	100%	54%	26%
$5-$15,000	21	43	16	0	15	23
$15-$30,000	4	11	22	0	31	32
$30-$50,000	0	7	13	0	0	6
$50-$100,000	8	0	15	0	0	6
Over $100,000	4	4	5	0	0	6

* Number of employees in the office.

Source: "AMS Survey: Records Management Practices," *Administrative Management* (October, 1964), p. 60.

Calculating precisely the cost of records management becomes a complicated task because of the variability of cost factors such as salaries, office rent, and the estimated life of the equipment. However, certain basic factors can be determined. For example, in one firm each file clerk is responsible for 15 four-drawer file cabinets, and for every ten file clerks there is one supervisor. A file clerk is paid $4,000 a year, on the average, and a supervisor, $6,000. Each four-drawer file cabinet costs $100. Using these figures, the annual cost of maintaining one four-drawer file cabinet may be calculated as follows:

File clerk's salary	$267
Supervisor's salary	40
Floor space, 5½ square feet @ $6	33
Supplies, $8 per cabinet	8
Cost of cabinet amortized over 10-year period	10
Transfer file and supplies	25
Total annual cost of maintaining one file cabinet	$383

Savings Realized from Studies of Records Management

A number of firms have realized substantial savings through studies of their records management costs. An engineering company realized annual savings of more than $2,500 after the installation of a microfilm system.[14] Prior to installing the system one girl was

[14] "Microfilm Cuts Budget by Over $2,500," *Administrative Management* (October, 1969), pp. 28-30.

spending eight hours each week, or 416 hours each year, filing active records and transferring inactive materials from the central files to remote storage areas. Ten workers in the sales department were spending 182 hours each year in searching the files in remote locations. The annual cost of filing supplies was about $1,400; the 93 metal file cabinets in central and remote locations cost $9,300. The cabinets occupied 302 square feet of floor space at 75 cents per square foot for a total rental cost of $226.50. Following the installation of the microfilm system the following savings and advantages were realized: (1) search time and time required to refile documents were cut by at least 80 percent, with annual savings in search time amounting to about $300; (2) the number of new file folders purchased annually was reduced, bringing about an added savings of more than $1,000; (3) 70 of the firm's 93 cabinets were emptied of their contents and shifted to other departments, thus eliminating the need to buy more cabinets; and (4) annual savings contributed by floor space vacated is about $140. The company spent $2,600 for the microfilm system installation, and at the present rate of savings the new system equipment will be amortized in less than ten years.

A nationally known oil company with offices in many cities was persuaded to follow the recommendations of a file specialist in one of its offices. The result was a saving of about 50 percent floor space—enough to make room for 20 stenographers; a salvage of about 185 steel filing cabinets; and a release of five personnel out of ten for other duties. The payroll savings alone paid for the entire cost of the change in little more than a year.

A newly developed system for information handling, a combination of computers and microfilm into a device known as COM (Computer Output Microfilm), offers huge potential savings in the office. (The COM device was described in Chapter 8.) One application of the COM system is illustrated by the paper-work flow at the National Bank of Detroit. Rather than purchase its own COM system, the bank purchases the time of a service bureau that obtains the bank's internally produced magnetic tapes and converts them into plain language on microfilm. The service bureau's equipment prints at rates up to 20,000 lines per minute, which is 20 to 30 times faster than conventional line printers.[15] A binary code index, which includes the account

[15] "COM: What It Costs and How It's Used," *Administrative Management* (March, 1971), p. 22. For additional information about COM, see *Computer Output Microfilm,* published by National Microfilm Association, Suite 1101, 8728 Colesville Road, Silver Spring, MD 20910. Also, the October, 1970, issue of *The Office* contains several articles that describe the state of the art to date and what can be expected in the future as well as how several firms are now utilizing COM systems.

number and transaction date to be used for information retrieval, is recorded on each film image as the microfilm is produced. As a result of using the COM system, the bank has released 57 four-drawer file cabinets and six typewriters for other purposes; seven clerks who formerly handled the referencing and filing of records in the trust department have been reassigned other duties.

In the cost accounting department of a manufacturer of office machines and equipment, the 125,000 cost records were formerly maintained in open tub files. After the installation of a mechanized filing system using a work station approach, space needs were reduced by 60 percent. Prior to using the new system, nearly three times as much floor space and considerably more employee movement by the five file clerks were required. Under the new system each work station operator is assigned to one file and is responsible for approximately 25,000 cards. The new files have the capacity for a 35 percent expansion and can be adapted easily to hold punched cards instead of conventional file cards should there be a change in the system. The space freed by the new files has been used to install an electronic data processing system along with several cost analysis functions that had been inconveniently located in other areas or did not previously exist.[16]

In one company the contents of four-drawer file cabinets are periodically transferred to inactive storage cases on steel racks that extend to the ceiling in the storage area. One steel rack occupies 17.5 square feet, holds the contents of ten four-drawer file cabinets, and costs $50. The calculation of annual savings under this approach is shown below:

Filing Costs in Four-Drawer File Cabinets in Active Storage		Filing Costs After Materials Are Transferred to Inactive Storage	
1 file cabinet @ $100, amortized over ten-year period	$10.00	1/10 steel rack @ $50, amortized over ten-year period	$ .50
5½ square feet @ $4	22.00	6 cardboard containers @ .25	1.50
Overhead and maintenance, 5½ square feet @ $2	11.00	1/10 of 17.5 square feet @ $1	1.75
		Overhead and maintenance, 1/10 of 17.5 square feet @ $1	1.75
Total costs	$43.00	Total costs	$5.50

Annual savings when contents of one four-drawer file cabinet are transferred to inactive storage: $43.00 − $5.50 = $37.50.

[16] With permission of Mr. R. A. Saunders, Advertising Manager, Diebold, Incorporated, February, 1970.

A few years ago when a firm of records control specialists investigated the records kept by the American Cyanamid Company, it was able to reduce the company's annual record-keeping costs by some $85,000. Rental of the space occupied by each office file cabinet, plus amortization of the initial cost of the cabinets, was costing Cyanamid $8.72 a year. Each file cabinet in storage was annually costing $2.76 to maintain. The firm of records specialists tossed out 54 percent of the storage records and either destroyed or transferred to storage 26 percent of the office records.[17]

Cost-Reduction Suggestions

Among the procedures that the office manager may use to reduce the costs of records management are:

1. Centralize those files used by all departments. In the data processing department, a data librarian should be appointed to keep track of each data item by means of visible files and control boards.
2. Constantly study the filing systems in use to make sure that the systems are adaptable to the records being filed.
3. Use work-facilitating equipment such as file racks, sorting racks, sufficient file guides, and colored folder labels.
4. Provide a layout for the filing department that will insure a smooth and efficient flow of work to and from the files.
5. Schedule the collection and distribution of the materials to be filed or to be delivered from the files.
6. Develop a sound method of transferring inactive records from the files and a workable schedule for records retention and destruction.
7. Use special file cabinets, such as map files and voucher files, for papers or records that do not fit into regular letter-size or legal-size file drawers. Punched cards should be filed vertically to protect them against bending and folding so they will run smoothly through the high-speed processing equipment. Punched tapes can be filed in tape pockets attached to cards that list the data punched into them. Extra long tapes can be put on reels and stored vertically in cabinets or shelves.

   Magnetic tapes and discs must be protected from dust, heat, and humidity. Since dust and dirt deposits can cause loss

---

[17] "More Companies Turn to Experts to Clear Files, Store Records," *The Wall Street Journal,* February 23, 1965, p. 1.

or garbling of the data stored, the media should be filed in tight-fitting cases and stored in special cabinets that hold the reels vertically. To prevent damage to magnetic discs, they should be stored in cabinets that lock the disc packs in place so they will not slide around. Control panels can be stored vertically or horizontally so long as their delicate circuitry is protected.

8. Consider the microfilming of records in lieu of storing records in transfer cases. The cost of microfilming one cubic foot of records (about 2,000 documents) is about $20. This amount includes labor, film, developing, and depreciation or rental of equipment. By comparing the annual cost of storing the same number of documents in transfer cases with the cost of microfilming, a break-even point can be quickly established.
9. Develop a filing manual (see Chapter 23) for training employees and for controlling the filing work.
10. Carefully estimate and check on the volume of work that should be done in the filing department. Use workers from the mail department or other departments during rush periods in the filing department.
11. Purchase durable equipment and supplies. It is estimated that the average file drawer is opened and closed 100,000 times during its useful life. Cheap cabinets are wasteful because their poor construction prevents rapid filing. Supplies of poor quality interfere with efficient filing because they must be constantly replaced.
12. Do not hesitate to use the expert services of the companies manufacturing filing supplies and equipment, provided there is a qualified person in the firm to aid in the selection of the equipment and to supervise its operation after it has been installed. Otherwise, the installation may result in a waste of money for the firm.
13. Consider the employment of a records control specialist, who will analyze the files to see that outdated papers are disposed of, important ones retained, and papers that are neither useful nor important are kept in some location where they can be stored cheaply.

The suggestions given above should prove an excellent outline for the records management supervisor in reviewing his work and for the administrative office manager in evaluating the records management function. Instead of continuing to do an office routine such as filing in the same way that it has been done for years, all jobs should be studied so that common sense and business efficiency, not habit, are the reasons for following certain procedures. Answering the questions, "Why is this done?" "Is it necessary?" "If so, how can it be simplified or done at less cost?" will prove very helpful in reducing the costs of records management.

REDUCING THE COSTS OF REPRODUCTION SERVICES

Controlling the costs of reproduction services means not only keeping the costs at a minimum but also improving the quality of the work, increasing the volume of necessary work, and doing the work in the shortest possible time. Thus, it is necessary that those handling the work be familiar with the various methods of reproduction which are described in Chapter 9.

The Cost of Duplicating Processes

Duplicating processes, as distinguished from copying processes, require the preparation of some kind of master, stencil, or other medium from which final copies are made. Duplicators are generally used to make fairly long high-speed runs; the copying processes are rarely effective for making more than a few copies in a run, and these are produced at relatively slow speeds and more expensively. One exception in this comparison is the diazo unit that will produce hundreds of copies per hour at a fairly inexpensive rate.

The following suggestions for reducing the costs of duplicating services should be taken into consideration by the office manager, dependent upon the type of process utilized within his firm:

1. Plan and organize the daily work so as to encourage the reproduction department or service center to increase the quantity and quality of the work produced.
2. Search constantly for the best methods, materials, and equipment to increase the efficiency of the reproduction personnel. Consult the methods and procedures department, if one exists, or the salesmen of equipment and supplies to keep up-to-date on developments in duplicating equipment and processes.
3. Analyze and compare in-house reproduction costs periodically with the cost of having the work handled by outside firms. Occasionally ask for bids from three or four commercial

sources for a series of typical jobs. If the cost of sending the work out is less than or equal to the cost of doing it inside, it is probably best to direct the work to the commercial sources.

4. Require requisitions for all work orders, and control the approval of these requisitions. Only essential work should be performed by the duplicating department. Establish priorities for jobs to be done and see that the delivery dates are met and that the quality of the work is satisfactory. Check periodically the requisitions and sample the jobs being duplicated to see if the proper materials have been used, if the right processes have been selected, and if delivery dates have been met.
5. If an offset duplicator is used, review the duplicating needs to make sure there is enough work to keep the equipment busy. It may be less expensive to use a commercial printer or perhaps a stencil duplicator and still do the job satisfactorily.
6. If the purchase of an offset duplicator is being considered, make sure the correct size is purchased. Too small a press will result in backup work and delays. Too large a press, operating at speeds far in excess of actual needs, can cause wasteful down-time or needless printing in an attempt to justify the cost of the equipment and the salaries of the operators.

The Cost of Office Copiers

The real costs involved in the use of office copiers are the basic costs plus waste. The cost of waste may exceed 50 percent of the original cost of the materials, and some users claim that, as a practical matter, in the normal office situation one cannot expect to get below 10 percent waste. The basic cost factors to be considered in the purchase of office copying equipment are:

1. Price of the equipment. Here, the advantages of leasing versus purchase should be weighed.
2. Recurring costs of paper and chemicals. Paper costs will vary in accordance with quantity ordered and whether the dealer's policy is one of granting discounts.
3. Amount of time and effort needed to run the copier.
4. Costs of cleaning and repairs and the availability of ready maintenance.
5. Silent waste-causing factors such as reaction of chemicals to extremes of cold and heat, care required in exposing papers to

room light, speed with which papers spoil, and voltage variations that may affect copy quality.

To reduce and to control copying costs, the administrative office manager must be aware that there is a copying problem and that cost reduction can be made. The following cost-reducing suggestions are offered:

1. Eliminate as many self-service copiers as possible and establish satellite copy centers staffed with operators and messengers. Pick-up and delivery stations can be set up on each floor where work to be copied can be dropped off and delivered. Messengers can make pick-ups and deliveries at these stations on an hourly basis.

   In each satellite copy center that is established, assign one person who is trained in the operation of each copier to do all the copying on that machine. This person should keep a log of all materials copied, showing the kind of documents copied and the number of copies made. Examination of the log may show in relation to the volume of copies made that another kind of equipment should be used for reproducing certain documents.
2. If centralized copying operations that require the full-time services of one or more operators cannot be justified, consider the use of an administrative substation that contains a centralized copying operation as well as an office supplies center. When the operator is not busy copying, she can dispense office supplies and take care of other assigned duties.
3. If self-service and desk-top copiers are scattered throughout the general offices in an attempt to shorten waiting and traveling time, close control must be exercised over the machines to avoid abusive uses such as using the machines for personal use, wasting copies because of improper adjustments, making more copies than are actually necessary, and making copies that could be reproduced more economically by some other method. Users should be instructed by means of a notice posted near each machine that no more than a specified number of copies, say ten, should be made of any one original.
4. Adopt specific controls for the production of multiple copies by restricting single-copy machines to making one to five copies, and multiple-copy machines, to six to ten copies. Establish a copy center for reproducing, say, 11 to 40 copies and provide a reproduction service for more than 40 copies.

5. Install key locks and meters on copiers so that each machine is inoperable unless a key is used.[18]
6. Establish guidelines for copying versus typing carbons versus cutting a stencil. In many instances since the material has to be typed anyway before being distributed, preparing carbon copies or cutting a stencil may be more economical.

REDUCING THE COST OF INTERCOMMUNICATIONS

The office manager must be constantly on the alert for improved methods of using his present intercommunications equipment or of installing new equipment. The installation of a modern intercommunications system can result in lower office costs. Among the methods that can be applied to accomplish this goal are:

1. Use of an intercommunications system, Private Automatic Exchange (PAX), or CENTREX system wherever it will relieve the work of the regular office telephones. It is important that incoming calls not be "held" at the switchboard. The CENTREX system allows incoming calls to bypass the company switchboard and to ring directly at the telephone of the person called. (The various kinds of intercommunications systems are discussed in Chapter 7.)
2. Use of an electric paging system where its cost of operation is proven more economical than other systems in use.
3. Comparative cost studies and instructions in the use of mail, telephone, and telegraph for intercommunications. Instruct those who dictate and type telegraphic messages on how to prepare and use the services. These instructions may form a part of the employees' communications manual, as described in Chapter 23. Rate sheets and word count forms may be obtained from the local Western Union office. Particular attention should be paid to the proper wording of telegrams, proper selection of types of messages that can be sent at reduced rates, and elimination of extra charges by refraining from use of special symbols that increase the cost of the message.

[18] To learn how one firm reduced its copying costs from 20 to 50 percent by means of using copying machines on a metered, per-click usable-per-copy basis, see "Metering Reduces Lederle Laboratories' Copying Costs," *The Office* (March, 1971), pp. 66-77, 175. In this same issue also, see "Counters on Copiers Can Control Copying Costs," pp. 86-90. The November, 1970, issue of *The Office,* devoted to Copier-Duplicator Management, contains several articles illustrating: how the office administrator can determine his copy requirements and present productivity to meet current needs and to plan for the future; the manner in which the various copying and duplicating processes are being used today; and how one firm exercises tight control over its copying costs.

Messages should be checked periodically to make sure that instructions are being followed.

4. Controlling the use of telephones for personal messages. Obtain management support of the economical use of the telephone by periodically sending out announcements urging employees to keep personal calls at an absolute minimum.
5. Use of monthly budget figures and allocation of communications expense for control purposes. When division and department heads are required to budget all items of communications equipment and its use and to account for expenditures against this budget, they will be more cooperative in eliminating waste. The monthly summary of telephone expenses should cover the actual dollars allocated to each department for equipment cost, the amount of local messages assigned to each department, all long-distance calls charged to the department, other charges or credits assigned to the department, allocation of telegraph costs to departments using these facilities, and an accurate allocation of each department's use of special services such as WATS and Telpak.
6. Intercommunications costs should be studied in terms of the time of the employees—payroll cost—that is saved by the use of mechanical methods. Payroll cost is still the major item that must be controlled for an efficiently operating office. Everything else is merely a contingent or an indirect economy.

The ease with which the telephone can be used in the office often leads to a waste of time and money. Telephone usage is a costly office service, as brought out in a survey of 1,406 offices, which was conducted by the Telecommunications Committee of the Administrative Management Society.[19] In this survey it was found that the average local service telephone bill for offices with 25 to 100 employees is about $400 a month; for offices staffed by over 1,000 people but less than 5,000 the monthly bill is almost $7,000. For office staffs of more than 5,000, the monthly telephone service costs about $68,000. The survey also revealed that out of all industry groups, the insurance firms participating in the study had the lowest average monthly cost per telephone station—$9.05. The largest monthly cost, an average of $19.35 per station, was found in educational institutions.[20] The wide range of costs among industries can be accounted for by the nature of the businesses—some requiring more

---

[19] "What Business Spends for Its Phone Service," *Administrative Management* (June, 1964), p. 66.

[20] *Ibid.*, p. 67.

telephone communications than others and some utilizing more sophisticated telephone equipment than others.

Some cost-reduction measures for the use of the telephone are: [21]

1. Relieve the switchboard operator of other office duties so that undivided attention may be given to the placing and receiving of calls.
2. Have the person called answer the telephone himself instead of through a third party—usually the secretary. This saves much time in most offices.
3. Be sure that telephones are answered promptly, thus eliminating the necessity for needless additional calls.
4. Request each user of the telephone to make his own calls instead of asking the switchboard operator to make them all.
5. Have experienced, well-trained operators at the switchboard. Qualified personnel can be obtained directly from telephone company employment offices, or one of the firm's own operators may be trained by the telephone company.
6. Maintain and use an up-to-date house telephone directory to expedite the handling of interoffice and incoming calls.
7. In the information or service departments, locate the files and writing shelves near the telephone to expedite giving the information requested.
8. Be sure that the telephones are located where they are needed the most. Handy telephone installations save much time in walking back and forth. The cost of additional telephones is much less than the cost of time lost in traveling. Two employees at adjacent desks with low-call volume may be able to share the same telephone.
9. Provide an effective means of controlling costs by checking on out-of-town or toll calls. Many calls, especially international calls, can be replaced by significantly less expensive methods such as airmail letters or night letter cables.
10. Use instruction or pointer sheets to improve the use of the telephone.

COST CONTROL IN DATA PROCESSING CENTERS

In some firms having a data processing center, it will be found that the installation of automated data processing equipment has led

[21] For additional hints on how to reduce telephone costs, see "6 Do-It-Yourself Ways to Cut Telephone Costs," *Administrative Management* (September, 1970), pp. 67 and 68.

to a reduction in operating costs. In other firms, however, the data processing center has sent overhead costs soaring to new heights. Because of the speed with which automatic processing machines generate reports and analyses, managers may ask for more and more detailed machine-produced records in an effort to satisfy the center's insatiable demands for input data. The need for much of the newly produced output is questionable in relation to its contribution to management's ability to make more intelligent decisions. Costs are further increased as the result of the need to file, store, and maintain the newly produced records and reports.

Several suggestions for reducing costs in data processing centers are proposed:

1. Evaluate the importance of the data presently produced and the backlog of programs in varying stages of development. Each program that is planned for application by means of electronic data processing should be analyzed and priorities set in relation to which programs will yield the greatest savings to the firm.
2. Rather than increase the work load merely to utilize the idle time of equipment, allocate to the nonaccounting departments—research, engineering, marketing—the use of the equipment for special projects such as operations research studies, information retrieval, and statistical analyses. The level of present equipment usage can be determined by attaching meters to the central processing units and peripheral devices. Analysis of the usage records will indicate whether the cost of the present equipment can be justified.
3. Work flow, personnel, and machines should be synchronized by establishing rigid deadlines for completion of tasks at various stations. Bottlenecks in the manual work flow, such as in key-punch operations, should be eliminated in order to avoid backlogs in the automated processing procedures. Also, it should be determined whether key punching is the best method for providing input into the computer system. In some instances the installation of a typewriting operation to replace key-punch and key-verifying operations brings about greater accuracy, increases production, and reduces training problems. In such an installation an optical character reader, which translates the typewritten lists onto magnetic tape, may serve as input to the computer.[22]

[22] "17 Ways Companies Reduce EDP Costs," *Management Review* (February, 1971), pp. 8-17.

4. Control the labor costs of data processing by striving for a ratio of at least 1:2.5 for man-hours to machine-hours. Although the staff of the data center must grow to meet the expanded services demanded, the center should not grow without reason. The installation of work measurement and the development of standards should be considered, especially for the larger, more important repetitive tasks such as key punching. As a result of analyzing its productivity and accuracy, one firm was able to reduce its key punching costs by about 10 percent.[23] Through increased supervisory control over the work of the operators an additional 10 percent savings was achieved even after the increased supervision costs were taken into consideration.[24]

5. Determine what amount of error, or type of error, the company can afford to tolerate and decide at what point it becomes more expensive to prevent the errors than to correct them. Unless an error cut-off point is established, management may find that, to prevent errors from infiltrating its data processing center, a larger staff of people is being used than was employed when the data were processed manually.[25]

SCIENTIFIC MANAGEMENT AND BEHAVIORAL SCIENCE TOOLS OF COST CONTROL

At the beginning of this chapter it was stressed that to control the cost of office services, it is first necessary for the administrative manager to develop cost-conscious behavioral attitudes on the part of all employees. To lay the foundation for cost reduction as a continuous objective and function of each phase of work, the manager must subscribe to the basic concepts of scientific management and behavioral science. The scientific approach, which characterizes scientific management, must be followed in solving business problems and in advancing the development of behavioral science techniques. As described in an earlier chapter, scientific management employs an objective, experimental approach by first clearly stating the problem or the need. Next, the relevant data are collected, classified, and analyzed in order to formulate a tentative solution that may be tested to determine its validity or usefulness. Finally, the workable solution is put into action and periodically checked in order to

---

[23] *Ibid.*, p. 16.

[24] *Ibid.*

[25] Henry Schindall, "Trimming Data Processing Waste," *Administrative Management* (March, 1964), p. 60.

determine its effectiveness in achieving the desired goal. If necessary, the solution may be modified in light of any later findings or changed conditions.

The office manager is aided by several tools of cost control in applying the basic concepts of scientific management and behavioral science to the solution of office problems. Several of these tools are briefly described in the following paragraphs.

Quality Control

By use of several statistical techniques, the administrative manager can exercise control over certain types of repetitive office operations and thus obtain a warning of a decline in efficiency. In large offices, particularly in life insurance companies, increasing effort is directed toward improving and controlling the quality of the work. Under a *quality control program,* an attempt is made to recognize and to remove the identifiable costs of defects and variations from the standards that have been developed for the particular process or operation. For example, quality control may be exercised by means of individual error records that are completed from time to time or maintained continuously. From error records made each month, it is possible to prepare a summary table of the "Record of the Effect of Errors" for the year, showing the following: (1) errors of no consequence, (2) errors affecting the firm, and (3) errors affecting the customers. The amount and nature of the errors can be reduced to a monthly average, then analyzed, and preventive steps may be taken.

The cost of some types of quality control may be reduced by means of *probability sampling.* For example, rather than check the output of all billers and record all errors made, a randomly selected sample can be taken of the work produced by each biller. The sample size required to give valid and reliable findings can be statistically determined so that the costly checking of all records can be avoided. In one company a 60-day test was made using 100 percent checking and a 20 percent sample. The results were practically identical, and the firm is now using a 20 percent sample for its quality control program.[26]

[26] For an excellent application of probability sampling as a technique for reducing office costs, see "Sampling Improves Forms Control 6 Ways," *Office Systems in Action: Case Study Profiles,* Manual 2S-106, *Administrative Management* (1968), pp. 1-3.

Error Factor Analysis and Reduction

Aware that much quality control activity is concerned with inspection and control rather than prevention, the developers of the technique called *EFAR* (*Error Factor Analysis and Reduction*) have attempted to identify 12 causative areas external to the individual that are most responsible for errors.[27] One basic principle underlying the EFAR technique is that if a man or woman can perform a routine, repetitive clerical operation correctly 50 percent of the time, he can perform it correctly and probably more efficiently 60, 70, 80, or even 90 percent or more of the time; not 100 percent but approaching that level of performance.[28] The technique stresses that clerical work should be viewed broadly as a form of behavior and that the making of errors should be viewed as deficient behavior capable of being remedied in those workers who possess the required competence.

Zero Defects Plan

The *Zero Defects plan* is aimed at developing a constant, conscious effort on the part of each employee to improve performance continually in accomplishing his job so that he will do it correctly the first time. Someone has described the program as the personal search for perfection by everyone. The program utilizes what sociologists call group motivation to get individuals within the group to assign the same importance to their work activities as they do to their personal affairs.[29] At the Retail Credit Company, Atlanta, where the program is called "Target Zero," the objective is not just to detect errors but to get at their causes and to correct the causes. Error consciousness is encouraged among all employees and they are encouraged to do their jobs right the first time and every time. As a result of installing the Target Zero program, employees have been able to reduce mismailings by more than 40 percent, thus improving the speed of customer service. Also, the handling of the files has attained 98.5 percent accuracy.[30]

---

[27] For a complete discussion of the 12 causative areas, see William Exton, Jr., "Clerical Errors: Their Cost and Cure," *The Office* (December, 1970), p. 38.

[28] *Ibid.*, p. 37.

[29] For a description of the Zero Defects plan as one model example of group nonfinancial incentive plans, see Herbert G. Zollitsch and Adolph Langsner, *Wage and Salary Administration* (Cincinnati: South-Western Publishing Co., 1970), pp. 595-598.

[30] "Zero Defects Plan Reduces Mismails by over 40%," *Administrative Management* (July, 1970), p. 52.

Visual Control Boards

On a visual control board, a particular event in an office operation is plotted so that the person responsible for its completion is kept informed of the daily progress and is assured that plans are being carried out according to schedule. The development of the visual control board can be traced to the type of charts conceived by Henry Gantt, a pioneer in management science. The underlying principle of a *Gantt chart* is that the work planned and the work done are shown in the same space in their relation to each other and to time.

On the magnetic type of control board, such as that shown in Figure 21-3, the symbols, letters, and numbers are magnets themselves or are attached to magnets so that they may be easily moved about and placed in a path to illustrate graphically the facts needed to solve the problem at hand. Magnetic boards that make use of pegs, card inserts, grease pencils, or movable bars are also available.

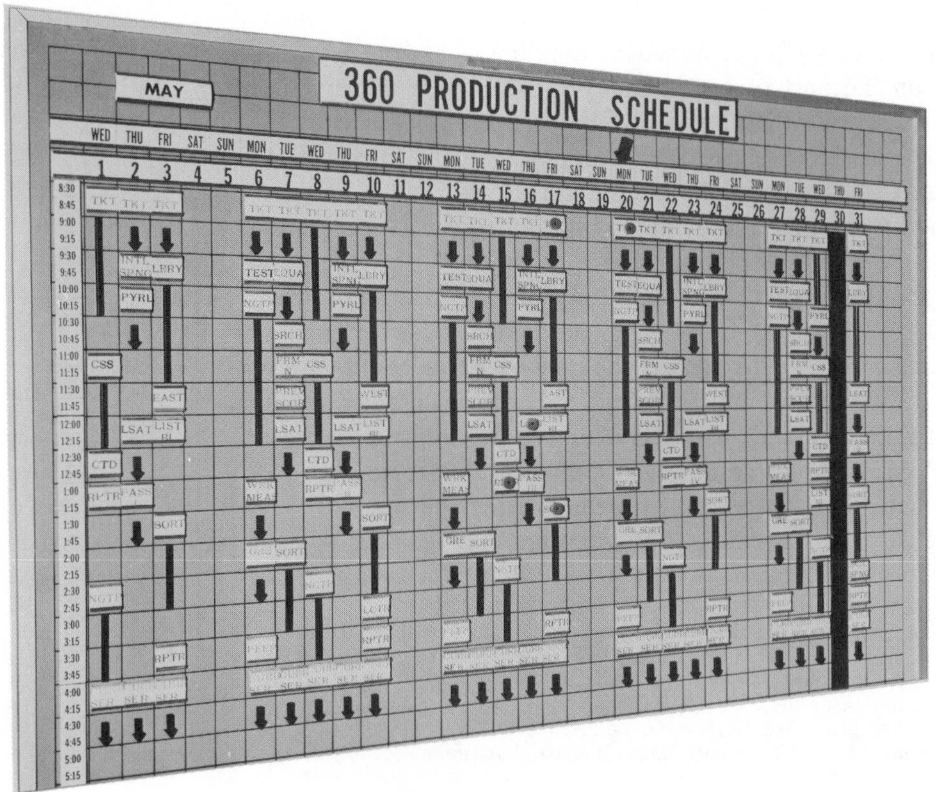

Fig. 21-3

Methods Research Corporation

Magnetic Control Board

On a control board used for scheduling, the "Today" line enables the user to know the exact status of any event, such as an order being processed, for a particular time period. Data pertaining to scheduling are usually represented horizontally, reading across the board from left to right, with the "Today" line running vertically from top to bottom. Events in the past are usually plotted to the left of the "Today" line; events of the future are plotted to the right of the line; those events in the column directly under the line pertain to the present.

A control board can be used to provide quickly and accurately many types of information, such as the following: [31]

1. Orders that are, or will be, behind schedule. (See Figure 21-3.)
2. Delivery dates that will be missed unless immediate action is taken.
3. Inventory status—where it will be short or long, and when.
4. Items which, if not quickly replaced, will stop production.
5. Salesmen and products behind or ahead of quota.
6. Overlooked or approaching maintenance checks.
7. Whether personnel are being utilized properly so that maximum output is gained.
8. Whether computer time is being properly scheduled and used.

PERT and CPM

Program Evaluation and Review Technique (PERT) is used for planning, scheduling, and controlling complex projects that involve a long series of steps and that have to be completed in the shortest possible time. In making use of PERT, a manager first sets a target date for the completion of a major task. Every event, large or small, that will occur in the completion of the job is defined. The events are linked together and plotted as a flow chart type of diagram. On the chart all the activities needed to achieve the events are shown as connecting arrows that form paths through what may be considered a network. The time required to complete each activity is estimated through a simple statistical technique by those responsible for the work. The time required to complete each activity

[31] "Control Boards from Pegs to PERT," *Administrative Management* (July, 1963), p. 41.

along every possible path through the network is then totaled. The longest path is labeled the *critical path* because no matter how quickly the events along the other paths are completed, the events along the longest path must be finished before the project can be terminated. The overall starting and completion dates are pinpointed, and target dates are established for each task. Unlike the Gantt chart, the PERT network, divided into the three aspects of time, cost, and performance, shows the sequence, interrelationships, and dependencies of individual tasks in the project. The PERT technique lends itself to use in computerized projects, and most computer manufacturers offer a PERT program along with their equipment. However, PERT can be utilized in other areas, such as book publishing, where no more than pencil and paper and the ability to do a little simple arithmetic are required.[32]

At about the same time the PERT technique was being devised a similar network control system, the *Critical Path Method (CPM),* was being developed. In the critical path technique the activities in a program are arranged in sequence, the time to complete each activity is estimated, and all factors are plotted on a network diagram. The objective is to determine the minimum elapsed time for completing the entire project. The time required to complete each activity is related to its cost and it is determined whether the time could be shortened by spending additional funds.

Operations Research (OR)

To improve their decision-making ability, managers have adopted some of the statistical methods of analysis used by scientists. One of these methods, *operations research,* was used by scientists and military experts during World War II to solve such strategic problems as the best program to follow for bombing, for mining enemy waters, and for searching out enemy ships. Operations research is "the application of scientific methods of analysis to executive-type problems involving the operations of man-machine systems in industrial organizations so as to provide those in control of the operations with optimum solutions to problems."[33] Involved in the techniques of operations research is the prediction of various courses of action that will provide a basis that a manager can use in making a choice

---

[32] "PERT, New Control for Production Management," *Book Production Industry* (March, 1965), p. 41.

[33] John R. Stockton and Charles T. Clark, *Introduction to Business and Economic Statistics* (4th ed.; Cincinnati: South-Western Publishing Co., 1971), p. 5.

between alternative courses of action. The principles of operations research can be applied to the solution of business problems concerned with determining the optimum procedure to follow with respect to site location, product mix, inventory scheduling, production planning, and shipments of goods to various markets from several far-flung warehouses. In conducting operations research, which often makes use of a team approach drawing upon persons from the fields of mathematics, statistics, physics, economics, and engineering, a model is usually formulated. The model, representing a simplified picture of the operation and containing all the factors of primary importance to the problem, is often set up in terms of mathematical equations.

One of the most effective techniques of operations research is *linear programming,* wherein a number of interdependent factors are mathematically related to one another in order to get the best results. Some objective function, such as the total cost incurred in a process is minimized (or maximized), subject to those constraints that exist within the framework of the problem. For example, by means of linear programming, it is possible to schedule job orders on several machines in such a fashion so as to obtain the minimum overall processing time, subject to constraints such as the number of machines or workers available. By means of an electronic computer, it is possible to solve business problems containing hundreds or thousands of linear restraint equations.

Another effective technique of operations research that can help the office administrator in making decisions regarding staff needs is *waiting-line,* or *queuing, analysis.* Several office services such as filing, bank teller operations, telephone switchboard work, typing pool services, or mail sorting and delivery usually must be performed promptly. People or customers do not like to wait in a long line to receive answers to their questions, to receive file folders requested, to have their memos typed, or to have entries recorded in their passbooks. It is not possible at all times to provide immediate service for each person in line unless extra people are employed. If additional help were provided, then when the waiting line grows short as a result of completing the work, there would be a few workers sitting idle. The problem facing the office administrator is to find the right balance—to have enough workers available to meet the needs of the queue but not to provide so many workers that at times some of them are idle.

In one application of waiting-line analysis to the Location File section of a medium-size utility company, it was found that several of the workers were idle at various times during the day.[34] The type of service rendered by the seven girls and their supervisor in this department consisted of answering calls from customers who want their power turned on, or a gas meter read, or an explanation of the last utility bill, or information about some other type of service. The number of incoming calls was charted by the supervisor and the length of each call was recorded in order to identify the patterns that emerged in customer calls arriving at the Location File and requiring service. Once these patterns were identified, the mathematical formulas of queuing analysis provided the information that the supervisor needed to render good service at minimal cost. As a result of this analysis, it was decided to reduce the staff from seven to five girls and to make use of their idle time by assigning them the job of stuffing envelopes.

IMPROVING EXECUTIVE CONTROL

In the preceding pages the means and methods of reducing the cost of office services are grouped according to the various office activities. But the force that initiates, carries out, and measures cost reduction is the administrative office manager and his supervisors. In order to perform the work in the office at lower costs, these executives should devise means and methods for improving their supervision, a topic that is discussed in Chapter 11. The use of office reports, one means whereby supervision may be improved, is further discussed in Chapter 22. These reports focus attention on what has been done, what is inefficient, what is good, and what is planned for the future.

Besides being present in the office, checking the work, and aiding the workers with his suggestions and instructions, there are other ways in which the office manager can bring about the production of better work. One of these methods requires the use of a series of office manuals, which are discussed in Chapter 23. If properly planned and produced at a small cost, these manuals reduce costs by standardizing the work and likewise reduce the time and effort required for employee instruction.

In large offices use may be made of the *management audit*, which is a thorough study of the planning, organizing, and supervising of the office services. The management audit is a broad analysis of the various jobs being done and the effectiveness of the work so that

[34] "The Use of Waiting-Line Analysis in Office Service Departments," prepared by AMS's National Operations Research Committee, F. B. Gardner, Chairman, *AMS Management Bulletin,* December, 1962, p. 2.

changes and improvements can be made immediately or planned for at some future date. While such an audit may seem to duplicate the work of systems and procedures analyses, the audit is much more comprehensive.

Management audits may assume several forms, such as the department audit and the functional audit. The *department audit* aims at gathering facts, developing recommendations, and striving to have the recommendations accepted and acted upon. For example, there may be an audit of the payroll department. All phases of the work of this department must be examined by means of interviews and questionnaires. The audit would cover such topics as the organization and line of authority, job analyses and descriptions, personnel practices, physical conditions, equipment requirements, and administrative procedures. On the basis of the audit, conclusions and recommendations will be given in the report. To be most effective, action must be taken on the report in order to justify the time and money spent on its preparation. In contrast to the limited department audit, a much more comprehensive study—the *functional audit*—is sometimes made. This audit is confined to one subject and cuts across department lines. For example, there may be an audit of the entire personnel function in the business firm, or perhaps of the training function if training is not included in the personnel function. The important questions that must be considered in using the audit tools in improving office operations are: (1) Who should perform the audit? (2) When or how often should the audit be performed? and (3) Will the results be used in improving the office work and in reducing costs?

QUESTIONS FOR REVIEW

1. What is the meaning of "cost consciousness"? How can the office administrator instill or develop cost-conscious behavioral attitudes among his employees?
2. In what ways may the standardization of equipment aid in reducing costs? Should the standardization of office equipment be rigidly adhered to? Explain.
3. Present a five-point plan for reducing the cost of office forms and supplies.
4. What are the objectives to be achieved in order to reduce the costs of correspondence? Which of the time and cost factors involved in creating a letter is the most expensive and offers the greatest opportunity for cost reduction?
5. How does the use of the AMS simplified letter aid in reducing costs?

6. What are some methods by which the costs of office mailing may be decreased? What types of equipment are available to expedite the work and to reduce costs in the mailing department?
7. In determining the costs of records management, what factors should be taken into consideration?
8. If the purchase of an offset duplicator is contemplated, what points should be kept in mind to make sure that duplicating costs will be kept at a minimum?
9. Explain why waste may represent a significant portion of the total cost of operating office copiers. How can the office manager guard against increased costs of waste in copying processes?
10. What methods may be followed to lower intercommunications costs?
11. How can the administrative office manager increase office efficiency by better use of telephone services?
12. What factors may contribute to an upsurge of costs when automated data processing equipment is installed? How may this potential increase in costs be prevented, or at least held within workable bounds?
13. How is the individual error record used as part of a quality control program? Does the use of such records follow the objective, experimental approach that characterizes scientific management? Explain.
14. What aspects of behavioral science underlie the EFAR and Zero Defects programs?
15. What is a visual control board? How might the visual control board be effectively used by the supervisor of a large reproduction department or the foreman of the in-plant printing department?
16. How are the tools of PERT and CPM used in business?
17. What is operations research? How can this statistical method of analysis help the office manager in reducing costs of office services?
18. Contrast the department audit and the functional audit as two means of improving executive control.

QUESTIONS FOR DISCUSSION

1. You have just assumed the position of administrative office manager in a firm employing 200 office workers. What phase of the office services would you first tackle with the hope of reducing costs? Why?
2. What is meant by a "letter clinic"? Should a letter clinic be conducted by the firm's executives or by some outside specialist?
3. If it is true that the greater the salary of an executive, the higher the cost of the letter, it would follow that the highest paid executives should spend a minimum of time writing letters. Is this true? Explain.

4. One basic piece of equipment in the mailroom is the mailing table and sorting rack, the cost of which seems disproportionately high. How might the office manager overcome this objection of cost?

5. Why is low-cost filing equipment false economy? Explain.

6. The Madison Office Machine Company has heard about "cost consciousness" in the office and has asked you, the office manager, to do something about it. After considerable thought, you have come to the conclusion that one good place to begin working on cost reduction is in the handling of customers' orders, since there are so many orders and so many employees working on them. Some of the orders are for a large number of completed machines; others, for a few repair parts. However, all orders go through the same procedure.

   Indicate how you would proceed with your workers in analyzing and in reducing the costs of this method of order handling.

7. The Faulkenberry Sales Company is moving to its new building. At its new address it plans to set up a centralized filing system, in contrast to the former decentralized system. On the basis of volume analysis and transfer policy, 400 four-drawer file units will be needed. However, as office manager, you feel that five-drawer file units will be more economical and efficient.

   Assume that the four-drawer file units cost $150 each, and the five-drawer units, $180 each. Each file unit occupies six square feet of office space, which rents for $8 a square foot per annum. Compute the probable savings that will accrue over a period of five years if your suggestion of purchasing five-drawer file units is approved.

8. In the Corelli Packing Company some of the office employees use the copying machines to reproduce birth certificates, wedding announcements, and even recipes clipped from the daily newspapers. As supervisor of reproduction services, what steps do you recommend be taken to stop the unauthorized use of the copying machines?

9. Several months ago the Nillson Company installed a typing pool in an effort to reduce the number of typists assigned to each of the firm's seven departments. However, the costs of operating the pool have been climbing rapidly each month and there never seems to be enough typists to do the work. An analysis of the workload has indicated that peak demands occur on Thursday and Friday of each week. How would you proceed to reduce the clerical costs in operating the pool?

PRACTICAL OFFICE CASES

Case 21-1 Reducing Stenographic Costs

As administrative manager for Rasmussen Marketing Research, you feel that the costs of typing and stenographic work are at least 30 percent too high. From your analysis of costs during the past six months, you attribute most of the high cost to: (1) the fact that beginning typists are poorly trained and have little knowledge of business requirements, grammar, and spelling; (2) inadequate supervision; (3) a certain amount of laxness in discipline; and (4) improper employee selection due to the shortage of qualified clerical help.

In order to improve the work and to reduce the cost of the typing and stenographic work, you plan to make certain improvements and changes.

■ By what methods do you think it would be possible to reduce the cost of stenographic work in this office? Outline your program of attack and indicate step by step how you would go about solving this program.

Case 21-2 Reducing Correspondence Costs

The Andover Manufacturing Company has a centralized correspondence department in which all letters except those of a specialized or confidential nature are handled and written. In recent months it seems that the cost of correspondence has increased unnecessarily. You, as administrative office manager, have decided to make a study of these costs with the purpose of finding ways in which the costs may be reduced.

You have decided that the letter-writing costs should be measured in terms of a single-page letter, and you find that the costs can be classified in the following categories: correspondents, transcription, filing, and mailing and messenger.

During the two-month period in which your study was undertaken, the production was 10,000 one-page letters; 1,000 two-page letters; and 500 three-page letters. The number of form letters sent out was 10,000, but these required only the insertion of an inside address and the preparation of an envelope for mailing. It is estimated that this operation required only one tenth of the time a transcriber used in preparing a one-page letter.

The costs compiled for the two months are as follows:

Cost Item	Correspondents	Transcription	Filing	Mailing & Messenger
Salaries	$16,000	$17,280	$ 800	$ 600
Supplies		700	90	
Postage				1,300
Depreciation:				
Equipment & machines	600	1,800	100	60
Furniture	880	820	710	20
Operating costs (rent, utilities, etc.)	520	750	600	350
Total	$18,000	$21,350	$2,300	$2,330

▪ Using the information given, compute the cost of a one-page letter. Suggest several methods by which you think the per-page cost of a letter might be reduced in the Andover Manufacturing Company.

Case 21-3 Reducing Reproduction Costs [35]

Rollins Machinery has several plants and offices in a number of cities. Several years ago the company decentralized its operations and made each division autonomous, with each division performing all its own management functions and processing of information. At the headquarters office in Philadelphia, the executives and staff, totaling about 2,500, are housed in eight floors of a large office building. When the divisions were being created as part of the decentralization program, each division set up its own reproduction shop. Each shop produces all its own forms, divisional instructions, reprints, charts, etc. There is no liaison between any of the shops.

Each of the five division reproduction shops is managed by a department head who has other functions and responsibilities that take precedence over his job of supervising the reproduction function. In the shops there are 15 printing presses comprising ten different models from four manufacturers, seven automated collators of which six models are from four manufacturers, six console electrostatic copiers from five manufacturers, and miscellaneous equipment from a variety of sources.

The total number of workers in the division shops is 58, consisting of six assistant supervisors, five clerks, 25 operators, and 22 collating clerks. The annual payroll for these workers is $250,000. About 25 percent of the time of the five department heads is devoted to reproduction, with their total time valued at $15,000. Thus, the annual expenditures for reproduction salaries is $265,000.

Annually about 35 million copies of work are delivered from the shops, which means that the average usable production per press is a little more than 2.3 million copies. However, purchase records indicate that 45 million sheets of paper were purchased and used last year. It has been concluded, as the result of a study, that the loss of ten million sheets of paper is due to: press operators who are wasting 20 to 25 percent daily, excessive paper being used in getting the presses ready to run, using more sheets than necessary when aligning the forms for printing, running paper through the presses to clean the printing blankets, overprinting the requisitioned number of sheets for many jobs, and using poor master copies from which to print.

Press operators are not given any formal training, and no production standards exist. Operators teach each other the use of the machines, and

[35] Adapted from "How to Reduce Office Reproduction Costs," from *The Office* (October, 1969), with permission of Office Publications, Inc.

turnover is excessively high because of a limited pay scale and no opportunities for advancement.

All types of masters (mats) are run, but about 40,000 of these are prepared on typewriter (direct image). Although there are master typists in each division, any typist or secretary can type masters; but most of these workers are not instructed in the proper typing of masters. About five percent of the masters sent to the reproduction shop must be retyped because of poor erasures and washoff of the image. Thus, much valuable press time, as well as paper, is wasted. About 10,000 masters are made on copiers, and usually five percent of these must be remade; 180,000 masters are made on platemakers, of which there are five in use. Each platemaker averages slightly more than 100 mats each day, making the cost of the mats excessively high.

In the reproduction shops the total number of copies made on copiers is about 360,000, including several thousand mats. Some 15 to 20 percent of the work run requires collating, which means that annually about six million sheets are collated.

Forty-seven different papers, many in several sizes, as well as ten colored papers, are stocked. Among other supplies, there are eight brands of ink, nine different sensitized plates from five sources, ten different direct-image mats from four sources, and ten brands of copier paper and chemicals. There are several brands of most of the miscellaneous items. Along with the work produced in each plant, each division purchases work from eight outside suppliers at an annual cost of about $300,000.

Throughout the general offices there are 14 electrostatic copiers. No control is maintained on the use of these copiers, and thus a substantial number of copies for personal use are made. At each copier there is a notice stating that no more than ten copies should be made of any one original; these notices are ignored.

In the secretaries' offices there are seven desk-top electrostatic copiers (five different brands) that are used by 12 secretaries. These copiers are really status symbols; for after one secretary was permitted to obtain a copier, copiers were subsequently installed in each of the other secretaries' offices. The number of copiers in use, including those in the reproduction shops, totals 27; and these consist of 17 different models from ten manufacturers. The records of copier use are neither complete nor accurate. Annual usage totals 2.1 million copies for all copiers, with the secretaries' private copiers averaging less than 500 copies each month.

■ After you have carefully studied the facts given above, prepare a report in which you outline your step-by-step proposal for saving both personnel time and money.

22

Budgetary Control and Report Preparation

In every phase of business operation, executives must look ahead and estimate the expected operating conditions of their firms. On the basis of their estimates they plan the policies and procedures to be installed and carried out, either on a short-term basis of a few months or a year or on a long-term basis of three to five years. The activities thus planned relate to new products, sales income, expansion plans, and operating costs. The success of operating a business often depends upon the reliability of future plans that show the estimated income and operating costs.

One of the major groups of operating costs is the administrative office costs or expenses. *Fixed costs* do not change even though the volume of business increases. They include such items as rent of space, real estate taxes, certain insurance costs, and depreciation of buildings and equipment. Over a short period of time, the administrative office manager has little or no control over fixed costs. The more important and controllable office costs are known as *variable costs*, which fluctuate with the change in the volume of business. In controlling the variable costs, the administrative office manager shows his managerial skill, since he must constantly strive to develop methods and procedures to reduce these costs.

To control costs and to obtain financial information quickly, briefly, and completely, management relies upon budgets and reports received from various department heads. The *budget* is a carefully planned program of estimated future operating conditions over both short and long terms. The important phase of budgetary control is not merely the preparation of the plan, but the periodic comparison of the actual operating data with the planned or budgeted data so that the causes of variances can be identified and, where possible, rectified. Through the use of budgets and periodic reports, top management can provide supervisory personnel with factual measures of achievement and fix responsibility, thus improving the cost consciousness of the entire office staff. The objectives of effective budgetary control are: (1) to provide an organized procedure for future planning; (2) to provide a means of coordinating the activities of the various components of a business organization; and (3) to provide a basis for managerial control.

BUDGETARY CONTROL OF OFFICE COSTS

Just where the administrative office manager fits into the scheme of budgetary control and report preparation is not the same in each firm. In some organizations, he is a service department head; in others, he may be a controller or a vice president. Many office managers are considered primarily as the heads of service departments because they are responsible for coordinating the major activities of accounting, administrative services, finance, production, and sales. Since a service function is an activity that runs vertically through an organization, it consists of specific types of work that are present in carrying on the work of all major divisions of business. Examples of service functions are correspondence, data communications, records management, and data processing.

If the office manager is a service department head, his reports will be essentially those prepared to budget the office activities for the period or to report on the production and cost of the office work for a definite period. The reports he prepares will be more detailed than those summarized for presentation to top management. The further down the administrative ladder the executive is located, the greater the amount of detail given in the report. The reports to be prepared by or for the office manager who is a service department head may include:

1. Estimated (budgeted) expenses for the various office services under his control, such as dictating, transcribing, records

management, and mailing. The annual report is supported by schedules or data prepared by first-line supervisors.

2. Operating reports showing in detail the actual costs along with the budgeted figures.

3. Analytical reports showing the breakdown of costs in each department. The filing department supervisor, for example, may prepare a report showing the cost of filing every one hundred papers; the correspondence department supervisor may prepare reports on the average cost of each letter written.

4. Special reports, most of which are surveys prepared at the request of some company official or initiated by the office manager in an attempt to improve some phase of his responsibility. For example, a report may be prepared comparing machine and stenographic transcription work, or a survey may be made of forms costs and control.

If the office manager is a controller or a vice president (and these titles imply a larger office staff than in the former illustration), he will receive detailed reports from his various department heads, such as the supervisors in charge of records management, correspondence, transcription, mailing, and accounting. The office manager must examine these reports, consolidate and condense them into a report covering all the office activities, and then submit the final report to the executive to whom he is held accountable. These reports will be further summarized and consolidated by the executive in charge of the budget, who may have the responsibility for developing the following reports and financial statements:

1. Master budget for the fiscal accounting period.

2. Summaries of the actual versus budgeted figures.

3. Interim or annual balance sheets and income statements. These financial reports may be prepared monthly for the company directors, and quarterly, semiannually, or annually for the stockholders. The reports for the stockholders are usually printed and distributed by mail if the corporation is very large. The financial report is usually prepared for or by the president of the company, after he has received the accounting report from the certified public accountants who have audited the books and prepared the financial statements. The pattern of these reports is fairly uniform and includes some or all of the following data:

a. Title page.

b. Page devoted to a listing of the board of directors, executive committee, officers, transfer agent, registrar, and accountants.

c. Letter of transmittal.

d. Body of report, which covers:

   (1) Discussion of financial history for the period and the financial condition at date of report.

   (2) Discussion of company policies and practices.

   (3) Discussion of company products and services.

   (4) Auditor's certificate and statements.

   (5) Miscellaneous statistical data usually presented in tabular or graphic form.

PRINCIPLES OF PREPARING A BUDGET OF ADMINISTRATIVE OFFICE EXPENSES

A well-prepared administrative office expense budget helps the office manager and his superiors plan where they want to go and how to get there and gives them the financial data needed for decision making. The budget aids the office manager in heading off crises, directs his attention to less profitable office activities, and provides a yardstick for measuring the progress in every area. But the office manager must remember that his office expense budget will get results in direct proportion to the skill, understanding, and effort that he has invested in its preparation.

In the preparation of an office expense budget, the office manager should pay close attention to each of the following principles.

Principle of Responsibility

The initial phases of preparing the budget should be assigned to key personnel at the operational level so that budgets flow upward from the departmental supervisors to the office manager.

By beginning the budget-making process at the operational rather than the staff level, cost consciousness is developed among all employees and a mutuality of understanding about the budget is provided. The budget estimates are made by those who are close to the work and thus a sense of participation is offered to those who will have to live with the budget later. If the budget originates at the top level and is imposed from above, the effects of the budget may be punitive in many instances. The responsibility for summarizing, combining, and consolidating the departmental budgets into a master budget should be assigned to an executive who has breadth of vision, versatility, a background in finance, an understanding of the corporate structure, and the ability to see the overall financial picture and all its components.

Principle of Objectivity

The budget should be realistic and show as objectively as possible what each department is capable of doing.

A sound budget can be neither unduly optimistic nor pessimistic, but must measure in an absolutely objective fashion what the office can do. Records of previous periods may be used as guides, but the budget maker should not be bound to the past, for cost factors may be changing constantly.

Principle of Target Setting

The budget prepared for each department, or for the office as a whole, should reflect the attainment of a specific target.

After a company target, such as a five percent increase in its share of the market, has been established and translated into sales dollars and number of units to be produced, a specific target should be set for each service department, or for the entire office, in order to achieve the overall company goal. At the operational level, standards of past performance for each employee should be reviewed and adjusted accordingly so that the overall performance of the department is geared to the newly established company target.

Principle of Flexibility

The budget should be sufficiently flexible and contain a "safety valve."

A flexible budget provides measures for emergency action that can be taken in case the company experiences a sharp reduction in income, a major strike, or a sudden move by competitors. The budget must not become so rigid that it stifles progress and prevents timely decisions. If, after a budget has been prepared, it is discovered that some objectives cannot be realized or that they are impractical, the conflicts must be resolved or budget directives may have to be changed to agree with the reality of the situation. Although budget directives serve as standards, they should never become straight jackets.

One of the most common approaches to budgeting, known as the "tight but attainable" philosophy, is based on better than average performance. Any unfavorable variances are critically reviewed since this approach usually includes allowances for less than ideal performance.[1] The "ideal performance" approach to budgeting, on the other hand, presumes that nothing will go wrong in the company's operations; it allows for no alterations or "slides" in schedules and contains no provisions for contingencies.[2] Another budgeting method, termed the "suicide" approach, is characterized by managers who set a budget that is practically impossible to meet and who push hard enough so that overruns are kept to a minimum. Often the impossible is accomplished and the budget is met. The disadvantage of this method is its pessimistic attitude, for managers soon learn that such a budget is an impossible goal and stop trying.[3]

Principle of Adherence

The completed office expense budget, as adjusted by the master budget, must be accepted and adhered to by supervisors and their subordinates at the operational level.

How the budget is accepted and adhered to at each level depends upon the tone set by top management. If top management is neutral about budget making and "budget following," it is not to be expected that supervisors and their subordinates will be much concerned about adhering to the planned goals.

Principle of Review

The budget should be reviewed frequently in order to determine variances that can be overcome before the budget has lost its effectiveness.

Delay in relating actual costs to estimated costs can be extremely costly. To overcome such delay, a program of reliable measurement

---

[1] William R. King, C.P.A., "How Cost Management Is Used by Business Today," *The Office* (February, 1971), p. 43.
[2] *Ibid.*
[3] *Ibid.*

and reporting of actual performance must be established. In some firms, computers are used on a daily basis to spot favorable and unfavorable variances from the budget. At the departmental level, written explanations may be required to explain the significant deviations from the budget; at the operational level, oral explanations may be given by the employee to the supervisor.

PREPARING THE BUDGET OF ADMINISTRATIVE OFFICE EXPENSES

The *budget of administrative office expenses* usually has a direct relationship to the income or sales of the firm. As indicated earlier, certain office costs are fixed and do not change regardless of the sales volume; other costs have a direct relationship to sales income. Furthermore, some office costs are controllable, while others are not. All these factors must be considered in preparing the office expense budget. The extent to which administrative office expenses are analyzed depends upon three factors:

1. The cost accounting training of the office manager.
2. The relative size of the office force as compared with sales and manufacturing activities.
3. The amount of money represented by office expenses in relation to sales income.

Kinds of Office Expenses

A large life insurance company or a public utility would be more interested in studying and reducing office costs than a firm whose employees consist mostly of factory workers and a sales force. It is assumed in the following discussion that office expenses are a major charge against the income of the firm. The usual office expenses are listed below:

1. Rent or real estate taxes.
2. Office salaries and payroll taxes.
3. Depreciation of office machines and equipment.
4. Cost of central machine dictation department.
5. Cost of central transcribing department.
6. Cost of data processing center.
7. Filing costs.
8. Telephone and telegraph.

9. Postage and mailing.
10. Insurance.
11. Personnel department expense.
12. Printing and stationery.
13. Miscellaneous expenses.

For most effective control, the office expenses should be classified under the headings of fixed, semivariable, and variable. For example, rent or real estate taxes might be considered as fixed; supervision, as fixed or semivariable; filing costs, as variable. With a grouping of this kind, the executive can analyze the semivariable and variable expenses which offer the best opportunities for control.

Allocating Office Expenses

To analyze the office expenses from a budgetary viewpoint, it becomes necessary to prepare departmental budgets of operating expenses. Some expenses originate in and are chargeable directly to one department. The direct departmental expenses are: (1) depreciation of machines and equipment in a particular department, and (2) salaries of the workers in a given department. Other expenses are general in nature and must be allocated on some logical basis. Expenses, whether budgeted or actual, that must be allocated, and their bases of allocation, are:

1. Local telephone expense, on the basis of the number of telephones in each department.
2. Telephone and telegraph toll service, which is directly chargeable to each department.
3. Cost of central dictation department, either according to the number of dictators in each department or on the basis of the number of hours of dictation.
4. Rent or taxes, on the basis of the area occupied by each department.
5. Printing and stationery expense, on the basis of requisitions filled.
6. Filing department expense, on the basis of the number of papers filed and retrieved by the filing department.
7. Data processing center costs, on the basis of processing hours used by each department.
8. Postage and mailing, on the same basis as the central dictation department for first-class mail; otherwise, on the basis of direct charge.

Comparing Budgeted with Actual Costs

The purpose of a budget is to make a comparison of estimated costs with actual figures and to analyze any variances so that controllable causes of increasing expenses may be eliminated. Table 22-1 shows one type of form prepared monthly by each department for this purpose.

Table 22-1

ACTUAL VERSUS BUDGETED EXPENSES

Sales Department: For Month of June, 19--

Expenses	Budget	Actual	Gain (+) or Loss (—)
Salaries	$4,000	$4,000	$ 0
Rent (or taxes)	200	200	0
Insurance	75	75	0
Depreciation of equipment	300	300	0
Printing and stationery	210	187	−23
Transcribing costs	180	160	−20
Data processing costs	400	425	+25
Filing costs	40	60	+20
Telephone and telegraph	92	100	+ 8
Postage and mailing	60	68	+ 8
Totals	$5,557	$5,575	$ +18

The cumulative figure may indicate more accurately than a monthly figure the nature of the comparison of the budgeted and the actual figures. Some concerns therefore expand the comparison form to show the accumulated budget and the actual figures to date. Such a cumulative form is illustrated in Table 22-2.

Table 22-2

ACTUAL VERSUS BUDGETED EXPENSES
Sales Department: For Month of June, 19--

Expenses	Budget Month	Actual Month	Monthly Variance + or −	Budget Year to Date	Actual Year to Date	Year-to-Date Variance + or −
Salaries	$4,000	$4,000	$ 0	$24,000	$24,000	$ 0
Rent (or taxes)	200	200	0	1,200	1,200	0
Insurance	75	75	0	450	450	0
Depreciation of equipment	300	300	0	1,800	1,800	0
Printing and stationery	210	187	−23	1,260	1,115	−145
Transcribing costs	180	160	−20	1,110	1,125	+ 15
Data processing costs	400	425	+25	2,500	2,450	− 50
Filing costs	40	60	+20	240	360	+120
Telephone and telegraph	92	100	+ 8	600	540	− 60
Postage and mailing	60	68	+ 8	360	420	+ 60
Totals	$5,557	$5,575	$+18	$33,520	$33,460	$− 60

The Master Budget

The preparation of the overall company budget, or the *master budget* as it is called, is usually placed under the supervision of the budget director, who may be the administrative office manager, the controller, or some other executive. In addition to the office or administrative expenses commonly classified under the heading "General Expenses," the master budget includes estimates of sales, cost of goods sold, and selling expenses. The budget may be prepared on a yearly basis and then subdivided into monthly, quarterly, or semi-annual figures for better analysis and control. Whenever a master budget is used, there must be provision for a periodic comparison of

PLAN FOR PREPARING A MASTER BUDGET

Step 1. Preparation of sales budget:
- a. By products.
- b. By territories, districts, departments, or salesmen if necessary.
- c. By months.

Step 2. Preparation of cost of goods sold or cost of production budget, depending upon whether the firm is classified as mercantile or manufacturing. To be most practical, the preparation of this budget should follow the pattern of the sales budget.

If a mercantile company, this pattern will be:
- a. By products.
- b. By months.

If a manufacturing company, the cost of production budget will show the data subdivided into cost of material, labor, and manufacturing overhead.

Step 3. Preparation of selling expense budget. Later, the sales budget may have to be revised to conform with the manufacturing budget.

Step 4. Preparation of general expense budget, which includes administrative office expenses.

Step 5. Preparation of consolidated budget and estimated income statement based upon Steps 1 to 4.

Step 6. Periodic compilation of actual figures in order to make a comparison with budgeted figures.

Step 7. Changes in business organization and administration or revision of budgeted figures to reduce the variation between budgeted and actual figures.

Fig. 22-1

Steps in Preparing a Master Budget

the actual with the estimated figures so that variations may be noted and proper managerial control may be exercised.

The master budget, of which the office expense budget has come to play an increasingly important part, may be prepared as indicated by the seven steps listed in Figure 22-1. On the basis of these steps, an estimated (*pro forma*) income statement, similar to the one shown in Figure 22-2, may be prepared for comparison with actual operating results.

Fig. 22-2

ESTIMATED INCOME STATEMENT

For the Year Ended December 31, 19--

		Percent of Sales
Estimated net sales	$1,000,000	100.00
Product A	630,000	63.00
Product B	120,000	12.00
Product C	250,000	25.00
	$1,000,000	100.00
Cost of goods sold:		
Product A	$ 420,000	42.00
Product B	84,000	8.40
Product C	150,000	15.00
	$ 654,000	65.40
Gross profit	$ 346,000	34.60
Operating expenses:		
Selling expenses:		
Sales salaries and commissions	$ 60,000	6.00
Advertising expense	43,000	4.30
Shipping expense	28,000	2.80
Traveling expense	16,700	1.67
Miscellaneous selling expense	2,800	0.28
Total selling expenses	$ 150,500	15.05
General expenses:		
Administrative and office salaries	$ 50,000	5.00
Office supplies	8,900	0.89
Depreciation--office equipment	7,200	0.72
Uncollectible accounts expense	6,400	0.64
Miscellaneous general expense	4,300	0.43
Total general expenses	$ 76,800	7.68
Total operating expenses	$ 227,300	22.73
Net income before income tax	$ 118,700	11.87
Income tax	50,476	5.05
Net income after income tax	$ 68,224	6.82
Dividends	$ 50,000	5.00
Estimated increase in retained earnings	$ 18,224	1.82

Estimated Income Statement

Problems of Cost Analysis Arising Through Budgetary Control

Among the various problems arising in cost analysis through the use of a budget, two stand out: (1) the need for standards, and (2) handling fluctuations in the volume of office work as a result of periodic or seasonal factors.

Work measurement and the development of work standards have been discussed in Chapter 19. By having work standards and knowing the estimated volume of sales and other office activities, it is possible to prepare a more reliable office expense budget.

Most firms attempt to operate with a minimum number of employees who are able to perform the usual volume of work without too much idleness, with little or no overtime, and still without too much pressure being placed on the average employee. But many firms are characterized by periods during which there are peak loads that must be considered in preparing and using an office expense budget. For example, during certain periods of the week, the payroll must be prepared and this swells the work load. Statements must be prepared and sent to customers. Quarterly or annual financial reports and statements must be prepared; inventories must be taken periodically. Although occurring with a certain amount of regularity, these activities complicate the planning, scheduling, and estimating of office costs, especially when the tasks must be completed by a definite date.

Recognition of the problem of peak-load fluctuations must be made by management, and the most efficient manner of controlling them must be followed. Office managers have used some or all of the following means to control the costs of peak-load fluctuations in office work:

1. *Overtime work.* This is an expensive method that increases costs 50 percent. Overtime work is best used where the overload is unexpected, or of short duration, and not expected to recur with any degree of regularity.
2. *Cycle billing.* By means of cycle billing, it is possible to average out the volume of accounts receivable work that must be completed. Cycle billing was discussed in Chapter 17.
3. *Split-payroll dates.* By having different payroll dates for the different departments, peak-load fluctuations in the preparation of the payroll occurring once or twice a month may be minimized. For example, in one firm it was decided to pay the clerical force and workers in the shipping and packing departments every two weeks; the exempt personnel continued to be paid twice a month on the 15th and the 30th. Thus,

the peak load that formerly occurred on the 15th and the 30th was smoothed out and the services of the personnel in the payroll department are more effectively utilized throughout the entire month.

4. *Part-time help.* There are instances where the employment of part-time workers is most satisfactory. There are other occasions when because of the special nature and continuity of the work, the employment of part-time help may result in errors, confusion, and higher costs.
5. *Floating or traveling units.* Under this method, office workers "float" from one peak-load area to the other as the need arises. This method can be employed only where there are many departments affected, and the peak loads occur with a certain amount of regularity, but not on the same date.
6. *Outside service bureaus and data processing centers.* The increase in the number of "peak-load" service bureaus and data processing centers indicates that many business firms find these sources to be an answer to the periodic overloads of office work. The high degree of skill, the confidential nature of their work, and the comparatively low cost have much to recommend this method for establishing cost and managerial control over the peak-load problems.

PRINCIPLES OF REPORT PREPARATION

Reports, usually generated through the use of financial, accounting, and logistics systems, are prepared to reflect past, present, and future positions or operating results; to evaluate people and their performance; and to serve as tools in controlling future operations. Reports are used by managers to aid in making decisions and to obtain records for placing responsibility, for modifying policies, or merely as a matter of history. Reports deal with facts. For example, an executive may want a report on the sales volume of the various departments for the past year; or in the area of administrative office expenses, he may want a report of what each department is presently doing, or what it is planning to do in the coming year. In some reports, the opinions or recommendations of experts may be used in addition to the facts, but these must be predicated upon the basic facts.

The organizational structure of a firm determines the nature and frequency of reports. In a small organization financial reports from the accounting records monthly or at a longer interval usually suffice. As the organization grows, however, the work becomes functionalized, departments are provided with supervisors, and it becomes necessary to keep all executives informed by more frequent reports.

Any classification of reports, such as those on pages 712-714, indicates that there is wide variation not only in their nature but also in their content. Therefore, whatever principles are given for the preparation of a report must be of a general nature.

Principle of Purpose

The report must have a sound and specific purpose which may be translated into more effective business management.

The main reason for writing a report is to tell someone something in the hope that action will be taken as a result of the conclusions reached in the report. Those who will read the report should be kept in mind when the report is written. Reports, as a rule, serve management in two ways: (1) they form the basis for a discussion of the facts and for recommendations, and (2) they serve as a historical record of that phase of the business activity.

Those charged with the preparation of reports to management must determine the minimum information requirements of each manager in relation to his needs to make his particular decisions. Often a manager may not know his needs exactly and may request more information in order "to play it safe." Thus, those charged with the responsibility of report preparation must make sure that they are meeting the needs, as opposed to the wants, of management.

Principle of Organization

The report should be well planned and well organized.

Since business reports differ widely in content, the organization of reports also varies. The report of operations is usually an accounting report supported by financial statements and schedules. Other reports are statistical, and still others are surveys or investigations that present answers to specific questions. The organizational plan of most reports includes:

1. *Purpose:* The introduction, which states the reason for the report, the information it contains, and the method employed in collecting the data.
2. *Summary:* A summary of the conclusions reached in the report. Many executives prefer the summary at the beginning of the report since placing it first saves their time by not having to read the entire report. If they believe it necessary, they can examine the supporting details.

3. *Problems and Solution:* The body of the report, consisting of a logical development of the subject matter, treated either historically, chronologically, or as the *status quo.* A report dealing with present transcription methods, for example, should show the present methods and costs of transcription by use of shorthand, the average cost of each letter under this method, a description of the proposed machine method of dictation and transcription, the expected costs under this method, the advantages and disadvantages of each method, illustrations of firms using each method, and recommendations. The logical sequence of such a report is apparent to the reader. This type of report deals with present conditions or the *status quo* and is based upon research. Solving the problem deals with analyzing and interpreting the data that were presented in order to substantiate the assumptions.

   The content should be developed as objectively as possible. The report writer should avoid extravagant statements such as saying "many" when "only two" is meant.
4. *Recommendations:* Whenever a report results in recommendations for action, these should be stated positively, clearly, and completely. The recommendations may be stated in the form of a summary at the end of each section, or they may be part of the summary at the beginning of the report.
5. *Appendix:* Exhibits should be included whenever the textual narrative of the report needs amplification. Appendix items may be in the form of supporting letters, memorandums, charts, layouts, tabulations, or statistics. The supporting data should be carefully chosen and must be relevant.

A very long, formal report may include additional elements such as preliminary pages consisting of the flyleaf, a title page, the copyright page, the foreword, acknowledgments, contents, and a list of tables and charts; a bibliography; and an index.

Principle of Brevity

The report should be kept short.

The old adage, "If I had more time, I would have written less," applies to report writing. A verbose report creates a bad impression and raises the question of its necessity. Quick attention can be captured by reducing or eliminating a lot of the introductory material.

Reports should be reasonably brief because: (1) they are expensive to prepare; (2) long reports are complicated, are difficult to analyze, and usually indicate poor planning; (3) verbosity is usually an indication of too much emphasis on minor details or irrelevant matters; (4) undue length evokes the criticism of inefficiency.

Principle of Clarity

Simple language should be used for fast and easy understanding.

The report writer should avoid long, involved sentences. Words should be carefully selected so that the meaning intended by the writer can be clearly communicated to the reader. New, technical terms that may create misunderstanding should be defined in order to eliminate communications "static," which may detract from the purpose of the message.

Principle of Scheduling

Reports should be scheduled so that they can be prepared without undue burden on the staff and with sufficient time to do the work well.

The interval between the compilation of data and the finished report should not be so long, however, that the material will have become obsolete by the time it is presented. Today, with the availability of "real-time" information through the use of "on-line" terminals connected to a computer (see Chapter 2), management is greatly aided in scheduling and preparing business reports. Modern management information systems provide the facility of answering a user's question immediately with up-to-the-minute information so that much educated guesswork is eliminated in the decision-making process. For example, managers cannot control those unusually high costs that have already been incurred; but by means of timely reports a manager is able to detect cost deviations before they reach excessive proportions.

Principle of Cost

The preparation and the use of a report should be worth its cost.

Cost estimates for the preparation of an average report run as high as $20 per page. From time to time some executive should examine the reports prepared within the firm to determine whether their cost of preparation and use justifies their continuance. Definite procedures should be established for approving the preparation of any new reports. With today's high-speed printers, undoubtedly many managers are flooded with useless reports that go under the guise of useful information.

PRESENTING DATA IN TABULAR AND GRAPHIC FORM

To aid the reader of business reports, many of the facts explained in quantitative form should be presented in some organized manner if their significance is to be understood. When a small number of items is being presented, the tabular form is the most common method of presenting the statistical data. Although all types of data can be depicted graphically, a graph is inferior to a table as a means of presenting data, since the reader can obtain only approximate values from a chart. The advantage of the chart, however, is that it emphasizes certain facts or relationships more dramatically than a table of figures.

Presenting Data in Tabular Form

The major parts of a table are the title, main body, footnotes, and source. In the main body of the table, the data are arranged in columns and rows. The heading of a column is referred to as a *caption;* the explanation of the material in a row is called a *stub.*

The *title* of the table should be brief, yet clearly indicative of the contents of the table. Information of secondary importance is often placed in a subtitle, as shown in Table 22-3.

Table 22-3

CONSIGNMENT SALES OF STOCK NO. BT-4: 1962 TO 1972
Home Office and Branch Offices

Year	Sales				
	Total	Home Office	Tacoma	San Jose	Tucson
1962	3,780,000	2,206,000	705,000 [1]	500,000	369,000
1963	4,162,000	2,475,000	772,000	506,000	409,000
1964	4,034,000	2,380,000	765,000	498,000	391,000
1965	4,218,000	2,533,000	763,000	487,000	435,000
1966	4,569,000	2,969,000	692,000	493,000	415,000
1967	4,551,000	2,994,000	701,000	502,000	354,000
1968	4,903,000	3,306,000	713,000	513,000	371,000
1969	4,988,000	3,401,000	719,000	525,000	343,000
1970	4,642,000	3,185,000	604,000	478,000	375,000
1971	4,820,000	3,268,000	623,000	540,000	389,000
1972	4,994,000	3,410,000	638,000	547,000	399,000

[1] Data for last nine months of year only.

The central point in the construction of a table is the arrangement of the data in columns and rows, which make up the *main body*. In most instances the classifications of data should be put in rows rather than in columns, for a column requires more space than a row. However, it is easier to make comparisons between figures when they are arranged in columns. It seems more natural for the eye to read down a column of figures than to read across a row. For example, in Table 22-3, it is somewhat easier to compare sales for 1972 with those for 1971 than to compare Home Office and Tacoma Branch Office sales for any year.

Footnotes are used to explain in more detail or to qualify the information and data contained in the title, stubs, captions, or in the main body. In Table 22-3 the footnote indicates that the 1962 data for the Tacoma Branch Office cover only the last nine months of that year. Both numbered and lettered footnotes are commonly found in business tables. Certain letters, however, have come to take on a fairly standard meaning in tabular construction. Thus, "*e*" is used to indicate estimated amounts; "*p*," preliminary data; and "*r*," revised figures.

In the preparation of some reports, data may be obtained from a source outside the firm. The *source line* indicates the organization or individual that originally collected the information shown in the table. In the preparation of a table, such as Table 22-3, for which the data are obtained from within the firm itself, a source line is rarely used. In some instances when the information used has been copyrighted by the original collector or publisher, the source line is used to acknowledge permission to reproduce the tabular material. Information contained in the source line also enables the reader to turn to the source if he desires further detailed facts or wishes to verify the accuracy of the information presented.

Whenever possible, the tabular information should be laid out so that it is unnecessary for the reader to turn the report sideways in order to read the data. White space should be generously used so that the table may be more easily read and so that certain parts of the table will stand out in relation to one another. The amount and type of ruling used in tables varies with the person designing the layout. In some tables no rulings are used; instead, white space is generously provided to set off totals or to emphasize certain sections of data. The important point is that whether or not rulings are used, the relationships depicted in the table should be clear and easy to see.

Presenting Data in Graphic Form

Several types of charts are used to analyze data and to emphasize facts and relationships much more vividly than tabular presentations. For added emphasis and dramatic effect, many charts make use of color.

Bar Chart. Vertical and horizontal *bar charts* are very commonly found in business reports, especially when growth or decline is being shown over a period of time. The scale that marks off the quantity should be so constructed and identified that the reader is able to interpret easily and quickly the significance of the length of the bars, as shown in Figure 22-3.

Fig. 22-3

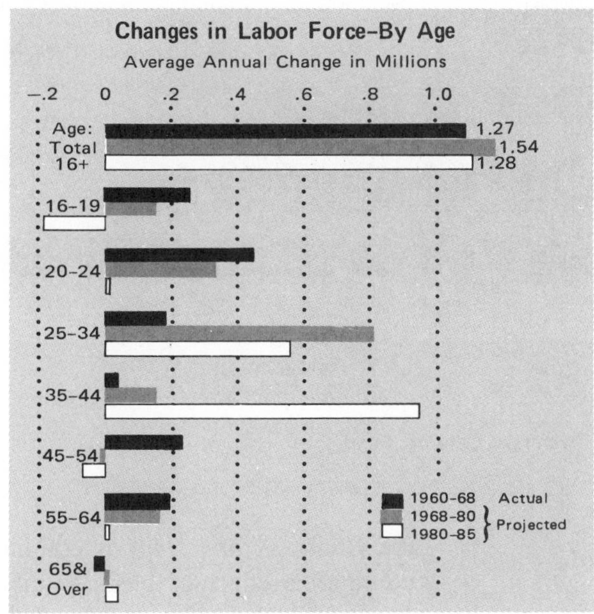

A Bar Chart

Source: Road Maps of Industry No. 1660, The Conference Board, February 15, 1971.

Pictogram. In a *pictogram*, each picture symbol represents a given magnitude. Although pictorial charts offer additional attractiveness in data presentation, accuracy in showing the information should not be sacrificed merely in order to gain attention. In Figure 22-4, the increase in productivity is shown by symbols, each of which represents 50 cents, at 1960 prices, of national income per man-hour of private employment. The pictogram shows that by 1975 each worker will be producing almost 12 times as much as the worker of 1850.

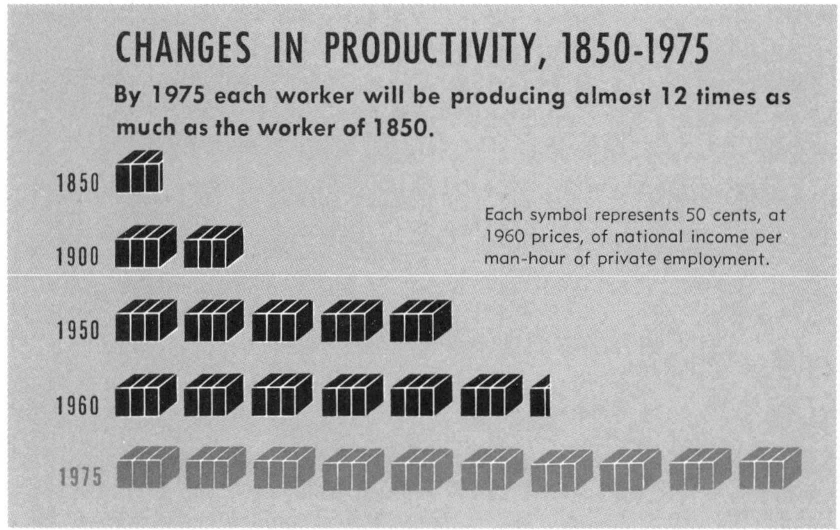

Fig. 22-4

A Pictogram

Source: The Twentieth Century Fund.

Line Chart. A *line chart* is commonly used to indicate a trend or a cumulative effect of business information. Both scales on the line chart are quantitative and the data plotted in relation to points on these scales are connected by straight lines. When time series data are plotted, the time classification is always laid out on the horizontal scale as shown in Figure 22-5. The data pertaining to each time period are plotted on the vertical scale.

Component Parts Chart. When the parts of a distribution of data are being compared with the total of that distribution, a *component parts chart* is often used to show the comparison graphically. Figure 22-6 illustrates the *divided bar chart,* and Figure 22-7, the *circle and sector,* or *pie, chart.*

Fig. 22-5

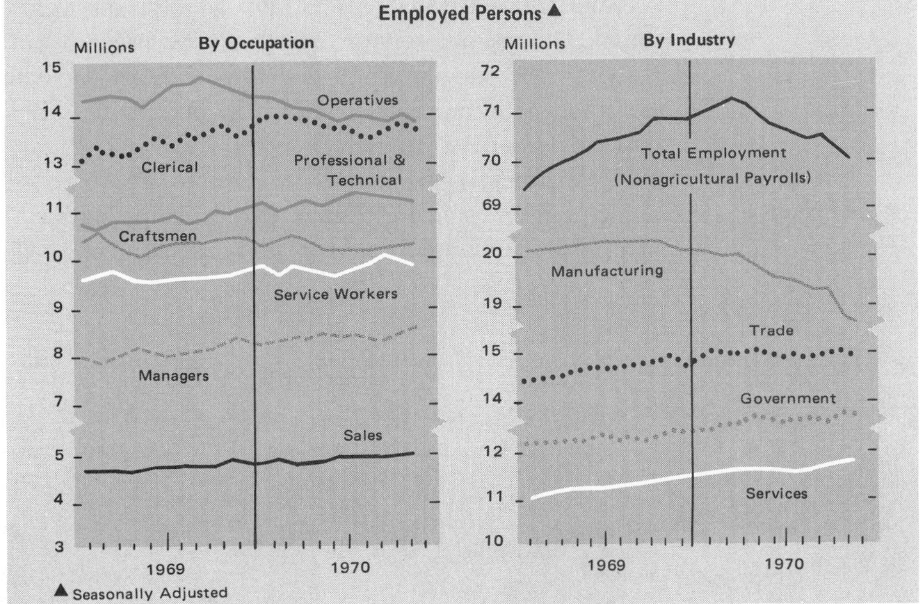

Line Charts

Source: Road Maps of Industry No. 1659, The Conference Board, February 1, 1971.

Fig. 22-6

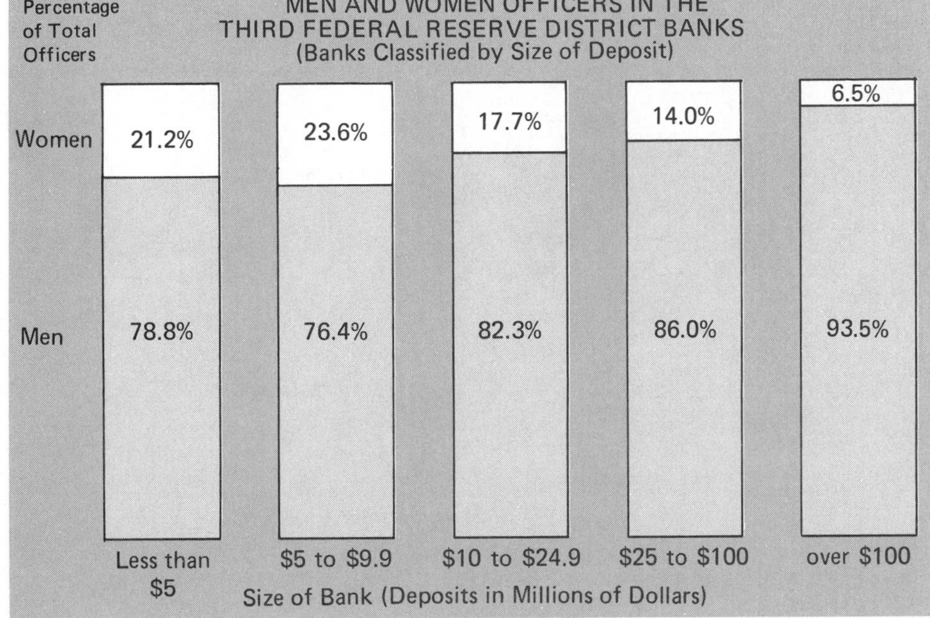

A Divided Bar Chart

Source: "Business Review," Federal Reserve Bank of Philadelphia, July, 1969, p. 14.

Map Chart. In the presentation of information for different geographical divisions, a *map chart* may be used to aid the reader in analyzing the concentration and dispersion of the data. Figure 22-8 shows the location of mining activities and plant and office operations of a major mining company.

The principles of report preparation and of presenting data in tabular and graphic form have excellent application in the development of office manuals, which are discussed in the following chapter.

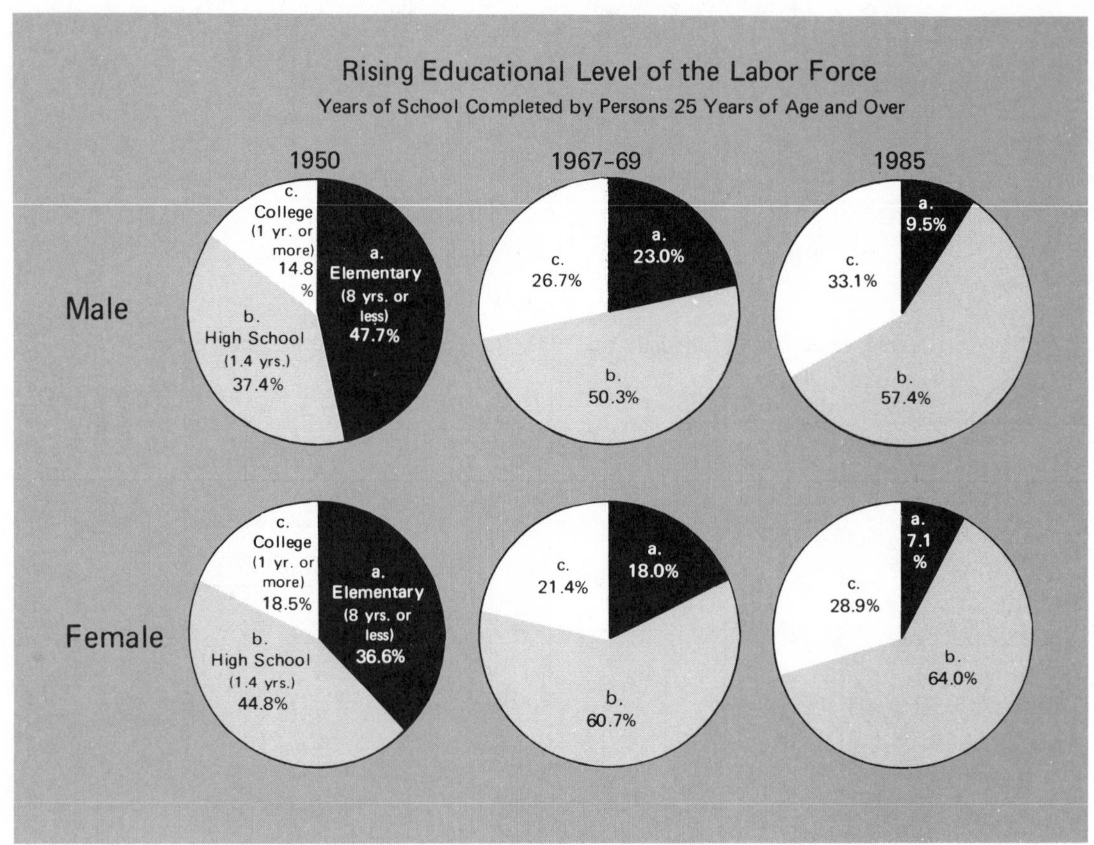

Fig. 22-7

Circle and Sector Charts

Source: Road Maps of Industry No. 1660, The Conference Board, February 15, 1971.

Fig. 22-8

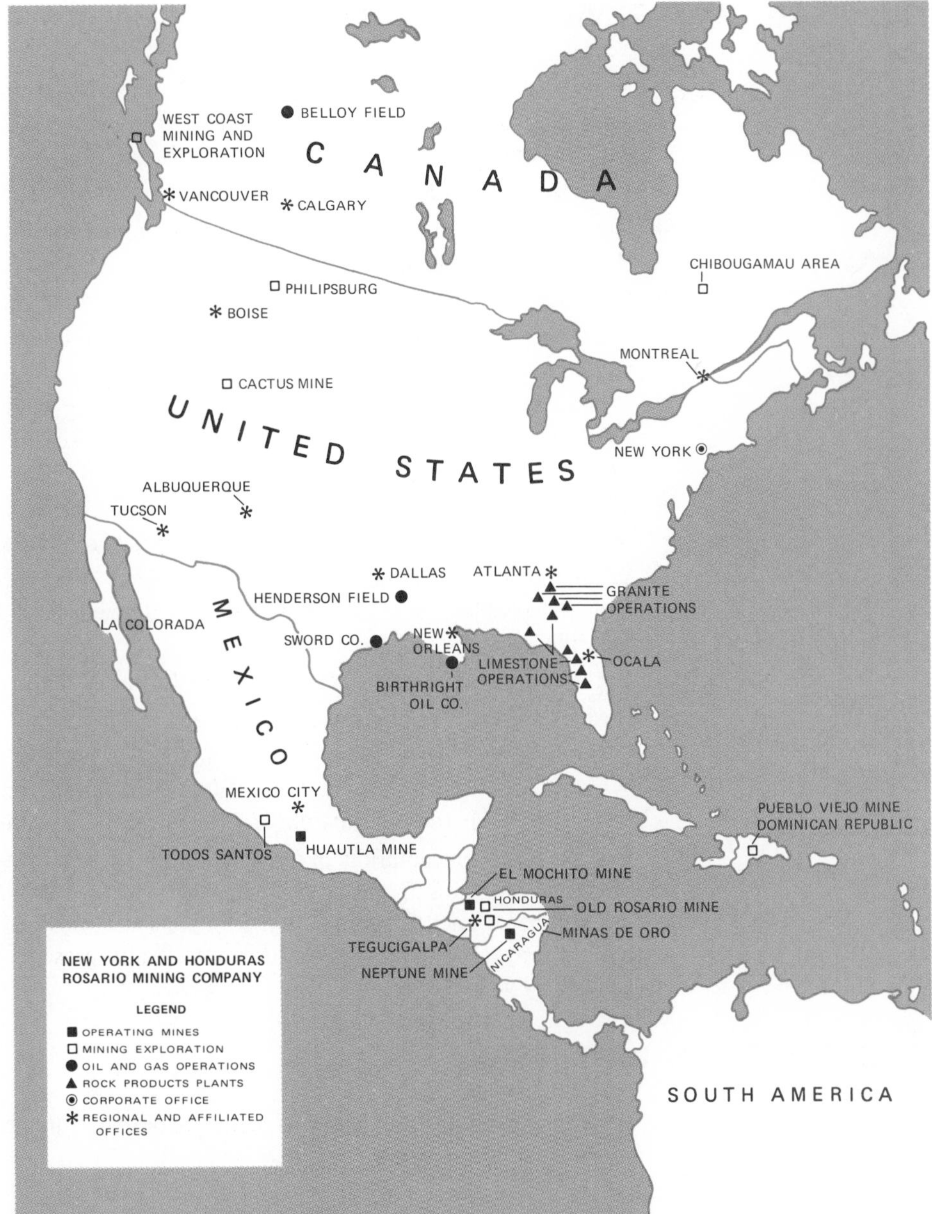

A Map Chart

Source: New York and Honduras Rosario Mining Company, 89th Annual Report, 1969.

QUESTIONS FOR REVIEW

1. What are the fundamental purposes of budgeting?
2. Why is it necessary to segregate office costs into two groups—fixed and variable?
3. What kind of data are usually contained in annual financial reports?
4. How does a well-prepared budget of administrative office expenses help the office manager in his daily work?
5. For what reasons should a budget contain a "safety valve"?
6. What factors determine the extent to which administrative office expenses will be analyzed and budgeted?
7. What is the usual basis for allocating the following kinds of expenses: (a) local telephone expense, (b) property taxes, (c) filing department expenses, and (d) postage?
8. What is a master budget? What is the relationship between the budget of administrative office expenses and the master budget?
9. What means are at the disposal of the office manager who is faced with the problem of controlling the costs of peak-load fluctuations in the office work?
10. What are the characteristics of a good business report?
11. Business reports usually follow a standard outline. What are the points covered in such an outline?
12. What is communications "static"? What principle of report writing is concerned with the elimination of communications "static"?
13. Compare the presentation of data in tabular form with the portrayal of the same data in graphic form. What are the advantages and limitations of each form? Which form has the most dramatic impact upon the average reader? What form generally presents the data most accurately?

QUESTIONS FOR DISCUSSION

1. What is meant by budgetary control? Compare the term *budgetary control* with *managerial control.*
2. A budget requires that a business firm use it for a long period of time before it actually becomes an effective tool of management. Explain the meaning of this statement.
3. A budgetary program has certain limitations. If this were not so, a business executive who was positive and correct in his prognostications could make a great financial success on Wall Street. Explain the limitations of this statement.
4. The effectiveness of a budgetary program is measured by making each departmental executive responsible for the departmental figures. Explain.

5. Should reports be prepared from the viewpoint of the writer or the recipient of the report? Why?
6. The number of copies of a report that must be made often has an influence on the form of presentation or reproduction of copies. Explain what this statement means.
7. What approaches should be used by the administrative office manager in an attempt to reduce the number of costly reports to his superiors?
8. A manager of office services was recently overheard commenting about many of his workers' complete lack of knowledge about company operations. He indicated that although his workers received a copy of the firm's annual report each year, still they did not know how much business the company was doing, where the branch offices are located, how many persons are employed, etc. What steps do you recommend the manager take to educate his workers more thoroughly on company operations, profitability, employment picture, etc.?
9. In most offices the types of reports and their purposes often determine the nature of their preparation. Some reports are made for an immediate superior or the top echelon in management. Others are directed at a group on lower managerial levels. Furthermore, it must be determined *why* the report is wanted. It is also necessary to determine before the preparation of a report what the reader will expect to get from the report and in what way he will use the information. Your analysis of reports indicates that there are two methods of preparation:

TWO METHODS OF REPORT WRITING

The Deductive Method	The Inductive Method
1. Purpose—why undertaken	1. Purpose
2. Scope—subject matter	2. Scope
3. Conclusions and/or recommendations	3. Facts
4. Facts	4. Fact analysis
5. Fact analysis	5. Conclusions and/or recommendations

Discuss the conditions under which you would use each of these methods in report preparation.

PRACTICAL OFFICE CASES

Case 22-1 Preparing the Budget of the Correspondence Department

The budget of administrative office expenses is prepared by the office manager at the end of each year for the ensuing year. This budget is a composite of all the functional departments under his supervision. Each department head is asked to prepare on a standard form the estimated budget figures for the year. These are analyzed on a monthly basis. Some of the costs submitted are fixed and are not affected by the volume of work to be done; others vary either constantly or gradually with the volume of work.

The budget of the variable and apportioned costs for the correspondence department of the Wilson Supply Company for the three months ending March 31, 19—, was:

	JANUARY	FEBRUARY	MARCH
Salaries of correspondents	$10,000.00	$10,000.00	$10,000.00
Stenographic costs	4,500.00	4,600.00	4,600.00
Postage	4,000.00	4,200.00	4,500.00
Telephone and telegraph	3,000.00	3,000.00	3,300.00
Supplies	1,000.00	1,000.00	1,100.00
Maintenance and repairs	100.00	100.00	100.00
Miscellaneous expenses	150.00	160.00	165.00
Share of administrative expenses	500.00	500.00	500.00
Share of personnel department costs	200.00	200.00	200.00
Rent	300.00	300.00	300.00
Light and heat	200.00	190.00	180.00
Depreciation of equipment	250.00	250.00	250.00
Insurance	100.00	100.00	100.00
F.I.C.A. tax	520.00	520.00	520.00
Federal unemployment comp. ins.	50.00	50.00	50.00
State unemployment comp. ins.	270.00	270.00	270.00

The actual costs for the three-month period were:

	JANUARY	FEBRUARY	MARCH
Salaries of correspondents	$ 9,800.00	$10,000.00	$10,200.00
Stenographic costs	4,300.00	4,500.00	4,600.00
Postage	3,800.00	3,800.00	3,950.00
Telephone and telegraph	2,800.00	3,000.00	3,100.00
Supplies	1,200.00	1,100.00	1,200.00
Maintenance and repairs	110.00	80.00	85.00
Miscellaneous expenses	165.00	140.00	175.00
Share of administrative expenses	500.00	500.00	500.00
Share of personnel department costs	200.00	200.00	200.00
Rent	300.00	300.00	300.00
Light and heat	188.00	178.00	168.00
Depreciation of equipment	250.00	250.00	250.00
Insurance	100.00	100.00	100.00
F.I.C.A. tax	509.60	520.00	530.40
Federal unemployment comp. ins.	49.00	50.00	51.00
State unemployment comp. ins.	264.60	270.00	275.40

■ Prepare a three-month comparison of budgeted and actual figures and do the following:

1. On each month's statement show the cumulative total of budgeted and actual figures to date.
2. Indicate possible causes of variance between actual and budgeted figures.

3. Compute the cost of each letter for each month for each expense if the volume of production for the department, after making allowances for form letters, fill-in letters, and interdepartmental communications, was equivalent to: January, 15,000 letters; February, 16,000 letters; and March, 16,500 letters.

Case 22-2 Preparing a Report on the Reduction of Correspondence Costs

George Lind is the office manager of the Futuristic Manufacturing Company. Most of the sales are made by mail-order, with direct-mail correspondence being used rather than catalogs. Frequently there are many problems of adjustment, complaints, dissatisfaction, and even direct selling. All of this requires a staff of 30 full-time correspondents. Because of the volume of correspondence, Lind feels that particular attention should be given to this phase of the work so that its cost may be reduced. You have been asked to analyze the stereotyped and redundant phrases used by the correspondents that could be eliminated to reduce the length of letters, improve their effectiveness, and reduce costs.

Some of the data you have collected for the month of March are:

Number of letters written during month	28,800
Average length of each letter	12 lines
Dictation costs	$19,500
Cost of transcription	$25,000
Cost of mailing and messenger service	$ 3,000
Cost of filing	$ 2,500
Cost of office supplies	$ 600

Among 8,000 letters that were studied, the frequency of poor, trite expressions was as follows:

"Enclosed you will find"	400 times
"As per your letter"	500 times
"Awaiting your further wishes"	1,500 times
"Acknowledging your letter of March 10, we wish to state that"	400 times
"We trust you will give this matter your earliest attention"	300 times
"The enclosed check for $00.00 is being sent with this letter"	250 times

Other trite expressions covered more than 15,783 words.

■ You, as supervisor of correspondence, are asked to prepare a report for submission to George Lind, giving the facts of your study and your recommendations. Set up the data in tabular or graphic form and indicate your interpretation of the data compiled. Also include a letter of transmittal.

Case 22-3 Preparing a Report of the "Real Costs" of Office Operations

You have just read an article wherein you learn that in a survey by a management consultant team it was found that a group of office employees studied were only 55 percent productive. During their usual 37½-hour week, they spend about 20 hours at work. In this same article you note that the average fringe benefit cost, according to a 1970 study by the U.S. Chamber of Commerce, is about 27.9 percent of the employee's hourly pay.[4]

Although you have not yet undertaken any detailed studies of nonproductivity in your own office, you feel that the following factors are at work to account for less than 75 percent productivity: time spent in getting underway on the job each morning; prolonged coffee breaks; unnecessary socializing on the job; extended lunch hours; boredom with the repetitive, unchallenging work; declining output at the end of the day; and early preparation for leaving at the end of the day.

You have brought together the following data that cover the hourly rate range for workers in your office, the cost of fringe benefits based on the Chamber of Commerce study, and the "real costs" of your workers, assuming three different levels of productivity:

Hourly Rate	Fringe Benefits at 27.9%	25% Non-productive	35% Non-productive	50% Non-productive
$2.00	2.56	3.41	3.94	5.12
2.25	2.88	3.85	4.43	5.76
2.50	3.20	4.27	4.92	6.40
2.75	3.52	4.69	5.42	7.04
3.00	3.84	5.12	5.91	7.68
3.25	4.16	5.55	6.40	8.32
3.50	4.48	5.97	6.89	8.96
3.75	4.80	6.40	7.38	9.60
4.00	5.12	6.83	7.88	10.24

▪ Prepare a report for the controller of your firm in which you show clearly and vividly what the nonproductive costs in your office may amount to, assuming the three levels of nonproductivity given above. The purpose of your report is to convince top management that funds should be expended to bring in a group of consultants to study the hidden costs of your office operations, with the aim of realizing significant savings. In your report present the tabular data in a graphic format so that the reader will be immediately impressed by the "real costs" of office operations.

[4] "Program Your Optimum Staff Needs," *Administrative Management* (November, 1970), p. 25.

23

Office Manuals-- A Tool of Cost Control

Some banks, insurance companies, department stores, and public utilities employ thousands of office workers. Many concerns operating branch offices on a national scale also employ a large number of office workers. The vastness of the organization and the large number of persons affected make it desirable, if not necessary, that general information, instructions, and regulations be put into writing. Having definite procedures in printed form saves time for the worker and overcomes the need for constant repetition of instructions. This is one of the purposes of office manuals. Because printed instructions may be made clear and complete and may be studied, a manual benefits not only the employer but also the employee.

Office manuals are used not only to fix responsibility for performing certain duties, but also to set up procedures for the performance of those duties. By having in written form instructions, rules, and regulations, each employee receiving a manual can be held responsible for them and for the manner in which they are carried out. An office manual that describes each step in the performance of a certain duty is sometimes referred to as a *manual of standard practice*. One bank has prepared a series of eight manuals covering the method of performing the work in the various departments, such as Credits and Loans, Foreign Exchange, and Trust Division. These manuals of standard practice possess the advantages that go with standardization, such as definite procedures, fixed responsibilities, and uniform requirements.

The office manual is an aid in the training of new employees because it gives them in readily available form the established systems, procedures, and duties. Office manuals can also serve in connection with refresher training courses for older employees. To be of greatest value, an office manual must give information regarding the policy, organization, and procedures of those whom it is intended to serve.

TYPES OF OFFICE MANUALS

Office manuals may be classified under a variety of headings. One grouping that is frequently used consists of four different types of manuals: (1) policy manual, (2) organization manual, (3) administrative practice manual, and (4) departmental practice manual. This classification is used here, and each of these types of office manuals is explained in the following paragraphs.

In some businesses, material may be selected from one or more of the basic types of manuals and brought together in the form of a *handbook,* which is distributed to all newly employed workers. Through the use of employees' handbooks, personnel policies, rules, and regulations can be explained to all new as well as older employees. The use of handbooks helps both management and the workers to eliminate the friction and misunderstandings that arise when policies and practices are not put into writing. Although the subjects that should be included in such handbooks are not uniform, the more progressive companies try to show their interest and sincerity by making the contents very comprehensive. A suggested table of contents for such a handbook is given in Figure 23-1.

Policy Manual

A *policy* is a definite course of action or a principle of procedure. A *policy manual* contains decisions, resolutions, and pronouncements of the board of directors establishing the policies of the company. Practically all organizations have general principles of practice to govern the conduct of their affairs. Policies should be somewhat elastic and not rigid; they should take into consideration the conditions that may prevail in the future.

Organizations may have several manuals embodying a consideration of all their policies. However, many companies, especially

Fig. 23-1

SECTION

I. Introduction
- Message from president
- Purpose of the handbook

II. The Company
- Organization
- Plant
- Products

III. Employment
- Change of address
- Discipline
- Employee contract and patent agreement
- Employee evaluation
- Employment procedure
- Follow-up of the new employee
- Gate passes
- Layoffs—reducing forces
- Promotions
- Relatives
- Release
- Seniority
- Tool checks
- Transfers

IV. Hours and Wages
- Attendance
- Bonus
- Clock cards—tardiness
- Holidays—Sundays
- Job analyses
- Job classifications
- Overtime
- Pay advances
- Pay reductions
- Paydays
- Rate changes
- Vacations
- Wage payment plan
- Work guarantee
- Working hours

V. Safety—Health—Insurance
- Accident prevention
- Fire brigade
- Group insurance
- Mutual aid
- Hospitalization and surgical insurance
- Physical examinations
- Safety awards
- Safety equipment

SECTION

V.

(Continued)
- Safety organization
- Safety regulations
- Shop hospitals
- Smoking
- Uniforms for female factory workers
- Workmen's compensation insurance

VI. Education and Training
- Apprentices
- Bulletin boards
- Co-ops
- Correspondence study
- Educational features
- Foremen's conferences
- Library
- Public school opportunity
- Suggestions

VII. Employee Organizations and Activities
- Annual affairs
- Credit union
- Department clubs
- Grievances
- Picnics
- Recreation
- Employees' associations
- Employees' store
- Service clubs

VIII. General Information
- Cafeteria
- Use of company name
- Gambling, betting, cards
- Gifts
- Liquor
- Lost and found articles
- Parking
- Passes for articles
- Personal debts
- Personal mail
- Personal property
- Personal work
- Salesmen
- Solicitations
- Use of telephone and telegraph
- Visitors
- Welfare

Table of Contents of a Comprehensive Employees' Handbook

smaller ones, embody all possible classifications of office manuals under one cover. Materials pertaining to such matters as the history of the company, the story of its products or services, its financial record, all matters that may be of possible value in orienting new employees most effectively into its employment, and material that might be of value to its stockholders should be included in some of its manuals. Probably the most effective place is either in the policy manual or in the organization manual.

Organization Manual

The *organization manual* explains the organization, the duties, and the responsibilities of the various departments and their respective divisions. Each section of the organization manual might consist of a description of the duties and responsibilities of the office or department treated in that section, the organization chart, and a listing of the administrative officers of the office or department.

The organization manual should be made accessible to at least departmental, if not divisional, heads. The level of authority and responsibility of each executive should be indicated in the manual, which, in effect, is interdepartmental. In other words, an organization manual represents the company as a whole and is an aid in determining procedures that govern the major segments or departments of the concern. Charts that show possible promotional lines for the entire company may be included in the organization manual.

Administrative Practice Manual

The *administrative practice manual* contains procedures that affect all departments. Standard methods or procedures are explained for carrying on the company's work. Such a manual gives an overview of procedures to be used in each of the various departments and divisions; much of this material is broken down and becomes the content of departmental practice manuals, as well as handbooks. An administrative practice manual might consider such topics as employees' education and training; instructions relating to correspondence and reports; personnel and public relations; and instructions for the preparation and administration of the budget.

Departmental Practice Manual

The *departmental practice manual* is intradepartmental and contains procedures for a particular department. The manual deals with the internal policies, organization, and procedures of one department. The use of any special departmental practice manual is limited to the particular department for which it was originally prepared. Each department is charted, and the organization chart is usually accompanied by a departmental, divisional, or sectional write-up.

Mailing Manual. Some large firms use mailing manuals as one means of training the mailroom personnel in their work. These manuals, prepared by the supervisor and similar to those used by the stenographic and filing departments, give minute instructions in all phases of handling both incoming and outgoing mail. If the messenger service is closely linked with the mailing department, as is often the case, instructions regarding pickup of mail from each department are also included.

Filing Manual. Most business concerns find that a filing manual is an invaluable aid in facilitating supervision, training new employees, standardizing the filing work, and speeding up filing. In short, the manual is of great assistance in making the files an effective instrument of service. Such manuals set forth the requirements for proper filing and list such rules and regulations as may seem desirable. All present employees in the filing department should study the manual carefully so as to be thoroughly familiar with the procedures and methods. New employees are assisted in their "breaking-in" training by studying this manual. If the filing work is decentralized, the manual has the advantage of making the work uniform in all departments where filing is done.

Since the rules and regulations for filing vary from company to company according to the system used, the methods of indexing, and the procedures for charging out and follow-ups, it would be impracticable to present here such a manual in its entirety. Instead, certain general principles followed by many business concerns in the organization and functioning of their filing departments are presented in the partially illustrated filing manual in Figure 23-2 on pages 744 to 749. The illustrative filing manual also lists the basic rules for alphabetic indexing and filing. In using indexing and filing in business, certain fundamental principles governing their use should be noted:

1. The rules must be written.
2. They must be strictly observed.

3. When opinion differs as to the proper method, one rule must be selected and adhered to consistently.
4. The rules should be amplified as individual experience requires.

FILING MANUAL

Program for records retention

The records retention schedule for each department shows each important record, the number of months it is to be held in the local files, and the number of years it is to be kept in dead storage.

PROGRAM OF RECORDS RETENTION

GENERAL FINANCIAL	NUMBER OF MONTHS: TO BE HELD IN LOCAL FILES	NUMBER OF MONTHS: TO BE HELD IN DEAD STORAGE
A. Expense vouchers (travel expense invoices, receipted bills, etc.)	12	72
B. Vouchers covering premium and dividend refunds (same period as accounting entries)	12	60
C. Premium entries, compensation and misc. liability (It should be noted that the underwriting folders containing copies of these entries are to be retained for 10 years.)	24	24
D. Salary department records:		
1. Notices of payroll change	15	57
2. Cash book records (i.e. carbon copy of check.)	6	114
3. Payroll lists (Names of persons and amount of salary.)	24	60
4. Original checks, paid through bank	12	108
5. Salary record cards (history of individual's salary account):		
Present Personnel	Permanently	
Former Personnel	120	Permanently

Storage vault commitment

The storage vault commitment card shows the period of retention and accompanies each batch of records sent to storage.

Filing Manual (Continued)

Fig. 23-2

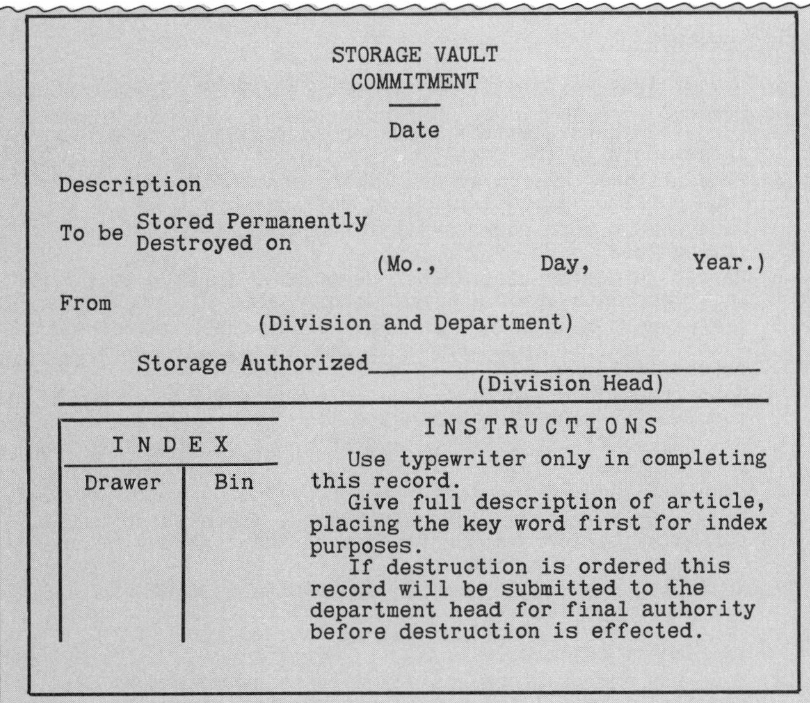

STORAGE VAULT
COMMITMENT

Date

Description

To be Stored Permanently
Destroyed on
(Mo., Day, Year.)

From
(Division and Department)

Storage Authorized____________________
(Division Head)

INDEX	
Drawer	Bin

INSTRUCTIONS

Use typewriter only in completing this record.

Give full description of article, placing the key word first for index purposes.

If destruction is ordered this record will be submitted to the department head for final authority before destruction is effected.

Fig. 23-2

General instructions

1. Follow instructions exactly. If you have a suggestion for improvement in the filing methods, refer it to the file supervisor, who will duly authorize a change in the manual if the new method is simpler and more efficient.
2. Do not discuss the contents of files with fellow employees or outsiders nor give out information or papers to persons whose duties have no relation to the material requested.
3. All special instructions must be given by the supervisor. Any problems that arise outside the regular routine of filing must be decided by the supervisor, not by a fellow clerk.
4. You are responsible for your own errors; thus, refrain from asking other workers for instructions. No one is more interested in helping you in your training than your supervisor. This is her job.
5. Accuracy is the first essential in filing; make it your primary consideration, and speed, the secondary. Accurate filing assures quick finding, and quick finding is the real test of your efficiency.
6. Familiarize yourself with office details other than those in your department wherever such knowledge will promote your understanding of how materials should be filed.

Filing Manual (Continued)

Daily work hints

1. A desk tray labeled "TO BE FILED" should be kept accessible.
2. Place all papers within a folder according to date, the latest date to the front.
3. Type all headings on gummed labels and affix on folder tabs. Neatness and legibility pay.
4. Always mend torn papers with transparent tape before filing them.
5. Handle guides by the sides. Never pull forward or push back the contents of a drawer by pressing the guide tabs.
6. Always pull the folders part way or entirely out of the drawer when filing in order to avoid placing papers between folders.
7. Keep the file drawers closed. Close every drawer as soon as you have finished using it.
8. Use rubber finger tips instead of a sponge or moistening your fingers in your mouth.
9. Keep headings to the left, face forward.
10. Except in extreme or irregular cases, there is no reason for material to remain unfiled more than one day after it comes to the department.
11. No papers may be put away in desk or table drawers. All papers pertaining to the work of the filing department must be in orderly, plainly labeled groups, in sorters or on desks.
12. Keep the number of papers actually being worked on at one time as small as possible; never take from the sorter at one time more papers than you can file in 15 minutes.
13. Experience has shown the following mistakes in filing to be the most common. Guard against them.
    a. Too few guides.
    b. Drawers and folders too full.
    c. Material in miscellaneous folders not filed alphabetically.
    d. No charge-out system.
    e. Transfers not made at regular periods.
    f. Papers improperly indexed.
    g. Work not kept up-to-date.
    h. Material stapled together that does not belong together.

Summary of rules for alphabetic indexing*

NAMES OF INDIVIDUALS

1. Order of Indexing Units. Each part of the name of an individual is considered to be a separate indexing unit. For filing purposes, the parts of an individual's name are considered in this order: (1) surname, or last name; (2) first name or initial; (3) middle name or initial.

---

*Ernest D. Bassett, Peter L. Agnew, and David G. Goodman, Business Filing and Records Control, (3d ed.; Cincinnati: South-Western Publishing Company, 1964).

Fig. 23-2

Filing Manual (Continued)

2. Surname Particles. A surname particle (sometimes called a prefix) is considered to be part of the surname, not a separate indexing unit. Examples of particles are D', Da, De, Del, Des, Di, Du, Fitz, La, Le, Les, Mac, Mc, O', Van, Vanden, Van der, Von, and Von der.
3. Compound Surnames. A compound surname (Campbell-Jones, for example) is treated as two indexing units. The hyphen is disregarded in filing.
4. Initials and Abbreviations. An initial is considered to be an indexing unit. It precedes all names in the same unit beginning with the same letter as the initial. An abbreviated first or middle name or a nickname is considered as if it were written in full if the full name is known.
5. Titles with Personal Names. A personal or professional title (such as Mr., Mrs., Miss, Dr., Father, Mayor, Professor, Rabbi, Reverend, Senator) or degree (such as D.D., Ph.D., D.V.M., M.D.) is usually not considered in determining alphabetic order, but is written in parentheses at the end of the name for identification purposes. A name consisting of a title followed by only a first name or by only a first and middle name is indexed in the order in which it is written.
6. Identical Personal Names. When the full names of two or more individuals are identical, addresses are used to determine alphabetic filing order. Location names are not considered to be indexing units, but merely a secondary means of determining alphabetic sequence.
7. Seniority Titles in Identical Names. A seniority designation, such as "Junior" and "Senior" or "II (Second)" and "III (Third)," used for what would otherwise be identical names, is not considered to be an identifying element for the name.
8. Names of Married Women. If the legal name of a married woman (her first name and maiden surname with her husband's surname, or her first and middle names with her husband's surname) is known, it is used for filing purposes rather than her husband's name. "Mrs." is placed in parentheses at the end of the name but is not considered in filing.
9. Unusual Names. When it is difficult to decide which part of an individual's name is the surname, the last part of the name as written should be considered to be the surname.
10. Order of Indexing Units. The general rule is that the units of a business name are considered in the order in which they appear and are read, the first word being the first unit. When the name of an individual (except a surname only) appears in a business name, the units in the individual's name are transposed in the same manner as the units in an individual's name considered by itself. Sometimes, however, a business name that contains the name of an individual (Marshall Field and Company, for example) is so widely known that confusion would be caused by such transposition. For this reason the units in such a name are indexed in the order in which they appear in the name.
11. Words Disregarded. Minor words--English articles, conjunctions, and prepositions (such as the, and, &, of, to, for, by, and in)--are generally not considered

Fig. 23-2

Filing Manual (Continued)

to be units for indexing purposes, but are enclosed in parentheses so that they will not be confused with the indexing units that are considered in filing. When the article "The" is the first word in a firm name, it is written in parentheses at the end of the name.

12. Abbreviations. An abbreviation in a business name (such as Okla. Refining Co. and U.S. Testing Service) is considered as if it were written in full.
13. Single Letters. A single letter in a business name, including an abbreviation for a word that is unknown and cannot be ascertained, is considered to be a separate filing unit. It precedes all names in the same unit beginning with that same letter.
14. Hyphened and Compound Names and Words. When actual or coined names, words, or word substitutes are combined with a hyphen, each part is considered to be a separate indexing unit. A single word written with a hyphen (a word containing a particle or prefix, such as ante-, anti-, bi-, co-, de-, dis-, inter-, mid-, non-, pan-, per-, pre-, re-, trans-, tri-, un-) is considered to be one indexing unit. When separate words in a business name may be written as one single word, the words are considered to be one indexing unit. (The use of a hyphen is of no significance.) Examples of such words are airport, carload, crossroads, downtown, eastside, goodwill, halfway, mainland, railroad, seaboard, and points of the compass words such as northeast, northwest, southeast, and southeastern.
15. Titles in Business Names. A title in a business name is considered to be a separate indexing unit and is indexed in the order in which it appears in the name.
16. Numbers. A number in a business name is considered to be in written-out form. It is indexed as one unit regardless of the length of the number of digits in the number.
17. Possessives. When a possessive ends with "apostrophe s" ('s), the final "s" is disregarded in that indexing unit. When the ending is "s apostrophe" (s'), the final "s" is considered to be part of the word.
18. Identical Business Names. When the names of two or more businesses are identical, location names and addresses are used to determine alphabetic filing order. Location names are not considered to be indexing units, but merely a secondary means of determining alphabetic sequence.
19. Compound Geographic Names. Each word in a compound geographic name is considered to be a separate indexing unit and the name is indexed as it is written.
20. Compound Foreign Names. Each separately written word in a compound foreign name is considered to be a separate indexing unit. A foreign article or particle is combined with the word following it, and the particle and word are considered to be one indexing unit. Obscure foreign business names are processed as written.

OTHER NAMES

21. Hotels and Motels. The name of a hotel or a motel is indexed in the order in which it is written unless some word other than the first word in the name more clearly identifies it. If the word "Hotel" or "Motel" appears first in the name, it is transposed to follow the most clearly identifying word.

Fig. 23-2

Filing Manual (Continued)

22. Elementary and Secondary Schools. The names of elementary and secondary schools are indexed (a) according to the names of the cities in which the schools are located and (b) according to the most distinctive words in the names of the schools. When the name of the city is the first word of the school name, the city name is used only once in indexing.
23. Colleges and Universities. The name of a college or a university is indexed according to the most clearly identifying word in the name. City names, unless they are part of the college names, are not considered except as identifying elements when identical college names are involved.
24. Churches and Synagogues. The names of churches and synagogues are indexed in the order in which they are written unless some word other than the first word in the name more clearly identifies the organization. If the name of the denomination is part of the church name, that name is used as the first indexing unit. For example, in the name "First Congregational Church," the primary indexing unit would be "Congregational" rather than "First." The word "Church" is never used as the first indexing unit.
25. Clubs and Service Organizations. The name of a club or a service organization is indexed according to the most clearly identifying unit in the name. A city name appearing in the name of an organization is treated as an indexing unit.
26. Newspapers and Periodicals. The name of a newspaper is indexed in the order in which it is written unless it does not contain the name of the city of its publication. In the latter case, the name of the city of publication is inserted before the newspaper name and is considered the first indexing unit.

    The name of a periodical is indexed in the order in which the name is written. (A cross reference may be made for the name of the publisher of a periodical so that this information will be available if and when needed.)

GOVERNMENTAL NAMES

27. Federal Government Offices. The parts of the name of a federal government office are considered in the following order: (a) United States Government--three indexing units, (b) the principal word or words in the name of the executive department, (c) the principal words in the name of the bureau, and (d) the principal words in the name of the division.
28. Political Subdivisions. The parts of the name of an office in a state, county, city, or other political subdivision are considered in the following order: (a) the principal word or words in the name of the political subdivision, followed by its classification such as "State," "County," or "City," and (b) the principal word or words in the name of the department, board, or office.
29. Foreign Government Names. Names of agencies or offices of foreign governments are indexed in a manner similar to that for American government offices; (a) the name of the country, (b) the name of the executive department, (c) the name of the office, bureau, or agency.

Fig. 23-2

Filing Manual (Concluded)

Correspondence Manual. The correspondence manual is a means of standardizing the methods and products of a correspondence department in a large firm. In some firms, the manual covers such topics as handling correspondence; structure and tone of letters; opening and closing of letters; intracompany correspondence; words, sentences, and paragraphs; punctuation; the outward appearance of letters; and the supervision of correspondence. To illustrate the contents of a correspondence manual, the table of contents taken from a manual used by a company having branches throughout the United States is shown in Figure 23-3. This outline may serve as a guide for those anticipating the preparation of such an office manual.

Fig. 23-3

Table of Contents of a Correspondence Manual (Continued)

Fig. 23-3

Section VII: Punctuation

Marks of separation
The period
The comma
The semicolon
The colon
The question mark
Quotation marks
The dash and the parentheses
The apostrophe
The exclamation mark
Use of period other than as a punctuation mark
Division of words

Section VIII: Outward Appearance of Letters

Uniformity and good appearance
Typing and placement
Dateline
Address
Salutation
Body
Complimentary close
Signature
Signature identification and stenographic reference
Enclosures
Intradepartmental correspondence
Rubber stamps not to be used
Envelope address
Sample forms of letters

Section IX: Supervision of Correspondence

Periodical examination of carbon copies at district and division headquarters
Inspection of correspondence files at the offices
Suggestions to inspection officials
Talks at development meetings

Section X: Supplement

Grammar and sentence structure
Trite phrases to be avoided
Incorrect and correct use of certain words and phrases

Table of Contents of a Correspondence Manual (Concluded)

The use of manuals is particularly helpful in large offices or in firms having many branches, in each of which some correspondence is prepared. A definite, uniform policy is developed, goodwill is established with the public, and responsibility is fixed. In substance, the manual represents an up-to-date discussion of business English. Although much of this information is available in standard business English textbooks, it is better to prepare a correspondence manual that will set up company standards and solve the peculiar letter-writing problems of the company. Every correspondence manual should contain specific instructions relating to the writing of letters. See the partially illustrated correspondence manual in Figure 23-4 on pages 752 to 756. In this illustration the rules and discussions from a manual used by a large business firm are given in condensed form. Some firms may have particular practices or policies that they may wish to emphasize in such a manual. The illustration in Figure 23-4 is presented solely to indicate a plan of organization and content, subject to adaptation where changes are desired.

CORRESPONDENCE MANUAL

Section I: Handling Correspondence

Section II: Structure and Tone of Letters

Clearness and Correctness:

Clearness is assured only by strict adherence to the accepted rules of writing. Any deviation from these rules tends to waste the reader's time and to indicate a lack of concern for the reader.

Grammar:

In letter writing, grammar pertains to the simplest and clearest way of saying things, not to fancy writing. This does not mean, however, that fundamental principles should be ignored.

Conciseness:

Conciseness is courtesy because it saves the reader's time. In letters it is as much a matter of concise and well-planned thought as it is a matter of words.

Courtesy:

Courtesy is more than the frequent use of "please." Courtesy is a matter of all the fundamental principles of letter writing. It denotes neatness and correctness, for a lack of either conveys the impression that the customer is not worth the trouble of writing simple, correct English. Courtesy is clearness, for obscurity wastes the customer's time.

Fig. 23-4

Section III: Opening and Closing

The Opening of a Letter:

The opening of a letter must clearly indicate the subject of the letter but not merely in the nature of a date reference. The opening should be woven into a cordial introduction that conveys the same cordiality with which a friendly interview is opened.

The Negative Opening:

Keep to a minimum negative words and ideas in the opening paragraph. Avoid such openings as "In reply to your letter of the 15th, I am writing to tell you that we cannot make shipment because you failed to tell us the size. . . ."

The Cordial, Positive Opening:

"Just as soon as you let us know what sizes you want, we will be glad. . . ." Such an opening goes directly to the point and produces the best possible effect.

The Participial Close:

Never use such archiac closes as "Trusting that," "Hoping that," and "Thanking you in advance." The last is especially poor because it presupposes that the requested favor is not worth thanks afterwards.

Correspondence Manual (Continued)

Fig. 23-4

Section IV: Intracompany Correspondence

Section V: Words

The Right Word:

The choice of the proper words is partly a matter of an adequate vocabulary, partly of discriminating choice from available word material, and partly of the faculty of putting ourselves in the place of the reader and visualizing how he will understand what we are trying to say to him. It might be added that it is also a matter of being willing to hunt for the proper word.

Long Words Vs. Short Words:

In business communications, short words are to be preferred because they form a letter that can be understood at a glance by the busy executive. Long words may be strange words to be puzzled over angrily.

Section VI: Sentences and Paragraphs

Length of Sentences:

Long, involved sentences waste the reader's time and tend to irritate him. A series of short, abrupt sentences gives an appearance of brusqueness. Judicious use of short and longer sentences, none longer than five lines, insures the best results.

Paragraphing:

Paragraphing is used to indicate a change in thought and to get letters read. A letter that looks hard to read is in danger of not being read attentively, if at all.

Length of Paragraphs:

Confronted with long paragraphs, a reader is likely to skip through the letter or lay it aside for "later reading." Short paragraphs, on the other hand, produce a choppy effect. Use a judicious mixture of short and long paragraphs.

Section VII: Punctuation

Marks of Separation:

The period, the comma, and the semicolon, which are essential marks of separation, provide the means of separating sentences, clauses, and phrases from each other so that each can be read in its proper relation to the context.

The Period:

A dot, or a period, indicates the point of separation between two or more thoughts, such as after "report," "long," and "complete" in the following: "I have just received the report. It is long. It is not complete."

Correspondence Manual (Continued)

The Comma:

The comma eliminates the jerkiness produced by a series of short sentences, as in the preceding paragraph. It is used to group together closely related thoughts into longer and more complicated sentences. The three sentences above thus become: "I have just received the report, which is long, though not complete." Many other uses for the comma have also been developed.

The Semicolon:

The semicolon indicates a separation more complete than that afforded by the comma and not quite as definite as that produced by the period. The semicolon is used when a sentence contains phrases already marked off by commas and a more distinct division between the two major sentence members is desired. It is also used to bring two closely related thoughts, which would otherwise be separated by a period, into more intimate contact so as to emphasize their relation or contrast.

The Colon:

The only approved uses of a colon in business letters are after the salutation, before a quotation, and to indicate that an enumeration or listing is to follow.

The Question Mark:

The question mark is placed at the end of a direct inquiry. It is not used after indirect questions or in the so-called question of courtesy: "Will you please report as soon as you can."

Fig. 23-4

Section VIII: Outward Appearance of Letters

Uniformity and Good Appearance:

Whereas a good appearance of letters gives a definite impression of good service and courtesy, careless looking letters are likely to be taken as indications of carelessness in other details of business.

Typing and Placement:

Letters must be neat without overwritten words or characters. There should be no crowding in of words in a line, and no letters typed above the line because of omissions. No ink or pencil correction is permissible. Letters should be typed with generous margins, with the width of the margin and the general placement on the sheet depending upon the length of the typed matter. The left-hand margin, of course, will be even. Care must be taken to see that the right-hand margin is not ragged, though naturally it will be somewhat irregular.

Dateline:

Type the date in full, such as August 1, 1966, starting at the left margin. Place the date on the second line below the city and state names printed on the letterhead.

Correspondence Manual (Continued)

Address:

Type each line of the address (the name and the full post office address), starting at the left margin. Type the address four to twelve single spaces below the date, depending on the length of the letter. The ZIP Code should be typed on the same line as the state name, with two spaces separating the state name and the number.

Avoid using abbreviations unless the balance would otherwise be destroyed. Do not use "City" in the address of a letter being sent to a person in the same city. Write the name of an individual exactly as it is signed, and the name of a firm as it appears on the letterhead.

Use the correct title before the name: Mr. for a man, Mrs. for a married woman, Miss for an unmarried woman, and Ms. if the marital status of a woman is unknown. Avoid using Messrs. and Mesdames; instead, use the name of the firm as it appears on the letterhead.

Abbreviate, if necessary, titles such as Dr., Rev., Prof., and Hon.

Avoid writing a single initial before a person's surname, unless the person signs his name that way. If there is no second initial, write out the first name in full. Never use the last name alone, as in Mr. Holmes. Refer to previous correspondence for the full name.

Do not use No. or # before a street number. Numbers designating streets should be written out. For street numbers above ten, figures may be used.

Fig. 23-4

Salutation:

Type the salutation at the left margin, two spaces below the last line of the address. A colon only follows the salutation. Two spaces separate the salutation and the body.

Gentlemen is approved for a company or other group of individuals; Ladies for two or more women; Ladies and Gentlemen if the group addressed is composed of both men and women.

In addressing an individual, Dear Sir or Dear Mr. Holmes is correct for a man; Dear Madam or Dear Mrs. Holmes, for a woman.

Body:

Type the first line of each paragraph at the left margin. Lines should be single-spaced, with double spacing between paragraphs. In the case of short, single paragraph letters, the body may be double-spaced.

Complimentary Close:

Always use a complimentary close. "Yours very truly" is the accepted closing in our correspondence. The close should be typed at the left margin. Only the first word is capitalized.

Correspondence Manual (Continued)

Signature:

Since the company name appears in our letterhead, the name should not be typed as part of the signature.

Type the dictator's name on the fourth line below the complimentary close, starting at the left margin. Place the dictator's title on the line below the dictator's name.

Signature Identification and Stenographic Reference:

Type the initials of the dictator, followed by your initials, at the left margin two spaces below the dictator's title, as: KLB:CJ

Enclosures:

When an enclosure is being sent with the correspondence, note this fact by typing Enclosure at the left margin two spaces below the reference initials. If more than one enclosure is being sent, indicate the number of enclosures, as Enclosures 3.

Intradepartmental Correspondence:

Type both the names of the person addressed and the writer at the beginning of the letter. Omit the salutation and complimentary close. Be sure that your initials are typed two spaces below the dictator's typewritten signature.

Rubber Stamps Not to Be Used:

Do not use rubber stamp signatures, except on form fill-in notices originating in the collection department. Similarly, no rubber-stamped dates or other information are permitted.

Envelope Address:

Write the envelope address exactly as the address on the letter.

Additional general instructions for the handling of your firm's correspondence are condensed on the following pages. Our forward-looking letters become advertisements of the company and those principles of business conduct for which it stands.

Fig. 23-4

Correspondence Manual (Concluded)

Communications Manual. The objective of preparing a communications manual is to guide employees in selecting a suitable communications service at the least cost to the company. Within the manual, an attempt should be made to impress upon the employees that communications media are in competition with each other, and thus the most economical and satisfactory medium should be selected to meet the needs of the communication at hand. The various media, such as telephone and telegraph, should be illustrated, along with the various types of services rendered by each. One portion of a communications manual, the rules and instructions relating to preparing and sending telegrams, is shown in Figure 23-5, on pages 757 to 760.

COMMUNICATIONS MANUAL

Fig. 23-5

Section II: How to write telegrams

1. The class of service should be marked in the box at the upper left-hand corner of the telegraph blank. The point of origin and the date should be written in at the upper right side of the blank. Indicate whether the telegram is sent "Paid" or "Collect" by writing one of these words in the upper left-hand corner of the blank. When the amount is to be charged to an account, the name of the account should be placed in the space provided for that purpose. See the example of a correctly prepared telegram on the following page.

   Both domestic and international messages may be sent without prepayment by holders of Western Union credit cards. The cards will also be honored for messenger errand service at any Western Union office. The arrangement is especially convenient for business representatives and other travelers "on the road" who can wire and "charge it" at hotels and motels, airports, railroad stations, on trains, or over customer teleprinters wherever they might happen to be, by merely giving the name and account number.

2. The telegraph company makes no extra charge for long addresses, except in unusual cases. For example, in a telegram addressed to "John Doe or Henry Roe," the words "or Henry Roe" are charged for.

3. The name of the person, firm, or corporation tc whom a telegram is to be delivered should be written below the upper left corner of the blank. In addressing telegrams, include all information that will be helpful in locating the addressee quickly. There is no extra charge, for instance, for the address: "Henry P. Dodson, Arthur Mfg. Co., 75 Madison Place, Toledo, Ohio." Although the ZIP Code number may be given as part of the address, the number is not normally transmitted. A telephone number, the business title of the addressee, or "Mr. and Mrs. John Roe and family," may be used without extra charge. Code addresses are not permissible in domestic telegrams.

4. In replying to a telegram when no street address is known, write "Answer date" or "Answer" after the name of the addressee, and address the telegram to the city and telegraph office from which the original telegram was sent. The originating branch office is indicated by one or two letters that may appear immediately preceding the "place from" in the dateline of the telegram received. For example: "Joe Jones, Answer Date MS, New York City."

5. Use firm names and room numbers in addresses such as "John Jones, Empire State Building, New York City," since there are thousands of people employed in that building. The address "11 Forty-Second Street, New York City," may necessitate attempts at delivery on both East and West Forty-Second Street.

Communications Manual (Continued)

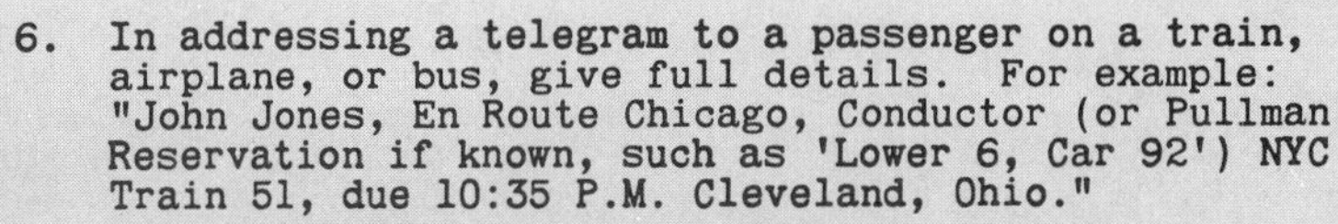

6. In addressing a telegram to a passenger on a train, airplane, or bus, give full details. For example: "John Jones, En Route Chicago, Conductor (or Pullman Reservation if known, such as 'Lower 6, Car 92') NYC Train 51, due 10:35 P.M. Cleveland, Ohio."

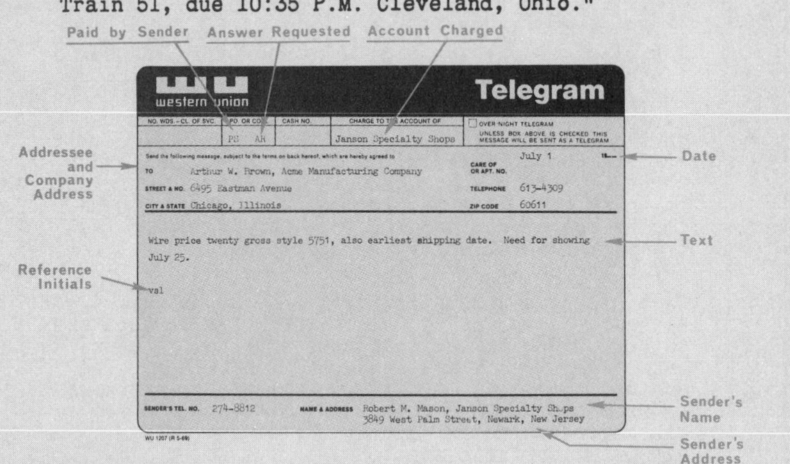

western union **Telegram**

NO. WDS.–CL. OF SVC.	PD. OR COLL.	CASH NO.	CHARGE TO THE ACCOUNT OF	OVER NIGHT TELEGRAM UNLESS BOX ABOVE IS CHECKED THIS MESSAGE WILL BE SENT AS A TELEGRAM
	PS AR		Janson Specialty Shops	

Send the following message, subject to the terms on back hereof, which are hereby agreed to July 1 19__

TO Arthur W. Brown, Acme Manufacturing Company CARE OF OR APT. NO.
STREET & NO. 6495 Eastman Avenue TELEPHONE 613-4309
CITY & STATE Chicago, Illinois ZIP CODE 60611

Wire price twenty gross style 5751, also earliest shipping date. Need for showing July 25.

vsl

SENDER'S TEL. NO. 274-8812 NAME & ADDRESS Robert M. Mason, Janson Specialty Shops 3849 West Palm Street, Newark, New Jersey

WU 1207 (R 5-69)

Every telegram you prepare should include each of the elements pointed out in the telegraph blank above.

Fig. 23-5

7. If a report on delivery is desired, the words "Report Delivery" should be written as part of the address, immediately following the addressee's name, thus: "John H. Brown, Report Delivery, 516 West Martin Drive, Tulsa, Oklahoma."

   These words, which are charged for, are then wired to destination, and a report is wired back "Collect," stating to whom and when the telegram was delivered.

8. The keynote of a well-worded telegram is conciseness. The message should be stated clearly and briefly. The ideal is for every word to be necessary to the meaning of the message, but no word should be omitted when such omission would make the meaning of the telegram doubtful.

   Conciseness should not be carried to a point where the meaning is obscured or where the valuable time of the sender is wasted in rewriting with only the object of saving a few cents. It is always better to use a few extra words when they add to clarity or the emphasis of a message. Many words can be omitted without any loss simply by eliminating such words as "the," "that," "and," "I," and "a." Nouns and verbs convey ideas and meanings more concisely than other parts of speech. In phrasing a telegram, therefore, nouns and verbs are used more freely than adjectives and adverbs.

   Be careful to avoid ambiguous phrases such as "Arrive on 2 P.M. plane. Please meet me." This message leaves the recipient in doubt as to whether the plane left its starting point at 2 P.M. or will arrive at its destination at that time. The text should read: "Arrive Eastern Flight 402 2 P.M. Saturday International Airport. Please meet plane."

Communications Manual (Continued)

9. Do not use salutations and complimentary closes such as "Dear Sir" and "Yours truly."

10. In typing telegrams, avoid dividing a word at the end of a line.

11. Telegrams written in paragraph form will be transmitted and delivered in paragraph form without extra charge. Paragraphs may therefore be used whenever they should normally be used.

12. In dictating a telegram from a telephone, avoid phonetic errors by pronouncing each letter of a difficult word. For example, if the word "Sioux" is being sent, say S as in Sugar, I as in Ida, O as in Ocean, U as in Union, and X as in X-ray.

Fig. 23-5

Section III: How to count chargeable words

The following practices are observed in determining the number of chargeable words in domestic telegrams to all points within the United States and to points in Canada and Saint Pierre-Miquelon Islands:

1. One address and one signature are free.

2. Dictionary words from the English, German, French, Italian, Dutch, Portuguese, Spanish, and Latin languages are counted as one word each, regardless of length. Any word or group of letters not forming a dictionary word in any of these eight languages is counted at the rate of one word for every five letters or fraction of five letters. Words in other languages are subject to the five-character count.

3. Proper names in any language are counted according to the way they are normally written. Examples:
   United States.................. 2 words
   North Dakota................... 2 words
   New York City.................. 3 words

4. Abbreviations and letter groups are counted at the rate of one word for each five letters. Examples:
   LB (for POUND).................. 1 word
   A.M. (if written without spaces). 1 word
   A. M. (if written with spaces)... 2 words
   PM (if written without periods and spaces)..................... 1 word
   LOSA (for LOS ANGELES).......... 1 word

5. Personal names are counted in the way they are normally written. Examples:
   Du Bois........................ 2 words
   Van Dyke....................... 2 words
   Van der Gross.................. 3 words
   Vandewater..................... 1 word

   Initials, when separated by spaces, are counted as separate words; but when written together as J.O.R. in the case of J.O.R. Smith, they are counted at the rate of one word for each five letters.

Communications Manual (Continued)

6. Punctuation marks, such as a period (or decimal point), comma, colon, semicolon, dash or hyphen, parentheses, question mark, quotation marks, and apostrophe are neither counted nor charged for, regardless of where they appear in the text of the message.

   Words such as "stop" and "quote" and the words "comma" and "period" used in lieu of punctuation marks, are counted and charged for as one word each.

7. Except for the punctuation marks enumerated in No. 6 above, the only additional signs that can be transmitted in domestic messages are: $, &, /, #, ' (for feet or minutes), and " (for inches or seconds). These are counted in accordance with No. 8 below.

   The symbols for ¢ and @ cannot be transmitted, and should be written out. The percent sign % is transmitted as 0/0 and counts as three characters.

8. Groups of figures, including the signs mentioned in No. 7 above, and mixed groups of figures and letters are counted in accordance with (a) and (b) below:

   (a) In messages between points within the United States and to points in Mexico, such groups are counted at the rate of one word for each five figures (including signs) and letters. Examples:

   12345 (5 characters)......... 1 word
   #78964 (6 characters)........ 2 words

   (b) In messages between points in the United States and points in Canada, and Saint Pierre-Miquelon Islands, each figure and sign is counted as one word. Each group of letters written together is counted at the rate of one word for each five letters or fraction of five letters. Examples:

   BC-AD (4 letters; hyphen is punctuation)................ 1 word
   12345 (5 figures)........... 5 words

Fig. 23-5

Communications Manual (Concluded)

PREPARING OFFICE MANUALS

Who is to supervise the preparation of the office manual? The answer to this question will depend upon the answers to the following questions relating to the policy to be adopted in the matter of manuals. Does the firm plan to have a complete series of manuals involving a general summary of each departmental activity, and a manual of procedure for each department? Does the firm plan to have just a few manuals for the special use of the mailing department, the correspondence and transcribing department, and the records management department? Answering the last question first, it is apparent that where only departmental practice manuals are to be prepared, the work is usually initiated and supervised by the person in charge of that department. For example, the head of the correspondence or transcribing department will direct the preparation and revision of the correspondence manual.

Where a more elaborate use of manuals is planned, one person, usually an executive from the coordinating department, will assume complete charge of planning the series of manuals; of outlining the procedure to be used in their preparation; and of supervising, collecting, editing, publishing, distributing, and revising the manuals.

Steps in Preparing Office Manuals

When a complete series of manuals of policy, practices, and instructions is to be issued, the following procedure is suggested:

1. *Preparation of an outline of the subjects to be covered by the manuals.* These subjects might include the following topics:
   History of the company and its products.
   Corporate policy in dealing with others.
   Office rules affecting office hours, vacations and holidays, use of telephones, and personal calls or letters.
   Departmental practices.
   Job sheets for specific tasks not otherwise covered.
2. *Organization of a committee on manual preparation.* It is customary to include the functional departmental heads for whom manuals are to be prepared. The personnel director will be responsible for the preparation of manuals of office practices and regulations; records management, mailing, accounting, and correspondence department heads should be part of the committee if their functions are to be covered by the manuals of departmental practice.
3. *Determination of how many manuals are to be prepared and the content of each manual.* This step will be accomplished by the committee under the direction of its chairman, who may be known as the Manual Supervisor.
4. *Preparation of questionnaires necessary for the study of the flow of work within each department and of the job analysis of each position.* The questionnaires and job analyses should be carefully planned, following the principles set forth in Chapter 18. The information presented in these questionnaires is basic in manual preparation and should include organization charts and flow charts as well as job descriptions.
5. *Assembling of data called for on the questionnaires.* After the questionnaire or inquiry blank has been approved, the forms are distributed to those who should receive copies. The information on the completed questionnaires should be classified and recorded under proper headings.
6. *Study of data by the committee to determine overlapping of jobs or duplication of functions.* After the data have been

properly broken down under the desired headings, the information should be studied to determine the *status quo.*

7. *Preparation and editing of manuals.* Since the first copies of the manual are tentative, subject to revision or correction, it may be wise to have the first set of manuals mimeographed or offset printed. Subsequent revisions may be printed. Whether manuals should be in permanently bound form or in loose-leaf form depends somewhat on the use made of them.

Writing the Office Manual

In writing an office manual, it is not easy to achieve a simple, direct style, nor to reduce its preparation to a fixed set of rules. However, there are a few basic principles that should be followed in order to improve the quality of the manual and to make its use more effective. Among these principles are:

1. Use the "command" style. In other words, talk directly to the person who reads the manual—not "it is done" but "DO"; not "it must be remembered" but "REMEMBER."
2. Break up the copy into short sentences.
3. Be careful of punctuation, and underline or capitalize statements or words which are to be emphasized.
4. Build each paragraph around a single point and include: (a) statement of the point, (b) elaboration of the point, and (c) conclusion of the point.
5. Use correct spelling and grammar. Although this principle should go without saying, it needs repetition.
6. Use terminology and expressions in keeping with the vocabulary of the persons who are to use the manual.
7. Express ideas in a positive rather than a negative manner.
8. Be concise in giving procedure directions.
9. Get top management backing to approve and enforce the rules and regulations given in manuals.
10. Keep the manuals up-to-date.

If the manual is to have effective use, it should be given an interesting or stimulating title. Such titles as "Your Work at the A B C Company," or "Working with the A B C Company," or "Our Company," or "Information for Staff Members" are much more desirable than a title such as "Rules" or "Regulations." The last two titles create a slight amount of resistance and may destroy the spirit of cooperation that is being sought.

The language and style of the material presented in the manual should be interesting, not critical. The presentation should convey the idea that all employees are working together for their mutual benefit and that the purpose of the manual is to create an interest in the firm's activities so that everyone will be happier in his work.

A statement of the firm's philosophy or principles of operation should be carefully made and inserted where it will not be overlooked, such as inside the front cover, inside the back cover, or immediately after the table of contents.

Revising the Office Manual

The preparation of office manuals can become an expensive undertaking. The Administrative Management Society estimates that private industry has spent more than $250 million on handbooks and manuals to get people to communicate with each other. Unless some provision for revision is made at the outset, much of the usefulness of the manuals is wasted. The contents soon become obsolete. Workers, following the manual and finding the contents obsolete, soon discard the manual entirely.

The department that originally created the manual should be held responsible for keeping it up-to-date. Revisions should be made as often as seems practical. If the manuals are in bound form, the revision becomes more difficult and expensive; if in loose-leaf form, substitute pages can be prepared more frequently. Business is not static; therefore, unless specific provision is made for revising the manuals and for placing responsibility for their changes, most manuals can conveniently be omitted as being impractical.

Distributing the Office Manuals

The policy to be followed in distributing manuals should be determined before the manuals are prepared. Employee handbooks, of course, are distributed to all employees. Organization manuals should probably be restricted to the major executives and, in a few instances, to those with lesser responsibility if justified by their area of authority. Departmental practice manuals are distributed to those employees or departments directly affected by the work and procedures described.

No manuals should be withheld from any employees if they are in a position to benefit by the use of the manual in their work. Some firms maintain all the more important manuals in a library so that employees realize that the manuals are the property of the firm, not of the individual employee. The distribution of revised sheets or supplements should be centrally controlled and supervised so that all manuals will be kept up-to-date. Some firms periodically inspect the manuals to be sure that they are in most recent form.

USING OFFICE MANUALS

No matter how good manuals are and how much time and money have been spent in their preparation, their value is lost unless some means is found for encouraging workers to study and to use them. This is partly the job of the supervisor of the particular department in which the work is being done. One method has already been suggested; namely, periodic inspection of manuals for completeness. Another method is to audit the work of various departments periodically to rate the employees on the extent to which their work conforms to the procedures outlined in the manuals. Demerit rating of employees making serious errors because of failure to follow the manuals can also be used. Not quite so severe as this approach would be the procedure of returning to the workers their materials that do not conform to the manual requirements. Quiz contests may be used in some departments to stimulate interest in the manuals. Where a formal training program exists for new employees, it is possible to have a series of examinations to cover the material contained in the manuals.

Advantages of Using Office Manuals

The importance of using office manuals may be brought out in a discussion of their advantages and disadvantages. The need for manuals has already been indicated, but it must still be determined whether the advantages sufficiently outweigh the disadvantages to make the use of manuals practical.

One of the first advantages, and the one that must be basic in installing any business procedure, is the saving of money for the firm. The reduction of time required to explain instructions to new employees decreases costs of training. Consequently, manuals designed to provide ready instructions for a large number of employees should bring about an appreciable savings in both time and money.

A second advantage is that manuals place responsibility—a basic principle governing all successful management—which tends to reduce errors. By using the principles "avoid verbal orders" or "put it in writing," employees can read exactly what or how work is to be done, as well as by whom.

The scientific study of many departments that is usually made when a manual is being prepared is a third advantage of having such books of rules and regulations. This study should result in greater efficiency as a result of standardizing procedures; eliminating overlapping functions and needless duplication of work; creating a smoother flow of work; compelling greater cooperation within a given department and within the organization as a whole; and, finally, presenting the most effective method of instruction, which can be tested, revised, and improved from time to time.

Disadvantages of Using Office Manuals

Wherever there are advantages, there are also certain disadvantages. In the balance of executive control, the advantages and disadvantages must be weighed. If the result is positive—that is, if the advantages of having a manual make for greater profits—then it should be prepared and used. Otherwise, it is questionable whether or not the preparation and use of an office manual is a good policy.

One of the disadvantages that should be considered is the cost of preparation. To prepare a manual of even the most limited size costs money; therefore, the savings through its use must more than equal its cost.

Manuals may have a further disadvantage of so standardizing the work that individual initiative is restrained. This may or may not be true depending somewhat upon the interpretation of the nature of office manuals. Certain methods and procedures must be standardized and should not permit deviation since that would lessen the means of executive control. Even with manuals that are permanent, there should be occasion for periodic review and changes; at such times suggestions and new methods may be inserted. The largest number of office workers will usually be content to be told how the work is to be done. They will not, for the most part, be very concerned about improvements or alterations. For the small number who may want to make suggestions for changes, provision for doing so should be made available.

EVALUATING OFFICE MANUALS

The following comments contain several criteria by which the effectiveness of office manuals may be evaluated.[1]

---

[1] Adapted from an address by John F. Pierce before the Office Management Conference of the American Management Association, New York City.

The first question is, "Is the manual usable?"

No matter how authoritative a manual may be, how completely it may be indexed, how well it is bound, how convenient its size, or how attractive its appearance, it cannot be used unless it is available. This statement is not new or astounding. It is merely true and speaks for itself. No manual can be said to serve its purpose if it is not put where it can be used. I do not mean that every employee should have a personal copy. Every office should have a copy, and this copy should be kept where it may be used at the convenience of the personnel.

The second question to be answered in judging a manual is similar to the first: "Is it used?"

At first sight it may seem that there is little or no difference between the usableness of a manual and the degree of its use. But there is a difference. A manual may have all the qualities which make up the usable manual and still not be used. Take this instance as an example: Suppose you have a satisfactory manual but issue instructions from day to day through the avenue of bulletins, memorandums, and other informational releases. Which will the employee use, the manual or the bulletin which passes over his desk? He will, of course, use the latter, for some worthwhile material will not be contained in his manual. Here we have a theoretically usable manual which is unused because of the other avenues by which procedural information may be issued.

Manuals are sometimes used infrequently because the employees are not educated to use them. There are perhaps employees in your organizations who wouldn't recognize your office manual if confronted with it. To be judged as good, the office manual must be used.

"Is the manual comprehensive in scope?" This is the third standard by which all manuals can be evaluated. To be acceptable, a manual must cover all necessary subjects. The details of the office manuals depend upon the nature of the organization and the type of personnel employed. If the office manual deals with a highly routinized procedure, it is necessary that every step be listed. If information is given concerning the routing of a form, no essential detail can be omitted. If the provisions of or exceptions to a regulation are being listed, none must be passed over. Nothing is more disillusioning than the symbol, "etc." in manual material. It makes the reader wonder if the items listed are as unimportant as the anonymous group which are left to conjecture. And yet there is a danger in comprehensiveness, and that is confusing completeness. Too much detail is a fault. It must be kept in mind that the manual must be usable, and that if too broad in its scope, that purpose is defeated. Vitally connected with completeness is clarity. Manual material must be clear. It must be couched in a style that requires no explanation beyond the statement of fact. Words by Milton and phrases by Johnson are taboo in the office manual. The simple phraseology is the clearest.

Although I list this next standard of judgment fourth, it's probably the one you would think of first: "Is the method of producing the manual economical?" It goes without saying that the cost of the manual should not overweigh its advantages.

The fifth and last criterion for judging the office manual is the method by which it may be changed to meet changing procedures. The question is this: "Can the manual be revised easily?" No manual should be issued as purely temporary or permanent. The manual cannot be static, and it is economically unwise to issue one of a temporary nature. Instead, the manual must be planned for the future. It must be so outlined as to care for future problems and so designed that revisions may be made with a minimum of effort and expense. It must be flexible enough to meet the needs of changing procedures, yet with enough internal strength to keep it from becoming a catchall.

QUESTIONS FOR REVIEW

1. The use of office manuals benefits not only the employer but also the employee. Explain how this is possible.
2. What is a policy? What kinds of policies are in a policy manual?
3. Organization manuals are primarily prepared for the benefit of management. Why?
4. Since organization manuals are primarily designed for the benefit of management, the care in their preparation and the need for revision are affected accordingly. Explain this statement.
5. What material should be contained in an administrative practice manual?
6. What activities are typically covered by a communications manual?
7. Because of the constant changes in interoffice and external communication methods, a communications manual requires frequent revision and updating. How do you feel this matter should be handled?
8. What preliminary considerations must be determined before establishing a program of office manuals?
9. One of the frequently overlooked managerial considerations in an office manuals program is the determination of policy for revising the manuals. What factors must be considered in agreeing upon a revision policy for office manuals?
10. The objective of certain office manuals is "uniformity of office procedures." What manuals usually serve this purpose? Why is such uniformity desirable?

QUESTIONS FOR DISCUSSION

1. In a canvass of 337 business firms, a management consulting organization found that the large companies have written policies covering 50 percent of their operations. It was observed that the smaller the company, the lower the percentage of coverage of policies in written form. Smaller organizations often feel that a policy manual costs too much and claim that it is easier and less expensive to write letters and memorandums.

Discuss the advantages that large companies realize as the result of having their policies in written form. Is it easier and less expensive for small firms to write letters and directives than to develop their policies in written form?

2. The Ayers Insurance Company employs 1,500 office workers in its main office building. As a consultant on management problems, you are asked to list *in order of importance* the names and the contents of the manuals that should be prepared for proper control of the office work. Since these manuals are to be listed in their order of importance, the last one would be eliminated first should it become necessary to reduce the number of manuals to be used. Discuss your idea of the types of manuals that should appear on this list.

PRACTICAL OFFICE CASE

Case 23-1 Preparing a Correspondence Manual

The Dietz Furniture Company has a large central office located on four floors of an office building in Detroit, Michigan. In addition, the company maintains 15 sales offices throughout the United States. In each of these sales offices there are five executives or sales representatives who have a considerable amount of correspondence to handle. To achieve a high-quality uniformity in letter writing, you, as office manager of the firm, have proposed the preparation and use of a correspondence manual.

■ Prepare a formal report to the president of the company, Jacques Dietz, in which you present the suggested contents of a correspondence manual that will standardize the outgoing correspondence. In your report you will want to cover such topics as:

1. Who is to use the manual.
2. Purposes for which the manual is to be used.
3. Minimum content to be included to insure its efficient use.
4. Periodic review and updating of the manual.
5. Cost of preparing the manual.
6. Reproducing and binding the manual.

24

Punched-Card and Integrated Data Processing Systems

A system was defined earlier as the framework of the personnel, forms, records, machines, and equipment involved in completing a major phase of office work. In the systems and procedures described up to this point, the work has been accomplished by manual means, supplemented by the use of mechanical equipment such as the accounting board, adding and calculating machines, numeric and alphanumeric accounting machines, and posting machines. Data processing systems, which are accounting systems of one form or another, are essential parts of any management information system. (Management information systems are discussed in Chapter 25.)

The end product, or the output, of any system is information—valid, reliable data that are supplied to management for timely use in decision making. Because of the dynamic nature of business operations today and management's constant need for fast, accurate processing of data, automated systems of information handling have become a major part of the total office concept. An automated system of data processing has been defined as "a process, largely self-regulating, in which information is handled with a minimum of human effort and intervention."[1] There are two types of automated systems used

[1] S. J. Wanous, E. E. Wanous, and A. E. Hughes, *Introduction to Automated Data Processing,* (Cincinnati: South-Western Publishing Co., 1968), p. 1.

in the processing of data. One is the punched-card system, which is discussed in this chapter, and the other is the electronic data processing system, which is discussed in the next chapter.

NATURE OF THE PUNCHED-CARD SYSTEM

In processing data by the punched-card system, numeric and alphabetic data and special symbols are converted into a code language that can be understood by all the machines and equipment used in the system. At the heart of the system is the punched card, the layout of which calls for a great deal of skill. If the system is properly planned and installed, it can prove extremely valuable and can supply accurate records and in more detail than the manual and other mechanical systems described in earlier chapters.

The three steps that make up the punched-card system of processing data are concerned with: (1) input, (2) processing, and (3) output.

Input

Input consists of data that are recorded manually or typewritten on source documents such as invoices, purchase orders, time cards, checks, and stock control records. As the first step in the punched-card system, the data on a source document are recorded in punched cards, the *input media.* Because a punched card is usually prepared to record information about each unit or item appearing on the source document, the term *unit record system* is used synonymously with punched-card system.

Punched Cards. A standard punched card has 80 columns in which to record data. In the past an 80-column card was used with IBM systems and a 90-column card with the Univac systems. Since Univac no longer makes the 90-column-card equipment, both systems now use standard 80-column cards which are identical in makeup and appearance. In addition, IBM has designed a 96-column card for use with its small, low-cost System/3 computer. This card, about one-third the size of a standard card, uses round holes to represent the data and holds 20 percent more information than the conventional 80-column card.

The equipment described in the remainder of this section is designed for use with the standard IBM 80-column punched card. Figure 24-1 shows how digits, letters, and special characters are recorded on a standard punched card. Each of the digits 0 through 9 is represented by one punch in the corresponding row. Only one punch is used in each column to indicate a digit. Thus, a two-digit number requires a punch in each of two columns; a three-digit number requires a punch in each of three columns; etc. When recording alphabetic data in punched cards, two additional rows known as the 12 punch position and the 11 punch position are required. For each letter of the alphabet, two punches are made in each column. Thus, as shown in Figure 24-1, the letter *A* is recorded by a punch in the 12 position and a punch in the 1 row. The letter *J* is recorded by a punch in the 11 position and a punch in the 1 row. Special characters are recorded by one punch or a combination of two or three punches in each column.

Fig. 24-1

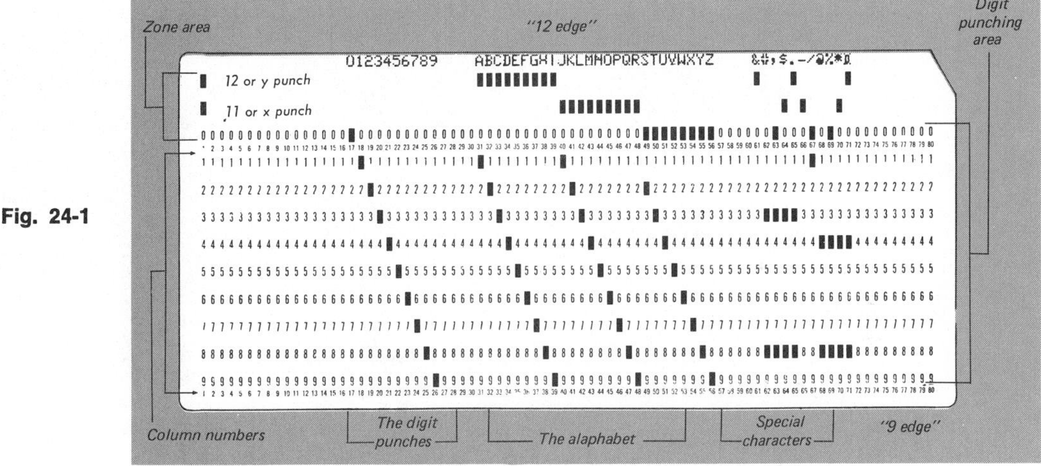

Digits, Letters, and Special Characters Recorded on a Standard IBM Punched Card

To conserve space on the punched card, alphabetic data are often abbreviated, and marks of punctuation may be omitted. For example, the name Williams Company, Incorporated, may be abbreviated and punched as Williams Co Inc. The names of the months are coded from 01 through 12; thus, a date such as December 15, 1972, is punched as 121572.

The nature of the final reports to be completed or the forms to be filled in determines the amounts and kinds of data to be punched into cards. The cards must be properly planned to accommodate all the data to be recorded and to make sure that on all cards the data will be recorded in the same location. The 80 available columns on a card are laid out in *fields,* with each field being assigned a sufficient number of columns for recording the greatest number of digits or letters to be accommodated in that field. In the punched card shown in Figure 24-2, columns 18 through 23 are set aside as the Date field. The recording of a date, after it has been coded, will not require more than six columns. The invoice number 9893 is recorded as 09893 in columns 24 through 28, the Invoice No. field. Since successive invoice numbers will shortly require five columns for their recording, the need for an extra column has been anticipated in laying out the field. In a similar fashion, a business must anticipate the greatest number of digits or letters to be accommodated in each of the various fields such as Stock Number, Unit Price, and Amount.

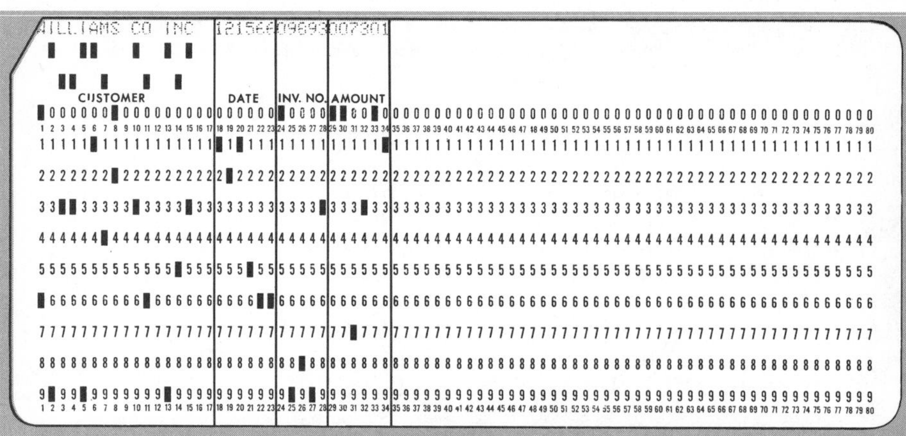

Fig. 24-2

Sales Data Recorded on a Standard IBM Punched Card

In addition to serving as the input media for data to be processed, punched cards may be used for recording programs—the instructions for machine operations and the processing of the data. The following list indicates some of the operations that may be punched into cards:

1. Add itself to, subtract itself from, multiply itself by, or divide itself into another amount.
2. List, reproduce, classify, select itself.
3. Print itself on another punched card.
4. Produce an automatic balance forward.
5. File or post itself.

6. Reproduce and print itself on the edge of the card.
7. Punch from a pencil mark on the card.
8. Print a total.
9. Compare itself with something else.
10. Cause a form to feed to a predetermined position, or to eject automatically, or to space from one position to another.

Marginal Punched Cards. In addition to the punched cards described above, there are several marginal punched cards on the market; one of those commonly used is the Keysort card. *Keysorting* is a patented mechanical and manually operated system for sorting data recorded on specially designed and coded cards. After the data are recorded on a Keysort card, the card is punched, or notched, along the four edges so that it may be accurately sorted into any required order. It is ideal for analytical work applied to sales, orders, payrolls, costs, inventories, vouchers, and checks.

In punching the card to designate a number, a group of four holes is required for each digit in the numeric code. If the numeric code uses a units digit only, a group of four holes is required. The holes have the numeric values of 7, 4, 2, and 1. By using the holes in each group of four singly or in combination, it is possible to designate all numbers from 0 to 9. Note in Figure 24-3 how the Job or Acct. No. 4209 has been punched along the top edge of the card.

Sorting of cards is accomplished by using a long, specially designed "needle." This needle is passed through the holes in the stack

Fig. 24-3

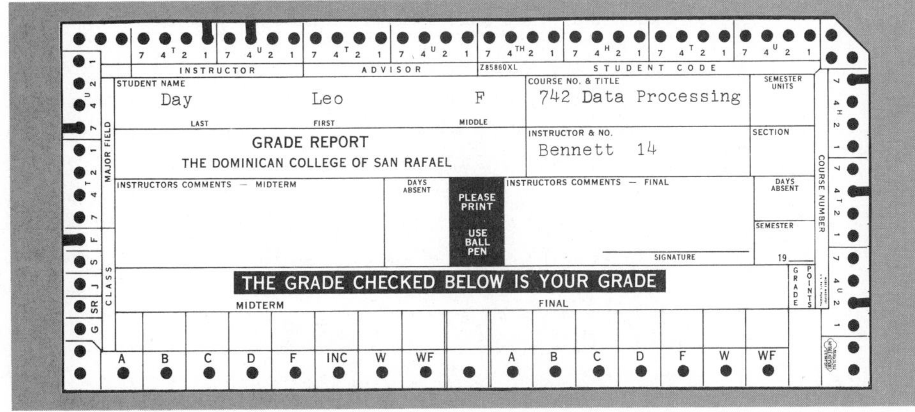
INSTRUCTOR | ADVISOR | Z85860XL | STUDENT CODE
STUDENT NAME
Day Leo F
LAST FIRST MIDDLE
COURSE NO. & TITLE
742 Data Processing
SEMESTER UNITS
GRADE REPORT
THE DOMINICAN COLLEGE OF SAN RAFAEL
INSTRUCTOR & NO.
Bennett 14
SECTION
MAJOR FIELD
INSTRUCTORS COMMENTS — MIDTERM
DAYS ABSENT
PLEASE PRINT
USE BALL PEN
INSTRUCTORS COMMENTS — FINAL
DAYS ABSENT
SEMESTER
SIGNATURE
19
COURSE NUMBER
CLASS
THE GRADE CHECKED BELOW IS YOUR GRADE
MIDTERM
FINAL
GRADE POINTS
A B C D F INC W WF
A B C D F W WF

Automated Business Systems, Division of Litton Industries

Data Recorded on Keysort Card

of cards designated by the code of the classifications or sorts desired. When the needle is raised, the cards in the classification sought fall from the stack of cards being sorted since the edges of the holes representing the classification sought have been notched out. An instant check of accuracy of the cards sorted is always available, since a missorted card shows up as a break in the line of notches.

Mark-Sensed Cards. *Mark-sensed cards* are specially designed cards used for recording information with an "electrographic" (graphite) pencil. The cards, although containing only 27 vertical marking columns, are very similar to the 80-column punched cards since the digit positions are the same on both types of cards. When a mark is made to record data on a card, the mark representing each digit of the amount covers three regular card columns. These cards are processed on equipment that senses and converts the graphite marks into punches.

Meter readers commonly use mark-sensed cards to record readings as they go from meter to meter. When the cards are returned to the offices of the utility, the same cards, or new ones, are punched automatically. The mark sensing of data is usually limited to the recording of numeric data containing few digits. Although alphabetic information can be recorded on the cards, a user such as a meter reader would have to carry with him the alphabetic code in order to mark such information on the cards. Alphabetic information recorded on mark-sensed cards is usually confined to items containing but a few letters of the alphabet, as shown in Figure 24-4.

Fig. 24-4

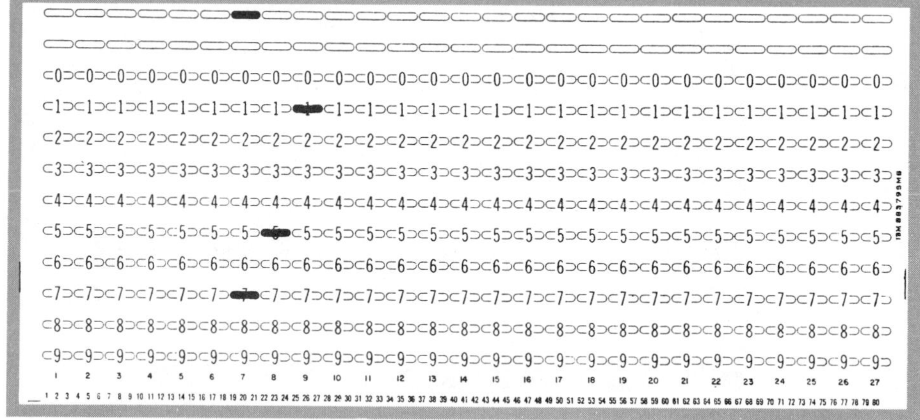

Mark-Sensed Card Showing the Recording of the Stock Number G51

The Key Punch. Data are recorded on punched cards by means of a *card-punch machine,* commonly called a *key punch.* The key-punch operator reads the data from a source document and presses the keys of the keyboard to punch the cards. (See Figure 24-5.) Two types of keyboards are used—one that records numeric data only, and one that records both numeric and alphabetic data. Blank cards are placed in the hopper and after the first two cards have been punched, automatic feeding of the remaining cards is achieved. When a key is depressed, the card moves automatically to the next column. The printing card punch automatically "reads" or "interprets" the punched information and prints it on the card.

On key-punch equipment having an electronic buffer, data are keyed directly into a storage area prior to being punched into a card. While one card is being punched, the next card is keyed into the buffer. In this way errors can be corrected before the characters are punched into cards; the operator simply backspaces and retypes a character, a field, a word, or an entire record to make a correction.

Small manually operated key punches are available for use in recording data at the point of origin as in the warehouse or in the plant. Most of these portable key punches record numeric data only and do not print as they punch.

Fig. 24-5

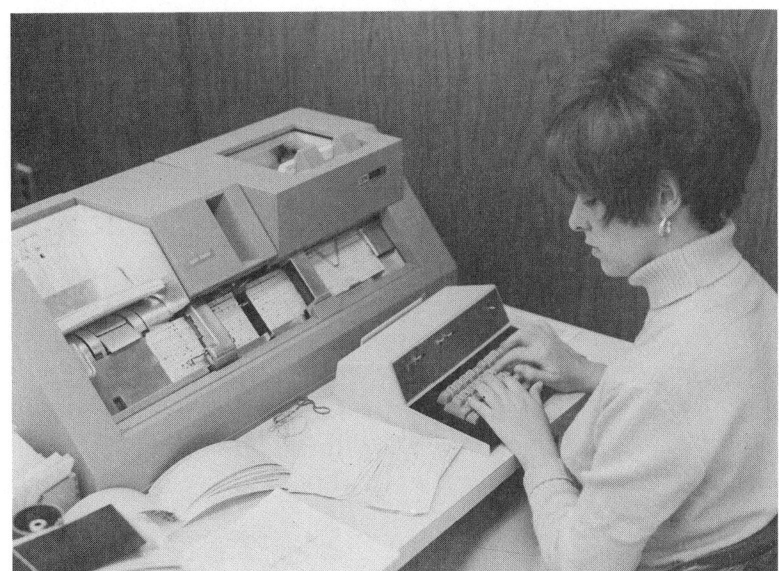

Orange and Rockland Utilities, Inc.

Using a Key Punch to Record Data from Source Documents

Fig. 24-6

Verifier

The Verifier. Since the use of punched cards usually involves a large volume of data to be processed, it is necessary to be sure that the data have been punched accurately. Therefore, a second operator checks the work of the key-punch operator by performing a similar operation on a *verifier,* shown in Figure 24-6. On the previously punched cards the verifier operator simulates the original keypunching, using the source documents. If the code for the depressed key agrees with the code punched into the card, the machine releases to the next column. If a disagreement occurs, the machine locks. In this event, the operator repeats the operation to be absolutely certain an error really exists. If an error exists, it is indicated by a mark in the appropriate column. A correct card is indicated by a notch punched into the edge of the card. On the buffered key punch described earlier, the verifying and punching can be combined in one unit. Also, the duplication of amounts and information and the skipping from column to column are done at electronic rather than mechanical speeds.

Punched cards may also be verified by reading the data printed at the top of the card during the punching operations and comparing the printed data with those appearing on the source document. The data may also be printed from the cards and then proofread.

Processing

After the punching has been completed, the cards are usually in miscellaneous order. The next step in the punched-card system is to arrange the cards in sequence by some desired classification—that is, to group them according to the information punched in them.

The Sorter. The *sorter* is used to arrange the punched cards according to a desired sequence. (See Figure 24-7.) The operation of the sorter is based on the position of the punched hole in a vertical column of the card. As the cards pass through the machine, a brush contact is made through the hole, causing an electrical circuit to close. This momentary circuit causes the card to be directed to a receiving pocket that corresponds to the position of the punched hole. For example, a card punched "9" in the column on which the sort is being made is directed to the 9 pocket; a card punched "6" in the same column is directed to the 6 pocket; and so on.

Automatic sorting is made on one column at a time. Therefore, to arrange a group of cards in numeric sequence according to the data punched in a three-column field, the deck of cards is passed through the sorter three times. The sort is made first on the units column, then on the tens column, and finally on the hundreds column.

International Business Machines Corporation

Fig. 24-7

Sorter

International Business Machines Corporation

Fig. 24-8

Tabulator

Output

As the last step in the punched-card system, the processed data, known as the *output,* are printed out on business forms and reports. Business forms and reports such as checks, invoices, sales analyses, stock control records, and punched cards, upon which the output appear are known as *output media.*

The Tabulator. The automatic compilation of punched data into printed reports and forms is accomplished by the *tabulator* (Figure 24-8), also known as the *accounting machine.* (Because the punched-card system is characterized by the use of tabulating or accounting machines, it is sometimes known as the *tabulating system* or the *electric accounting machine* [*EAM*] *system.)* The tabulator reads only one input medium—the punched card. It operates through the use of a control panel which is wired for each job. The tabulator is made up of three units: the reading unit, the calculating unit, and the printing unit.

The Reading Unit. As the punched cards pass through the machine, this unit senses the holes in the cards and transmits this information to the calculating and printing units in the form of electrical impulses.

The Calculating Unit. The various addition and subtraction counters in this unit are actuated by the information received from the reading unit. This unit is capable of accumulating and totaling in one operation the numeric data punched into cards.

The Printing Unit. This unit prints the summarized data resulting from the calculations on forms such as a withholding tax statement (W-2), employee's earnings paycheck, sales invoice, expense distribution sheet, or almost any other report or record requiring printed and numeric data. The tabulator positions continuous paper forms automatically to the line where the data are to be printed. It can also punch summarized data into cards when it is connected with another machine capable of *summary punching.*

Peripheral Equipment

To provide more flexibility in processing data by the punched-card system, peripheral equipment is available to perform the following operations: (1) print information on a punched card; (2) duplicate or reproduce the data in punched cards, (3) collate the cards when more than one type of card is used for a data processing operation, and (4) perform calculating operations.

The Interpreter. Whenever a manual check must be made of the data punched into a card or if the card is used as a business form, an interpreter is used to print information on the punched card. The machine translates the punched holes and then prints this information on the card, usually at the top edge.

The Reproducing Punch. A *reproducing punch* is used to punch automatically the data from one deck of cards into another deck of cards. For example, the reproducing punch is used in extracting constant data from a deck of prepunched master cards for use in a subsequent accounting period; as in the preparation of weekly earnings cards from a deck of employee master cards; or subscription renewal cards for magazine publishers; or billing cards for public utility companies. Firms using the reproducing punch for billing operations often send out a punched-card bill with a 22-column stub. When the customer remits his payment, he also returns the stub, which is used to reproduce automatically an 80-column card for mechanized cash accounting.

In other forms of duplication mark-sensed cards may be reproduced into punched cards, several detail cards may be punched from one master card (*gang punching*), or prepunched sales tickets may be fed through a specially designed machine and converted to standard punched cards for processing.

The Collator. Sometimes the data required for a printing operation must be obtained from two or more punched cards. For example, in preparing W-2 forms, the name and address may appear on one card, followed by other cards showing the social security account number, the gross earnings, and the taxes withheld. To use the punched-card machines most effectively, each series of cards must be arranged in the same sequential order. This arrangement can be accomplished by feeding the cards through a *collator,* which is similar to a four-pocket sorter. The collator performs four functions—merges the cards, matches the series of cards, checks the sequence, and makes special selections where desired.

The Calculating Punch. Mathematical calculations are performed by means of a *calculating punch.* The difference between a calculating punch and a tabulator is that the calculating punch can perform all mathematical operations whereas the tabulator can perform addition and subtraction only. This punch makes calculations from two or more punched cards and punches the result in one of the cards or on a following summary card. Sometimes a series of two machines known as an *electronic calculating punch* is used. Here, one machine does the calculating, and the other, the card punching.

Summary of the Steps in the Punched-Card System

Figure 24-9 shows in diagrammatic form the steps involved in a basic punched-card system. These steps are summarized as follows:

Input:

1. Source data are converted into punched-card form. Card punches range from simple portable units to the printing card punch, which prints information on the cards as it punches.
2. A reproducing punch, like an automatic copier, automatically transfers data from a set of source cards into another set. The two sets of cards are fed through the reproducing punch at the same time.
3. A sorter is used to group cards in sequence within desired classifications prior to use on other data processing machines.

Processing:

4. A collator is used to merge or combine newly punched cards with an existing file of cards into one file of a given sequence.
5. Arithmetic operations (multiplication, division, addition, and subtraction) are performed on the calculator. Cards produced by the calculating punch can be fed into the tabulator to obtain final printed reports.

Output:

6. The tabulator, or accounting machine, sums up automatically the data recorded on cards and prints various reports.

A PUNCHED-CARD SYSTEM—PAYROLL ACCOUNTING

In a punched-card payroll accounting system, all data required to prepare payroll records and reports are entered on punched cards. The cards are used to compute automatically all required amounts and to print all records and reports at high speed with any desired combinations of totals and balances. In a typical punched-card

Fig. 24-9

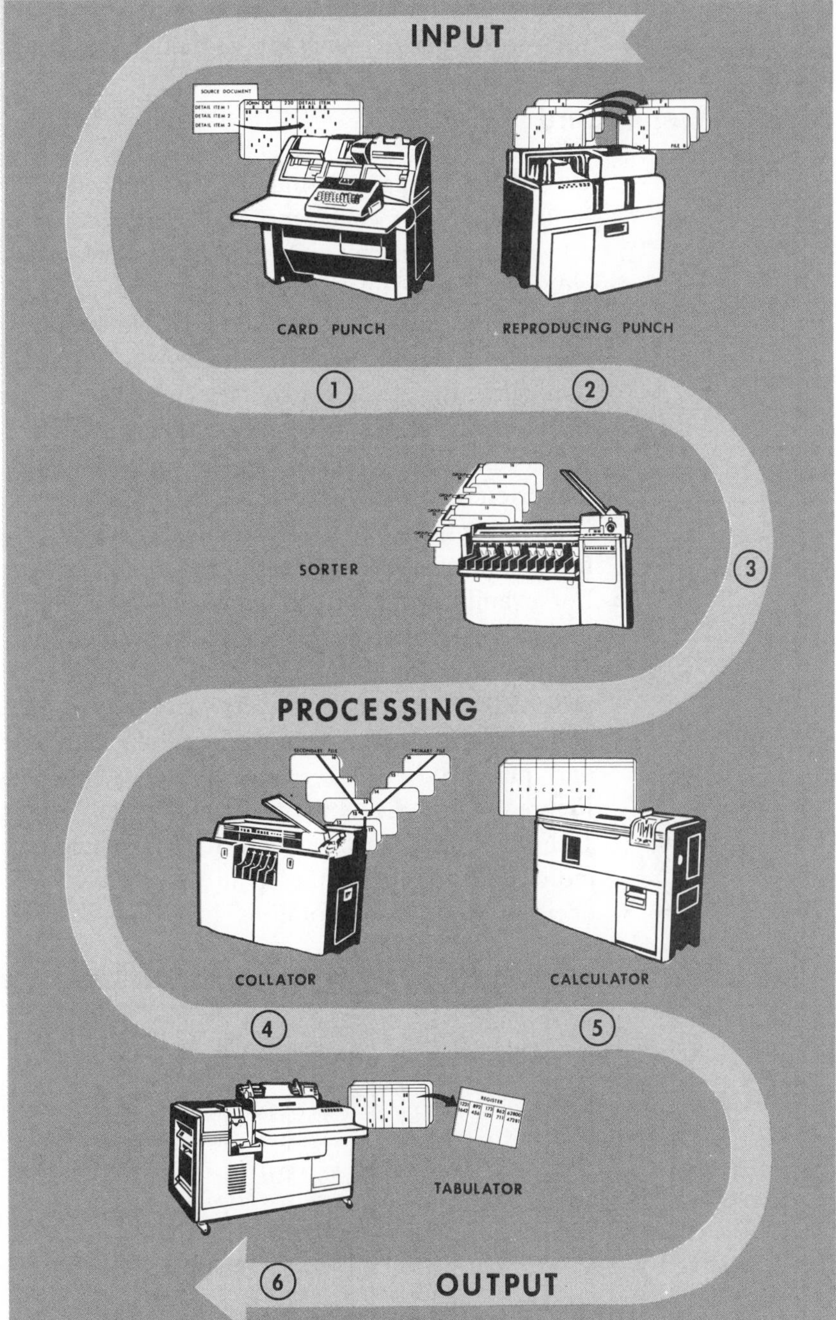

Basic Steps in the Punched-Card System

payroll accounting system, the punched cards commonly used are the payroll master card, the deduction card, and the time card.

Payroll Master Card

In converting information to punched-card form, the first step is to prepare for each employee a *payroll master card* that contains all constant payroll information—name, social security number, clock or badge number, and hourly rate or salary. Data for preparing the master card may be obtained from personnel records such as a notification of employment form. Additional information, such as date of birth, date employed, and marital status, which may be of interest to the personnel department, may be included.

Ordinarily, to speed up the payroll accounting procedure, a numeric code is assigned to all information punched into the master card, except the employee's name, which is retained in its alphabetic form, and of course, all data that originally exist in numeric terms. For example, rather than punching Tool Designer as the job occupation for which the employee was hired, this occupation may be assigned a code number such as 25, and that number would be punched into the card. However, the date of employment, such as November 16, 1963, would be retained in its original numeric form and punched as 111663. In the payroll master card shown in Figure 24-10, the employee's name has been punched in columns 1 through 12. However, since some employee's names will require more columns than these, in the initial planning stages it was decided to set aside columns 1 through 24 for recording employee

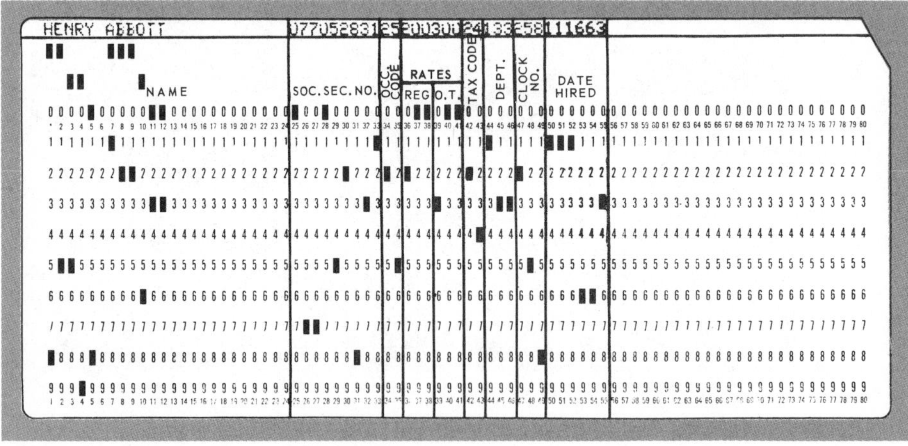

Fig. 24-10

Payroll Master Card

names. At the time of punching this name into the card, the key punch also printed or "interpreted" the name in the columnar heading at the top of the card. Other information recorded in the card and the fields occupied by these data are as follows:

Columns	*Description of Data*	*Data Recorded*
25 - 33	Social security number	077 05 2831
34 and 35	Occupation code number	25
36 - 41	Hourly rates	
	Regular	2.00
	Overtime	3.00
42 and 43	Tax code (the first number indicates marital status; the second, the number of exemptions)	24
44 - 46	Employee department number	133
47 - 49	Employee clock number	258
50 - 55	Date hired	November 16, 1963

Deduction Card

After the master card has been prepared, the next step is to create a *deduction card* for each employee to cover those payroll deductions requested by the employee. The employee usually signs an authorization form covering deductions to be made from earnings for such items as savings bonds, hospitalization insurance, charitable donations, lunch tickets, and union dues. In the payroll deduction card shown in Figure 24-11, the employee has authorized the monthly

Fig. 24-11

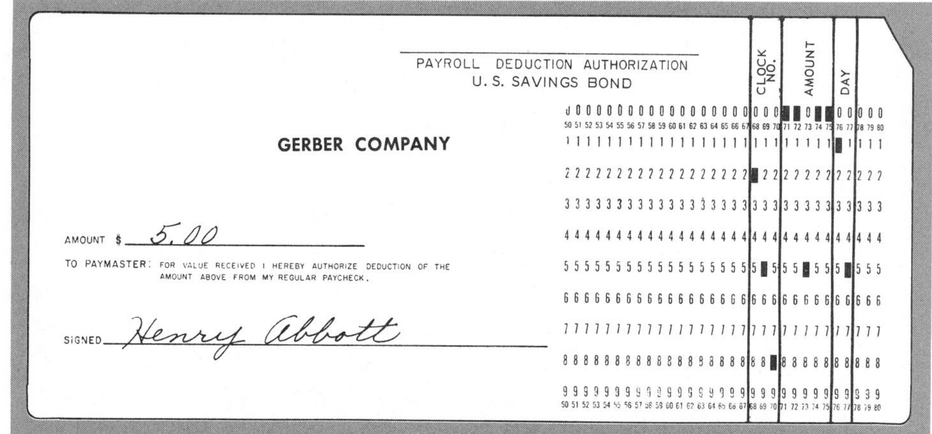

PAYROLL DEDUCTION AUTHORIZATION
U. S. SAVINGS BOND

CLOCK NO. | AMOUNT | DAY

GERBER COMPANY

AMOUNT $ 5.00

TO PAYMASTER: FOR VALUE RECEIVED I HEREBY AUTHORIZE DEDUCTION OF THE AMOUNT ABOVE FROM MY REGULAR PAYCHECK.

SIGNED Henry Abbott

Payroll Deduction Card

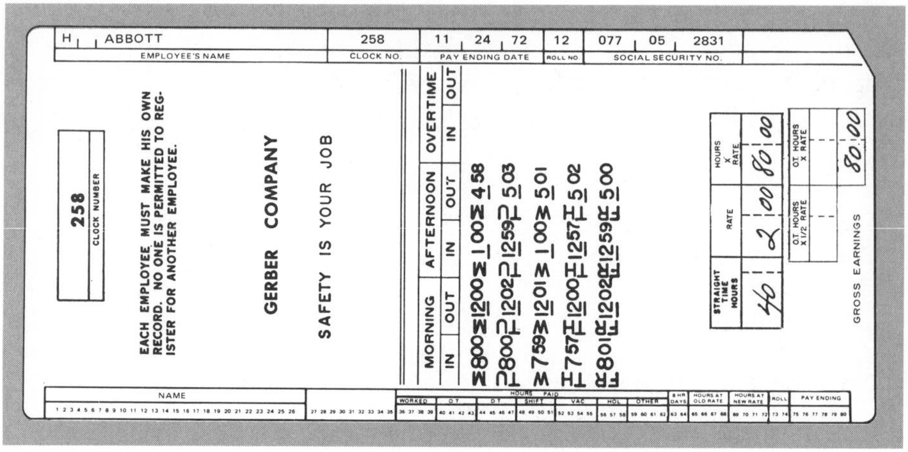

H. ABBOTT	258	11 24 72	12	077 05 2831
EMPLOYEE'S NAME	CLOCK NO.	PAY ENDING DATE	ROLL NO.	SOCIAL SECURITY NO.

258 CLOCK NUMBER

EACH EMPLOYEE MUST MAKE HIS OWN RECORD. NO ONE IS PERMITTED TO REGISTER FOR ANOTHER EMPLOYEE.

GERBER COMPANY

SAFETY IS YOUR JOB

MORNING IN OUT | AFTERNOON IN OUT | OVERTIME IN OUT

STRAIGHT TIME HOURS	RATE	HOURS X RATE
40	2.00	80.00

GROSS EARNINGS 80.00

Fig. 24-12

Weekly Attendance Time Card

deduction of $5 from his paycheck to cover the purchase of U.S. savings bonds. Such deduction cards, based upon authorization forms completed by the employee, can be predetermined by the payroll department and kept in the master file for reuse at each pay period.

Time Card

Under any payroll system, the basis for all payroll computations is the time and attendance record. In some systems, time and attendance records may be kept manually. In many payroll systems, however, mechanical equipment is used to record time on the job. Figure 24-12 shows but one type of weekly attendance card of the many kinds commonly used with a punched-card payroll accounting system. (Two other types of time cards are illustrated in Figure 17-4, page 542.) Attendance time is the basis upon which the employee's pay is figured, except when piecework or incentive plans are used. When an incentive or piecework plan is used, the employee's pay is calculated on the basis of units produced.

The time card may be either a "daily" time card or a "pay period" card, such as that shown in Figure 24-12. At the end of the pay period, the attendance time is figured and multiplied by the hourly rate to determine gross earnings. The extension of hours times rate may be accomplished on desk calculators or on other automatic equipment that is a part of the punched-card system. These data are then punched into a *gross earnings* card, similar to that shown in Figure 24-13.

Fig. 24-13

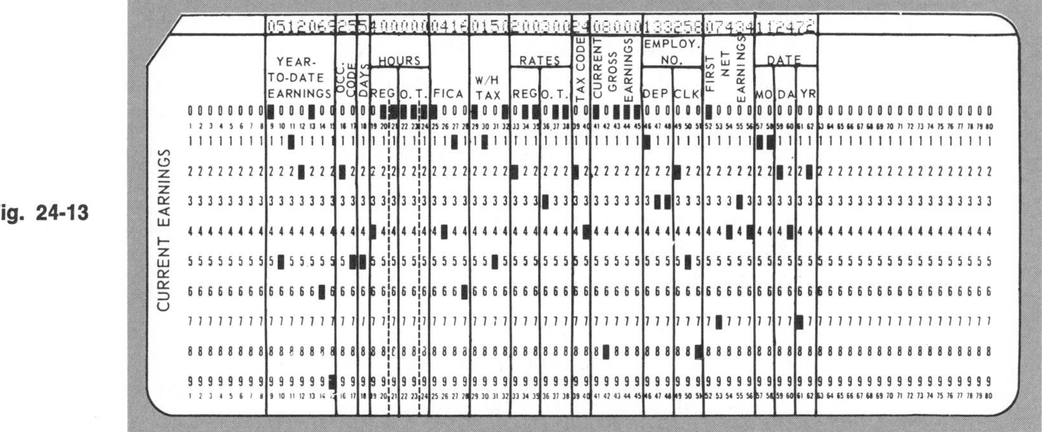

Gross Earnings Card

Output

The master card, the deduction cards, and the gross earnings card are then merged to prepare automatically the *payroll register.* As shown in Figure 24-14, the payroll register lists for each employee his social security number, clock number, hours worked, earnings, deductions, and net pay.

The file of punched cards may then be used to prepare automatically the payroll checks. If payments are made in cash, the data recorded on the payroll envelopes may be obtained from the payroll register. Statements of gross earnings, net earnings, and deductions may also be tabulated at this time. For example, usually a separate register is compiled for each type of deduction. Thus, the preparation

Fig. 24-14

SHEET 1 OF 6

GERBER COMPANY

PAYROLL REGISTER

DATE Nov. 24, 1972

NAME / DESCRIPTION	EMPL. NO.		TAX CODE	DAYS	BASE RATE	HOURS		CURRENT GROSS EARNINGS	DEDUCTIONS			CURRENT NET PAY	YEAR TO DATE		
	DEPT.	CLOCK				REGULAR	OVERTIME		F.I.C.A.	WITH. TAX	OTHER		EARNINGS	F.I.C.A.	WITH. TAX
HENRY ABBOTT	133	258	24		2 00										
SAVINGS BOND											5 00				
				5		40 0		80 00	4 16	1 50	5 00	69 34	5 120 68	266 28	273 60
MILTON ADMAN	131	100	23		2 80										
SAVINGS											7 50				
				5		40 0	2 0	120 40	6 26	10 30	7 50	96 34	5 280 70	274 60	330 10
GERALD ALTON	131	145	24		2 15										
SAVINGS											5 50				
SAVINGS BOND											5 00				
				5		40 0	2 0	92 46	4 81	3 20	10 50	73 95	5 903 12	306 96	393 60

Payroll Register Automatically Prepared from Punched Cards

of a register showing total withholding taxes becomes invaluable for reference purposes and for a basis of remitting to the appropriate government agency money deducted from employees' wages.

The punched-card payroll accounting system described above is depicted in chart form in Figure 24-15. In this system it is possible to prepare automatically these records and reports, which play an essential role in effective control of payroll accounting procedures:

1. Payroll register.
2. Deductions registers.
3. Payroll checks or envelopes.
4. Employees' pay statements.
5. Social security statement.
6. State and federal income tax reports.
7. State unemployment compensation wage reports.
8. Employee's earnings records.
9. State workmen's compensation reports.

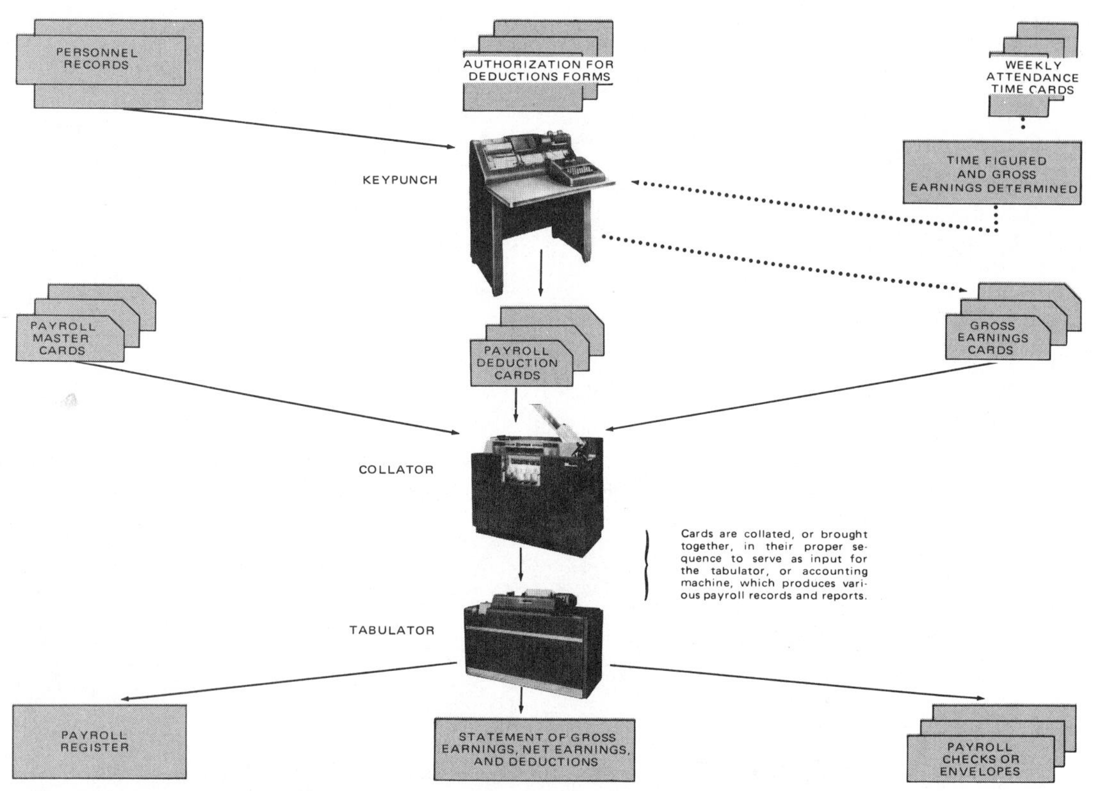

Fig. 24-15

A Punched-Card Payroll Accounting System

Additional reports more related to managerial control than to the accumulation of accounting data may be obtained. For example, from the information punched into the payroll master card, deductions cards, and gross earnings cards, management is able to obtain such data as the average hourly earnings per employee, average number of hours worked, labor turnover, departments in which turnover is excessive, number of employees contributing to charitable organizations, and amount of absenteeism.

INTEGRATED DATA PROCESSING (IDP)

Integrated data processing (IDP) is a comprehensive system of *originally* recording business information in a machine language and subsequently reproducing it for all purposes by means of compatible machines and equipment. The small company may achieve the economies of IDP by using punched paper tape and writing the data once, whereas larger firms may expand the system to include the use of punched cards and more sophisticated input media, as described in the following chapter.

The success of any data processing system depends on the amount and the quality of the *planning* that has preceded the installation. In planning the installation of an IDP system, a firm should study each of the office systems, such as the accounts payable system (purchasing), the accounts receivable system (sales), and the payroll system. The objective of the study is to determine whether it is economically feasible to apply data processing equipment to the existing company operations. For example, a study might first be made of the procedure for processing a customer's order. This study would follow the steps in a feasibility study (see Chapter 2) and would entail work simplification techniques and the construction of flow process charts such as those described in Chapter 15. The flow process chart can be used to determine what steps can be eliminated or combined; what sequence can be changed; and what work can be simplified. The analysis of each present system should result in the preparation of a flow chart of a proposed system that would reduce costs by simplifying the work and eliminating all duplications and other faults of the present system. A conference should be arranged with forms manufacturers and office equipment specialists to determine what equipment is available to meet the needs of the revised system. The advice of forms specialists is very important since the common-language information must be reproduced in the same manner and in the same location on each form.

Common-Language Tape

Integrated data processing *mechanizes* the writing of repetitive information by means of a *common-language tape*. This punched paper tape works on the same coding principle as that used in the music rolls on a player piano. Paper tape has been used for years in teletypewriters, which transmit written conversations just as the telephone transmits vocal conversations. Standard teletypewriter equipment, in conjunction with tape-punching and tape-reading equipment, can produce punched paper tape as a by-product of the typing operation. The data punched in tapes can be automatically transmitted to other teletypewriters that will print out the information or punch tapes identical to the one transmitted, or select and print out certain data from the tape transmitted. (The use of the teletypewriter as a means of office communications was discussed in Chapter 7.)

Since repetitive data are processed on several different types of office machines, such as typewriters, adding-listing machines, addressing machines, and electronic equipment, each machine must be "programmed" or controlled so that all units "read" the same code in the punched-hole positions. Although 5-, 6-, 7-, and 8-channel tapes are available (see Figure 24-16), the 5-channel (or 5-level) code is primarily used in various telegraph systems. With a 5-level code, shown in Figure 24-17, 32 combinations are mathematically possible. By means of a shift mechanism on the teleprinter keyboard, the number of combinations is extended to 62. Of these, 26 are assigned to the letters of the alphabet, with the rest to numerals, punctuation marks, and machine control functions.

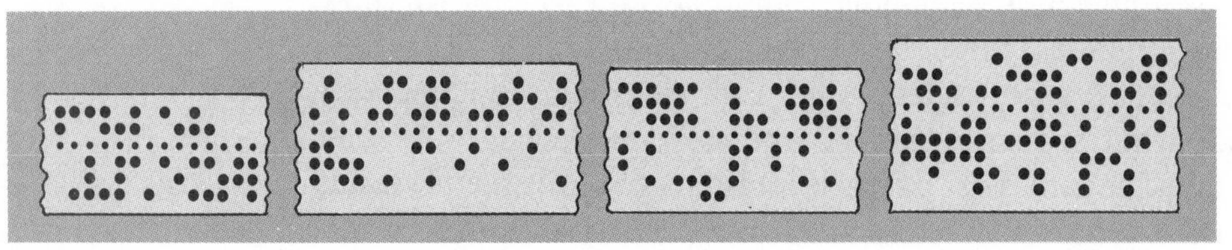

Fig. 24-16

Friden, Inc.

Common-Language Tapes

Handling computer input-output situations and moving huge quantities of data quickly, as discussed in the following chapter, require a code more flexible than the 5-level code. Thus, most Teletype data terminals now operate on an 8-level code. The first seven

Fig. 24-17

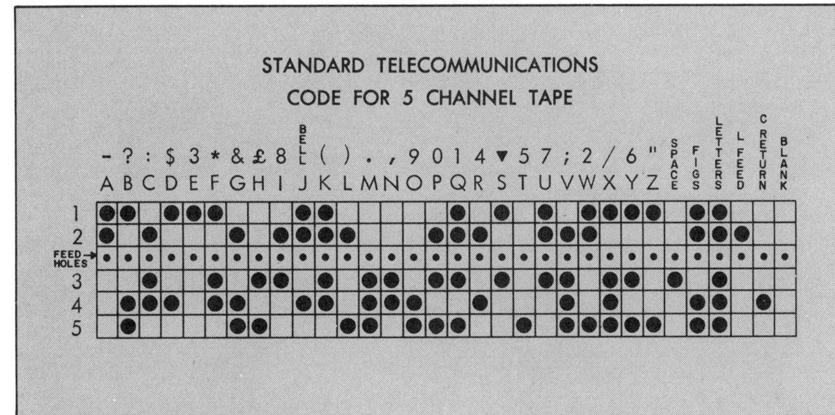

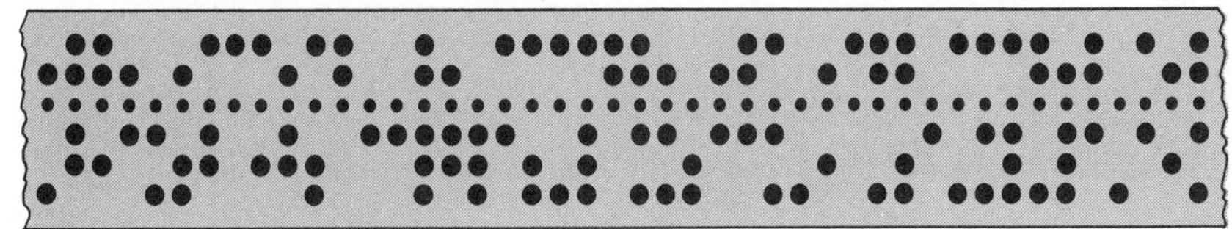

5-Channel Tape and Its Coding Arrangement

levels of this code offer the mathematical possibility of 128 combinations, with the eighth level being used for error detection.

Common-Language Machines

The punching or reading of paper tape can be adapted to many kinds of business machines, several of which are described below.

1. *Tape-punching typewriter.* Types business documents and simultaneously prepares a common-language tape of all or some of the typed data. (See Figure 24-18.)
2. *Card-punching typewriter.* Similar to the tape-punching typewriter, but prepares edge-punched cards of all or selected data, using the common-language code. (See Figure 24-19.)
3. *Card-reading and tape-reading equipment.* Automatically types data from punched cards and tapes, producing documents and tapes, or punched cards. (See Figure 24-18.)
4. *Sending and receiving equipment.* Using teletypewriter arrangements, input from punched tapes, cards, or typewriters reproduces simultaneously tapes, cards, or business forms at different locations. (See Figure 7-7 on page 189 and the accompanying discussion.)

Fig. 24-18

Dura, Division Intercontinental Systems, Inc.

Electronic Typewriter Comprised of a Punch, a Reader, and a Printer

Fig. 24-19

Friden Division, The Singer Company

The Computyper Data Processor

5. *Tape-to-card or card-to-tape converting equipment.* Reproduces input data from tapes to punched cards, or reproduces input punched cards into punched tapes.
6. *Addressing machines.* Embosses address plates or data automatically from punched tapes. (See Figure 17-7 on page 546 and the accompanying discussion.)
7. *Accounting machines.* Data typed on forms by means of accounting or bookkeeping machines are reproduced on common-language tapes for additional processing. (See Figure 24-20.)

Fig. 24-20

Burroughs Corporation

Alphanumeric Accounting Machine

IDP Using Common-Language Tapes [2]

The method of handling orders in one chemical company before the installation of an IDP procedure was as follows:

1. When orders were received, they were edited and approved; shipping dates were set, and the orders were sent to the order department, which prepared a 9-part order form on an electric typewriter. Two copies of each order were filed in the order department by customer name and shipping date.
2. After the material was shipped, the shipping department returned one copy to the order department, which then destroyed the shipping-date copy. The copy filed by customer's name was then sent to the accounting department along with the shipping department copy.
3. The accounting department priced and extended the order, computed the salesman's commission and other charges, and prepared a 5-part invoice. This invoice had to be checked before distribution to the various persons and departments concerned. One copy of the invoice was sent to the code clerk, who coded the entire invoice for punched-card preparation for various statistical reports.

When an integrated data processing system was installed to eliminate the large amount of repetitive writing, the flow of paper work had

[2] Courtesy of Moore Business Forms, Inc.

to be modified only slightly. The use of electric typewriters in conjunction with common-language paper tape was recommended. The new procedure, which is charted in Figure 24-21, is as follows:

1. Preparation of master card and tape for each customer, which contains the following *constant* information: sold to name and address, ship to name and address, terms, number of invoice copies, F.O.B. point, material, test specifications, grade, freight charges, special instructions, and freight rates required.
2. When an order is received, the master card and tape and the customer's order are given to the typists for preparation of a 10-part order form. The typist inserts the master tape in the

INTEGRATED DATA PROCESSING

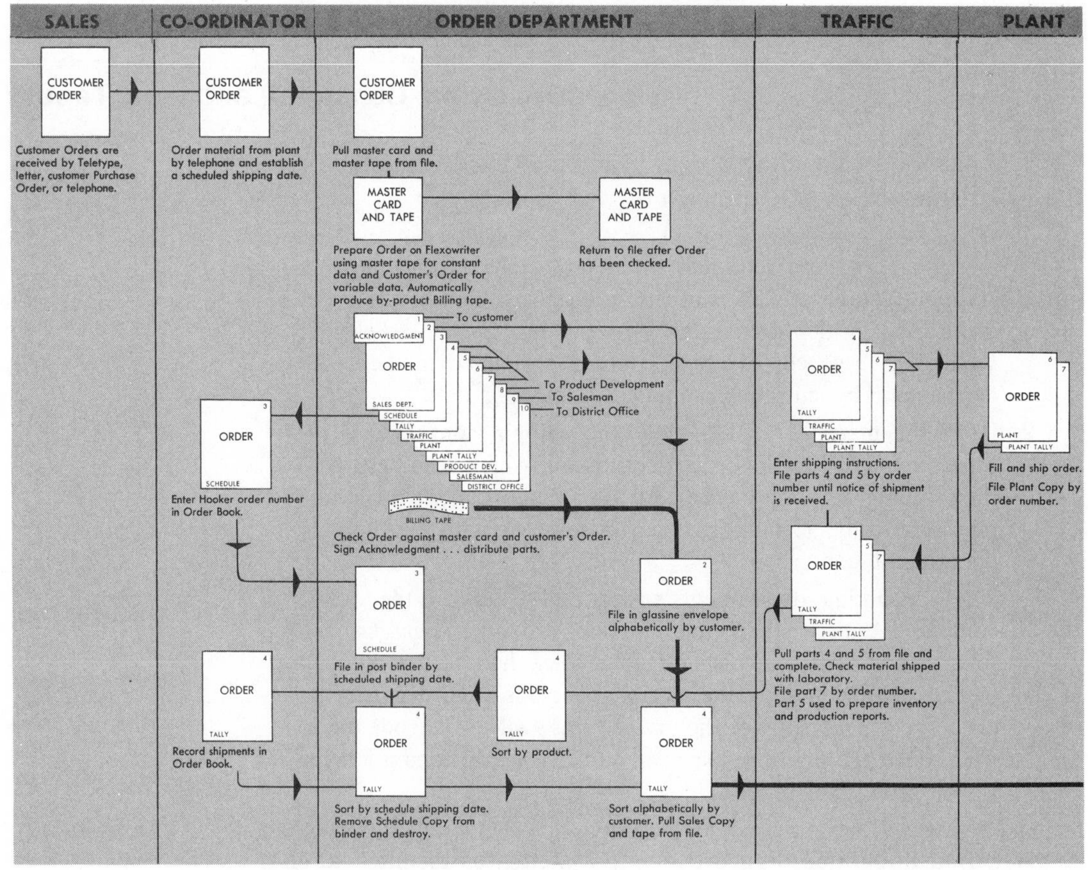

Fig. 24-21

tape-reader, and the typewriter automatically reproduces on the form all the constant information and codes. Where necessary, the typist enters manually the *variable* information from the customer's order. In this operation, the following data are recorded: customer's order number, customer's requisition number, date of order, shipper's order number, scheduled date, quantity, and special instructions. While each order is being prepared, a by-product tape (common language) is punched automatically to be used later to prepare the invoice. Since the constant data are reproduced automatically, only the variable information must be checked before the copies are distributed.

USING COMMON LANGUAGE TAPES

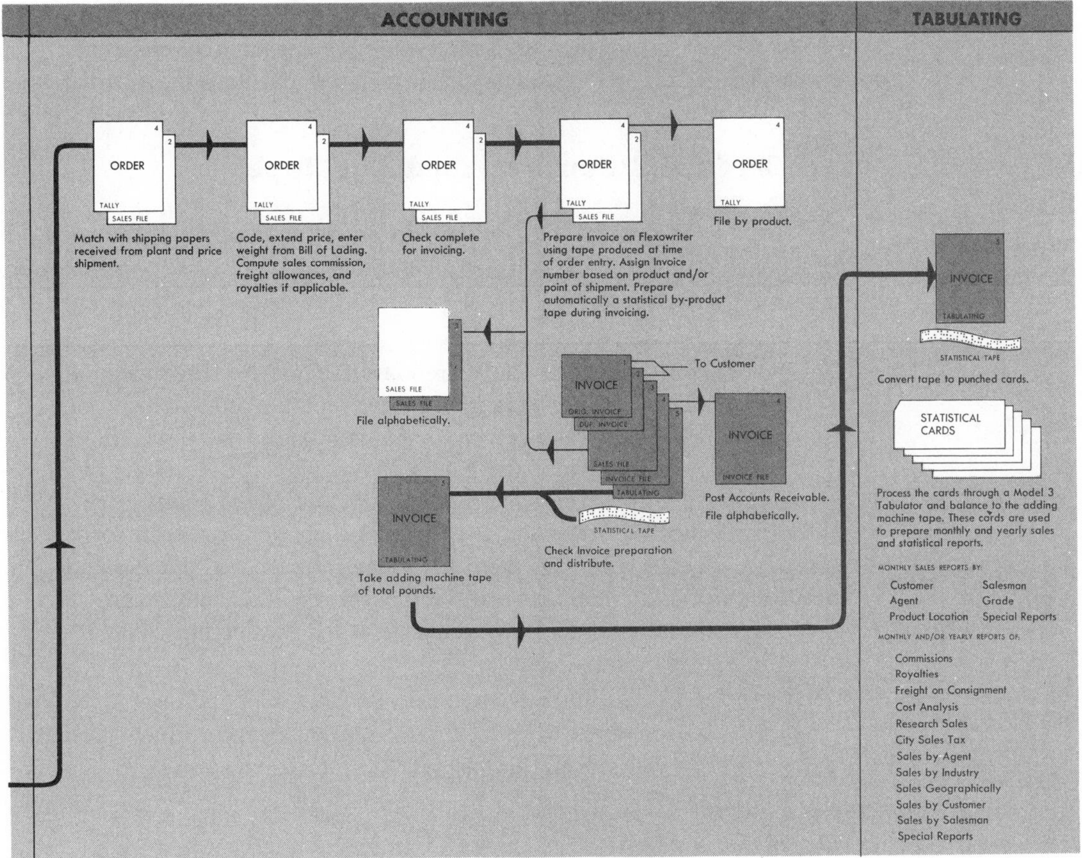

Integrated Data Processing System in a Chemical Company

3. The by-product tape to be used for preparing the invoice is filed until the notification of shipment is received. When the order has been shipped, the tally copy is returned promptly to the order department, then attached to the sales department copy and the billing tape, and forwarded to the accounting department. This department rechecks the prices, extends them, computes the various charges and commissions, and gives the document to the typist who assigns an invoice number.
4. The typist inserts the billing tape in the reader and typewriter, and a 5-part invoice is reproduced automatically. The variable information is typed manually. While the invoice is being prepared, a by-product common-language tape is automatically punched. Copies of the invoice are distributed and the statistical tape is forwarded to the tabulating machine department.
5. The tabulating machine department converts the statistical tape to punched cards by means of a tape-to-card converter. The cards are then used to prepare regular monthly and yearly reports as well as any special analyses that may be required.

IDP Using Punched Cards and Common-Language Tapes [3]

Prior to the installation of integrated data processing, the method of order handling and billing used by a power tool manufacturer was as follows:

> This manufacturer has warehouse facilities in three locations throughout the United States with three separate order areas where customer's orders were received. At each one of the three offices, a 13-part order-invoice was typed. Three copies were sent to the area warehouse, from which, upon shipment of the goods, a copy of the shipping order and the bill of lading were returned to the office. The invoice was then completed in a second typing operation. For accounting and statistical purposes, a tabulating card was punched for the order entered and later for the shipment billed.

In order to eliminate the repetitious manual paper work, to give customers better service, and to gain control over production scheduling and inventory, an integrated data processing system was installed as described below. The operation of this system is diagrammed in Figure 24-22.

1. By means of teletypewriters, all orders are received at the main office. Thereafter, all sales order data are produced on all

[3] Courtesy of Standard Register Company, Dayton, Ohio.

required records *mechanically*. The integrated data processing procedure integrates punched-card accounting with five-channel common-language tape transmission of records on teletypewriters.

2. Prepunched tabulating cards store the major part of all repetitive data that are to appear on a given order. The clerk simply pulls cards for "charge to" name and address, "ship to" name and address, and the product description and price of each item on the order. Pertinent information relating to only one order such as "our order number" is punched into miscellaneous data cards. The quantity order is mark sensed on the product card by a clerk who verifies all cards against the customer's order.
3. The deck of cards for an order is fed into a card-to-tape converting machine to obtain a five-channel common-language punched tape, programmed for teletypewriter operation. Orders are grouped by warehouse districts, thus providing a tape for continuous transmission to each.
4. Punched cards are available for tabulating a daily report of orders entered. Each order deck is placed in a backlog tub file pending shipment. The sending teletypewriter at the main office writes a three-part set of forms for each order: sales copy (placed in numeric file), customer acknowledgment copy and salesman copy (both of which are mailed). In the warehouse, the receiving teletypewriter simultaneously types a three-part form for shipping order, warehouse file, and packing list.
5. The shipping order is posted to the stock records in the warehouse and then used in typing a four-part bill of lading, which includes a *duplicating master* for printing labels. Upon shipment, the warehouse airmails the shipping order with original copy of bill of lading to the main office.
6. In the main office the numeric file is relieved of all papers if the shipment is complete. The order deck of cards is pulled out by order number from the backlog tub file for tabulating an invoice. In case of partial shipment, product cards for items not shipped are separated and processed through the system again. For completed shipments, the punched cards are put in an accounting machine to prepare a 10-part invoice. The same cards are used to prepare daily reports of shipments billed.

Advantages of IDP

The results achieved in integrated data processing systems vary with different concerns, depending upon the extent to which the system is used. One firm not only reduced its costs of clerical work by some 40 percent, but also was able to process orders more

IDP USING PUNCHED CARDS

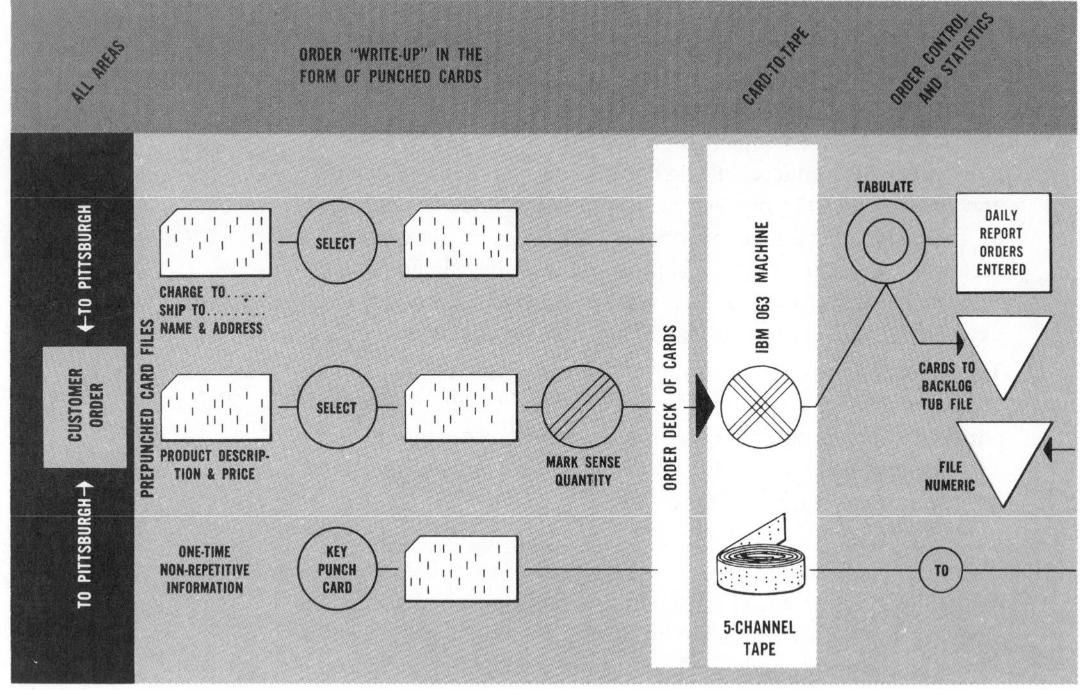

Fig. 24-22

rapidly, ship goods more promptly, bill more quickly, notify customers of their order status more rapidly, and centrally maintain better inventory records and control for a number of widely dispersed warehouses. Another firm was able to obtain prompt, accurate, and automatic preparation of reports for management covering such information as raw material requirements, inventories, plant work loads, and shipment schedules.

The outstanding advantages resulting from integrated data processing may be summarized as:

1. *Savings of as much as 80 percent of normal typing time* by using customer record punched tapes or cards (common language) for all basic information on regular reorders. Item description tapes and cards can be used for sales orders, invoices, requisitions, and purchase orders. Tapes and cards punched as a by-product of the typing of orders can be used to produce punched cards or to retype the information on an invoice, and information on punched cards may be transferred to punched

AND COMMON-LANGUAGE TAPES

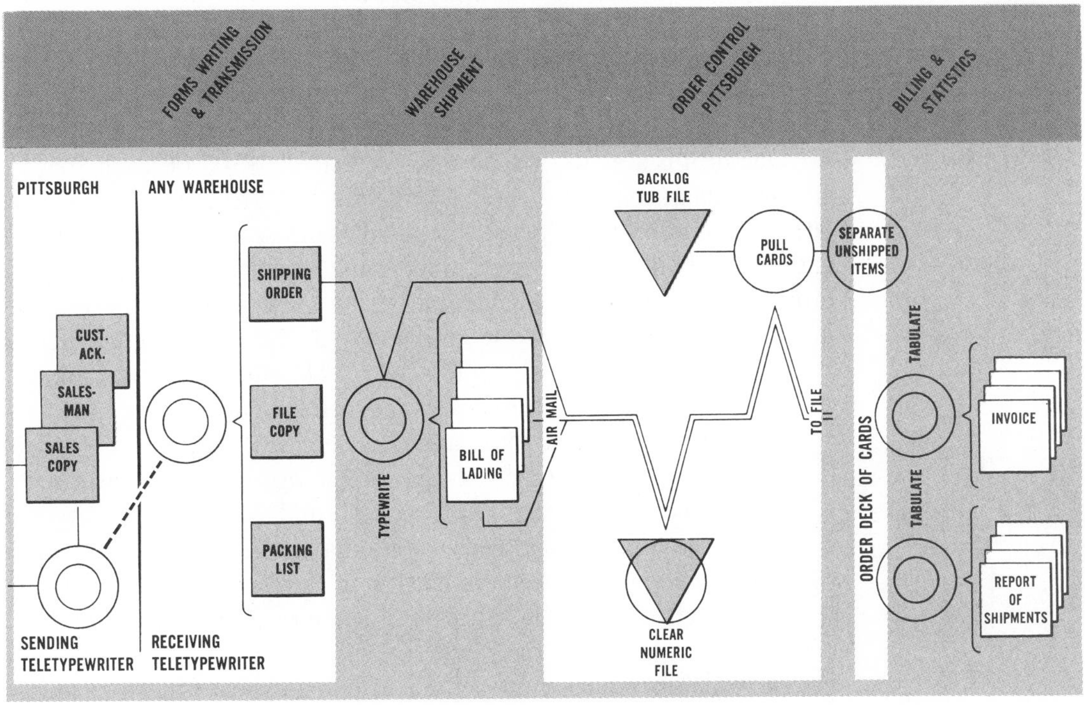

Integrated Data Processing System in a Power Tool Manufacturing Company

tape for teletype transmission. Addressograph plates may be produced automatically from punched tape for mailing lists, or for heading up a variety of forms.

2. *Distance can be eliminated* in communication, centralized record keeping, and accounting. Through teletype, IDP can encompass widely separated sales offices, warehouses, and plants in the procedures of original recording and subsequent processing. Reproduction of printed records at a distance can be handled by mailing tape records to a point desired, and the same record can also be sent to more than one receiving point at a time—such as to the order department and to the shipping department.
3. *Accuracy* is a distinct advantage of IDP because automatic reproduction of data is more dependable than manual in such instances as typing detailed technical descriptions, embossing metal plates, and producing punched cards.
4. *Speed* is evidenced by the time saved in reproduction and transmission of data.

Data Communication and Punched-Card Systems

A number of companies are able to improve their operations, provide faster delivery of their products, and reduce costs by using telephonic data transmission facilities as a direct link to their customers.

One firm is able to save its customers about $30,000 each year by enabling them to reduce their inventories and the clerical details related to the purchasing procedure. This firm uses card-reader devices and Data-phone sets for machine-to-machine transmission of sales orders by telephone. (See Chapter 7 for other examples of data communication systems.) In the operation of the automated ordering system, each customer is supplied with cards that contain a picture of items described and priced in the catalog. When the customer wishes to order, he selects the appropriate card for the item needed, dials the telephone number of the supplying company, inserts the card into the connecting card reader, and registers the desired quantity. The card reader feeds these data to the Data-phone, which converts the data to tones suitable for transmission over the regular telephone network. In the offices of the supplier, a data-set receiver converts the incoming tones into impulses that are fed into a key punch, which produces punched cards that duplicate the transmitted data. In the tabulating department, the cards are rapidly processed into orders, shipping lists, and acknowledgments.

The more sophisticated data communication systems that utilize electronic equipment and components are discussed in Chapter 25.

QUESTIONS FOR REVIEW

1. For what reasons may a business automate the processing of its accounting and statistical data?
2. Why is the punched card considered to be the heart of the punched-card system of processing data?
3. Briefly describe each of the three steps that make up the punched-card system.
4. Explain the use of mark-sensed cards in punched-card accounting.
5. What is the function of each of the following: (a) key punch, (b) verifier, (c) sorter, and (d) tabulator?
6. What three types of punched cards are commonly used in a typical punched-card payroll accounting system? For what reason is each type of card prepared?
7. What is integrated data processing?
8. What is the nature of the common language by which IDP machines communicate with one another?

9. The teletypewriter is one of the most important machines used in integrated data processing. Under what conditions can it be most effectively applied?
10. What types of business transactions lend themselves most suitably to integrated data processing? Why?

QUESTIONS FOR DISCUSSION

1. Some writers state that keypunching is slowly becoming a dirty word and that users today demand a more sophisticated approach to data preparation, such as optical scanning. Others argue that for the small firms with standard data, keypunching remains the most efficient procedure. What evidence can you advance to justify these two points of view? What do you see as the future role of keypunching?
2. "Frequently installations of punched-card equipment have been made that have proven impractical." What are some of the limitations of punched-card machines with which the administrative office manager should be familiar?
3. Keysorting is a manual process used in some accounting work. It is also considered an adjunct to the records management function in the office. Indicate how both accounting and records management may be expedited by means of keysorting.
4. What steps are prerequisite to the installation of an IDP procedure? Why are these steps necessary?
5. How might an IDP procedure be used at the point of sale in a large department store?
6. Why have punched-card procedures found such widespread use in modern business offices?
7. Punched-card equipment may be either purchased or leased. Which approach should a firm follow if it plans to use the equipment in recording and analyzing its sales and inventories? Why?

PRACTICAL OFFICE CASES

Case 24-1 Applying IDP to the Processing of Customers' Orders

The order processing procedure of the Mathews Manufacturing Company is as follows:

1. As customers' orders are received, they are edited, specifications are approved, and shipping dates are assigned by the sales coordinator. Orders are then forwarded to the Order Department and each customer's master card is pulled. A separate master card is on file for each customer for each product purchased.
2. From the customer's order and the master cards, a 9-part order form is prepared on electric typewriters. After being carefully

checked, the copies are distributed to the various destinations. Two copies are retained in the Order Department, one filed by scheduled shipping date and the other by customer name.

3. After the material has been shipped, the Traffic Department returns one copy of the order form to the Order Department as notification of shipment. The copy filed by scheduled shipping date is pulled from the file and destroyed. The copy filed by customer name is pulled and sent to the Accounting Department along with the Traffic Department copy.
4. The Accounting Department prices and extends the order, computes the salesman's commission and calculates the freight allowances. After checking these computations, a 5-part invoice is prepared on electric typewriters. One copy of the invoice is sent to a code clerk who codes the entire invoice for key punching. The punched cards are used later in preparing various statistical reports.

■ After much study, the company realizes that there is too much waste in repetitive writing. As office manager, you have been assigned the job of exploring the possibility of applying automation through integrated data processing. Discuss the possible procedures that you might follow in integrating the processing of customers' orders to make the procedure more efficient.

Case 24-2 Applying IDP to the Handling of a Branch Payroll

Tyler Mobile Homes, with its main office in Louisville, Kentucky, has two plants in this location, where there are 2,500 employees. A branch plant employing 450 workers is located in Syracuse, New York, and another plant employing 180 workers is located in Tyler, Texas.

In the home office there is a punched-card accounting and processing department in which the payroll for the Louisville employees is prepared. The size of the Syracuse and Tyler payrolls, however, does not warrant the employment of a full-time payroll clerk in either branch office. The cost of calculating the branch payrolls therefore has been getting way out of line.

The long-established custom of this firm requires that employees be paid each Wednesday for the preceding week's work. The company is seeking to reduce the branch payroll work and at the same time maintain accuracy in accounting and promptness in payment.

■ As the newly employed office manager in the home office, you have been asked to devise a suitable integrated data processing system for handling the branch payrolls, using, if possible, centralized punched-card accounting. In your report, present a reasonable description of the kinds of equipment, forms, and procedures involved in your recommended plan.

25

Electronic Data Processing Systems

Electronic data processing (EDP) is the use of a computer in the processing of facts and information that have been converted into a code consisting of electrical impulses. This code may be based upon binary language, a numbering system that uses two as its base instead of ten as in the decimal system. Or the code may be based on the octal system, using a base of eight, or the hexadecimal system, which uses a base of 16. Data (input) are read into a central processing unit by means of direct keyboard, magnetic tape, paper tape (either punched or inked), optical scanners, or punched cards, and are then treated mathematically, classified, sorted, and stored. Output is called out from the central processing unit as needed and recorded in magnetic tape, paper tape, or punched cards; or automatically printed on business forms and reports; or displayed on cathode ray tube (CRT) output terminals; or transferred from magnetic tape to microfilm for storage; or transmitted orally to the user via telephone (voice response).

The growth and development of the computer industry, the world's fastest growing major business, has been phenomenal since its birth in the 1950's. By the end of 1971, according to a study undertaken by the Diebold Group, Inc., some 90,000 computers will have been installed; the same study predicts that by 1975 there will be 160,000 computer systems in operation [1] and that the following amounts will be expended for various computer components: hardware, $15.5 billion; software, $2.6 billion; information services, $6.4 billion; and support services, $3.5 billion.[2] Virtually nonexistent in 1970, the area of information services is expected to experience the most impressive growth. The basic function of information services is to provide much of the data that is now offered only in a limited way by today's data processing techniques. The Diebold study foresees these services taking two forms: on-line computation, and sales and distribution of information through a communications network.[3] The market for the smallest computers (mini-computers), estimated at $150 million in 1970, is expected to increase fivefold to $750 million by 1975.[4] It is predicted that sometime in the 1980's, electronic data processing will become the world's biggest business, surpassing both the petroleum and the automotive industries.[5]

In the United States the manufacture of computers is dominated by International Business Machines Corporation. Other computer manufacturers include: Burroughs, Control Data Corporation, Digital Equipment Corporation, Honeywell, National Cash Register, Univac Division of Sperry Rand Corporation, and Xerox Data Systems. Most of these firms, along with other leading manufacturers, also produce the greater part of peripheral equipment such as input and output units and additional storage units.

HISTORY OF THE COMPUTER INDUSTRY

The growth, innovation, and technological change within the computer industry may be broken down into roughly defined time periods referred to as generations.

First Generation (1950-1955)

The first truly electronic computer, ENIAC (Electric Numerical Integrator and Computer), and other early models made use of vacuum tubes. Input consisted primarily of punched cards, and

[1] "Census of Computers," *The Office* (February, 1970), p. 80.

[2] *Ibid.*

[3] William D. Smith, "Computers' Gain Seen to Top Spot," *The New York Times*, February 8, 1970, p. 19.

[4] "Mini-Computers: EDP's Mighty Lightweight," *Administrative Management* (June, 1970), p. 37.

[5] Smith, *loc. cit.*

programs stored within the computer were pretty much limited to magnetic drums and cores. The development of temporary storage devices known as *buffers* enabled the ordering of input, output, and movement of data and instructions within the computer according to a kind of seniority system so that the data, instructions, and calculations would not commingle and thus become meaningless. This time period was also marked by the processing of data at random rather than in serial or sequential order. Most firms utilized the early computers in converting from their existing manual and mechanical accounting and clerical systems in order to obtain savings in the number of personnel required to do the work, to secure increased accuracy, to simplify their procedures, and to provide for computer capacity that would absorb anticipated increased workloads.

Second Generation (1955-1964)

Computers developed during this time period were marked by the use of transistors and diodes, which are much smaller and more compact and require much less air conditioning than vacuum tubes. Further, transistors offer the advantages of reliability since they last almost indefinitely, and of speed since they are characterized by their fast switching ability. Technological advances of the second generation also included the further perfection of high-speed magnetic tape units with massive amounts of data stored on reels of magnetic tape for later processing on the computer at high speeds, expanded magnetic core memories, removable disc packs to permit nearby storage of data, symbolic languages, and modularity or the building-block principle whereby small and medium-size computer systems could be expanded with compatible equipment into large systems. Coming upon the scene was the application of on-line real-time data processing to new management information systems and applications in the areas of management science. By means of on-line real-time systems, data can be fed into the computer, processed, and returned to the user in time for him to have immediate access to the desired information, thus enabling timely decision making.

Third Generation (1964-1971)

During this period transistors began to give way to microminiaturized circuits in still smaller, more compact units that increase the reliability of operations and decrease the maintenance costs. With the perfection of micromonolithic circuitry, complete circuits were produced in one manufacturing operation. The third generation was also marked by massive computer disc storage, multiprogramming, time-sharing, refined on-line real-time capabilities, companywide systems, and the total systems approach.

Fourth Generation (1971-   )

In the early 1970's computer manufacturers and users anticipate further simplification of systems and programming analysis, with increased reliability, flexibility, and confidentiality of computer systems. Computers of this time period will increasingly handle specialized functions by means of *microprogramming*—a system in which the programmer uses the basic, built-in instructions of a computer to construct other instructions. Also predicted is the development of gigantic memories that will utilize laser beams and cost less than present systems. Fourth-generation computers will be characterized by *polymorphism*—the ability of the computer to keep going even if one of the circuits is broken. Thus, when one circuit breaks, rather than an instant collapse of the computer, a series of progressive failures occurs over a period of time, with the vital circuits functioning for the longest period of time. Coming upon the scene will be computers that economically and practically handle graphic, nondigital information such as engineering drawings, designs, and legal documents. The computer will be able to receive, store, process, and print images as such rather than having them translated into machine language first.[6]

The fourth stage of computer development will be marked by the *distributed information system,* which utilizes a network of compatible systems, all interconnected by data-voice (and possibly picture) communications systems.[7] Four levels of capability will be provided for the information systems in the network of central, regional, local, and individual user locations. Also forecast is the concept of "public utility" computers, whereby time sharing will become possible on a far vaster scale. Huge installations will be provided for use by hundreds of companies on a basis similar to electricity and telephone systems. Such computer installations, in addition to serving as data banks, may offer processing capabilities as well. Simplified machine operations are anticipated, with man having less and less to do with

---

[6] "Forecasts for the Fourth EDP Generation," *Computers: How to Buy and Use Them,* Administrative Management Manual 1E-101 (New York: Geyer-McAllister Publications, 1968).

[7] "Fourth EDP Generation Is Here," *Administrative Management* (April, 1970), p. 21.

the computer. It is predicted that the fourth-generation computers will be able to handle increased amounts of work automatically; and vast numbers of personnel, who formerly spent time in working out programs, will be freed for more creative undertakings.

THE ELECTRONIC COMPUTER

Electronic computers are classified as: (1) digital, and (2) analog. *Digital* computers count numbers (sales totals, analyses, costs, and other numeric data); the results of one calculation can be retained and used again for further computation. *Analog* computers are used primarily in scientific research for measuring physical variables such as voltage, speed of sound, rotation, and air resistance. These computers solve problems by translating physical conditions such as flow, temperature, and pressure into mechanical or electrical quantities. For example, an analog computer is used by the National Aeronautics and Space Administration (NASA) to measure the speed, direction, and trajectory of manned space vehicles.

This discussion will be confined to digital computers since this kind of computer is the one most often used by business in the processing of its information. Digital computers may be classified according to functional application such as scientific, general purpose, or business, as well as in terms of size such as large scale, medium scale, small scale, and mini. The classification according to size is not precise nor clearly defined, but generally computer installations may be scaled to size as follows: [8]

Size	*Monthly Rental*
Large scale	$30,000 and over
Medium scale	$10,000 to $30,000
Small scale	$ 3,000 to $10,000

Mini-computers have smaller capacities and their functions are more limited than the three standard sizes cited above. Mini-computers seldom sell for more than $100,000 and generally the monthly rental is no more than $1,500. As the newest type of computer on the market, the mini-computer is suitable for those tasks (accounts payable, sales statistics, interests and yields, freight billings, etc.) that are too complex for the desk calculator but too simple for the large-scale computer. With a small investment in a mini-computer a firm

[8] Carl Heyel, *Computers, Office Machines, and the New Information Technology* (London: The Macmillan Company, 1969), p. 94.

may commence converting its operations to computerized systems and at a later date expand its computing power as needed by adding new mini-computer work stations, increasing the storage capacity, or adding various peripheral pieces of equipment. Because of their economy of cost, several mini-computers may be purchased and each one utilized for a specific business application. Often each desk-top computer is assigned to one person such as a researcher, a mathematician, or an analyst. According to the Diebold Research organization, in the future mini-computers will serve primarily in the areas of process control, data communications, and instrumentation, with their success not affecting materially any developments in business electronic data processing.[9]

Components of the Computer System

The equipment and devices that form a computer system and its peripheral equipment are known as *hardware*. The five components of the system are: (1) input, (2) processing, (3) storage, (4) control, and (5) output. Each of these components may be an individual unit, and one or more of the components may be located a few feet or hundreds of miles away from the central processing unit. Data may be recorded in the input unit at their source of origin and transmitted via telephone or telegraph lines to the processing unit.

Input. Input consists of the *data* to be processed and the *instructions* to process the data. "Feeding" the data into the computer system for processing requires the services of trained technicians, known as *programmers,* who plan the conversion of original data into a medium that is acceptable to the computer, such as punched cards, punched paper tape, or magnetic tape. The programmer plans the logical arrangement, sequence, and correlation of data taken from several sources. The sequence of instructions to the computer is called the *program*. For example, in an analysis of sales, the data may be partially contained on a tape prepared from the invoices and partially contained on a tape prepared from the shipping records. The data on the two tapes must be correlated and arranged in their proper sequence. Similarly, in the processing of payroll data, one tape may show the hours worked and the hourly rates; another, the social security status and related data; another, the withholding tax deductions; etc. Reading the information in proper sequence into the

[9] AMemo, *Administrative Management* (January, 1971), p. 76.

computer is part of the input operation and also part of the second phase, processing.

The following forms of input may be used in a computer system:

1. *Punched cards,* with the data being translated into a computer language by means of a card reader.
2. *Punched paper tape* with a code that uses from five to eight channels. Data on punched paper tape are translated into computer language by means of a paper tape reader.
3. *Magnetic tape,* upon which data are recorded as magnetized spots to create the electrical impulses. A tape unit may be used to translate the data from magnetic tape into the computer language. Or by means of key to tape, as shown in Figure 25-1, the data are entered directly onto the magnetic tape for immediate processing by the computer. In key to cassette, the data are recorded on a small magnetic tape cassette and then later converted to full-size magnetic tape for acceptance by the computer.

Fig. 25-1

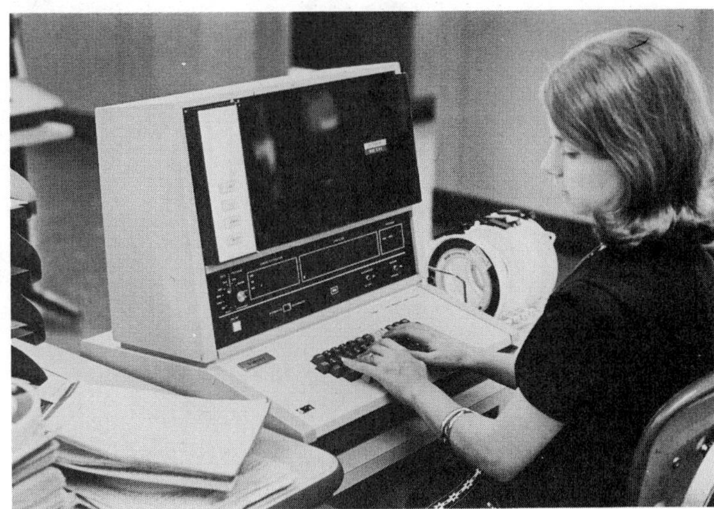

Key to Tape Input

4. *Magnetic discs and drums.* A *magnetic disc* is a thin metal disc coated on both sides with a recording material. Data are recorded on a disc in the form of magnetized spots located in concentric tracks on each recording surface. A *magnetic drum*

is a steel cylinder whose coated surface is the actual storage medium upon which data are recorded in the form of magnetized spots. By means of key to disc or shared processor, the data are keyed onto a random access storage disc or drum that is built around a central processor. The output is on a magnetic tape that is compatible with the computer. In the KeyProcessing System shown in Figure 25-2, data are entered through as many as 32 individual keystations for processing by the system's shared computer and stored on magnetic discs in locations unique to the keystation of original entry. Completed batches of data may be automatically transferred in any desired sequence from the disc onto a single reel of magnetic tape.

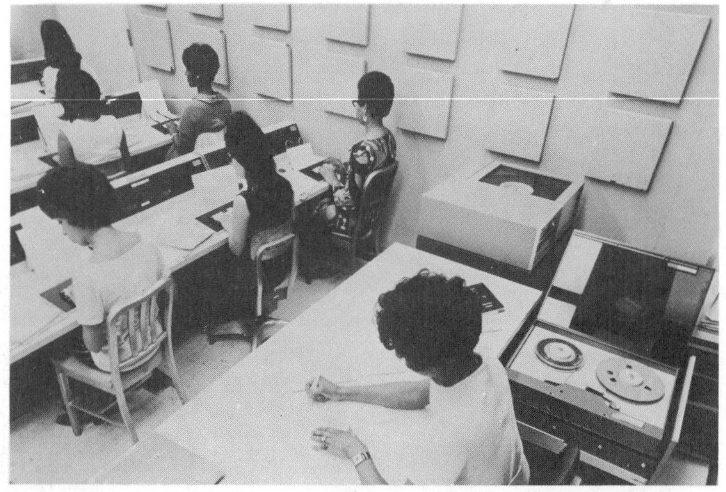

Computer Machinery Corporation

Fig. 25-2

KeyProcessing System Showing Recording of Data on Keyboards and Storage on Magnetic Discs

5. *Optical scanners* that read documents printed or handwritten in an alphanumeric font transmit the data directly to a computer, thus bypassing human data preparation.
6. *Magnetic ink character readers* that read characters specially printed in magnetic ink.
7. *Console typewriters and data terminals* which are used for manual direct keyboard input of data, for updating data already stored in the computer, and for querying the computer. The data terminal illustrated in Figure 25-3 is a compact, portable terminal with paper tape and edge-punched card input/output capabilities.

Fig. 25-3

Dura Division, Intercontinental Systems, Inc.

Data Terminal

Some input media may be read directly into the control and the processing units, but in other systems it is necessary to convert the data on punched cards or punched tape to magnetic tape in order to speed up the operations, or to adapt the input media to the type of electronic equipment used. Use of magnetic discs, as input media, permits random access—the retrieval of data from any portion of the record. When other input media such as punched cards or punched paper tape are used, it may be necessary to sort through a deck of cards or run through unwanted portions of tape in order to locate the desired data. Punched cards and punched tapes possess the advantages of low cost and adaptability to use on much of today's automated equipment; their disadvantages include their bulk, inability to hold large volumes of data, and susceptibility to damage. Both punched cards and punched paper tape are relatively slow in the speed with which data recorded in these media can be transferred to the storage unit of the computer. Magnetic tape possesses the advantages of both punched cards and punched paper tapes, but, in addition, magnetic tape may be erased and reused.

Processing. In the *processing unit,* sometimes called the *arithmetic unit,* the data are mathematically manipulated. Arithmetic and comparison operations are performed on the data according to the instructions that have been programmed into the computer by means of the input media.

When data are to be processed by the computer, they are converted into electrical impulses that are based upon the binary code. In the binary code, all letters and numbers are represented by two symbols, "0" and "1," in various combinations. These two symbols mean respectively, "no pulse" and "pulse," or "no charge" and "charge," or more simply, "off" and "on." The position of the "on" indicates the number, and in binary notation the value of a digit is doubled each time it is moved one place to the left. To accommodate all the decimal digits from 1 through 9 requires four binary digits, as shown below.

Decimal Digit	*Binary Notation*
	8|4|2|1
0	0000
1	0001
2	0010
3 (1 + 2)	0011
4	0100
5 (4 + 1)	0101
6 (4 + 2)	0110
7 (4 + 2 + 1)	0111
8	1000
9 (8 + 1)	1001

As shown in Figure 25-4, a row of four electric light bulbs, like a row of magnetic cores or transistors, forms the digits 1 to 9 by being turned "on" and "off" (or 1 and 0) in a variety of combinations.

Larger decimal digits, letters of the alphabet, and special symbols are expressed in binary code by providing additional binary digits. For example, by adding two binary digits to the basic four in the binary-coded decimal system, 64 combinations are made possible. Since there are 26 letters in the alphabet and 10 decimal digits, a

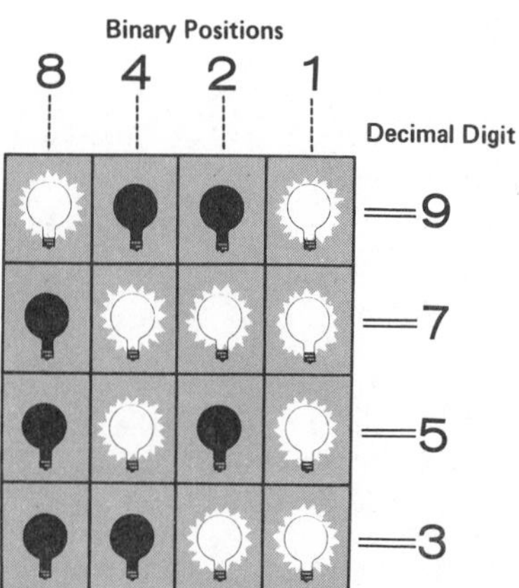

Fig. 25-4

Using the On and Off Symbols to Express Binary Symbols

total of 36 combinations is needed to express these characters. So, 28 combinations remain for the representation of special symbols.

Using six binary digits, the following code may be developed:

Digit, Letter, or Symbol	*Binary Notation*
	32|16| |8|4|2|1
1	00 0001
2	00 0010
3	00 0011
9	00 1001
A	01 0001
B	01 0010
C	01 0011
D	01 0100
E	01 0101
$	11 1011
%	11 1100

The smallest unit of information in the binary code is expressed in the electronic computer system as a *bit,* which is the contraction for "binary digit." For example, each zero and each number one (nonpulse and pulse) is known as a "bit." Each magnetic core in the storage unit of the computer is capable of storing either a binary one or a binary zero. A series of adjacent bits, operated on as a unit and usually shorter than a word, is known as a *byte.* A series of cores is used to store a word—either an *instruction word* that directs the computer to perform some function, or a *data word,* upon which the computer has been directed to perform some operation.

Storage. The *storage unit,* sometimes called the *memory,* retains the input in coded form until the data are called forth for processing or for "read out." The data, as instructed by the program, move back and forth between the storage unit and the processing unit.

The data may be stored internally or externally. Data are stored internally by means of magnetic cores, as shown in Figure 25-5. This type of storage makes use of tiny doughnut-shaped rings called *cores,* which are strung on frames to form a matrix. An electrical current is passed through the cores to charge them in a positive or a negative direction, thus accomplishing the recording of data in, or the reading of data from, the memory unit. When data are stored externally, they are retained in the form of punched cards, punched paper tape, magnetic drums, magnetic discs, magnetic tape, or magnetic cards,

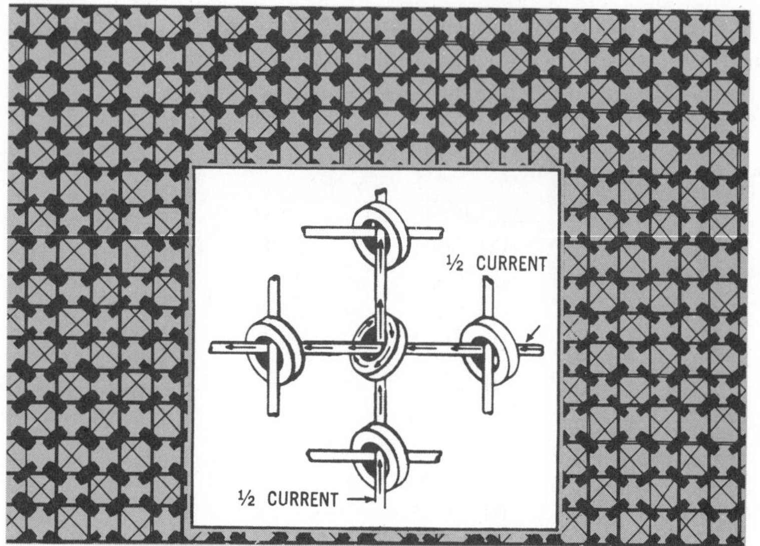

Fig. 25-5

Internal Storage by Means of Magnetic Cores

ready for reading into the computer at any time. The storage of data in magnetic tape files is shown in Figure 25-6.

Technological advances foresee plated wire magnetic thin-film memories, large-scale integrated solid-state memories, and magnetic bubble devices taking the place of magnetic core memories.[10]

Fimaco, Inc., Philadelphia

Fig. 25-6

Magnetic Tape Files

---

[10] AMemo, *Administrative Management* (March, 1970), p. 96.

Fig. 25-7

International Business Machines Corporation

Core-Storage Memory Unit

All data and instructions must be assigned specific locations (*addresses*) within the storage unit so that they may be readily located when needed in the processing operations. In any computer system, one of the major considerations is the speed with which the data and the instructions can be extracted from their location in the memory unit and transported to the desired location. This speed, called *access time,* is measured in thousandths of seconds (milliseconds), millionths of seconds (microseconds), or billionths of seconds (nanoseconds). The data stored in the computer are not erased when they are transported to another location nor when they are "read out"; the data are erased only when the computer is given instructions to store new information in the same location as the old data. Because of the speed of access to data in magnetic core storage and its storage capacity, core storage is often the most economical means of storage in terms of cost per machine calculation. In Figure 25-7, arrays of core-storage planes (resembling small screen doors) are mounted in units to provide up to two million characters of information. Multiple units can be linked into the computer system to place each of more than eight million characters at the direct command of the programmer in eight-millionths of a second.

Control. The *control unit* interprets the instructions recorded on the input media, directs the various processing operations, and checks to see that the instructions are properly carried out. The control unit directs the receipt of information in the storage unit, stores the intermediate results of the operations, and releases the information as needed in the arithmetic operations.

Output. After a program has been "run," the results of the computer operations, the *output,* are communicated to its user. The instructions fed into the computer indicate the location in the storage unit of the output that is to be printed out, where it is to be printed, and the manner in which it will be printed. If the end use of the processing is a formal report or a business document, the results will be printed in planned report form or on a business form such as a statement or a check. If the output is to be used in subsequent processing, it may be recorded on punched cards or magnetic tapes to be used later in the input unit for further calculations.

The major kinds of output devices are:

1. *Impact printers* that produce two to ten very legible copies on virtually any kind of paper stock.
2. *Nonimpact printers* that "squirt-print" charged microparticles of ink at the paper stock. Entirely electronic jet printers are very fast (up to 5,000 lines per minute with 250 characters per line), can be used with business forms and gummed labels, and eliminate the noise associated with the mechanical output equipment in which hammers are striking the paper.
3. *Cathode ray tube (CRT) terminals* that provide one-time information on television-like screens. CRT terminals have proved very popular because of their speed (160 characters per second, outputting a 72-character line, about 30 lines per "page" or screen image), their cost (many models available for less than $100 monthly rental), their peripherals (text editing capabilities, erase codes, and yes-no communications), and their convenience (ease of installing the sets which are no larger than mini-television sets). Figure 25-8 shows a bank of CRT display terminals that perform normal editing functions as well as transmit messages to other display stations.
4. *Voice response units* that represent the most convenient means of accessing data for certain kinds of businesses such as airlines, transportation companies, and financial institutions. Through the use of public telephone networks, voice response units can be made very portable and lightweight.

5. *Computer output microfilm (COM) systems* in which digital signals, read from magnetic tape or the computer's core storage, are translated into human understandable alphanumeric language and written directly on microfilm at up to 90,000 characters per second. (See pages 229-230 for additional discussion of COM systems).

Fig. 25-8

Orange and Rockland Utilities, Inc.

Cathode Ray Tube (CRT) Display Stations

Each of the components of a computer system and their interrelationships are diagrammatically illustrated in Figure 25-9.

Steps in the Electronic Computer System

The heart of an electronic computer system is its program. In computer programming, the first step is to define and analyze the particular problem or procedure that the program is to handle. Programming involves a complete analysis of each problem, beginning with the source data and ending with the final reports. Programming entails long, analytical study and the preparation of instructions broken down in sequential steps so that every eventuality can and will be considered. Otherwise, the data and the reports will be incorrect and faulty, thus involving much expense and delay.

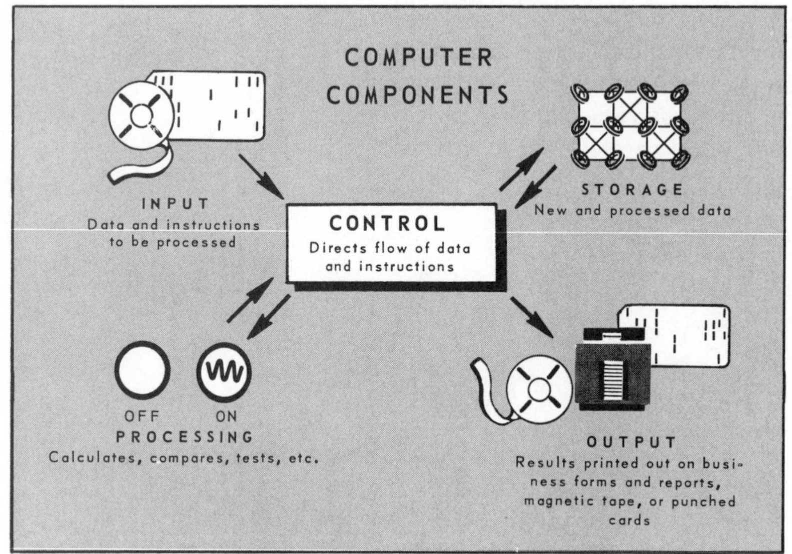

Fig. 25-9

Components of the Computer System

The basic steps in an electronic computer system may be outlined as follows:

1. A person with a problem, such as a systems analyst, describes the problem. It may be the preparation of monthly statements, the preparation of payroll checks, an accounting problem, or a problem of managerial decision making with which the business is faced.
2. Complete information about the problem is given to a programmer, who analyzes and studies the problem and breaks it down logically into all its steps and substeps in the form of a program. After the program has been translated into a computer language, the program is tested by running it on a computer. The purpose of the testing operation is to make sure that the program works and to provide for all predictable contingencies. At this stage, *debugging*—the process of making corrections—commences. Debugging is an important step in the programming process, consuming an average of 15 to 20 percent of the time the programmer spends working on the program.[11]
3. Detailed instructions for the computer are recorded on input media, such as magnetic tape. These are the instructions

[11] "Programming: You Can Master It," *Administrative Management* (October, 1969), p. 39.

prepared by the programmer and are used in connection with the problem data, which are recorded on a separate magnetic tape (Step 4). The instructions that may be recorded on the computer program cover four basic operations:

a. Arithmetic instructions (+, —, ×, or ÷).
b. Logical or sequential instructions such as "Read In" or "Halt."
c. Data transport instructions, indicating where to store or transport a result of sequential and arithmetic instructions.
d. Machine control instructions such as "Halt" or "Repeat."

4. The problem data are recorded separately on a magnetic tape so that they may be fed into the computer.
5. The computer, following the instructions on the magnetic tape, performs the calculations arising from the problem data recorded on the separate magnetic tape.
6. The computed results are recorded on magnetic tape.
7. The results on the magnetic tape (Step 6) are converted to printed form.

Block Diagramming (Flowcharting)

Much of the preliminary work of programming involves the preparation of block diagrams. The *block diagram* is a schematic presentation in English-language form of all the steps involved in a problem being solved on the computer. The preparation of a block diagram enables the programmer to check upon the adequacy of the instructions and to make sure that all steps have been set forth logically and completely.

As a relatively simple example of the kind of work involved in programming, the problem of taking a physical inventory of stock on hand will be analyzed, presented in a step-by-step form, and illustrated by means of a block diagram. In this example, it will be assumed that after the inventory has been taken, the following data are to be recorded in punched cards: (1) part number, (2) inventory count in units, and (3) unit price.

The cards are to be keypunched, sorted, and then processed by a computer to provide the needed information. The following steps are involved in completing the problem:

1. A separate punched card will be prepared for each part number. Punches will be made for the part number, number of units of that part in stock, and price per unit.
2. The cards will be sorted into part number order.

3. The sorted cards will be fed into a computer which is to multiply for each inventory item the units on hand times the unit price. Also, the computer is to print for each item the part number, units on hand, unit price, and total value of each stock item on hand adjusted to the nearest cent.
4. The report on which the foregoing information is to be printed is to show a heading line at the start of each page.
5. On the final page of the report, the total value of all stock on hand is to be printed following the caption FINAL TOTAL.

The block diagram of the computer program shown in Figure 25-10 indicates that all the foregoing conditions are met; the program starts with Step 3. Note that such conditions as end of page, last card, and final page have been taken into consideration.

The basic flow of this diagram is to print the page heading, read a card into storage, perform the necessary calculations, print these calculations along with other data, test to see if the last card has been processed, and if so, print the final total and halt. If it is not the last card, the computer must test for the end of the page; if it is not the end of the page, the computer reads another card into storage and repeats the process. The routine is changed when a new page is needed and when all the cards have finally been processed.

Computer Languages

To perform all its different activities, the computer system must be programmed in "language" that will be understood by all the units that make up the system. To program a computer in its own binary-code language, with symbols that represent different possible actions, is a tedious process that requires the programmer to remember the codes for all the steps in an operation as well as the storage location of all data and instructions. To overcome the difficulties involved in writing a program in actual machine language, synthetic programming systems were developed. Such systems represent a cross between our normal language and the numerical language of the machines. With the functions of computer systems becoming increasingly specialized, along with the need for users to be able to "talk" to their computers in terms peculiar to their own businesses, more than 100 different specialized languages have come into existence. However, according to the president of Worldwide Computer Services, today there is a retrenchment in the number of languages used, for most people are not willing to change their language as often as they

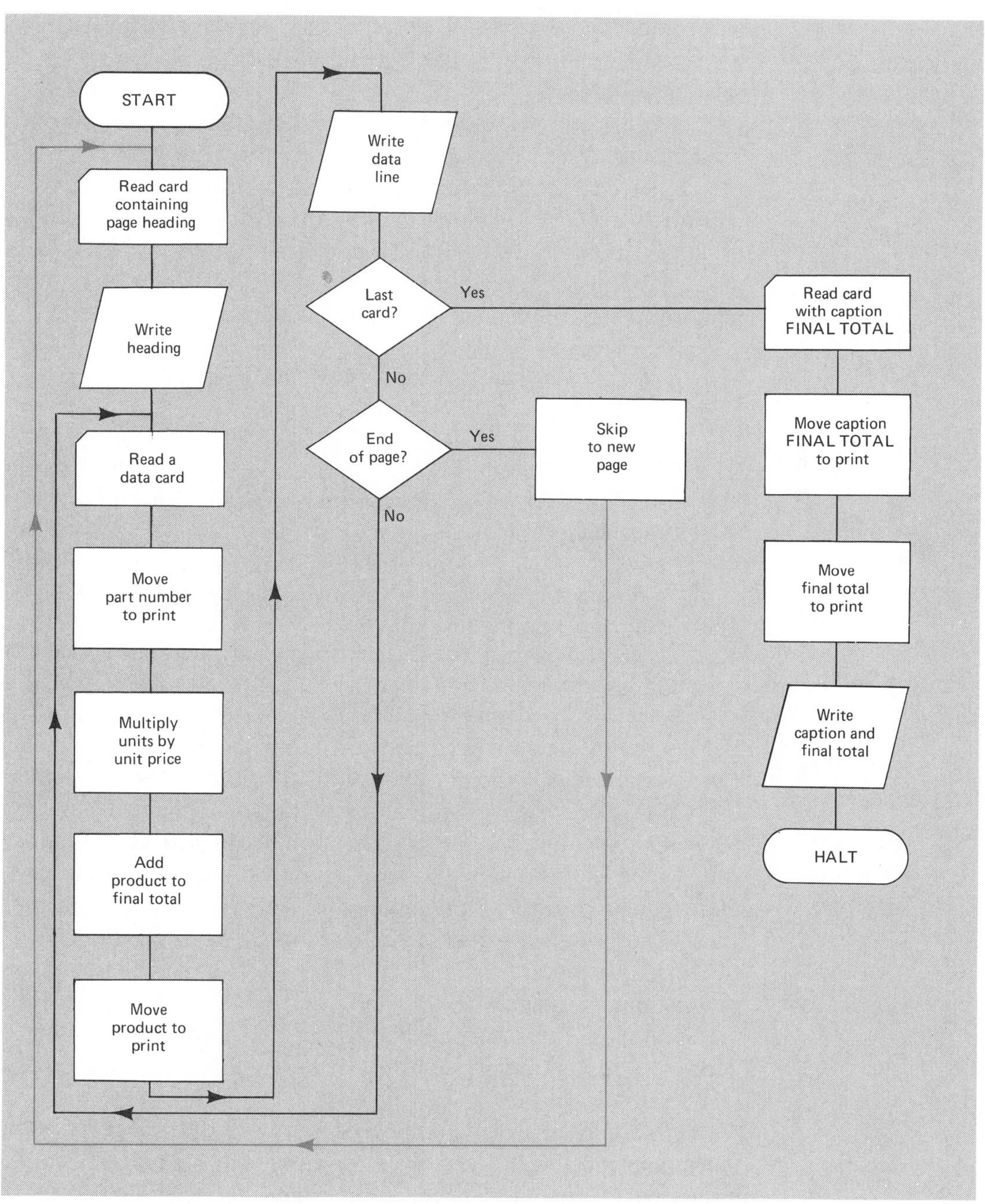

Fig. 25-10

Block Diagram for Solving an Inventory Problem

once did.[12] The extensive number of languages is evidenced by the great variety of ready-made programs that have been developed by software producers.

Software is a set of coded instructions that are written into a program to direct the hardware operations. The program directs the actual computations or organizes the hardware operations into an orderly sequence while at the same time maintaining efficient use of logic circuits, memory, and peripheral equipment. The reasons advanced for the increased popularity of ready-made programs supplied by the computer manufacturer include: [13]

1. The greatly increased number of computers in use requires more software than ever before.
2. With the increased sophistication of computers, there is a shortage of sufficiently skilled programmers. Thus, well-planned software packages enable the user to obtain fuller computer capability.
3. Many firms want to use their computers for more complicated problems such as those encountered in management information and employee information systems, which require a high level of systems design and programming skills often not available within the firm.

Because of the factors cited above, International Business Machines Corporation now has more than 3,000 program packages available to its users. These programs consist of those supported by the computer manufacturer and tested on its own equipment as well as those contributed by customers who have developed the programs as part of their regular operations in conjunction with the computer manufacturer. The prices of software packages range from $500 for a relatively simple program up to $100,000 for a highly complicated programming system.[14]

Several of the synthetic languages offered as part of software packages are very briefly described below.

SPS (Symbolic Programming System). In this language which uses mnemonic substitutes for operation codes, each instruction is written on a separate line of a special coding sheet. After the complete program has been written, each line in the coding sheet is punched into a separate SPS program card. The program, coded in SPS and

[12] "Is Your Fortran Rusty?" *Administrative Management* (April, 1971), p. 36.
[13] Anthony D. K. Carding, "A Hard Look at Packaged Software," *Administrative Management* (August, 1969), pp. 58-62.
[14] *Ibid.*

punched into cards, is referred to as the source program. A processor program, supplied by the computer manufacturer, translates the source program prepared by the programmer into an object program, which is then in actual machine language.

Autocoder. This system of coding is somewhat more advanced than, but very similar to, SPS. More freedom is provided the programmer, for fewer restrictions in preparing the coding sheets must be kept in mind. The major difference between the two systems lies in the format of the instructions sheets.

COBOL. The *Co*mmon *B*usiness-*O*riented *L*anguage, abbreviated as COBOL, is one of the most widely used languages designed primarily for use in processing business data. The language can be used in scientific applications also. One objective of those who created COBOL was to develop a program language that would be usable on any manufacturer's equipment. Thus, the computer user would be provided with flexibility when he changes from one model of equipment to another or when a new piece of equipment is added. COBOL uses ordinary words such as "ADD," "SUBTRACT," "TOTAL," and the computer manufacturer makes available a *compiler*—a deck of punched cards or magnetic tape—that converts these English words into the computer's numeric-code language.

FORTRAN. This computer language, whose name was created from the two words FORmula TRANslation, was prepared to aid in the programming of scientific, mathematical, and engineering problems. FORTRAN relies upon what might be called mathematical English and uses symbols for operations, such as = for EQUALS and + for PLUS. Numerous *subroutines,* which are segments of a standard program, are provided for frequently performed mathematical operations and are used to avoid rewriting those sections of programs that keep recurring as parts of a major program.

ALGOL (ALGorithmic-Oriented Language). Similar to FORTRAN, this language ranks closest to the symbolism used in mathematical and statistical notation. The language is used for expressing problems in the form of algorithms—series of well-defined arithmetic steps that are followed in obtaining a desired result. ALGOL was originally developed to standardize communications among mathematicians throughout the world and has been promoted by technical groups particularly outside the United States.

PL/1 (Programming Language-1). This language, incorporating features of FORTRAN, COBOL, and ALGOL, was created in response to requirements brought about by advances in computer technology, such as mass storage, teleprocessing, and multiprogramming. The language was developed by International Business Machines Corporation for use in its System/360 computer, which is described later, and allows one language to be used by both scientific and business users.

BASIC (Beginner's All-Purpose Symbolic Instruction Code). BASIC is the language used in the Honeywell time-sharing system described later in this chapter. Resembling ordinary mathematical notation, the language has a simple English vocabulary and few grammatical rules. The language is versatile, for it can be used for business and statistical problems as well as for engineering and scientific calculations.

RPG (Report Program Generator). This programming system aids in organizing random data into orderly printed reports. Using abbreviated English terms and special source statements, called "specifications," the programmer states his problem in terms of an input, a calculation, and an output, such as "Field A is to be multiplied by Field B; put results in Field C." Four forms, resembling the instruction sheets used with accounting machines, are filled in to set up a job. The filled-in information is punched into cards and fed into the computer along with the Report Program Generator. The computer then generates its own program to process the data. The program can also be punched into cards for later use.

ILLUSTRATIVE EDP SYSTEMS

The following descriptions of EDP systems are designed to tie together the principles and concepts of punched-card data processing presented in Chapter 24 and the preceding discussion in this chapter.

Burroughs Corporation's L5000 Magnetic Record Computer

The Burroughs magnetic record computer, a mini-computer, enables the user to read, store, and retrieve data on magnetic memory records and to produce a variety of accounting records and comprehensive management reports. Data on the magnetic memory records are provided in both printed and electronic forms. The memory

Burroughs Corporation

Fig. 25-11

Burroughs Corporation's L5000 Magnetic Record Computer

records may be randomly accessed from an unlimited file for automatic updating or for immediate visual reference. Through automatic selective electronic reading of the statistical data provided by the memory records, timely and detailed reports can be produced.

Users can refer to the magnetic memory records visually, use them as input to the computer for updating accounting records, and process them through an automatic magnetic record reader for many types of reports useful for effective management control. Data stored electronically in the memory contribute directly to speed, accuracy, and processing productivity. For example, in invoicing with accounts receivable and inventory updating, the name and address are read from the customer's memory record and automatically printed in the "Sold To" portion of the invoice. The inventory memory record automatically provides product description, pricing, discount, and other data for automatic completion of the invoice. The customer and inventory memory records are updated automatically.

Functional Units. The magnetic record computer, shown in Figure 25-11, operates with a variety of input and output peripheral devices that increase accounting and management reporting flexibility. The automatic magnetic record reader provides for automatic retrieval of data stored on the memory records and is an important adjunct to the computer. The reader performs many time-consuming jobs automatically with electronic accuracy.

Readers for input of information include a punched paper-tape reader, an edge-punched card reader, and an 80-column punched-card reader. Devices for output include a punched paper-tape punch, an edge-punched card punch, and an 80-column card punch.

The computer is programmed internally and has monolithic circuitry, magnetic disc memory, advanced logic for decision-making ability, and fourth-generation techniques called micrologic. *Micrologic* consists of strings of micro-instructions stored in the computer's disc memory and provides complete internal control of computation, print formatting, printer positioning, forms movement, and console and peripheral data input and output.

Software. Forty-eight standard application programs, written in COBOL, are available for such businesses as manufacturing, contracting, credit unions, hospitals, automobile dealers, banks, and government.

Singer System Ten

The Singer System Ten is a small- to medium-scale highly modular general-purpose system that is adaptable to a variety of business uses. The system features on-line disc storage capacity and hardware control of multiprogramming for up to 20 users.

Functional Units. The central processing unit consists of core storage, an arithmetic and control unit, and input-output channels. Storage in the system consists of from one to 11 core modules, each of which contains 10,000 characters of storage. Input-output devices, some of which are shown in Figure 25-12, consist of a card reader, card punch, line printer, work station, paper tape reader, paper tape punch, and a display device. The card reader, which reads 300 standard punched cards per minute, automatically transfers the information into the system. The card punch converts System Ten data into punched cards for storage or additional processing at the rate of 100 cards each minute. The line printer, a drum type that has a 132-character line, prints from 225 to 450 lines of information each minute and will accommodate up to six-part forms. By means of the work station, a printer-keyboard, the operator can converse back

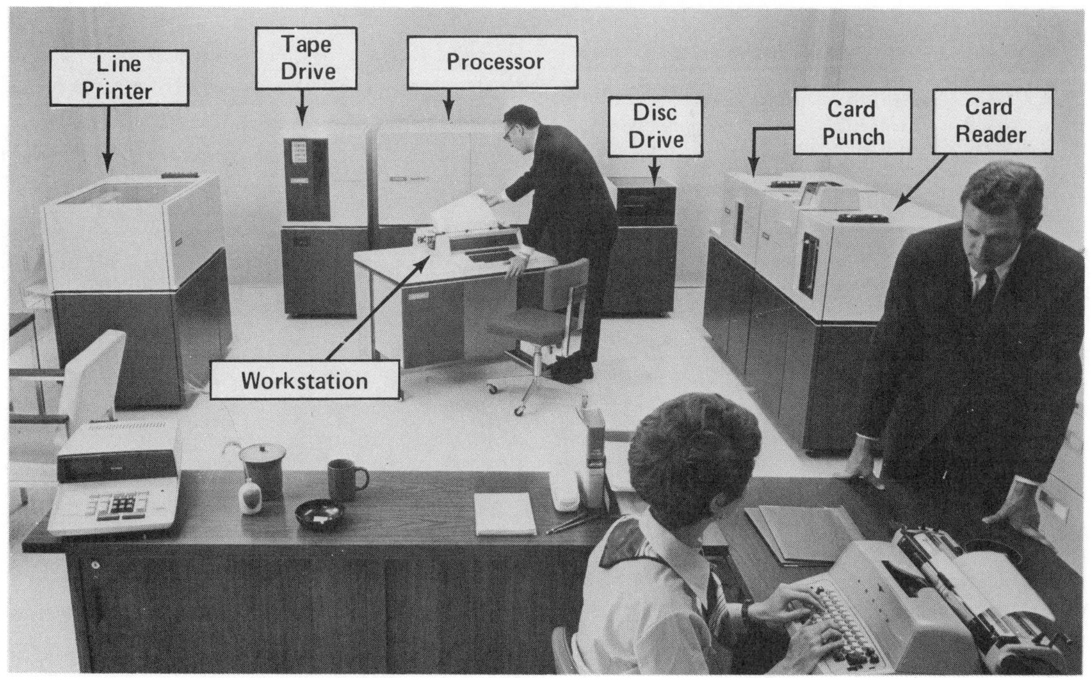

Friden Division, The Singer Company

Fig. 25-12

Singer System Ten

and forth with the system. The paper tape reader and paper tape punch, offered as alternatives to the card reader and card punch, employ the system's code on standard paper or polyester punch tape. Disc storage for the system is furnished with a disc drive, and the system can support as many as ten drives, for up to 100 million characters of storage.

Up to 20 work stations may be utilized with a single processor and distributed throughout the office where needed. Each of the 20 jobs can proceed independently just as if the operator has the computer all to himself. With System Ten a firm can purchase a minicomputer and then expand as the needs grow. New applications may be added merely by installing an additional terminal.

Software. The operating system is provided completely through hardware, for there is no software operating system, nor is one needed. The only programming language facility offered is an assembly language that converts symbolic source documents into machine language.

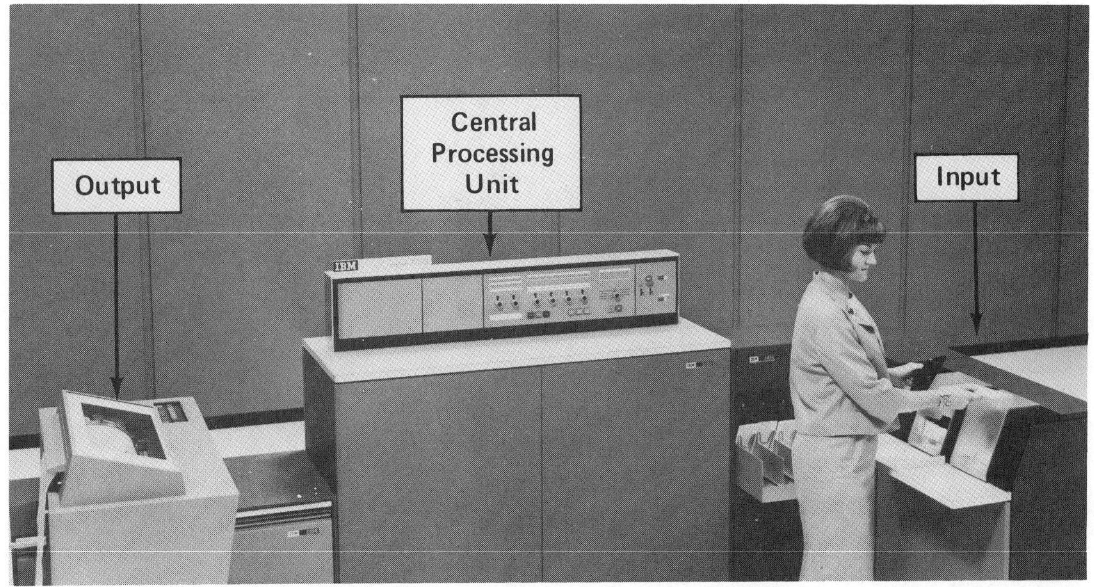

International Business Machines Corporation

Fig. 25-13

System/360 Model 20 Electronic Data Processing System

IBM System/360 Model 20

The IBM System/360 Model 20 is especially designed to meet the data processing needs of small and medium-size businesses. This system is illustrated in Figure 25-13.

Functional Units. The Model 20 system is essentially a punched-card-oriented data processing system to which has been added the speed and versatility of a stored-program computer. Input is provided by punched-card readers that read and transfer data to the central processing unit at speeds ranging from 500 to 1,000 cards per minute. The data are stored in the central processing unit at addressable locations from which they may be moved when needed. The stored program, which is the series of instructions in the sequence necessary to complete a given procedure, is also stored in the processing unit. The control aspect of the processing unit comes from individual commands in the program. These commands are instructions to the various units to perform a specified function.

The functions of addition, subtraction, multiplication, and division are accomplished in the central processing unit under command of the stored program. Certain logical decisions can be made and acted upon as the situation requires. Based on whether a stated condition exists or not, the processing unit can be instructed to get to one series of instructions or another. For example, when an inventory withdrawal quantity is subtracted from the stock balance and the balance becomes negative, the processing unit can test for this condition and, noting the negative balance (out of stock), branch to a series of instructions (a subroutine) that will print out notification of the condition.

Output is in the form of punched cards and/or printed reports. Printers operate at speeds of from 200 to 750 lines per minute, and from punches at rates of 90 to 500 cards per minute.

By means of a multifunction card machine (labeled "Input" in Figure 25-13), all the facilities of a card reader, a card punch, a summary punch, a collator, an interpreter, and a card document printer are placed under the control of the stored program. In one pass of the punched cards through the machine, cards may be collated, gang punched, reproduced, summary punched, calculated, printed, and classified. Use of the multifunction card machine reduces significantly the card passes, card handling, and operator time and results in a simpler, more efficient procedure.

Software. A number of routine operations are required frequently of every computer installation. Such operations range from the printing or punching of information in storage to the placement of a program in storage so that the computer may take its instruction from that program. Each of these operations can be performed by the computer itself under control of a simple program. In order to save programming and computer time, the computer manufacturer provides a standard set of utility programs to perform these functions. The system also utilizes Report Program Generator, which was described on page 822. In addition to these programs, a basic assembler program is available for use in translating the source program into the machine-language program for use by the computer.

ILLUSTRATIVE EDP APPLICATION

The following application of a fully integrated EDP system shows the role played by forms specialists in designing the output form—the customer's monthly electric bill—for processing on an optical scanner tied in with a computer system.[15]

---

[15] Through the courtesy of The Standard Register Company, Dayton, Ohio, and Raymond F. Czinger, Systems and Procedures Department, Cleveland Electric Illuminating Company, Cleveland, Ohio.

Requirements of the Output Form

In the company operations described below, the billing procedure requires the processing of 560,000 bill forms each month and the printing of approximately 27,000 bills each day on a 21-day month. A similar numbers of forms must be reconciled with customer payments.

In designing the new bill to be used with the newly installed computer system, the forms specialists had to meet many requirements. First, the bill must hold all the information necessary to the internal operations of the electric company, and the information must be presented in a logical, easily understood format for the customers. Second, since the bill is processed on a variety of automated equipment, the bill must be compatible in layout and construction with the specifications of all equipment used. Third, the bill must be of material and design to withstand an amount of punishment not ordinarily required by other types of forms. Finally, the appearance of the bill must be modern in approach and acceptable to customers.

Preparing the Electric Bills

The revenue accounting system of the electric company incorporates mark-sense reading cards, computers, high-speed printers, and optical scanning equipment. The preparation of the electric bills, which makes use of the first three of these pieces of equipment, is outlined below.

1. The issuance of a bill starts with the reading of a meter. As each meter is read, the meter reader checks the proper information on a mark-sense card.
2. The mark-sense cards are returned to the electric company office where they are run through the mark-sense reader that converts the markings to holes in punched cards.
3. The deck of punched cards is processed on an IBM computer system to convert the information to magnetic tape.
4. The magnetic tape is processed through an IBM computer system to compute the bill for each customer and to update the customer master file, which is also kept on magnetic tape. Billing and customer record tapes are also prepared.
5. The billing tapes are fed through the computer system and bills are produced on the high-speed printer. The bill form, shown in Figure 25-14, is a single-part, marginally punched form that is printed two-wide on the high-speed printer.

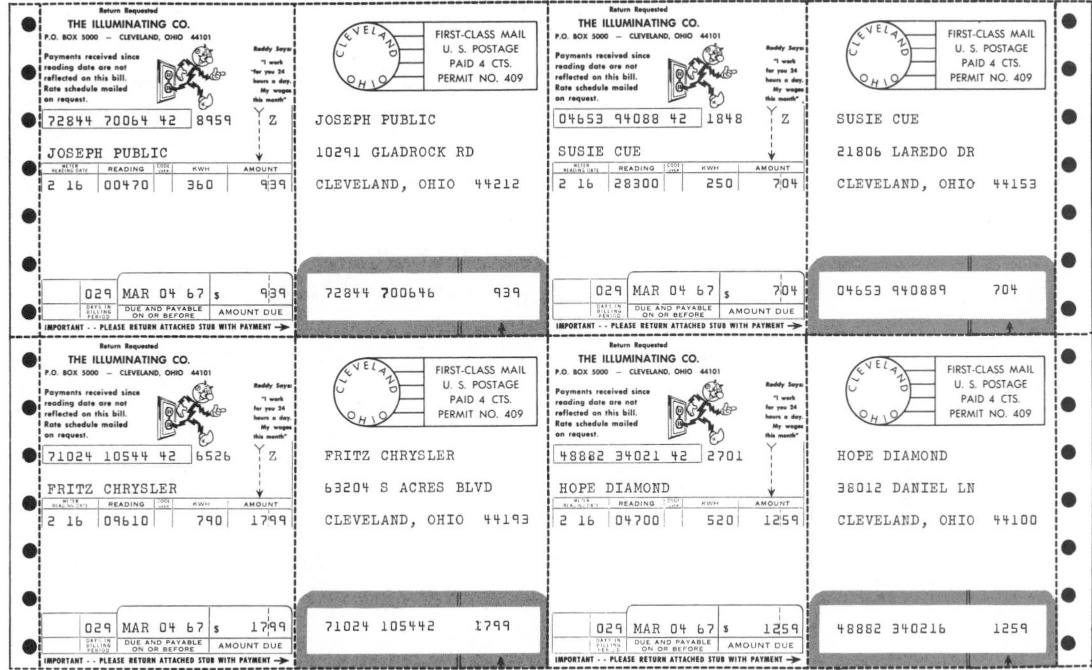

Return Requested
THE ILLUMINATING CO.
P.O. BOX 5000 — CLEVELAND, OHIO 44101
Payments received since reading date are not reflected on this bill. Rate schedule mailed on request.
Reddy Says: "I work for you 24 hours a day. My wages this month"
72844 70064 42 | 8959 | Y Z
JOSEPH PUBLIC

METER READING DATE	READING	CODE	KWH	AMOUNT
2 16	00470		360	939

DAYS IN BILLING PERIOD	DUE AND PAYABLE ON OR BEFORE	AMOUNT DUE
029	MAR 04 67	$ 939

IMPORTANT - - PLEASE RETURN ATTACHED STUB WITH PAYMENT →

CLEVELAND OHIO
FIRST-CLASS MAIL U. S. POSTAGE PAID 4 CTS. PERMIT NO. 409
JOSEPH PUBLIC
10291 GLADROCK RD
CLEVELAND, OHIO 44212
72844 700646 939

Return Requested
THE ILLUMINATING CO.
P.O. BOX 5000 — CLEVELAND, OHIO 44101
Payments received since reading date are not reflected on this bill. Rate schedule mailed on request.
Reddy Says: "I work for you 24 hours a day. My wages this month"
04653 94088 42 | 1848 | Y Z
SUSIE CUE

METER READING DATE	READING	CODE	KWH	AMOUNT
2 16	28300		250	704

DAYS IN BILLING PERIOD	DUE AND PAYABLE ON OR BEFORE	AMOUNT DUE
029	MAR 04 67	$ 704

IMPORTANT - - PLEASE RETURN ATTACHED STUB WITH PAYMENT →

CLEVELAND OHIO
FIRST-CLASS MAIL U. S. POSTAGE PAID 4 CTS. PERMIT NO. 409
SUSIE CUE
21806 LAREDO DR
CLEVELAND, OHIO 44153
04653 940889 704

Return Requested
THE ILLUMINATING CO.
P.O. BOX 5000 — CLEVELAND, OHIO 44101
Payments received since reading date are not reflected on this bill. Rate schedule mailed on request.
Reddy Says: "I work for you 24 hours a day. My wages this month"
71024 10544 42 | 6526 | Y Z
FRITZ CHRYSLER

METER READING DATE	READING	CODE	KWH	AMOUNT
2 16	09610		790	1799

DAYS IN BILLING PERIOD	DUE AND PAYABLE ON OR BEFORE	AMOUNT DUE
029	MAR 04 67	$ 1799

IMPORTANT - - PLEASE RETURN ATTACHED STUB WITH PAYMENT →

CLEVELAND OHIO
FIRST-CLASS MAIL U. S. POSTAGE PAID 4 CTS. PERMIT NO. 409
FRITZ CHRYSLER
63204 S ACRES BLVD
CLEVELAND, OHIO 44193
71024 105442 1799

Return Requested
THE ILLUMINATING CO.
P.O. BOX 5000 — CLEVELAND, OHIO 44101
Payments received since reading date are not reflected on this bill. Rate schedule mailed on request.
Reddy Says: "I work for you 24 hours a day. My wages this month"
48882 34021 42 | 2701 | Y
HOPE DIAMOND

METER READING DATE	READING	CODE	KWH	AMOUNT
2 16	04700		520	1259

DAYS IN BILLING PERIOD	DUE AND PAYABLE ON OR BEFORE	AMOUNT DUE
029	MAR 04 67	$ 1259

IMPORTANT - - PLEASE RETURN ATTACHED STUB WITH PAYMENT →

CLEVELAND OHIO
FIRST-CLASS MAIL U. S. POSTAGE PAID 4 CTS. PERMIT NO. 409
HOPE DIAMOND
38012 DANIEL LN
CLEVELAND, OHIO 44100
48882 340216 1259

Cleveland Electric Illuminating Company

Fig. 25-14

Electric Bills Printed Two-Wide on High-Speed Printer

Two-wide printing enables the company to obtain the required number of bills in half the amount of machine running time necessary if a "one-up" form were used.

The information on the face of the bill includes the customer's name and address, and all the billing information such as reading date, code numbers, kilowatt hours, and amount. Data are printed in a type font designed especially for ease in optical scanning. The back of the bill is preprinted with an explanation to the customer of the codes used.

6. The customer record tape is processed through the high-speed printer to produce a record that shows the latest billing, accounts receivable, and service information concerning the customers just billed.

Since the stubs of the customer bills are read on an optical scanner, the printing quality on the bill forms must be assured. The electric company checks the quality of the printing by printing a one to two percent sample at the beginning and at the end of each run of printing the bill forms. The sample bills are sent through the scanner to check the accuracy of registration as well as proper printing and inking quality. If the scanner accepts 99 percent of the stubs, the bills are released for mailing. On rare occasions, if the bills do not pass the 99 percent test, they must be reprinted.

Processing Customer Payments

When the customer pays his electric bill either to the company or to its authorized agent, such as a local bank, the payment must be accompanied by the right-hand stub of the bill, which is read by the scanner. The steps in processing customer payments are:

1. The customer payment stations total the daily payments received and forward this tape, with the stubs, to the central office of the electric company.
2. Stubs are sent in batches to the scanning equipment. The pay station number and its total for the day are typed on batch cards for use in later checking.
3. The scanning equipment senses the printed figures at a speed of 300 documents a minute, prints the results on an output paper tape, and feeds the information through a card-punching machine to create punched cards. The data on three customer stubs can be recorded in one punched card.
4. The punched cards are fed into the computer system to update customer and company records.
5. Mutilated or unreadable stubs are rejected by the optical scanner and sent to a typist pool, where electric typewriters with optical scanning fonts are used to prepare substitute stubs.
6. The replacement stubs are entered into the scanner system. If there are no rejects on this run, the total of the output tape of the scanner should balance with the tape total from the pay stations. If the two totals do not balance, another run of stubs is made. If the balance still does not check out, a visual search is made through the cards to find the error.

With its new computer system, the company has noted gains in internal efficiency, a reduction of human error to the minimum, and a higher degree of accuracy than ever possible before.

COMPUTER SERVICE CENTERS

An entirely new industry—the service center—was created as the result of the growth in computer usage. There are about 800 data processing or service organizations in this country and in Canada. Included in this number are those centers that are operated independently and those that function as departments or subsidiaries of the computer manufacturers. The use of the service center is especially suited to small and medium-size businesses that do not have computers. The service center provides access to its data processing services, which may include applications involving payroll, accounts receivable, accounts payable, inventory, and production statistics; financial and sales analyses; and the microfilming of business records.

It is not necessary for the customers of the service center to prepare punched cards as the data processing input, for other types of input media such as magnetic tape, punched paper tape, forms with optical scannable type font, and magnetic stripe ledger cards, can be produced on office machines as a by-product of daily operations. By sending such by-product input media to the service center, the small business obtains timely, up-to-date data. For example, in a typical automated system designed by the National Cash Register Company, a cash register is combined with a punched-tape output and a computer to provide timely reports on accounts receivable and the aging of accounts receivable. The key to the system, as shown in Figure 25-15, is the cash register, which punches out, as a by-product of ringing up the charge sales and payments on account, a punched tape showing the amount and the customer's account number. For retail systems involving 35 to 40 cash registers, register tape with a stylized optical print, rather than punched tape, is often more economical to use. Stores that do not have a computer or an optical scanner to process the punched tape or printed tape can send their tape output to a data center for processing.

Automatic Data Processing, Inc., of Clifton, New Jersey, provides another example of a computer service center. As one of the country's leading data processors, the firm makes available to its clients the following payroll services: computation of all elements of wages and salaries and all statutory and voluntary deductions; preparation of individual earnings statements and payroll checks, departmental labor analyses, weekly personnel and year-to-date earnings reports, individual employee ledger cards, quarterly FICA reports, required data for state unemployment insurance and disability reports, and federal, state, and city withholding statements; and production of special payroll reports as required. The service center includes as part of its payroll service the pick-up and delivery of the client's payroll. The client firm is provided with a preprinted transmittal form on which the hours worked by each employee are recorded. The transmittal

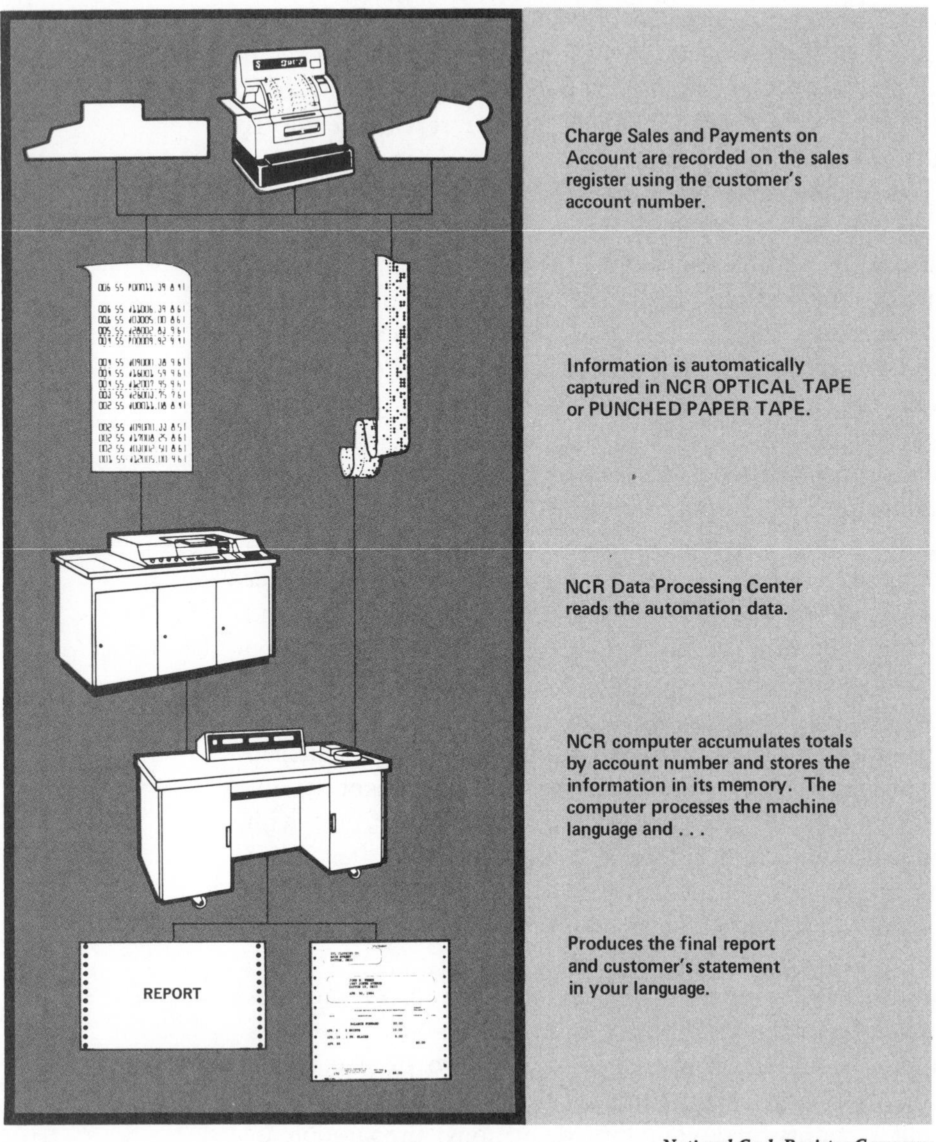

Charge Sales and Payments on Account are recorded on the sales register using the customer's account number.
Information is automatically captured in NCR OPTICAL TAPE or PUNCHED PAPER TAPE.
NCR Data Processing Center reads the automation data.
NCR computer accumulates totals by account number and stores the information in its memory. The computer processes the machine language and . . .
Produces the final report and customer's statement in your language.
REPORT

Fig. 25-15

National Cash Register Company

Flow Chart Showing the Handling of a Retailer's Accounts Receivable and Age Analysis by a Service Center

form is picked up and the completed payroll delivered by the company's fleet of radio-equipped vehicles. Each client's payroll is kept confidential, for security is built into every procedure. Any internal payroll "leaks" in the client's firm are lessened since the physical payroll processing is removed from the client's premises.[16]

The total accounting and management reporting system called Direct Dial Data System, developed by General Computer Service, Inc., of El Paso, provides more than 14 million different reports for its customers. As shown in Figure 25-16, the data are entered into the Direct Dial Data System via a touch-tone card dialer telephone in the customer's office. (See pages 191-192 for a description and illustration of the card dialer). The telephone is connected to a dealer's office (service bureau), where data sets on standard dial-up rotary lines accept the input from touch-tone phones from any point in the country. Next, a translator accepts data from the data set and translates the data into key-tape language. The signals emitted from the translator make the key tape a data collection device for the daily transmittal of data to a regional data center for processing. After processing, the tapes are sent back to the dealer's office for printing in his office and daily delivery to the customer.[17]

Augmenting the popularity of the service center has been the development of "line of business" package systems created by accounting machine manufacturers, computer manufacturers, and the data processing centers themselves. As a result, some data processing centers are devoted exclusively to particular lines of business such as automobile dealers, hospitals, and trucking firms. One of the leading suppliers of forms for automobile dealers has developed a package system based upon well-designed source documents including sales invoices, repair orders, cash receipts, and voucher checks. Data on these forms are recorded daily on an adding machine that produces by-product punched tape, or in the newer installations, optically scannable printed type. Each day the tapes are mailed to the service center where they are converted to punched cards that serve as the input media for the computer. Computer output for the automobile dealers consists of daily operating controls, customer statements and aged accounts receivable each month, detail journals periodically during the month, and general ledgers and supporting schedules following the receipt of the last tape for the month.

Banks have entered into the operation of computer service centers by joining together in intra-industry arrangements. For example, the First Western Bank and Trust Company, with its 68 branch offices

---

[16] Information supplied the authors by E. William Donahoe, Manager, Advertising/Communications, Automatic Data Processing, Inc., Clifton, New Jersey, January, 1970.

[17] Information supplied the authors by Paul H. Stevens, Marketing, General Computer Service, Inc., El Paso, June, 1971.

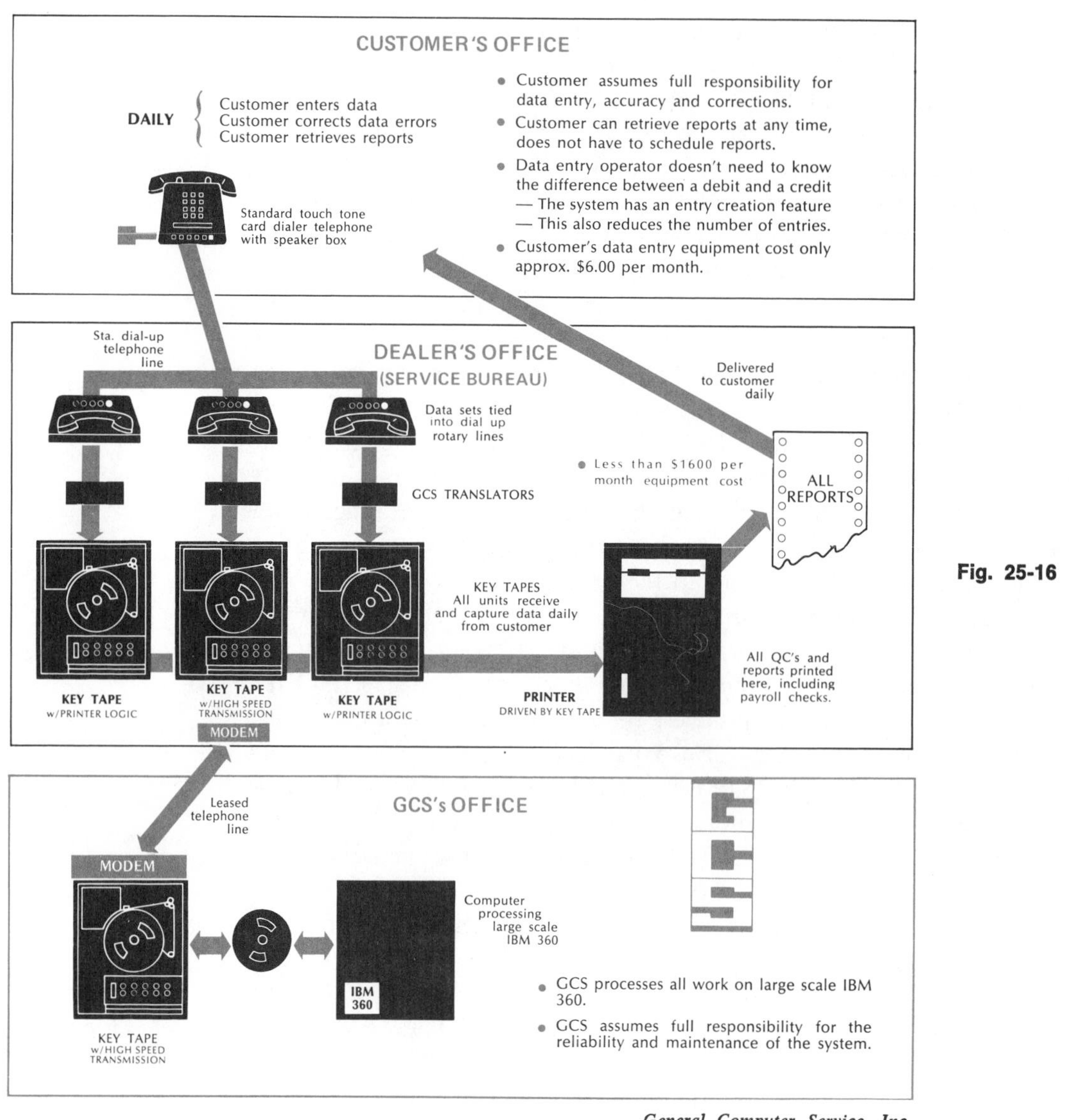

General Computer Service, Inc.

Fig. 25-16

The Direct Dial Data System—a Total Accounting and Management Reporting System

in California, operates a data processing center in San Francisco that provides complete computerized services to its depositors and to other customers. The Savings and Loan Bank of the State of New York, which acts as a central reserve and service bank for New York's state-chartered savings and loan associations, operates a state-wide communications system to handle the data processing for as many as 255 savings and loan associations.

Involved in the decision to use the services of a data processing center are the major factors of *cost* and the *needs* of management. In the analysis of costs to find out if any dollar savings will result from the use of a service center, the amount presently being spent on clerical operations that would be taken over by the service center must be determined. In calculating the cost for processing the records of a company, the service center may base its charges on the number of punched cards or entries processed, or on an hourly or flat contract basis. For processing data on electronic computer systems, the service centers commonly charge by the hour, with costs ranging from $25 an hour for small computers to $550 and more for large computers. Additional volume that may result from expansion of work in the office can often be handled at a lesser cost by the service center than by the company that must add more employees to handle the increased work load. In some instances, management needs more speed and accuracy in obtaining its periodic reports. In order to meet these needs, the decision may be made to use a data processing center even though no dollar savings are anticipated.

TIME SHARING

By means of *time sharing,* many users, each of whom has been assigned a segment of time within the computer's central processor, have simultaneous access to a single computer. The users have data terminals, usually teletypewriters, at their desks through which they can communicate with a remote computer whenever they wish. The data terminals are connected to the computer via telephone lines and thus can be located wherever there is a telephone. Associated with the concept of time sharing is *multiprogramming,* whereby several programs may be operated at one time within a single computer. Information needs or problem solutions can be received within seconds at the user's desk in printed form or on punched paper tape. The high speed of the system in compiling several programs and in performing computations thus allows many users to share the same system at the same time. Each user experiences the feeling of exclusive control of the computer system.

With an easy-to-use conversational language available for communicating with the system, scientists, engineers, accountants, and managers find that, after a few hours of instruction, they can develop and run their own programs. Because problem solutions are available when needed, people can use their time more effectively and complete their projects more rapidly.

With the advent of time sharing, commercial time-sharing service bureaus have come upon the scene. This type of operation differs from the data processing service bureau's operation in that the time-sharing bureau sells only its services to the computer via a communication terminal. The time-sharing services vary, with the usual service being that of straightforward computations. The service bureau may or may not offer an array of programming languages, debugging aids, and specialized programs for its clients.

General Electric, whose Information Systems Equipment Division was merged into Honeywell Information Systems, lists the following benefits of time sharing:

1. Increases efficiency and productivity of people.
2. Provides immediate access to a computer from desk-side terminals.
3. Improves response time to information needs and problem solutions.

Honeywell Information Systems

Fig. 25-17

Honeywell 430 Time-Sharing System

Fig. 25-18

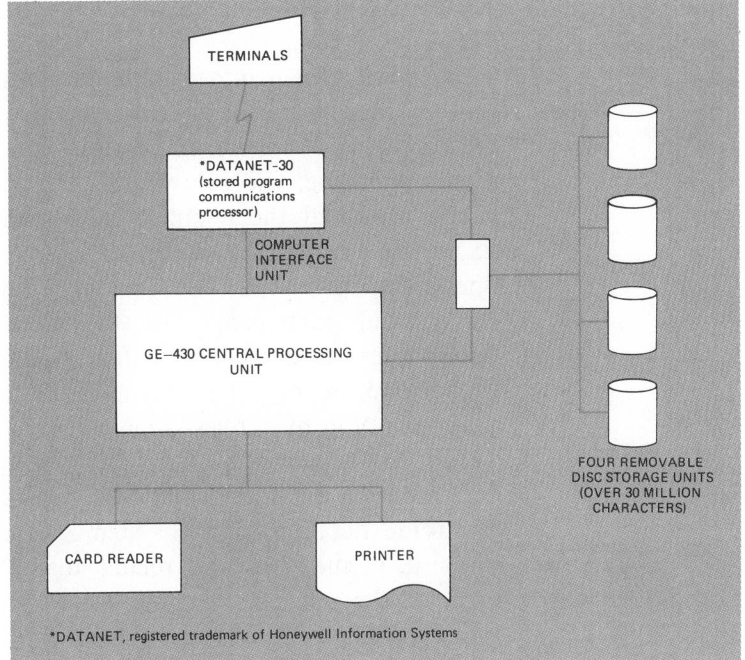

Honeywell Information Systems

Basic Components of the Honeywell 430 Time-Sharing System

4. Noncomputer-oriented personnel can quickly learn the user-oriented language required to operate the system.
5. More advanced languages are provided for solving difficult computational problems.
6. New programs and applications are developed directly from terminals.
7. Programs are stored for reuse.
8. Library routines can be stored for general use by all users.
9. At user's discretion, private libraries can be established.
10. Shared computer facilities reduce computing costs for all users.

One of the several time-sharing systems developed by Honeywell is illustrated in Figure 25-17. The basic components of this system, which serves up to 30 users simultaneously via telephone dial-up connection, are schematically shown in Figure 25-18.[18]

---

[18] From information supplied the authors by Ernest J. Lassen, Merchandising, Marketing Communications, Honeywell Information Systems, Inc., Phoenix, Arizona, July, 1969, and September, 1971.

MANAGEMENT INFORMATION SYSTEMS

A *management information system (MIS),* operated either manually or through mechanical or electronic means, has as its purpose the supplying of timely information to management for use in planning, organizing, and controlling. A management information system encompasses all the communications methods within and external to an organization by which data are recorded and processed for operational purposes. The data may be obtained by telephone, by contact with other people, by studying an operation, as well as from data processing units. The system exists to provide information that supports top managers in directing the total enterprise in the accomplishment of its objectives. Supplementing this purpose are the processing of the data and the keeping of historical records. In a study of 112 firms, it was found that over one half of the objectives of their electronic data processing systems were financial in nature; about one fifth of the objectives related to the information itself. The first eight of the measurable goals listed by these companies included: improved clerical savings, reduced data processing costs, lower administrative or overall costs, better service to customers, greater timeliness of information, increased speed of information, improved accuracy of information, and greater efficiency.[19]

A successful, cost-effective management information system is characterized by the following five criteria:

1. The system and the information supplied by it must be *relevant* to purposeful needs of the business. Lying behind the current explosion of paper work is the presence of electronic devices of a bewildering array and variety, all dedicated—paradoxically—not just to production, but to reproduction, duplication, and permanent storage of vast quantities of irrelevant data, which companies seem determined to retain.[20] Thus, the objective of the system and its byproducts must be clearly stated at the outset; and it must be determined who will use the information, how they will relate to the system, and in what fashion the system will satisfy the stated aims. Today the task is to discover more effective ways of using present systems, as well as developing new systems. The objective of the system must center about the information, not the data, and about the understanding of relationships drawn

---

[19] M. Valliant Higginson, "Managing with EDP, A Look at the State of the Arts," AMA Research Study 71 (New York: American Management Association, 1965), pp. 32-33.

[20] Quoted from *The Office* in "Are We Drowning in Data?" *Management Review* (September, 1970), p. 48.

from the information, not the mere retention of permanent records.

2. The system must be *economically feasible,* and its cost must be compatible with the results to be achieved. Huge sums of money are being spent on information systems; and information, like any asset, must be managed with skill and efficiency in order to yield the greatest return on investment.
3. The information system must provide adequate controls to assure *accuracy*. A firm may currently have a computerized system that is not being utilized and also have a duplicate manual system which, although recognized as inefficient by its users, is necessary in order for the managers to perform their functions. Such a situation represents one of the worst kinds of cost ineffectiveness and is not uncommon.[21] The development of this situation can be prevented by carefully considering the requirements for systems control at the time of designing the system.
4. The system must provide a high degree of *flexibility* to handle normal growth for the future and to handle the inevitable changes in the planning process or in the company's operations. To aid in providing flexibility, general and operating managers must play a more prominent role in the designing of the system to make sure that the system is tailored to the company from the top down.[22]
5. The system must provide for timeliness through its response time. The increasing complexity of business and the speed up in decision making made possible by electronic devices demand that the output of meaningful information be accelerated. The quantity of data is not enough; the data must be accurate, logical, and timely. The quality of the output information depends upon the quality of the input data. No information system, especially a computerized system, can convert faulty basic data into logical results.

QUESTIONS FOR REVIEW

1. What are the major characteristics of the four generations of growth, innovation, and technological change in the computer industry?
2. Since the capacities of mini-computers are relatively small and their functions are somewhat limited, why might a small business be motivated to rent one or more mini-computers?

---

[21] Burton J. Cohen, *Cost-Effective Information Systems* (New York: American Management Association, 1971), p. 15.

[22] William M. Zani, "Blueprint for MIS," *Harvard Business Review* (November-December, 1970), p. 96. This very fine article presents a general scheme for relating systems to the jobs they are really supposed to do.

3. (a) Describe the five components of a computer system. (b) With which of these units is the programmer's work most closely related? (c) With which is the administrative office manager most concerned?
4. Compare the advantages and disadvantages of punched cards and magnetic tape when used as input media.
5. Data may be stored internally or externally in a computer system. Explain the major differences between these two types of storage.
6. Briefly describe each of the major kinds of output devices and the media produced.
7. Why may a programmer prepare a block diagram as part of his preliminary work in defining and analyzing a particular problem?
8. What factors account for the development of synthetic programming systems?
9. What are some of the uses of the magnetic memory records produced by Burroughs Corporation's L5000 Magnetic Record Computer?
10. What is the purpose of the work station in Singer's System Ten data processing system?
11. In the IBM System/360 Model 20 computer system, what functions are handled by the multifunction card machine?
12. In the revenue accounting system for the electric company, as described in this chapter, why are the design and the quality of printing of the utility bill of such great significance?
13. What types of services do data processing service centers make available to small and medium-size businesses that do not have computers?
14. Define time sharing. What advantages may be realized by the company that avails itself of the services offered by a time-sharing bureau?
15. What is a management information system? Summarize briefly the criteria by which the cost effectiveness of a management information system may be determined.

QUESTIONS FOR DISCUSSION

1. How great a financial return should management expect to make on its investment in an electronic data processing system?
2. How can the administrative office manager make sure that he will not be "stuck" with an inflexible electronic data processing system?
3. Why is the job of the programmer so important in an EDP system?
4. The R. W. Hale Company, a large construction company, has building projects going on all over the country. At present, one job, 1,300 miles away from the home office, has 200 men on the payroll. The company is considering the advisability of having daily payroll records prepared in the main office, where there is punched-card equipment capable of tape-to-card and card-to-tape preparation of data for the

electronic computer. Discuss the possible use of a teletypewriter hook-up for the preparation of all payrolls in the main office to save time and cost. Indicate the procedure that you think should be followed.

5. The Yonkers Elevator Company has installed an electronic computer at a cost of $250,000 to watch over the 35,000 items in the stock-room. About 20,000 entries are fed into the computer daily. The inventory is valued at more than $10 million. This massive inventory is necessary because no two elevators are exactly alike, and the firm is prepared to service any elevator that it has installed. Discuss the reasons that must have guided this firm in making the computer installation and the possible procedure for using this equipment.

PRACTICAL OFFICE CASES

Case 25-1 Processing Customer Complaints [23]

You are the administrative manager of a growing manufacturing company which has sharply increased its sales volume over the last year. It has come to your attention that there have been an increasing number of customer complaints in recent months regarding poor service. An example of a typical complaint is indicated in the letter shown in Figure A from the Johnson Machine Works, a small customer.

Upon investigation, you learned that all parties had followed prescribed procedures—which consisted mainly of preparing the proper forms for keypunching and verification. The punched cards prepared by keypunching then were used to enter updated information into the computerized order, inventory, and accounting system.

You determined that the growing number of complaints could not be attributed to clerical or procedural errors, and that under normal work loads the present system of handling customer complaints was adequate. You also decided that the increasing difficulties in processing complaints efficiently was directly related to the rapidly growing sales volume, and the greatly increased number of unique or "exception" complaints resulting from that volume.

■ What would your recommendations be to correct this situation?

Case 25-2 Undertaking a Feasibility Study and Converting to Computerized Operations

■ Refer to Case 11-3, "Working with Supervisors on a Feasibility Study," pages 360-362, and after you have become familiar with the information contained in the case, prepare a report for Mr. Linn in which you discuss the following questions:

---

[23] AMS News (January, 1971), p. 3. This case originally appeared under the title "The Persistent Computer."

Gentlemen:

On January 3, I received a shipment of 100 (one hundred) #10 widgets from your company. I refused to accept the shipment since my order had been for 10 (ten) #100 widgets. I telephoned Jack Deegan, your sales representative, and he assured me that the error would be corrected. On January 5, I received a computer-prepared bill for 100 #10 widgets, which represented the erroneous shipment. I ignored the bill based on my conversation (and assumption) that corrective action would be taken by Mr. Deegan.

In subsequent weeks, the situation was further confused by the following events:

1. In a second telephone conversation with Mr. Deegan on January 26, I asked him why I still had not received my correct shipment and indicated that there was an urgent need for the parts ordered. He indicated that verification had been requested from the Shipping Department and he did not know why I hadn't received the corrected order. He then promised to expedite matters by cancelling my old order and resubmitting the order, which would be handled by the newly automated Order Department.

2. On January 29, I received a past-due notice for the 100 #10 widgets. I telephoned Mrs. Jones of your Billing Department and she said that all billing adjustments had to originate at the warehouse with Mr. James, who is responsible for keypunching and adjustments.

3. I subsequently called Mr. James and found that in order to correct my account I would have to call Mr. Smith in the Shipping Department.

4. I next tried to contact Mr. Smith and was informed that he was on vacation.

5. On February 5, I received my correct order of 10 #100 widgets.

6. On February 11, I received a bill for the 10 #100 widgets, and a notice of payment past-due for the 100 #10 widgets, along with a threat of legal action.

Fig. A

1. How would you proceed in undertaking the feasibility study? Would there be much merit in looking at Beck's computer installation and attempting to learn more about their operations? In order to perform a feasibility study, what executives and supervisors would you appoint to your committee? Should the company president be a member of this committee?
2. As a result of the feasibility study, what office work would you anticipate should be first converted to computer operations? Would this area of office work, when computerized, represent the most profitable changeover from the standpoint of long-term growth?
3. Do you believe that the results of the feasibility study will indicate that a computer should be installed in the offices of Linn's Toys?

Index

A

D

E

F

G

H

M

N

O

P

Q

R

S

U

V

W

Y

Z